Standard History Of The City Of Washington

WILLIAM TINDALL

Standard History of the City of Washington, W. Tindall
Jazzybee Verlag Jürgen Beck
86450 Altenmünster, Loschberg 9
Deutschland

ISBN: 9783849671815

www.jazzybee-verlag.de
admin@jazzybee-verlag.de

Printed by Createspace, North Charleston, SC, USA

CONTENTS:

CHAPTER I.

The Period Prior to the Adoption of the Site on the Potomac for the Permanent Seat of Government.

AS the beholder looks upon the Capital of the Nation today, with its wide, shaded streets, magnificent buildings, restful parks, costly monuments, and thousands of trees, it requires a vigorous play of the imagination to picture the swamps and forests which they have replaced and to realize that where is now the teeming population of a metropolitan city were once the tepees and campfires of the primitive Indian inhabitants.

Some of the ancient Indian village sites in the present District of Columbia named by archaeologists are: one at Little Falls on the west bank of the Anacostia; one between First and Second Streets, southeast; one on the crest of the hill on the Virginia side of the Potomac at Chain Bridge; another opposite the foot of Analostan Island on the Virginia side; another at the mouth of Four Mile Run; and yet another at the south end of Long Bridge; while the abundance of flint debris on hills bordering Rock Creek, show that vicinity to have been a popular Indian resort for making arrow-heads.

The site where our National Capital now spreads its streets and avenues was formerly the center of the one-time powerful Algonquins, the sub-tribe of this great family having their village here being the Powhatans. They were in possession when Captain John Smith explored the region and had been for hundreds of years previous to that time. All the tribes of the Algonquins met in council here and the place of these national meetings was on the delta between the Potomac and its Eastern Branch. The council-house stood at the foot of the very hill on which now stands the lofty American Capitol. The Indians also came here in great numbers during the fishing season and called the vicinity their "fishing ground."

The first white men to explore the Potomac, though they do not appear to have come as far up as the present site of Washington, were in all probability Spaniards.

The story of the first Spanish settlement as gathered from the Spanish records by Buckingham Smith is related by the Catholic historian Shea in a paper contributed by him to the New York Historical Society. The story as thus given is that a Spanish vessel came up the Potomac in the first half of the Sixteenth Century and carried away to Mexico the brother of the Chief of Axacan. Giving to the letter "x" its Spanish pronunciation approaching the German " ch, " the Spanish name Axacan becomes almost the exact equivalent of the English Occoquan. This Indian was baptized in the Christian Church and sent to Spain. In 1566 the Spanish Admiral Pedro Menendez sent a vessel with two Dominican fathers to set up a mission at Axacan but the party was frightened away. The enterprise was taken up four years later by a party of Jesuits under Father Segura. The latter expedition reached Axacan September 10, 1570, bringing with them the Indian who had been taken away by the Spaniards years before and who had been given the name Luis de Velasco, and who was relied upon to protect the party from the attacks of the Indians. Velasco 's wild nature reasserting itself, he deserted the missionaries and participated in their slaughter by the Indians. In the following spring a Spanish vessel arrived with supplies for the mission and carried the news of its fate back to Menendez who proceeded to Axacan and hung at the yard arm eight of those who had participated

1

in the killing of the missionaries, though Velasco had escaped to the mountains. With Menendez the Spanish flag departed forever from the Potomac. The Spaniards named the Chesapeake the Bay of St. Mary and the Potomac the Espiritu Santo.

Parkman in his "Pioneers of New France" mentions letters from Menendez to Philip II of Spain reciting that in 1565 and for some years previous the French above the Gulf of St. Lawrence had received buffalo skins — six thousand in two yean — from the Indians who had brought them down the Potomac and up the coast in canoes. Mr. Hugh T. Taggart in a paper read before the Columbia Historical Society argues that the voyage from the Potomac to the St. Lawrence in heavy laden canoes was an impossibility and that the French must have done their trading with the Indians on the Potomac.

Captain John Smith, probably the first Englishman to explore the Potomac, as well as other rivers emptying into the Chesapeake Bay, said in his valuable and remarkable "General History of Virginia, New England and the Summer Isles:"

"The fourth river is called Patawomecke, 6 or 7 myles in breadth. It is navigable 140 myles, and fed as the rest, with many sweet rivers and springs, which fall from the bordering hils. These hils many of them are planted, and yield no lesse plentie and varietie of fruit, then the river exceedeth with abundance of fish. It is inhabited on both sides. First on the south side at the very entrance is Wighcocomoco and hath some 130 men, beyond them Sekacawone with 30. — The Onawmanient with 100. And the Patawomekes more than 200. Here doth the river divide itself into 3 or 4 convenient branches. The greatest of the last is called Quiyouh, trending Northwest, but the river itselfe turneth Northeast, and is still a navigable streame. On the Westerne side of this branch is Tauxenent with 40 men. On the North of the river is Secowocomoco with 40. Somewhat further Potapaco with 20. In the East part is Pamacaeack with 60. After Moyowance with 100. And lastly, Nocotchtanke with 80. The river aboue this place maketh his passage downe a low pleasant valley overshadowed in many places with high rocky mountaines; from whence distill innumerable sweet and pleasant springs. "

Some historians deny that Captain Smith saw the present site of Washington and others assert that it is very uncertain, but whether he stood on the exact site of this city or not, it is reasonably certain that he came this far north on the Potomac. He tells of being entertained near the present site of Mt. Vernon, at Toags, which place appears on his map as Tauxenent on the Virginia side of the river; at Mayaones opposite, on the Maryland side; and at Nacotehtant or Nacotchtanke, which was situated within what is now the District of Columbia.

He went on up the river until his navigation was prohibited by immense rocks over which the water poured, so that it appears he went to or nearly to the falls.

William Stith, writing in 1746, tells of Captain Smith's voyage up the Potomac River, his encounters with tribes of Indians, the finding of the antimony mine, et cetera, and then says:

"Towards the Falls of Patowmack, they met several Parties of Indians in Canoes, loaded with the Flefh of Bears, Deer, and other wild Beafts."

This early navigator and explorer was one of the most striking and interesting characters of our Country's history, although he is accused of exaggeration and even of prevarication in recording his own deeds. One writer calls him "an egotist and a braggart, " but the same accuser says later: "If John Smith, in his many writings, sometimes boasted more than other men, he had also done more," and one to do was the sort of person needed then, as at all times. Smith was truly brave or he would not and could not have faced all the dangers to be met in exploring a country of savages, many of whom were unfriendly to the white people.

Nor were his explorations made simply for adventure. He drew a map of Virginia, very accurate, considering all the difficulties in his way, and preserved many valuable records of the country and Indian tribes that would be lost to the world but for his pen.

His descriptions of some of the natural advantages of Virginia in those early days, which country includes the Potomac and its cities, are interesting. "This Virginia," he says, "is a country in America betweene the degrees of 34. and 45. of the North latitude. The bounds thereof on the East side are the great Ocean ■. on the South lyeth Florida: on the North nova Francia: as for the West thereof, the limits are vnknowm' Of the climate he said:

"The sommer is hot as in Spaine; the winter colde as in Fraume or England. The heat of sommer is in Iune, Iuly and August, but commonly the coole Breeses ass wage the vehemencie of the heat. The chiefe of winter is halfe December, Iunuary, February, and halfe March. The colde is extreme sharpe, but here the proverbe is true that no extreme long continueth.

"In the yeare 1607 was an extraordinary frost in most of Europe, and this frost was founde as extreame in Virginia. But the next yeare for 8. or 10. daies of ill weather, other 14 daies would be as Sommer." In general praise of Virginia he said:

"The mildnesse of the aire, the fertilitie of the soile, and the situation of the rivers are so propitious to the nature and vse of man as no place is more convenient for pleasure, profit and mans sustenance," and concluding a chapter of praise in 1612, he wrote:

"So then here is a place a nurse for souldiers, a practise for marriners, a trade for merchants, a reward for the good, and that which is most of all, — a businesse (most acceptable to God) to bring such poore infidels to the true knowledge of God and his holy Gospell."

He tells of the soil and shows considerable knowledge of its properties, as he does of nearly everything that comes under his observation. This vigorous pioneer, trying to build a successful colony, was observant of every advantage in the new country, and when he was placed at the head of the colony his work and reports all tended to the good of the English settlement, regardless of individuals, some of those considering themselves gentlemen above the indignity of labor, bringing forth reprimand from the practical Captain, and contemptuous remark in liis reports of the proceedings of the colony. He forced every man to work or go without provisions, a law he realized to be necessary if the settlers were to be kept from starving. He showed his impatience with the would-be idlers when he wrote, in 1608:

"At this time were most of our chiefest men either sick or discontented, the rest being in such dispaire, as they would rather starue and rot with idlenes, then be perswaded to do anything for their owne relief e without constraint." Captain Smith gives us a very good conception of the Indians of this part of the country in the Seventeenth century. Of their dress the Captain tells us:

"For their apparell, they are some time couered with the skinnes of wilde beasts, which in winter are dressed with the haire, but in sommer without. The better sort

3

vse large mantels of deare skins not much differing in fashion from the Irish mantels. Some imbroidered with white beads, some with copper, other painted after their manner. . . . We have seen some vse mantels made of Turkey feathers, so prettily wrought and wouen with threads that nothing could be discerned but the feathers, that was exceeding warme and very handsome. . . . They adorne themselves most with copper beads and paintings. Their women haue their legs, hands, breasts and face cunningly imbrodered with diuerse workes, as beasts, serpents, artificially wrought into their flesh with blacke spots. In each eare commonly thy haue 3 great holes, whereat they hange chaines, brace. lets, or copper. Some of their men weare in those holes, a smal greene and yellow coloured snake, neare halfe a yard in length, which crawling and lapping her selfe about his necke often times familiarly would kiss his lips. Others wear a dead Rat tied by the tail . . . he is most gallant that is most monstrous to behould. " Of their houses:

"Their buildings and habitations are for the most part by the rivers or not farre distant from some fresh spring. Their houses are built like our Arbors of small young springs (sprigs) bowed and tyed, and so close covered with mats or the barkes of trees very handsomely, that not withstanding either winde raine or weather, they are as warme as stoones, but very smoaky; yet at the toppe of the house there is a hole made for the smoake to goe into right over tie fire."

In these houses or arbors he says of the sleepers that "they lie heads and points one by the other against the fire: some covered with mats, some with skins, and some starke naked lie on the ground; from 6 to 20 in a house. "

"For their musicke they vse a thicke cane, on which they pipe as on a Recorder. For their warres they haue a great deepe platter of wood. They cover the mouth thereof with a skin, at each corner they tie a walnut, which meeting on the backside neere the bottome, with a small rope they twitch them togither till it be so taught aud stiff e, that they may beat vpon it as vpon a drumme. But their chief e instruments a Rattels made of small gourds or Pnmpion shels. Of these they haue Base, Tenor, Counter-tenor, meane and Trible. These mingled with their voices sometimes 20 or 30 togither, make such a terrible noise as would rather affright than delight any man." He tells too of their terrible sacrifices, some of them so horrible as to make the reader shudder. Indian characteristics are summed up in these words:

"They are inconstant in everything, but what feare constraineth them to keepe. Craftie, timerous, quicke of apprehension, and very ingenuous. Some are of disposition fearefull, some bold, most cautelous, all Savage. . . . They are soone moued to anger, and so malicious, that they seldome forget an injury: they seldome steale one from another, lest their coniurers should reveale it, and so they be pursued and punished." Robert Beverly gives us a picture of the physical Indians of those days in these words:

"They are ftraight and well proportioned, having the cleaneft and most exact Limbs in the World: They are so perfect in their outward Frame that I never heard of one Angle Indian that was either dwarfish, crooked, bandyleg 'd or otherwife miffhapen." He also tells of finding in a sack

"some vaft Bones, which we judged to be the Bones of Men, particularly we meafured one Thigh-bone, and found it two foot nine Inches long."

The next Englishman to ascend the Potomac as far as Washington, of whom we have authentic record, was Henry Fleet, an English fur-trader and explorer.

Fleet was a man of sense, and brave almost to the point of fool-hardiness. He mixed with the Indians a great deal and became familiar with their language and customs, which enabled him to preserve, in his journal and letters, much of the history of his time, as well as to encourage the people of England to emigrate to the new world. We learn most that is known of his explorations in New England and Virginia from his journal.

July 4, 1631, he wrote:

"We weighed anchor from the Downes, and sailed for New England, when we arrived in the harbour of Pascattowaie the 9th of September, making some stay upon the coast of New England. From thence, on Monday the 19th of September, we sailed directly for Virginia, where we came to anchor in the bay there, the 21st of October, but made little stay. Prom thence we set sail for the river of Potowmack, where we arrived the 26th of October at an Indian town called Yowaccomoco, being at the mouth of the river. . . . Here I was tempted to run up the river to the head, there to trade with a strange populous nation, called Mohaks, man-eaters, but after good deliberation, I conceived many inconveniences that might fall out."

He has much to say of his New England explorations but nothing more of Virginia until April, 1632, when he mentions having difficulty in getting to Virginia. May 16, 1632, he wrote: "We shaped our course for the river Potowmack, with the company of Captain Cleybourne, being in a small vessel."

He described the trip up the river and in June he arrived at the rushing part of the river, or falls, now known as Little Falls, four miles above Washington, and described the locality, thus: "This place without all question is the most pleasant and healthful place in all this country, and most convenient for habitation, the air temperate in summer and not violent in winter. "

He traveled yet further up the river:

"The 27th of June I manned my shallop and went up with the flood the tide rising about four feet in height at this place. We had not rowed above three miles but we might hear the Falls to roar about six miles distant."

It must have been on his way back from this expedition that Captain Fleet was captured by Indians or chose to stay at a village on the Piscataway creek, and there, two years later, some English explorers under Leonard Calvert found him. These explorers landed at a point near the present Colonial Beach, then further up at Marlborough Point on Potomac creek, where they were treated in a friendly manner by the Indians. After a visit they sailed on the Piscataway creek, where they encountered "the natives armed and assembled upon the shore to the number of five hundred, ready to dispute his landing, but they succeeded in convincing the savages that they had only friendly intentions. After this adjustment of intentions they were hospitably treated by the Indians and Captain Fleet, who acted as interpreter, and good feeling was established all around.

The Englishmen, who were seeking a place in which to settle, decided that this point was too far up the river and returned to Blackistone's Island, near the mouth of the river, taking Fleet with them. The Captain acted as friend, guide and interpreter, he by this time being thoroughly familiar with the wild Indian country through which they traveled. Some of his descriptions of the upper Potomac, which were later published in England, caused many immigrants to turn to the new country overseas.

Captain Fleet ever continued to be interested in the growing colonies and in 1638 we find him a member of the Maryland House of Assembly and later, 1652, a member of the Virginia House of Burgesses.

We do not read of other white settlers visiting the site of the District of Columbia until the close of the Seventeenth Century, when a company of Irish and Scotch came over and started a colony in Maryland within the present limits of the District. Of the land ceded to these settlers three tracts lay within the boundaries of the City of Washington.

These refugees seem to have been good managers and to have succeeded accordingly. They called their new home New Scotland and worked their farms in peace and quiet, little dreaming that land where their produce grew would one day be the territory of one of the proudest cities of one of the greatest nations of earth's history.

One of these early proprietors, Robert Troop, called his farm "Scotland Yard," and it comprised what is now Southeast Washington. Another, Francis Pope, named his place Rome, and called a small stream at the foot of his hill, Tiber River. It is told of this dreamer, that he predicted a greater capital than Rome would occupy that hill and that later generations would command a great and flourishing country in the new world. He related that he had had a dream or vision, in which he had seen a splendid parliament house on the hill, now known to us as Capitol Hill, which he purchased and called Rome, in prophetic honor of the great city to be.

His title to the land may be somewhat convincive of his prophecy, as it was deeded under the name "Rome," June 5, 1663. It reads:

"Layd out for Francis Pope of this Province Gentleman
a parcel of land in Charles County called Rome lying on
the East side of the Anacostian River beginning at a
marked oak standing by the riverside, the bounded tree of
Captain Robert Troop and running north by the river for
breadth the length 200 perches to a bounded oak standing
at the mouth of a bay or inlet called Tiber."
His furrows have long since given place to streets and
buildings; his stream still flows in the old course, less glorious,
perhaps, though more useful, as it now serves the modern use
of a city sewer.

Some of the descendants of those early Scotch and Irish farmers were among the first proprietors of the City of Washington and many of their descendants have continued to help build the capital and the country to the present day.

Many of the great men and women of our Country have come down from these old Scotch-Irish pioneers, who settled not only on this site, but all along the Potomac River and other parts of the then known country. They were people who had been persecuted in their own country, and their determined efforts for freedom and prosperous homes, together with like determination in other home-makers of the different colonies, gathered in force and importance, making a people of sturdy mold, of like desires and of democratic principles, who were, at a later day, to break all bans and form a new country on the earth, — a country of freedom for all people.

The Seventeenth Century closed and the Eighteenth advanced many years without any remarkable event disturbing these workers, living their contented lives, with plenty of work to occupy them and much beauty to behold in the great woods, hills and rivers, on which floated majestic swans in great numbers, fish abounded in the waters, and birds of the air, now no longer known to this region, often passed overhead in flocks of thousands and tens of thousands during migrating seasons.

As time progressed and English subjects were occupying their plantations and smaller tracts in the new world, the French were broadening their claims until finally encroachments on their part caused Britain 's children to become alert and question their safety if encroachment continued unmolested. So, as preparation against possible invasion, ammunition and other army supplies were sent to Virginia, which colony then occupied large territory in the West.

The English governor, Robert Dinwiddie, a Scotchman, was ordered in 1753 to write a protest to the French Commandant, which done, the Governor looked about for a trustworthy messenger to carry the message. A young man then only twenty-one years of age, George Washington, who had already served his country in several useful capacities, was selected for the important duty, and history tells of his successful trip through" almost insurmountable difficulties.

Chevalier de St. Pierre received the young envoy with courtesy, but his reply to the English protest was a refusal to comply with the request, which unwelcome answer Washington was compelled to carry back through the winter woods, a trip through which in those early days, was almost Herculean. It is recorded that an Indian guide attempted to shoot Washington during this return trip and that his life was also endangered by a fall into the Alleghany River, at that time filled with floating ice.

It is known how, after this failure to bring about amicable relations, the English, in 1754, sent the ill-fated expedition under General Braddock against the French, which was the beginning of hostilities that ended only after years of fighting, in English victory. This long French and English war is matter of history, mentioned here only to bring forward George Washington, who then played a conspicuous part and was later to take such active part in the history of his country.

Governor Dinwiddie's choice shows the esteem in which the young Washington was held at twenty-one, and this respect of his elders began at a much earlier age. During his early years George Washington was learning to be a surveyor, gaining rough and valuable experience in Virginia wilds with Indians and other woods inhabitants. At sixteen Lord Fairfax engaged him to survey his lands of thousands of acres and the lad proved himself capable of such a performance. The government surveyors engaged in laying out the Appalachian forest reserve have recently reported finding the marks left by Washington in running the lines of Lord Fairfax's lands.

These early incidents of Washington's life had an important if indirect bearing upon the subsequent establishment of the National Capital. As will be noted later, one of the important considerations which determined the selection of the present site was its accessibility to the country west of the Allegheny Mountains by way of the Potomac River, the Cumberland Pass, and the headwaters of the Ohio River. It was this route which Washington traversed in the occasion of his mission to the French and again in company with the Braddock expedition. After the close of the Revolution he again, in 1784, journeyed across the mountains by the same route. His familiarity with the importance of the Western Territory and of the advantages of the Potomac route which he acquired on these trips was doubtless an important factor among the influences which brought Congress to adopt the site on the Potomac for the Federal City.

CHAPTER II.

The Adoption of the Site on the Potomac

THE Capital City of the United States is the only national capital the establishment of which was to a material degree due to or influenced by the purpose of the national authority to protect itself from its own citizens.

It will be recalled that near the close of the Revolutionary War a body of dissatisfied soldiers of the American Army marched to Philadelphia where the Continental Congress was then holding its sessions, and with threats of violence demanded of that body the satisfaction of certain demands, chief among which was that for the settlement of arrears of pay due the soldiers. This was in June of the year 1783. The immediate result of this action on the part of the revolutionary soldiers was that on June 21, 1783, the Continental Congress passed the following resolution:

"Resolved, That the President and supreme executive council of Pennsylvania be informed that the authority of the United States having been this day grossly insulted by the disorderly and menacing appearance of a body of armed soldiers about the place within which Congress were assembled, and the peace of this city being endangered by the mutinous disposition of the said troops now in the barracks, it is, in the opinion of Congress, necessary that effectual measures be immediately taken for supporting the public authority.

"Resolved, That the committee, on a letter from Colonel Butler, be directed to confer, without loss of time, with the supreme executive council of Pennsylvania, on the practicability of carrying the preceding resolution into effect; and that in case it shall appear to the committee that there is not a satisfactory ground for expecting adequate and prompt exertions of this State for supporting the dignity of the Federal Government, the President on the advice of the committee be authorized and directed to summon the members of Congress to meet on Thursday next at Trenton or Princeton, in New Jersey, in order that further and more effectual measures may be taken for suppressing the present revolt, and maintaining the dignity and authority of the United States.

"Resolved, That the Secretary at War be directed to communicate to the commander in chief, the state and disposition of the said troops, in order that he may take immediate measures to dispatch to this city such force as he may judge expedient for suppressing any disturbances that may ensue. "

On June 21, a committee consisting of Mr. Hamilton and Mr. Ellsworth was appointed for the purpose of conferring with the Supreme Executive Council of Pennsylvania with a view to obtaining the protection of Congress by the militia of the State of Pennsylvania, and on June 24 that committee returned a lengthy report in which the attitude of the authorities of that State was set forth as follows:

"That the council had a high respect for the representative sovereignty of the United States and were disposed to do everything in their power to support its dignity. That they regretted the insult which had happened, with this additional motive of sensibility, that they had themselves had a principal share in it. That they had consulted a number of well-informed officers of the militia and found that nothing in the present state of things was to be expected from that quarter. That the militia of the city in general were not only ill provided for service but disinclined to act upon the present occasion. That the council did not believe any exertions were to be looked for from them, except in case of further outrage and actual violence to person or property. That in such case a respectable body of citizens would arm for the security of their property and of the public peace; but it was to be doubted what measure of outrage would produce this effect, and in particular, it was not to be expected merely from a repetition of the insult which had happened. " Without going at length into the methods by which the mutiny was dealt with, and the equanimity of Congress, which had removed to Princeton, restored, it is sufficient to note that the immediate effect of the incident was the commencement of a series of discussions which was destined to last through a period of seven years looking to the establishment of the seat of government to be under the exclusive jurisdiction of Congress. The matter first came up in definite form when, on October 6, 1783, the order of the day having been called for and read, it was resolved "that the question be taken in which state buildings shall be provided and erected for the residence of Congress, beginning with New Hampshire and proceeding in the order in which they stand." The question upon each state passed in the negative, no state having received more than four votes, New Jersey and Maryland having each received that number.

The first consideration of a proposal to acquire territory for the establishment of a new capital city, and apparently the first consideration of the Potomac River as the site thereof appears in a motion by Mr. Gerry of Massachusetts, seconded by Mr. Howell of Rhode Island, on Tuesday, October 7, 1783, as follows:

"That buildings for the use of Congress be erected on the banks of the Delaware, near Trenton, or of Potomac, near Georgetown, provided a suitable district can be procured on one of the rivers as aforesaid for a Federal town, and the right of soil and an exclusive or such other jurisdiction as Congress may direct shall be vested in the United States."

Omitting a review of the long series of motions, countermotions and debates relating to the proposed Federal city which constituted a very considerable portion of the proceedings of the Continental Congress, it is worthwhile to call attention to the fact that repeatedly the motions for the adoption of one site or another contained the proviso found in Mr. Gerry's motion, namely that "the right of soil and an exclusive or such other jurisdiction as Congress may direct shall be vested in the United Stated."

It is interesting to note the striking and fundamental difference between this language and that later adopted by the Constitutional Convention, to which the question of providing for a permanent capital was shifted. By Section eight of Article 1 of the Constitution Congress is given power:

"To exercise exclusive legislation, in all cases whatsoever, over such district (not exceeding 10 miles square) as may, by cession of particular States, and the acceptance of Congress, become the seat of the Government of the United States, and to exercise like authority over all places purchased by the consent of the legislature of the State in which the same shall be, for the erection of forts, magazines, arsenals, dockyards, and other needful buildings." It will be observed that with regard to the seat of government, that the Constitution makes provision for "exclusive legislation," only, over such District as may by cession of particular states and the acceptance of Congress become the seat of government. As to sites for forts, magazines, arsenals, dockyards and other needful buildings, the Constitution gives Congress like authority

9

over all places " purchased by the consent of the legislature of the state in which the same shall be." It is evident from the language used in the Constitution, that as to places acquired for forts, magazines, arsenals and dockyards, its framers contemplated not only that Congress should exercise exclusive legislation over such places, but that the title to the land acquired for such purposes should be in the United States. The land was to be purchased not from the State in which it might be situated but from its individual owners, with the consent of the state legislature.

But as to the territory to be acquired as the seat of government, it is evident from the language used in the Constitution, that there was no thought of any purchase of title to the land further than of such as might be necessary for government purposes. The territory was to be acquired not by purchase but "by cession of particular states." By this cession the states were to transfer to the United States merely their sovereignty over the territory ceded — not the ownership of the land. The ownership of the land was to remain in the individual proprietors and only so much of the land to be purchased by the United States from such proprietors, as should be needed for government purposes. In line with this thought, the act of cession of Virginia of December 3, 1789, and the Act of Maryland of December 19, 1791, ratifying the cession of that State, both contained provisos to the effect that nothing therein contained should be construed to vest in the United States any right of property in the soil or to affect the rights of individuals therein otherwise than as the same should or might be transferred by such individuals to the United States.

This proviso of the Maryland and Virginia Acts, as well as the spirit of the Constitutional provision for the Federal Territory, are notably different from the underlying idea involved in Mr. Gerry 's original motion for the establishment of a Capital City on the Potomac River and embodied in nearly all of the motions and resolutions on the subject of the location of a permanent capital discussed by the Continental Congress. In the propositions considered by the Continental Congress, the almost invariable language: " provided a suitable district can be procured * * * and the right of soil and an exclusive or such other jurisdiction as Congress may direct shall be vested in the United States," indicates that the consideration of primary importance during that period was that the Federal Government should own the soil itself. The matter of exclusive jurisdiction was then regarded as of secondary importance, as is clearly to be gathered from the repeated use of the alternative provision, — provided an exclusive or such other jurisdiction as Congress may direct, shall be vested in the United States.

The reversal of the attitude of the founders upon the question of the respective importance of these two considerations was of fundamental consequence in its bearing upon the future relationship between the Federal Government and the District of Columbia. Whether this has worked to the detriment or to the advantage of the latter, it is impossible to say; but it is safe to assert that if the Constitution had provided for the acquisition not only of jurisdiction but also of the "right of soil" by the United States as provided for in the motions considered by the Continental Congress, and if these requirements had been observed in the acquisition of the site for the Federal city, Congress would not have taken between seventy and eighty years to come to a realization of its obligations toward the development of the District of Columbia, nor, having come to that realization be constantly holding over the District the menace of a reversal of its attitude. As proprietor of all the land, it would at least have felt and could not have evaded the responsibilities incident to the ownership of the land. Whether the opportunities for outsiders to move in and assist in building up a beautiful capital city would have been so favorable, and whether the burden upon the population as lessees of the government would have been greater or less than as owners of the land, it is impossible to say; but in any aspect of the case the National Government would have been compelled to recognize from the outset its primary responsibility for the municipal expense of the District, regardless of the measures to be adopted by it in seeking contribution or reimbursement from the local population.

Immediately upon the assembling of the Congress provided for by the Constitution, the question of the establishment of a permanent seat of government was taken up. The discussion was marked, as it had been during the sessions of the Continental Congress, by a divergence of sentiment between the Northern and Southern states, — the former favoring a city to be established upon either the Delaware or the Susquehanna, and the latter a city to be established upon the Potomac. The discussion at times was exceedingly acrimonious as is evidenced by Mr. Madison's remark in the course of a debate, that had a prophet started up in the Constitutional Convention and foretold the proceedings of that day, he verily believed that Virginia would not then have been a party to the Constitution.

The final determination to locate the Capital City upon the Potomac River was probably ascribable to a number of important considerations. Its location there was in a measure a compliment to General Washington and had the further advantage of being the most nearly accessible to both the Northern and Southern states of any site that could have been selected. Another geographical reason which played a highly important part, in the adoption of that location, was the fact that the Potomac River allowed of a site, which could be reached by ocean navigation, the farthest inland of any to be found on any of the rivers of the Atlantic seaboard, and at the same time afforded the shortest line of communication with the vast undeveloped region to the west, the most important point of which at that time was the present site of the City of Pittsburg. The head waters of the Potomac and the head waters of the Ohio River approach so close to each other that these two rivers afford an almost continuous potential water passage from the Atlantic Ocean to the Ohio Valley. General Washington had as has already been told traversed this route on several occasions prior to the Revolutionary War and in the fall of 1784 had again traversed it on the occasion of a trip to the Western country. He was an ardent believer in the feasibility of utilizing this route as a great commercial highway when developed by means of canals. He had in fact organized the Potowmack Company in 1785 for the purpose of clearing the channel of the Potomac and building canals around the Great and Little Falls, and the work was in course of prosecution while the debates on the site for the federal city were in progress. It was expected that the region west of the Allegheny Mountains would rapidly become populated and developed, and with this expectation in mind, the importance of placing the National Capital where it could be most easily reached by the population which should settle in this new Western country was obvious to everyone.

In the records of the proceedings of Congress for September 14, 1789, appears the following discussion which will serve to indicate the force of this argument in determining the question where the Capital City should be placed:

11

"Mr. Scott, of Pennsylvania, observed that the question seemed to lie between the Susquehanna and the Potomac. He gave a geographical description of those rivers, in relation to their advantages of communication with the Western territory; he considered Pittsburg as the key of that territory. The result of his detail was clearly in favor of the Potomac. That there is no comparison between the advantages of one communication and the other, with respect to the Ohio country. The Potomac will, no doubt, one day be a very important channel into those regions. That though he thought that the Potomac was nearer the center of communication between the Atlantic and the Ohio than the Susquehanna, as there was no prospect of a decision in favor of the former he should give his vote for the Susquehanna. In this situation, as he was a native of Pennsylvania, there was a certain duty which he owed to his country, and which he should now perform." Mr. Madison, in debate (on the 4th of September), observed —

"if there be any event on which we may calculate with tolerable certainty, I take it the center of population will continually advance in a southwestern direction. It must then travel from the Susquehanna, if it is now found there. It may go beyond the Potomac; but the time will be long first; and, if it should, the Potomac is the great highway of communication between the Atlantic and the Western country, which will justly prevent any attempts to remove the seat farther south. I have said, sir, that the communication to the Western territory is more commodious through the Potomac than the Susquehanna. I wish all the facts connected with this subject could have been more fully ascertained and more fully stated. But if we consider the facts which have been offered by gentlemen who spoke, we must conclude that the communication through the Potomac would be much more facile and effectual than any other." Mr. Madison stated the probable distance by land from the seat of government, if fixed on the Potomac, to Pittsburg, at 170 or 180 miles; if by the river, 250 miles; and from the seat of Government, if fixed on the Susquehanna, by land, 250; by the river, 500.

"Whether, therefore [he said], we measure the distance by land or water, it is in favor of the Potomac; and if we consider the progress in opening this great channel, I am confident that consideration would be equally favorable. It has been determined, by accurate research, that the waters running into the Ohio may be found not more than 2 or 3 miles distant from those of the Potomac. This is a fact of peculiar importance." The journal kept by William Macklay, Senator from Pennsylvania, who was an ardent advocate of the site on the Susquehanna River, recites that a decisive argument in favor of the site on the Potomac was an estimate of the expenditure which would be required to render the Susquehanna navigable. On the other hand, the Potowmack Company of which President Washington was the moving spirit had already demonstrated the practicability of opening to navigation the Potomac and its tributaries from their headwaters to tidewater at Georgetown and had carried this project well toward completion.

All of the considerations above noted, however, would probably have failed to bring about the selection of the Potomac River as the site for the Federal Capital, owing to the reluctance of the Northern States to place the seat of government so far south, had it not been for an additional consideration less legitimate but undoubtedly much more powerful than the others. The Northern States were exceedingly anxious to have the Federal Government assume the debts contracted by the several states in the prosecution of the Revolutionary War, and a measure to this effect had been ardently championed by Alexander Hamilton as part of the general fiscal scheme which he was endeavoring to put in operation. The Southern States were opposed to this measure, and finally agreed to its passage, but only when the consent of the Northern States to the location of the Capital City on the Potomac River had been pledged. The manner in which the final compromise was brought about is interestingly related by Mr. Jefferson in the collection of notes which he entitled his "Ana," as follows:

"Hamilton was in despair. As I was going to the President's one day, I met him in the street. He walked me backwards and forwards before the President's door for half an hour. He painted pathetically the temper into which the legislature had been wrought, the disgust of those who were called the creditor States, the danger of the secession of their members, and the separation of the States. He observed that the members of the administration ought to act in concert, that tho' this question was not of my department, yet a common duty should make it a common concern; that the President was the center on which all administrative questions ultimately rested, and that all of us should rally around him and support with joint efforts measures approved by him; and that the question having been lost by a small majority only, it was probable that an appeal from me to the judgment and discretion of some of my friends might affect a change in the vote, and the machine of government, now suspended, might be again set in motion. I told him that I was really a stranger to the whole subject; not having yet informed myself of the system of finances adopted, I knew not how far this was a necessary sequence; that undoubtedly if its rejection endangered a dissolution of our Union at this incipient stage, I should deem that the most unfortunate of all consequences, to avert which all partial and temporary evils should be yielded. I proposed to him, however, to dine with me the next day, and I would invite another friend or two, bring them into conference together, and I thought it impossible that reasonable men, consulting together cooly, could fail, by some mutual sacrifices of opinion, to form a compromise which was to save the Union. The discussion took place. I could take no part in it but an exhortatory one, because I was a stranger to the circumstances which should govern it. But it was finally agreed that whatever importance had been attached to the rejection of this proposition the preservation of the Union and of the concord among the States was most important, and that therefore it would be better that the vote of rejection should be rescinded, to effect which some members should change their votes. But it was observed that this pill would be peculiarity bitter to the Southern States, and that some concomitant measure should be adopted to sweeten it a little to them. There had before been propositions to fix the seat of government either at Philadelphia or at Georgetown on the Potomac; and it was thought that by giving it to Philadelphia for ten years and to Georgetown permanently afterwards this might, as an anodyne, calm in some degree the ferment which might be excited by the other measure alone. So two of the Potomac members (White and Lee, but White with a revulsion of stomach almost convulsive) agreed to change their votes, and Hamilton undertook to carry the other point.

"In doing this, the influence he had established over the Eastern members, with the agency of Robert Morris with those of the Middle States, effected his side of the agreement and so assumption was passed, and twenty millions of stock divided, among favored states, and thrown in as a pabulum to the stock-jobbing herd. This added to the number of votaries to the treasury, and made its chief the master of every vote in the legislature which might give to the Government the direction suited to his political views. "

Two letters written by Mr. Madison to Mr. Monroe within a space of six weeks preceding the final decision of the question in Congress give a very good idea of the apprehension which Mr. Madison felt that the measure for which he had labored so earnestly to locate the Capital City on the Potomac would be defeated. Under date of June 1, 1790, he writes:

"You will see by the enclosed paper that a removal from this place has been voted by a large majority of our House. The other is pretty nearly balanced. The Senators of the three Southern States are disposed to couple the permanent with the temporary question. If they do so, I think it will end in either an abortion of both, or a decision of the former in favor of the Delaware. I have good reason to believe that there is no serious purpose in the Northern States to prefer the Potomac, and that if supplied with a pretext for a very hasty decision, they will indulge their secret wishes for a permanent establishment on the Delaware. As Rhode Island is again in the Union and will probably be in the Senate in a day or two, the Potowmac has the less to hope and the more to fear from that quarter." Under date of June 17, 1790, he writes:

"You will find in the enclosed papers some account of the proceedings on the question relating to the seat of government. The Senate have hung up the vote for Baltimore, which, as you may suppose, could not have been seriously meant by many who joined in it. It is not improbable that the permanent seat may be coupled with the temporary one. The Potomac stands a bad chance, and yet it is not impossible that in the vicissitudes of the business it may turn up in some form or other." At the time of the passage of the Act of July 16, 1790, the Acts of cession of Maryland and Virginia were already in existence. The Act of Maryland approved December 23, 1788, was a model of brevity, and provided merely:

"Be it enacted by the General Assembly of Maryland, That the representatives of this State in the House of Representatives of the Congress of the United States, appointed to assemble at New York on the first Wednesday of March next, be, and they are hereby, authorized and required, on behalf of this State, to cede to the Congress of the United States any district in this State not exceeding ten miles square, which the Congress may fix upon and accept for the seat of government of the United States." The somewhat more extensive Act of Virginia, approved December 3, 1789, was as follows:

" I. Whereas the equal and common benefits resulting from the administration of the General Government will be best diffused and its operations become more prompt and certain by establishing such a situation for the seat of said government as will be most central and convenient to the citizens of the United States at large, having regard as well to population, extent of territory, and free navigation to the Atlantic Ocean, through the Chesapeake Bay, as to the most direct and ready communication with our fellow citizens in the Western frontiers; and whereas it appears to this assembly that a situation combining all the considerations and advantages before recited may be had on the banks of the river Potomac above tide water, in a country rich and fertile in soil, healthy and salubrious in climate, and abounding in all the necessaries and conveniences of life, where, in a location of ten miles square, if the wisdom of Congress shall so direct, the States of Pennsylvania, Maryland, and Virginia may participate in such location:

"II. Be it further enacted by the General Assembly, That a tract of country, not exceeding ten miles square, or any lesser quantity, to be located within the limits of this State, and in any part thereof as Congress may by law direct, shall be, and the same is, forever ceded and relinquished to the Congress and Government of the United States, in full and absolute right and exclusive jurisdiction, as well of soil as of persons residing or to reside thereon, pursuant to the tenor and effect of the eighth section of the first article of the Constitution of the Government of the United States.

"III. Provided, That nothing herein contained shall be herein construed to vest in the United States any right of property in the soil, or to affect the rights of individuals therein, otherwise than the same shall or may be transferred by such individuals to the United States.

"IV. And provided also, That the jurisdiction of the laws of this Commonwealth over the persons and property of individuals residing within the limits of the cession aforesaid shall not cease or determine until Congress, having accepted the said cession, shall by law provide for the government thereof, under their jurisdiction, in the manner provided by the article of the Constitution before recited." The result of the debate on this subject was the passage of the Act approved by President Washington July 16, 1790, accepting a site to be later more definitely located, which should lie upon the Potomac River at some point between the Eastern Branch and the Conogocheague, the latter being a small stream emptying into the Potomac from the Maryland side near Williamsport, about eighty miles above the present site of Washington and near the Battlefield of Antietam. This act passed the Senate on Thursday, July 1, 1790, by a vote of fourteen to twelve. It passed the House of Representatives on Friday, July 9, 1790, by a vote of thirty-two to twenty-nine.

The text of the Act is as follows:

"AN ACT for establishing the temporary and permanent seat of the Government of the United States.

"Section 1. Be it enacted by the Senate and House of Representatives of the United States of America in Congress assembled, That a district of territory, not exceeding ten miles square, to be located as hereafter directed on the river Potomac, at some place between the mouths of the Eastern Branch and the Connogochegue, be, and the same is hereby, accepted for the permanent seat of the Government of the United States: Provided nevertheless, That the operation of the laws of the State within such district shall not be affected by this acceptance, until the time fixed for the removal of the government thereto, and until Congress shall otherwise by law provide.

"Sec. 2. And be it further enacted, That the President of the United States be authorized to appoint, and by supplying vacancies happening from refusals to act or other causes, to keep in appointment as long as may be necessary, three commissioners, who, or any two of whom, shall, under the direction of the President, survey, and by proper metes and bounds define and limit a district of territory, under the limitations above mentioned; and the district so defined, limited, and located shall be deemed the district accepted by this Act for the permanent seat of the Government of the United States.

"Sec. 3. And be it (further) enacted, That the said commissioners, or any two of them, shall have power to purchase or accept such quantity of land on the eastern side of the said river, within the said district, as the President shall deem proper for the use of the United States and according to such plans as the President shall approve, the said commissioners, or any two of them, shall, prior to the first Monday in December, in the year one thousand eight hundred, provide suitable buildings for the accommodation of Congress and of the President, and for the public offices of the Government of the United States.

"Sec. 4. And be it (further) enacted, That for defraying the expense of such purchases and buildings, the President of the United States be authorized and requested to accept grants of money.

"Sec. 5. And be it (further) enacted, That prior to the first Monday in December next, all offices attached to the seat of the Government of the United States, shall be removed to, and until the said first Monday in December, in the year one thousand eight hundred, shall remain at the city of Philadelphia, in the State of Pennsylvania, at which place the session of Congress next ensuing the present shall be held.

"Sec. 6. And be it (further) enacted, That on the said first Monday in December, in the year one thousand eight hundred, the seat of the Government of the United States shall, by virtue of this act, be transferred to the district and place aforesaid. And all offices attached to the said seat of government, shall accordingly be removed thereto by their respective holders, and shall, after the said day, cease to be exercised elsewhere; and that the necessary expense of such removal shall be defrayed out of the duties on imposts and tonnage, of which a sufficient sum is hereby appropriated.

"Approved, July 16, 1790. (1 Stats., 130.)" The Act of Congress of July 16, 1790, notwithstanding it was officially entitled "An Act for establishing the temporary and permanent seat of the Government of the United States," was generally referred to as the Residence Act, by reason of its purpose to establish a residence for the Government. It is by the latter name that it is mentioned in all the correspondence of the times, and the generality of the use of that name justifies its adoption for the sake of brevity in future references to the Act herein.

It is a matter of interest in connection with the proceedings leading up to the passage of this law, that evidence of the President's interference with the deliberations of Congress is singularly meager. This is doubtless owing to the fact that, notwithstanding the keen interest which he must have entertained towards the proposition to establish the seat of government on the Potomac, his invariable recognition of the proprieties made him reluctant to obtrusively use his influence in support of a measure in which he necessarily had so strong a personal concern.

That he was nevertheless, a close observer of the course of events, and that he was in conference with and probably helped to furnish arguments to Mr. Madison, who seems to have led the fight for the site on the Potomac, is attested by the following letter to Mr. Madison under date of August 18, 1788:

"I am clearly in sentiment with you that the longer the question respecting the permanent Seat of Congress remains unagitated, the greater certainty there will be of its fixture in a central spot. But not having the same means of information and judging that you have, it would have been a moot point with me, whether a temporary residence of that body at New York would not have been a less likely means of keeping it ultimately from the center (being further removed from it) than if it was to be at Philadelphia; because, in proportion as you draw it to the center, you lessen the inconveniences and of course the solicitude of the Southern and Western extremities; — and when to these are superadded the acquaintances and connections which will naturally be formed — the expenses which more than probably will be incurred for the accommodation of the public officers — with a long train of et ceteras, it might be found an arduous task to approach nearer to the Axis thereafter. These, however, are first thoughts, and may not go to the true principles of policy which govern in this case."

Again, in a letter to Madison, under date of September 23, 1788, he writes:

"Upon mature reflection, I think the reasons you offer in favor of Philadelphia, as the place for the first meeting of Congress, are conclusive; especially when the farther agitation of the question respecting its permanent residence is taken into consideration."

If any further proof of Washington's interest in the premises were required, it is found in the untrammeled authority with which the Residence Act invested the President in carrying out the purpose of that Act coupled with the undivided responsibility for the success of the undertaking, which the statute imposed upon him, obviously in accordance with his preference.

CHAPTER III

Selection of the Site and Acquisition of the Land for the City

WITH the passage of the Residence Act, Congress imposed upon President Washington the task of evolving out of the wilderness, within the space of ten years, a city equipped and ready for the reception of the National Government. It is difficult at this day to bring the mind to a just conception of the magnitude of this task. It was not in the mere administrative proceedings necessary to its performance, though these were formidable, that its chief difficulties lay. The great obstacle to be overcome was the devising and carrying out of a plan whereby the necessary ground should be acquired and the expense of laying out the city and erecting the public buildings be provided for; and this in the face of doubt, distrust, and jealous opposition in every quarter. The President in accomplishing this end was to find his resourcefulness, his great tact and unfailing patience, and his marvelous executive faculties taxed to the uttermost. It is indeed by no means unlikely that the votes necessary to the decision in favor of the Potomac would not have been forthcoming but for the secret conviction in the minds of many that, shorn as the Act was of any appropriation, it imposed upon the President the accomplishment of an impossibility. Certainly the task was one which none but a man of Washington's extraordinary capacity for achievement could hope to accomplish, and which none but a brave man could face without dismay.

From the outset President Washington was fortunate in having the enthusiastic and disinterested encouragement, and advice of his Secretary of State, Mr. Jefferson. It is interesting to speculate as to how far he would ever have gotten in carrying the Residence Law into effect but for the aid which Mr. Jefferson rendered during the early period when the wheels of the federal establishment were being put in motion. While it is impossible from the evidence at hand to be certain where to apportion the credit for what was done, the careful investigator will be forced to conclude that there is at least strong evidence tending to indicate that the solutions of many of the most difficult problems which confronted President Washington were the product of the restless and versatile mind of Mr. Jefferson.

Perhaps the most satisfactory aspect of the association of these two men in this undertaking was the complete harmony that existed between them. President Washington, at all times reserving to himself the final decision, yet gave to the suggestions of Mr. Jefferson the most respectful and thorough consideration; and Mr. Jefferson, while advancing his ideas with the earnestness of an enthusiast, nevertheless did so with the utmost diffidence; and when overruled yielded with a completeness that gave grace even to his reluctance.

That Mr. Madison, also, was an active worker for the new federal seat after the passage of the Residence Act, as he had been in advocating the adoption of the site on the Potomac, is strongly suggested by the evidence at hand, though this evidence is much more fragmentary and incomplete than that which testifies to the activities of Mr. Jefferson.

In putting the Residence Act into operation a number of important questions at once presented themselves to President Washington for his action. It was necessary in the first place to decide at what point on the Potomac River between the Eastern Branch and the Conogocheague the federal territory should be located, and to

18

determine upon the extent and general outlines of the territory. It was necessary at an early date to select three Commissioners fitted for the difficult task of laying out the new city and preparing the public buildings for the reception of the government. It was necessary to devise ways and means for acquiring title to such land as should be needed for government purposes and for obtaining the funds with which to erect the public buildings. Finally, it was necessary to determine upon the location and general plan of the city which was to be established within the federal territory. These matters demanded the personal attention of President Washington. The carrying out of such plans and methods of procedure as he should determine upon would rest in the main with the Commissioners to be appointed by him under the provisions of the Act.

The first active steps by President Washington toward carrying the Residence Law into effect appear to have been taken in the course of a trip to Mount Vernon in the interim between sessions of Congress during the months of September, October and November, 1790. On this trip he was accompanied by Mr. Jefferson and Mr. Madison.

There can be little question that from the outset the President had a very clear idea as to the general location for the federal territory upon which he expected to decide. He was not unfamiliar with the country to which Congress had confined his selection. Five years before the passage of the Act for establishing the seat of government he had organized the Potowmack Company which was to improve the navigation of that river and its tributaries so that the products of the upper country could be brought down the Potomac to communication with deep water shipping at Georgetown. He believed that the point of junction of the upper river navigation with ocean going vessels was destined to be a great commercial center. This point was at or near Georgetown, and the probabilities are that he gave little serious consideration to any other locality than the vicinity of that port, although, as will appear, he did in fact make an investigation with respect to the claims of the regions about the Monocacy and Conogocheague Rivers.

The President was greatly aided in his efforts by the fact that he was well acquainted with the prominent men residing near the Potomac within the limits prescribed by the Residence Act. Many of them had served under him in the Revolutionary Army, and others had been and were then associated with him in the affairs of the Potowmack Company.

During the course of the President's visit td' Mount Vernon he proceeded energetically to ascertain the sentiment of the land owners at various points along the Potomac with regard to concessions they were willing to make with a view to obtaining the establishment of the federal city in their respective neighborhoods. It is evident that even at this time the President had given much thought to the problem of making some arrangement with the owners of the land which would provide for the financing of the city by means of sales of lots to be platted from land which should be conveyed by the original proprietors to the public on terms very favorable to the latter. The subject was in all probability much discussed between the President and Mr. Jefferson, for in a series of notes in Mr. Jefferson's handwriting of proceedings to be had under the Residence Act appears the following query:

"When the President shall have made up his mind as to the spot for the town, would there be any impropriety, in his saying to the neighboring landholders 'I will fix the town here if you will join and purchase and give the lands?' They may well afford it from the increase of value it will give to their own circumjacent lands." Further on, going into the question of the legality of such a proceeding under the terms of the Residence Act, he says:

"6. The completion of the work will depend on a supply of the means. These must consist either of future grants of money by Congress which it would not be prudent to count upon — of State grants — of private grants — or the conversion into money of lands ceded for public use which it is conceived the term 'use' and the spirit and scope of the Act will justify. " Having in mind this solution of the financial problem, the plan seems to have been early decided upon of playing the different localities against each other with a view to quickening among them a spirit of rivalry which should result in the most advantageous terms possible being granted to the public. On this point we again have the evidence of Mr. Jefferson's notes wherein he suggests:

"2. That the President inform himself of the several rival positions; leaving among them inducements to bid against each other in offers of land or money, as the location when completed by the survey will not be mutable by the President, it may be well to have the offers so framed as to become ipso facto absolute in favor of the U. S. on the event which they solicit."

On their arrival at Georgetown, President Washington, Mr. Jefferson and Mr. Madison proceeded to ascertain the views of those owning property between Georgetown and the Eastern Branch. Two gentlemen in whom the President appears to have reposed considerable confidence were William Deakins and Benjamin Stoddert. Another was Charles Carroll. For the substance of the interviews with these gentlemen we are again indebted to Mr. Jefferson's notes. He says:

"In conversation with Mr. Carroll, Mr. Stoddert and Mr. Deakins they were properly impressed with the idea that if the present occasion of securing the Federal seat on the Potowmack should be lost, it could never more be regained, that it would be dangerous to rely on any aids from Congress, or the Assemblies of Virginia or Maryland, and that therefore measures should be adopted to carry the Residence Bill into execution without recourse to those bodies; and that the requisites were 1st land enough to place the public buildings on; and 2ndly money enough to build them, and to erect moreover about 20 good dwelling houses for such persons belonging to the Government as must have houses to themselves, about as many good lodging houses, and half a dozen taverns.

'To obtain this sum, this expedient was suggested to them. To procure a declaration from the proprietors of those spots of land most likely to be fixed for the town, that if the President's location of the town should comprehend their lands, they would give them up for the use of the U. S. on condition they should receive the double of their value, estimated as they would have been had there been no thought of bringing the federal seat into their neighborhood. It was supposed that 1500 acres would be required in the whole, to-wit, about 300 acres for public buildings, walks, etc., and 1200 acres to be divided into quarter acre lots, which, due allowance being made for streets, would make about 2000 lots, the vacant lots in Georgetown now sell at £200, those of Alexandria, at £600. Suppose those of the new town should bring only £100 clear this would produce £200,000 a sum adequate to the objects before mentioned. It was further supposed that the Assembly of

Maryland would interpose to force the consent of infant or obstinate proprietors for a reasonable compensation.

" It was also suggested as a more certain means of ensuring the object, that each proprietor within the whole ten miles square should cede one-half his lands to the public, to be sold to raise money; perhaps this would be pushing them too far for the reputation of the new government they were to come under, and further than is necessary when we consider the sum which may be raised by the sale of lots, the donation of 120,000 dollars by Virginia, and the possible donation of an equal sum by Maryland; at least it might show a commendable moderation not to push this proposition until experiment should prove the other resources inadequate; great zeal appeared in the gentlemen before mentioned, and they seemed to approve the proposition for the 1500 acres; that for a moiety of all the lands within the ten miles square was hazarded only to Mr. Carroll; they will probably proceed immediately to make the best arrangements practicable and to come forward with them to the President."

After visiting with the President at Mount Vernon, Mr. Jefferson and Mr. Madison appear to have visited with General Stevens Thomson Mason, who then owned and resided on Analostan Island, such at least being the probable identity of the person referred to in Mr. Jefferson's account of their visit in a letter to President Washington written from Fredericksburg, Va., on September 17, 1790, wherein he says:

" Sir: In the course of the visit we made the day we left Mount Vernon we drew our host into conversation on the subject of the federal seat. He came into it with a shyness not usual in him. Whether this proceeded from his delicacy as having property adjoining Georgetown or from what other motive I cannot say. He quitted the subject always as soon as he could. He said enough however to show his decided preference of Georgetown. He mentioned shortly in its favor these circumstances: 1. Its being at the junction of the upper and lower navigation where the commodities must be transferred into other vessels: (and here he was confident that no vessel could be contrived which could pass the upper shoals and live in the wide waters below his island). 2. The depth of water which would admit any vessels that could come to Alexandria. 3. Narrowness of the river and consequent safeness of the harbor. 4. Its being clear of ice as early at least as the canal and river above would be clear. 5. Its neighborhood to the Eastern Branch whither any vessels might conveniently withdraw which should be detained through the winter. 6. Its defensibility, as derived from the high and commanding hills around it. 7. Its actual possession of the commerce and the start it already has.

"He spoke of Georgetown always in comparison with Alexandria. When led to mention the Eastern Branch he spoke of it as an admirable position, superior in all respects to Alexandria."

Not feeling justified in confining his attention to the vicinity of Georgetown and the Eastern Branch, President Washington later took a trip up the river for the purpose of investigating the advantages of the various available sites in that region. The Georgetown newspapers of October 26, 1790, state that the previous Friday President Washington had arrived in town and that in company with the principal gentlemen of the town he had set out to view the adjacent country in order to fix upon a future situation for "the Grand Columbian Federal City," and that he left on

Saturday for the Great Falls and Conogocheague. In this work he enlisted the services of Francis Deakins, the brother of Col. William Deakins, whom he commissioned to make a plat of the lands in the neighborhood of the Monocacy and the Conogocheague and to obtain such propositions as the land owners might see fit to put forward. Mr. Deakins reported the results of his efforts in the following letter to the President at Mount Vernon:

"Monocacy, November 12th, 1790. " Sir: I now enclose you a draft of the Lands you viewed about this place, with the offers the proprietors has made for the use of the public buildings, etc. You'l please to Consider our neighborrs as retired Industrious planters having no income but the produce of their farms; not more than a moderate Support for their families, as a Reason why they have not been more Liberal.

"I expected Mr. Williams to have sent me some papers and notes about the mouth of Conogocheague which has not come to hand, his Brother Genl. Williams, was up immediately after you, who I suppose will make that return to you.

"Having no assistance in laying down the plats — much other business on hand and a faint expectation of its possessing superior advantages to any other place, I hope will in some degree apologize for the roughness of it.

"I have the honor to be Sir,

Your most obedt Servt

Francis Deakins. "

In the meantime Col. William Deakins had been active among the proprietors of the lands lying between Georgetown and the Eastern Branch with the result that on November 3rd he wrote from Georgetown to the President at Mount Vernon:

"Sir: The day after you left this place we employed a Surveyor to lay down our Situations, but it has taken more time than we expected, to ascertain the exact Quantity of Land held by each proprietor within the lines laid down. I expect on Sunday or Monday next to hand you the plan and proposals from the holders of the land. "I am, very respectfully,

Sir, Your obdt Servt

Will Deakins, Junr. "

The proposal from the owners of the land to which Mr. Deakins referred was in the following language:

"We, the subscribers, do hereby agree and oblige ourselves, our heirs, Executors and Administrators, to sell and make over by sufficient Deeds, in any manner which shall be directed by General Washington, or any person acting under him, and on such terms as he shall determine to be reasonable and just, any of the Lands which we possess in the vicinity of George-Town, for the uses of the Federal City provided the same shall be erected in the said vicinity.

"Witness our hands this thirteenth day of October, 1790. Robt. Peter, for One hundred Acres, should so much of mine be tho't necessary.

Thos. Beall of Geo.

Benj. Stoddert. "

Uriah Forrest.

Will Deakins, Junr.

John Stoddard, Any land on the north side of my meadow.

J. M. Lingan, George Beall, Anthony Holmead."

Accompanying this proposal was a lengthy statement setting forth the merits of Georgetown as an harbor and place of residence, the opening and closing of which recited:

"The object of the subscribers to the paper annexed, is to accommodate, — they will cheerfully consent to any other arrangement, that may be thought reasonable, should their Lands, or any part of them, be selected for the Federal City.

" They are induced to make the offer of their Lands under the idea that if the Federal City should be erected on navigation, no place in the small distance from the mouth of the Eastern Branch, to the highest Tide water, offers so many advantages and that to none there can be so few solid objections, as to George Town and its immediate vicinity.

"The subscribers cannot but be of opinion (and where their observations are just, they will not bear less weight for coming from men interested) that the speediest means of extending the town all over and between the Country between Georgetown and the Eastern Branch, would be, to erect the Federal Buildings adjacent to George-Town — in such an event no doubts could be entertained of the rapid improvement of the City and Country around it. — No buildings would be omitted in consequence of apprehensions that the Seat of Government might not after all be on Potowmak, for all men would be satisfied that if disappointed in this favorite object, their improvements would still afford them ample compensation for their expenses, from being in a large Commercial Town."

The plat which had been prepared for the proprietors as mentioned by Mr. Deakins was probably one by Beatty and Orme, reference to which will later be found in President Washington's correspondence with Messrs. Stoddert and Deakins.

The President appears to have requested of Mr. Deakins to procure an extension of this plat to include Georgetown and to have taken up with the proprietors the question of a conveyance from them to the public on the basis of every third lot being reconveyed to the proprietors, for shortly after Mr. Deakins' letter of November 3rd we find him writing to the President who was just about to start on his return to Philadelphia:

"Geo. Town, Novr. 18th, 1790. "Sir: I saw my brother a few days ago and he tells me he will have the Platts for the Situations above Lodged in my hands by Monday next, to be delivered on your way through this place and I will also have another plan of our situation with the Streets of Georgetown and its additions Laid down for your Information.

"If the second proposition of the proprietors should be preferred, that is for them to retain every third Lott in the Federal Town you may Extend the Limits to 3,000 As. "I am with every Sentiment of Respect and Esteem, Your obt servt,

Will Deakins, Junr."

While the negotiations with the proprietors of the land were going on the President was proceeding with the other duties imposed upon him by the Residence Act. One of those duties was the naming of the three Commissioners to carry on the work of preparing the new federal seat for the reception of the Government. Diverse considerations were to be weighed in this connection. On this subject Mr. Jefferson's notes are again a source of valuable information and throw much light upon the considerations by which the President was influenced in making his selection.

With regard to the Commissioners to be appointed Mr. Jefferson says:

"3. Commissioners to be appointed.

"I suppose them not entitled to any salary.

"(If they live near the place, they may, in some instances, be influenced by self-interest, and partialities; but they will push the work with zeal; if they are from a distance and northwardly, they will be more impartial, but may affect delays.) "

Further on he continues:

"The act for establishing the temporary and permanent seat of Government of the U. States requires the following steps for carrying the latter into effect.

"1. The appointment of three Commissioners of sufficient respectability having good will to the general object without any particular bias of private interest.

"Should it be advisable after securing a majority near at hand to make an appointment with a view to attach particular parts of the Union to the object. N. England particularly Massachusetts, first occurs — and next, S. Carolina and Georgia. Mr. Ellicot (Mr. Gorum, Mr. Bull) Mr. Fitzhugh (of Chatham) Mr. 0. Wolcott, Mr. Tucker, Mr. Lloyd (of Annapolis), Mr. ———— of R. I., Mr. Baldwin, Rev'd. Mr. Lee Massey." And again:

"The Commissioners should have some taste in Architecture, because they may have to decide between different plans.

"They will however be subject to the President's direction in every point."

The result of the President's deliberations was the selection of Thomas Johnson, Daniel Carroll and David Stuart, and the issuance of a commission to them in the following form:

"(Seal) George Washington, President of the United States.

"To all who shall see these presents, Greetings: "Know ye, that reposing special trust and confidence in the integrity, skill, and diligence of Thos. Johnson and Daniel Carroll, of Maryland, and David Stuart, of Virginia, I do, in pursuance of the powers vested in me by the act entitled 'An Act for establishing the temporary and permanent seat of the Government of the United States, approved July 16, 1790, hereby appoint them, the said Thomas Johnson, Daniel Carroll, and David Stuart, commissioners for surveying the district of territory accepted by the said act for the permanent seat of the Government of the United States, and for performing such other offices as by law are directed, with full authority for them, or any two of them, to proceed therein according to law, and to have and to hold the said office, with all the powers, privileges, and authorities to the same of right appertaining each of them, during the pleasure of the President of the United States for the time being.

"In testimony whereof I have caused these letters to be made patent and the seal of the United States thereto affixed.

"Given under my hand at the city of Philadelphia, the twenty-second day of January, in year of our Lord one thousand seven hundred and ninety-one and of the Independence of the United States the fifteenth.

George Washington.

By the President:

Thomas Jefferson."

Thomas Johnson was a resident of Frederick, Maryland, and an old friend of President Washington. Prior to the Revolutionary War he had been interested with the latter in the project of rendering the upper Potomac and its tributaries navigable by a series of improvements in the channel and the construction of canals around the Great and Little Falls. As one of the Representatives of the State of Maryland in the Continental Congress he had nominated Washington to be Commander-in-Chief of the Continental Army and he had later served under General Washington in the Army. After the Revolutionary War he had taken an active part with Washington in reviving the project of improving the navigation of the Potomac, and after the organization of the Potowmack Company for that purpose in 1785, had given special attention to the supervision of the work which the company undertook. He had been the Governor of his State, and at the time of his appointment as Commissioner was its Chief Justice. Shortly after his appointment as Commissioner, President Washington appointed him to the Supreme Court of the United States to take the seat vacated by Mr. Rutledge. He continued to serve as Commissioner while holding his place on the Supreme Bench. He was of a brusque, impetuous temperament, and was strongly addicted to swearing, though he is spoken of as generous and warm hearted.

President Washington probably was moved by a number of considerations to name Mr. Johnson as one of the Commissioners. He knew that the latter 's residence near the location of the new city and his interest in the Potowmack Company would give him a strong incentive to push the development of the city. He knew from observation of Mr. Johnson's efforts in directing the work of the Potowmack Company that he was a man of great energy and executive capacity. He knew him to be an astute lawyer, thoroughly grounded in the Maryland laws and he doubtless anticipated that such a man would be invaluable as legal adviser to the Commission and particularly in preparing the conveyances which would be required in carrying out his scheme for acquiring the site for the proposed city and in drafting such legislation as would be needed to facilitate the work of the Commission.

Daniel Carroll was a resident of Carroll Springs, Montgomery County, Maryland. He was born at Upper Marlboro, and with his brother John Carroll had received a finished education abroad. His brother entered the priesthood and later became the first Catholic Bishop of Baltimore and the founder of Georgetown Academy — afterwards Georgetown University.

Daniel Carroll had been a member of the Continental Congress and of the Constitutional Convention and at the time of his appointment as Commissioner was a member of the United States House of Representatives from Maryland. On this account he declined to accept the appointment as Commissioner until the expiration of his term in Congress on March 4, 1791, when a new Commission was sent him. He was commonly spoken of as Daniel Carroll of Rock Creek to distinguish him from Daniel Carroll of Duddington.

David Stuart was President Washington's family physician, and a resident of Alexandria, Va. He had married the widow of John Parke Custis, the son of the President's wife. He had long been the trusted advisor of President Washington whose correspondence during the early years of his presidency contains numerous letters to Dr. Stuart explaining the President's attitude on public questions, inquiring as to the state of public opinion and soliciting the Doctor's views and advice. In a sense the Doctor may be regarded as having been the President's personal representative in the Commission.

The Commission was directed to Mr. Carroll with a letter notifying him of his appointment. A similar letter was sent to the other appointees. These letters are in the handwriting of Mr. Jefferson by whom they were probably prepared. That to Mr. Carroll reads:

"Philadelphia, January 24th, 1791.

"Dear Sir: The President of the United States desirous of availing himself of your assistance in preparing the federal seat on the Potomac is in hopes you will act as one of the Commissioners directed by the Law for that purpose. I have the honor now to enclose a joint commission for yourself and two others, together with a copy of the Proclamation meant to constitute your first direction. The President will from time to time communicate such further directions as circumstances shall call for.

" I have the honor to be with great esteem.

Dear Sir, Your most obt and most h'ble servt.

Honorable Daniel Carroll."

The organization of the Commission as a whole was delayed owing to the doubt expressed by Mr. Carroll as to his qualifications for the position during his term as Congressman. Mr. Jefferson, however, wrote to the other two, calling attention to the provision in the law which authorized two Commissioners to act and they took steps looking to the organization of the Commission prior to Mr. Carroll's qualifying for the position. The first full meeting occurred on April 12, 1791.

While the President was deciding upon the selection of the Commissioners he was devoting much thought to the determination of the exact location, extent and outlines of the territory not exceeding ten miles square within which the Federal City was to be located.

As to the question of extent, the probabilities are that President Washington at no time gave serious consideration to the acquisition of less than the full quantity of land allowed by the Residence Act, though Mr. Jefferson was for a time at least disposed to regard an area five miles each way as sufficient. Both President Washington and Mr. Jefferson, however, quickly perceived the extreme desirability of including both shores of the Eastern Branch, Mr. Jefferson going so far as to strongly advocate the inclusion of Bladensburg, which at that time was an important point for the shipment of tobacco. President Washington was also desirous of including the town of Alexandria.

The difficulty in carrying out this plan was the provision in the Residence Act requiring the federal territory to be located above the Eastern Branch. A means of surmounting this difficulty was, however, soon devised and is set forth by Mr. Jefferson in his notes on the Federal City, where, in his enumeration of the steps to be taken under the Residence Act he includes:

"3. That the President direct the Survey of the District which he shall ultimately elect. It seems essential that the District should comprehend the water adjoining the establishment and eligible that it should comprehend the opposite shore. The legality of this seems to be decided by the clause confining the purchase or acceptance of land for the use of the U. S. 'to the East side of the river within the said district' which imply that the whole district was not necessarily to be on that side. Quer: whether it will not be convenient to accept in the first instance so much less than ten miles square as will allow places to be afterwards taken in, which may not now be obtainable, or it may not be prudent now to accept."

Further on in a series of queries he suggests the solution which was eventually adopted. He asks:

"Would it not be well if a position below the little falls should be decided on, to begin the ten miles just above the commencement of the canal; and accept from Maryland, for the present, only from thence down to the Eastern Branch, supposed about seven miles; and to accept from Virginia ten miles beginning at the lower end of Alexandria, and running up as far as it will extend, which probably will be as far up as the commencement of the Maryland side this being accepted, and professedly (as to Maryland) in part only of their session, when Congress shall meet they may pass an amendatory bill authorizing the President to complete his acceptance from Maryland by crossing the Eastern Branch and completing the ten miles in that direction, which will bring the lower boundary on the Maryland side very nearly opposite to that on the Virginia side — it is understood that the breadth of the territory accepted will be of five miles only on each side." The plan outlined by Mr. Jefferson in being put into operation was modified in that instead of limiting the sides of the territory to five miles and locating the territory below the Little Falls, the sides were given the full length of ten miles allowed by the law and the territory made to extend a considerable distance above the Little Falls. Conformably to this plan President Washington on January 24, 1791, issued his proclamation announcing the location of one part of the district by running as "lines of experiment" the lines which he expected would constitute the boundaries of the District when finally designated.

The text of this proclamation follows:

"By the President of the United States of America.

A PROCLAMATION.

"Whereas the General Assembly of the State of Maryland, by an Act passed on the 23rd day of December, 1788, entitled, 'An Act to cede to Congress a district of ten miles square in this State for the seat of Government of the United States,' did enact, that the representatives of the said State in the House of Representatives of the Congress of the United States, appointed to assemble at New York on the first Wednesday of March then next ensuing, should be, and they were thereby, authorized and required, on the behalf of the said State, to cede to the Congress of the United States any district in the said State not exceeding ten miles square, which the Congress might fix upon and accept for the seat of Government of the United States.

"And the General Assembly of the Commonwealth of Virginia, by an act passed on the 3rd day of December, 1789, and entitled 'An act for the cession of ten miles square, or any lesser quantity of territory within this State, to the United States in Congress assembled, for the permanent seat of the General Government,' did enact, that a tract of country not exceeding ten square miles, or any lesser quantity, to be located within the limits of the said State, and in any part thereof, as Congress might by law direct, should be and the same was thereby forever ceded and relinquished to the Congress and Government of the United States, in full and absolute right, and exclusive jurisdiction, as well of soil as of persons residing or to reside thereon, pursuant to the tenor and effect of the eighth section of the first article of the Constitution of Government of the United States:

"And the Congress of the United States, by their act passed the 16th day of July, 1790, and entitled 'An act for establishing the temporary and permanent seat of the Government of the United States,' authorized the President of the United States to appoint three commissioners to survey under his direction, and by proper metes and bounds to limit a district of territory not exceeding ten miles square on the river Potomac, at some place between the mouth of the Eastern Branch and Conogocheague, which district, so to be located and limited, was accepted by the said Act of Congress as the district for the permanent seat of the Government of the United States.

" Now, therefore, in pursuance of the powers to me confided, and after duly examining and weighing the advantages and disadvantages of the several situations within the limits aforesaid, I do hereby declare and make known that the location of one part of the said district of ten miles square shall be found by running four lines of experiment in the following manner, that is to say: Running from the court house of Alexandria, in Virginia, due southwest half a mile, and thence a due southeast course till it shall strike Hunting Creek, to fix the beginning of the said four lines of experiment.

"Then beginning the first of the said four lines of experiment at the point on Hunting Creek, where the said southeast course shall have struck the same, and running the said first line due northwest ten miles; thence the second into Maryland, due northeast ten miles; thence the third line due southeast ten miles; and thence the fourth line due southwest ten miles, to the beginning on Hunting Creek.

"And the said four lines of experiment being so run, I do hereby declare and make known that all that part within the said four lines of experiment which shall be within the State of Maryland, and above the Eastern Branch, and all that part within the same four lines of experiment which shall be within the Commonwealth of Virginia, and above a line to be run from the point of land forming the Upper Cape of the mouth of the Eastern Branch due southwest, and no more, is now fixed upon, and directed to be surveyed, defined, limited, and located for a part of the said district accepted by the said Act of Congress for the permanent seat of the Government of the United States; hereby expressly reserving the direction of the survey and location of the remaining part of the said district, to be made hereafter contiguous to such part or parts of the present location as is or shall be agreeably to law.

"And I do accordingly direct the said commissioners, appointed agreeably to the tenor of the said Act, to proceed forthwith to run the said lines of experiment, and, the same being run, to survey and, by proper metes and bounds, to define and limit the part within the same which is hereinbefore directed for immediate location and acceptance, and thereof to make due report to me under their hands and seals.

"In testimony whereof I have caused the seal of the United States to be affixed to these presents, and signed the same with my hand-presents and city of Philadelphia the 24th day of January, in the year of our Lord 1791, and of the Independence of the United States the fifteenth.

George Washington.

By the President:

Thomas Jefferson."

The President, having had a number of these proclamations printed, sent them to Messrs. Stoddert and Deakins, with the following letter requesting the publication of them:

"Gentlemen: I enclose you several proclamations expressing the lines which are to bound the District of ten miles square for the permanent seat of the General Government, which I wish you to have made public with all expedition, and in the most general and extensive manner that you can to prevent any kind of speculation, let them be published in the newspapers — put up in public places and otherwise so disposed as to answer my object as fully as possible. The proclamations are this moment struck off and the mail is about to be closed, which prevents me from adding more at this time; but I shall write you more fully upon this subject in a few days.

I am, sir, Your most obt servt,
George Washington.
United States, January 24, 1791."

This proclamation the President sent to Congress with the following letter suggesting the enactment of a law so amending the Residence Act as to permit him to carry out the object sought:

" Gentlemen: In execution of the powers with which Congress were pleased to invest me by their act entitled, ' An Act for establishing the temporary and permanent seat of the Government of the United States' and on mature consideration of the advantages and disadvantages of the several positions within the limits prescribed by the said Act I have, by a proclamation bearing date this day directed Commissioners, appointed in pursuance of the Act, to survey and limit a part of the territory of ten miles square on both sides of the river Potomac so as to comprehend Georgetown in Maryland and to extend to the Eastern Branch. I have not by this first act given to the said territory the whole extent of which it is susceptible in the direction of the river; because I thought it important that Congress should have an opportunity of considering whether by an amendatory law they would authorize the location of the residue at the lower end of the present location so as to comprehend the Eastern Branch itself and some of the country on its lower side in the State of Maryland, and the town of Alexandria in Virginia; if however they should think that the federal territory should be bounded by the water edge of the Eastern Branch, the location of the residue will be to be made at the upper end of what is now directed. A copy of the proclamation is enclosed for your more particular information. I have thought it best to await a survey of the territory before it is decided in what part of it the public buildings shall be erected." The result of the President's request was the passage by Congress of an amendatory Act, approved March 3, 1791, repealing so much of the original Residence Act "as requires that the whole of the district or territory, not exceeding ten miles square shall be located above the mouth of the Eastern Branch," and making it lawful "for the President to make any part of the territory below the said limit, and above the mouth of Hunting Creek, a part of the said district, so as to include a convenient part of the Eastern Branch, and of the lands on the lower side thereof, and also the town of Alexandria. " The Act closed with a proviso to the effect that nothing therein contained should authorize the erection of the public buildings otherwise than on the Maryland side of the river Potomac.

Previous to the passage of this Act steps had been taken looking to a survey of the ten miles square.

On February 1st, 1791, President Washington wrote to Mr. Jefferson:

"Tuesday Evening. "My dear Sir: Nothing in the enclosed letter superseding the necessity of Mr. Ellicott's proceeding to the work in hand I would thank you, for requesting him, to set out on Thursday; or as soon after as he can make it convenient: Also for preparing such instructions as you may conceive it necessary for me to give him for ascertaining the points we wish to know; first, for the general view of things and next for the more accurate and final decision. Yrs. Sincerely and affly.,

George Washington. "

Pursuant to this request Mr. Jefferson wrote to Major Ellicott "to proceed by the first stage to the Federal Territory on the Potomac for the purpose of making a survey of it. "

Andrew Ellicott was a native of Pennsylvania, born January 24, 1754, and was consequently just entering his thirty-eighth year when this commission was given him. He had served in the Revolutionary Army, rising to the rank of Major. At the time of his appointment to the task of surveying the Federal Territory he had just come from the completed surveys of boundary lines of the great central states of New York, Pennsylvania, Maryland and Virginia, in most of which important and responsible work he was chosen Commissioner as well as astronomer and surveyor. The determination of the west boundary of the State of New York, it being the limit of the Massachusetts claim and a subject of National import was made by him pursuant to a joint resolution of the old and the new Congress, under the direction of President Washington. From this duty Maj. Ellicott came to the Federal District, directly in the line of his continuing official duty as Geographer General, and not as one engaged for the occasion.

On February 14, Major Ellicott arrived in Alexandria and wrote his wife:

"I have been treated with great politeness by the inhabitants, who are truly rejoiced at the prospect of being included in the Federal district. I shall leave this town this afternoon to begin the rough survey of the ten miles square. "

On the same day he wrote Mr. Jefferson telling him of the progress of his work, ending with the lines:

"You will observe by the plan which I have suggested for the permanent location a small deviation with respect to the courses from those mentioned in the proclamation. The reason of which is that the courses in the proclamation strictly adhered to would neither produce straight lines nor contain quite the ten miles square besides the almost impossibility of running such lines with tolerable exactness. "

Major Ellicott was assisted in the work of laying off the Federal Territory by Messrs. Briggs and Fenwick, his brother Benjamin Ellicott, and the negro astronomer and mathematician, Benjamin Banneker, a free negro who had already attracted the attention of Washington and Jefferson by his wonderful mathematical ability. He was a protege of Major Ellicott and of his father, Joseph Ellicott. His knowledge of the exact sciences was remarkable, and he was able on a number of occasions to indicate errors in the "Nautical Almanac" which had before passed unnoticed.

Major Ellicott had at first little appreciation of the site that had been selected for the Federal Territory, a letter to his wife during the period ending:

"The country intended for the Permanent Residence of Congress, bears no more proportion to the country about Philadelphia and German-Town, for either wealth or fertility, than a crane does to a stall-fed Ox! "

In order to provide for Major Ellicott 's expenses the President, pursuant to a previous understanding, wrote to Thomas Beall, the Mayor of Georgetown, as follows:

"Philadelphia, February 3rd, 1791.

"Sir: In consequence of your letter of the 26th of January to Daniel Carroll, Esquire, informing him that the order of the President of the United States upon you as Mayor of Georgetown, would be paid on sight, I have to request that you will answer the demands of Andrew Ellicott, Esquire, within the sum of fifty guineas, as he may have occasion to make them without further advice from Your most obedient servant,

George Washington. "

In the meantime Major Pierre Charles L' Enfant had been selected by the President to make a preliminary survey of the site of the proposed city. About the first of March, the letter bearing date, merely March, 1791, Mr. Jefferson wrote to Major L 'Enfant as follows:

"Sir: You are desired to proceed to Georgetown where you will find Mr. Ellicott employed in making a survey and maps of the Federal Territory. The special object of asking your aid is to have the drawings of the particular grounds most likely to be approved for the site of the Federal town and buildings. You will therefore be pleased to begin on the Eastern Branch and proceed from thence upwards, laying down the hills, valleys, morasses, and waters between that, the Potomac, the Tiber, and the road leading from Georgetown to the Eastern Branch, and connecting the whole with certain fixed points on the maps Mr. Ellicott is preparing. Some idea of the height of the lands above the base on which they stand would be desirable. For necessary assistance and expenses be pleased to apply to the Mayor of Georgetown who is written to on this subject. I will beg the favour of you to mark to me your progress about twice a week, by letter, say every Wednesday and Saturday evening, that I may be able in proper time to draw your attention to some other objects which I have not at this moment sufficient information to define. " I am with great esteem, Sir,

Your most obedient humble sevt.,

Th. Jefferson.

Majr L 'Enfant."

Major L 'Enfant had come to America in the fall of 1777, with Monsieur Ducoudray. He was promoted to a Captaincy of Engineers, February 18, 1778, and after the war granted the rank of major by brevet on his own application. He had been wounded at the siege of Savannah and made a prisoner at Charleston. He is stated to have been born in France, August 2, 1755. He would thus have been only twenty-two years of age on his coming to this country — scarcely old enough to have had any engineering experience — and thirty-six at the time of his employment on the Federal City. Subsequent to the Revolution he lived for a time with the Calverts, near Marlboro, Maryland. Going back to France on a mission connected with the

Order of Cincinnati and again returning to America he obtained employment as an architect in the reconstruction of the building at New York for the meeting of the first Federal Congress. He is described as fully six feet tall erect and of a military bearing, with a finely proportioned figure and prominent nose.

The work of L 'Enfant in connection with the remodeling of the New York Capitol building had come to the notice of President Washington. His attention had been further drawn to the French Engineer by a direct application by the latter for appointment to the task of laying out the new Federal city. In making this application, L 'Enfant had taken time by the forelock, as the Act fixing the site on the Potomac was not passed until nearly ten months later.

In his letter, which bore date September 11, 1789, in which, from the quality of the English employed, he doubtless had the aid of an amanuensis, as his other letters display a very defective knowledge of the idiomatic nature of the English language, he said:

"The late determination of Congress to lay the foundation of a city, which is to become the Capital of this vast empire, offers so great an occasion of acquiring reputation to whoever may be appointed to conduct the execution of the business that your excellency will not be surprised that my ambition and the desire I have of becoming a useful citizen should lead me to wish a share in the undertaking.

"No nation, perhaps, had ever before the opportunity offered them of deliberately deciding on the spot where their capital city should be fixed or of combining every necessary consideration in the choice of situation, and although the means now within the power of the country are not such as to pursue the design to any great extent it will be obvious that the plan should be drawn on such a scale as to leave room for the aggrandizement and embellishment which the increase of the wealth of the nation will permit it to pursue at any period, however remote. Viewing the matter in this light, I am fully sensible of the extent of the undertaking, and under the hope of a continuance of the indulgence you have hitherto honored me with I now presume to solicit the favor of being employed in this business." The letter continued with a recommendation that the preparation of a system of coast fortifications be at once commenced and a request for appointment to the Engineer Corps where he could engage in the fortification work as well as in such work of a civil character as might require his attention.

Concerning the arrival at Georgetown of Majors Ellicott and L 'Enfant, the Georgetown Weekly Ledger of March 12, 1791, says:

"Sometime last month arrived in this town Major Andrew Ellicott, a gentleman of superior astronomical abilities. He was appointed by the President of the United States to lay off a tract of land ten miles square on the Potomac for the use of Congress. He is now engaged in this business and hopes soon to accomplish the object of his mission. He is attended by Benjamin Banniker, an Ethiopian, whose abilities as a surveyor and astronomer clearly prove that Mr. Jefferson's concluding that race of men were void of mental endowments was without foundation.

"Wednesday evening arrived in this town Major Longfont a French gentleman employed by the President of the United States to survey the lands contiguous to Georgetown where the Federal city is to be built. His skill in matters of this kind is justly extolled by all disposed to give merit its proper tribute of praise. He is earnest in the business and hopes to be able to lay a plat of that parcel of land before the

President upon his arrival in this town. " Major L 'Enfant wrote to Mr. Jefferson on March 11, 1791, reciting his arrival on the 9th and his review of the ground the following day, the Mayor of Georgetown having offered his assistance in procuring three or four men to attend him in the surveying. It is evident that even in this brief view of the ground he grasped many of the possibilities which it offered, for he says:

"As far as I was able to judge through a thick fog I passed on many spots which appeared to me really beautiful and which seem to dispute with each other who command. In the most extensive prospect on the water the gradual rising of the ground from Carrollborough toward the Ferry Road, the level and extensive ground from there to the bank of the Potomac as far as Goose Creek present a situation most advantageous to run streets and prolong them on grand and far distant point of view. "

Previous to Major L 'Enfant 's appointment, and while Major Ellicott was preparing to make his survey of the ten miles square President Washington had been continuing his efforts to obtain suitable terms from the owners of such land as he deemed necessary for the Federal town.

By this time it is evident that the President had come to the conclusion that little could be accomplished so long as he worked in the open to reach an agreement with the land owners, as the prospect of a speedy inflation of the values of their lands had aroused a degree of cupidity in the owners which no appeal to their public spirit was effective to counteract. Accordingly he determined to abandon his tactics of direct approach and to endeavor to make terms with the proprietors through secret agents who should adopt the appearance of being engaged in a speculation of their own. For this purpose he selected Messrs. Deakins and Stoddert who had acted far him before in making arrangements with the land owners. To these gentlemen he wrote from Philadelphia under date of February 3, 1791:

"Philadelphia, February 3rd, 1791. " Gentlemen: In asking your aid in the following case permit me at the same time to ask the most perfect secrecy. "The Federal Territory being located, the competition for the location of the town now rests between the mouth of the Eastern Branch and the lands on the river below and adjacent to Georgetown.

"In favor of the former, Nature has furnished powerful advantages. In favor of the latter is its vicinity to Georgetown which puts it in the way of deriving aids from it in the beginning, and of communicating in return an increased value to the property of that town. These advantages have been so poised in my mind as to give it different tendencies at different times. There are lands which stand yet in the way of the latter location and which, if they could be obtained for the purposes of the town, would remove a considerable obstacle to it, and go near indeed to decide what has been so long on the balance with me.

"These are, first, the lands on the S. West side of a line to be run from where the road crosses Goose Creek in going from Georgetown to the Eastern Branch to the corner of Charles Beatty's lot; including by the plat of Beatty and Orme the house of William Peerce; or if the whole of this parcel cannot be obtained, then secondly, so much as would lie within a line to be run from the said ford, or thereabouts, to the middle of the line of cession which extends from the corner of Beatty's lot, as above mentioned, to its termination on Goose Creek; thirdly, the lands of Mr. Carroll between Goose Creek, the river and Mr. Young, to the same ford of the creek.

"The object of this letter is to ask you to endeavor to purchase these grounds of the owners for the public, particularly the second parcel, but as if for yourselves, and to conduct your propositions so as to excite no suspicion that they are on behalf of the public.

"The circumstances of the funds appropriated by the States of Virginia and Maryland, will require that a twelve months credit be stipulated, in order that they may cover you from any inconvenience which might attend your personal undertakings. As the price at which the lands can be obtained would have its weight also with me, I would wish that in making your bargains you should reserve to yourselves a fortnight's time to consider, at the end of which you should be free to be off or on, but the seller not so. This will admit your writing to me and receiving my definitive answer.

" A clear purchase is so preferable to every other arrangement, that I should scarcely think any other worthy attention.

"I am obliged to add that all the dispatch is requisite which can consist with the success of your operations, and that I shall be glad to hear by post of your progress, and prospect of the accomplishment of this business, in whole or part.

"I am, Gentlemen, Your most Obe'd Hble, &c,

George Washington.

Messrs. Deakins and Stoddart.

"P. S. — That my description of the lands required in the foregoing letter may be more clearly understood, and my wishes further explained, I enclose you a rough (and very rough indeed it is) copy of the ceded tracts, roads, etc., of Messrs. Beatty and Orme's Survey — adding thereto lines of augmentation. To obtain the lands included within the lines A, B and C is my first wish, and next to that the lands within the lines D, E and F; but those within the lines D, E, and along the Creek to G, are indispensably necessary; and being not over 250 acres might, I suppose, be easily obtained. It ought to be the first essay and I wish to know as soon as possible the result of it, before any others are directly attempted. G. W. "

It is difficult to gather from this letter the precise areas to which the President referred, the sketch to which it relates being apparently no longer in existence; yet it is evident that he was endeavoring to extend the limits of the proposed cessions as far as possible to the northeast. He had at the same time been making every effort through Deakins and Stoddert to acquire the land of David Burnes and other proprietors nearer Georgetown. These lands then appeared to be indispensable, owing to the unwillingness of the proprietors of the lands near the Eastern Branch to come to satisfactory terms. Accordingly President Washington, on February 17th wrote to Deakins and Stoddert:

" Gentlemen: I have received your favor of the 9th and 11th inst. and shall be glad if the purchase from Burns should be concluded before you receive this at £18 or £12 — 10 as you choose, but as you mention that should he ask as far as £20 or £25, you will await further instructions before you accept such an offer. I have thought it better, in order to prevent delay, to inform you that I would wish his lands to be purchased even at those prices, rather than not obtain them." Mr. Burnes, however, appears to have been obdurate, and the President resolved to adopt the tactics suggested in Mr. Jefferson's notes of "leaving them inducements to bid against each other." Accordingly the President wrote Messrs. Deakins and Stoddert on February 28th:

" Gentlemen: If you have concluded nothing yet with Mr. Burns nor made him any offer for his land that is obligatory I pray you to suspend your negotiations with him until you hear further from me.

"With much esteem, I am, Gen'n. Yrs. &c,

G. W."

Following this letter to Deakins and Stoddert, Mr. Jefferson about March 1st wrote his letter of instructions to Major L 'Enfant before quoted, directing him to "begin on the Eastern Branch and proceed from thence upwards," the purpose being to thereby convey to Mr. Burnes and the other proprietors having lands towards Georgetown the impression that it had been determined to locate the Federal buildings near the Eastern Branch. In explanation of these instructions to Major L 'Enfant the President on March 2nd wrote to Deakins and Stoddert for their private information as follows:

"Philadelphia, March 2nd, 1791. "Gentlemen: Major L 'Enfant comes on to make such a survey of the grounds in your vicinity as may aid in fixing the site of the Federal town and buildings. His present instructions express those alone which are within the Eastern Branch, the Potomac, the Tiber, and the road leading from Georgetown to the ferry on the Eastern Branch; he is directed to begin at the lower end and work upwards, and nothing further is communicated to him.

The purpose of this letter is to desire you will not be yourselves misled by this appearance, nor be diverted from the pursuit of the objects I have recommended to you. I expect that your progress in accomplishing them will be facilitated by the presumption which will arise on seeing this operation begun at the Eastern Branch, and that the proprietors nearer Georgetown who have hitherto refused to accommodate, will let themselves down to reasonable terms. I have referred Maj. L 'Enfant to the Mayor of Georgetown for necessary aids and expenses. Should there be any difficulties on this subject, I would hope your aid in having them surmounted tho' I have not named you to him or anybody else, that no suspicion may be excited of your acting for the public.

I am, gentlemen. (No signature on letter press copy.) Messieurs Stoddert and Deakins. " At this point it is necessary to call attention to the fact that within the territory lying between Georgetown and the Eastern Branch were two unincorporated towns — known respectively as Hamburgh and Carrollsburgh. Hamburgh was a platted town laid out by Jacob Punk, and was known also as Punkstown. It contained 130 acres, subdivided into 287 lots, and was located with a frontage on the Potomac River, just above the mouth of what was then Goose or Tiber Creek. It was bounded on the north by a line about on the present location of H Street, northwest, on the east by a line about midway between the present locations of Eighteenth and Nineteenth Streets, west, and on the west by a line approximately on the line of the present location of Twenty-third Street, west. The plat is recorded at Marlborough, Maryland, under date of October 28, 1771. The land appears to have been purchased by Funk from Thomas Johns in 1765.

Carrollsburgh was located between the north bank of the Eastern Branch and James Creek. It was bounded on the north by a line from a point on James Creek a few feet north of the present N Street bridge over that stream to a point on the

Eastern Branch about midway between the terminations of N and Streets, south. It contained approximately 160 acres, subdivided into 268 lots under terms of a deed of trust recorded at Marlborough, November 20, 1770. This deed runs from Charles Carroll, Jr., to Henry Kozier, Daniel Carroll and Notley Young, and authorized the grantees to subdivide Duddington Manor and Duddington Pasture, and to sell the lots except six, to be selected by the grantor, his heirs or assigns, and to draw the lots or cause them to be drawn for by ballot or lottery. The deeds of conveyance to the lots in Carrollsburgh, which are numerous, recite the fact that the lots had been drawn by the grantees respectively, in a lottery of the same. The drawing of lots by lottery was in accordance with a custom which at that time was quite prevalent.

On his way to Philadelphia the preceding November, President Washington had requested Messrs. Deakins and Stoddert to make inquiries as to the ownership of the Hamburgh lots. The results of their investigation were set forth in the following letter to the President under date of December 9, 1790:

"Sir: Immediately after we had the honor of seeing you on your way to Philadelphia, we sent up to Jacob Funk in Washington County for a particular state of the situation of the lots in Hamburgh, and never till yesterday received his answer.

"We find there are 287 lots laid out upon 130 acres of land and as far as we can judge from the book of sales kept by Funk which he sent us, the whole of the lots are in the hands of about 150 proprietors principally Dutchmen residing in Frederick and Washington Counties, and in Pennsylvania, who have heretofore held them in but reasonable estimation; and we have reason to believe that the far greater part of them might now be purchased at little more than the original cost, which was five pounds each lot; tho' there can be no doubt that if the seat of government should be fixed so as to comprehend these lots, a much higher value would be instantly set upon them. And on this account we had once determined to commence an immediate purchase of them, meaning to accommodate the public without any private advantage, but we were deterred from carrying this into effect by the consideration, that if they should not be wanted by the public, they would remain a considerable loss on our hands. To leave nothing undone that we could consistently do, we are now making application to our Legislature through the delegates from this county for a law to pass condemning any land that may be chosen for the seat of government at the reasonable valuation of disinterested men, in cases where the proprietors will not agree to the terms offered, and where they reside at a distance — and, as like difficulties occur at almost every possible place on the river, we have no doubt such a law will pass, and we imagine in the course of next week, there being a disposition in the majority of both houses, to promote the residence on the Potomac.

"We have the honor to be, with the highest respect and esteem Sir, Your most Obed. Servts.,

Will Deakins, Junr.,

Ben Stoddert."

Coming to a consideration of the question of the Hamburgh lots the President, in his letter to Deakins and Stoddert of February 17, 1791, in which he urges them to purchase the lands of David Burnes, continues:

"The Maryland Assembly has authorized a certain number of acres to be taken without the consent of the owners on making compensation as therein provided, this will be principally useful as to the old lots of Hamburgh. However by purchasing up these lots or as many as we can, we shall be free to take on the terms of the Act so much of any other lands in our way, and consequently those whose proprietors refuse all arrangement. I will therefore beg the favor of you to take measures immediately for buying up all the lots you can in Hamburgh on the lowest terms you cannot exceeding the rate of twenty-five pounds the acre. I leave it to yourselves to dispatch a private agent for this purpose to treat with the proprietors wherever to be found, or to do it by any other means which in your discretion shall appear not too expensive and which may not excite suspicions of their being on behalf of the public. I am, with great esteem, gentlemen, your most obd't humble serv't. (No signature on letter press copy.)

Messrs. Deakins and Stoddert. "

A number of circumstances tend to indicate that at about this period the President's concern with regard to the importance of Hamburgh was accentuated by a strong inclination to make this the site of the principal Federal buildings. The President at this time was planning to stop at Georgetown in the course of a trip through the Southern States, and on the same day that the President wrote to Stoddert and Deakins with regard to the owners of lots in Hamburgh — Mr. Jefferson wrote to Major L 'Enfant to desist from his work on the Eastern Branch, if uncompleted, and prepare, for the inspection of the President on the occasion of his contemplated visit, a plan of the land in the neighborhood of Hamburgh. His letter, the postscript to winch is particularly significant, reads:

"Philadelphia, March 17, 1791. " Sir: Your favor of the 11th inst. has been duly received. Between the date of that and your receipt of the present, it is probable that the most important parts of the ground towards the Eastern Branch will have been delineated. However, whether they are or not, as the President will go on within two or three days, and would wish to have under his eye, when at Georgetown, a drawing also of the particular lineaments of the ground between Rock Creek and Tiber, you are desired, immediately on the receipt of this, to commence the survey of that part, beginning at the river, and proceeding towards the parts back of that till his arrival. If the meanders of those two creeks and of the river between them should not have been before laid down either by yourself or by Mr. Ellicott, it is desired that Mr. Ellicott should immediately do this while you shall be employed on the interior ground, in order that the work may be as much advanced as profitable on the arrival of the President, and that you will be so good as to notify this to Mr. Ellicott.

I am with great esteem sir, your most obedt humble servt.

(No signature on letter press copy.)

"P. S. — There are certainly considerable advantages on the Eastern Branch: but there are very strong reasons also in favor of the position between Rock Creek and Tiber independent of the face of the ground. It is desired that the proper amount should be in equilibrio between those two places till the President arrives, and we shall be obliged to you to endeavor to poise their expectations. Major L 'Enfant."

A further highly important item of evidence on this point is to be found in a document drawn by Mr. Jefferson preparatory to the President's departure from Philadelphia. This is a draft of the Proclamation which the President intended to issue after reaching Georgetown, setting forth the complete limits of the Federal Territory. At the close of this draft Mr. Jefferson added in brackets the following, which he said, being conjectural, would be rendered conformable to the ground when more accurately examined:

"the highest summit of lands in the town heretofore called Hamburgh, within said territory, with a convenient extent of grounds circumjacent, shall be appropriated for a capitol for the accommodation of Congress, and such other lands between Georgetown and the stream heretofore called the Tiber, as shall on due examination be found convenient and sufficient, shall be appropriated for the accommodation of the President of the U. S. for the time being, and for the public offices of the Government of the U. S."

Accompanying this draft was a plan giving an accurate illustration of Mr. Jefferson's ideas regarding the proposed city as it would be if located in accordance with the quoted portion of the draft. This plan showed the town facing south and extending along the north bank of the mouth of Tiber Creek with the President's house located on Observatory Hill and the Capitol about at the present location of the White House or Treasury Department.

At the mouth of Tiber Creek was the note: "no water here for commerce and a fine open prospect for those attached to the government." Along the shore between Tiber Creek and Rock Creek was the notation: "This part will suit merchants because of the depth of water." On the stretch of land lying on the Potomac below Tiber Creek and extending toward Young's (now Arsenal) Point was remarked: "To be laid off in future."

In a letter to Major L 'Enfant of April 4, 1791, President Washington enclosed this plan with others explaining that it had been prepared under an idea that no offer worthy of consideration would come from the land-holders in the vicinity of Carrollsburgh, from the backwardness which appeared in them, and therefore was accommodated to the grounds about Georgetown.

On the 11th of March Messrs. Deakins and Stoddert had written to the President that the owners of Hamburgh lots in Washington County, Maryland, were willing to sign a paper ceding their lots on being requested by any person under the President's direction. In order to take advantage of this disposition on their part the President wrote the following letter which he sent to Stoddert and Deakins to be used in obtaining the desired agreements:

"Philadelphia, March 17, 1791. "Gentlemen: On passing through Georgetown I propose to examine the ground between that town and the Eastern Branch, and on that examination to fix on a site for the public buildings. Should there be any circumstances in favor of the ground next adjoining to Georgetown, I foresee that the old town of Hamburgh will be a considerable obstacle, as the streets of that will probably not coincide with those which might be proposed for the Federal City; on behalf of the public I should be much pleased if the proprietors of lots in that town would voluntarily consent to cede them at such price as may be set on the adjacent lands which have been or shall be ceded. I will ask the favor of you to have application made to them in time for their decision to meet me at Georgetown.

(No signature on letter press copy.)

Messieurs Deakins and Stoddert." This letter was enclosed with a private communication to Deakins and Stoddert in which, after requesting them to dispatch his letter to the owners of the Hamburgh lots with the necessary propositions in form, he says: "I am aware that by this means it will become known that you are acting for the public; but there will be no reason for keeping this longer secret after my arrival at Georgetown."

Deakins and Stoddert, pursuant either to this request or possibly to a former one to the same effect, procured from such of the owners of Hamburgh lots as were convenient to Georgetown the following agreement, the date of which appears to make the instrument antedate the President's request:

"Whereas, It would be a desirable circumstance to the Subscribers, that the Federal City should be laid off so as to Comprehend within its lines, the Town of Hamburgh, lying in Prince Georges County — And whereas, the president of the United States, has the power under an Act of the General Assembly of Maryland to Condemn one hundred and thirty Acres of Land, anywhere in the State of Maryland for the purpose of the Federal City — and it is reasonable to Suppose that if a Situation for the Federal City should be Chosen, so as to Comprehend Hamburgh, as aforesaid, the President of the United States would find it necessary to have, the whole of the Lotts in said Town condemned, unless the same could be had by purchase from the Proprietors — Now we the Subscribers, proprietors of Lotts in Hamburgh, in consideration of the premises, as well as for the Consideration hereafter mentioned, Do hereby agree and bind ourselves, our heirs, Executors and Administrators to sell to the President of the United States, or to a Commissioner or Commissioners, Appointed, or to be Appointed by him, the Lotts which we respectively hold in Hamburgh, for the uses of the Federal City, and for such price for each Lott, as each of those Lotts shall be valued at, which may be condemned under the Act of Assembly aforesaid, it being probable that the whole of the proprietors of Lotts in Hamburg, may not agree to Sell, and that it will therefore be necessary, that a Condemnation should take place, with respect to some of them.

'In Witness whereof We have hereunto set our hands and seals this Twenty-first day of February, 1791.

Thos. Cramphin (Seal).

Witness.

Benj. Stoddard — for Thomas Cramphin — x2 lotts No. 150: 239.

Chas. Beatty (Seal).

Benj. Stoddard— for Charles Beatty— 4 Do. 286: 115 243

Robt. Peter (Seal)

Benj. Stoddard— for R. Peter— 83: 84: 170: 225

Wm. Robertson (Seal)

Benj. Stoddard — for Wm. Robertson, either No. 277.

Thos. Beall of Geo. (Seal)

Benj. Stoddard— for Thos. Beall— 1 lott 233.

Markham Waring (Seal)

Benj. Stoddard— for M. Waring— 1 lott 76.

John Montz (Seal)

Will Deakins — for John Montz — No. 1.

Thomas Johns (Seal)

Will Deakins Jr. — for T. Johns. Will Deakins Jr. — for F. Kokindoffer for 4 lo 248: 252—3 lotts No. 85: 86: 157—

Jas. M. Lingan (Seal)

Will Deakins for J. M. Lingan— 9 Lotts No. 8 27: 187: 218: 211: 247: 269.

Henry Hilliarys Sen'r (Seal)
ditto for H. Hilliarys— No. 102.
Will Lydebotham (Seal)
ditto for Wm. Lydebotham — No. 155.
Thos. O. Williams(Seal)
ditto for T. 0. Williams— No. 26: 222.
Evan Thomas (Seal)
ditto for Evan Thomas — No. 81.
Lawrence O'Neale (Seal)
ditto for L. O'Neale— No. 274.
12x23 Anthony Holmeade (Seal)
Jno. Suter Jr. for Wm. Magrath.
William Magrath (Seal)
2 lotts No. 83 & 208
Forrest and Stoddard. (Seal)

Eight lotts, two of which are improved, the value of the improvements must be paid, and may be ascertained by any person appointed by the President. No. 32: 91: 92: 44: 45: 167: 55."

President Washington had kept in communication with Mr. Carroll respecting his proposed visit to Georgetown and finally, under date of March 17, 1791, wrote to him from Philadelphia fixing definitely the date when he should expect to meet the Commissioners. The letter which follows is interesting for the light it sheds upon the length of time required for traveling before the advent of steam railroads:

"Philadelphia, March 17, 1791.

"To Daniel Carroll, Esq. — Georgetown.

"Dear Sir: The enclosed letter (requesting Mr. Carroll to send an express to Mr. Johnson to notify him of the proposed meeting) was written to go by the post yesterday but was omitted to be put to the office in season.

"I have thought best upon further consideration to fix on Monday next for the time of my departure from this City — in which case I expect to be four days in Travelling to Baltimore, and as I shall be under the necessity of going by way of Annapolis, I must calculate upon three days more for my journey from Baltimore to that place, and my stay there. One day will carry me from thence to Georgetown, which will bring it to Monday the 28th of this month, at which time if no accident intervenes, I shall expect to meet the Commissioners at that place, of which I will thank you to give them notice.

With very great regard, I am, dear Sir,

Your most obedient servant, G. Washington."

Evidence of the continuing interest of Mr. Jefferson in the new Federal seat and of the methodical bent of his mind is found in a memorandum prepared by him for the President's use entitled "Objects which may merit the attention of the President at George T."

This memorandum enumerated as matters to be attended to by the President, the following: The Commissioners to be called into action; deeds of cession to be taken from the landholders; site of the Capitol and President's house to be determined on; proclamation completing the location of the territory and fixing the site of the Capitol; town to be laid off; squares of reserve to be decided on for the Capitol,

President's house, offices of government, town house, prison, market and public walks. Other squares for present sale designated. Terms of sale to be settled.

He also recommended that the President form a Capitulary of such regulations as he might think necessary to be observed until there should be a town legislature to undertake that office. His legal training manifested itself in the observation that this Capitulary should be indented, signed, sealed and recorded according to the laws of conveyance of Maryland, and be referred to in every deed for conveyance of lots to purchasers, so as to make a part thereof, an alternative being suggested that the same thing might be effected by inserting special covenants for various regulations in every deed.

Continuing, Mr. Jefferson says he cannot help again suggesting one regulation formerly suggested, to wit, "to provide for facilitating the extinguishment of fires and the openness and convenience of the town by prohibiting houses of excessive height, making it unlawful to build on any one's purchase any house with more than two floors between the common level of the earth and the eves, nor with any other floor in the roof than one at the eves."

In his notes on the Residence Act he had remarked that in Paris it was forbidden to build a house beyond a given height, saying "it is admitted to be a good restriction, it keeps the houses low and convenient, and the streets light and airy, fires are much more manageable where houses are low."

Mr. Jefferson further suggested that the President should consider in what way contracts for the public buildings should be made and whether as many bricks should not be made that summer as might employ brickmakers in the beginning of the season of 1792 till more could be made in that season. He closes by setting forth at much length the desirability of and a proposed method for including Bladensburgh in the Federal Territory by a rearrangement of the boundary lines of the Federal Territory as then determined.

This paper is of special interest as constituting a methodical outline of almost the precise steps followed by President Washington and afterwards by the Commissioners in the work of laying out the city.

The President kept true to his schedule, though after a trip accompanied with some vicissitudes, among them being stuck on the bar at the mouth of the Severn River and being compelled to spend the night in his cloak and boots in a berth too short by the head.

What transpired during his stay at Georgetown is best told in his own words. In his diary he writes:

"March, 1791, Monday, 28th. Left Blandensburgh at half after six, & breakfasted at George Town about 8; where, having appointed the Commissioners under the Residence Law to meet me, I found Mr. Johnson one of them (& who is Chief Justice of the State) in waiting — & soon after came in David Stuart, & Danl. Carroll Esqrs. the other two. — A few miles out of Town I was met by the principal Citizens of the place and escorted in by them; and dined at Suter's tavern (where I also lodged) at a public dinner given by the Mayor & Corporation — previous to which I examined the Surveys of Mr. Ellicot who had been sent on to lay out the district of ten miles square for the federal seat; and also the works of Majr. L 'Enfant who had been engaged to examine & make a draught of the grds. in the vicinity of George

Town and Carrollsburg on the Eastern Branch making arrangements for examining the ground myself tomorrow with the Commissioners.

" Tuesday, 29th. In a thick mist, and under strong appearances of a settled rain (which however did not happen) I set out about 7 o'clock for the purpose above mentioned — but from the unfavorableness of the day, I derived no great satisfaction from the review.

"Finding the interests of the Landholders about Georgetown and those about Carrollsburgh much at variance and that their fears and jealousies of each other were counteracting the public purposes & might prove injurious to its best interests whilst if properly managed they might be made to subserve it — I requested them to meet me at six o'clock this afternoon at my lodgings, which they accordingly did. To this meeting I represented that the contention in which they seemed to be engaged, did not in my opinion comport either with the public interest or that of their own; that while each party was aiming to obtain the public buildings, they might by placing the matter on a contracted scale, defeat the measure altogether; not only by procrastination but for want of the means necessary to effect the work; that neither the offer from George-Town or Carrollsburgh separately, was adequate to the end of insuring the object. That both together did not comprehend more ground nor would afford greater means than was required for the Federal City; and that, instead of contending which of the two should have it they had better, by combining more offers make a common cause of it, and thereby secure it to the district — other arguments were used to show the danger which might result from delay and the good effects that might proceed from a Union.

"Dined at Colonel Forrest's to day with the Commissioners and others.

"Wednesday, 30th. The parties to whom I addressed myself yesterday evening, having taken the matter into consideration saw the propriety of my observations; and that whilst they were contending for the shadow they might lose the substance; and therefore mutually agreed and entered into articles to surrender for public purposes, one half of the land they severally possessed within bounds which were designated as necessary for the City to stand with some other stipulations, which were inserted in the instrument which they respectively subscribed.

" This business being thus happily finished and some directions given to the Commissioners, the Surveyor and Engineer with respect to the mode of laying out the district — Surveying the grounds for the City and forming them into lots — I left Georgetown — dined at Alexandria and reached Mount Vernon in the evening." The instrument subscribed by the proprietors and referred to in President Washington 's diary was as follows:

"We, the subscribers, in consideration of the great benefits we expect to derive from having the Federal City laid off upon our Lands, do hereby agree and bind ourselves, heirs, executors, and administrators, to convey, in Trust, to the President of the United States, or Commissioners, or such person or persons as he shall appoint, by good and sufficient deeds, in Fee simple, the whole of our respective Lands which he may think proper to include within the lines of the Federal City, for the purposes and on the conditions following:

"The President shall have the sole power of directing the Federal City to be laid off in what manner he pleases. He may retain any number of Squares he may think proper for public Improvements, or other public Uses, and the lots only which shall be laid off shall be a joint property between the Trustees on behalf of the public, and each present proprietor, and the same shall be fairly and equally divided between the public and the Individuals, as soon as may be, after the City shall be laid off.

"For the streets the proprietors shall receive no compensation; but for the squares or Lands in any form, which shall be taken for public buildings, or any kind of public improvements, or uses, the proprietors, whose lands shall be so taken, shall receive at the rate of twenty-five pounds per acre, to be paid by the public.

"The whole wood on the Lands shall be the property of the proprietors.

"But should any be desired by the president to be reserved or left standing, the same shall be paid for by the public at a just and reasonable valuation, exclusive of the twenty-five pounds per acre to be paid for the Land, on which the same shall remain.

"Each proprietor shall retain the full possession and use of his land, until the same shall be sold and occupied by the purchasers of the Lots laid out thereupon, and in all cases where the public arrangements as to streets, lotts, &c, will admit of it, each proprietor shall possess his buildings and other improvements, and graveyards, paying to the public only one-half the present estimated value of the Lands, on which the same shall be, or twelve pounds ten shillings per acre. But in cases where the arrangements of the streets, lotts, squares, &c, will not admit of this, and it shall become necessary to remove such buildings, Improvements, &c, the proprietors of the same shall be paid the reasonable value thereof, by the public.

"Nothing herein contained shall affect the Lotts which any of the parties to this Agreement may hold in the Towns of Carrollsburgh or Hamburgh.

"In witness whereof we have hereunto set our hands and Seals, this thirteenth day of March, 1791.

"Signed & sealed in presence of us — Mr. Thos Beall, making an exception of the Lands he sold Abraham Young not yet conveyed.

Witness to all the subscribers including William Young

Signed

Robert Peter (Seal)
David Burnes (Seal)
Jas. M. Lingan (Seal)
Uriah Forrest (Seal)
Benj. Stoddert (Seal)
Notley Young (Seal)
etc. etc.

Under the same date as the foregoing, a number of identical instruments were circulated among and signed by the owners of lots in Carrollsburgh. These instruments were in the following form:

"We the Subscribers holding or entitled to Lots in Carrollsburgh agree with each other and with the President of the United States that the lots and lands we hold or are entitled to in Carrollsburgh shall be subject to be laid out at the pleasure of the president as part of the Federal City and that we will receive one half the Quantity of our respective Lots as near their present Situation as may agree with the new plan and where we may be entitled now to only one Lot or otherwise not entitled on the new plan to one entire lot or do not agree with the President, Commissioners or other person or persons acting on the part of the public on an adjustment of our interest we agree that there shall be a sale of the Lots in which we may be interested respectively and the produce thereof in money or Securities shall be equally divided one half as a Donation for the Use of the United States under the Act of Congress, the other half to ourselves respectively. And we engage to make Conveyances of our respective Lots and lands af'd to Trustees or otherwise whereby to relinquish our rights to the said Lots & Lands as the president or such Commrs or persons acting as af'd shall direct to secure to the United States the Donation intended by this Agreement.

"Witness our hands this thirtieth Day of March, 1791.

N. B. See the alteration of these Subscriptions.

Th. Johnson,

Daniel Carroll,

Will Deakins, Jun'r.,

William Bayly,

Daniel Carroll for Th., Morton,

Notley Young,

Notley Young for Mary,

Young and Eliz. Carroll."

President Washington appears to have been much elated over his success in procuring the execution of these agreements, and justly so. They outlined a plan whereby the Federal City should finance itself. The ground necessary for the streets was to be donated to the Federal Government, and while such land as should be needed for public reservations and buildings was to be paid for by the Federal Government at the rate of £25 Maryland currency or $66 2-3 per acre, nevertheless the arrangement whereby the Federal Government should divide with the original proprietors all the platted squares gave to the former a source of revenue which it was anticipated would suffice not only to pay for the public reservations but also for all the Federal expenses in connection with the city for many years to come. While the disposal by the Federal Government of its proportion of the lots assigned to it was afterwards severely criticized as improvident, nevertheless the funds so obtained sufficed eventually to pay for all the land laid out for Federal buildings and reservations and provided for the erection of the Federal buildings and for their reconstruction after they had been destroyed by the British in the War of 1812.

The whole transaction is succinctly characterized in a report by Mr. Southard, Chairman of the Senate Committee on the District of Columbia, presented to the Senate February 2, 1835, in which he says:

"For this large extent of land (i. e. the public reservations) equal to all its present and prospective wants, the Government paid, nominally, the sum of $36,099 to the proprietors of the soil; but in reality nothing. This sum was not drawn from the general Treasury, nor one cent of it contributed by the people of the United States. The whole of it was taken out of the proceeds of the sales of the building lots, which had also been secured by the Government in the contract with the landowners. It thus appears that the people of the United States have paid nothing for all their public lots, nor for the property in the streets. They procured them, and now own them, without the expenditure of a single dollar." This agreement was in after years made the basis of litigation in the case of Van Ness v. City of Washington (4 Peters 232). The Supreme Court, replying to the contention that the portion of the land taken by the Government for streets and public reservations was clothed with a trust that they should remain such and that upon any change in their character the title should revert to the original proprietors, said: "It is not very material, in our opinion, to decide what was the technical character of the grants made to the government; whether they are to be deemed mere donations or purchases. The grants were made for the foundation of a Federal City; and the public faith was necessarily pledged when the grants were accepted to found such city. The very agreement to found a city was of itself a most valuable consideration for these grants. It changed the, nature and value of the property of the proprietors to an almost incalculable extent. The land was no longer to be devoted to mere agricultural purposes but acquired the extraordinary value of city lots. In proportion to the success of the city would be the enhancement of this value; and it required scarcely any aid from the imagination to foresee that this act of government would soon convert the narrow income of farms into solid opulence. The proprietors so considered it. In this very agreement, they state the motive of their proceedings in a plain and intelligible manner. It is not a mere gratuitous donation from motives of generosity or public spirit; but in consideration of the great benefits they expect to derive from having the Federal City laid off upon their lands. For the streets they were to receive no compensation. Why? Because those streets would be of as much benefit to themselves, as lot-holders, as to the public. They were to receive £25 per acre for the public reservations; 'to be paid' (as the agreement states it) 'by the public' They understood themselves, then, to receive payment from the public for the reservations. It makes no difference, that by the subsequent arrangements they were to receive this payment out of the sales of the lots which they had agreed to convey to the public, in consideration of the government's founding the city on their lands. It was still contemplated by them as a compensation; as a valuable consideration, fully adequate to the value of all their grants. It can, therefore, be treated in no other manner than as a bargain between themselves and the government, for what each deemed an adequate consideration. Neither considered it a case where all was benefit on one side, and all sacrifice on the other. It was, in no sense, a case of charity, and was never so treated in the negotiations of the parties. But, as has already been said, it is not in our view material, whether it be considered as a donation or a purchase, for in each case it was for the foundation of a city." There is, however, another side to this question. As will later appear, the work of effecting divisions between the public and the proprietors was slow and the sales of the property equally so. It was many years before some of the proprietors were able to dispose of any considerable quantity of their lots. In the meantime their farms were no longer a. source of income. One of them Daniel Carroll of Duddington, in a letter to Mayor Brent written July 24, 1837, replying to an inquiry on this very point said:

"In answer to yours, I fear the deeds will fully express the relinquishments of right in the streets to the government. I nevertheless perfectly remember that the general opinion was that so great was the gift that the citizens would never be subject to taxation for the improvement of the streets — having relinquished every alternate lot to the government. Indeed, some were so wild as to suppose the donation was so great the government might pave the streets with ingots of gold or silver. After nearly a half century the result is now fully known; the unfortunate proprietors are generally brought to ruin, and some with scarcely enough to buy daily food for their families.

The subject is so truly frightful to me that I hate to think of it, much less to write of it." Another proprietor, David Burnes, was so sorely pressed

for money to pay his bills while the divisions between the Government and the proprietors were being made and the lots sold that he repeatedly appealed to the Commissioners for even partial payments upon the land taken from his tract for public reservations, with the result that the Commissioners as a measure of relief to him assumed the payment of some of his most pressing debts.

On the same day with the execution of the foregoing agreements, President Washington issued his proclamation finally setting forth the boundaries of the ten miles square. This proclamation recited the publication of the first proclamation, the passage of the amendatory Act of Congress allowing both sides of the Eastern Branch and the Virginia shore as far as Hunting Creek to be included within the Federal Territory and proceeded to define the boundaries of the latter as follows:

"Beginning at Jones' Point, being the upper cape of Hunting Creek, in Virginia, and at an angle in the outset of forty-five degrees west of the north, and running in a direct line ten miles, for the first line; then beginning again at the same Jones' Point, and running another direct line at a right angle with the first, across the Potomac ten miles, for the second line; thence from the termination of said first and second lines, running two other lines of ten miles each, the one crossing the Eastern Branch aforesaid and the other the Potomac, and meeting each other in a point. "

Major L 'Enfant 's first report, which is undated, was probably delivered to the President at the time of his presence in Georgetown when he secured the signing of the preliminary agreement by the proprietors. After describing the general characteristics of the land and of the waters adjoining it, he gives some of his ideas as to the locations for public buildings. He suggests a bridge over the Eastern Branch at a point about a half mile above Evans' Point where the deep channel terminates, and one across the Potomac above Georgetown "at the place of the two Sisters w(h)ere nature would effectually favor the undertaking." He proposes the placing of wharves and the establishing of a naval store, arsenals and warehouses on the Eastern Branch. As to the locations most favorable for the public buildings he says:

"there w(h)ere the level ground on the water and all around w(h)ere it descend but most particularly on that part terminating in a ridge to Jenkin's Hill and running in a parallel with and at half mile off from the river Potowmack separated by a low ground intersected with three grand streams — many of the most desirable position offer for to erect the Publique Edifices thereon — from these height every grand building would rear with majestic aspect over the Country all around and might be advantageously seen from twenty miles off which Contigeous to the first settlement of the City they would there stand to ages in a Central point to it, facing on the grandest prospect of both of the branch of the Potowmack with the town of Alexandry in front seen in its fullest extent over many points of land projecting from the Maryland and Virginia shore in a manner as add much to the perspective at the end of which the Cape of great Hunting Creek appears directly w(h)ere a corner stone of the Federal District is to be placed and in the room of which a majestic colum or a grand Perysomid being erected would produce the happyest effect and compleatly finish the landscape — " He suggests opening "a direct and large avenue from the bridge on the Potowmack to that on the Eastern Branch the which should be well level passing across Georgetown and over the most advantageous ground for prospect trought the Grand City, with a middle way paved for heavy carriage and walk on each side planted with double Rows of trees."

The idea of laying out the city in regular squares according to the plan of Philadelphia he somewhat contemptuously dismisses in the following:

" * * it is not the regular assemblage of houses laid out in square and forming streets all parallel and uniform that is so necessary for such plan could only so on a level plain and w(h)ere no surrounding object being interesting it become indifferent which way the opening of street may be directed, but on any other ground a plan of this sort most be defective and it never would answer for any of the spots proposed for the Federal City, and on that held here as the most eligible it would absolutely annilate every of the advantage enumerated and the seeing of which will alone injure the success of the undertaking, such regular plan indeed however answerable as they may appear upon paper or seducing as they may be on the first aspect to the eyes of some people most even when applayed upon the ground the best calculated to admit of it become at least tiresome and insipide and it never could be in its orrigine but a mean continuance of some cool imagination wanting a sense of the real grand and truly beautifull only to be met with w(h)ere nature contribut with art and diversify the object."

The four or five days following the execution of the agreement by the proprietors were spent by President Washington at Mount Vernon mainly in attending to his private affairs and preparing for his coming Southern trip. The Federal City, nevertheless, appears to have been quite constantly on his mind, for during that period he wrote a number of important and interesting letters.

The day following his arrival at Mount Vernon he wrote to Mr. Jefferson enclosing the Proclamation defining the limits of the Federal Territory and explaining the omission therefrom of the provision in Mr. Jefferson's draft designating the sites for the public buildings on the land near the mouth of the Tiber, and explaining also the non-inclusion of Bladensburg within the ten miles square. He said:

"Mount Vernon, March 31, 1791. "Dear Sir: Having been so fortunate as to reconcile the contending interests of Georgetown and Carrollsburg, and to unite them in such an agreement as permits the public purposes to be carried into effect on an extensive and proper scale, I have the pleasure to transmit to you the enclosed Proclamation, which you will cause after annexing the Seal of the U. S. and your countersignature to be published.

"The terms entered into by me, on the part of the United States, with the Landholders of Georgetown and Carrollsburg are that all the land from Rock Creek along the river to the Eastern Branch and so upwards to, or above the ferry including a breadth of about a mile and a half, the whole containing from three to five thousand acres is ceded to the public on condition, that when the whole shall be surveyed and laid off as a city (which Major L 'Enfant is now directed to do) the present Proprietors shall retain every other lot — and for such part of the land as may be taken for public use, for squares, walks, &c, they shall be allowed at the rate of twenty-five pounds per acre — the Public having the right to reserve such parts of the wood on the land as may be thought necessary to be preserved for ornament. The landholders to have the use and profits of all the grounds until the City is laid off into lots, and sale is made of those lots which, by this agreement, became public property — nothing is to be allowed for the ground which may be occupied as streets or alleys.

"To these conditions all the principal Landholders, except the purchaser of Slater's property who was not present, have subscribed, and it is not doubted that the few who were not present will readily come into the measure, even the obstinate Mr. Burns.

"The enlarged plan of this agreement having done away the necessity and indeed postponed the propriety of designating the particular spot on which the public buildings should be placed until an accurate survey and subdivision of the whole ground is made, I have left out that paragraph of the proclamation.

"It was found on running the lines that the comprehension of Bladensburg with the district must have occasioned the exclusion of more important objects — and of this I am convinced as well by my own observation as Mr. Ellicott's opinion.

"With great regard and esteem, I am dear Sir Your most obd't Servt.,

Copy to Mr. Jefferson.

" Signed G. W.

The writing of this letter probably reminded the President of the matter of building regulations, with the importance of which he seems to have been much impressed, and which he had overlooked in the multitude of matters which claimed his attention while at Georgetown; for the following day he took up the subject with Messrs. Stoddert and Deakins, saying:

"Mount Vernon, April 1st, 1791. "Gentlemen: Being accustomed to write to you respecting the grounds for the Fed'l City, I continue the practice.

"It may be Tuesday or Wednesday next before I shall leave this place, — by which (say by Monday's Post) I should be glad to hear what progress has been made, and what still remains to be done in the business which so happily commenced on Tuesday last under the accommodating spirit which then prevailed.

"The subscription paper has been, I presume, deposited in the hands of the Commissioners, for the purpose of drawing conveyances. I should be glad nevertheless to receive a copy of it with the names of the subscribers annexed thereto for my own satisfaction — the general tenor of the agreement was, I well remember, pleasing to me, and, in my opinion reciprocally beneficial to all the parties, but I do not now recollect with precision whether it is fully expressed that the lots left to the disposal of the several proprietors by the conditions of their grants are subject to all the rules and regulations (with respect to the buildings, &c, &c.) as the public ones are. This unquestionably ought to be the case — it was evidently my meaning that they should be so — and unless it is so, one of the great objects — to wit — uniformity and beauty — may be defeated.

"The mail of Wednesday brought me a letter from Mr. Jefferson, dated the 27th ulto. in which is the following paragraph: ' A bill was yesterday ordered to be brought into the house of representatives here for granting a sum of money for building a Federal hall, house for the President, &c.' This (though I do not wish that it should be expressed as my sentiment) unfolds most evidently the views of P ———— at the same time that it proves in a striking manner the propriety of the measure adopted by the Georgetown and Carrollsburgh proprietors on Wednesday last — As also the necessity of their completing the good work they have begun in a speedy, and, in an effectual manner that the consequent arrangements may take place without delay.

"With esteem and regard, I am, Gent'n, Y. obd. Hbl. Serv.,

G. Washington."

President Washington was at this time especially anxious that the work of completing the survey and laying off the city as well as that of completing the arrangements with the proprietors of the land by means of formal conveyances and to the proper trustees, the divisions between the Government and the proprietors, and the sales of lots should proceed vigorously. Even at this period, the efforts of other localities to obtain the location of the permanent seat of government had not ended. Baltimore, which had raised a large fund for the erection of Federal buildings, was still protesting against the establishment of a new city in the wilderness; and Philadelphia, which was to be the seat of the Government during the ten years allowed for the laying off of the city and the erection of the public buildings, was still hopeful of becoming the permanent seat of the National Capital. To this end as President Washington's letter just quoted mentions, the Pennsylvania legislature was then considering a bill to appropriate a sum of money for the erection of buildings for the use of the Government. President Washington consequently felt very strongly that delay or embarrassment in establishing the city on a substantial basis would be exceedingly prejudicial to its interests. His eagerness in this particular is evidenced by a letter which he wrote to the Commissioners from Mount Vernon, under date of April 3, 1791, in which he again alluded to the bill pending in the Pennsylvania legislature. He said:

"Mount Vernon, April 3rd, 1791. "Gentlemen: As the Instrut. which was subscribed at George Town by the Landholders in the vicinity of that place and Carrollsburg, was not given to me, I presume it has been deposited with you. It is of the greatest moment to close this business with the proprietors of the land on which the Federal City is to be that consequent arrangements may be made without more delay than can be avoided.

"To accomplish this matter so as that the Sales of the lots, the public buildings &c. may commence with as much facility as the nature of the case will admit, would be I conceive advisable under any circumstances — perhaps the friends of the measures may think it materially so, from the following extract of a letter from Mr. Jefferson to me, dated the 27th ulto. 'A bill was yesterday ordered to be brought into the House of Representatives here for granting a sum of money for building a Federal hall, house for the President, &c.' This, (though I do not want any sentiment of mine promulgated with respect to it) marks unequivocally in my mind the designs of that State and the necessity of exertion to carry the Residence Law into effect agreeably thereto.

"With great and sincere esteem and regard, I am gentlemen, your most obedt. and Hbl. Servt.,

George Washington.

Thos. Johnson, David Stuart, Danl. Carroll, Esqrs.

On April 4th, the President wrote to Major L'Enfant enclosing Mr. Jefferson's and another sketch of the proposed town, saying:

"Mount Vernon, April 4th, 1791.

"Sir: Although I do not conceive that you will derive any material advantage from an examination of the enclosed papers, yet, as they have been drawn under different circumstances, and by different persons, they may be compared with your own ideas of a proper plan for the Federal City under the prospect which now presents itself. For this purpose I commit them to your private inspection until my return from the tour I am about to make. The rough sketch by Mr. Jefferson was done under an idea that no offer, worthy of consideration, would come from the Landholders in the vicinity of Carrollsburg; form y. backwness. wch. appd. in them; and therefore was accommodated to the grounds about George Town. The other is taken up upon a larger scale, without reference to any described spot.

"It will be of great importance to the public interest to comprehend as much ground (to be ceded by individuals) as there is any tolerable prospect of obtaining from them. Although it may not be immediately wanting, it will nevertheless increase the Revenue; and of course be beneficial hereafter not only to the public but to the Indiv. also, inasmuch as the plan will be enlarged, and thereby freed from those blotches which otherwise might result from not comprehending all the lands that appear well adapted to the general design and which in my opinion, are those between Rock Creek, Potomac River and the Eastern Branch, and as far up the latter as the turn of the Channel above Evans' Point; these including the flat, back of Jenkins' Heights; thence to the road leading from Georgetown to Blandensburg as far Easterly along the same as to include the branch which runs across it, somewhere near the exterior of the Georgetown Session — thence in a proper direction to Rock Creek at, or above the ford, according to the situation of ground. Within these limits there may be lands belonging to persons incapacitated though willing to convey on the terms proposed; but such had better be included than others excluded the proprietors of which are not only willing but in circumstances to subscribe. I am, Sir,

Yr. most obdt. Servt.,

G. Washington.

To Majr. L 'Enfant."

This letter is of importance because the instructions therein given to Major L 'Enfant relative to the extent of territory to be included in the city were the basis of the controversy which soon afterwards arose over the execution of the formal conveyances by the proprietors.

On the same day that President Washington wrote the foregoing letter to Major L 'Enfant the Major wrote to Mr. Jefferson, who, he probably had been informed, had collected the plans of a number of European cities during the period, from 1784 to 1789, of his sojourn there as the American Minister Plenipotentiary to arrange treaties of Commerce. The letter reads:

"George Town, April 4th, 1791. "Sir: I would have reproached myself for not having written to you as regularly as you had desired. I should were it not circumstances to which you will I doubt not attribute this seeming neglect in approving of the considerations which made me give the whole of my time to forward as much as possibly could be the business I had to perform. Great as were my endeavors to that end, it still remained unfinished at the moment of the President's arrival at this place where I could present him no more but a rough drawing in pencil of the several surveys which I had been able to run — nevertheless the President's Indulgent disposition making him account for the difficulties encountered, I had the satisfaction to see the little I had done agreeable to his wishes — and the confidence with which he has been pleased since to Honor me in ordering the Survey to be continued and the delineation of a grand plan for the local distribution of the city to be done on principles conformable to the ideas which I took the liberty to hold before him as proper for the establishment being so highly flattering to my ambition to fail exerting the best of my ability. It shall be from this moment my endeavor to answer the President's expectation in preparing those plans and having them ready for the time of his return from the Southern tour.

"I shall in the meanwhile, Sir, beg for every information respecting all what may in your judgment appear of most immediate importance to attend to as well as relating to every desirable establishment which it will be well to foresee although delaying or perhaps leaving the execution thereof to a natural succession of time to effect.

"The number and nature of the public buildings with the necessary appendix I should be glad to have a statement of as speedily as possible — and I would be very much obliged to you in the meantime if you could procure for me whatever may 'fall within your reach — of any of the different grand cities now existing such as for example — as London — Madry — Paris — Amsterdam — Naples — Venice — Genoa — Florence together with particular maps of any such sea-ports or dock-yards and arsenals as you may know to be the most complete in their improvement for notwithstanding I would reprobate the idea of limiting and that contrary having this intention it is my wish and shall be my endeavor to delineate on a new and original way the plan the contrivance of which the President has left to me without any restriction soever — yet the contemplation of what exists of well improved situation, given the parallel of these with ineffective ones, may serve to suggest a variety of new ideas and is necessary to refine and strengthen the judgment particularly in the present instance when having to unite the useful with the commodious and agreeable viewing these will by offering means for comparing enable me the better to determine with a certainty the propriety of a local which offer an extensive field for combinations.

"I have the honor to be, with great respect, Your most humble and most obedient servant,

P. C. L 'Enfant.

Mr. Jefferson, Secretary of State. "

The suggestion has been advanced that Mr. Jefferson may have been piqued at not being accorded greater recognition in the laying out of the city. Whatever of force there may be in this suggestion it is not borne out either in his reply to the President's letter informing him of the signing of the agreements by the proprietors nor in his response to Major L 'Enfant 's request, though the letter to Major L'Enfant gives evidence that some of Mr. Jefferson's ideas had failed to meet with the President's approval. Both letters testify to his love for and familiarity with the study of architecture.

The letter to the President, so far as it relates to the Federal City, reads:

"The acquisition of ground at Georgetown is really noble. Considering that only £25 an acre is to be paid for any grounds taken for the public, and the streets not to be counted, which will in fact reduce it to about £19 an acre, I think very liberal reserves should be made for the public. Your proclamation came to hand the night of the 5th. Dunlap's & Bache's papers for the morning of the 6th being already filled, I could only get it into Brown's evening paper of the 6th. On the 7th the bill for the Federal buildings passed the representatives here by 42 to 10, but it was rejected yesterday by 9 to 6 in the Senate, or, to speak more exactly, it was postponed till the next session. In the meantime spirited proceedings at Georgetown will probably, under the continuance of your patronage, prevent the revival of the bill. I received last night from Major L 'Enfant a request to furnish him any plans of town I could for his examination. I accordingly send him, by his post, plans of Frankfort-on-the-Mayne, Carlsruhe, Amsterdam, Strasburg, Paris, Orleans, Bordeaux, Lyons, Montpelier, Marseilles, Turin, and Milan, on large and accurate scales, which I procured while in those towns respectively. They are none of them however comparable to the old Babylon, revived in Philadelphia, and exemplified. While in Europe I selected about a dozen or two of the handsomest fronts of private buildings of which I have the plates. Perhaps it might decide the taste of the new town were these to be engraved here and distributed gratis among the inhabitants of Georgetown. The expense would be trifling."

The letter to Major L 'Enfant after mentioning the sending of the plans asked for, proceeds:

"I will beg your care of them and to return them when no longer useful to you, leaving you absolutely free to keep them as long as useful. I am happy that the President has left the planning of the town in such good hands and have no doubt it will be done to general satisfaction. Considering that the grounds to be reserved for the public are to be paid for by the acre, I think very liberal reservations should be made for them, and if these be about the Tiber and on the back of the town it will be of no injury to the commerce of the place, which will undoubtedly establish itself on the deep waters towards the Eastern Branch and mouth of Rock Creek; the waters about the mouth of the Tiber not being of any depth. Those connected with the government will prefer fixing themselves near the public grounds in the center, which will also be convenient to be resorted to as walks from the lower and upper town. Having indicated to the President before he went away, such general ideas on the subject of the town, as occurred to me, I make no doubt that, in explaining himself to you on the subject, he has interwoven with his own ideas, such of mine as he approved: for fear of repeating therefore what he did not approve, and having more confidence in the unbiased state of his mind, than in my own, I avoid interfering with what he may have expressed to you. Whenever it is possible to prepare plans for the Capitol, I should prefer the adoption of some one of the models of antiquity which have had the approbation of thousands of years; and for the President's house, I should prefer the celebrated fronts of modern buildings which have already received the approbation of all good judges. Such are the Galerie du Louvre, the Gardes meubles, and two fronts of the Hotel de Salon."

On April 12, 1791, the first meeting of the full Board of Commissioners was held, the record thereof reciting the fact that:

"The form of the conveyance to Trustees, to be executed by the proprietors of the Lands between the Eastern Branch and Rock Creek, prepared agreeably to the directions of the President of the United States, and pursuant to the tenor of the agreement signed by the proprietors, was presented by Mr. Johnson, and agreed to by the Commissioners — but there was this difference between the deed from Mr. Young and the deed from the other proprietors, as then agreed upon, that the word 'Garden' should be inserted after the word 'Building' in two places in the deed from Mr. Young."

Meanwhile arrangements for the survey of the boundaries of the Federal Territory were going forward. On March 31, the day following President

Washington's departure from Georgetown, the Commissioners addressed a communication to Major Ellicott requesting him to supply himself with tents, provisions and other articles necessary to expedite the running of the lines of the ten miles square. Major Ellicott at once proceeded with the preliminary work of this survey with the result that two weeks later the following entry was made on the records of the proceedings of the Commissioners:

"At a meeting of the Commissioners, at Alexandria, in the State of Virginia, on Friday the 15th day of April, 1791. "Present, David Stuart and Daniel Carroll. The Surveyor, Mr. Andrew Ellicott, having before this time under the directions of the Commissioners run a line from the court house in Alexandria due southwest half a mile, and thence southeast course to Hunting Creek, to find the beginning of the four lines of experiment, agreeably to the President's proclamation of the 24th of January last, the Commissioners attended by the surveyor, and a large concourse of spectators, proceeded to Jones' Point on the uppermost Cape of Hunting Creek, and fixed a stone at the same place, it being the beginning of the four lines of experiment." On April 13, the President wrote to the Commissioners from Richmond where he had arrived in the course of his journey through the South, again urging them to hasten the securing of the conveyances from the landowners. He mentioned that it had been intimated to him that the proprietors of Georgetown were desirous of being comprehended within the limits of the Federal City and suggested that if the measure was seriously contemplated the present was the fit moment for carrying it into effect in order that it might be included in Major L'Enfant 's plan.

In the meantime trouble was brewing which was to delay for nearly three months the execution of the conveyances from the proprietors which the President was so anxious to obtain and which eventually was to require the personal attendance of the President before the execution of the conveyances could be effected.

It will have been noted that at the time he brought about the signing of the preliminary agreements by the proprietors he omitted to include therein a specific statement of the boundaries of the city, though his views on this point were probably conveyed to the Commissioners. When the proprietors were shown the draft of the deeds prepared by Mr. Johnson, a number of the proprietors refused to sign deeds conveying the extensive area provided for in the description set forth in the form of deed which Mr. Johnson had prepared. The halt in the proceedings and its cause are thus set forth in the record of the proceedings of the meeting of the Commissioners on April 14:

"The Commissioners having met on Tuesday last, in consequence of the President's letter, for the purpose of preparing and receiving conveyances: proceeded as far as to prepare the draft of a conveyance, which they communicated to several of the subscribers, and which in the frame of it appeared generally agreeable; but in fixing the extent to the Northeastward, several of the subscribers were willing only to insert a line drawn from Evan's point to the road half a mile from Rock Creek, a little above the ford. The Commissioners seeing the writing, in the terms of it, subjects 'the whole of the respective subscribers' lands, which the President might think proper to include in the lines of the Federal City for the purposes and on the conditions therein expressed,' and being of opinion from several circumstances, happening since the entering into that engagement, that the President has an idea to extend the city further, on that side: think themselves not at Liberty to accept conveyances, containing that description, and therefore resolve to forbear taking conveyances for the present, as they conceive it their duty not to do any act which may tend to narrow or restrain the President's views in the plan or extent of the city. A letter was received from Robert Peter and others, of this date, also one from George Walker, and others; which were enclosed with a copy of the above resolution in a letter from the Commissioners to the President. There was enclosed in their letter also, a plat of the lands between Rock Creek and the Eastern Branch with several different back lines and a copy of the agreement entered into by the proprietors of the said lands and the President." The letter from Robert Peter and others reads:

"Georgetown, April 14th, 1791.

"Gentlemen: When the President communicated his ideas to the proprietors of land within both the offers, of the insufficiency of either; and the necessity of an union of interests, he was requested to explain his views with respect to the form and extent of territory he would wish for the Federal City — and his reply was, to the best of our recollection — that he would desire to begin at Evans' Point on the Eastern Branch and run from there over Goose Creek some distance above the fording place, to intersect the road leading from Georgetown to Bladensburg about half a mile from Rock Creek — thence to Rock Creek, and with the Creek, River, and Branch to the beginning — supposing that about 3500 acres would be comprehended — but, upon some explanations by some of the proprietors it seemed to be understood that more would be included and probably 4000 acres or upwards.

" In compliance with the views of the President, an agreement was prepared, in which the lines as mentioned by him, were omitted to be inserted, in the fullest confidence that tho' not mentioned in the agreement, they would be adhered to — or at least if they were varied, it would not be to include any considerably greater quantity of land, which we conceive; besides taking land we never had it in contemplation would be required, would only tend to lessen the value of the rest, without any real benefit to the public — as the price of lots would diminish in proportion as the number for sale increased.

"The deed which you now present for signing goes far beyond our idea of what was the spirit of the agreement, — we would therefore wish to decline singing it — and hope it will answer every purpose of the President to confine the lines of the city agreeably to his explanation on the height of the union of interests, when there will be no difficulty on our part to making the proper conveyances.

"We have the honor to be with high respect, Gent'l. Yr. Most Obed. Servts., Robt. Peter, Notley Young, Jas. M. Lingan, Forrest & Stoddert."

The letter from George Walker and others reads:

"Georgetown, April 14th, 1791.

" Gentlemen: We are extremely sorry to find you are at this time prevented from taking deeds and conveyances of the lands granted to the President of the United States, by the respective proprietors, who signed and sealed the agreement made with him on the 30th day of March last; owing to some of these gentlemen now alleging that they had conceived the President should be confined to certain bounds and limits, as well as extent of territory, in laying out the Federal City.

"We however conceiving that, according to the before mentioned agreement, the President has a right to lay out the city upon our lands, where and in what manner he pleases, are ready and willing on our part fully to confirm by deed and conveyance what we have already ratified by our hands and seals: And we confide that you will not accede to any system, that may mutilate, disfigure or render inconvenient the great Metropolis of America.

"Whatever might drop from the President in course of conversation, concerning the lands to be occupied by the city, we do not consider conclusive, as it could not then be expected he could with precision determine, what might be proper to include within its limits; the great object in view, being the founding an elegant, convenient, and agreeable Capital for the Union. Indeed it was our expectation, that after the different interests of Georgetown and Carrollsburgh were happily reconciled, that no further cause of discontent would arise; neither did we expect, that it was ever imagined, the President should be excluded from accepting of such grants as should be made him, for the purposes of erecting the public buildings.

"We hope, therefore, that nothing will be done to frustrate the views of the President, in accomplishing the important object of establishing the residence of Congress upon the Potomac — and are respectfully, gentlemen, Your Mo. Ob. Servants, (Signed) Chas. Beatty,

George Walker now proprietor of the lands lately belonging to Overton Carr, and Thos. Beall of Geo.

Saml. Davidson now proprietor of the land lately belonging to Edwd. Pierce.

The Commissioner."

Supporting this letter Thomas Beall wrote the following day:

"Georgetown, April 15th, 1791.

"Messrs. Johnson, Stuart and Carroll:

"Gentlemen: When I signed the agreement with the President of the United States by which I ceded half of the land I might possess within the limits of the Federal City it was then my opinion as well as now that the President should run the line where he might see proper and include as much land as he might think necessary. "I am respectfully, Your Mo. Obt. Sr.,

(Signed) Thos. Beall, of Geo.

P. S. — My excepting against the land I sold Mr. Abraham Young will prove the above assertion.

(Signed) Thos. Beall of Geo."

It was these three letters which the Commissioners enclosed with one from themselves to the President explaining the situation. Evans' Point on the Eastern Branch was at about the present eastern end of Massachusetts Avenue. A point on the Georgetown and Bladensburg Road (Florida Avenue) half a mile from Rock Creek would be a short distance above the intersection of Massachusetts Avenue with that stream. The dispute, therefore involved the question of the inclusion or exclusion of practically the entire portion of the original area of the city north of Massachusetts Avenue. President Washington was anxious to include this territory and had so indicated in his letter to Major L 'Enfant of April 4th. The contention of the protesting land holders amounted almost to an accusation that he had taken an unfair advantage of them by inducing them to sign the preliminary agreement of

March 30, under the representation that the limits of the city would stop short of this territory, and he replied with considerable spirit as follows:

"Charleston, May 7th, 1791.

"Gentlemen: I have received your letter of the 14th of last month.

"It is an unfortunate circumstance in the present stage of the business, relative to the Federal City, that difficulties unforeseen and unexpected should arise to darken, perhaps to destroy, the fair prospect which it presented when I left Georgetown — and which the instrument, then signed by the combined interest (as it was termed) of Georgetown and Carrollsburg, so plainly describes. The pain which this occurrence occasions me is the more forcibly felt, as I had taken pleasure during my journey through the several states to relate the agreement, and to speak of it on every proper occasion, in terms which applauded the conduct of the parties, as being alike conducive to the public welfare, and to the interest of individuals,, which last it was generally thought would be most benefited by the amazing increase of the property reserved to the land holders.

"The words cited by Messrs. Young, Peter, Lingan and Forrest and Stoddard may be nearly what I expressed; but will these gentlemen say this was given as the precise boundary, or will they, by detaching these words, take them in a sense unconnected with the general explanation of my ideas and views upon that occasion or without the qualifications, which unless I am much mistaken, were added of running about so and so — for I had no map before me for direction. Will they not recollect my observation that Philadelphia stood upon an area of three by two miles and that, if the Metropolis of one State occupied so much ground, what ought that of the United States to occupy? Did I not moreover observe that before the city could be laid out and the spot for the public buildings be precisely fixed on, the water-courses were to be levelled, the heights taken, &c, &c?

"Let the whole of my declaration be taken together, and not a part only, and being compared with the instruments then subscribed, — together with some other circumstances which might be alluded to, let any impartial man judge whether I had reason to expect that difficulties would arise in the conveyances.

"When the instrument was presented I found no occasion to add a word with respect to boundary, because the whole was surrendered upon the conditions which were expressed. Had I discovered a disposition in the subscribers to contract my views, I should then have pointed out the inconveniences and the impolicy of the measure.

"Upon the whole I shall hope and expect that the business will be suffered to proceed — and the more so as they cannot be ignorant that the further consideration of a certain measure in a neighboring State stands postponed — for what reason is left to their own information or conjectures.

"I expect to be with you at the time appointed, and should be exceedingly pleased to find all difficulties removed. "I am, with great esteem, gentlemen

Your most obedient servant,

George Washington.

Messr. Johnson, Stuart and Carroll, Georgetown."

Before starting on his Southern trip President Washington, whose itinerary had been carefully worked out in advance, arranged to meet with the Commissioners on June 27, by which time it was calculated he would have returned to Mount Vernon.

After spending a week at Mount Vernon on the conclusion of his trip, riding over his farms and receiving visitors, he went to Georgetown as per appointment on June 27th, the particular business in hand being to bring the proprietors into line with his ideas as to the boundary line which should be adopted for the northeastern limits of the city and to obtain the execution of conveyances from them which should incorporate a description adopting the boundary so determined. Among those who had protested against the description in the deed as originally drawn was Col. Stoddert who owned a tract of land near the Eastern Branch and lying just within the boundary as contemplated by the President. Upon this tract was a spring known as Gibson's or Cool Spring which delivered a copious flow of water and headed a stream which flowed eastward to the Eastern Branch. This stream was located just east of the present intersection of Fifteenth and E Streets, northeast, and is now used by the Hygienic Ice Company. Col. Stoddert desired to have this spring excluded from the limits of the proposed city, and apparently this was the basis of his opposition to the form of the deed as first drawn. At any rate the President, according to his own version of the affair, had little difficulty in bringing the proprietors into line except that, either by way of compromise or as a favor to his old friend, he agreed to so draw the boundary line of the city as to exclude Col. Stoddert 's spring. The line as finally agreed upon, instead of continuing straight to the Eastern Branch on the course it took at the crossing of Reedy Branch of Goose Creek (9th and Florida Avenue) takes a course due south at Fifteenth Street and Florida Avenue, northeast, continuing to C Street, northeast, and following the line of the last named street to the Eastern Branch, thus forming the right angled notch which appears on the maps of the city at that point. The incidents of the President's stay are recited in the following extracts from his diary for that period:

"Monday 27, June, 1791: Left Mount Vernon for Georgetown before six o'clock; and according to appointment met the Commissioners at that place by nine. Then calling together the proprietors of those lands on which the Federal City was proposed to be built who had agreed to cede them on certain conditions at the last meeting I had with them at this place but from some misconception with respect to the extension of their grants had refused to make conveyances and recapitulating the principles upon which my comns to them at the former meeting were made and giving some explanations of the present state of matters and the consequences of delay in this business they readily waived their objections and agreed to convey to the utmost extent of what was required.

" Tuesday, 28th: While the Commissioners were engaged in preparing the deeds to be signed by the subscribers this afternoon, 1 went out with Majors L 'Enfant and Ellicott to take a more perfect view of the ground in order to decide finally on the spots on which to place the public buildings and to direct how a line which was to leave out a spring (commonly known by the name of the Cool Spring) belonging to Major Stoddart should be run.

"Wednesday, 29th: The deeds which remained unexecuted yesterday were signed today and the Dowers of their respective wives acknowledged according to law. This being accomplished, I called the Several Subscribers together and made known to them the spots on which I meant to place the buildings for the P: and Executive departments of the government — and for the Legislature of D. A Plan was also laid before them of the City in order to convey to them general ideas of the City — but they were told that some deviations from it would take place — particularly in the diagonal streets or avenues, which would not be so numerous; and in the removal of the President 's house more westerly for the advantage of higher ground. They were also told that a Town house, or exchange wd be placed on some convenient ground between the spots designed for the public buildings before mentioned, and it was with much pleasure that a general approbation of the measure seemed to pervade the whole. "Thursday, 30th: The business which brot me to Georgetown being finished and the Commissioners instructed with respect to the mode of carrying the plan into effect I set off this morning a little after four o'clock in the prosecution of my journey to Philadelphia." It was either while the President was at Georgetown on this occasion or on the occasion of a visit of Major L 'Enfant to Mount Vernon that the latter laid his second report and tentative plan before the President.

Major L 'Enfant 's report was dated June 22, 1791. In this report the Major goes quite fully into his explanation of the system of avenues which was to characterize his plan, saying:

"having first determined some principal points to which I wished making the rest subordiante I next made the distribution regular with streets at right angle north, south and east, west but afterwards I opened others on various directions as avenues to and from every principal places, wishing by this not merely to afford a greater variety of pleasant seats and prospect as will be obtained from the advantageous ground over the which the avenues are mostly directly but principally to connect each part of the city with more efficacy by, if I may so express, making the real distance less from place to place in menaging on them a reciprocity of sight and making them thus seemingly connected promot a rapide stellement (settlement) over the whole so that the most remot may become an addition to the principal while without the help of these divurgents communications such settlements if at all attempted would be languid, and lost in the extant would become detremental to the main establishment."

He further spoke of his system of avenues as "being combined to injure (insure) a rapide Intercourse with all the part of the City to which they will serve as does the main veins in the animal body to diffuse life through smaller vessels in quickening the active motion of the heart."

With respect to the points selected by him for the locations of the public buildings, he says:

"After much menutial search for an elligible situation, prompted I may say from a fear of being prejudiced in favour of a first opinion I could discover no one so advantageously to greet the Congressional building as is that on the west end of Jenkins heights (Capitol Hill) which stand as a pedestal waiting for a monument, and I am confident, were all the wood cleared from the ground no situation could stand in competition with this. Some might perhaps require less labour to be rendered agreeable but after all assistance of arts none ever would be made so grand and all other would appear but of secondary nature. "

He then proceeds to discuss the location for the President's house, in the selection of which President Washington had apparently had some voice. He says:

"that where I determine the seat of the presidial palace, in its difference of nature may be view of advantageous to the object of adding to the sumptuousness of a palace the convenience of a house and the agreeableness of a country seat situated on that ridge which attracted your attention at the first inspection of the ground on the west side of the Tiber entrance it will see 10 or 12 miles down the Potowmack front the town and harbor of Alexandria and stand to the view of the whole city and have the most improved part of it made by addition to those grand improvements for which the ground in the dependenly of the palace is proper." After remarking that he does not anticipate that any disadvantage will result from the distance between the Capitol and President's House, he continued:

"to make however the distance less to the other offices I placed the three grand Departments of State contiguous to the principle Palace and on the way leading to the Congressional House the gardens of the one together with the park and other improvement on the dependency are connected with the publique walk and avenue to the Congress house in a manner as most form a whole as grand as it will be agreeable and convenient to the whole city which form (from) the distribution of the local will have an early access to this place of general resort and all along side of which may be placed play houses, room of assembly, academies and all such sort of places as may be attractive to the learned and afford diversion to the idle." In this he evidently referred to his scheme for the development of the Mall.

Other explanations set forth his plans for developing the Tiber Canal and the park south of the President's house and indicate his intention to place "a grand Equestrian figure" of President Washington on the present site of the Washington Monument.

The deeds of which President Washington had secured the execution recited that in consideration of five shillings and of the uses and trust thereinafter mentioned, the proprietors conveyed all their lands within the defined boundaries of the city, except such as lay within the limits of Carrollsburgh or Hamburgh, to Thomas Beall, son of George, and John Mackall Gantt, in trust to be laid out into such streets, squares, parcels and lots as the President might approve, for the purpose of the Federal City. They provided that the trustees should convey to the Commissioners all of the streets and such of the squares, parcels and lots as the President should deem proper, the residue of the lots to be equally divided between the proprietors. The half thus apportioned to the public were to be sold to raise money with which to erect the public buildings, but the first proceeds were to be applied to reimburse the proprietors for the land taken for the public reservations at the rate of £25 ($66) per acre, no payment being made for the land taken for streets.

The full text of the deeds follows:

"This indenture, made this 29th day of June, in the year of our Lord one thousand seven hundred and ninety-one, between (here is inserted the name of the grantor), of the State of Maryland, of the one part, and Thomas Beall, of George, and John M. Gantt, of the State of Maryland, of the other part, witnesseth: That the said — (the grantor), for and in consideration of the sum of five shillings, to him in hand paid by the same Thomas Beall, of George, and John M. Gantt, before the sealing and delivery of these presents, the receipt whereof he doth hereby acknowledge, and thereof doth acquit the said Thomas Beall, of George, and John M. Gantt, their executors and administrators; and also, for and in consideration of the uses and trust hereinafter mentioned, to be performed by the said Thomas Beall, of George, and John M. Gantt, and the survivor of them, and the heirs of such survivor, according to the true intent and meaning thereof, hath granted, bargained, sold, aliened, released, and confirmed, and by these presents doth grant, bargain, sell, alien, release, and confirm unto the said Thomas Beall, of George, and John M. Gantt, and the survivor of them, and the heirs of such survivor, all the lands of him, the said (grantor) lying and being within the following limits, boundaries, and lines, to wit: Beginning on the east side of Rock Creek, at a stone standing in the middle of the main road leading from Georgetown to Bladensburg; thence along the middle of the said road to a stone standing on the east side of the Reedy Branch of Goose Creek; thence southeasterly, making an angle of 61 degrees and twenty minutes with the meridian, to a stone standing in the road leading from Bladensburg to the Eastern Branch ferry; thence south, to a stone eighty poles north of the east and west line already drawn from the mouth of Goose Creek, to the Eastern Branch; then east, parallel to the said east-andwest line, to the Eastern Branch; thence by and with the waters of the Eastern Branch, Potomac River, and Rock Creek to the beginning, with their appurtenances, except all and every lot and lots of which the said ——— (the grantor) is seized or to which he is entitled in Carrollsburgh or Hamburgh; to have and to hold the hereby bargained and sold lands with their appurtenances to the said Thomas Beall of George and John M. Gantt, and the survivor of them, and the heirs of such survivor forever: To and for the special trust following, and no other; that is to say: That all the said lands hereby bargained and sold, or such part thereof as may be thought necessary or proper to be laid out, together with other lands within the said limits, for a Federal City, with such streets, squares, parcels, and lots as the President of the United States for the time being shall approve; and that the said Thomas Beall of George and John M. Gantt, or the survivor of them, or the heirs of such survivor shall convey to the Commissioners for the time being, appointed by virtue of the act of Congress entitled 'An act for establishing the temporary and permanent seat of the Government of the United States,' and their successors, for the use of the United States forever, all the said streets and such of the said squares, parcels, and lots as the President shall deem proper, for the use of the United States; and that as to the residue of the said lots, into which the said lands hereby bargained and sold shall have been laid off and divided, that a fair and equal division of them shall be made. And if no other mode of division shall be agreed on by consent of the said — (the grantor and the Commissioners for the time being, then such residue of the said lots shall be divided, every other lot alternate to the said ——— (the grantor), and it shall, in that event, be determined by lot, whether the said ——— (the grantor) shall begin with the lot of the lowest number laid out on the said lands or the following number. "And all the said lots which may in any manner be divided or assigned to the said — (the grantor) shall, thereupon, together with any part of the bargained and sold lands, if any, which shall not have been laid out in the said city, be conveyed by the said Thomas Beall of George and John M. Gantt, or the survivor of them, or the heirs of such survivor, to him, the said ——— (the grantor) , his heirs and assigns. And that the said other lots shall and may be sold at such time or times, in such manner, and on such terms and conditions as the President of the United States for the time being shall direct; and that the said Thomas Beall of George and John M. Gantt, or the survivor of them, or the heirs of such survivor, will, on the order and direction of the President, convey all the said lots so sold and ordered to be conveyed to the respective purchasers in fee simple, according to the terms and conditions of such purchases; and the produce of the sales of the said lots when sold as aforesaid shall in the first place be applied to the payment in money to the said ——— (the grantor), his executors, administrators, or assigns, for all the part of the land hereby bargained and sold which shall have been laid off into lots, squares, or parcels, and appropriated as aforesaid to the use of the United States, at the rate of twenty-five pounds per acre, not accounting the said streets as part thereof.

"And the said twenty-five pounds per acre, being so paid, or in any other manner satisfied, that then the produce of the same sale, or what thereof may remain as aforesaid, in money or securities of any kind, shall be paid, assigned, transferred, and delivered over to the President of the United States, for the time being, as a grant of money, and to be applied for the purposes and according to the act of Congress aforesaid. But the said conveyance to the said ——— (the grantor), his heirs or assigns, as well as the conveyance to the purchasers, shall be on, and subject to such terms and conditions as shall be thought reasonable, by the President, for the time being, for regulating the materials and manner of the buildings and improvements on the lots, generally, in the said city, or in particular streets, or parts thereof, for common convenience, safety, and order: Provided, Such terms and conditions be declared before the sales of any of the said lots, under the direction of the President. And in trust further, and on the agreement that the said ——— (the grantor), his heirs or assigns, shall and may continue his possession and occupation of the said lands hereby bargained and sold, at his and their will and pleasure, until they shall be occupied under the said appropriations for the use of the United States as aforesaid, or by purchasers; and when any lots or parcels shall be occupied under purchase or appropriations as aforesaid, then, and not until then, shall the said ——— (the grantor) relinquish his occupation thereof. And in trust also, as to the trees, timber, and wood, on the premises, that he the said ——— (the grantor) his heirs or assigns, may freely cut down, take, and carry away, and use the same as his and their property, except such of the trees and wood growing as the President or commissioners aforesaid may judge proper, and give notice, shall be left for ornaments, for which the just and reasonable value shall be paid to the said ——— (the grantor), his executors, administrators, or assigns, exclusive of the twenty-five pounds per acre for the land.

"And in case the arrangements of the streets, lots, and the like will conveniently admit of it, he the said ——— (the grantor), his heirs or assigns, if he so desire it, shall possess and retain his buildings and graveyard, if any, on the hereby bargained and sold land, paying to the President at the rate of twelve pounds ten shillings per acre for the lands so retained, because of such buildings and graveyards, to be applied as aforesaid, and the same shall thereupon be conveyed to the said ——— (the grantor), his heirs or assigns, with his lots. But if the arrangements of the streets, lots, and the like will not conveniently admit of such retention, and it shall become necessary to remove such buildings, then the said ——— (the grantor), his executors, administrators, or assigns, shall be paid the reasonable value thereof in the same manner as squares or other ground appropriated for the use of the United States are to be paid for. And because it may so happen that by deaths or removals of the said Thomas Beall, of George, and John M. Gantt, and from other causes, difficulties may occur in fully perfecting the said trusts, by executing all the said conveyances, if no eventual provision is made, it is therefore agreed and covenanted between all the said parties, that the said Thomas Beall, of George, and John M. Gantt, or either of them, or the heirs of any of them, lawfully may, and that they, at any time, at the request of the President of the United States for the time being, will convey all or any of the said lands hereby bargained and sold, which shall not then have been conveyed in execution of the trusts aforesaid, to such, person or persons as he shall appoint, in fee simple, subject to the trusts then remaining to be executed, and to the end that some may be perfected.

"And it is further granted and agreed between all the said parties, and each of the said parties doth for himself, respectively, and his heirs, covenant and grant to and with the others of them, that he and they shall and will, if required by the President of the United States for the time being, join in and execute any further deed or deeds for carrying into effect the trusts, purposes, and true intent of this present deed. In witness whereof the parties to these presents have hereunto set their hands and affixed their seals the day and year first above written.

Signed by the grantor.

——— ——— [Seal.]

Signed, sealed, and delivered in the presence of — "

The question of the authorship of these deeds, from which the greater part of the titles to land within the original limits of the city are commonly regarded as dating, is a subject for interesting speculation. Mr. Johnson undoubtedly drew them. In his letter to the Commissioners of April 3rd, almost immediately following the execution of the preliminary agreement by the proprietors, President Washington wrote:

"The form of the conveyances as drawn by the Attorney General will, I presume, require alteration or a counterpart, as the present agreement essentially differs from the former. If Mr. Johnson could conveniently undertake to prepare such a deed as he thinks would answer all the purposes both of the public and the Grantees I am sure it would be efficiently done. If this cannot be, then it might be well to furnish the Attorney-General of the United States with a copy of the agreement with the papers I left with you and such other information as will enable him to do it." Following this letter is the record of the proceedings of the Commissioners from April 12, 1791, before quoted, wherein it is recited, that the form of the conveyance to Trustees was that day presented by Mr. Johnson and agreed to by the Commissioners.

The letter from President Washington to the Commissioners, however, indicates that a form of deed had already been prepared by the Attorney General, Edmund Randolph, and to what extent Mr. Johnson used this form in drawing the deed it is difficult to say.

The participation of the Attorney General is further indicated by a note from President Washington to Mr. Jefferson dated Sunday, March 6, 1791, wherein he says:

"The President would thank Mr. Jefferson for placing all, or such of the enclosed papers (after he has perused them) in the hands of the Attorney General as he shall deem necessary for the purpose of drawing the several documents of the Ceded Lands or, the form of one. If the former, it is conceived further information than the enclosures contain is wanting. If the latter, the agreement, and perhaps the plat to which it refers, is all that is necessary; but the plat referred to, does not apply to the subsequent purchasers. "

But while the evidence would thus strongly tend to show the joint authorship of the deeds to have been in Mr. Randolph and Mr. Johnson, there is evidence worthy of serious consideration indicating the possibility of Mr. Jefferson's having had a hand in this as in so many other matters connected with the task of starting the city on its road to actual existence.

In the letter which Mr. Jefferson wrote to the President on September 17, 1790, relating the results of his and Mr. Madison's interviews with General Mason, he enclosed a memorandum setting forth the substance of a proposed deed which he desired the President to forward to Mr. Charles Carroll with whom the subject had been discussed. This memorandum was evidently drawn with the idea that the proprietors would sell their lands outright, as the scheme of a division between the proprietors and the government is not provided for therein. Nevertheless, the provisions set forth in Mr. Jefferson's memorandum are so similar to those of the deeds in trust as finally prepared that the conclusion is almost irresistible that Mr. Jefferson's memorandum was in large measure used either by the Attorney General or by Mr. Johnson as the foundation upon which the deeds were framed. It reads:

"The Conveyance to be executed, according to the form of the laws of Maryland, by the Proprietors of the land designated by the President for the Federal seat.

"The preamble to recite the substance of that part of the Residence Act which authorizes the President to receive grants of lands or money for the use of the United States and to declare that the object of the conveyance is to furnish both Land and money for their use. The body of the deed to convey the lands designated for the city (suppose 1500 acres) to A and B and their heirs in trust for the following purposes:

"1. To reconvey to the commissioners their heirs and successors to be named by the President, such portions of the said lands as the President shall designate for the site of the public buildings, public walks, streets, &c, to remain for the use of the United States.

"2. To reconvey the residue of such lands, to such persons, and on such conditions as the Commissioners shall direct, for the purpose of raising money, and the money when received to be granted to the President for the use of the United States according to the Residence Act.

"The effect of this last clause will be such that the President (without any further legislation from Congress) may proceed to lay out the town immediately into 1, public lots; 2 public walks and gardens; 3 private lots for sale; 4 streets. The 1, 2 and 4th articles to be reconveyed to the Commissioners, and the 3rd to private purchasers as above proposed. It is understood that this conveyance will have been preceded by articles of agreement signed by all the proprietors of the lands in and about those several spots which have such obvious advantages as render it presumable to everyone that some one of them will attract the President's notice and choice." Not all the land within the city was conveyed to the Trustees at the time the first deeds were executed. The record of the proceedings of the Commissioners for that day (June 29, 1791) recites that the deeds of trust .executed by Robert Peter, Notley Young, Benjamin Stoddard, James Pierce, Anthony Holmead, Daniel Carroll of Duddington, James M. Lingan, David Burnes, Jonathan Slater, Samuel Davidson, William Young, Abraham Young, Charles Beatty, Clement Woodward, and George Walker, were lodged in the care of the Commissioners and they directed their Secretary to have them recorded in due time in the General Court Records. The proceedings for the same day recite that Messrs. U. Forrest, Wm. Bayly, Philip R.

Fendall and Wm. Deakins, Junior, entered into an agreement to convey about five hundred acres under the terms of the other deeds of trust as soon as required after obtaining deed from John Warring and that Jonathan Slater previous to executing his deed entered into an agreement that if the contract he had made with John Prout should not take effect he would subject the land concerning which it was made to the same terms as the other lands were by the proprietors subjected within the proposed limits of the Federal City, and that whether the contract should take place or not he would subject his land reserved out of that contract to the same terms.

On September 3, 1791, Mr. Johnson submitted to the Commissioners the form of the deeds to be used for the Hamburgh and Carrollsburgh lots and rapid progress was made in securing the execution of the deeds by such of the owners as were competent and could be located. These deeds conveyed all the general grantors' lots in Hamburgh and Carrollsburgh subject to the trusts named in the other deeds and provided that one half the quantity of land thereby bargained and sold should be conveyed as near the old situations as possible to the grantors so that each respective former proprietor should have made up to him one-half of his former quantity in as good a situation as before, but that if from appropriations for the use of the United States one-half could not be assigned in like situation as before, satisfaction should be made in ground in the city to be agreed upon or if the proprietors and commissioners could not agree the proprietors should be compensated in money to be raised by a sale of such parts of the lots conveyed as should remain clear of appropriations, the proceeds to be applied first to compensate the proprietors and the remainder to go to the President as a grant of money for the purposes of the city, the sales to be subject to such building regulations as might be established.

By means of the various deeds above mentioned all the lands within the limits of the city, except such as belonged to persons incompetent to convey or to such as could not be reached, came eventually into the hands of the Trustees Beall and Gantt, the Commissioners by a memorial to the Maryland Legislature dated September 8, 1791, reporting as follows:

"That within these Limits (i. e. as outlined in the deeds of trust) your memorialists do not know nor have reason to believe that there are any proprietors and possessors who have not come into the common terms of agreement except Elizabeth the wife of Aquilla Wheeler who is said to be insane and whose husband is willing her land should be subjected in the same manner as the land of others, the minor Children of Stephen West, whose nearest friends have agreed to subscribe for their own parts and wish the lands of the minors to be put on the same footing, and the heirs of Joseph Coones and some of the persons entitled to Lands in Carrollsburgh and Hamburgh though but a few of them considering their dispersed situation. That some lots belonging to persons absent, and may have been transmitted by descent and devise, the heirs and devisees in some cases being minors."

The titles to such parcels of land as were not conveyed to the trustees, Beall and Gantt by the deeds before described were acquired under the provision of an Act of Maryland to be later referred to more at length.

It is a matter of interest that the execution of the deeds to the greater part of the property within the boundaries of the city, on June 29, 1791, occurred approximately one year after the passage of the act to establish the temporary and permanent seat of Government. Within that time President Washington, notwithstanding the manifold public matters of gravest import which claimed his attention as Chief Executive of the new Republic, and which enforced his presence the greater part of the time at Philadelphia, had inspected the entire territory mentioned in the Act, selected the site and determined upon the boundaries of both the Federal Territory and the Federal City; had brought about the acquisition of the greater part of the land for the city, and had seen the planning of the city well advanced towards completion. Such an achievement furnishes some idea of the extraordinary caliber of the man.

CHAPTER IV.

The First Board of Commissioners

WHEN President Washington left Georgetown on June 30th, 1791, the day after the execution of the deeds in trust by the conciliated proprietors, he in large measure shifted the burden of responsibility for the progress of the city from his own shoulders which up to that time had chiefly borne it, to the shoulders of the Commissioners.

The President in dealing with the proprietors of the land had found his task no easy one, but the eagerness of the latter to have the city located upon their lands, added to President Washington's prestige and the force of his personality, had enabled him to overcome all difficulties without serious opposition. The case with the Commissioners was different. The prospect of funds from the sale of lots, upon which President Washington calculated for the prosecution of the public works, fell far short of materialization. The expectations of a rapid development and settling up of the city and of early wealth to accrue to the proprietors therefrom, which had been President Washington's chief argument in dealing with the proprietors, proved to have been founded on an undue optimism. Misunderstandings and quarrels resulted in breaches between the Commissioners and their most important subordinates, which, added to their shortage of funds, contributed greatly to hinder the prosecution of the work. Among the proprietors were some whose disappointment, joining with the hostility of the enemies of the city, manifested itself in criticism and abuse amounting at times almost to vilification.

Through these tribulations the Commissioners pursued their course with a singleness of purpose and a devotion to the object of their appointment which has placed the nation under an obligation to them which has been singularly overlooked. Frequent mention is heard of the desirability of according recognition, by some adequate memorial, to the designer of the plan of the Capital City, and it is indeed fitting that this should be done. But equally fitting would be some appropriate acknowledgment of the debt which is owing to the Commissioners who bore the brunt of the administrative labor of preparing the city and public buildings for the reception of the government. Particularly is such recognition due to the three original Commissioners, Daniel Carroll, Thomas Johnson and David Stuart, who organized the administrative details of the work and continued in control of it until the processes of establishing the Federal City were fairly on the way to success.

In following the story of the founding of the city, it is gratifying to note one bright and compensating aspect of the Commissioners ' connection therewith; namely, the unwavering loyalty which President Washington at all times displayed towards them. In every contingency he sustained their dignity and authority and insisted upon their being accorded recognition as his accredited and plenipotentiary agents. With a few rare exceptions when especial exigencies or the slowness of communication made it necessary for him to vary his rule, he refused to consider matters coming within the scope of their functions until passed upon by the Commissioners and their recommendations made; and practically without exception sustained their acts and decisions.

In following the proceedings of the Commissioners it is well to bear in mind that none of the three original members of the board lived at the scene of operations. Mr.

Johnson lived at Frederick, Maryland, Doctor Stuart at Alexandria, and Mr. Carroll near the present station of Forest Glen, Maryland. The Commissioners usually met once a month, and their meetings often lasted for a week or longer. Communications requiring special action were generally sent to Mr. Carroll as most convenient to Georgetown; and he in turn summoned his colleagues by express messengers.

At the first meeting of the Commissioners on April 12, 1791, John M. Gantt was appointed Secretary. On June 30, William Deakins was appointed Treasurer; his compensation to be one per cent of the amount of money paid out by him. He was required to give bond in the sum of £10,000 ($26,600) and qualified with Benjamin Stoddert and Thomas Beall as his bondsmen. He was directed, in the event of the anticipated establishment of a bank of deposit or branch of the bank of the United States of Alexandria, to lodge there all moneys beyond eight hundred dollars which should come to his hands, subject to be drawn by him as wanted. On October 22nd, Thomas Cooke was appointed clerk and bookkeeper.

The Commissioners served for nearly two years without salary until March 4, 1793, when on the recommendation of the President it was resolved that they be allowed one thousand dollars per year each.

The task which it became the duty of the Commissioners to superintend, aside from completing the acquisition of the land within the limits of the city, which, it will be remembered, had been only partly accomplished by President Washington, may be summarized as consisting first, in the perfection of the plan of the city; second, in surveying, platting and marking the streets, reservations, squares and lots; third, in effecting divisions of the lots with the proprietors; fourth, in raising the money needed for the erection of the public buildings and for the expenses of administration — this by collecting the Virginia and Maryland grants, by the sale of lots, and by negotiating loans; and lastly, in the erection of the public buildings and the completion of such other public improvements as the needs of the city dictated and the means at hand permitted.

Tt was deemed imperative by the President to hold a sale of lots at the earliest possible date, and when he left the Commissioners after obtaining the execution of the deeds of trust on June 29, it was with instructions to proceed vigorously with that purpose in view.

Accordingly at their meeting the day after his departure, the following advertisement was directed to be published in the Georgetown Weekly Ledger:

"Georgetown, 30th June, 1791. " The President having approved the sites of ground for the public buildings to be erected in pursuance of the Act of Congress for establishing the Temporary and permanent seat of Government of the United States, the Commissioners appointed in virtue of that act will meet at George Town on Thursday the seventeenth day of October next and proceed to sell at vendue a number of Lots in the best Situations in the Federal City. A deposit of eight per cent will be required. The residue to be on bond with security payable in three equal yearly payments. The regulations as to the manner of Improvements and other circumstances will be made known at the sale.

Thomas Johnson,
David Stuart,
Danl. Carroll,
Commissioners.

"Printers throughout the United States are requested to insert the above in their papers. "

Meanwhile, Major L 'Enfant was proceeding vigorously with his work of laying out the city, with the assistance of Major Ellicott who had been called in from the work of running the boundary lines of the ten miles square in order that the survey of the city might be sufficiently advanced for the October sales. As to the manner in which the basis for the survey of the city was established, the legend upon Major L 'Enfant 's map entitled "Observations Explanatory of the Plan," affords the following interesting information:

"First. The positions for the different grand edifices, and for the several grand squares or areas of different shapes, as they are laid down, were first determined on the most advantageous ground, commanding the most extensive prospect, and the better susceptible of such improvements as the various intents of the several objects may require.

"Secondly. Lines or avenues of direct communication have been devised to connect the separate and most distance objects with the principal, and to preserve through the whole a reciprocity of sight at the same time. Attention has been paid to the passing of those leading avenues over the most favorable ground for prospect and convenience.

"Thirdly. North and south lines, intersected by others running due east and west, make the distribution of the city into streets, squares, etc., and those lines have been so combined as to meet at certain given points with those divergent avenues, so as to form on the spaces first determined the different squares or areas, which are all proportioned in magnitude to the number of avenues leading to them." L 'Enfant then states how these lines were drawn.

"In order to execute the above plan, Mr. Ellicott drew a true meridional line by celestial observation, which passes through the area intended for the Congress House. This line is crossed by another line due east and west, which passes through the same area. These lines were accurately measured and made the bases on which the whole plan was executed. He ran all the lines by a transit instrument, and determined the acute angles by actual measurement, and left nothing to the uncertainly of the compass." The line due east and west mentioned by L 'Enfant was doubtless the same line as that referred to in the deeds in trust as "the east and west line already drawn from the mouth of Goose Creek to the Eastern Branch."

The "Observations" furnish the further information that in the space now occupied by Lincoln Square near the terminus of East Capitol Street, it was proposed to erect "a historic column, also intended for a mile or itinerary Column, from whose station (a mile from the Federal house) all distances of places through the continent are to be calculated."

Much speculation has been indulged in as to the reasons for the adoption of the diagonal avenues as a feature of the plan, and as to the source from which L 'Enfant obtained the idea of employing them. On the former question it has been suggested that the diagonals centering upon the open reservations were designed to facilitate movements of troops from one part of the city to another in the event of riots; the park spaces affording room for concentration. L 'Enfant however, makes no reference to such a purpose in any of his official communications, extracts from which, bearing upon this question were quoted in the preceding chapter. Whether

68

the idea of employing these diagonals in his plan originated in his own mind or was suggested by plans of other cities is problematical. Mr. Glenn Brown, in an illustrated article in Volume 6, of the Records of the Columbia Historical Society, suggests that either Sir Christopher Wrenn's plan for the rebuilding of London after the fire, or the plans of Annapolis, Maryland, or Williamsburg, Virginia, may have furnished the idea. From the illustration given by Mr. Brown of the plan of Annapolis, the conclusion is hard to resist that it was from this source, if from any other than his own mind, that L 'Enfant received his inspiration. This plan shows two centers: the State House Circle and the Church Circle, highly suggestive of L 'Enfant 's centers at the Capitol and President's House, each having its radiating system of streets and both lying in the course of one of the chief thoroughfares of the town. The plan is startlingly suggestive of L 'Enfant 's plan for the federal city. L 'Enfant was doubtless familiar with the town, or at least had access to a plan of it; whereas there is no evidence that he ever saw Sir Christopher Wrenn's proposed plan for the rebuilding of London. Letters quoted in the preceding chapter, show that in his request to Mr. Jefferson for the plans of foreign cities which had been collected by the latter, he mentioned that of London; but Mr. Jefferson, in his letter enumerating the plans sent to L 'Enfant in response to this request, makes no mention either of the plan of London or of Sir Christopher Wrenn's proposed plan of it.

The result of the labors of those engaged in this work was that by the middle of August Major L 'Enfant had completed his plan which he took to Philadelphia for the President 's inspection. With his plan, Major L 'Enfant submitted a lengthy statement largely consisting of a very cogent argument in favor of a postponement of the contemplated sale of lots. In setting forth the state of progress of the federal city he allows his characteristic enthusiasm to manifest itself in the following:

"Brought to the point as matters do now stand enough is done to satisfy everyone of an earnestness in the process of Execution — and the spots assigned for the Federal House and for the President's palace in exhibiting the most sumptuous aspect and claiming already the suffrage of a crowd of daily visitors both natives and foreigners, will serve to give a grand idea of the whole, but nevertheless it is to be wished more may be done to favor a sale — this being to serve very little towards evidencing the beauties of local (ities) reserved for private settlements all being absolutely lost in the chaos of pulled timber without possibility to judge of the advantages of relative conveniency much less of agreement, to be derived from improvements intended in a surrounding local of which but few can form an idea when after inspecting a map.

"The Grand avenue connecting both the palace and the federal House will be most magnificent and most convenient, — the Streets running west of the upper square of the federal House, and which terminate in an easy slope on the canal through the tiber which it will overlook for the space of above two miles will be beautiful above what may be imagined — those other streets parallel to that canal, those crossing over it and which are as many avenues to the grand walk from the water cascade under the federal House to the President's Park and dependency extending to the bank of the Potomac, and also the several Squares or area such as are intended for the Judiciary court — the national bank — the grand church — the play House — the Market and exchange — all through will offer a variety of situations unparalleled in point of beauties — suitable to every purpose and in every point convenient; both are devised for the first offset of the City and combined to command the highest price in a sale."

This plan, it may be here stated, was submitted by the President to Congress for its inspection on December 13, 1791, with the following brief comment:

"Gentlemen of the Senate and House of Representatives: 1 place before you the plan of the city that has been laid out within the district of ten miles square, which was fixed upon for the permanent seat of the Government of the United States." It was shortly after withdrawn to be used by Major L 'Enfant in preparing the draft for the engraver.

While Major L 'Enfant was in Philadelphia with his plan he was requested by the President to hold a conference with a number of persons interested in the new city, among them Mr. Jefferson and Mr. Madison. As the result of this conference it was decided that Mr. Madison and Mr. Jefferson should stop at Georgetown on their way to Virginia a little later and obtain the views of the Commissioners relative to the matters which had been discussed at the Philadelphia conference. Pursuant to appointment, Mr. Madison and Mr. Jefferson met with the Commissioners at Georgetown on September 8th, 1791 and went at length into many details with reference to the policy to be followed in establishing the City. Mr. Jefferson came equipped with a set of questions, which with the answers agreed upon by the Commissioners, are set forth in the record of the meeting.

Mr. Jefferson's report to the President of the action taken by the Commissioners is but one of the many testimonials to be found to the complete liberty of judgment and action on the part of the Commissioners upon which the President at all times insisted. Writing on September 8, 1791, the day of the meeting, Mr. Jefferson says:

"We were detained on the road by the rains so that we did not arrive here till yesterday about ten o'clock; as soon as horses could be got ready we set out and rode till dark, examining chiefly the grounds newly laid open, which we found much superior to what we had imagined, — we have passed this day in consultation with the Commissioners, who having deliberated on every article contained in our paper and pre-admonished that they should decide freely on their own view of things, concurred unanimously on, I believe every point with what had been thought best in Philadelphia." From the record of the Commissioners' meeting for that day, it appears that Major L 'Enfant 's recommendations in favor of a postponement of the coming sale were considered and overruled; that the question of attempting to effect a loan on the security of the public's share of the lots in the city was discussed and decided to be impracticable until the approximate value of the property should be established at a sale, as well as being of doubtful legality without previous legislation; that it was decided to increase the ready money deposits on sales of lots to one-fourth; that the building of a bridge over the Eastern Branch, the digging of the Tiber Creek Canal and the construction of wharves on the river below Rock Creek as had been proposed by Mr. Peter of Georgetown were postponed for want of funds; that no wooden houses should be allowed in the town; that it was concluded (doubtless in accordance to Mr. Jefferson's pronounced views on the subject) that liberty should be allowed as to the distance of buildings from the streets, but some limit placed upon their heights — no house wall to be higher than thirty-five feet in any part of the town and none lower than that on any of the avenues; that it was determined that the digging of earth for bricks the coming fall was indispensible, the procuring of

70

other materials to depend upon the funds; that it was thought advisable to advertise a prize for the best plans for the public buildings; that encroachments in the streets such as stoops or projections of every kind should be prohibited; that the plan of the city should be engraved; that the names of the streets should be alphabetical one way and numerical the other, the former to be divided into north and south letters, the latter into east and west numbers from the "Capitol;" that lots with springs on them should be appropriated to the public if practicable without too much discontent, the springs not to be sold again; that the public squares should be left blank except that for the Capitol and one for the executive department, which should be considered as appropriated; that soundings of the Eastern Branch should be made and a post road established through the city; and lastly that the name of the city and territory should be "City of Washington and Territory of Columbia."

On September 9, 1791, the day following this meeting, the Commissioners wrote to Major L 'Enfant at Philadelphia:

"We have agreed that the federal District shall be called 'The Territory of Columbia,' and the federal City 'The City of Washington,' the title of the map will, therefore, be 'A Map of the City of Washington in the Territory of Columbia.'

"We have also agreed the streets be named alphabetically one way, and numerically the other; the former divided into North and South letters, the latter into East and West numbers from the Capitol."

On Major L 'Enfant 's return from Philadelphia the Commissioners, by a resolution dated September 24th, 1791. instructed him to employ on the first Monday in October next one hundred and fifty laborers to throw up clay at the President's House and the house of Congress and in doing such other work connected with the post road and the public buildings as he should think most proper to have immediately executed. He was also instructed to have three hundred copies of the plan of the federal city transmitted to such parts of the Northern states as he should think proper and to keep the remainder subject to the directions of the Commissioners. The time set for the first sale of lots was rapidly approaching and was doubtless looked forward to with much concern by both the President and the Commissioners, for the result of this sale was to be an indication of the probable success or failure of the scheme for financing the city from the sale of lots. Major L 'Enfant and Major Ellicott with their assistants were bending every energy to completing the survey of a number of squares in preparation for the sale. Pursuant to a recommendation which Major Ellicott had made, the lots which it was decided to offer were to be those in the neighborhood of the Capitol and President's House, these being deemed the most desirable.

On October 14, the Commissioners met and adopted the form of the bond to be given by purchasers to secure the deferred payments on the lots purchased and also the form of the certificate of sale to be furnished to purchasers of lots; and had a quantity of both forms printed for use at the sale. On October 16, the Commissioners adopted the following building regulations which were promulgated over the President's name at the sale the following day:

"1st. That the outer and party walls of all houses within the said city, shall be built of brick or stone.

"2nd. That all buildings on the streets shall be parallel thereto, and may be advanced to the line of the street, or withdrawn therefrom, at the pleasure of the improver: but where any such building is about to be erected, neither the foundation or party wall shall be begun, without first applying to the person or persons appointed by the commissioners to superintend the buildings within the city, who will ascertain the lines of the walls to correspond with these regulations.

"3rd. The wall of no house to be higher than forty feet to the roof, in any part of the city; nor shall any be lower than thirty-five feet on any of the avenues.

"4th. That the person or persons appointed by the commissioners to superintend the buildings, may enter on the land of any person to set out the foundation and regulate the walls to be built between party and party, as to the breadth and thickness thereof: which foundation shall be laid equally upon the lands of the persons between whom such party walls are to be built, and shall be of the width and thickness determined by such person proper; and the first builder shall be reimbursed one moiety of the charge of such party wall, or so much thereof as the next builder shall have occasion to make use of, before such next builder shall any ways use or break into the walls. The charge or value thereof, to be set by the person or persons appointed by the commissioners.

" 5th. As temporary conveniences will be proper, for lodging workmen, and securing material for building, it is to be understood that such may be erected, with the approbation of the commissioners: but they may be removed or discontinued by the special order of the commissioners.

"6th. The way into the squares, being designed, in a special manner, for the common use and convenience of the occupiers of the respect squares, the property in the same is reserved to the public, so that there may be an immediate interference on any abuse of the use thereof by any individual, to the nuisance or obstruction of others. The proprietors of the lots adjoining the entrance into the squares, on arching over the entrance, and fixing gates in the manner the commissioners shall approve, shall be entitled to divide the space over the arching, and built it up with the range of that line of the square.

"7th. No vaults shall be permitted under the streets, nor any encroachments on the footway above, by steps, stoops, porches, cellar doors, windows, ditches, or leaning walls, nor shall there be any projection over the street, other than the eaves of the house without the consent of the commissioners.

"8th. These regulations are the terms and conditions under and upon which conveyances are to be made, according to the deeds in trust of the lands within the city.

George Washington."

The seventh regulation was amended on July 7th, 1794, to permit of area ways seven feet in breadth secured by a freestone wall raised eighteen inches above the surface having a neat iron palisading four feet high in the center thereof.

Before the sale commenced, the Commissioners issued the. following announcement:

"All the Lots purchased at this sale are to be subject to the Terms and conditions declared by the President pursuant to the deeds in Trust. The purchaser is immediately to pay one-four part of the purchase money; and to secure the payment of one Third yearly with six per cent interest on the whole by bond with good security: But if any payment is not made at the date the whole is to be recovered in one suit and execution.

"The purchaser is to be entitled to a deed on the whole purchase money and Interest being paid and not before. No bid under twenty Shillings to be received." Before the sale began the Commissioners announced that every facility the public convenience would admit of would be given to purchasers, and that the latter would meet with that disposition in the Commissioners; but that if the terms of sale were not complied with nor any accommodation agreed upon for the convenience of the purchaser, the sale should be binding or not at the option of the Commissioners.

The sale continued from the 17th to the 19th of October with James McKenna acting as vendue master. The result was that thirty-one lots were sold at prices ranging from sixty-five pounds Maryland currency ($173), to one hundred and fifty pounds ($400). The Commissioners in reporting the results of this sale to the President stated that to accommodate some strangers they were obliged to agree that the land should stand as security subject to forfeiture of the one-fourth paid down if the other payments were not made. They gave in explanation of this course the fact that the gentlemen in town had come to a resolution not to go security for purchasers which they conceded was perhaps almost necessary, and that as a result it had happened that the purchasers had no acquaintances of whom they could ask such a favor. The Commissioners suggested that it was worth considering whether in future the terms ought not on this account to be varied. The President, writing to the Commissioners, expressed himself as encouraged by the outcome of the sale, not so much by reason of the number of lots sold as because of the fact that the Commissioners had been able to keep up the prices.

It was at this sale that the first serious indications of trouble between Major L 'Enfant and the Commissioners manifested themselves. The Major, it will be remembered, had from the first opposed the holding of a sale at this time; his letter to President Washington of August 19, being devoted largely to an argument in favor of a postponement. At the sale he conceived the idea that it would tend to induce speculation to permit purchasers to see the plan of the city, the draft of which he had completed while in Philadelphia. Accordingly, he refused the request of the Commissioners to exhibit it at the sale, and the Commissioners were compelled to indicate the locations of lots to purchasers as best they could. This circumstance the Commissioners reported to the President in a letter of October 29, 1791. The President's reply, addressed to Dr. Stuart, is an interesting document, by reason of the insight which it furnishes of his intimate knowledge of human nature, and of the skill and tact which made him so successful in handling men. It is important also as refuting the premise upon which Major L 'Enfant based his subsequent controversies with the Commissioners, to wit, that it was by virtue of the President's instructions to him that he was independent of the authority of the Commissioners. The letter is of still further interest as indicating that the President was now beginning to feel that the establishment of the city, while not completely out of danger, was yet in a much more secure state than it had been a few months before. The letter reads:

"Philadelphia, November 20th, 1791. " Dear Sir: I had heard before the receipt of your letter of the 29th of October — and with a degree of surprise and concern not easy to be expressed — that Major L'Enfant had refused the map of the Federal City when it was requested by the Commissioners for the satisfaction of the purchasers at the sale. It is much to be regretted, however common the case is, that men who possess talents which fit them for peculiar purposes should almost invariably be under the influence of an untoward disposition, or are sottish, idle, or possessed of some other disqualification by which they plague all those with whom they are concerned. But I did not expect to have met with such perverseness in Major L 'Enfant as his late conduct exhibited.

"Since my first knowledge of this Gentleman's abilities in the line of his profession, I have viewed him not only as a scientific man but one who added considerable taste to professional knowledge and have thought that, for such employment as he is now engaged in, for prosecuting public works, and carrying them into effect, he was better qualified than anyone who had come within my knowledge in this country, or indeed in any other, the probability of obtaining whom could be counted upon.

"I had no doubt, at the same time, that this was the light in which he considered himself; and, of course, that he would be so tenacious of his plans as to conceive that they would be marred if they underwent any change or alteration; but I did not suppose that he would have interfered further in the mode of selling the lots, than by giving an opinion with his reasons in support of it; and this perhaps it might be well always to hear, as the latter would stamp the propriety or show the futility of it. To advise this I am the more inclined, as I am persuaded that all those who have any agency in the business have the same objects in view, although they may differ in sentiment with respect to the mode of execution; because, from a source even less productive than L 'Enfant 's may flow ideas that are capable of improvement; and because I have heard that Ellicott, who is also a man of uncommon talents in his way, and of a more placid temper, has intimated that no information had been required either from him, or L 'Enfant on some point or points (I do not now particularly recollect what) which they thought themselves competent to give.

" I have no other motive for mentioning the latter circumstance than merely to show that the feelings of such men are always alive, and where their assistance is essential that it is policy to humor them or to put on the appearance of doing it.

"I have, however, since I have come to the knowledge of Major L 'Enfant 's refusal of the map, at the sale, given him to understand through a direct channel, though not' an official one as yet, further than what casually passed between us, previous to the sale, at Mount Vernon, that he must in future look to the Commissioners for directions; that he having laid the foundation of this grand design, the Superstructure depended upon them; that I was perfectly satisfied his plans and opinions would have due weight, if properly offered and explained; that if the choice of Commissioners was again to be made I could not please myself better, or hit upon those who had the measure more at heart, or better disposed to accommodate the various interests and persons concerned; and that it would give me great concern to see a goodly prospect clouded by impediments which might be thrown in the way, or injured by disagreements which would only serve to keep alive the hopes of those who are enemies to the Plan. But that you may not infer from hence he has expressed any dissatisfaction at the conduct of the Commissioners towards him, it is an act of justice I should declare that I never have heard, directly or indirectly, that he had expressed any. His pertinacity would, I am persuaded, be the same in all cases, and to all men. He conceives, or would have others believe, that the sale was promoted by withholding the general map, and thereby the means of comparison; but I have caused it to be signified to him, that I am of a different opinion; and that it is much easier to impede, than to force a sale, as none who knew what they were about would be induced to buy — (to borrow an old adage) 'a Pig in a Poke.'

"There has been something very unaccountable in the conduct of the Engraver, yet I cannot be of the opinion the delays were occasioned by L 'Enfant. As soon, however, as a correct draught of the City is prepared, the same, or some other person shall be pressed to the execution. I say a correct draught, because I have understood that Mr. Ellicott has given it as his opinion it was lucky that Engravings did not come out from the first plan inasmuch as they would not have been so perfectly exact as to have justified a sale by them.

"It is of great importance, in my opinion, that the City should be laid out into squares and lots with all the dispatch that the nature and accuracy of the work will admit. And it is the opinion of intelligent and well informed men, now in this City, who are friends to this measure, that for this purpose, and to accommodate the two great interests of George Town and Carrollsburg, it would be advisable, rather than delay another public sale until the Whole can be completed to lay all the ground into squares which shall be West of the Avenue leading from George Town to the President's House, thence by the Avenue to the House for Congress, thence by a proper Avenue (I have not the plan by me to say which) to the Eastern Branch, comprehending the range of Squares next to and bounding on the said Avenues on the East side; and to appoint as early a day, for the sale as a moral certainty of their completion will warrant.

"When I speak of the importance of dispatch, it does not proceed from any doubt I harbor, that the enemies to the measure can shake the establishment of it; for it is with pleasure I add as my opinion that the roots of the permanent seat are penetrating deep and spreading far and wide. The Eastern States are not only getting more and more reconciled to the measure, but are beginning to view it in a more advantageous light as it respects their policy and interests; and some members from that quarter who were its bitterest foes while the question was pending in Congress, have now declared in unequivocal terms to various people and at various times, that if attempts should be made to repeal the Law they would give it every opposition in their power. These sentiments of the Eastern people being pretty well known, will, I am persuaded, arrest the design, if a repeal had been contemplated; but it will not prevent those who are irreconcilable, from aiming all the side blows, when in their power at it; and the rumor which was spread at the Sale, that Congress never would reside there, is one of the expedients that will be exerted in all its force, with a view to discourage the Sales of the Lots, and the buildings thereon, that the accommodations may be unfit for the Government when the period shall arrive that the removal is to take place.

"When I see Major L 'Enfant, who it is said will shortly be here, I shall endeavor to bring him to some explanation of the terms on which he will serve the public and will also impress upon him the necessity of dispatch, that as early a Sale as circumstances will admit may ensue.

"When I began this letter, and until I had got to the present stage of it, it was intended as an answer to yours of the 29th of October; but on reperusal of that of the 21st of the said month from the Commissioners, I find it will serve as an answer to both; and, as it is of an enormous length, and my head and hands during the

Session of Congress are fully employed, I pray you at the first meeting of the Commissioners to lay these sentiments before them for their private information.

"I forward the enclosed, as I did a former communication from the same person, that the Commissioners may be apprised of the circumstances attending the land which is the subject of the letter. No acknowledgment of this, or the former, has been made by me.

"With very great esteem and regard I am, Dear Sir, Your most obt. and Affecte, Humble Servant.

G. Washington."

Close upon the controversy which arose over the refusal of Major L 'Enfant to permit the inspection of his plan at the October sale of lots, came a new and more serious one which arose over the demolition by Major L 'Enfant of the house of Daniel Carroll of Duddington. So serious was this latter controversy that, notwithstanding peace was eventually re-established, relations were strained to such a degree that only one further incident of a similar character was required to create a situation which made it necessary for the President to decide whether he should dispense with the services of the Major or with those of the Commissioners. Much has been written and told of these quarrels and of their outcome, and an impression more or less general has prevailed that the Major was harshly treated. This must necessarily be a matter of individual opinion. The interest which attaches to the circumstances leading up to the severance of Major L 'Enfant 's connection with the city, however, justifies a full statement of the entire affair.

With reference to the circumstances attending the demolition of Mr. Carroll's house much testimony has been furnished by the various participants in the episode. In trying to effect a settlement with Mr. Carroll, President Washington found it necessary to obtain the opinion of his Attorney General, Edmund Randolph, and to this end called upon the Commissioners for a full statement of the facts. The statement, as it appears copied in the Commissioners' letter book is as follows: (blank spaces probably being due to the illegibility in the original). In reading it the difference of identity between Daniel Carroll, the Commissioner, and Daniel Carroll of Duddington, must be kept in mind to avoid confusion.

"Daniel Carroll's Case. In 1790, the cellar of his house was walled up and stood so the Winter — 30th of March, 1791, he signed the agreement subjecting his property marked A. — 27th or 28th of June, 1791, he executed a deed in trust to carry the agreement into effect. The original is in the Office at Annapolis where it was lodged to be recorded, but the paper B is a copy of the trust part of that and the other deeds. (B). In the latter end of August a day or two before Major L 'Enfant set out for Philadelphia the northern part of the street was run and struck the house about —— feet. Major Ellicott (and several of his Assistants then present) told D. C. that the street was originally intended 110 feet wider but that Major L 'Enfant had said to save the building if that would do it, he would reduce the street to 100 feet. Major Ellicott and all the Assistants seem to have been impressed with and given the idea that a — alteration conveniently could and would be made to leave the house clear. Fenwick's Dep. C — Mr. Carroll sometime before. Daniel Carroll of Duddington, resumed his building fell in company with him near the Camp. The latter complained that he had been disappointed in not having the location of his house ascertained agreeable to reported promises given him that he had his workmen under engagements in consequence thereof and could not delay any longer. Mr. Carroll being — both in private and public account went immediately to Camp in hopes of seeing Major L 'Enfant, but not finding him there requested Major Ellicott to communicate the above to him with his earnest wish and that all misunderstanding might be avoided by explanation or a conference. Previous to this Mr. Carroll from — conversations with Major Ellicott was under impressions that a very short time would suffice to ascertain the location of the house and — conversation with Major L 'Enfant he had taken up the same idea, but he said at the same time something of the plan, to be approved of by the President. Mr. Carroll afterwards hearing the line of the street had struck the house called on Major Ellicott — Major L 'Enfant having set off for Philadelphia and informed him that he intended to write to the President, that if an alteration could not be made with convenience and propriety Daniel Carroll of Duddington, might have notice and desist. On which Major Ellicott answered that an alteration might be made without the least injury to the plan and that he would be answerable that Daniel Carroll of Duddington, would be safe. Mr. Carroll confiding in this did not trouble the President on the subject. This conversation has been acknowledged by Major Ellicott in the presence of Doctor Stewart and Mr. Gantt. Doctor Stewart is under the fullest impression from various conversations he had with Major Ellicott on the subject of Daniel Carroll of Duddington house and more especially the particular one in Mr. Gantt 's Office when Major Ellicott was called upon expressly to give information on the subject: that he gave it as his decided opinion that when the work was concerted Daniel Carroll of Duddington house would not be effected by the street. As a proof of this he frequently repeated that the plan at that time was mere fancy work, and would be very different when completed, that therefore, it was idle to be alarmed at what was then doing. On Friday the 13th of November, Doctor Stewart and Mr. Carroll met as Commissioners and agreed to meet again the Friday following. After the adjournment Major L 'Enfant meeting with Dr. Stewart told him that he had wrote to Daniel Carroll of Duddington, informing him that his house must come down. Doctor Stewart told him that he hoped he wrote in an accommodating manner, the Major said he had and feeling in his pockets said he was sorry he had not the letter with him. Dr. Stewart told the Major the Commissioners were to meet the following Friday and that if Mr. Carroll did not choose to pull his house down, to lay the letters before the commissioners.

"The Tuesday following the demolition began, whilst it was in progress Daniel Carroll of Duddington having obtained an injunction showed it to Mr. Roberdeau and Mr. Orme, who were at the spot overseeing the work and read it, as alleged. See D. C. letter of the 7th of Jan. — D. Major L 'Enfant at the time of showing the injunction was in Virginia. Friday, the 25th, Dr. Stewart and Mr. Carroll met as Commissioners, see their letters to Major L 'Enfant. — E. and Mr. Roberdeau and Benjamin Ellicott. — H. See also Major L 'Enfant 's letter of the 6th of Dec. to the Commissioners. G. which shows that after his return from Virginia and his recit of the Commissioners' letter to him he resumed and completed the demolition which had been suspended in his absence. Daniel Carroll of Duddington, has laid before the Commissioners Major L 'Enfant 's letter of the 13th of November, 1791.— G. his letter 21st of November. — H. and Daniel Carroll of Duddington account. — I. The paper K. is a statement of what Major L 'Enfant refers to, as to Mr. Carroll's not acting. "Respecting Major L 'Enfant 's letter about Daniel Carroll. Something being said in Major L 'Enfant 's letter to the Commissioners of ——— respecting one of them.

Mr. D. Carroll, he deems it proper to acknowledge, he said in the presence of Major L 'Enfant, that if there was occasion he would appear as an evidence not as a Commissioner on this subject, and further, to remark that such was his intention with the permission of the other Commissioners on such an event. That there was not a Board on this occasion without him, that circumstance made it appear to him proper to act, that Major L 'Enfant did not mention this to Dr. Stewart on the conversation between them which has been mentioned, Dr. Stewart adds for this, that knowing Daniel Carroll's intention on this subject, he had in conversation with Major L 'Enfant informed him that if an occasion should arise Mr. Johnson and himself would be ready to give their determination."

The first information of Major L 'Enfant 's action to reach the President, was conveyed by Mr. Carroll of Duddington, who laid the entire matter before him in a letter of November 21st. The President, with his characteristic loyalty to the Commissioners, stated in his reply that he would rather Mr. Carroll had made his appeal to the Commissioners, but feeling that the exigencies of the occasion made it highly important to bring about a speedy settlement of the affair before it should give rise to rumors of controversy in connection with the federal city, he took the matter up in person and proposed two alternatives for Mr. Carroll's choice; first, to have the Commissioners complete the demolition of the building and rebuild it, the following spring, in line with the street, to the height it had attained; second, to let Mr. Carroll rebuild it at his own expense and occupy it six years, at which time it should be removed; allowance to be made only for the value of the walls at the time they were torn down.

In the meantime the Commissioners wrote to the President on November 25th, the following account of the affair up to that time:

"Sir: We are sorry to be under the disagreeable necessity of mentioning to you an Occurrence which must wound your feelings. On our meting here to-day, we were to our great astonishment informed that, Maj'r L 'Enfant, without any authority from us, and without even having submitted the matter to our consideration, had proceeded to demolish, Mr. Carroll's house, Mr. Carroll who had received some letters, from the Maj 'r on the subject, fearing the consequence obtained an injunction from the Chancellor, for him to desist: with a summons to Maj'r L 'Enfant to attend the Court of Chancery in December, to receive his decision on the subject, but before his return the house was in part demolished. Tho' this circumstance is sufficiently unfortunate of itself it is particularly so with respect to the time at which it has happened. We had just sent up a memorial to the Assembly, on several subjects which we had deemed of importance to the Federal City. We therefore fear it may produce unfavorable impressions in the members respecting the several matters prayed for, Tho' we have taken every step in our power to prevent it. As soon as we met we issued directions to Maj'r L 'Enfant and the persons acting under him in his absence, to desist till he received our instructions which might have obtained, what was proper in the Case, without any disagreeable consequences. As he cannot pretend to have Acted from any authority from us, we have been much hurt at insinuations, that he acted by authority from you. Being fully convinced that these were unfounded, we have not hesitated to declare that they were so. The Maj'r is at Dumfries, so that we have had no opportunity, of communicating, with him on the subject or learning his reasons and justifications, anticipating your feelings on this subject, and fully apprised of the Maj'rs fitness for the work he is employed in, we cannot forbear expressing a hope that the affair may be still so adjusted that we may not lose his services." On receipt of this letter the President wrote to Major

L 'Enfant, who had advised him of the action he had taken:

"Philadelphia, Dec. 1, 1791. "Sir: I have received with sincere concern the information from yourself as well as others, that you have proceeded to demolish the house of Mr. Carroll of Duddington, against his consent, and without authority from the Commissioners or any other person. In this you have laid yourself open to the laws, and in a country where they will have their course. To their animadversion will belong the present case. In future I must strictly enjoin you to touch no man's property, without his consent, or the previous order of the Commissioners. I wished you to be employed in the arrangements of the federal city. I still wish it: but only on condition that you can conduct yourself in subordination to the authority of the Commissioners, to the laws of the land, and to the rights of its Citizens.

"Your precipitate conduct will, it is to be apprehended, give serious alarm and product disagreeable consequences. Having the beauty and regularity of your plan only in view, you pursue it as if every person, and thing, was obliged to yield to it; whereas the Commissioners have many circumstances to attend to, some of which, perhaps, may be unknown to you; which evinces in strong point of view the propriety, the necessity, and even the safety, of your acting by their directions.

"I have said, and I repeat it to you again, that it is my firm belief that the Gentlemen in Office have favorable dispositions toward you, and in all things reasonable and proper will receive and give full weight to your opinions and ascribing to your zeal the mistakes that have happened I persuade myself under this explanation of matters, that nothing in future will intervene to obstruct the harmony which ought to prevail in so interesting a work." Major L 'Enfant 's position is set forth in a letter which he wrote the Commissioners on December 6, after the destruction of the house had been completed. In the course of this letter he says:

"The peculiar circumstance attending the undertaking of Mr. Carroll of Duddington, together with his manifested disposition to contravene his engagement and oppose the progress of operating being sufficiently known you could not but be satisfied that I acted with propriety in proceeding as I have done. Had that house been one of those improvements the removal of which in complyance with the compact between the individuals and the public would have required a previous estimate of its value, I would have doubtless referred the circumstance to the consideration of your board and would have suspended the operation until matter had been adjusted between you and the individual concerned, but this not being necessary in the case of Mr. Carroll of Duddington, a different mode of process was expedient and proper and the mode I pursued it must be allowed has been more delicate than was his right to expect — having offered him a fair opportunity to oppose at least contest an immediate operation.

*****

"The measure was necessary and expedient to be proceeded to with allacrity it was proper — I proceeded to it of right as well as I do in directing trees to be cut

79

down or rock to be removed where obstructive to the operations or impediments in the streets, and if the way of process is made or any individual injured it is to me and not to the people employed to whom opposition is to be made and lead in my steps with due regard to the public as well . as to the individuals rights. Complaints from any of them when founded on raison have and will always meet me ready to redress and whenever the matter will be of a nature as to require your interference you will always find me disposed to respect the hotority vested in you by law.

"In this instance the magnitude of the object to remove only constituted its importance — the novelty of the case has I conceive rised your apprehension and I account how one of the gentlemen of your board close connection with Mr. Carroll of Duddington, most have interested you to the event and lead you to conceive the undertaking delicate and of consequence for you to determine upon.
*****

"The removing of the building Mr. Carroll of Duddington, had erected in contrariety to the plan was doing justice to them all and it has been effected without a violation of the right of property a difference and a wide one too being to be made in this case from that of touching a man's property without his consent. This exposal of the considerations and reasons which was and ever will made the rue of my conduct being wholly to convince you I have acted consistently I hope from this explanation of the matter that nothing in future will intervene to disturb the harmony and good understanding which it is desirable may prevail amongst all concerned in so interesting a work." Mr. Carroll, having considered the President's alternative propositions, accepted the one providing for the reconstruction of his house by the Commissioners; but when this became known to the other proprietors, they addressed a vigorous protest to the Commissioners who referred it to the President, by whom it was in turn referred, together with the statement of the case previously quoted and other pertinent documents, to the Attorney General.

The result of the Attorney General's consideration of the case was an agreement to pay Mr. Carroll the value of the materials in his house at the time of its destruction. The matter was later. (June 4, 1792) settled by the payment of £1679, 12 sh, 3 d.

On Christmas (1791) Major L 'Enfant started for Philadelphia to prepare the plan of the city for engraving. He left in charge of operations two young men, Isaac Roberdeau and Balentine Baraof, to whom he gave instructions as to the work to be attended to in his absence. Under his instructions Mr. Roberdeau took twenty -five of the men engaged in the city work to the stone quarry at Aquia Creek. The Commissioner, thinking it more important that the work of digging up the clay for bricks should be pushed during the Winter season, requested Mr. Roberdeau to attend their meeting to receive their instructions. Instead of complying with their request Mr. Roberdeau proceeded to Aquia Creek. The Commissioners at the same time directed Mr. Baraof to discontinue the work in the city in which he was engaged and to discharge the hands, settle their accounts, take care of the tools, and sell a horse purchased at the public expense. Instead of obeying he went to Virginia to consult Mr. Roberdeau and on returning ordered a supply of bread for the men preparatory to renewing operations. In consequence of this proceeding the Commissioners gave Mr. Baraof peremptory orders to turn over the public property in his charge to Capt. Elisha Williams and warned him that if he presumed to interfere in digging the soil or doing any act on the land as of his own or under any kind of public authority they would order actions of trespass against him. The patience of the Commissioners was now being rapidly exhausted as the following recital of events sent by them to the President under date of January 7th, 1792, will show.

"From what we collect from the Commissary of provisions there are now retained in service about laborers

and their overseers in the City and that Major L 'Enfant has ordered 25 of them to be withdrawn from there to be employed in the Stone Quarry under the direction of Mr. Roberdeau, who has left George Town on that business though previously told by two of the Commissioners separately and by the third on his way that his presence was desired at the meeting and we have reason to believe that he proceeded, to avoid orders from us, independent of this mortifying treatment we think it advisable, from the nature of the season, for the present at least, to put everything we can on piece work and to discharge the hands engaged on time wages and provisions, and employed in digging. For though pains were taken on our part to get brick clay turned up this Fall, we have no knowledge or reason to believe, that a spade of clay has been turned up for that purpose, but labor diverted to other objects which may correspond with Major L 'Enfant 's designs respecting the Capital and Palace, but we do not conceive that there is certainly enough of the adoption of unprepared plans to warrant the cost of digging long, deep, wide ditches in the midst of the Winter, which if necessary at all might be done much cheaper at some other season. These impressions though we wish to avoid a step in Major L 'Enfant 's absence, which he may possibly think wanting in delicacy, have occasioned us to discharge the hands. The produce of our funds and the public expense must be brought into view and comparison by us: for supposing as we do, that we are not answerable in our private characters for debts incurred within the line of our Office, our honor is concerned, that the engagements entered into with our approbation should be faithfully complied with nor can we suffer ourselves to be led from these objects: it will hence be necessary that we know and approve the thing to be done and the means and calculations to effect it. We flatter ourselves we need not declare to you that we shall be glad to receive advice, as such at all times, for we are conscious that we need that assistance, and that we ever sincerely wish an unreserved intercourse, and are yet disposed to meet in measures to that end. But without remaining over disagreeable occurrences Major L 'Enfant and Major Ellicott both must if we do business with them consult us in the future. We exceedingly regret the necessity we feel ourselves under in interrupting the too few moments you have of leisure and shall truly lament if it so happens the loss of Major L 'Enfant 's taste and professional abilities, of which we with yourselves have a high opinion: but we owe something to ourselves and to others which cannot be given up."

After issuing orders to Mr. Roberdeau on January 10th, to turn the public property over to Capt. Elisha Williams, the Commissioners, thinking everything settled for the time, dispersed to their homes. The day following their departure Mr. Roberdeau, collected hands and resumed the digging operations. The Commissioners were summoned by express and making their way to where Mr. Roberdeau was carrying on the work, were informed that he was determined to execute Major L 'Enfant 's orders in opposition to theirs. On the arrival of mail from Philadelphia he announced that by reason of a communication from Major L 'Enfant he held it necessary for his justification to submit to an arrest, which the Commissioners proceeded to cause. He informed the Commissioners that Major L 'Enfant had directed him to desire the Commissioners not to have any clay turned up for bricks at the President's House.

On receipt of information of these proceedings the President both in person and through others endeavored to bring the Major, who was then at Philadelphia, to adopt his views as to the Major's functions.

On February 22, 1792, Mr. Jefferson at the President's instance tactfully informed Major L 'Enfant that his continuation in the work would be desirable to the President, but that the law required it should be in subordination to the Commissioners who would from time to time receive his propositions and submit them to the President to be approved or disapproved, and that when they should be returned with the President's approval, the Commissioners would place in the Major's hands the execution of such parts as should be arranged with him.

This statement of his position was not satisfactory to the Major and after a series of interviews and communications back and forth Major L 'Enfant and the President came to a deadlock; the Major refusing without qualification to finish the work in a capacity subordinate to that of the Commissioners. Regretfully the President was compelled to face the necessity of dispensing with the Major's services, his decision being conveyed in the following letter to the Major from Mr. Jefferson:

"Philadelphia, Feb. 27, 1792.

"Sir: Prom your letter received yesterday in answer to my last, and your declaration in conference with Mr. Lear, it is understood that you absolutely decline acting under the authority of the present Commissioners. If this understanding of your meaning be right, I am instructed by the President to notify you that notwithstanding the desire he has entertained to preserve your agency in the business, the condition on which it is to be done is inadmissible, and your services must be at an end.

Your most obedient humble servant, Major L 'Enfant.

Thomas Jefferson."

Writing the Commissioners under date of March 6, 1792, the President recites the efforts made by him to reach a friendly understanding with Major L 'Enfant. The pertinent portions of his letter follow:

"Matters are at length brought to a close with Major L 'Enfant. As I had a strong desire to retain his services in this business, provided it could have been done upon a proper footing, I gave him every opportunity of coming forward and stating the mode in which he would wish to be employed, always, however, assuring him that he must be under the control of the Commissioners. But after keeping open the communication with him as long as any reasonable means could be found of doing it, he chose to close it by declaring that he could only act in a certain way, — which way was inadmissible. His services, therefore, must be no longer calculated upon. Altho' his talents in designing, and the skill which he is said to possess in the execution of this kind of business may occasion the loss of his services to be regretted; yet I doubt, upon the whole, whether it will be found in the end that his dereliction will be of real disservice to the undertaking; for so unaccommodating is his disposition that he would never suffer any interference in his plans, much less would he have been contented under the direction of the Commissioners. I am convinced, Gentlemen, that in your transactions with Major L 'Enfant you must have suffered much from his temper; — and if my approbation of yr. conduct in this business can afford you pleasure, you may be assured you have it. Even if I had no corroboration of the fact, I should be persuaded, from what I have known of his disposition on the recent occasion, that there would scarcely be a possibility of acting harmoniously in concert with him. "As Mr. Jefferson has, in his letter, mentioned the particular objects to which your attention will probably be turned — I shall only observe here that I am impressed in the strongest manner, with the necessity there is of carrying on this business with as much vigor as the nature of the thing will admit. It has been observed by intelligent and well informed men, (not however of the class most friendly to the measure) that the whole success of the federal City depends upon the exertions which may be made in the ensuing season towards completing the object; for such is now the state of the public mind on this subject that it appears as if it were in an equilibrium, and will preponderate either for or against the measure as the progress of the thing may be. And there are not wanting those who, being interested in arresting the business, will leave no means unessayed to injure it. By the proposition for a loan which Mr. Jefferson transmits to you, you will see what prospect you have of funds in addition."

In all of his controversies with the Commissioners, Major L 'Enfant had enjoyed the support and sympathy of most of the proprietors, to which cause, it is very easy to believe, may probably be ascribed, in part at least, the obstinancy which he displayed. On hearing of the Major's dismissal a number of the proprietors wrote to Mr. George Walker, who was in communication with Mr. Jefferson, the following letter for Mr. Jefferson's attention:

"Georgetown, March 9, 1792.

" Sir: We are obliged by your communication of the letter from the Secretary of State.

"We cannot but lament extremely that the misunderstanding between the Commissioners and Major L 'Enfant, has ended in the dismission of the latter — for, having from our own knowledge of his Conduct, formed the highest opinion of his Talents, his unwearied zeal, his firmness, (though sometimes perhaps improperly exterted, in general highly useful), his impartiality to this or to that end of the City; or to the views of those proprietors, with whom he has been in Friendship or otherwise —— and from his total disregard for all pecuniary considerations, we greatly doubt whether a successor can be found in this country, or indeed in any country, qualified to be so eminently useful to the object in which we are all so Interested, — and certainly none can be found possessing in a higher degree, the public confidence, a circumstance which we cannot help thinking of very great importance in the business where as much depends on public opinion. Thus thinking, we anxiously hope that some mode will yet be devised by the friends of this place at Philadelphia, to secure to the City, the benefit of Major L 'Enfant 's future services.

"The Commissioners we presume, would do everything they could do, consistently with their duty, to accommodate to his views, and however he may have been misled by the warmth of his Temper, we are persuaded from his well-known attachment to the object, which has employed so much of his time and study, that he will on cooler reflexion and on knowing the highest confidence placed in him by the Bulk of the proprietors, stand less on Punctilio than he has hitherto done; especially if he could have assurances, that in things really in his province (and in which from his Scientific knowledge and approved Taste, He would be most competent to Decide) he would be left without controul.

"As you are in correspondence with the Secretary of State, and as it is but justice to Major L 'Enfant that the Opinion the proprietors entertain of his merit, from their own observation, should be known to those to whom he owed his appointment, we request you will enclose this letter with your own.

"We are, Sir,
Your most obed servts,
Robert Peters, Ben Stoddert,
John Davidson, Uriah Forrest,
Sam Davidson, Win. Prout,
Jas. M. Lingan, Overton Carr,
Abraham Young, David Burnes,
Wm. King, Eliphaz Douglas."

The President's determination to dismiss Major L 'Enfant was not reached without serious consideration of the possible consequences to the city, not only by reason of the loss of the Major's services, but through the loss of public confidence which was likely to result therefrom, and the consequent strengthening of the claims of Philadelphia for the permanent retention of the Seat of Government at that place.

According to a letter which he wrote to Dr. Stuart shortly after the dismissal of Major L 'Enfant, the President was strongly apprehensive that either the Major or his friends would come out with a public announcement, to quote the President, "that he found matters were likely to be conducted upon so pimping a scale that he would not hazard his character or reputation on the event under the controul he was to be placed; " and that it would require the most vigorous exertions on the part of the Commissioners looking to the prosecution of the work along the lines of Major L 'Enfant 's plan, to prevent the chrystallization of public sentiment in favor of an abandonment of the project.

The question of the compensation to be offered Major L 'Enfant for his services was determined by President Washington after consultation with others in his confidence at Philadelphia. In his letter to Doctor Stuart, just referred to, he says "the plan of the city having met universal approval (so far as my information goes) and Major L 'Enfant having become a very discontented man, it was thought that less than from 2,500 to 3,000 dollars, would not be proper to offer him for his services." "Instead of this," he suggests, "suppose five hundred guineas, and a Lot in a good part of the City were to be substituted? I think it would be more pleasing, and less expensive." Previous to his discharge the Major had received six hundred dollars and his expenses, but had persistently refused, though several times requested by the Commissioners, to name the compensation he would expect. Acting upon the President's suggestion, the Commissioners wrote to the Major advising him that they had sent an order in his favor for five hundred guineas and would add to it a lot in the city.

Major L 'Enfant wrote briefly in reply that without inquiring into the principles upon which they based their offer he should only testify his surprise thereupon, and decline to accept it.

What amount he regarded as requisite to adequately compensate him for his services he does not appear at the time to have indicated either to the Commissioners or to the President. In 1800 he presented a claim to the then members of the commission in which, without naming any specific sum, he enumerated the following items:

"1st. Of a Salary of my Agency commensurate with the magnitude and importance of the Object and of the Affairs managed.

"2ndly. Of payment for the delineation of the City Plan on an estimation expected such as the Sentiment of a work of genious alone can suggest and — differencing the production of the artist from that of the mere artisan or virtuoso, making also the price comport with the benefit in the end to result to the Nation.

"3rdly. Of the proceed from the printing of the City Plan or an equivalent for being taken away the property thereof.

"4th. Of the great additional perquisite necessarily to have devolved to me from the agency." By way of furnishing a basis for estimating what the additional perquisites would have come to, he cites the relinquishment of other engagements which would have yielded him a clear gain of $50,000. His prospective profits in sales of maps he calculated upon a probable sale of from fifteen to twenty thousand maps at from two or three dollars each.

His claim being rejected by the Commissioners, was presented to Congress in much the same form. As stated in a committee report of that body, returned in 1802, the items were estimated to be:

For labor for one year $8,000; anticipated profits from sales of maps, $37,500; perquisites, $50,000; total, $95,000.

In 1804, a law was passed authorizing the Superintendent of the City, who was the successor to the Commissioners, to make a settlement with L 'Enfant, but the money was levied upon by a creditor. In 1810, Congress in response to a further memorial from L 'Enfant, appropriated $666 with interest from March 1, 1792, the total coming to $1,394.20. This was the last financial reward the designer of the city ever received for his services.

After leaving the service of the city Major L 'Enfant accepted various employments, but the extravagant and visionary trend which had enabled him in his mind's eye to picture in the forests and swamps which lay before him the streets, avenues, parks and public buildings of the future City of Washington, proved in the more practical affairs with which he became connected, to be a handicap, which, coupled with the overbearing temper which remained with him, prevented him from attaining any considerable amount of private business or degree of professional success. Obtaining employment with a Jersey manufacturing concern, he was shortly dismissed "for mistakes and a Quixotic invention" The faith of the public in his abilities accordingly fell. Not knowing of his discharge, Robert Morris had employed him to design and superintend the construction of a house which he contemplated building in Philadelphia — giving him carte blanche as to his expenses. L 'Enfant 's plan of this building was upon a most expensive scale and was changed so frequently and at such increase of cost as to drive the owner to desperation.

Oberholtzer, in his life of Morris, says "the Financier frequently denied, as his misfortunes accumulated and the folly of his undertaking became very manifest, that he had given L 'Enfant authority to lay the plans on so extravagant a scale." At all events, after four years of building up and tearing down, on August 15, 1796, Mr. Morris wrote L 'Enfant:

"It is with astonishment I see the work of last fall now pulling down in order to put more marble on my house, on which there is already vastly too much. The difficulty and cost of getting money is vastly greater than you can conceive, and if you persist in exposing yourself to censure and me to ridicule by alterations and additions, you will force me to abandon all expectations of getting into the house and to stop the work which I am unwilling to do, if it can be avoided, and which can only be prevented by economy and dispatch."

Mr. Morris, continues the same authority, "rolled sheet iron at his works at Morrisville to take the place of slate upon the roof in order that the rain might not beat in, but in May, 1797, although upon his own estimate he had expended ten times as much as he was told the house would cost, the roof covered only a portion of the building and not a single floor was laid, nor a single wall plastered. In this house Morris never lived."

Major L 'Enfant was later tendered a position as an instructor at West Point but declined it, apparently conceiving that an acceptance would prejudice his claim for compensation as the designer of the city. His after life was embittered by what he considered the lack of public appreciation of his work. In his later years he was invited by Mr. William Dudley Digges to make his home with the latter at his estate "Green Hill," in Prince George's County, Maryland, and it was there his death occurred on June 14, 1825, at the age of seventy years.

In 1908, Congress appropriated one thousand dollars "to remove and render accessible to the public the grave of Major Pierre Charles L 'Enfant." On April 22, 1909, the remains were taken from the grave and on April 28 were taken under military escort to the rotunda of the Capitol where for three hours they lay in state, being then borne upon a caisson at the head of a procession nearly a mile in length to the National Cemetery at Arlington. Before the firing of the three volleys over the new grave and sounding of "taps" by the bugler, Monsignor William T. Russell, Pastor of Saint Patrick's Church, performed the rites of the church, and concluded with an eloquent and fitting tribute to the service which Major L 'Enfant had rendered the country of his adoption.

Much has been said about the lack of public recognition of L 'Enfant 's work, and it is impossible to contemplate the tragedy of his after life without a sense of regret. Yet, upon a dispassionate view of the case, the conclusion can hardly be resisted that he was himself chiefly responsible for the troubles which overtook him.

So far as the question of the adequacy or inadequacy of his compensation is concerned, those who lived at the time were in a position to estimate more accurately the propriety of the sum offered him than it is possible to do today. President Washington thought the sum adequate; indeed he shows by his letter to Dr. Stuart that in fixing on that amount he had been influenced by a desire to avoid arousing a sentiment against the new city by any evidence of lack of appreciation of L 'Enfant 's work. The tone of his correspondence throughout, as well as that of the Commissioners, shows an entire absence of any personal feeling on the part of any of them against the Major; and President Washington, in all his dealings, was the last of all men to allow such consideration to influence him. A moment's reflection, too, must lead to the conviction that the items of anticipated profit which Major L 'Enfant later enumerated in his claim were essentially visionary and in all probability would not have been, even approximately, realized. As to the merits of his quarrel with the Commissioners, the record fails to show any fair reason why he could not have continued his work of supervising the work of laying out the city, in the most complete harmony with the Commissioners but for the fact of his inability to comprehend that both under the law and as a matter of practical necessity it was requisite that the President be represented by some such administrative body, and that in the nature of the case its authority in directing the work of establishing the city must be superior to his as its designer. The Commissioners throughout evinced toward the Major a highly conciliatory spirit and a desire, founded upon a genuine appreciation of his abilities, to reach a working agreement with him which should be conducive to the best interests of the city. For his sake it is regrettable that the bringing about of such an agreement was impossible of accomplishment. So far as the interests of the public were concerned, it had little to lose. Major L 'Enfant had for all practical purposes fulfilled his mission when he finished the design which will arouse the wonder and admiration of men for all time to come.

It will be remembered that Major L 'Enfant at the time of his dismissal, was in Philadelphia, whither he had gone for the purpose of preparing the map of the city. According to his account, he had, before leaving Georgetown, requested Benjamin Ellicott to delineate on paper all the work which had been done in the city, which, being accurately measured and laid down on the ground, he intended to make the basis of a drawing from his original plan upon a reduced scale for engraving. Not having this with him on his arrival in Philadelphia and experiencing some difficulty in finding a good draughtsman and engraver, he met with some delay in the preparation of the map and finally requested Benjamin Ellicott to assist him, giving the latter for the purpose a sketch which had already been prepared. L 'Enfant superintended this work until told by Major Ellicott that the latter had been instructed by Mr. Jefferson to attend to that business and had engaged an engraver to do the work. L 'Enfant paid no further attention to the matter at the time, thinking it impossible for Ellicott to complete the work without reference to L 'Enfant 's large plan which the latter had in his possession; expecting, however, to be called upon to review and correct the plan when completed. After some days he went to Ellicott 's home and found the draught nearly finished but, as he states, "most unmercifully spoiled and altered from the original plan to a degree indeed evidently intended to disgrace me and ridicule the very undertaking."

L 'Enfant, desiring to correct the plan, sent to Major Ellicott for it, but the latter refused to deliver it up; upon which L 'Enfant, on February 17, 1792, wrote to Mr. Lear, the President's private secretary, reciting the facts as above stated and protesting against the publication of the plan as Mr. Ellicott had drawn it.

Whether Major L 'Enfant 's version of the matter is correct, or whether as would appear from President Washington's and Major Ellicott 's statements to the Commissioners, the trouble was the result of another instance of Major L 'Enfant 's captiousness, it is not easy to decide. President Washington, in his letter of March 6, 1792, wrote:

"It is impossible to say with any certainty when the plan of the City will be engraved. Upon Major L 'Enfant 's arrival here, in the latter part of December I pressed him in the most earnest manner to get the plan ready for engraving as soon as possible. Finding there was no prospect of obtaining it through him (at least not in any definite time) the matter was put into Mr. Ellicott's hands to prepare about 3 weeks ago. He has prepared it, but the engravers who have undertaken to execute it, say it cannot certainly be done in less than two — perhaps not under 3 months. There shall, however, be every effort made to have the thing effected with all possible dispatch." Major Ellicott, writing on February 23, 1792, said:

" On my arrival at this City, I found that no preparation was made for an engraving of the plan of the City of Washington. Upon this representation being made to the President and Secretary of State, I was directed to furnish one for an engraver; which with the aid of my Brother was completed last Monday and handed to the President. In this business we met with difficulties of a very serious nature. Major L 'Enfant refused us the use of the Original! What his motives were, God knows. The plan which we have furnished, I believe will be found to answer the ground better than the large one in the Major's hands. I have engaged two good artists, (both Americans) to execute the engraving, and who will begin the work as soon as the President comes to a determination respecting some small alterations. "

The result of Major Ellicott's execution of the plan, whatever the circumstances may have been, resulted in its being published to the world, apparently as his design. Major L 'Enfant 's plan contained in the upper left-hand corner a title legend giving his name as the author. It also, as previously noted, contained the statement crediting Major Ellicott with the astronomical work incident to the execution of the plan on the ground. Major Ellicott, in his map, omitted Major L 'Enfant 's name as well as a large part of the explanatory matter, but left the reference to himself as it appeared on L 'Enfant 's plan, placing it prominently at the lower right hand corner, embracing his name in enlarged letters, in such a manner as upon a casual glance to give the impression, without expressly setting forth such a claim, that Major Ellicott was the author of the plan.

Ellicott's draft, notwithstanding L 'Enfant 's charge that it unmercifully spoiled and altered the original, in fact adhered quite closely to the latter. The most easily noted alterations consist in the straightening of Massachusetts Avenue, which in L 'Enfant 's plan takes a sharp break to the southeast from the point where it crosses New Jersey Avenue, and in the elimination of four or five short avenues which appear in L 'Enfant 's plan. It also omits the designation of any of L 'Enfant 's public reservations except those for the President's House and Capitol. These alterations, while they may have improved rather than injured the original, were not such as to justify Ellicott in seeking to obtain public recognition as the author of the design.

It is evident from the fact that the names of the avenues are given upon Ellicott's map that they were determined upon during the time of its preparation in Philadelphia; for they do not appear on L'Enfant's plan, and Pennsylvania Avenue is mentioned by Major Ellicott, in a letter to the Commissioners written in December, shortly before he went to the latter place, as the diagonal leading from the President 's house to the Capitol.

The work of engraving Ellicott's map was entrusted to two firms, Thackara and Vallance, of Philadelphia, and S. Hill, of Boston. Though both products were referred to generally as the "Engraved Plan," the former was more particularly designated as "The Philadelphia Plate," and the latter as "The Boston Plate." The Philadelphia Plate was about twice the size of the Boston Plate and was much preferred because of the fact that it gave the soundings of the Potomac River and Eastern Branch which were forwarded too late to be incorporated in the other.

The Boston Plate was completed in time to be exhibited at the second public sale of lots on October 8, 1792, the Philadelphia Plate not being received by the Commissioners until the 13th of the following November.

The difficulties of the Commissioners with Major L 'Enfant were but the prelude to a series of annoying and long drawn controversies with his successor, of a nature even more acrimonious and personal than the quarrels with the eccentric Frenchman.

While the discussions between President Washington and Major L 'Enfant were going on and Major Ellicott was engaged in preparing the draft of the plan of the City, the latter, by his own statement appears to have been anticipating the possibility of his appointment as Major L 'Enfant 's successor. In his letter to the Commissioners of February 23, above quoted from, he says:

"In several conferences which I have had with the President, and Secretary of State, on the subject of the City of Washington, he wrote the Commissioners, I have constantly mentioned the necessity of system in the execution of the business: without which there can be neither economy, certainty, nor decision. — The Major has both a lively fancy and decision; but unfortunately no system; which renders the other qualifications much less valuable, and in some cases useless. I suspect the measures are now taking, which will either reduce the Major to the necessity of submitting to the legal arrangements or deserting the City. " On receiving notice of Major L 'Enfant 's dismissal the Commissioners on March 14, 1792, wrote to Major Ellicott placing him in charge of the surveying department and offering to employ his brothers as his assistants. They notified him that they had already employed a Mr. McDermott as an assistant. The latter, whose real name was James R. Dermott, was an Irishman whose reputation in Alexandria as a mathematician had come to the attention of Doctor Stuart who had mentioned his name to the other Commissioners with the result indicated in their letter to Major Ellicott. On the 3rd of August following, Mr. George Fen wick was appointed an assistant surveyor, and shortly after was detailed to the work of placing stones at the corners of squares as laid off in the City.

During the summer and fall of 1792, Major Ellicott and his force, besides their work in laying out and dividing squares in the city, had been engaged in the survey of the boundary of the federal territory. This work being completed by the first of the new year, Major Ellicott submitted to the Commissioners the following report of his work, upon the receipt of which the Commissioners by their proclamation issued on the same day, authenticated the boundary as laid out by Major Ellicott to be the boundary of the federal territory. Major Ellicott 's report, the wording of which in its essential points is closely followed in the Commissioner's proclamation, after reciting the surveying of the boundary according to the President's proclamations relating thereto, continued:

"A space has been opened and cleared forty feet wide, that is twenty feet on each side of the lines limiting the territory: and, in order to perpetuate the location of the Said Territory, I have set up squared mile-stones, marked with the number of miles progressively, from the beginning on Jones's point to the west corner, thence from the west corner to the north corner, thence from the north corner to the East corner; and from thence to the place of beginning on Jones 's point: except in a few cases where the miles terminate on declivities or in waters, in such cases the stones are placed on the nearest firm ground, and their true distances in miles and poles marked on them. On the sides of the stones facing the Territory, are inscribed the words 'Jurisdiction of the United States.' On the opposite sides of those placed in the commonwealth of Virginia, is Inscribed 'Virginia' and on those in the State of Maryland, is Inscribed 'Maryland,' and on the third and fourth sides, or faces are Inscribed the year in which the stone was set up and the present variations of the magnetic needle at that place. In addition to the foregoing work, I have compleated a Map of the four lines (with an half mile on each side) including the said District of territory, with a survey of the different waters.

"Witness my hand this first day of January, 1793.

Andw. Ellicott."

It was about the time of the making of this report that the first definite signs of the trouble between Major Ellicott and the Commissioners began to display themselves.

Apparently complaints had been made to the Commissioners, by some of the proprietors, of slowness in the prosecution of the survey of the city; a circumstance for which Major Ellicott, engaged as he was in the survey of the boundary lines of the territory, was perhaps not to blame. In two letters of January 4, 1793, replying to the Commissioners representations, he sets forth his explanation of the delay and at the same time evinces almost as much sensitiveness to criticism as his predecessor, saying:

" In the execution of the Plan of the City of Washington, I have met with innumerable difficulties on account of its extreme complexity; and from its extent, the labor becomes augmented, to such a degree, that it can only be judged of, by those intimately acquainted with such business. Those causes, and not want of exertions, may possibly have produced an apparent delay, in the execution of the Plan.

* * *

"If it should be your pleasure, you may rest assured that it will be mine, to quit the further execution of the Plan of the City of Washington by the first day of May next. You may probably find some person, more capable both to execute the work, and give satisfaction." The Commissioners having directed his attention to the complaints of some of the proprietors who were demanding surveys of their lands, he continued:

"I shall not pretend to say, but that every proprietor of lands in the City of Washington, has an equal right to have his property prepared for sale; but as the work cannot be executed in an instant; some must be accommodated before others: and this accommodation must depend upon the system, proper to pursue, in executing the work.

"From both experience, and reflection, I am now convinced, that in the very beginning of the business, it would have been better; to have proceeded regularly from some particular point, to the extremities of the City; than to have worked in detached pieces, which in executing the general plan, will all have to be gone over again: This is the case with part of Mr. Walker's property, and many others, and I know of no way that they can be particularly accommodated but at an extra public expense." In the latter part of January of the same year, 1793, a publication appeared in one of the Baltimore papers criticizing Major Ellicott for his alleged dilatoriness in pushing the survey of the city. Upon seeing this, Major Ellicott, on January 29, wrote to the Commissioners demanding an investigation of his conduct of the office and also requesting that Mr. Dermott be directed to deliver up to him all the papers in his possession relating to the Surveyor's office, in order that Major Ellicott might be enabled to complete a general return of the work executed, by the first of the following May.

This request was communicated to Mr. Dermott, whose reply has an important bearing upon the charges which Major Ellicott soon after made against him. Referring to the request which had been communicated to him he said:

"I have received a letter from the Commissioners yesterday desiring some papers which you wanted. They did not specify any therefore did not know what to send. If you had only hinted to me that you wanted any papers in my possession, either public or private; they should have been delivered, as soon to your order as theirs. "

After explaining the state of his work and offering to put his notes in shape to be understood if desired, he concluded: "Any other direction you'll please to send here shall be complied with, as soon as I return, which will be in a few days"

Major Ellicott made no reply to this letter nor any further demand upon Dermott but soon after laid him off for the winter.

To Major Ellicott 's demand for an investigation the Commissioners replied that they did not consider that there was any occasion for it; remarking that they felt no animosity against him, and that they were much more concerned than gratified at the address to him in the Baltimore papers. They, however, requested of the Major either a personal communication or a report on the condition of affairs of his office; to which he replied that he would make a report on May first when it was his intention to resign. A few days later Major Ellicott completed a map of the federal territory which had been requested of him by the President; and on February 11, the Commissioners sent him with this map to Philadelphia, writing at the same time to Mr. Jefferson that they had had some explanations with him which rendered them better satisfied than at the time of their last writing a short time previously.

On leaving for Philadelphia, Major Ellicott agreed to meet with the Commissioners at their next meeting in March. On his way to this meeting, Doctor Stuart met Dermott in Virginia, when the latter repeated a statement which he had previously made while in a state of intoxication, alleging that a number of discrepancies existed between the measurement of the squares on the ground and as returned in the Surveyor's office. At Doctor Stuart's request Dermott attended the meeting and presented his charges in writing. After waiting nearly a week for Major Ellicott 's return, the Commissioners ordered Mr. Geo. Fenwick one of the surveying staff, to remeasure the squares where Dermott had alleged the errors to exist; and a number of errors were found. A day or two later, Major Ellicott returned and was requested to make a written statement explaining the errors. This he refused to do saying that Dermott had stolen a number of important papers necessary for a complete statement, among them the draft of L 'Enfant 's plan, but offering to make a verbal statement. The Commissioners refused to accept a verbal statement saying:

"We think it very far from a work of Time to give us the satisfaction required and in the manner we desired, and from 10 to 110 Feet of Land in a Square not so trifling a Difference, between Seller and Buyer as not to draw at least their attention. The work cannot with propriety nor shall proceed, till what is done has been examined and Mistakes endeavored at least to be rectified." Having procured the L 'Enfant map, which was a partial copy made by Mr. Hallett from the original, from Mr. Dermott, they advised Ellicott the next day that "Mr. Dermott has shown no signs of Concealment of any papers. He acknowledged his having possession of Major L 'Enfant 's old Draft without any hesitation, and has given it to us, and without request another paper or two."

The Commissioners after an extensive interchange of ideas with Major Ellicott, proceeded on the 14th of March, 1793, to announce a set of regulations pertaining to the conduct of the office, which outlined the system under which the survey of the city was completed. The squares were to be remeasured by Mr. Fenwick. Dermott who had previously laid down the lines of Hamburgh upon the plat of that part of the city was directed to do the same with regard to Carrollsburgh. His spare time was to be devoted to dividing squares into lots as certified to him by the measurers, and to report any disagreements between the measurements returned to him and those on the general plan. Major Ellicott was directed to proceed with the work of laying off the streets, avenues and squares on the ground. Under this arrangement the work continued for about two weeks when Major Ellicott, who, still smarting under the criticism directed against him, made a personal statement of his grievances to President Washington, who was passing through on his way to Mount Vernon, and invoked the aid of the latter in obtaining an investigation. The President promised to ask this of the Commissioners, taking occasion, nevertheless, to advise Ellicott that his attitude towards the Commissioners, so far as appeared from the correspondence, had not been respectful; and emphasizing his indisposition to interfere with the functions of the latter. The following day he kept his promise, submitting to the Commissioners, in his usual tactful manner, the question whether an investigation would not be advisable rather than a newspaper altercation, which he thought likely to follow a refusal of it.

In compliance with this letter the Commissioners spent several days in going over the affairs of the surveying department with Major Ellicott, with the result that an agreement was reached and set forth in an order dated April 9, providing that Major Ellicott was to direct the field work and be answerable for its accuracy and dispatch. He was required as soon as squares should be finished and marked out on the ground, to deliver to the Commissioners' Clerk at their office, certificates to that effect; giving the location and measurements of the square. The work from time to time was to be added on the large plat, which was to be considered as a record. It was stated that the Surveyor ought to have the work certified to him by his assistants for his own protection, as the Commissioners would look only to him. The work of platting and dividing squares, left as before to Mr. Dermott, was stated not to be considered within the surveying department. Major Ellicott was made head of the surveying department, with Isaac Briggs, Benjamin Ellicott and Geo. Fenwick, as his assistants.

Taking up the regulations to govern Mr. Dermott 's work, the Commissioners on the following day directed that Dermott should apply from time to time to their Clerk and take minutes of the squares from certificates returned by the surveyor. From these he was to plat the squares on a scale of forty feet to the inch and divide them into lots. In one corner of the paper he was to write down the substance of the certificate. Shortly afterwards Dermott was further directed to make out three plats for each square; one for recording with the Clerk of the District, one for the Commissioners' office, and one for the proprietors.

Owing to the discrepancies which had been found between the squares as platted and as laid out on the ground, it had previously been ordered that the surveyor who should be directed to lay out any lot should at the same time measure and mark out all lots on the same line of the square of which it was a part, and if he should find any excess to divide it, or if a deficiency, to abate in each lot for the deficiency pro rata. It was also ordered that all divisions of squares between the proprietors and the public thereafter made, should contain a stipulation agreeing to the arrangement just mentioned for prorating any excess or deficiency.

On July 19, 1793, Major Ellicott went to Philadelphia to engage in other work, advising the Commissioners on his departure that his personal attention to the survey would not be required for some time, and that he would leave the work in charge of his assistants, Isaac Briggs and Benjamin Ellicott during his absence. The surveying was carried on by these two during the summer and fall; reports of its progress being required of them by the Commissioners at each of their meetings. Almost without exception, in making these reports, Briggs and Ellicott took occasion to make disparaging statements with reference to Dermott; to charge him with having moved stakes; with being a disreputable character; and with having boasted while drunk that he had "put the affairs of the city on such a train they would never be right again. "

To these assertions the Commissioners for a long time paid no attention. Finally, their patience became exhausted, and they wrote on October 17, 1793, to Briggs, inviting him to meet with them and if possible substantiate his charges against Dermott.

The meeting developed into a stormy interview, at the end of which Briggs was dismissed from the service, and Benjamin and Joseph Ellicott with George Fenwick were left in charge of the survey. Under the latter arrangement matters went on smoothly until the 9th of December, when Major Ellicott returned and informed the Commissioners that he had re-established himself at the head of the department. The Commissioners replied that as matters had proceeded much more satisfactorily in his absence than before, and as they had not had his services during the summer months when they would have been most useful, they would not add to the expense of the establishment by employing him during the winter. They continued Major Ellicott 's brothers in their employ, but peace was impossible so long as Major Ellicott remained in Georgetown. He spent his time voicing his complaints to the residents of the latter place and stirring up dissatisfaction with the Commissioners among them. With his brothers, too, he made his influence felt; instigating them to revive the old story of the theft of the L 'Enfant draft by Dermott, which they did by inserting in the Georgetown paper the following advertisement:

"Six Dollars Reward

Stop the Thief! "

Was stolen from the Surveyor's office, sometime in the latter part of the year 1792, a manuscript draft, or Plan of the City of Washington, given, in trust, to me by Major L 'Enfant, The person formerly suspected for this infamous conduct was a certain James Mac Dermott 'alias' James R. Dermott, who has twice acknowledged the theft.

" He is a native of Ireland, well made, about five feet ten inches high, has a remarkably red face, an impudent brazen look, dark-colored hair, which he commonly wears tied behind. Whoever will take up the said Thief and commit him to any jail in the United States, so that he may be brought to condign punishment shall receive the above reward from Benjamin Ellicott. "

In the same issue they published over Benjamin's name, an open communication to the Commissioners, stating the manner in which Ellicott had come into possession of the map; that his brother had told him that it had been stolen; that it had appeared from an extract of a letter of the Commissioners published a few days previously in the same paper (this was at their own instigation) that the Commissioners had received it; and that "in this public and pointed manner" he requested that it be immediately given up as he was determined to prosecute with the utmost rigor of the law, the person who had taken it.

The result of this publication was that on March 31, 1794, the Commissioners ordered the Ellicotts "to deliver over to George Penwick all papers and everything else in the surveying department. " They added " This will terminate your official employment and our official discussions with you."

Sometime after this the attention of the Commissioners was drawn by the President to two lengthy letters which had been addressed to the President by Andrew Ellicott, Isaac Briggs and Benjamin Ellicott on June 29, 1793, and February 28, 1794. These letters set forth at length the complaint of the writers against the Commissioners and Dermott. The Commissioners' reply under date of March 23, 1794, which sets forth at length the history of their relations with Ellicott contains many facts in connection with this unfortunate quarrel of particular interest because they refer to the man who later prepared the so-called "Tin Case" or Dermott Map of the City, which was officially authenticated by Presidents Washington and Adams as delineating the streets and reservations of the city. In the course of this letter they say:

"Nor is the Major better grounded in his charge against Dermott of habitual Drunkenness. We were unwilling to Take his malice or the mouthing of some of the people of Georgetown as Evidence of it, we were well informed that he had now and then drank to access and when inebriated that he is unruly and quarrelsome but we did not perceive that its frequency injured the business he was engaged in; we made inquiry and formed an opinion not that he was the most discreet nor faulty in this particular to a very uncommon degree; he has since tabled at Sims's for near a year with Gentlemen of much sobriety and propriety of conduct in every respect as any in George Town, who speak well of him. The Major would be far from gaining by placing his moral character in one Scale and Dermott's in the other.

"The Major is always giving verbal evidence of his attachment to the interest of the City but neither he nor any body introduced by him has purchased a Lot. Dermott says nothing about his attachment that we have ever heard, but out of his savings, on moderate wages tho' a Drunkard, has purchased several Lots, and is improving according to his ability. "

* * *

"Major Ellicott cannot but remember that more than once he spoke of Dermott as the readiest calculator he had but with and though in the Succeeding Summer he employed him wholly or nearly so as an Overseer to overlook the negroes in cutting down the Trees in the Streets and Avenues previous to the Sale in the fall and preparatory to it he employed him in calculating the Areas and dividing the Squares.

"The Commissioners saw the impropriety of employing Dermott to overlook the cutting down the Avenues and Streets at his wages and especially as he was an European he had probably never had anything to do of the kind they perceived too Dermott's uneasiness at his Situation and were glad to see that Ellicott had changed it."

* * *

"On Major Ellicott 's evading the delivery of the papers we went with Colo Deakins to Prouts house where he then kept his Office and made a personal demand of them. He then told us that Dermott had stolen a plan of the City describing it. Mr. Johnson remarked it was a severe charge for which he ought to be well grounded before he made it. Major Ellicott said he had stolen it, that it was in his Trunk and he could prove enough to obtain a Search Warrant, and if we could break open his Trunk we should find it. Mr. Johnson replied that the end might perhaps be answered by milder measures without going to that violence. On turning off he proposed to Dr. Stuart and Mr. Carroll to send for Dermott immediately on their return and question him about the plat and if he denied his having it to desire him to submit his Trunk to their Search. It was agreed to. Dermott was sent for and attended Mr. Johnson asked him if he had the plat, describing it. He answered yes — where is it? In my Trunk — The Commissioners wish to see it — I will bring it to you immediately Sir. Major Ellicott knows very well I have it and that I would deliver it to him at any time he'd ask for it. He expressed astonishment at Major Ellicott 's making, in his expression, a fuss about it for he knew he offered to deliver him any papers he had, and that Major Ellicott said it was no matter it would do as well some other time." Taking up Ellicott 's and Briggs' charge of the removal of stakes by Dermott, they say:

"Another charge against Dermott was his changing and maliciously misplacing stakes. We heard nothing of that 'till we perceived the greater part of a succeeding Summer was spent in going over the work of the preceding, and then the excess was, that somebody had altered the situation of stakes, and it must be maliciously done because the alteration was so systematic that the greater part of a season was spent before it could be discovered. Dermott was said to know nothing of the system, but it was Dermott because he was malicious, and he was malicious because he did it. It was first suspicious, afterwards certain, it was first several stakes, afterwards one, and now amongst all Dermott 's crimes, this the most capital is omitted. Briggs at several times mentioned to Dr. Stuart that Dermott had altered the Stakes, the Doct. inquired if he had any proof of it Briggs acknowledged that he had not but suspected it, the Doctor remarked that it was a very delicate thing and that it would be unjust to act on suspicion. When in Briggs' altercation with the Commissioners he recurred again to the Story of the Stakes as an Evidence of Dermott 's infamous conduct, Dr. Stuart lost his Temper and spoke to him very roughly. The truth is the Commissioners had their suspicions too whether ill or well-founded they cannot say but they suspected that the whole story was invented to cover a mistake which had happened accidentally or for want of care. If the charge of altering the work, of stealing or maliciously Secreting a paper; or misplacing a stake was substantiated the result would surely be against Dermott. We have seen strong marks of candor in this

Man we have no reason to suspect his telling us a lie. He shows an attention to the public Interest in his divisions, has his business in good order and gives us and others such ready answers that he must have the clearest and most comprehensive view of his department." Immediately after the close of the L 'Enfant incident President Washington urged the Commissioners, as part of the general policy of vigorously prosecuting the affairs of the city, to hold another sale of lots at the earliest possible date and in response to his request the Commissioners on June 2, 1792, published an advertisement of a sale to be held in October, approximately one year after the first sale. In preparation for this sale and to avoid any charge of favoritism on the part of the proprietors, they directed Major Ellicott on September 1st to prepare divisions, between the public and the proprietors, of several squares near the President's House, the Capitol, the Commissioner's house (a building for their own accommodation which they contemplated erecting) the Judiciary, the Market, on the Canal, on the Mall and on the Eastern Branch, doing this when it was possible on the different proprietors' lands near each of the places named. The sale continued from October 8th to 10th.

For more than a year the subject of giving the Commissioners authority to dispose of lots at private sale had been under consideration by the President and shortly before the second public sale, he empowered them after that sale to sell or agree for the sale of lots in such terms as they might think proper. This course had been decided on largely as the result of the interest taken by Mr. Samuel Blodget, Jr., of Boston, who had engaged the attention of a number of wealthy men of that place as well, as of New York and Philadelphia, in the opportunity which the new city offered for real estate investments. Shortly after the public sale in October 1792, Mr. Blodget and a party of friends, John Templeman, Nathan Bond, a Mr. Killand, Peter Gilman, Thomas Metcalf and Benjamin Blodget, purchased fifteen lots at one hundred pounds each. Before he left, Mr. Blodget was commissioned to effect private sales in the northern and eastern cities, and so energetically did he execute his commission that on January 26, of the following year he reported the sale of fifty lots, saying "I have no doubt of making as many sales as will be prudent for I tender to all my obligation to receive again for my own Private a/c any or all such Lots as may be returned by the purchaser on any dislike that may occur within ten years from the date of the contract. 50 Lotts are sold already on these terms (the particulars of which I will send you) in which I believe I am very safe as they are chiefly to sanguine, moneyed, Influential men just such as we want."

A number of desultory sales of lots were made from time to time, but nothing of consequence in that line occurred until the execution of the famous Greenleaf contract, and its outgrowth, the Greenleaf, Morris and Nicholson transaction, to which reference will hereinafter be more fully made.

While on the subject of Mr. Blodget, however, it is proper to make some reference to the two lotteries which he fathered.

Mr. Blodget was undoubtedly a man of remarkable resourcefulness and ingenuity as well as of almost unlimited enthusiasm. Almost as soon as the Commissioners had entered upon the performance of their duties his interest in the new city began to manifest itself in the proposal to Mr. Jefferson of a scheme to buy up and build upon an entire street. So forcibly did this suggestion impress Mr. Jefferson that upon the latter 's recommendation the Commissioners directed that the surveying and platting of squares should be confined to those on the diagonal between the President's House and the House of Congress in the anticipation of the materialization of Mr. Blodget 's scheme. During his presence with his friends at Georgetown in October, 1792, Mr. Blodget unfolded to the Commissioners and received their consent to a plan for a lottery commonly mentioned as the hotel lottery, and hereinafter more fully set forth, for the purpose of stimulating interest in the new city. Mr. Blodget on returning to Philadelphia, lost no time in putting his lottery under way.

This lottery, it should be remarked was solely Mr. Blodget 's private affair so far as the profits and the responsibility for the payment of prizes was concerned, notwithstanding the fact that the announcement of it proclaimed it to the Public as being held by the Commissioners. At the solicitation of Mr. Blodget, Col. Deakins was joined with him in the management of the lottery. The tickets were bought up with avidity in Georgetown, Baltimore, Philadelphia, New York and Boston, with the result that in April, 1793, Mr. Blodget proposed a new lottery. The Commissioners were in some doubt as to the advisability of a second lottery and nothing further was done about it at the time.

When the time for drawing prizes arrived, much dissatisfaction appeared among the public with the manner of drawing the prizes. Rumors became current that the Commissioners had leagued with Blodget to take advantage of the people by delay in drawing prizes, thus enabling them to buy in prizes at a great discount. Among the poorer people doubts arose as to whether the prizes could be paid; and it was asserted by some that the "Capitals" had not been put into the wheel. Alarmed by those signs of dissatisfaction, the Commissioners on September 20, 1793, obtained from Blodget and Deakins an agreement reciting that the Commissioners were in no way connected with the lottery, and promising severally to indemnify the latter against all claims on account of prizes drawn against tickets sold by Blodget and Deakins respectively. Early in December, 1793, Blodget informed the Commissioners that he had sold several thousand tickets in a new lottery. To the holding of this the Commissioners at first demurred, then flatly forbade any representation of themselves as having anything to do with it, writing him on the 21st of December:

"It may be, that many, and indeed most you converse with, may be fond of another Lottery and may to you, approve the Manner of Conducting of the present, but the Majority of those who speak to us on this subject express very different sentiments and many of them friends of the City as well as ourselves. We certainly shall never give countenance to a Lottery further than mere naked consent, as was designed in the present, nor that, unless proper security is given before any tickets are disposed of. This is not from any suspicion of you but from a sense of propriety which ought to make the Rule universal." Notwithstanding this manifestation of displeasure with his new scheme, Mr. Blodget on the first of the new year — 1794 — came out with a publication of his second lottery offering $400,000 in prizes, the most important of which were a $50,000 prize consisting of a $20,000 dwelling house with $30,000 in cash, and lesser prizes, consisting of less expensive dwelling houses accompanied with cash prizes, ranging from $40,000 down to $10,000; the scheme of giving houses as prizes being, as in the case of the Hotel, both to furnish a pretext for and to give an official coloring to the lottery, and to induce the consent of the Commissioners to Blodget 's giving to the lottery the appearance of its being held under their auspices.

Both the Commissioners and the President becoming thoroughly farmed at the prospect of a public scandal to result from non-payment of prizes in either or both of these schemes, the Commissioners on January 28, 1794, obtained from Blodget a conveyance to Thomas Johnson, Jr., and Thomas Peter of a large amount of property which he owned in the federal territory, including the tract known as "Jamaica" which he had purchased in January, 1792, of Philip P. Fendall, together with 7,160 shares which he held in The Insurance Company of North America; this conveyance being in trust to secure the payment of the prizes in the hotel lottery. The closing up of the lottery was put in the hands of Mr. George Taylor, Chief Clerk of the office of the Secretary of State and Mr. Richard Harrison, Auditor of the Treasurer, who devoted some months to the task of examining the tickets and certifying the payment of prizes as made. While this was being attended to Blodget continued his efforts to put the second lottery before the public as a project of the Commissioners. The latter required him on May 29, 1794, to sign a written statement which recited:

"In order to remove any doubts which may have arisen or that may hereafter arise I do hereby declare that it is not now nor has it ever been considered by me that the Commissioners of the City of Washington were ever responsible either in their Public or their private capacities for the Lottery N 2 or the conducting thereof, I having proceeded on the Sales at my own private risque under their express declaration that they would not be held responsible directly or Indirectly for this Business in any event or in any manner whatever.

Sam'l Blodget."

Even the execution of this statement failed to put a check on Blodget's attempts to publish the second lottery as sanctioned by the Commissioners, with the result that they finally published their disavowal of it in both the Philadelphia and Baltimore papers. Several open communications between them and Blodget passed through the same channels with the result that Blodget appears finally to have become discredited by the public. The hotel though partially erected was never completed by Blodget and the holder of the prize, Robert S. Bickley, was compelled to bring suit against Blodget in Pennsylvania for damages resulting from its non-completion. Having recovered a money judgment in this suit he brought proceedings in the District of Columbia to collect the same out of the property conveyed by Blodget to Johnson and Peters to secure the payment of the lottery prizes. The litigation lasted as late as the year 1818. The hotel stood on the northwest corner at Seventh and E Streets, northwest, and in 1800 was partially reconstructed as the United States Theatre, the first theatre in the new city.

The practical effect of the hotel lottery upon the affairs of the city was summed up by the Commissioners in a letter to Mr. Randolph, the Secretary of State, written at the time of the execution by Blodget of the deed to Johnson and Peter, wherein they say: " We feel ourselves relieved and easy on the present Lottery which though it has occasioned anxiety to us, has, we are satisfied on the whole been useful in bringing the City into general view and contemplation."

While the controversy between the Commissioners and Major L'Enfant, relative to the destruction of Mr. Carroll's house, was going on, the Maryland Act of December 19, 1791, ratifying the cession of the federal territory to the United States was passed. This act, while its primary purpose was as just indicated, was in fact of an omnibus character and dealt with a multitude of matters relating to both the federal territory and the federal city. In connection with two supplemental acts passed by the Maryland Legislature it, with the deeds in trust, constitutes for all practical purposes the foundation upon which all titles to land within the original limits of the city of Washington rest. Its importance justifies more than a passing notice.

The necessity for an act ratifying the cession of the federal territory to the United States had been suggested by Mr. Jefferson so far back as March, 1791, in the memorandum entitled "Objects which may merit the attention of the President at George T.," which he handed the President previous to the latter 's visit to Georgetown which resulted in the preliminary agreement signed by the proprietors on March 30, 1791. In the course of this memorandum Mr. Jefferson says: "That State (Maryland) will necessarily have to pass another act confirming whatever location shall be made, because her former act authorized the delegates then in office to convey the land. But as they were not located, no conveyance has been made, and those persons are now out of office and dispersed." The argument advanced by Mr. Jefferson explains the reasons for the portion of the act ratifying the cession, which portion reads as follows:

"Whereas in the cession of this State, heretofore made, of territory for the Government of the United States, the lines of such cession could not be particularly designated; and it being expedient and proper that the same should be recognized in the acts of this State —

"2. Be it enacted by the General Assembly of Maryland, That all that part of the said territory called Columbia which lies within the limits of this State shall be, and the same is hereby, acknowledged to forever ceded and relinquished to the Congress and Government of the United States, and full and absolute right and exclusive jurisdiction, as well of soil as of persons residing or to reside thereon, pursuant to the tenor and effect of the eighth section of the first article of the Constitution of Government of the United States: Provided, That nothing herein contained shall be so construed to vest in the United States any right of property in the soil as to affect the rights of individuals therein, otherwise than the same shall or may be transferred by such individuals to the United States: And provided also, That the jurisdiction of the laws of this State over the persons and property of individuals residing within the limits of the cession aforesaid shall not cease or determine until Congress shall, by law, provide for the government thereof, under their jurisdiction, in manner provided by the article of the Constitution before recited." The act then proceeds to make provision for the vesting of title in the trustees Beall and Gantt and the platting and division between the proprietors and the public of such lands as had not been conveyed to the trustees by deeds. It recited the fact that most of the land in the city had been conveyed to the trustees and that on the strength of that fact the city had been designated by the President, and stated it as the sense of the Maryland Assembly that it appeared just that all the lands within the city should contribute in due proportion to the means which had already greatly enhanced the value of the whole; and provided two methods by which the Commissioners should be empowered to bring about that end. The first had reference to the lands belonging to minors, persons absent out of the State, married women, or persons non compos mentis, and lands belonging to the State. As to the lands of such owners within the limits of Carrollsburgh and Hamburgh the Act provided that they should be subjected to the terms and conditions contained in the deeds already executed by many of the owners of lots in those towns. As to all other lands within the limits of the city belonging to the several classes of owners mentioned the act provided that they should be subjected to the same terms and conditions as those contained in the deeds from Notley Young, Daniel Carroll of Duddington and others. As to the divisions of lots between the public and such proprietors the act went on to provide that where the proprietor was incompetent or failed to attend on three months' advertisement of notice in the Maryland Journal and Baltimore Advertiser, the Maryland Herald, and the Georgetown and Alexandria papers, the Commissioners might allot the portion of such proprietor as near the old situation as possible where his land lay in Carrollsburgh and Hamburgh, and that as to the other lands within the city the Commissioners should make such allotment in alternate lots; provided that in cases of coverture and infancy the husband, guardian, or next friend might agree as to the allotment, and that in eases of contrary claims, where the claimants would not agree, the Commissioners might proceed as if the proprietors were absent. As an additional method of compelling the cession of the unconveyed lands the Commissioners were vested with power to condemn the lands of any who should not have executed conveyances within three months of the passage of the act, by means of a special jury of five, the lands when condemned and paid for to vest in the Commissioners in trust to be disposed of by them or otherwise employed to the use of the city of Washington. This section repeals the former act of Maryland "to condemn lands for the public buildings of the United States," which had been passed in 1790 for the purpose of authorizing the condemnation of the lots in Hamburgh.

The next section of the act was designed to render incontrovertible the titles acquired by purchasers, whether from the public or from the proprietors. It provided that purchases of lots from the United States, or purchases or leases from private persons, claiming to be proprietors who, or those under whom they claimed, had been in possession of the lands purchased or leased in their own right for five years next before the passage of the act, should be "good and effectual for the estate, and on the terms and conditions of such purchases and leases, respectively, without impeachment, and against any contrary title now existing." In the ease of a conveyance by any person not having the right to make it the act provided that the true owner might recover all money received by the person making the conveyance both for land appropriated by the United States and for that sold or leased.

The next section was passed with a view to inducing wealthy foreigners to invest their money and settle in the new city. It gave to foreigners the same right to take and hold lands within that part of the federal territory lying within the State of Maryland, and to dispose of them, as if they were citizens of the State, providing, however, that no other privileges of citizenship should be thereby conferred.

The act then provided for a recorder of deeds, and for the acknowledgment of deeds and required that no deed thereafter made or lease for more than seven years should be effectual unless recorded within six months.

Another section provided for builders' liens, and authorized the Commissioners, until Congress should exercise jurisdiction over the federal territory, to license and regulate the building of wharves, to make regulations for the discharge of ballast, for landing and laying building materials and the disposal of earth dug from cellars, wells, and foundations, for ascertaining the thickness of walls of houses, and the retailing of distilled spirits. As to the latter, it is curious to note that the act defines retailing as selling in quantities of less than ten gallons to the same person.

The financial needs of the Commissioners were given consideration in the act by a provision that the treasurer of the Western shore should be required to pay the seventy-two thousand dollars agreed to be advanced to the President in sums as they might come into his hands on the appointed funds without waiting for the day appointed in the original act for the payment thereof.

The authorship of this act is undoubtedly to be credited to Mr. Johnson, the record of the proceedings of the Commissioners for September 8, 1791, reciting that a draft of the law had been that day submitted by Mr. Johnson. It was a painstaking work, going into minute detail to provide for every contingency that might arise under any of the subjects to which it referred; and in its preparation, as in that of the deeds of trust, Mr. Johnson vindicated the President's selection of him as one of the Commissioners. One provision of the act was probably the result of Mr. Jefferson's influence, viz. — the provision for workmen's liens. Justice White, in his dissenting opinion in the Potomac Flats cases, calls attention to the fact that this provision was foreign to the English law but well known to the civil law which prevailed in France. It is more than likely that Mr. Jefferson became familiar with it during his four years' stay in the latter country. The authority for all the provisions of the act, except that ratifying the cession, is found in the clause in the Act of Congress of July 16, 1790, for establishing the temporary and permanent seat of the Government of the United States ("the Residence Act"), which provides that "the operation of the laws of the State within such district shall not be affected by this acceptance until the time fixed for the removal of the government thereto, and until Congress shall by law otherwise provide."

Under authority of this act the Commissioners on January 6, 1792, appointed John Mackall Gantt, Clerk for recording deeds of lands within the Territory of Columbia.

Two supplements to this act were later passed by the Maryland legislature. The first arose out of a doubt as to whether it was necessary that deeds to property within that part of the Territory of Columbia ceded by Maryland should, in addition to being recorded according to the provisions of the original law, be recorded in conformity to the laws of the State as they existed prior to the passage of that law. The supplement, which was passed December 23, 1792, provided that deeds recorded agreeably to the original law should be as effective as if also recorded in the manner prescribed by the laws of the State existing prior to the passage of the original law.

The second supplement, passed December 28, 1793, was designed to meet a number of exigencies which had arisen in connection with the disposition of property in the city.

The first section made it unnecessary for the Commissioners to execute formal deeds to the purchasers of public lots in the city, by providing that the certificates of the Commissioners acknowledging the receipt of the purchase money should be effectual without a formal conveyance. The second section resulted from the difficulty experienced in collecting the deferred payments due on lots purchased from the Commissioners and authorized the Commissioners to resell at public sale on sixty days' notice lots purchased of the public where any deferred payments should not be met within thirty days from the time they became due, paying over to the original purchaser any balance of the purchase price after deducting the amount due from him with costs of sale.

The third enabled the Commissioners to make divisions between the public and the owners of all lots in Carrollsburgh and Hamburgh after three weeks' publication as if the proprietors lived out of the state, the latter class being provided for in the original act. The fourth section authorized a seal of office for and the collection of fees by the Clerk for recording deeds within the "District of Columbia," this being, it is believed, the first legislative employment of that name.

"With the exception of having some of the clay thrown up from the foundations of the Capitol and President's House in the fall of 1791, the first step looking to the erection of those buildings was taken on March 14, 1792, when an advertisement was ordered to be published in the principal towns of the United States announcing that five hundred dollars or a medal of that value at the option of the party would be given for the most approved plan submitted before July 15, next, for a President's House. It was added that it should be a recommendation of any plan if the central part of it might be detached and erected for the present with the appearance of a complete whole and be capable of admitting the additional parts in future, if they should be wanted.

A premium of a lot and five hundred dollars or a medal of that value was offered for the most approved plan for the Capitol and two hundred and fifty dollars or a medal for the plan deemed next in merit, the building to be of brick and to contain the following compartments:

"A conference room, a room for the representatives, sufficient to accommodate 300 persons each; a lobby or antechamber to the latter, a senate room of 1200 square feet area, an ante-chamber or lobby to the latter, these rooms to be of full elevation. 12 rooms of 600 square feet area each for committee rooms and clerk's offices to be of half the elevation of the former."

On July 16 and 17, 1792, President Washington met with the Commissioners and examined the plans which had been submitted. No decision was reached as to the plans for the Capitol as none of those submitted was regarded as satisfactory. For the President's house the plan of James Hoban of Charleston, S. C, was given first prize, he electing to receive a gold medal of the value of eight or ten guineas and the balance in money. A second prize of one hundred and fifty dollars was awarded to John Collins. Mr. Hoban was at once employed at a salary of three hundred guineas per year to make drawings and superintend the execution of his plan of the "palace" and of such other works of that kind as might be in execution. The day following the adoption of Hoban 's design the Commissioners, in company with Mr. Hoban went to the ground intended for the site of the President's House for the purpose of laying out the plan of the foundation on the ground. Major L 'Enfant had previously staked out the lines of the foundation upon considerably larger dimensions than those contemplated in Mr. Hoban 's design and the Commissioners, being at a loss how to adjust the discrepancy, awaited the return of the President who had proceeded to Mount Vernon.

On August 2nd, the President rejoined Commissioners Carroll and Stuart and on the following day went over the ground with them. The fixing of the exact site of the building caused the President no inconsiderable difficulty. His final conclusion was that instead of dividing equally on all sides the difference between Hoban 's and L

'Enfant 's ground areas, the north front of the building should be brought up to the point fixed therefore by Major L 'Enfant, the chief reason for his decision being that in this position the building would be "most in view to the diagonals, and on E. W. Street, though not so much so, from the Capitol, as might be wished."

On October 13th, following, according to the record of their proceedings for that date "the Commissioners, accompanied by a numerous collection of free-masons, architects and inhabitants of the cities of Washington and Georgetown, went in procession and laid the first corner stone of the President 's House. "

At the time of the adoption of Mr. Hoban's design it was thought desirable to increase the size of the building one-fifth, and Mr. Hoban accordingly enlarged his plans as directed in this particular. The expense of the enlarged plan he estimated by comparison with the cost of the Dublin Exchange at £77,900 Sterling. Somewhat taken back by these figures, the Commissioners submitted to the President, along with a statement of the financial prospects for the coming year, the question of reverting to Mr. Hoban's original plan. The President's reply under date of March 3, 1793, illustrates the intensely practical turn of his mind. He said:

"It was always my idea (and if I am not mistaken Mr. Hoban coincided in the propriety and practicability of it) that the building should be so arranged that only a part of it should be erected at the present; and upon such a plan as to make the part so erected an entire building and to admit of an addition in future as circumstances might render proper, without hurting but rather adding to the beauty and magnificence of the whole as an original. I was led to this idea by considering that a House which would be very proper for a President of the United States for some years to come, might not be considered as corresponding with other circumstances at a more distant period: and therefore, to avoid the inconvenience which might arise hereafter on that subject, I wished the building to be upon the plan I have mentioned."

Notwithstanding their recommendation in favor of the reduced plan, the Commissioners upon further reflection, reversed themselves and finally determined to construct the building upon the enlarged plan. Their decision and the grounds therefor, were set forth in a communication to Mr. Hoban under date of March 14, 1793, wherein they say:

"On reflecting on all circumstances we believe it will be best to begin the President's House on the large plan with a present intention of dropping a story in the execution. It will according to your idea described bring it on a whole, to much about the same expense as in the smaller, length and breadth, with the addition of the story. It will certainly not sink the neighboring buildings so much and perhaps the beauty of the whole may be increased. Besides if the funds should serve out and opinion should lend to it in the progress of the work the large scale may be carried through. " The reference to "dropping a story" is believed to have arisen from an original purpose to make the President's House three stories high. This idea is born out by a letter from Mr. Hoban to the Commissioners dated October 15, 1793, wherein he says:

"The whole of the Stone Cutters now in employ are preparing Ashler, and Architraves, calculated to suit the President's House; either to finish with two Storys on the present basement agreeable to your Idea given me some time ago; or to finish with three Storys, so as to accord with the plan. * * * N. B. Should the President's

House be found Sufficient for the purposes intended, with two Story 's on the present basement, still retaining the same proportions as the Original design, I am of opinion in point of Ellegance it will have a better effect." The selection of a design for the Capitol proved to be a much more difficult task than was the case with that of the President's House.

After the consideration and rejection by the President and the Commissioners of the plans submitted in response to the Commissioners' advertisement, Mr. Stephen Hallett, a Frenchman, whose plan had received much approbation, was requested to come on from Philadelphia at the expense of the city and view the ground in the expectation that this would enable him to improve upon his original design. On his arrival he made so favorable an impression that the Commissioners requested him to direct his efforts to perfecting a plan in line with certain notes which they furnished him, assuring him that in any event he should not suffer by reason of a loss of his time.

In the meantime Dr. William Thornton, of Philadelphia, who had been anxious to take part in the competition but had been prevented therefrom by his absence on a trip to the West Indies, finding on his return that no selection had been made, submitted his plan to the President in Philadelphia. The latter submitted the plan to the judgment of others with the result that the unanimous verdict was in favor of its adoption, and the President through Mr. Jefferson so notified the Commissioners. The latter were naturally in a position of some delicacy by reason of their engagement with Hallett, as is evident from their reply of July 7, 1793, in which they tell Mr. Jefferson: "Though we are much pleased that we shall at length be furnished with a plan of a Capitol so highly satisfactory to the President, and all who have seen it, we feel sensibly for poor Hallett, and shall do everything in our power to sooth him. We hope he may be usefully employed notwithstanding."

The tact with which they announced the news to Hallett was exceeded only by the loyalty with which they assumed and relieved the President of the responsibility for the decision. Their letter dated March 13, 1793, which follows, is worthy of restoration from the seclusion in which it has rested.

"The plan you first offered for a Capitol appeared to us to have a great share of merit, none met with entire approbation, yours approaching the nearest to the leading ideas of the President and Commissioners. Your time has been engrossed in unremitted efforts under your hope and our wishes that you would have carried the prize. Our opinion has preferred Dr. Thornton's, and we expect the President will confirm our choice. Neither the Doctor nor yourself can demand the prize under the strict terms of our advertisement, but the public has been benefited by the emulation existed, and the end having been answered we shall give the reward of 500 dollars and a lot to Dr. Thornton. You certainly rank next, and because your application has been exited by the particular request, we have resolved to place you on the same footing as near as may be, that is to allow a compensation for everything to this time, £100 being the value of a lot and 500 dollars. "

The President sent Doctor Thornton to the Commissioners with a letter of introduction, wherein referring to the Doctor's design, he said: "Grandure, simplicity and convenience, appear to be so well combined in this plan of Doctor Thornton's, that I have no doubt of its meeting with the approbation from you, which I have

104

given it upon an attentive inspection and which it has received from all others who have seen it and are considered as judges of such things. "

The difficulties with regard to the plan for the Capitol were not ended with the adoption of Dr. Thornton's design. The Commissioners believing it prudent to have the design thoroughly understood by whomsoever should be entrusted with its execution, requested Mr. Hallett to make a study of it. Mr. Hallett found many features of it which he reported were incapable of practical execution; and of his own initiative prepared a revision of it so greatly simplifying and abridging the original as to reduce the estimated cost of the building approximately, one half. This revised, or as it was afterwards termed, "reformed" plan, being favored over the original by Mr. Hoban and others, the Commissioners sent Mr. Hallett with it to Philadelphia to confer with the President who after consulting with Mr. Jefferson, submitted the decision on the criticisms of Dr. Thornton's plan to two builders of Philadelphia chosen by the Doctor for that purpose. The result is set forth by the President in the following letter to the Commissioners, under date of July 25, 1793:

"I enclose for your information, the copy of a letter from the Secretary of State to me, on the subject of the objection made to Doct. Thornton's plan of a capitol. By that Letter you will see that after a candid discussion it was found that the objections stated, were considered as valid, by both the persons chosen by Dr. Thornton as practical Architects and competent Judges of things of this kind.

"And one of them (Mr. Carstairs) who appeared to have studied the matter with the most attention, pronounced them irremediable without an alteration of some parts of the plan: — the other (Colo. Williams) proposed Certain other methods of obviating some of the objections, but in what manner you will see, by the enclosed letter. The plan produced by Mr. Hallet, altho' preserving the original ideas of Doct. Thornton and such as might upon the whole be considered as his plan, was free from those objections, and was pronounced by the Gentlemen on the part of Doctr. Thornton, as the one which they, as practical Architects, would chuse to execute. Besides which you will see that, in the opinion of the Gentlemen, the plan executed according to Mr. Hallet 's ideas would not cost more than one-half of what it would if executed according to Doct. Thornton's. "After these opinions, there could remain no hesitation how to decide; and Mr. Hoban was accordingly informed that the foundation would be begun upon, the plan as exhibited by Mr. Hallett, leaving the recess in the East front open for further consideration. If this meets your Ideas, the work of that building will progress as fast as circumstances will permit. It seems to be the wish that the Portico of the East front, which was in Doctor Thornton's original plan — should be preserved in this of Mr. Hallet 's. The recess which Mr. Hallet proposes in that front, strikes everyone who has viewed the plan, unpleasantly, as the space between the two wings or projections is too contracted to give it the noble appearance of the buildings of which it is an imitation; and it has been intimated that the reason of his proposing the recess instead of a portice, is to make it in one essential feature different from Doct. Thornton's plan. But whether the portice or the recess should be finally concluded upon, will make no different in the commencement of the foundation of the building, except in that particular part — and Mr. Hallet is directed to make such sketches of the Portico, before the work will be affected by it, as will shew the advantage thereof. The ostensible objection of Mr. Hallet to the adoption of Doctr. Thornton's East front is principally the deprivation of light and air, in a degree to the apartments designed for the Senate and representatives. " After the decision to adopt Mr. Hallett 's "reformed" plan, Mr. Hallett was directed to put it in shape for use in the erection of the building. He appears, however, to have developed a disposition not unlike that of Major L 'Enfant, for he had not been long engaged in the task allotted to him, before he became involved in a dispute with the Commissioners over the question of his authority in connection with the supervision of the construction work which had been delegated to Mr. Hoban. The Commissioners politely informed Mr. Hallett that he was not to interfere with Mr. Hoban. Mr. Hallett thereupon refused to allow the use of the plans, claiming them as his own, and the Commissioners retained Mr. Philip B. Key to replevin them. The matter was finally adjusted without a suit and the services of Mr. Hallett dispensed with.

The laying of the corner stone of the Capitol took place on September 18, 1793, with masonic ceremonies over which the President, as Master pro tempore of the Alexandria lodge, presided. The proceedings which included a formal procession to the Capitol, were enlivened by the maneuvers and salvos of a company of Virginia volunteer artillery. President Washington laid upon the corner stone which was located at the southeast corner of the building, a silver plate upon which was engraved the circumstances of the occasion; after which he made an appropriate address. The ceremony was followed by a barbecue.

The difficulties which confronted the Commissioners in connection with the erection of the public buildings was not confined to the selection of plans. For these works it was necessary to institute vigorous measures to find labor, tools and material; and the story of the efforts which the Commissioners made to obtain these essentials forms an interesting chapter in the city's history.

Immediately following the sale of lots in October, 1791, the Commissioners began to take active steps to procure both labor and materials. In October, 1791, they requested Major L 'Enfant to purchase in his own name the stone quarries on Higgington's Island at Aquia Creek which had been advertised for sale by the trustees of Robert Brent, at not more than eleven pounds, Virginia currency, per acre. The Brent Trustees demanded £2,200 for the tract. Thinking this figure too high the Commissioners obtained leases on two neighboring tracts, whereupon the price on the Brent property was reduced to £1,300, and the Commissioners purchased it at that figure, the deed being dated February 19, 1792.

On November 25, 1791, the Commissioners contracted for two thousand logs, thirty-six feet long, hewn on three sides to square twelve inches for use in building wharves.

Earlier in the summer the Commissioners had received a letter from Francis Cabot soliciting an agency for the purchase of materials. They had declined to employ him at the time owing to the unfavorable financial outlook but had later taken the matter up with him and on November 26, 1791, they voted the sum of one thousand dollars to send Mr. Cabot into the Eastern States for the purpose of informing himself minutely of the terms on which men and materials might be obtained. Mr. Cabot was to report from time to time so that the Commissioners might avail themselves of his information in making contracts.

The item of tools was an important one. Apparently there were no large stocks of such articles which could be purchased for immediate delivery. Everything had to be made under special contract. Wheelbarrows being needed for getting the clay out of the foundations with which to make brick for the buildings, the Commissioners on January 10, 1792, contracted with Henry Upperman for fifty to be delivered by March 1st at fifteen shillings apiece. On the 30th of March, the Commissioners contracted with John Mountz for ten sledge hammers, five hundred wedges of different sizes, twenty picks and ten trimming hammers, "of the best iron and to be well steeled" for the sum of eleven pence current money per pound. They also contracted with Mountz for ten mattocks and six axes of the best quality for ten shillings each.

On April 14, Captain Elisha Williams was directed to purchase thirty or forty thousand feet of lumber at not over one dollar per thousand and to build a lumber yard for storing it. In preparation for working the quarries at Aquia, Captain Williams was directed on March 15, to go down to the quarries and engage persons to erect four huts for the accommodation of the workmen. On April 10, an agreement was entered into with William Wright of Alexandria to act as superintendent of the stone quarry on Higginton Island, "the men to be found provisions by the Commrs., that is one pound good pork or one pound and a half of beef and one pound of flour per day all days included."

In addition to the working of the Aquia quarries, the Commissioners made several private contracts. On October 21, 1791, they contracted with Philip R. Fendall and Lewis Hipkins for 4,000 perches of foundation stone. On June 6, 1792, they contracted with William Smith for four hundred perches of foundation stone, and on December 10, 1792, with John Mason for three thousand perches. On March 22, 1793, finding the deliveries from the quarry which they had purchased at Aquia Creek not sufficient for their needs, they signed leases with John Gibson for stone land adjoining the quarry. The deliveries of stone still continuing unsatisfactory the Commissioners on July 30, 1794, contracted with James Smith and John Dunbar for its delivery at the rate of four dollars per ton for freestone and three and two-thirds dollars per ton for Ashler. To facilitate matters John Watson, one of the foremen on the work in the city, was directed to work part of his hands at the quarry and "to increase the amount of liquor in extraordinary cases at his discretion."

In 1793, the Commissioners discovered that an extensive bed of foundation stone existed at the "Key of all Keys," and thereafter a large quantity of this material was obtained from that source.

On September 24, 1791, the Commissioners instructed Major L'Enfant to employ one hundred and fifty laborers to throw up clay at the President's House and the House of Congress in anticipation of brick-making the following summer. This order, it will be recalled, was the occasion of one of the quarrels between the Major and the Commissioners. On May 3rd, 1792, the Commissioners entered into contracts with William Hill and Anthony Hoke for the manufacture of 1,100,000 bricks of statutory size near the site of the President's House, the Commissioners to furnish the clay already dug.

The matter of lime was for a time a subject for concern to the Commissioners. Mr. Cabot and others with whom they were in communication were requested to make special inquiries in the east with reference to this commodity. A source of supply, was, however, soon discovered to exist in the vicinity of Frederick, Maryland, and on May 4, 1792, Commissioner Johnson was requested to arrange with the lime burners in that neighborhood for the delivery of a quantity of unslackened lime. A quantity of oyster shells were at one time purchased for making poorer grades of lime but did not prove satisfactory.

The heavy timbers of white oak and yellow poplar, twenty to thirty-five feet long and squaring fifteen inches, for use in the construction of the Capitol and President's House were acquired from the White Oak Swamp in Westmoreland County, Virginia, through the good offices of Mr. William Augustine Washington, who assisted in negotiating the purchase of the timber. It was rafted up the river from Monroe Creek.

The procuring of skilled workmen was a subject of probably even greater concern to the Commissioners than that of obtaining materials, though common labor was not hard to obtain, as many of the residents of both Maryland and Virginia were glad of the opportunity of hiring their slaves to the Commissioners. The chief difficulty was to find masons, stone-cutters and carpenters.

Major L 'Enfant and Major Ellicott had been instructed on October 6, 1791, to have several huts erected for the accommodation of the workmen. On April 13, 1792, the Commissioners resolved to hire good laboring negroes by the year, the masters clothing them well and finding each a blanket, the Commissioners finding them provisions and paying them twenty-one pounds a year wages. They stipulated that if the negroes absented themselves a week or more such time would be deducted. On December 3, 1792, they authorized Mr. Brent to hire for work on the quarries twenty-five able bodied negro men slaves at a price not exceeding fifteen pounds, Virginia currency per year, feeding and clothing. On October 16, 1794, they advertised for a number of slaves to work in the brick-yards, stone-quarries, etc., for which generous wages would be given, and on December 3, 1794, Captain Williams was requested to obtain one hundred negro men at sixty dollars a year, findings and provisions, the masters to clothe well and find each a blanket, the same provision as before with respect to deduction in pay to apply in case the negroes should absent themselves a week or more.

To obtain such skilled labor as stone-cutters, brick-layers, masons and carpenters the Commissioners at first looked to the Eastern States. Mr. Cabot was instructed to look out for workmen of this character, particularly brick-makers in Philadelphia. On September 4, 1792, the Commissioners gave notice that they were desirous of engaging masons who could also work in brick, and that those who cut stone would have employment immediately and during the winter, applications to be made to Mr. Colin Williamson who was Superintendent of the mason work. On December 5, 1792, they announced that they wished to employ four sets of sawyers immediately, one set to be well acquainted with the sawing of mahogany.

It had become apparent, however, before this that the supply of such labor would be hard to fill, and the question of importing foreign labor was taken up. Accordingly on July 5, 1792, the Commissioners published an offer to pay the passages of not exceeding one hundred Scotch stone-cutters, masons and other mechanics.

This publication proving barren of results the President wrote to the Commissioners on December 18, 1792:

" Your letter to the Secretary of State dated if I recollect rightly the 5th instant intimating among other things that you had failed in an attempt which had been made to import workmen from Scotland, equally with that for obtaining them from

Holland, fills me with real concern; for I am very apprehensive if your next campaign in the Federal City is not marked with vigor, it will cast such a cloud over this business and will so arm the enemies of the measure, as to enable them to give it (if not its death blow) a wound from which it will not easily recover.

"The more I consider the subject, the more I am convinced of the expediency of importing a number of workmen from Europe to be employed in the Federal City. The measure has not only economy to recommend it, but is important by placing the quantity of labor which may be performed by such persons upon a certainty for the term for which they should be engaged.

"Upon the whole it will readily be perceived in what a serious light I consider delay in the progress of the public buildings, and how anxious I am to have them pushed forward. In a word, the next is the year that will give the tone to the City, — if marked with energy, individuals will be inspirited, — the sales will be enhanced — confidence diffused and emulation created. Without it I should not be surprised to find the Lots unsaleable, and everything at a stand. "

In response to this urgent request from the President the Commissioners decided to make their offer more attractive, agreeing to advance the passage money, to provide for the transportation of the men's wives and to give assurances of their social standing on arrival and some idea of the steadiness of their employment and of the wages to be paid. Accordingly on January 3, 1793, they published the following "Terms for Mechanicks. "

"The Commissioners will advance in Europe as far as thirty shillings Sterling each for expenses there so that they may by laying it out prudently be the more comfortably accommodated. The Commissioners will also pay them money on their arrival. In some instances, the fewer the better, it may be necessary and the Commissioners will make the advance for the wife. The mechanic to be allowed the same wages as there is of the same qualifications now in the Country. Their wages as in other places will fluctuate on circumstances though not in greater degree; and from what must happen, the expenditure of 2,000,000 of Dollars in the course of eight years there's no probability of any considerable decline of wages. At present stone-cutters and good masons have from 4/6 to 5 Stirling for their actual working time by time book. There's no idea of considering mechanics in any other light than the respectable of our own Country. They will draw one-half of their wages weekly and the other half to be retained till the advance and passage money is satisfied. Stone-cutters in the different branches are most wanted, masons and brick-layers are also though not so much wanted. Those who pay their own passage will be immediately employed at the same time rate given to such workmen in the Country."

Mr. Jefferson interested himself actively in the solution of this problem. He had previously imported a number of German tenants through a firm in Amsterdam to whom on his recommendation the Commissioners wrote stating their needs. Through a contractor in Philadelphia, Mr. Jefferson was able to put the Commissioners in touch with an agent of the latter in Scotland who had sent numbers of workmen to America, and to this agent also the Commissioners applied. They further addressed a memorial to the municipality of Bordeaux through the mediumship of a Mr. Fenwick.

The Amsterdam firm replied that they had in past experienced so much trouble as the result of their efforts to send immigrants to America that they were compelled to decline the undertaking. The Scotch correspondent replied that the demand for such workmen in Scotland and England was at that time so heavy that it would be impossible to send any to America. Mr. Fenwick wrote from Bordeaux that the laws against emigration, resulting from the war in which France was engaged, would make it impossible to secure any workmen from that country.

The Commissioners were, therefore, compelled to look to the American cities for their workmen, and it was from this source that the greater part were eventually procured, largely through the efforts of Mr. Colin Williamson, the Superintendent of the workmen at the Capitol.

On February 8, 1793, the Commissioners, on Mr. Williamson's request, agreed with Mr. Hunter, one of the masons who was about to go to Philadelphia for his wife, to pay Mr. Hunter one day's wages for each good mason, not exceeding twenty in all, approved by Mr. Williamson, who should come on Mr. Hunter's recommendation; agreeing also that the workmen should be entitled to their wages while coming, provided they should be approved on arrival.

To accommodate the workmen, the Commissioners allowed them to build temporary frame dwellings; and later the Commissioners themselves erected a number of temporary brick houses, two stories high, for this purpose. Evidently some of the workmen were accompanied with families, for in October, 1793, the Commissioners gave permission for the erection of a temporary school building on one of the public lots. For the accommodation of the sick, Mr. Hoban was directed on December 24, 1793, to erect a temporary hospital on some of the public squares near a good spring; and on January 10, 1794, the Commissioners appointed Dr. John Crocker physician to attend the laborers, about forty-six in number, employed by them in the city, at a salary of twenty-five pounds per year. The following April, Mr. Hoban was directed to select some public grounds in the City suitable for a burying ground.

The Commissioners were not free from the troubles which attend nearly all large employers of labor. The most serious occurred as the result of some conflict of authority between Mr. Hoban and Mr. Williamson relative to the masonry work at the Capitol. The matter coming to the attention of Col. Stoddert, he on May 26, 1794, wrote to Commissioner Carroll with a view to preventing the spread of the disaffection of the workmen. In the course of his recital of the occurrence he says:

"Twelve or fifteen of the masons employed in the City, have already gone off in very great disgust in consequence of some late change in the manner of conducting the work and twenty some odd more are going. These men wherever they go, spread disaffection to the City among the mechanics, and it will be found very difficult, if not impossible to get Tradesmen to carry on the business. The Tradesmen who arrived at Norfolk destined for the City, have stopped on their way, some at Alex, and some at other places — some who have come to the City have gone back. Those men who went off a few days ago, have already published in the Bait, paper a warning to Tradesmen how they came to the City, where they represent the usage as very bad." The account of the public work undertaken by the first Commissioners would be incomplete without some reference to two other projects to which they directed their attention: viz., the Canal and the Rock Creek Bridge.

In September, 1792, a canal between tidewater on James Creek and tidewater on Goose Creek, twelve feet wide at the bottom and fifteen feet wide at the top, the bottom to be two feet below common level water, was projected to facilitate the drainage of the lower parts of the city. Its completion for purposes of navigation was not undertaken until a number of years later when it became the subject of private enterprise.

The construction of a bridge over Rock Creek near its mouth together with a causeway along the bank of the river above the bridge, was thought of sufficient importance to justify the Commissioners in undertaking it as a matter relating to the interests of the city, and a contract therefor made on March 29, 1792.

In September, 1794, the bridge proved so unsafe that it became necessary to rebuild it.

Almost immediately on effecting their organization, the Commissioners took steps, looking to the realization of funds with which to carry on their operations. Congress had made no appropriation for this purpose. An attempt to include an appropriation of one hundred thousand dollars in the Residence Law had been voted down in the Senate the day before the final passage of the act by that body.

The only sources to which the Commissioners could look for immediate funds were the grants which had been voted by the States of Maryland and Virginia. The Maryland legislature had by a resolution adopted on the tenth day of December, 1789, agreed to advance the sum of $72,000, payable in three annual instalments. The State of Virginia had on December 27, 1790, voted a grant of $120,000, also payable in three annual instalments.

When in Richmond in the course of his southern trip the President had consulted with Governor Beverly Randolph of Virginia with a view to obtaining part of the Virginia grant for immediate use. The Virginia treasury was at the time practically empty, but Governor Randolph made arrangements to let the Commissioners have one thousand dollars at once on the order which the President had already drawn for the first instalment of $40,000, and wrote to Dr. Stuart on April 15, 1791, suggesting to the Commissioners to obtain an order from John Hopkins, the State Commissioner of Loans, upon the Collector of Alexandria. Accordingly, the Commissioners on May 9th, drew on the auditor of Public Accounts of Virginia for one thousand dollars in favor of their Treasurer, William Deakins — this being the first money which came into their hands. The Commissioners also promptly applied to Thomas Harwood, the Treasurer of the Western Shore of Maryland, who had the custody of the fund from which the Maryland grant was to be paid, asking him to pay all or part of the first instalment on the grant from that State, in advance of the 1st of January, 1792, the date fixed by law for the payment. Although the Executive Council of Maryland recommended compliance with this request, and the full amount of £9,000 or $24,000 was on hand, the Treasurer of the Western Shore declined to pay it over until the date fixed by law. In the meantime the Commissioners obtained six thousand dollars more from Virginia; and with this sum, reinforced by their personal credit and that of their Treasurer, Col. Deakins, they managed to tide over the summer, finding it necessary, however, to decline entering into a number of important engagements respecting the public works. In an early communication they advised the President that on a rough estimate they expected to have to pay between five and six thousand dollars in October, not including Major L'Enfant's compensation.

The financial problem continued to be at all times a serious one with the Commissioners. Although instalments of the Maryland donation, subsequent to the first, were paid considerably in advance of the dates originally intended, the instalments of the Virginia Donation were very tardy and only collected piecemeal and after repeated importunings from the Commissioners not only to the Executive but to the Legislature of that State. An idea of the embarrassment caused by the tardiness with which the Virginia payments were made is furnished by the following letter from the Commissioners to Governor Henry Lee of that State, which is typical of many which the Commissioners were compelled to send. On September 23, 1793, they said:

"It is with regret we feel ourselves under the necessity of applying to you again on the subject of the Virginia Donation. Our situation makes it proper for us to tell you frankly that we shall not be able to carry on the public buildings unless we can soon have what is behind of the last sum, the receipt of which we made ourselves certain of long before this time. We entreat Sir, that the executive may take effectual measures to throw the balance into our Hands for there's no calculating the injury to the Business should we unhappily be obliged to delay the payment of any just demand. The last sum will be wanted punctually and we assure ourselves that you will urge to the assembly of Virginia, the propriety of an early and adequate provision."

Early in 1792, Mr. Blodget had proposed a plan for placing a half million dollar loan upon the lots in the City owned by the public; the loan to be made in instalments of $50,000 each; and the Commissioners had in April of that year gone as far as to execute five hundred notes to cover the first instalment, when their hopes were disappointed by a serious financial crash in Boston, New York and Philadelphia, resulting from the failure of a Mr. Duer. Mr. Blodget furnished $8,000, and disposed of $2,000 more, but further attempts to push the project were at first postponed until the fall and finally abandoned entirely.

The funds derived from the sales of lots did little to reinforce the Maryland and Virginia grants. The sales up to the time of entering into the Greenleaf contract on September 23, 1793, hereinafter mentioned, were not of any considerable extent, and buyers in the majority of instances were very slow in meeting the deferred payments on their purchases.

In October, 1793, the President, at the request of the Commissioners for an auditing of their accounts, appointed Col. Robert Townsend Hooe of Alexandria, and David Ross of Bladensburg, for the purpose. In their report dated October 31, 1793, they state that the Commissioners were chargeable to that date with £30,000 ($80,000) from Virginia, £27,000 ($72,000) from Maryland, £6,005 ($16,000) from lots and other articles sold; that their expenditures were £50,502, leaving a nominal balance on hand of £12,503 of which £5,760 was a balance on an order made on Virginia but not yet actually received.

On April 22, 1794, shortly before Mr. Johnson and Doctor Stuart went out of office as Commissioners, Col. Deakins, the Treasurer to the Board, furnished them with the following statement of the financial condition and prospects of the city at a time when the only actual funds in sight consisted of the then long overdue third instalment of $40,000 of the Virginia Grant. Col. Deakins says:

"All the money that had been lodged in the Treasury was expended about the first of February last. Since then I have been obliged to have recourse to the Bank of Maryland and the Office of Discount and Deposite at Baltimore. The 1st February I had my notes discounted there for 8000 Dollars at 60 days. These notes were taken up the 1st April by further discount of my notes for an equal sum at 60 days which notes will grow due and must be taken up the 1st of June next. These 8000 Dollars are now expended and I am in Advance about 2000 Dollars and must again have recourse to the Banks for immediate demands.

" I have laid before you Mr. John Hopkin 's letter respecting the President's Order on the Executive of Virginia for 40,000 Dollars due the first of January last, from which you will find, we can have no well-grounded hopes of receiving any part of that Order in all the present year.

"From a Moderate Calculation, I suppose your Expenditures during the Summer and Fall will not be less than 10,000 Dollars P month (exclusive of your contracts for Timber, Mahogany, &c, and you can best judge what sum will be wanted for those Objects.

"The following payments if made into the Treasury, may answer the Demands for the Monthly expenditures, say

"The first payment 1st May, next to pay what may then be due and for the expenditures in that month 14,000.

"2nd payment, 1st June 8000 Dollars to take up my Notes in Bank then due and the further Sum of 10,000 Dollars for the Expenditures in that Mo 18,000.

"For the Months of July, Augt., Septr., October and Novr., 10,000 P Month 50,000.

during the Winter Months the Expenditures will be reduced, and funds may then be expected from the order on the Executive of Virginia. All the Delinquents for the Lotts purchased at public sale have been Wrote to but few or none of them have yet come forward to make the payments. You will consider what had best be done to Compel payment." The Maryland Legislature on December 28, 1793, passed an

act authorizing Samuel Blodget, Jr., William Deakins, Jr., Uriah Forrest, John Mason, James Maccubbin Lingan, Francis Lowndes, Marsham Warring, Peter Cassanave, William Burrell Magruder, Joseph Forrest, Thomas Peter, John Templeman and Benjamin Stoddert, to open subscriptions for ten thousand shares of stock in a bank, at one hundred dollars per share.

Under authority of this act the Bank of Columbia was established in Georgetown, and the Commissioners under authority of the act subscribed one thousand dollars of the stock, in the expectation of being thus enabled to obtain loans of moderate amounts as need from time to time.

On September 23, 1793, the Commissioners contracted with Mr. James Greenleaf of New York, to sell him three thousand lots at the price of £25 per lot to be paid in seven annual instalments beginning May 1, 1794. By the terms of this contract Mr. Greenleaf was to erect ten houses two stories high each year. He was to make no sale prior to January 1, 1796, without stipulating that on every third lot purchased of him a house should be built within four years from the date of sale. Greenleaf further agreed that if so required by the Commissioners, he would lend them one thousand pounds Maryland currency, each month until the completion of the public buildings, but not later than January 1, 1800. For the purpose of securing the loans they were to set apart by way of mortgage one lot for each £25 advanced by Greenleaf. Shortly after this Mr. Robert Morris agreed to join with Greenleaf in the speculation and gave the latter authority to contract with the Commissioners for a like number of lots. Greenleaf contracted on Morris' behalf for three thousand lots at thirty-five pounds each with similar building requirements to those in the Greenleaf contract, These two contracts were on December 24, 1793, merged in a single contract between the Commissioners on the one hand, and Morris and Greenleaf on the other, for six thousand lots, stipulated to average 5,265 square feet in area, at thirty pounds each; in all, one hundred and eighty thousand pounds Maryland currency ($480,000), in seven annual payments to begin May 1, 1794.

Morris and Greenleaf agreed to build twenty two-story brick houses each year until one hundred and forty houses should be built, the same to conform to the building regulations of the city. The same provision was included, as in the Greenleaf contract, relative to sales by Morris and Greenleaf. It was stipulated that four thousand five hundred of the lots should be southwest of Massachusetts Avenue and the remaining fifteen hundred to the northeast thereof. A number of provisions limited the locations from which the lots could be selected and the manner of selecting them. Everything relating to a loan in the original Greenleaf contract was referred to a new contract with Greenleaf. John Nicholson was associated in this enterprise as a silent partner with Morris and Greenleaf.

On July 9, 1794, the Commissioners, pursuant to an agreement that day entered into by them with Greenleaf for the purpose of facilitating a loan for which he was negotiating in Holland, issued certificates to him for three thousand lots to be used by Greenleaf as security for the loan. The amount for which Greenleaf was negotiating was three hundred thousand pounds Maryland currency, ($800,000), and the arrangement between Greenleaf and the Commissioners was that the city was to receive one-third of this amount. This was one of the last acts of the original Board of Commissioners. The transactions growing out of this contract play a prominent part in the early history of the city and will be set forth as part of the history of the administrations of the succeeding Commissioners.

CHAPTER V.

Conclusion of the Establishment Period.

TOWARDS the close of "the year 1793 it became evident that a due attention to the affairs of the city demanded that the Commissioners should reside close to the scene of operations. Commissioners Johnson and Stuart were unwilling to remove to Georgetown. The former, moreover, was desirous of entering into business ventures largely in connection with real estate in the new city, and such an undertaking he considered as incompatible with his capacity as Commissioner. In the fall of 1793, the Commissioners advised Mr. Blodget that Mr. Johnson and Doctor Stuart were continuing in office solely for the purpose of closing up the affairs of the Hotel lottery. The last meetings of the old Board, with Commissioners Carroll and Stuart present, were held from July 27 to 31, 1794, from which date an adjournment was taken to September 15. During this interim the President appointed in the places of Commissioners Johnson and Stuart, Gustavus Scott of Baltimore and Doctor William Thornton, of Philadelphia. Mr. Scott's commission was dated August 23, 1794; Doctor Thornton's, September 12, 1794.

Gustavus Scott was born in Prince William County, Virginia, and educated at King's College, Aberdeen, Scotland. When his friend, Sir Robert Eden, was appointed Royal Governor of Maryland he removed to that province and entered upon the practice of law in Somerset County. He was a delegate to the Maryland Convention of 1774, 1780 and 1784. He also had been a member of the association of the freemen of Maryland who signed the pledge in 1775 to throw off the proprietary authority and assume a provisional government. In 1784 he was elected a delegate to Congress, serving only one term. He was one of the organizers of the Potowmack Company.

William Thornton was born at Tortola, West Indies, and was educated as a physician. He lived for many years in Philadelphia and held a high position in scientific circles. His taste for architecture had been demonstrated in his design for the Philadelphia library building in 1790. As the designer of the Capitol he was thought to be specially fitted for membership on the Commission, one of the chief duties of which was to bring about the completion of that building. After the abolishment of the Commission he was appointed first Superintendent of the Patent Office and served in that capacity until his death in 1827.

The first meeting of the new Board was held September 15, 1794, with Mr. Carroll and Mr. Scott present. Doctor Thornton joined the Board the following day. Mr. Carroll continued on the Board until May 21, 1795. He was succeeded by Alexander White of Virginia whose commission bore date May 18, 1795.

Mr. White was born in Rappahannock County, Virginia, in 1738. He took an active part in the political agitation which preceded the Revolution, being noted for his eloquence and patriotism. He was a delegate to the Continental Congress from 1786 to 1788 and also to the first and second Congresses of the United States. It was he to whom Mr. Jefferson, in the passage from his Ana previously quoted, refers as having reluctantly voted in favor of the Funding Bill in order to make possible the adoption of the site on the Potomac for the federal seat. Mr. White was one of the directors of the Potowmack Company. At the time of his appointment, his home was at Woodville, near Winchester, Virginia, where he died in 1804.

The salaries of the Commissioners under the new arrangement were raised to $1600 per year in recognition of the fact that their entire time was to be devoted to the city's affairs. Mr. Thomas Johnson, Jr., a nephew of the former Commissioner Johnson, who had succeeded Mr. Gantt, continued for some time as Secretary to the Board and was succeeded by Mr. Thomas Munroe. On July 28, 1796, the Commissioners abolished the office of Treasurer on the ground that the continued presence of the members of the Commission at the scene of operations rendered the office no longer necessary.

At the time the new Board came into office the Chief Surveyor was Thomas Freeman. In May, 1796, Mr. Freeman was appointed by President Washington to run the line between the territory of the United States and Spain. His place was taken by Mr. Dermott. On January 3, 1798, the Board resolved that they had no further occasion for the services of Mr. Dermott. What the cause of this action was does not appear, though a letter from Dermott 's successor Nicholas King to the President some years later recites that it was for misconduct.

Commissioner Scott died on Christmas day, 1800, and on January 14, 1801, his successor, William Cranch, presented his Commission and took his place on the Board. Mr. Cranch was born in Weymouth, Massachusetts, in 1769. After practicing law three years in Massachusetts and New Hampshire, he came to Washington in 1793 as the agent of James Greenleaf. He resigned his Commission on March 3rd, 1801, after serving six weeks on the Board, to accept an appointment as one of the judges of the Circuit Court of the District of Columbia, of which he became Chief Justice in 1805, serving in that capacity until his death in 1855.

Mr. Cranch was succeeded on March 10, 1801, by Tristram Dalton. Mr. Dalton was born in Newburg, Massachusetts, in 1738. He was an ardent patriot, a delegate to the convention of committees of the New England provinces which met at Providence in 1776, a member of the Massachusetts Legislature, and a short-term Senator from Massachusetts in the first Congress of the United States. He died in Boston in 1817.

With the coming into office of the new Commissioners a noticeable change took place, not only in the manner of administering the affairs of the federal establishment, but in the matters to which the activities of the Commissioners were directed.

The first Commissioners had been the pioneers in the work of establishing the new city and their term was characterized by those struggles with primitive conditions which are the inevitable incidents to all pioneering endeavor. To them had belonged the task of devising ways and means and inventing methods for carrying on a work which not only was without precedent at the time they were called upon to perform it, but stands today as unique among the achievements of men. The work of the succeeding Boards, so far as their administrative functions were concerned, consisted mainly in carrying out what the original Board had begun.

In another field, however, their task was far heavier and involved exertions and responsibilities of a character and magnitude which were unknown to the members of the original Board. The latter, despite the disappointments which they met in their efforts to raise money from sales of lots, had been able to carry on their work with the funds provided in the Maryland and Virginia donations. But these resources had, with the exception of the last installment of the Virginia donation, been exhausted by the time the new Commissioners came into office. Their task involved, therefore, not only the carrying out of the work which had been started, but the procuring of the money with which to do it. How desperate the city's affairs at that time were; how intimately they were involved with matters of national and even international consequence; and at what labor and devotion on the part of the Commissioners they were rescued and continued to a successful outcome, are matters which have passed largely into oblivion. If, as is sincerely believed, the memories of Commissioners Carroll, Johnson and Stuart are entitled to perpetuation because of the work which they performed in organizing and setting in motion the work of establishing the city, no less a debt is due to Gustavus Scott, William Thornton and Alexander White whose exertions preserved and made effective the results of their predecessors' labor.

An important circumstance attending the appointment of the new Commissioners was the fact that by the terms of their appointment they were required to remove to Georgetown. In consequence of their residence at Georgetown it was possible for the Commissioners to meet as often as the business demanded. On February 18, 1795, they announced that after the 20th day of March they would sit three times each week and as much oftener as the business might require. Prom recitals in their correspondence it is apparent that practically all their time not given to meetings was taken up with other matters connected with the affairs of the city.

One of the first measures. entered upon by the new Board was the collection of the final installment of the Virginia donation. This installment, amounting to $40,000, was then practically a year overdue, owing largely to the expense of guarding her frontiers from the Indians. Finally, in response to the repeated applications of the Commissioners, Mr. John Hopkins, the officer having charge of the collection of the State revenue, wrote on January 21, 1795, proposing to endeavor to obtain $14,000 from sales of the State's western lands and $10,000 from the sale of three hundred hogsheads of tobacco then in the treasury, for a commission of three per cent of the money obtained. The Commissioners were reluctant to lose the three per cent but finally consented to the proposition only because of their extreme need of money.

The next active step taken by the Commissioners looking to the procuring of funds was to send Doctor Thornton to Philadelphia in February of 1795, in conformity with a request of President Washington, for the purpose of endeavoring to negotiate a loan based upon the public property. Mr. Greenleaf had attempted to place a loan both in this country and in Holland upon the property which had been conveyed to him by the Commissioners for that purpose. His efforts in this country had been futile and the Commissioners had withdrawn from the plan of attempting to affect a joint negotiation.

Dr. Thornton sounded all the financial institutions of Philadelphia without success and after conference with the President and Mr. Randolph, the Secretary of State, it was decided to apply to the English financiers. Accordingly on March 20, 1795, a power of attorney, for this purpose was sent to four Americans then in England, William Allen Dear, Samuel Bayard, Joshua Johnson and William Murdoch. These gentlemen or any two or three of them, were authorized to negotiate a loan to the extent of £300,000 Sterling. At this period the Napoleonic wars were taxing the financial resources of all Europe to the limit, and funds were not available for investments of any character.

Pending the outcome of these applications, the operations of the Commissioners were seriously handicapped by the lack of funds. They were aided to some extent by the Bank of Columbia which advanced to them upon the personal notes of themselves and their Treasurer, Colonel Deakins, sufficient for indispensable expenditures, but at the close of the season of 1795 the outlook was little short of hopeless.

On September 27, 1795, the Commissioners wrote to President Washington:

"We see with equal indignation and grief the hour approaching fast when all our Operations must cease for want of a few thousand Dollars; this too when every material is collected and the season is most favorable for the rapid progression of the works. We are Daily in session exerting our best endeavors tho' hitherto in vain to form some probable scheme to raise thirty or forty thousand Dollars to continue the Operations on the public buildings till the middle of December. The various expedients Have been discussed, nothing bearing the Appearance of efficiency has Occurred." The continuation of the work through the fall of that year was made possible by the sacrifice of the stock held by the Commissioners in the Bank of Columbia.

It was at about this time that a suggestion, which ultimately proved to contain the solution of their difficulties, was made to the Commissioners by Colonel Forrest, one of the proprietors of the land embraced in the city, who was a member of the Maryland Legislature, and who had at all times interested himself actively in the city's affairs. On October 24, 1795, Colonel Forrest wrote to the Commissioners that he had suggested to a number of influential members of the Maryland Legislature the possibility of a loan of $200,000 of the United States six per cent stock held by the State of Maryland. This was the stock which the Federal Government had issued to the several states when it assumed the payment of their expenditures in connection with the Revolutionary War. It will be remembered that it was in return for the southern votes in favor of the law providing for this assumption that the northern members of Congress had agreed to vote for the placing of the federal seat on the Potomac River.

The United States stock held by the State of Maryland was paying that State $25,000 annually in interest, sufficient to meet all of its ordinary administrative expenses. Colonel Forrest wrote that he had convinced those with whom he had spoken that it was the same thing to the State of Maryland whether it received the interest payments on this stock from the general Government or from the City of Washington and gave it as his opinion that an application for a loan of a portion of this stock would meet with success. It developed, however, that a sufficient number of the members of the Legislature could not be convinced of the safety of such an investment of the State's funds with no other security than the public property in the City of Washington, the sales of which had thus far proved anything but encouraging.

Nothing remained but an appeal to Congress. This was a project which had been delayed as a last resort, and which was now determined upon with reluctance and doubt. As has already been mentioned, Congress had refused to make any appropriation at the time of the passage of the act fixing upon the Potomac as the site of the Federal City; and at that time the friends of the Potomac had given repeated assurances that the national Government would not be called upon for financial aid. To go to Congress now and ask for money was, therefore, a most unpleasant task for the Commissioners. Commissioner White, by reason of his former service and extensive acquaintance in Congress, was selected for the duty.

It may with much reason be said that upon the success or failure of Mr. White's efforts, at the time he accepted this responsibility, rested the fate of the new city. Unless help could be obtained from Congress it was not perceived then, nor is it apparent in the light of present available sources of information, whence the funds necessary for completing the public buildings were to be obtained. A suspension of the work meant the proclamation of the entire enterprise as a failure; and such an event would have been a strong inducement to Congress to declare an abandonment of the entire project.

Mr. White left for Philadelphia about the first of December, 1795. Two alternative lines of action appear to have been decided on: one, an application for an appropriation of money, either outright or by way of a loan; the other an application for an act guaranteeing a loan to be obtained elsewhere. From the time of his arrival at Philadelphia early in December, 1795, until the final passage of the so-called Guarantee Law on May 6, 1796, five months later, Mr. White was engaged unceasingly in urging upon the members of Congress the propriety of granting the aid he sought. Throughout this time he was in constant communication with his colleagues at Washington, advising them by nearly every post of the progress of affairs, and frequently calling on them for information regarding matters upon which he was mercilessly interrogated by the members of both houses of Congress. It is doubtful whether any other period or incident in connection with the establishment of the City of Washington is of more intensely dramatic interest than the experience of Mr. White and his colleagues as set forth in this correspondence, every letter of which breathes the alternating hopes and discouragements of the former and the suspense and anxiety of the latter. A month was spent in interviewing members of Congress, consulting the President and obtaining information upon matters as to which Mr. White wrote that he had foreseen he was "to be sifted like wheat." Finally, at the suggestion of President Washington, a memorial was signed by the Commissioners and forwarded to Congress on January 8, 1796, with a short message from the President, in which he said among other things:

" I have no doubt, if the remaining resources are properly cherished, so as to prevent the loss of property by hasty and numerous sales, that all the buildings required for the accommodation of the government of the United States may be completed in season without aid from the Federal Treasury."

The result of this application was the appointment of a Committee by the House of Representatives which on January 18, reported in favor of guaranteeing a loan of $500,000; but many other matters of importance were claiming the attention of Congress and delayed its action. On February 19, Mr. White wrote: " Monday is the President 's birthday when it is expected there will be a greater display of attachment than was ever yet exhibited on a similar occasion. * * * Report says that the British Treaty is arrived at Charleston on the General Pinckney — if so the course of the Post is expected to bring it to this city tomorrow — whether that circumstance will have any effect on the business, as some predict, time alone must determine."

Many members of Congress were disposed to criticize the buildings; particularly the President 's House, the extent and grandeur of which it was claimed were more in keeping with the idea of royalty than with that of American Republicanism; and one of the duties imposed upon the House Committee was to determine whether or not any change should be made in the buildings. The fact that Mr. Jefferson, whose democratic principles and taste in architecture were even then famous, had approved the plan of the public buildings, was largely influential in reconciling Congress to what had been done. Many charges of extravagance and poor administration were made.

On February 25, Mr. White wrote that the House of Representatives had recommitted the bill, adding:

"But what shall I say when I am asked for an estimate of the expenses of the Capitol. What a Field for cavil and declamation when it can be said that the plan of such a Building was accepted without any knowledge of the costs? If an estimate tolerably accurate could be sent on, it might possibly answer some good purpose. Do not Jefferson's letters show that both Plans were examined and approved by him? That circumstance would shut the mouths of some."

The attitude of the Committee towards the legislation of the State of Maryland, so far as it affected the titles to property conveyed under the deeds in trust and the security it would afford on a loan, proved a formidable obstacle. Alluding to this, Mr. White wrote:

"I attended the Committee at 7 o'clock last night the Attorney General was present. After much conversation they agreed to report a Bill, a rough copy of which is enclosed. I gave no information with respect to the title of the lots, but that the Trustees had never conveyed. Had I introduced the maze of Maryland Laws, we never should have got through them. They would certainly have been considered as void, and of no effect by a Committee who think that Congress cannot even direct the mode of executing a Trust created by individuals for the use of the United States. How then could the Legislature of Maryland take the lots out of the hands of the President and Trustees and give the sole power over them to another body of men, viz, the Commissioners?" On March 31, 1796, the House of Representatives by a vote of 72 to 21 passed the bill guaranteeing a loan of $300,000, and the task of getting it through the Senate was begun. Here an unlooked-for obstacle was met in the fact that the question of ratifying or rejecting the treaty with Great Britain, the arrival of which had previously been mentioned by Mr. White, was pending in the Senate. From Mr. White's account it is probable that upon the fate of this treaty depended not only the fate of the City, but the continuance of the Union of the States. The actuality of this crisis can most effectively be gathered from Mr. White's own words. Writing under date of April 18, 1796, he says:

"After writing you on Friday I waited on Mr. Henry to know what policy the Senate meant to pursue with respect to the Bill before them. He said he had proposed to Mr. King to report the Bill, but could not prevail on him to do it, and to report it against his will would occasion a quarrel which he wished to avoid, that he was of opinion that all the Members east of Maryland who were in favor of the Treaty would vote for postponing the Bill if it were reported till the event of the Treaty business was known, and if provision is not made for carrying it into effect, they would finally reject the Bill. On Saturday morning I waited on the President, he seemed rather disinclined to my leaving the City but said that it would be well to ascertain the real sentiments of Mr. King and other members of the Senate with respect to the Bill. * * * I waited on Mr. King, he avowed the Policy mentioned by Mr. Henry, he said he had no aversion to the measure, no objection to a City rising on the Potowmack, and the General Governments removing thither, that he never would do anything to obstruct it, and that if harmony prevailed in the United States he should have no objection to promoting and encouraging it, but that in his opinion, in the present state of things the bill ought not to be acted upon. That he did not expect this would influence the vote of any man or mean to use it in that way, but if the British Treaty should be rejected no matter by whom brought about, it would place us in such a state that he should think it improper to engage in any enterprise either of a public or private nature, or to pass any Laws except such as were necessary to keep up the form of the Government. In the evening I had a long conversation with Cabot of Massachusetts and Trumbull of Connecticut, they avowed the same sentiments with Mr. King. I consider them as really friendly to the measure as promotive of the interest of their States, but they declared they would not pass a Law which had the continuance of the Union for its sole basis during a Crisis which so seriously threatened its dissolution. Yesterday morning I mentioned the opinions of those gentlemen to Mr. Bradford of Rhode Island; he expressed his disapprobation in strong terms and said it was the first he had heard of it and did not believe the sentiment prevailed in the Senate, that he would enquire and inform me. I then called on Mr. Fowler, his Colleague — he said he always approved of the Seat of Government being on the Potowmack, and thought it ought to be promoted by Government, but that the inevitable consequence of rejecting the Treaty with Great Britain would be a War with that nation; that the Eastern States would not join in the War and to avoid it would separate from the Southern States, that he would acquaint himself with the sentiments of other members respecting the postponement and inform me, but on looking over the list he concluded there was a majority for postponing the Bill."

The treaty in question grew out of a treaty between the United States and certain Indian tribes which prohibited traders and hunters to reside with the Indians in this country without a license. This measure had grown out of the pernicious activities of the Canadians and English in inciting the Indians to violence against the Americans. England considered it to be in violation of the provision contained in the treaty of peace of 1784 securing free passage across the border to the citizens of both nations. The new treaty bound the United States not to impede this right of free access by any further treaties with the Indians. The matter will hardly seem at this date to have justified so close an approach to war, but its seriousness at the time was manifested by a hostile attitude in the House of Representatives which passed a resolution requesting President Washington to submit to that body the correspondence relating to the treaty and threatened to prevent its passage. President Washington in his reply, refusing compliance with this resolution, laid down the principle which has never since been questioned that since the treaty making power is by the Constitution confided to the President by and with the advice of the Senate, the House of Representatives is without authority to interfere.

The treaty was ratified by the Senate on May 9, 1796. The removal of the opposition to the treaty in the House of Representatives by President Washington's reply had made it possible to pass the Guarantee Bill through the Senate on May 6, by a vote of 16 to 7.

This law authorized the Commissioners to borrow from time to time such sums as the President should direct, not exceeding three hundred thousand dollars in the whole, nor two hundred thousand in any one year, at not exceeding six per cent interest, reimbursable at any time after the year 1803 in installments not greater than one-fifth of the whole sum borrowed in any one year. All the unsold public lots in the city, except those appropriated for public use, were pledged as security for the money to be borrowed; the deficiency, if any, after the sale of the lots, to be paid by the United States.

The passage of this law, however, was only one step towards the solution of the difficulties of the Commissioners. The problem now confronting them was where to obtain the money. Almost immediately following the passage of the law a power of attorney to procure a loan of five hundred and twelve thousand guilders in Holland was forwarded to the firm of Wilhelm and Jan Willink of Amsterdam, and in October brought the information that the French invasion of that country had resulted in the levying upon all persons of a tax of one-sixth of their estates, both in that and in the preceding year, with the result that the loan sought would be impossible of negotiation at that time. Following the receipt of this information on October 31, 1796, an application for a loan of $100,000 was made to the Bank of the United States at Philadelphia, but that institution was averse to making long time loans and, moreover, was much taxed to accommodate its local patrons, and declined to make the loan.

That the Commissioners were enabled to carry on their operations during that season was due to the accommodations granted by the Bank of Columbia. On July 22, an agreement was entered into between that bank and the Commissioners, reciting that the bank had already advanced $42,000 and that it undertook to advance $40,000 more in installments of $10,000 per month, beginning August 1st. For the total sum of $82,000 the Commissioners gave their personal short time notes endorsed by Robert Peter, Notley Young, Thomas Law, Uriah Forrest and Francis Loundes.

Upon the refusal of their application to the Bank of the United States, the Commissioners again turned to the Legislature of Maryland, and on November 21, 1796, they authorized Mr. Scott, whose acquaintance among the members of that body was large, to seek a loan from that State. President Washington at the same time wrote to Governor Stone in support of the Commissioners' application. Mr. Scott's efforts resulted in a resolution passed on December 14, 1796, authorizing the nominal loan of $100,000 of United States six per cent stock. By the act authorizing this loan, the Commissioners were required to give bond in their official capacity in the sum of $100,000, and in their individual capacities in twice that amount.

Referring to the passage of this act President Washington on December 26, 1796, wrote to the Commissioners: "The voice of Maryland as expressed by its Legislature, is flattering indeed, as it respects myself personally; and highly pleasing as it relates to their federal sentiments." But, referring to the provision requiring the Commissioners to render themselves personally liable, he added: "At the same time I must confess that the request has a very singular appearance and will not I should suppose be very gratifying to the feelings of Congress."

Immediately on receiving the transfer of this stock the Commissioners sold $20,000 of it back to the State of Maryland for $16,583.33. Shortly after this they accepted a proposition from the Bank of Columbia to deposit the stock with that institution and receive credit on its books against which on notice they might draw in amounts of between ten and twenty thousand dollars, the bank undertaking to dispose of the stock at the Philadelphia prices. About $84,000 was realized from this stock.

At the close of the ensuing season (1797) the Commissioners found themselves nearly as badly off as before. An application to the Bank of Columbia for temporary help resulted in the reply that the bank would lend them $3,000 " at a time when we are not accommodating any individual and the Banks of Baltimore are continually calling on us for specie." An application to the Bank of Alexandria resulted in a refusal.

It was finally decided to lay the matter before President Adams, and on November 25, 1797, the Commissioners addressed a memorial to him reciting the disappointments which had grown out of the Greenleaf and Morris contract, the difficulties which had been met in attempting to sell the public lots, and the failure of the attempted Holland loan, and stated that the only suggestion they had to make was the impracticable expedient of exposing the public lots at auction until the whole should be sold. Action upon this memorial was suspended upon receipt of a communication from Colonel Forrest to the effect that he believed that a decent majority of both houses of the Maryland Legislature, then in session, would favor a second loan of $100,000. Accordingly a memorial was drawn by the Commissioners and presented to the Maryland Assembly by Mr. Scott on December 13, 1797, with the result that on the 22nd of the same month a second loan similar to and upon the same conditions as the first was authorized by that body. The casting vote of the Speaker was required for its passage in the House of Delegates, owing to the activities of the friends of the Potowmack Company who were seeking aid for that enterprise.

This second loan from the 'State of Maryland was far from adequate to meet the requirements of the Commissioners for the ensuing season. With this prospect confronting them the Commissioners decided to make an appeal to Congress for direct financial assistance. Accordingly the memorial to President Adams was revived and Mr. White commissioned to proceed to Philadelphia to lay the facts before the members of Congress.

Mr. White arrived in Philadelphia early in February, 1798. He found President Adams unwilling to assume the responsibility of transmitting to Congress the memorial which had been addressed to him, with a message from himself asking the aid of that body; but agreeable to the idea of transmitting a memorial to be addressed to Congress by the Commissioners. This plan was adopted. The labors of Mr. White were arduous, but after two months and a half his persistence was rewarded by the passage on April 18, 1798, of a law authorizing the loan to the Commissioners of one hundred thousand dollars in two yearly installments, bearing interest at six per cent. All the unsold public lots in the city were declared to be subject to sale for the repayment of the loan.

Until the passage of this act the Commissioners had kept in communication with Messrs. Willink and Willink of Holland in the hope that conditions in Europe would so improve as to make it possible to place a loan there; but the continuation of the wars on the continent had prevented the consummation of this measure. Upon the granting of the loan by Congress, negotiations with that firm were closed.

This federal loan, together with such funds as were obtained from sales of lots, carried the operations, through the seasons of 1798 and 1799. Towards the close of the season of 1799 it became apparent that still further advances would be required in order to make it possible to have the public buildings ready for the accommodation of the government at the date set for its removal. The borrowing power of the public property had been exhausted by the three loans already obtained. It was necessary to obtain a loan upon other security, and for this purpose it was decided to ask the opinion of President Adams upon the question of pledging the public equity in the lots which had been contracted for but not fully paid for — principally those involved in the Morris and Greenleaf contract. Two letters were written to President Adams upon this point, but no reply being received it was on December 9, 1799, decided by a majority of the Board, in view of the urgency of the case and the rapidly approaching close of the session of the Maryland Legislature, to make the application without waiting for the President's approval. As on previous occasions the efforts of Colonel Forrest proved efficacious. The application was promptly answered by a resolution passed on December 23, 1799, authorizing a loan of $50,000 in United States stock to be bottomed upon such real and personal security as the Governor and Council of the State should approve. The terms of security required by the Maryland authorities were met by the execution on February 28, 1800, of a bond signed by Commissioners Scott and Thornton and joined in by Colonel Uriah Forrest and General James M. Lingan. In addition Colonel Forrest gave a mortgage upon a farm of four hundred and twenty acres of land in Montgomery County.

On July 1, 1802, the office of the three Commissioners was abolished by section 1 of "An act to abolish the Board of Commissioners in the City of Washington, and for other purposes," approved May 1, 1802, which directed the Commissioners to deliver all their official records and property relating to said city to an officer created by said act and styled "Superintendent," to be appointed by the President, and to succeed to all the powers and duties of said Commissioners. By that act the Superintendent was directed to sell sufficient of the public lots, which had been pledged under the Guarantee Act, to satisfy the two one hundred thousand dollar Maryland loans as fast as the interest and installments should come due under the terms of the Guarantee Act. The proviso was attached that if in the opinion of the President the sale of a sufficient number of lots could not be made without an unwarrantable sacrifice, so much money as might be necessary to provide for the deficiency should be paid out of the Treasury.

For the repayment of the last Maryland loan of $50,000 the same Act directed the Superintendent to sell all of those lots held by the Commissioners for default in the payment of the purchase price, which had been sold by them subsequent to the passage of the Guarantee Law, and provided for the payment of any deficiency out of the Treasury.

An account of the financial affairs of the Commissioners would be incomplete without some reference to their dealings with Morris and Greenleaf, and with Morris and Nicholson who succeeded to the interest of Morris and Greenleaf in the contract with the Commissioners.

The outcome of that contract, which had promised so much for the city, was a great disappointment to everyone concerned. Morris, Greenleaf and Nicholson fell far short of living up to their undertaking, and a large part of the energies of the Commissioners was devoted to efforts to obtain from those gentlemen a fair degree of compliance with the terms of their contract. Nevertheless the funds obtained as a result of that transaction, tardy and hard wrung though they were, aided materially in making it possible to complete the public buildings in time for the reception of the Government at the date set for its removal to the new seat.

Not long after the execution of the contract with Morris and Greenleaf, the Commissioners received a remittance of $16,000 from those gentlemen. On July 9, 1794, the Commissioners entered into an arrangement with Mr. Greenleaf separately, whereby they executed certificates to him for three thousand lots in the city, to be used as security for a loan of £300,000, one-third of which was to be for the benefit of the city. Many difficulties were met in obtaining the money, and finally the idea was given up and the 1000 lots intended to secure the city's share of the loan were reconveyed. Mr. Greenleaf succeeded in obtaining a portion of the loan sought in Holland on his own account. However, the matter of an advance was taken up with Morris and Greenleaf jointly, and on October 18, 1794, the Commissioners conveyed to the latter eight hundred and fifty-seven lots in return for their acceptance of bills of exchange sufficient to furnish the Commissioners an advance of $12,000, and other sums to be paid thereafter.

The expected funds were not realized, and after numerous futile applications to Morris and Greenleaf, the Commissioners stated the case to President Washington, who referred their communication to Mr. Morris. The reply of the latter stated that he had been making every possible effort to obtain the money, but that the financial stringency then prevalent in this country and the wars then engaging Europe, had made it impossible for him to do so.

When Mr. White went to Philadelphia to urge upon Congress the passage of the Guarantee Law, he was directed to endeavor to obtain funds from Morris, Greenleaf and Nicholson, and his letters to his colleagues show that much of his time and efforts were devoted to that end, although he was only able to obtain remittances amounting altogether to about $10,000. Mr. White's letters also show that the financial ruin which later sent Mr. Greenleaf into bankruptcy and Morris and Nicholson to the debtor's prison, was already fastening upon those gentlemen. The fact is that these bold adventurers had engaged upon a campaign of land speculation throughout the United States, of an almost incredible extent. From New York to Georgia they had bought up vast areas of wilderness. In the City of Washington they had not confined themselves to their contract with the Commissioners but had dealt extensively with the proprietors. The wars then raging in Europe and the depredations upon American commerce had created a shortage of money which made impossible any approach to compliance with their enormous obligations. Mr. Morris at the time of his eventual failure, was indebted to upwards of three million dollars.

Strictly speaking, Morris and Greenleaf were also completely remiss in the matter of compliance with their agreement with the Commissioners to build twenty houses each year. They did in fact erect thirty buildings under a contract with Daniel Carroll of Duddington, which were completed to the roofing in the year 1796, and the Commissioners accepted this as a partial compliance with their building engagement; but this was the extent of their operations in that direction. These buildings were generally referred to at the time as the "Twenty Buildings." Their location is described by Mr. Allen C. Clark, in his volume "Greenleaf and Law in the Federal City," as follows:

"On South Capitol street beginning at M, southward, were live houses each twenty -nine feet live inches front; then an alley twenty-five feet wide; then twelve houses each twenty feet wide; then an alley twenty feet wide, then five houses each twenty-nine feet five inches front, the most southern on the corner with N street. On N, were four houses each eighteen feet one inch front; then a vacant space; then four houses each eighteen feet nine inches front, the most western on the corner with Half street. The houses on South Capitol Street had 'breast summer fronts' and were 'capable of making a handsome row of fronts.' "

Following the unsatisfactory results of Mr. White's efforts, the Commissioners were compelled to place with a lawyer for suit, the bills of exchange aggregating in the neighborhood of $.35,000, on which they had made their conveyance to Morris and Greenleaf; but the bills were finally paid before suit was entered.

It had early become apparent that the only means of recovery open to the Commissioners was a resale of the lots which had been contracted for but not actually conveyed. The question arose as to whether it would be necessary to go into Chancery and obtain a decree of court authorizing such a sale or whether it would be competent for the Commissioners to proceed by the summary method of resale upon advertisement provided for by the Maryland act of December 28, 1794. This act had been passed four days after the execution of the contract with Morris and Greenleaf and it was contended by the latter that it could not operate retroactively so as to affect their contract. Mr. White while in Philadelphia in connection with the Guarantee Bill, obtained the opinion of Attorney General Charles Lee upon this point. Mr. Lee's opinion was that a sale under the Maryland act was proper and that the act could not be regarded as ex post facto since it did not alter the, contract but merely provided a speedy mode of preventing injuries which might arise from a breach thereof.

In the summer and fall of 1797 the Commissioners held several sales of lots, but the scarcity of money and the efforts of Morris and Greenleaf to create a belief among prospective buyers that the sales were unlawful, prevented the realization of any considerable amount of money.

In June, 1798, the Commissioners advertised a sale to be held in the following September, of a long list of Morris and Greenleaf 's lots to raise the sum of $120,000 then due from the latter and fortified themselves against the assaults of Morris and Greenleaf by a second opinion of the Attorney General, confirmatory of his first opinion, which they published before the sale. The sales on this occasion were more extensive than formerly, but still very disappointing.

In 1799 the Commissioners again advertised a sale but this time were stopped by an injunction brought by Mr. Greenleaf, after selling $41,000 worth of lots. In 1800 the sales amounted to nearly $60,000. In a letter written in November, 1799, to Colonel Stoddert, then Secretary of the Navy, the Commissioners say that $103,500 was then due from Morris and Nicholson. As five installments of $68,571 or $342,855 in all would have been then due under the terms of the contract, it would seem that the Commissioners had up to that time received in the neighborhood of $239,355 from the transaction. The funds derived from sales of lots were not confined to those received from the Morris and Greenleaf transaction, but the other sales were of comparative unimportance.

Morris, Greenleaf and Nicholson sold many of their lots to various purchasers, chief among whom was Thomas Law, an Englishman who had amassed a fortune in India and who settled in Washington and became one of its prominent citizens. An account of the ramifications of the transactions of this remarkable group of men in the City of Washington; their quarrels among themselves; their disputes with the Commissioners, and the varied, extensive and protracted litigation which arose out of their affairs, would be of great interest, but impossible in the limits of a volume devoted to the history of the City of Washington. It has been made the subject of the intensely interesting volume by Mr. Allen C. Clark, heretofore mentioned, "Greenleaf and Law in the Federal City."

It may be readily gathered from the review which has been given of the financial activities of the Commissioners that their operations involving the expenditure of the funds acquired by them must have been extensive. These were mainly confined to the completion of the Capitol and President's House upon the plans adopted by their predecessors, and the erection of the buildings for the executive offices. Enough has been said in the preceding chapter to give some idea of the difficulties attending the erection of the Capitol and President's House. Disputes with the workmen and with the superintendents in charge of the work were frequent and resulted eventually in the committing of the superintendence of all the public buildings to Mr. Hoban. An interesting letter is found from Samuel Smallwood, an employee, who complains of both the small pay, $15 per month, and the diet, which, he says, "are nothing more than salt meat for Brexfast, Dinner and Supper, which is neither palitable nor Constitutinal. "

The work upon the Capitol was confined, after the construction of the foundations, to the completion of the north wing. On June 20, 1801, following the removal of the Government to Washington, a contract was entered into with William Lovering and William Dyer to erect a temporary building on the elliptical foundation of the south wing for the accommodation of the House of Representatives.

After the roofing of the President's House the work upon that building was subordinated to that on the Capitol, but on November 15, 1800, a contract was entered into to finish it in one month.

On June 23, 1798, the Commissioners contracted with Leonard Harbaugh for the erection of a building for the Treasury Department, east of the President's House, for $39,511. The building was to be of brick exterior, 148 feet by 57 feet six inches in area. On August 6, 1799, the Commissioners contracted with Harbaugh for the erection of a similar building west of the President's House, for the accommodation of the other executive departments.

The matter of the location of these buildings was the occasion of some concern to the Commissioners. When President Washington induced the original proprietors to agree to the plan for ceding their lands to the Trustees he stated that the executive departments would be located near the President's House, and this was the location intended for them by the Commissioners. President Adams, however, expressed to Mr. White when the latter was in Philadelphia urging the federal loan, the opinion that these buildings should be near the Capitol in order to make them accessible to the members of Congress.

On hearing of this, Robert Peter and Samuel Davidson addressed a protest to the Commissioners on the ground that the arrangement proposed by President Adams was in violation of President Washington's representations. The Commissioners promptly took the matter up with President Adams, urging not only the grounds advanced by Peter and Davidson but also the fact that President Washington had personally indicated to them on the ground, the spots where he desired the buildings to be placed, and had given in support of the location near the President 's House the experience of the Executive Chiefs in Philadelphia who had been so hampered in their work by the visits of the members of Congress that they had been compelled to go to their homes and deny themselves to all visitors.

So important was the question regarded that the Commissioners invoked the opinion of General Washington, then in retirement at Mount Vernon, who replied with some warmth in support of the location of the buildings near the President's House. As a result of these representations President Adams acquiesced in that arrangement.

In November, 1795, the Maryland Legislature authorized Notley Young, Daniel Carroll of Duddington, Lewis Deblois, George Walker, William Mayne Duncanson, Thomas Law, and James Barry to hold two annual lotteries for raising the sum of $52,500 for the purpose of rendering navigable the Tiber Creek Canal which the first Board had begun. The persons named were required by the Act to give bond to the Commissioners in the sum of $200,000 for the payment of the prizes and faithful application of the moneys raised. The work of completing the canal was to be subject to the direction and superintendence of the Commissioners. The lottery was held and the tickets sold, but apparently entirely on credit. The Commissioners made repeated demands upon the managers of the lottery for an accounting, but the latter replied that despite their greatest exertions nothing could be collected.

Not the least important of the acts of the Commissioners during the period under discussion was the fixing of the designations of the streets and appropriations. As early as June 15, 1795, this work was put on foot by an order to Mr. Dermott to prepare a plat of the city "with every public appropriation plainly and distinctly delineated." It was intended that upon the completion of this plat the Trustees, Beall and Gantt, who held under the deeds in trust from the original proprietors, should execute a conveyance to the Commissioners of all the streets and public appropriations, as designated upon the plat. This conveyance, together with the map, were to constitute the evidence of the title of the United States to the streets and public grounds. For this purpose the Commissioners advanced the proposition that in their official capacity they should be incorporated to avoid the complications incident to their taking title as individuals, but this measure was not put into effect.

In the preparation of the Ellicott Map, all the designations of appropriations appearing on L 'Enfant 's Map, except those for the Capitol and President's House, were struck out, and after the publication of Ellicott 's Map many changes were made in the open spaces indicated but not referred to as appropriated to any particular object. These changes consisted mainly in reducing the sizes of these open spaces by the laying out of blocks which encroached upon them, as at the Arsenal Point on Notley Young's land, and at the site intended for a fort on Robert Peter's land, the present site of the Naval Hospital.

In the course of the preparation of Dermott's Map a controversy arose between the Commissioners and the proprietors relative to the question whether the open spaces created by the intersections of streets and avenues, together with the points of the adjacent squares which were taken off and included in the open spaces, were to be considered as streets or as public appropriations. The Commissioners contended they should be regarded as streets and therefore were to be donated free by the proprietors to the public under the terms of the deeds in trust. The proprietors contended that the entire areas, both streets and points of squares, were to be considered as appropriations and to be paid for at twenty-five pounds per acre under the terms of the deeds of trusts, or that the points of squares should be laid off into building lots and divided between the public and themselves.

The Commissioners wrote to President Washington on November 30, 1796, stating the issue in controversy and suggesting the plan of making the street area as large as possible relatively to the park area by laying out a street 160 feet wide around each of these reservations and enclosing the center as a park. President Washington recognized the justice of the claim made by the proprietors for pay for the points of land though not for the streets. He stated the case with his usual perspicacity in a letter to the Commissioners of December 26, 1796, wherein he said:

"With respect to the claim of individual proprietors, to be compensated for the spaces occasioned by the intersection of streets and avenues, I should conceive that they might, with equal propriety, ask payment for the streets themselves; but the terms of the original contract, or cession, if a dispute on this point should arise, must be recurred to, for I presume the opinion of the President, in such a case, would avail nothing. But if angles are to be taken off, at these spaces, the case is materially altered; and, without designing it, you make a square where none was contemplated, and thereby not only lay the foundation of claim for those angles but for the space also which is made a square by that act."

The settlement of this dispute failed to reconcile many of the proprietors to the adoption of Dermott's plan. Chief among the objectors was Samuel Davidson, who from the time of the appearance of Ellicott's map had protested that the alteration made by Ellicott in the north front of the President's Square, changing it from a semi-circle, as planned by L 'Enfant, to a square, was an unlawful confiscation of property thus included in the appropriation to which as the proprietor he would have been entitled under the plan laid out by L 'Enfant. He contended that the President's act in laying L 'Enfant 's plan before Congress in December, 1791, made that the official plan of the city. This contention being called to the attention of President Washington, he on February 20, 1797, wrote to the Commissioners in refutation of Mr. Davidson 's position, saying:

"That many alterations have been made from Major L 'Enfant 's plan by Major Ellicott, (with the approbation of the Executive) is not denied; that some were deemed essential is avowed; and had it not been for the materials which he happened to possess 'tis probable no engraving from Major L 'Enfant 's draught would ever have been exhibited to the public; for after the disagreement which took place between him and the late Commissioners, his obstinacy threw every difficulty it could in the way of its accomplishment.

"To this summary may be added, that Mr. Davidson is mistaken if he supposes that the transmission of Major L 'Enfant 's Plan of the City to Congress, was the completion thereof. So far from it, it will appear by the Message which accompanied the same that it was given as a matter of information, to show in what state the business was in, and the return of it requested. That neither house of Congress passed any act consequent thereupon. That it remained as before, under the control of the Executive. That afterwards, several errors were discovered and corrected, many alterations made, and the appropriations (except as to the Capitol and President's House) struck out under that authority, before it was sent to the engraver, intending that his work and the promulgation thereof, were to give it the final, and regulating stamp."

On June 22, 1797, the Commissioners wrote the Trustees, Beall and Gantt, requesting them to execute a conveyance of the streets and public reservations. Mr. Gantt in conversation stated that he deemed it advisable to await the completion of Dermott's plan and to then include in the conveyance a designation of the appropriations after having the President specifically certify them as such. Accordingly on January 31, 1797, the Commissioners forwarded to President Washington a draught of a proclamation designating the public appropriations and referring to them as being indicated on Dermott's map, which was recited as being attached. This proclamation was signed by President Washington on March 2, 1797, two days before the close of his administration, and in the press of business the affixing of the map was omitted.

For more than a year after this the Commissioners continued their efforts to obtain a deed from Beall and Gantt, who were alarmed by the contention of the proprietors that a conveyance according to the designations on Dermott's map would constitute a violation of their trust for which they would be personally responsible to the proprietors. Among other objections they raised the point that the map had not been attached to President Washington's proclamation. Accordingly the Commissioners on June 21, 1798, forwarded the Dermott map to President Adams with President Washington's original proclamation and the draft of another for execution by President Adams. The map was enclosed in a tin case from which circumstance it has come to be commonly referred to as the "tin case map." In their letter to President Adams, the Commissioners say: "As These acts are the authentic documents of the title of the public to the lands appropriated, we shall write to Mr. Craik or some other gentleman, to take charge of their return, rather than trust them to the mail."

Writing to Mr. William Craik on June 25, 1798, the Commissioners said:

"Some days ago, we sent the plan of the City of Washington to the President, in order to procure his direction to the Trustees to convey the streets and public property in the City to the Commissioners, the plan is enclosed in a tin ease too large to go by the ordinary conveyance of the mail. Mr. Joseph Nourse was so obliging as to take charge of it to Philadelphia, and we request the favor of you to bring it with you when you return, as the enclosure is of great importance, being the evidence of the public property in the City." On the receipt of President Adams' proclamation with the

map attached, the Commissioners again requested the Trustees to execute the conveyance, whereupon a letter was sent to the Trustees signed by David Burnes, William Prout, Robert Peter by Nicholas King his attorney, Samuel Davidson, for himself and the heirs of John Davidson, John Oakley for Ruth Ann Young and the minor children of William Young, deceased, Daniel Carroll of Duddington and James M. Lingan. This letter stated that it was the understanding of the signers that there was no duly authenticated plan of the city exhibiting the streets and appropriations "as heretofore acted upon and believed to exist;" and cautioned the Trustees at their peril not to convey the said streets and appropriations until there should be such a duly authenticated plan. The letter concluded by saying that if compulsory measures should be adopted to compel the Trustees to convey before such plan should be established, the signers engaged to defend the Trustees in a legal resistance thereto.

On the receipt of this communication the Trustees refused to execute any deed specifically designating the streets and appropriations but offered to convey in general terms, but without specific designation, all the streets, squares and parcels which had been laid off by the President pursuant to the deeds in trust. This form of conveyance not being acceptable to the Commissioners the question of instituting coercive measures was submitted to the President. In view of the opinion of the Attorney General, Charles Lee, however, to the effect that it was not material to the United States whether the Trustees conveyed public appropriations to the Commissioners or not as the title of the United States would be equally valid in either case, no further attempt was made to compel a conveyance.

It should be remarked that by reason of the proceedings here recited the Dermott map was accepted by the Supreme Court of the United States in the Potomac Flats cases, as the official and authentic map of the streets and reservations of the city.

A matter of interest connected with the disposition of the public appropriations was the attempt of the Commissioners to donate a tract of land to the Queen of Portugal as a site for the residence of her minister. The idea of making such a donation had been previously discussed with the Spanish Minister, but the first definite step after obtaining the consent of President Adams, was the addressing of an identical letter on May 3, 1797, to the British, Batavian and Portuguese Ministers offering each such quantity and location of ground as they should select, and expressing the hope that the transaction would tend to strengthen the ties of friendship with this country. The offer was taken up by the Portuguese Minister, Chevalier Cypriano R. Freire, and resulted in his coming to Washington and selecting a site for which the Commissioners, on May 25, 1798, executed a deed to the Queen of Portugal, describing the tract as the Square on the President's Square east of Square 171, 319 feet by 281 feet five inches. The deed was forwarded to President Adams for an endorsement of his approval and was brought to the attention of the Attorney General in connection with a memorial from a number of the proprietors protesting against various of the acts of the Commissioners. Charles Lee, the Attorney General, gave it as his opinion that since the Constitution gives Congress the power "to dispose of and make all needful rules and regulations respecting the territory or other property belonging to the United States," and since the lot in question, which was situated on one of the public reservations, was the property of the United States, it could not be lawfully conveyed without an Act of Congress. The Commissioners sought to procure an act sanctioning the conveyance but Congress failed to act in the matter and nothing further was done.

The date of the transfer of the seat of government to the District of Columbia was fixed by the first paragraph of section 6 of the act of July 16, 1790, as follows:

"And be it enacted, That on the said first Monday in December, in the year one thousand eight hundred, the seat of the Government of the United States shall, by virtue of this act, be transferred to the District and place aforesaid; " the place referred to being the portion of the District selected for the Federal City.

An act of Congress approved April 24, 1800, authorized the President of the United States to direct the removal of the various Executive Departments to the City of Washington at any time after the adjournment of the first session of the Sixth Congress and before the time fixed by the act of July 16, 1790, for the transfer of the seat of government to that place.

The date of the first meeting of Congress in the District was fixed by an act passed May 13, 1800, for the 17th day, or the third Monday, in November, 1800; but it actually met for the first time in the District on November 21, which was the first day of the session when a quorum of both Houses was present. The meeting was in the north wing of the Capitol, then the only completed part of the building. A quorum of the House of Representatives was present on the 18th of that month.

The personnel and records of the several Departments were transferred from Philadelphia to Washington about the same time, at an expense of $32,872.34, and those Departments were fully removed to the latter city by June 16, 1801. (Senate Doc. No. 238, second session, Fifty-fifth Congress.)

The Supreme Court held its first session in Washington on the 2nd of the ensuing February; but the first session at which a quorum of that court was present was held on the 4th of that month.

In a message to Congress on December 3, 1799, President Adams said:

"The act of Congress, relative to the seat of government of the United States, requiring that on the first Monday of December next, it should be transferred from Philadelphia to the district chosen for its permanent seat, it is proper for me to inform you, that the Commissioners appointed to provide suitable buildings for the accommodation of Congress, and of the President, and of the publick offices of the government, have made a report of the state of the buildings designed for those purposes in the city of Washington; from which they conclude that the removal of the seat of government to that place, at the time required, will be practicable, and the accommodation satisfactory."

President Adams left Philadelphia May 27, and arrived in the District of Columbia June 3, when he was met by a large escort, who conducted him to the Union Tavern in Georgetown, the Executive Mansion not yet being ready for his reception in Washington.

Christian Hines, in his "Early Recollections of Washington, " says:

"The vessels in which were brought the furniture, etc., landed and discharged their cargoes at Lear's wharf, and as the vessels were unladen their contents were carried away to the War and Treasury offices, the only two that were built at the time. Some of the furniture was stored away in the stone warehouse and afterwards taken away in wagons, it being too bulky to remove in carts. "

Abraham Bradley, Jr., the Assistant Postmaster General, wrote, June 2, 1800, his impressions of the new city to a friend, as follows:

"We arrived here on Friday last, having had a pleasant journey as far as we travelled by daylight. Captain Stevenson, with whom I agreed for a house before my arrival, was not ready to give possession, and the house was not convenient for us. I have, therefore, taken a large three-story house within a few rods of Blodget's Hotel, which will accommodate the office and my family and the Postmaster's office. It is about equidistant from the President's House and the Capitol. It is impossible that all the people attached to the public offices should be accommodated with houses, the few that have been left are at rents none under $250 and $300. Provisions are plenty, good enough, and cheaper than in Philadelphia. * * * For myself, I do not regret the removal. The situation of the city is beautiful."

In November, 1800, President and Mrs. Adams took possession of the far-from-finished President's Mansion, and Mrs. Adams has left graphic descriptions of her surroundings and feelings. In a letter to her daughter, she wrote:

"I arrived here on Sunday last, and without meeting with any accident worth noticing, except losing ourselves when we left Baltimore, and going eight or nine miles on the Frederic road, by which means we were obliged to go the other eight through the woods, where we wandered for two hours without finding guide or path. * * * Woods are all you see from Baltimore till you reach the city. * * * Here and there is a small cot, without a glass window, interspersed amongst the forests, through which you travel miles without seeing any human being. In the city there are buildings enough, if they were compact and finished, to accommodate Congress and those attached to it; but as they are, and scattered as they are, I see no great comfort for them." Describing the President 's House, she said: " The house is made habitable, but there is not a single apartment finished. We have not the least fence, yard or other convenience without, and the great unfinished audience room I make a drying room of, to hang up the clothes in. The principal stairs are not up and will not be this winter."

Mrs. Adams expressed the opinion that if the twelve year's work had been going on in New England it would have been better managed and completion much nearer its end; but she saw the possibilities of the new city, for she continued: "It is a beautiful spot, capable of any improvement, and the more I view it the more I am delighted with it. "

One of the Congressmen, John Cotton Smith, also described his impressions of the wilderness city after his arrival there in 1800, thus:

"Our approach to the city was accompanied with sensations not easily described. One wing of the Capitol only has been erected, which, with the President's house, a mile distant from it, both constructed with white sandstone, were shining objects in dismal contrast with the scene around them. Instead of recognizing the avenues and streets portrayed on the plan of the city, not one was visible, unless we except a road, with two buildings on each side of it, called the New Jersey Avenue. The Pennsylvania, leading, as laid down on paper, from the Capitol to the Presidential mansion, was then nearly the whole distance a deep morass, covered with alder bushes which were cut through the width of the intended avenue during the then ensuing winter. Between the President's house and Georgetown a block of houses had been erected, which then bore and still bear, the name of the six buildings." He also tells of other blocks in an unfinished, or rather a just-begun condition, in different directions, of buildings half-finished and abandoned for lack of funds, saying, "There appeared to be but two really comfortable habitations in all respects, within the bounds of the city, one of which belonged to Dudley Carroll, Esq., and the other to Notley Young."

An official statement of the number of dwelling houses in the city is to be found in a report made by the Commissioners to President Jefferson on December 4, 1801, wherein they say that on May 15, 1800, there were 109 brick and 263 wooden dwellings, and that on November 15, 1801, there had been added to these 84 of brick and 150 of wood, with 79 brick and 35 wooden houses unfinished; a total of 735. The probabilities are that many of these were the temporary structures which the Commissioners had allowed to be erected for the use of workmen and tradesmen. It should be noted that the original building regulations had been amended on June 25, 1796, so as to permit of the erection of frame dwellings until the first Monday of December, 1800.

Inhabitants of the new district showed their interest in the proceedings of Congress by sending to that body of law-makers a letter "expressive of satisfaction upon the first meeting of the national assembly at the permanent seat of government."

Before the Government was fairly settled in its new home a destructive fire occurred in the War Department building on Pennsylvania avenue, when many valuable government papers and records were destroyed. This misfortune occurred on November 8, 1800.

The loss occasioned by this fire was a severe blow to the Government, but matters had just fairly been put to rights, when a second destructive conflagration occurred in the Treasury Department on January 20, 1801.

CHAPTER VI

The Mayoralty Government of Washington; 1802-1871.

Charters.

On May 3, 1802, the first charter of the City of Washington was granted under an Act of Congress incorporating the inhabitants and dividing the city into three wards for the purpose of assessment. This charter provided for the government of the city by a Mayor, to be appointed annually by the President, and an elective Council of twelve members divided into a "first chamber" of seven members, and a "second chamber" of five members, the latter to be chosen from the whole number of councilors. The continuance of this charter was limited to a period of two years. It was renewed at its expiration by an act approved February 28, 1804, for an added term of fifteen years. The act of renewal changed the council to consist of two chambers of nine members each, both of which were to be chosen by popular election.

An act of Congress approved May 4, 1812, further amended the charter so as to provide for the election of the Mayor by the "Councils," which were to consist of a Board of Aldermen of eight members elected biennially, two from each ward, and a Board of Common Council, of twelve members, elected annually, three from each ward. This act provided for the redistricting of the city from time to time so as to equalize as nearly as possible the numbers of voters in the several wards.

An entirely new charter was created by an act of Congress approved May 15, 1820. This act contained many provisions relating to the powers and duties of the Corporation but made little change in the form of government except to provide for the election of the Mayor biennially by popular ballot and for the annual election alternately of one of the two aldermen from each ward. By this act the city was provisionally divided into six wards. The charter of 1820 was by its terms to continue in force for twenty years. It was amended in minor respects in 1824 and 1826, and as so amended continued in force until 1848. Up to this time the city officers, aside from the Mayor and members of the two boards of the Council, had been appointed under authority of ordinances creating their offices. In 1848 the charter was amended to make the offices of assessor, register, collector and surveyor, elective. The charter, as amended in 1848, continued in force under its own provisions for a period of twenty years with some amendments made in 1864 and 1865.

Upon the expiration of the term of this charter in 1868, it was continued for one year with an amendment making all officers who had previously been appointed by the Mayor, elective by the Mayor, Board of Aldermen and Board of Common Council in joint session. In 1869 these offices were again made appointive by the Mayor and in this form the charter continued in force until the Territorial form of government went into full effect on June 1, 1871.

The control of the property of the United States in the city remained until 1816, in the Superintendent who had succeeded to the original Commissioners on June 1, 1802. By an act approved April 29, 1816, the office of Superintendent was abolished and the duties thereof as well as those of the three Commissioners appointed by the President under the Act of February 13, 1815, to superintend the reconstruction of the public buildings after their destruction by the British in 1814, were imposed upon a single Commissioner. By act approved March 2, 1867, they were placed under the

135

Chief of Engineers of the Army, who designates for their immediate supervision an officer entitled the Officer of Public Buildings and Grounds.

On June 1, 1802, Robert Brent was appointed by President Jefferson to be the first Mayor of the City of Washington. Mr. Brent was an active and prominent citizen. He served as Justice of the Peace from 1801 to 1817; and as Judge of the Orphans' Court from 1806 to 1814. He was President of the Patriotic Bank and a member of the school hoard. He was reappointed nine times but resigned just before the close of his tenth term, upon the passage by Congress of the charter of May 4, 1812, which made his office elective.

Daniel Rapine was appointed to fill out Mayor Brent's unexpired term. Upon the expiration of that term, he was, on June 1, 1812, elected to succeed himself by the City Councils, in accordance with the new charter, and served one term. Dr. James H. Blake, who succeeded Mr. Rapine in June, 1813, was elected by the City Councils for four consecutive terms. Benjamin G. Orr was elected in the same manner in 1817 and served two terms. Samuel N. Smallwood was elected by the City Councils in 1819, being the last Mayor so elected.

In 1820 Mr. Smallwood was elected by popular ballot under the new charter of that year. Mr. Smallwood was followed in 1822 by Thomas Carberry, who served one term. Mr. Smallwood was again elected in June, 1824, but his term was cut short by his death on September 30 of that year. Roger C. Weightman was elected by the City Councils to succeed Mayor Smallwood on October 4, 1824, and in June, 1826, was elected by popular vote. He resigned on July 31, 1827, to become cashier of the Bank of Washington.

Joseph Gales, Jr., was elected by the City Councils on July 31, 1827, to fill out the unexpired term of Mayor Weightman, and in June, 1828, was elected by the people for one term. Mr. Gales was born at Eckington, near Sheffield, April 10, 1786, and died in Washington, D. C, July 21, 1860. He was educated at the University of North Carolina, went to Philadelphia to learn the art of printing, and in 1807 settled at Washington as the assistant and afterward as the partner of Samuel Harrison Smith, who in 1800 had removed the "Independent Gazetter" to Washington and changed its name to the "National Intelligencer." In 1810 Mr. Gales became sole proprietor of the journal, which was published tri-weekly. In 1812 he took into partnership his brother-in-law, Mr. William W. Seaton, and in January, 1813, began to issue the "National Intelligencer" daily. It was continued till 1867. Mr. Gales was succeeded in June, 1830, by John P. Van Ness who served two terms.

Mr. Van Ness was succeeded by William A. Bradley who served from June, 1834, to June, 1836, and was in turn succeeded by Peter Force, who served two terms from June, 1836, to June, 1840.

Mr. Force was a striking character. He had come to Washington in 1815, and from that year had remained one of the city's progressive workers. For nine years he was the forceful editor of a daily paper, the National Journal. When he had lived in the National Capital six years he was elected a councilman and then an alderman and was selected by his contemporaries as president of both these boards. He was prominent in military as well as in civic affairs and was successively elected Captain, Lieutenant-colonel, Colonel and Major-General in the District Militia. A scientific man, he was elected and served for several years as President of the National Institute.

His service to the city was inestimable in recording statistics and other historical facts, thus leaving much useful information for future historians and statisticians. He published the "National Calendar and Annals of the United States," which publication he continued to issue from 1820, for sixteen years, missing three years during the time. John Quincy Adams was a contributor to this paper and Henry Clay his warm friend and advocate.

Other of his writings were "Historical Tracts," and a series of American Archives. Of these, Mr. A. R. Spofford, the Librarian of Congress, said: "These archives constitute a thesaurus of original information about the two most momentous years of the Revolutionary Struggle, and especially concerning the Declaration of Independence, of inestimable value."

Mayor Force was one of the first American collectors of manuscripts and documents, and was untiring in securing files of Washington papers, "Army Orders" and other published records of American affairs, thus preserving unbroken successive historical information. After his death his collection of documents was purchased under an act of Congress for the Congressional Library.

Mr. Force was succeeded by William W. Seaton who held office for a full decade of five successive terms from June, 1840, to June, 1850. Mr. Seaton was born in King William County, Va., Jan. 11, 1785, and died in Washington, D. C, June 16, 1866. He successively edited the "Petersburg Register," the "North Carolina Journal" at Halifax, and the "Register" at Raleigh, N. C.; and in 1812 became partner with his brother-in-law Joseph Gales, Jr., in the "National Intelligencer" at Washington, which, after the death of Mr. Gales in 1860, he continued to edit alone till 1865. Prom 1812 to 1820 Gales and Seaton were the exclusive reporters as well as editors of their journal, one of them devoting himself to the Senate and the other to the House of Representatives. Their "Register of Debates" is one of the standard sources of American history.

Mr. Seaton was a Whig and was opposed to many measures of National policy, especially as regarded the banking system. His election by the city caused much dissatisfaction in Congress and brought about political turmoil between the City and National Governments. The Senate formed a bill to abolish the city charter and passed it to a third reading.

The District citizens were indignant over what they considered unjust treatment by Congress, and on July 27, 1840, a mass meeting was called in front of the City Hall for the purpose of discussing their wrongs and devising remedies. The new Mayor was made chairman of the meeting and Walter Lenox secretary.

Resolutions were taken to hold a convention in Washington August 10, following, for the purpose of adopting measures to right affairs in the District of Columbia, to which citizens of Georgetown and Alexandria were invited.

As not all of Congress had agreed to the measures taken against the District, the meeting adopted resolutions of thanks to Honorables William D. Merrick, Chairman of the District Committee of the Senate, and William C. Johnson, Chairman of the District Committee for the House, and to other members who had resisted the measures of Congress.

Georgetown also held an indignation meeting on July 21, in front of the Mayor's office, at which a committee was appointed to draw up resolutions to report at a meeting to be held July 23, in the Lancastrian school house.

All these meetings brought about a petition for a new charter, as that granted in 1820, had been stipulated to continue in force for twenty years, and that time had about expired. This petition, signed by nearly four hundred citizens, was presented to Congress, and was referred to a select committee, of which Mr. Norvell of Michigan was chairman.

The bill reported by the Committee was entitled, "An Act to Amend and Continue in Force the Act to Incorporate the Inhabitants of Washing-ton." It was really an act to amend only, and not one to "Continue in Force." To the satisfaction of the city, it was laid on the table after the third reading. One feature which made the bill unpopular was the clause abolishing slavery, a change not yet approved nor considered practicable by the District nor by many Congressmen.

Mayor Seaton was succeeded by Walter Lenox who served one term from 1850 to 1852, and who was in turn succeeded in June, 1852, by John W. Maury who served for one term. Mr. Maury was succeeded in June, 1854, by John T. Towers, who served one term until June, 1856, when he was succeeded by Dr. William B. Magruder.

In June, 1858, James G. Berrett, the late postmaster of this city, was elected by a vote of 3,688, as against 3,117 for Richard Wallach, formerly Marshal of the District. Mr. Berrett ran as the "Anti-Know-Nothing" candidate and Mr. Wallach as the Republican candidate. In 1860, the same candidates were opposed on the same issues, Mr. Berrett receiving 3,434 votes as against 3,410 for Mr. Wallach. Dr. Magruder, as an independent candidate, received 147 votes. Mr. Wallach gave notice that he would contest the election on the ground of fraud, hut the contest did not come to trial. On August 24, 1861, Mayor Berrett was arrested by a detail of the Provost Marshal's guard and taken to Fort Lafayette for refusing to take the oath of loyalty to the United States, which was prescribed by Congress. Two days later the City Councils at a special session elected Mr. Wallach to fill the office of Mayor until Mr. Berrett 's return. No proof of disloyalty being found against Mr. Berrett who maintained his attachment for the Union, he was released, but on September 14, resigned his office. A doubt then arising as to whether the previous election of Mr. Wallach by the Councils was valid, the question was submitted to the Corporation Attorney, Joseph H. Bradley, who gave as his opinion that Mr. Wallach was the regularly elected Mayor. To avoid any uncertainty the Council held another election on October 17, 1861 and reaffirmed their choice of Mr. Wallach to fill out Mayor Berrett 's unexpired term.

Mr. Wallach was elected by popular vote in June, 1862, again in 1864, and again in 1866, his term thus covering practically the entire period of the Civil War.

In the election which took place in June, 1868, negroes took part in the municipal elections of the City of Washington for the first time. The candidates were John T. Given, Democrat, and Sayles J. Bowen, Republican. On the face of the returns Mr. Bowen was elected. While the vote was being recounted by a joint committee of the City Councils the Republican members of the two boards declared Mr. Bowen elected Mayor, and the Democratic members declared W. W. Moore, Mayor, pro tempore. Mr. Bowen took possession of the Mayor's office and proceeded to act as Mayor. He held that position throughout the term but was defeated for re-election in June, 1870, by Matthew Gault Emory, who received a vote of 10,096 as against 6,877 for Mr. Bowen. Mr. Emory was the last of the Mayors. His term expired on

June 1, 1871, when the Territorial form of government, under the act of Congress approved February 21, 1871, went into full effect.

No provision for a salary for the Mayor appears to have been made until August 18, 1812, when an ordinance was enacted allowing him four hundred dollars per annum. This was, on August 8, 1815, raised to five hundred dollars, on June 20, 1820, to one thousand dollars, on May 8, 1850, to sixteen hundred dollars, on March 20, 1856, to two thousand four hundred dollars, and on December 28, 1863, to three thousand six hundred dollars.

By ordinance of May 30, 1807, provision was made for the appointment by the Mayor of Commissioners, from each of the four wards. They were officially designated " City Commissioners." Their number remained at four, notwithstanding the increase in the number of wards, until June 4, 1829, when they were increased to six, and denominated "Ward Commissioners." By ordinance of May 24, 1853, their number was reduced to four, and they were designated Commissioners of Improvements. As "City Commissioners" they constituted a board and were presided over by the Mayor. They were required to meet at least once each month. As " City Commissioners, " " Ward Commissioners " and " Commissioners of Improvements " their duties were to superintend the execution of the laws of the Councils and prosecute for violations thereof, to direct the expenditure of appropriations not particularly designated; to contract for and superintend the making of public improvements; to enforce the removal of nuisances, and perform various other services in connection with the police, fire, health and tax departments of the city.

The first act of the City Councils was the passage of an ordinance on July 20, 1802, adopting as the Seal of the city, "the representation of an edifice supported on sixteen columns, having the word 'Washington' at the top, the words 'City Seal' with the figures '1802' at the bottom, and the motto 'Union' beneath the dome. "

In 1802 ordinances were passed establishing the Center Market at the present site of the Washington Market and providing other public markets.

At frequent intervals ordinances were passed respecting nearly all matters which are the subject of municipal regulation today.

The regulations specifically concerning colored persons, both free and slave, during the early half century of the city's existence, formed no inconsiderable part of the laws enacted by the City Councils. Extensive ordinances were passed in 1812, 1821, 1827, 1836 and 1850. These enactments required the registration of the free negroes of the city and their families, the exhibition of evidence of their title to freedom and certificates of good character, and the furnishing of bond each year, with white sureties, for their good behavior, and provided for the issuing of annual licenses to such as complied with the requirements of the law in these respects.

The rules governing the conduct of free negroes were very strict. It was unlawful for one of them to give a dance at his house without written consent of the Mayor. They were forbidden to go at large after ten o'clock at night; and all meetings by them after that hour were prohibited. The sale of liquor to negroes after sunset was unlawful. They were not allowed to keep taverns or sell liquor, and no licenses could be issued to them except to drive hacks and carts.

By the charters of 1812 and 1820 offenses committed by slaves were made punishable by whipping, not exceeding forty stripes, or by imprisonment not exceeding six months for any one offense. This did not apply to free negroes. In

139

some eases it was provided by ordinance that the owner might relieve the slave from the penalty of whipping by paying the fine with which the offense would have been punishable if committed by a white person.

The first ordinance relating to the subject of cruelty to animals dates back to July 12, 1821, when it was made punishable with a fine of five dollars, or in cases of slaves, by not less than five nor more than ten lashes, to " cruelly beat or wantonly abuse any animal of the horse kind. "

For the enforcement of the city ordinances the office of Superintendent of Police at a salary of two hundred dollars per annum was created on September 20, 1803. This officer was required to visit every part of the city at least once a month and any particular part thereof at any other time when required by a householder, and to give information to some magistrate of and prosecute for all breaches of law. In addition to his salary he was to receive one-half the penalties received in cases in which he was the informer.

In 1805 this office was abolished and its duties transferred to an officer called the High Constable. The latter office was abolished in 1807 and its duties conferred upon the four Ward Commissioners. In 1808 the city was divided into two Police Districts, each presided over by a Police Officer. The latter office was abolished in 1811 and its duties transferred back to the Ward Commissioners and to constables appointed under the Act of 1807. The constables were legislated out of office in 1820 and were restored in 1821.

By an act approved August 23, 1842, Congress provided for a police establishment known as the Auxiliary Watch, or Auxiliary Guard. As first constituted that force consisted of a Captain and fifteen officers. In 1851 Congress increased the number of officers by fifteen. This force had the same functions as the police force of the city; it was subject to the Mayor's orders and was controlled by a set of regulations established by a board consisting of the Mayor, the United States District Attorney and the Corporation Attorney; it availed itself of the use of the headquarters of the city force at the City Hall; it was required to co-operate with and assist the city police force, and for all practical purposes was an integral part of the city police system, though receiving its pay from Congress. This dual police system continued in effect until the creation by Congress of the Metropolitan Police District in 1861.

By act of August 6, 1861, Congress created the Metropolitan Police District comprising the corporations of Washington and Georgetown and the County of Washington. By this act the President of the United States was authorized to appoint five commissioners; three from Washington, one from Georgetown and one from the part of the District of Columbia lying outside of those corporations. These Commissioners, with the Mayors of Washington and Georgetown, constituted the Board of Police, which was empowered to divide the District of Columbia into not more than ten precincts, establish stations, assign sergeants and patrolmen to exercise general supervision over licensed vendors, hackmen, cartmen, second hand dealers, intelligence offices, auctioneers of watches and jewelry, suspected private banking houses, "and other doubtful establishments."

By the act of July 23, 1866, an additional force was provided for and the offices of Mayor, Captain, Lieutenant, and Sergeant established. By act of March 2, 1867, previous service in the Army or Navy of the United States was made a condition of employment on the force, but this prerequisite was later revoked by court decision.

The Board of Metropolitan Police continued in existence until the establishment of the permanent form of government for the District under the act of Congress approved June 11, 1878, when its functions were transferred to the Board of Commissioners of the District of Columbia.

The disastrous fires in the two department buildings which occurred shortly after the removal of the Government to Washington, resulted in early action by the City Councils looking to provision for the prevention and extinguishment of fires. On January 10, 1803, an ordinance was passed requiring every proprietor of a dwelling or business house to provide as many leather two and one-half gallon fire buckets as there were stories to his house and imposing other duties upon citizens in connection with the prevention and extinguishment of fires.

On July 24, 1804, the city was divided into four fire wards and provision made for the organization of a volunteer fire company in each ward. In 1815 the sum of one hundred and seventy-five dollars was appropriated for the purchase of ladders, fire hooks, axes, crow-bars and buckets. In 1817 an annual appropriation of twenty-five dollars was provided for the upkeep of the several engines in the city. All citizens were made subject to service at the requirement of the commanders of the fire companies who were distinguished by a white wand five feet long and a speaking trumpet.

In 1853, provision was made for an Inspector of Fire Apparatus who was required to make monthly inspections of the apparatus of each company in the city which was expected to be found at all times to be of the value of at least five hundred dollars. By the same ordinance an annual appropriation of one hundred dollars was made payable to each company of not less than fifty members which in the opinion of the Mayor possessed an efficient organization. The governing body of the department consisted of the presidents of the several fire companies. Rivalry and friction between the fire companies was such a source of disorder that in 1857 the Mayor, to prevent conflicts, was authorized to prescribe limits beyond which it was unlawful for the apparatus of the several companies to be run.

On October 6, 1862, the fire companies were organized under the name of The Washington Fire Department. The governing body of the department consisted of five delegates from each company.

In 1865, the city purchased three steam fire engines and in 1867 added two more. The United States Government had previously acquired three steam engines for the protection of its property and these had commonly been used in co-operation with the city fire department. The Government disbanded its fire department in 1864.

The first measure relating to the public health appears to have been an ordinance approved May 1, 1811, making it punishable with a fine of one hundred dollars to voluntarily introduce or propagate smallpox in the city, and requiring the person in whose family it should be accidentally introduced to forthwith notify the Mayor under penalty of twenty dollars fine.

By ordinance of August 14, 1819, the Mayor was required to appoint a discreet and prudent citizen, being a member of the Medical Society of the District of Columbia, to be Health Officer of the City.

This officer was required to report nuisances, sources of disease, epidemics and contagious diseases, with his opinion as to means for restraining and preventing them and to keep a register of deaths and their causes upon weekly reports from the sextons of cemeteries based upon certificates of undertakers or personal inquiry.

On March 30, 1822, the office of Health Officer was abolished and a Board of Health created, to consist of one physician and one layman from each ward in addition to the physician attending the Washington Asylum. The powers and functions of the Board of Health were enlarged from time to time by numerous ordinances. On January 17, 1856, the office of Commissioner of Health who should be ex officio Secretary of the Board, was created with functions so extensive as to practically make that officer supersede the Board which was, however, still continued in existence.

The water supply of the city in its early years was drawn entirely from wells and springs. By an ordinance passed in 1812, the Mayor was authorized to sink wells upon petition of two-thirds of the residents of any neighborhood and assess the cost against the property thought by the ward assessors to be benefitted by the improvement. In 1818 similar provision was made for the construction of concrete reservoirs at the sites of hydrants.

The most prominent spring in or near the city was that located on the farm of J. A. Smith just north of the present pumping plant on North Capitol Street. This was one of the sources of Tiber Creek. In 1831 its waters were conducted in iron pipes from a reservoir which was created on the site of the spring to two basins, one on the east front of the Capitol and the other on the west front. This pipe still furnishes the water for the gold fish basin at the foot of the west front of the Capitol. A line of pipe from this spring was carried up Pennsylvania Avenue nearly as far as Fifteenth Street.

A spring in City Hall Park, about fifty feet west of the building supplied a line of pipe on Second Street and another on Louisiana Avenue as far as Seventh Street.

On C Street between Four-and-a-Half and Sixth Streets was another well-known spring. Another at the site of the Masonic Temple supplied a line of pipe on F Street and down Ninth and Tenth Streets. There was a spring in Franklin Square and another just outside the square. At the intersection of New Jersey and New York Avenues was the Carroll Spring. A spring on P Street near Rock Creek for many years furnished water to the Metropolitan street car stables in Georgetown by means of a pipe under the bridge. On Virginia Avenue between Twenty-sixth and Twenty-seventh Streets was a large spring. The Gibson spring at Fifteenth and C Streets, northeast, now utilized by the Hygienic Ice Company, was mentioned in a former chapter as having played a part in determining the location of the city boundary line at that point.

The desirability of procuring a more generous supply of water than was furnished by springs, was early recognized. In 1830 the subject was broached by Mr. Robert Mills, an engineer and architect, who suggested a system to be drawn either from the sources of Tiber Creek or from Rock Creek. Nothing was done, however, towards the establishment of a general water system until 1850 when Congress appropriated $500 for a preliminary investigation. In 1852 Congress appropriated $5,000 for a survey. In 1853 General Joseph G. Totten made a report to the Secretary of War as to the relative cost and feasibility of three alternative schemes; one to obtain the water from Rock Creek; another to obtain it from the Potomac River at the Little Falls, and a third to obtain it from the river at Great Falls. The latter plan was adopted. The work of construction was placed in charge of Captain Montgomery C. Meigs of the Engineer Corps of the Army.

The ceremony of ground breaking for this work on November 8, 1853, was quite elaborate. President Pierce attended with his cabinet at the scene near Great Falls and turned the first spadeful of earth. Others who participated were Jefferson Davis, Secretary of War, Senator Douglas, Mayor John W. Maury, and Ex-Mayor W. W. Seaton.

The completion of the work occupied about nine years, and involved an expenditure up to June, 1862, of $2,675,832.53. Most of the work was done under the supervision of Captain — afterwards General — M. C. Meigs.

The length of the conduit from its beginning at Great Falls to the north end of the Georgetown aqueduct is fourteen miles. Its construction involved the construction of Cabin John Bridge, famous as one of the longest single span arches in the world.

In 1859 Congress empowered the corporations of Washington and Georgetown to regulate the distribution of water within their respective limits and authorized Georgetown to borrow $50,000 and Washington $150,000 for the construction of mains.

Following the passage of that act the Washington City Councils created the offices of Water Registrar and Water Purveyor, directed the construction under the direction of the latter, of a system of mains, and established a water code for the city. The water system received no material extension from that time until after the establishment of the permanent Commission government in 1878.

As early as January 12, 1803, an ordinance was passed directing the Mayor to cause lamps to be placed on the most public avenues and streets, to supply them with oil and to employ persons to attend to lighting them and keeping them in order. In 1830 it was ordered, in the interest of economy, that the lamps should be lighted only from the first day of December to the thirtieth day of April each year.

The lighting of the city with gas was provided for in 1853. An ordinance passed June 3 of that year directed the Mayor to erect lamp posts upon the application of the owners of more than half the property in any portion of a street not less than a square, the cost to be borne by the property fronting on that portion of the street.

The chief works of a public character in the early years of the city consisted in the completion of the Washington Canal and the reclamation r A the low grounds lying between the canal and Pennsylvania Avenue.

The canal which had been partially cut for drainage purposes by the original Commissioners was deepened and widened so as to permit of navigation, by the Washington Canal Company, a corporation authorized by an act of Congress approved February 16, 1809. The canal was operated by this company until 1831 when in anticipation of the construction of the Chesapeake and Ohio Canal it was purchased by the city for $50,000. The city greatly improved it by widening and deepening, and by walling it with stone for the cost of which the city was reimbursed $150,000 by Congress.

The reclamation of the low lands adjoining the canal on the north commenced in 1816 when $2,000 was voted by the Councils for filling between Pennsylvania Avenue and the Canal from 7th to 12 Streets, the cost being assessed against the "squares which were overflowed by the tides." This canal began at a basin at 17th and B Streets, northwest, at the mouth of Tiber Creek, and extended thence east along B Street, north, to a point midway between 6th and 7th Streets, west; thence south to the center line of the Mall; thence east to 3rd Street west; thence south to Maryland Avenue; thence southeast to the center of South Capitol Street; thence south to a point midway between F and G Streets, south; thence southeast to near 2nd and K Streets, southeast, and thence to the Anacostia River or Eastern Branch. It was filled from Rock Creek to 17th Street and converted into a sewer from 17th Street to 3rd Street west, by the Board of Public Works. The remaining portions between 3rd Street west and the Anacostia River were filled by the Board of Commissioners at a cost of $70,000 which was appropriated by Congress in 1878, 1879, 1880 and 1881 to give employment to laborers in the periods of industrial depression which then prevailed.

In 1822 Congress authorized the city to sell certain public squares to raise funds for filling the low grounds on the borders of the Canal, and a board of four commissioners was provided for by ordinance to carry this law into effect. In 1823 the city appropriated $3,000 "for removing the nuisance which exists by the stagnant water and other sources of disease in that portion of the city lying between 7th and 12 Streets, west, and C Street north of the Canal," and $2,500 for filling the Center Market Square and forming a basin for the Canal at that point.

In 1820 the construction of the City Hall — the present Court House — at the head of Four-and-a-Half Street was commenced. The plans were drawn by George Hadfield, who had been one of the superintendents in charge of the construction of the Capitol under the original Commissioners. Hadfield 's first plan was rejected as involving too great a cost, but he modified it so that on July 14, 1820, proposals were called for with the idea of constructing so much of the building as the commissioners in charge of the work might deem expedient. The cornerstone was laid on the 24th day of August, 1820, with elaborate ceremonies. The cost of the building was originally expected to be $100,000, and it was proposed to raise this sum by lottery. The affair was known as the National or Gillespie lottery, and is referred to elsewhere. It proved very disastrous to the city, owing to the defalcation of one of the managers. In 1823, when the building was partly finished, Congress appropriated $10,000 to complete a portion of it for the accommodation of the United States Circuit Court, and the Clerk, Marshal, records and juries connected therewith. The total cost of the building was $148,451.29, of which sum about $105,000 was reimbursed to the city by Congress in various ways, largely through the eventual purchase in 1873 of the building as a whole for the use of the United States Courts and appurtenant officials.

The first attempt at street improvement under municipal control was an appropriation of $200 on November 19, 1802, for clearing and rendering passable Fourteenth Street from north F Street to the northern extremity thereof. The first cover for both carriageways and sidewalks was gravel. Later it became the practice to pave the gutters.

About 1814 the municipality began the use of curbstones and foot pavements, with paving brick and stone cross-walks at intersections.

In 1832 the United States Government macadamized Pennsylvania Avenue between First Street and 15th Street under a contract with Hugh Stewart. This pavement remained until replaced by wooden blocks in 1870.

The first paving of the carriageways appears to have been Seventh Street west from the south side of Virginia Avenue to H Street north, under an act of the Councils of April 23, 1845, and in accordance with the general ordinances of the Councils of April 17, 1845, for paving with stone blocks not more than four inches square, under which the cost of such improvements was paid wholly by the abutting property, except at the intersection of streets and at alley openings where the cost was borne by the ward funds.

Under an appropriation made in the civil and diplomatic appropriation law of August 31, 1852 (10 Stat. 94) and other laws, the carriageway of Pennsylvania Avenue from 17th Street to Rock Creek was paved with "round-stone."

By an ordinance of June 5, 1863, establishing a general rule for paving carriageways, the abutting property on each side of a street was taxed with only one-third of the cost of paving carriageways.

An ordinance approved May 7, 1869, legalized the "Smith and Burlew concrete (bituminous) pavement" for paving streets and sidewalks in the City of Washington whenever citizens preferred it to brick or stone as then provided by law.

Under an ordinance approved September 7, 1869, the carriageway of Vermont Avenue between H and I Streets, northwest, was paved with coal tar concrete by George Scharff under his patent, at the sole cost of abutting property. This pavement was as good and lasting as any bituminous roadway of any patent or material ever laid in the District.

Indiana Avenue for two or three blocks west of First Street west was paved in 1870 by the City of Washington with irregular blocks of Seneca sandstone, a sort of reddish stone from the shore of the Potomac a few miles above Great Falls.

In 1870, Pennsylvania Avenue from First Street to Fifteenth was paved with various kinds of wooden blocks. This pavement, with frequent repairs, continued until 1876. In 1876 and 1877 Pennsylvania Avenue was repaved by a commission appointed under Act of Congress, July 19th, 1876, consisting of two officers of the Engineer Corps of the Army and the Architect of the Capitol. The cost was divided among the United States, District of Columbia, private property, and the street railroad whose tracks were upon it.

The beginning of the sewer system of the city consisted of a twenty-two inch main on the north side of Pennsylvania Avenue from Four-and-a-Half Street to Second Street, west, for which the sum of one thousand dollars was appropriated in 1829, the cost of the sewer being assessed against the property fronting on that portion of Pennsylvania Avenue. This and a number of other small sewers which were created from time to time emptied into the Tiber Canal. No comprehensive sewer system was attempted until the establishment of the Territorial Government in 1871.

The early financial arrangements of the city included two interesting features, namely, a system of municipal lotteries, and a system of municipal due bills; both of which were long ago discontinued and have almost passed into oblivion.

Lotteries with the approval of the President " for the effecting of important improvements in the city which the ordinary revenue thereof will not accomplish " were authorized in amounts of not exceeding $10,000 in any one year by the charters of 1812 and 1820.

On November 23, 1812, a resolution was adopted by the City Councils to the effect that it was deemed expedient to raise $10,000 by lottery for building, establishing and endowing two public school houses on the Lancastrian system. On August 3, 1814, a similar lottery to raise funds for the erection of a workhouse and on May 10, 1815, one to raise funds for building a city hall were recommended. In 1816, 1817, 1818, 1819, 1820 and 1821, resolutions were adopted recommending the holding of lotteries to raise $10,000 for the purposes of building, establishing and endowing public schools, building a penitentiary or workhouse, and building a town house or city hall.

By act of July 24, 1815, John Davidson, T. H. Gillis, A. Way, Jr., Moses Young, William Brent, Daniel Rapine and Samuel N. Smallwood were appointed managers of the three lotteries authorized up to that time for raising a total sum of thirty thousand dollars. On November 17, 1818, an ordinance was passed authorizing the Mayor to appoint seven citizens to manage a lottery to raise a total sum of forty thousand dollars as provided for by the resolutions of 1816, 1817 and 1818. On January 4, 1827, an ordinance authorized the sale of the three pending lotteries, as well as any future ones to be authorized under the charter provision, the purchasers to assume the entire responsibility for the payment of the prizes.

It was under this ordinance that the management of the lotteries was taken over by David Gillespie and others. Gillespie defaulted with the main prize of $100,000, and other amounts, and, the managers being unable to pay the prizes, the city was subjected to judgments aggregating upwards of $198,000. No further attempts were made to raise money by this method.

The use of due bills as a medium of exchange grew out of the dearth of small change, to remedy which two ordinances were passed in 1814 authorizing the Mayor to issue due bills for sums of not less than one cent nor more than fifty cents in a total amount of not to exceed ten thousand dollars, redeemable in sums of not less than five dollars. In 1819 an issue of ten thousand dollars and in 1821 an issue of twelve thousand dollars in due bills in denominations of fifty cents, one dollar and two dollars, was authorized. In 1824, a measure was adopted providing for the use of this medium for raising fourteen thousand dollars largely to be used in public improvements and in 1832 an issue of fifteen thousand dollars was authorized to raise money for the general fund.

The indebtedness of the city was chiefly represented by registered certificates commonly termed "stock," which were in the nature of unsecured bonds.

In 1827 the city subscribed for one million dollars of the stock of the newly formed Chesapeake and Ohio Canal Company, and Georgetown and Alexandria each subscribed $125,000. The following year these three corporations authorized Richard Rush, who in addition to numerous other important offices had recently held that of Secretary of the Treasury, to negotiate a loan in Europe for paying up their subscriptions. Mr. Rush obtained a loan from the firm of Daniel Crommelin and Sons of Amsterdam in 1829. The loan was bottomed upon the property of the city which by an act of Congress had been made subject to a tax for repaying it. The approaching maturity of this loan in 1835 threatened the city with bankruptcy and resulted in an appeal to Congress for aid. The report of the Senate Committee on the District of Columbia in connection with this appeal, signed by Senator Samuel

Southard, of New Jersey, its chairman, furnishes a graphic description of the financial situation of the city at the time. Mr. Southard says:

"The city is involved in pecuniary obligations, from which it is utterly impossible that it can be relieved by any means within its own control, or by any exertions which it may make, unaided by Congressional legislation. Its actual debts now amount to the enormous sum of $1,806,442.59. * * * So perfectly exhausted have its resources become that it will very probably in a short time be driven to the surrender of its charter by neglecting to elect its corporate officers, and thus be left upon the hands of Congress to dispose of, govern, and sustain as may best suit their own views of what is proper for the capital of the Union. * * * A part of the engagements of the city, in relation to the stock which it holds in the Chesapeake and Ohio Canal, it is known to Congress, are of a kind which must be promptly satisfied or the property of the inhabitants exposed to sale in a few months under the orders of the Executive of the United States, and its creditors, who are foreign bankers, in all probability will become the owners of a great proportion of the property within the capital of the Union." * * *

Senator Southard's report is memorable by reason of its eloquent presentation of the cause of the city for recognition by the National Government of its obligation to share in the expense of maintaining the government of its Capital.

In the course of his report Senator Southard advanced the proposition which in 1878 was definitely adopted as the basis of the financial relations between the National Government and the city as to street improvements, that "the narrowest measure of justice would have required, and does now require, that the Government having in its private building lots and public reservations at least an equal interest in the improvement of the streets, should pay at least one-half of the expense of those streets. "

The result of Senator Southard's report was the passage by Congress of the Act approved May 20, 1836, authorizing the Secretary of the Treasury to assume on behalf of the United States the indebtedness of Washington, Georgetown and Alexandria on account of the Chesapeake and Ohio Canal loan upon the depositing with him by those cities of their holdings of stock in the Canal Company. The Secretary of the Treasury was by the Act given ten years in which to sell this stock under the most favorable terms for the purpose of reimbursing the United States the amount expended in taking up the loan. The passage of this Act, while it was a measure of vital relief to the residents of those cities, did not establish any permanent basis for contribution by Congress towards the expenses of the Capital City.

On May 31, 1871, the last day of the existence of the City of Washington as a separate municipality prior to the taking effect of the Territorial government, its debt was $5,237,533.87.

CHAPTER VII.

The Territorial Government; 1871-1874

It was an inevitable result of the Civil War that the interest of the nation in its Capital should be keenly awakened. Almost immediately upon the close of that conflict, public sentiment was directed to the problem of placing the city in a condition fitting its character as the seat of the government of the reunited country. The consideration of this question was crystallized into law by the act approved February 21, 1871, creating the so-called "Territorial" Government, which provided that on and after June 1 of that year the corporations of Washington and Georgetown, and the Levy Court of the County of Washington, which had jurisdiction over the portion of the District which was outside of those corporations, should no longer exist as such; and that beginning with that date the entire District of Columbia should constitute a single municipality under the name of "The District of Columbia." It was the passage of this act which gave the National Capital its full municipal impulse. From this time forward the municipal history of the City of Washington is identical with that of the government of the District of Columbia.

This legislation originated in the Senate by the introduction on February 25, 1870, by Senator Hannibal Hamlin of Maine, of Senate Bill 594, entitled " An Act to change the form of government of the District of Columbia." This bill was reported with amendment March 18, 1870; discussed on May 27 and passed by the Senate on May 28 of that year. It then went into a long stage of hibernation until January 20, 1871, when it was taken up and discussed in the House. On the 23rd of January it passed the House with amendment. It went to a conference committee whose report was adopted by the Senate on January 24 and by the House on February 17, 1871.

The new municipality consisted of a Governor; a Board of Public Works composed of the Governor and four other persons; a Secretary; a Board of Health; a Legislative Assembly, consisting of a Council of eleven members and a House of Delegates consisting of 22 members, and a Delegate in the House of Representatives of the United States.

The Governor, the Board of Public Works, the Secretary, the Board of Health, and the Council were appointed by the President of the United States, by and with the consent of the Senate. The members of the House of Delegates and the Delegate in the House of Representatives were elected by the qualified voters of the District of Columbia, whose qualifications are hereinafter described under the head of "Suffrage." The official term of the Governor, members of the Board of Public Works, the Secretary, and the members of the Board of Health, was four years; the term of the members of the Council and the Delegate to Congress two years, except that of those members of the Council first appointed, five were appointed for the term of one year, and six for the period of two years; and the term of the members of the House of Delegates one year. The compensation for all of these officials except the members of the House of Delegates, was paid exclusively out of the United States Treasury.

The general duties of the Board of Public Works were to have entire control of and make all regulations which they might deem necessary for keeping in repair, the streets, avenues, alleys, and sewers of the city, and all other works which might be entrusted to their charge by the Legislative Assembly or Congress. Special requirements were imposed upon the Board from time to time by Congress and the Legislative Assembly.

The Board had no power to make contracts to bind the District to the payment of any sums of money except in pursuance of appropriations made by law, and not until such appropriations had been made.

The law prescribed that the Governor should have resided in the District twelve months before his appointment and have the qualifications of an elector; that the members of the Board of Public Works, except one who was required to be a civil engineer, should be citizens and residents of the District, having the qualifications of electors therein. One was required to be a resident of Georgetown, and another a resident of the portion of the District outside of Washington and Georgetown. It was provided that the Secretary should reside in the District and possess the qualifications of an elector; that the members of the Legislative Assembly should have the qualifications of voters, and the Delegate to the House of Representatives of the United States, should be a citizen of the United States and of the District of Columbia and have the qualifications of a voter. No qualifications were prescribed for members of the Board of Health.

The Governor was empowered to grant pardons and respites for offenses against the laws enacted by the Legislative Assembly and to commission all officers elected or appointed to office under the laws of said assembly. He was required to take care that the laws be faithfully executed and to approve bills passed by the Assembly or return them with his objections. He was not empowered to grant pardons or respites for offenses against any of the laws of Congress in force in the District, nor against the ordinances of the City of Washington, Georgetown or Levy Court. His salary was $3,000.

Henry David Cooke, the first Governor, was born in Sandusky, Ohio, November 23, 1825, and died in Georgetown in the District of Columbia on February 24, 1881. He was graduated as an A. B. by Transylvania University, Kentucky, and was admitted to the bar of Sandusky and of Philadelphia. In 1845 he was attaché to the American Consul at Valparaiso, Chile. Subsequently he was a journalist. As representative of the firm of Jay Cooke & Co., he rendered inestimable service to the cause of the Union during the Civil War, by negotiating the sale of United States bonds in Europe. As Governor of the District of Columbia, he enthusiastically co-operated in the comprehensive measures undertaken by the Board of Public Works. His aid in giving his personal exertions and the influence of his name to floating the bonds of the District, whose proceeds furnished the funds with which the Board of Public Works began its task, was essential to the success of those projects.

He was an expert navigator and once navigated a ship from Cape Horn to San Francisco, when the Captain died. Gifted, generous, amiable, and irreproachable in every phase of his life, he worthily discharged the duties of his high office, and his responsibilities as a member of society.

The duties of the Secretary were to record and preserve all laws and proceedings of the Legislative Assembly, and acts of the Governor in his Executive Department, and to transmit copies thereof to the President and Congress of the United States. In case of the death, removal, resignation, disability or absence of the Governor from the District, the Secretary was vested with all powers and duties of the Governor's office. In the event of and during a vacancy in both offices of Governor and

Secretary, those powers became vested in the President of the Council and Speaker of the House of Delegates in the order named. The Secretary's salary was $2,000.

The first Secretary of the District was Norton P. Chipman, then a patent attorney, who was appointed to that office on March 2, 1871. When he was elected Delegate in Congress he was succeeded as Secretary on May 19, 1871, by Edwin L. Stanton, a lawyer, and the son of Edwin M. Stanton, Secretary of War during the administration of President Abraham Lincoln. He was succeeded on September 22, 1873, by Richard Harrington, who was also a lawyer, and whose term expired with the abrogation of the office on June 20, 1874.

Secretary Stanton was the only Secretary who had an opportunity to serve as acting Governor, which capacity he filled several times. The most notable of those occasions was the calling of a special session of the Legislative Assembly which passed the Act of October 18, 1871, appropriating $100,000 for the relief of the people of Chicago who were suffering from the disastrous fire of that year.

The Delegate in Congress was "entitled to the same rights and privileges as are exercised and enjoyed by the Delegates from the several Territories of the United States to the House of Representatives. " He was also to be a member of the Committee for the District of Columbia.

Norton P. Chipman was the only Delegate. He was first elected on April 21, 1871, and re-elected on October 14, 1873, which was the date fixed by the Act of the Legislative Assembly, approved June 20, 1872, for holding the annual elections. He was continued in that position until March 4, 1875, pursuant to a proviso in the Act of June 20, 1874, creating the temporary commission government.

Although the charter of the new government did not become effective entirely until the first of June, 1871, the Board of Public Works, which was created by it, organized and began the preparation of plans of municipal engineering development in May of that year, pursuant to a grant of authority in the deficiency act of April 20, 1871. Other preliminary measures under that charter were taken by the Board of Health; and others in the election of the members of the House of Delegates and the Delegate in Congress.

When the Territorial government was established, the offices of the Corporation of the City of Washington were housed in the City Hall at the north end of Four-and-a-Half Street. The Governor and the Board of Public Works deemed it advisable to discontinue the use of the City Hall as the municipal headquarters in order to avoid the possibility of being associated in reputation with what at the time was called "the City Hall Ring." The result was that the Governor rented for his office the building at the northwest corner of Pennsylvania Avenue and Seventeenth Street, northwest.

The Board of Public Works first met and organized in this building in May, 1871. At this meeting Alexander R. Shepherd was chosen Vice-President of the Board, though no such office was provided for by law. He acted as such until September 13, 1873, when he was appointed Governor, vice Governor Cooke. The Board subsequently established its offices in the "Columbia" or "Morrison" Building, located on the west side of John Marshall place, then 4th Street N. W., where it continued its headquarters during its entire remaining existence. This building was rented but the District authorities paid $57,787.18, or nearly what the entire building and site were then worth, in making alterations on it.

The first members of the Board were Governor Henry D. Cooke who as Governor was ex-officio, President of the Board; Alexander R. Shepherd; Samuel P. Brown; Alfred B. Mullett, civil engineer and at the time the Supervising Architect of the Treasury, and James A. Magruder. Governor Cooke was appointed on February 28, 1871, and the others on March 16, following. Mr. Mullett resigned and was succeeded on January 2, 1873, by Adolph S. Cluss, who was in turn succeeded by John B. Blake, on September 13, of the same year. Mr. Brown was succeeded by Henry A. Willard on May 22, 1873. Mr. Shepherd was appointed Governor of the District of Columbia on September 13, 1873, but no appointment was made to the vacancy in the Board thus created.

The first election for members of the House of Delegates of the District of Columbia and of a Delegate to the House of Representatives of the United States was held on Tuesday, the 20th of April, 1871. The law creating the Territorial government prescribed that the election should be held within sixty days after its passage. The election was held in accordance with that law and the rules and regulations prescribed by the Governor and Judges of the Supreme Court of the District of Columbia, acting under a requirement thereof. The Governor and Judges also appointed a board of registration and persons to superintend the election and returns thereof, prescribed the time, places and manner in which such election was conducted and divided the District of Columbia into twenty-two election Districts, for the election of delegates to the House of Delegates for a term of service of one year, "giving to each section of the District representation in the ratio of its population as nearly as may be. " An apportionment was also required to be made " as nearly equal as practicable, into eleven districts, for the appointment of the Council," but no such apportionment was made, although two of the members of the Council were appointed from Georgetown and two from the portion of the District of Columbia outside of Washington and Georgetown, as required by Section 5 of the Act.

The first meeting of the Council and House of Delegates, of the Legislative Assembly, was held on the 15th day of May, 1871, at 12 o'clock M., in the "Metzerott Hall Building," on the north side of Pennsylvania Avenue, between Ninth and Tenth Streets, northwest, in pursuance of the proclamation of the Governor, dated April 25, 1871, which was issued in accordance with the provisions of the fifth section of the act.

The Territorial government, by the terms of the law creating it, went into operation on June 1, 1871. On June 20 the Board of Public Works submitted to the Legislative Assembly estimates for improvements amounting in the aggregate to $6,578,397, to pay for which they recommended a bond issue of $4,000,000 and an assessment of $2,000,000 against the property specially benefitted. On July 10, the Legislative Assembly passed an act appropriating $4,000,000 for the improvements recommended by the Board of Public Works and authorizing an issue of twenty-year seven per cent, bonds for the purpose of obtaining a loan of this amount.

A number of citizens applied to the Equity Court of the District for an injunction against the issuance of these bonds. The injunction being granted by Judge Andrew Wylie, the Legislative Assembly, on August 11, 1871, passed a supplemental act appropriating $500,000 for the purpose of avoiding the technical objections raised by the applicants for the injunction, and work was at once commenced. The injunction was subsequently dissolved, and by a later act the Legislative Assembly reduced the amount of the appropriation by $500,000, thus making the total appropriation $4,000,000, as originally contemplated.

Pending the action of the Court, the Legislative Assembly passed another Act on August 19, 1871, submitting the question to the people at an election to be held November 22, 1871, at which the issue of $4,000,000 of "special improvement" bonds and payment of interest thereon was approved by an overwhelming majority.

The proceeds of these bonds, with the authority granted by the act of the Legislative Assembly, approved August 11, 1871, for the Governor to anticipate the collection of taxes to the extent of $500,000, and the authority in the 37th section of the Act of February 21, 1871, creating the Territorial government, to assess upon property adjoining and especially benefitted by an improvement not more than one-third of the cost of such work, constituted the resources with which the Board of Public Works began its tremendous task of converting the village-like status of the streets of Washington into a condition which should be appropriate to the highways of the Capital of a great Nation.

When the Territorial government was established Washington was just emerging from the stage of an overgrown country town into metropolitan responsibility. Nearly all of the streets were dirt roadways. Where these were improved they were rudely covered with gravel, from which, in dry weather, clouds of dust arose with the breezes or from the passing vehicles, and many of the streets were almost impassable in times of heavy rains. The few that were improved with a more durable surface, excepting the portion of Pennsylvania Avenue which was paved with wood, and the square on Vermont Avenue between H and I Streets which was paved by Mayor Bowen with coal tar concrete, were paved with the roughest of cobble or other irregularly shaped stones, destructive alike to the vehicles which traveled upon them, and to the nerves of those by whom these vehicles were occupied. As late as the fall of 1871, a fire engine was stalled up to the hubs in the soft roadway, in an effort to mount the short rise on 11th Street, between E and F Streets, northwest. Fire apparatus was occasionally obliged to travel on the sidewalk, in responding to alarms in unusually wet weather. The paved sidewalks were few and confined to the thickly built sections.

Tiber Creek ran from the boundary to the old canal along B Street as an open sewer with a brick arch across it at Pennsylvania Avenue, and rude wooden bridges at other points. The Washington canal was another open sewer, exposing a festering mass at low tide, and a scum covered surface when the water was high.

Through the northwestern parts of the city flowed Slash Run, and in other sections were other water courses, all of which were open sewers. Hundreds of acres in the extreme northwest were covered by Slash Run Swamp, whose nightly vapors rendered the bordering heights tenantable only at risk of malarial fevers. There was no systematic street tree system established, nor street parking of any sort.

On January 2, 1873, the Governor and Board of Public Works represented to Congress that $150,000 would be a fair value of the District's interest in the old City Hall. They were supported in this effort by the judges of the Supreme Court of the District, who submitted a statement showing that the Court needed all the room in the building.

On March 3, 1873, Congress adopted the following proviso in the deficiency appropriation act of that date:

"For the purchase by the United States of the interest of the District of Columbia in the present City Hall building in Washington, now used solely for Government purposes, such sum as may be determined by three impartial appraisers, to be selected by the Secretary of the Interior, not exceeding $75,000, the same to be applied by said District only for the erection of a suitable building for the District offices; and the Governor and Board of Public Works are authorized, if they deem it advisable for that purpose, to make arrangements to secure sufficient land fronting on Pennsylvania and Louisiana Avenues, between Seventh and Ninth Streets; provided that the Government of the United States shall not be liable for any expenditure for said land, or for the purchase money therefor, or for the buildings to be erected thereon, and no land or the use thereof is hereby granted for the purpose of erecting any building thereon for such purpose."

On March 18, 1873, an agreement was made between the Washington Market Company and the Board of Public Works to transfer as a site for a suitable building under that appropriation all the title of that company to the portion of the reservation at the intersection of Seventh Street and Pennsylvania Avenue, between the buildings of said company and Pennsylvania Avenue. In consideration of this concession, the District authorities agreed to reduce the annual franchise rental for the relief of the poor which that company was required to pay by its charter, from $20,000 to $7,500. This rental had previously been reduced from $25,000 to $20,000 by an Act of the Legislative Assembly, approved August 23, 1871, as follows:

"Be it resolved by the Legislative Assembly of the District of Columbia, That the Governor be authorized and required to act as one of the commissioners of the Washington Market Company, under the resolution of Congress, approved December twenty, eighteen hundred and seventy; and that he be requested to procure such alterations in the plan of the buildings to be erected by said company as shall transfer the proposed hall from Ninth Street wing to the main building on Pennsylvania Avenue, and also to secure a reduction from twenty-five thousand dollars to twenty thousand dollars of the annual rental required to be paid by said company, and which is now assessed by the company upon the stall-holders." The validity of the reduction in the franchise rental to $7,500 was determined in favor of the Market Company, in D. C. v. Washington Market Company (3 MacArthur 559), and D. C. v. Washington Market Company (108 U. S. 243).

The $75,000 appropriated to be applied in erecting a new building appears to have been paid to the treasurer of the Board of Public Works on the 27th day of August, 1873, in two installments, one of $25,000, and the other of $50,000. Five thousand dollars of this money was kept intact for the purposes for which it was appropriated, except such of it as was used to make a slight excavation for the new building on the site referred to. The remainder appears to have been used by the Board of Public Works in the prosecution of municipal street improvements, and the specific object of its appropriation protected, as the treasurer of the Board of Public Works testified before the Congressional committee of investigation, by the deposit in the bank, under the orders of said Board, of $80,000 in sewer certificates which were then worth about fifty cents on the dollar. After the Board of Public Works was abolished these sewer certificates were invalidated by the Act of Congress of June 20, 1874, which abolished the Territorial form of government, and were subsequently cancelled, leaving the District with nothing but a site with a small excavation in it and the unexpended balance of the $5,000, to show for the $75,000 it had received to commence the erection of a City Hall.

The treasurer of the Board testified that the Board used the money because it deemed it better to pay its debts to contractors with it, than to use for that purpose the sewer certificates which would bear eight per centum interest.

Among the features which were introduced by the Board of Public Works, was a public convenience station at the intersection of 7th Street and Louisiana Avenue where the monument to the organizer of the Grand Army of the Republic now stands; but public sentiment had not then become educated to the importance of the subject, and the station was removed by the successors of that Board in deference to public ridicule.

Although most of the work done by the Board of Public Works has disappeared through defects due to haste and experimental construction, and replacement to meet later requirements, except the grading of the streets, a few of the larger sewers, and the street tree system which was installed under the sagacious supervision of the parking commission appointed by the Board of Public Works, consisting of three experienced arborists, William R. Smith, John Saul and William Saunders, public sentiment has justly crowned the general result with approval.

The Legislative Assembly so far as its relation to the Board of Public Works was concerned was a subservient agency of that body. That relation was necessary, as both public sentiment and the President of the United States, to whom the Assembly was officially responsible, fully recognized that notwithstanding the faults of detail in the struggle to physically rehabilitate the National Capital, the national reputation was largely dependent upon the continuance of the work upon which the Board of Public Works was engaged.

The last Legislative Assembly enacted only one law. That was hastily passed on the last day of its existence and provided for the payment of the salaries of the members of the House of Delegates, and the subordinate officials of both the House and Council. The compensation of the members of the Council was provided by appropriation by Congress.

While among the members of the Legislative Assembly a few were not above reproach, they as a rule were competent, public spirited and honorable public representatives.

Some of them received, in the same spirit in which they had provided for their compensation, the information that the act of June 20, 1874, which ended their official existence, had passed, and forthwith began to appropriate to their own use the desks, chairs and other articles which their fancy led them to select as souvenirs of their recent official estate.

The Secretary to the Governor was at the time in his office at Seventeenth Street and Pennsylvania Avenue, and to him as the only one having any semblance of executive authority, the old colored watchman at the Legislative Assembly Hall came almost breathless with the exclamation, "Doctor Tindall! they's a-stealin ' the Legislative Hall! " After the Secretary learned the full meaning of his errand, he told him to hurry to the Superintendent of Police and tell him to have the depredations stopped.

154

He started with the message, but somehow the marauders got wind of his mission, and when the police reached the scene of distribution, the conscience-stricken relic-hunters had returned or were returning their plunder, and the affair had assumed more of the appearance of a donation-party than the pilfering bee which was in full blast when the faithful messenger left for help. One of those who was found *flagrante delictu* was a noted local politician who had slipped down his trousers' leg one of the official feather dusters which he could not "all conceal;" and he not only had to return it, but became the butt of the newspaper jesters of the times, and the occasion of the derisive nom-de-plume of "Feather-duster legislature," which will ever distinguish the last phase of the suffrage times.

It was said that one of the worthies who was elected to this legislature received the votes of a number of men who were not on the registration list; that a few minutes before the closing of the polls in one of the precincts in his district he learned from one of the trusty helpers whose appointments he had secured as superintendents of election, that about fifty persons had not voted. Nearly all of these were Democrats who would not vote with negroes. He got a sufficient number of colored men who were working under a District contractor nearby, to vote under the names of the fastidious Democrats. In some cases the Democrats called to vote, later in the day, but were astonished when informed by the election officials that they had already voted. In a few instances tardy Republicans were served in the same manner.

It used to be related of this member that when any one asked him to introduce or support a measure which proposed to involve an appropriation, he would ask the applicant, "How much of the hair on this dog is for me?"

It was a common practice in those days, to import from the tidewater Potomac regions of Maryland and Virginia, boat loads of negroes for voting purposes. On one of these trips one of the most notorious managers of these personally conducted trips was a light-colored negro named Tom Bowie, who fell off the barge and was drowned.

A recital of the progress made under the Territorial government would be deficient without some account of the notable work accomplished by the Board of Health during that period.

The Board of Health first met on April 6, 1871, and organized on the 13th of that month, and proceeded upon the performance of its duties, which were prescribed by the act creating it to be "to declare what shall be deemed nuisances injurious to health, and to provide for the removal thereof; to make and enforce regulations to prevent domestic animals from running at large in the cities of Washington and Georgetown; to prevent the sale of unwholesome food in said cities, and to perform such other duties as shall be imposed upon said board by the Legislative Assembly."

The first members were N. S. Lincoln, M. D.; Tullio S. Verdi, M. D.; Henry A. Willard; John M. Langston; and John Marbury, Jr., all of whom were appointed March 15 of that year. Dr. Lincoln resigned on the 22nd of that month and was succeeded on the 3rd of April by Christopher C. Cox, M. D. Mr. Willard declined to accept his appointment, and Dr. D. Willard Bliss was appointed on May 23, 1871, in his stead. No other changes were made in the personel of the Board until November 10, 1877, when Robert B. Warden succeeded Mr. Langston, who had resigned. Mr.

Langston was a light complexioned colored man of general culture and exceptional oratorical talent.

When the Board of Health was created, the facilities for the collection and disposal of garbage and other refuse were as crude and unsatisfactory as the other primitive features of municipal management. Garbage was fed to hogs in hog pens in almost every section of the city. Cowsheds also lent their influence to pollute the air. Chickens, geese, goats, cows and other cattle roamed at large in many localities. The scavenger service offended both sense and sentiment, and filled the night air with noisome odors, and the most noxious kinds of offal and refuse were daily dumped on the surface of the commons.

During the four years and two months of its existence, the Board performed a revolutionary and enduring service in the public behalf by eliminating most of the insanitary conditions and practices whose abatement fell within its purview; and placed the National Capital in the van of the cities of the world in matters of municipal hygiene. Practically all of its policies are yet standard guides so far as they apply.

This Board continued until July 9, 1878, when pursuant to Section 8 of the law of June 11, 1878, creating the permanent Commission government, it was abrogated by the appointment of Doctor Smith Townshend as Health Officer.

It is worthy of note that the conduct of this branch of the Territorial government was not criticized by the Committee of the House of Representatives which investigated in 1872 the government of the District of Columbia, nor by the Joint Select Committee of the Senate and House of Representatives which made a like investigation in 1874 and recommended the abolition of all of the features of that government except the Board of Health.

The dominant character of the Territorial epoch was Alexander Robey Shepherd. Concerning the part played by him the following expressions from the report of the Allison Committee, to be presently referred to, are eloquent:

"The 9th day of October, 1871, the board clothed the vice-president with authority as follows:

*****

" Ordered, That the vice-president of this board shall be the executive officer thereof; he shall be in attendance at the office of the board daily, between 1 o'clock p. m. and 4 o'clock p. m., to receive all persons having business with the board, and to dispose of such applications as may need immediate attention; he shall sign all orders of the board, and submit at each session thereof an abstract of all business transacted by him since the preceding meeting. It shall also be his duty to have all papers properly briefed and prepared for consideration by the board, and generally to arrange its business in proper shape for action; he shall see that the reports of the different officers are promptly made, and orders to them shall be issued through him; he shall require that the various officers properly perform their respective duties, and may dismiss any employee of the board, subject to its approval.

"All requisitions for work or material must be approved by him, said requisitions to specify the particular improvement for which it is needed, and the nature of the work for which it is to be used. He shall also perform such other duties as may, from time to time, be required of him by the board.

"Pursuant to this authority, for no other seems to have been relied upon, the vice-president ultimately came to be, practically, the board of public works, and exercised the powers of the board almost as absolutely as though no one else had been associated with him."

Governor Shepherd was born in the City of Washington, on January 31, 1835, in a frame house situated on the south side of G Street between 9th and 10th Streets, southwest, on parts of lots 26 and 27, in Square 390. This building has since been incorporated as part of a new one which is now designated as No. 926 Qt Street, southwest.

His father whose Christian name was Alexander, was small in size but an intelligent, energetic and successful business man. His mother's maiden name was Susan Davidson Robey. She was large and strong in person and correspondingly apt and forceful in mind. He obviously came fitly by his distinctive physical and mental powers.

His earlier education was acquired under a private tutor. He later attended Nourse's School on the south side of Indiana Avenue, between 3rd Street and John Marshall Place, and afterwards had the advantage of a short term at Columbian College then located on the west side of 14th Street Road a short distance north of what is now Florida Avenue.

His practical business life commenced as an employee of Mr. John W. Thompson, who was then the leading contractor for plumbing and gas-fitting in the District. He succeeded Mr. Thompson in that occupation, but in addition thereto became influential in banking circles, and a dominant factor in other lines of business, as is attested by numerous buildings still existing which were constructed through his enterprise.

When the Civil War began, he and his brother, Thomas M., enlisted on April 15, 1861, for three months, as privates in the company commanded by Captain John P. Smead, 3rd Battalion, District of Columbia Volunteers, and remained in that service until the term of enlistment expired.

Soon after his discharge from that military service, he became conspicuous in local public affairs. He was elected a member of the 59th, 60th and 61st Common Councils of the City of Washington, in June, 1861, 1862, and 1863, respectively. He was President of the 60th Council. He was elected a member of the Board of Aldermen in June, 1870. Mr. Crosby S. Noyes, who was one of his colleagues in the Common Council, often referred admiringly to the versatility of Mr. Shepherd in the performance of his duties in that body. The mutual friendship and respect which that association engendered continued through the lives of both. No man could have a more unassailable certificate of sterling qualities of character, than that he was the cherished companion and confident of such men as Mr. Noyes, Mr. Louis C. Clephane, and of Mr. Win. F. Mattingly who was his intimate life-long friend. He was appointed in 1867 a member of the Levy Court of the County of Washington, D. C.

He was married on January 30, 1862, to Miss Mary Grice Young, a daughter of Colonel William P. Young of this City. They had ten children, three of whom died in infancy.

He died at the city of Batopilas, in the State of Chihuahua, Mexico, at 7:45 A. M., September 12, 1902, as the result of an operation for appendicitis. His body arrived at the railroad station on the southwest corner of 6th and B Streets, northwest, a few minutes before 8 o'clock on the morning of May 4, 1903, and was escorted on that date to the New York Avenue Presbyterian Church, where obituary services were held at 4 P. M. of that day.

He is buried at Rock Creek Cemetery in the District of Columbia.

As Governor, Mr. Shepherd made no material changes in the policy or methods of administering the District government but was principally occupied in avoiding embarrassments in the conduct of the District's official business due to the inadequacy of the revenue which had been entailed by the demands for funds to meet the cost of executing street improvements.

His failure to control the complex conditions of his environment exemplified again that all men have their limitations; that greatness is a myth and that achievement is restricted to adventitious opportunity.

Ambition goads our powers, but to gain
Visions of heights we strive to reach — in vain.
The most we can achieve tends but to prove
The vanity of Pride. Life's goal is love.

His subsequent career was principally as a resident of Mexico engaged in the business of mining. During the years he was in public life, as a member of the Board of Public Works and as Governor, his official duties monopolized his time and energies to such an extent that his private business and fortune were practically sacrificed, so that he was obliged to begin his private business anew. He chose to accept the opportunity to engage in business in Mexico, which then presented the most promising field for his energies. He revisited the District of Columbia twice; the second time in 1887, and on the 6th of October of that year reviewed from a stand south of the Treasury Department Building, an imposing demonstration by the people of the District in his honor.

His merits were heroic. His failings those of superabundant physical strength and its temptations, and the ruthless impulse which is usually a concomitant of effective ambition in official or business life.

Whose eye is fixed upon the mountains head,
Recks not the gowan's rights beneath his tread,
Justice nor sentiment; nor praise nor blame,
Divert his steps, where Lust aspires to Fame.

He judged men by their merits alone. As an employer in private business as well as in public affairs, he was ever zealous to recognize and reward attentive and efficient service, but language could not provide him with expletives sufficiently numerous or intense to express his disapproval of careless or unfaithful performance of duty.

Like all successful leaders he owed much to tact.

As a friend he was devoted, considerate, constant and liberal to a fault; as a companion he was ideally unconventional, genial, jovial and democratic. Although a vindictive enemy, he did not go out of his way to indulge his animosities. In no sense a temperance man, he was neither an intemperate one nor a glutton. While he was too sensible to be a practical joker, he was promotive of joviality at all social gatherings, as he was a leader in other affairs of life; but on staid occasions, he displayed an inherent dignity upon which no frivolity or assurance cared to presume.

As a host he was ideal. The humblest guest received as considerate attention as the most consequential. In this as in all other phases of his social and domestic relations, he was gracefully assisted by the consummate tact and kindliness of his accomplished wife.

The temerity of his resolution, and the intrepidity by which it was sustained, were typically illustrated in the peremptory removal, by his orders, of the tracks of the Baltimore and Ohio Railroad from First Street, west, where they had been laid and used as military necessity, but without warrant of law, during the Civil War. This line of track extended from Long Bridge at the southern terminus of Maryland Avenue, along that avenue to First Street, west, then to Indiana Avenue, and thence to the Baltimore and Ohio Railroad station at New Jersey Avenue and C Street, northwest, and obstructed the work of improving the streets. When it is considered that Mr. John W. Garrett, the then President of that road, was at that time one of the most potent influences in the political and financial world, the audacity of that act, although in the discharge of a public duty, was a phase of moral grandeur.

Not less decisive was the destruction of the old Northern Liberty Market House at the intersection of New York and Massachusetts Avenues, northwest, where the Public Library Building now stands. This was accomplished during the evening of September 3, 1872. During the progress of the demolition of this structure two of the dealers went into it to secure their property and were accidentally killed there.

In both cases prompt action became necessary by the imminence of injunction proceedings which might have indefinitely delayed the progress of improvements. In fact, the constant threat of interference by the courts or by Congress was the stimulus to the feverish haste with which all of the work of the Board of Public Works was done, and a leading cause of its consequent expensiveness for which the Board is often reproached.

There were other giants of those days who were associated with Governor Shepherd in his great work. His case is no exception to the rule that the Hero's wreath which history weaves, is largely twined with laurels gathered through the thought and toil of others. But he pre-eminently possessed the talent and power for leadership. The responsibility and guidance were his, and public opinion has justly attached to the name of Governor Alexander Robey Shepherd, the dominant fame of effecting the improvements in the physical status of the National Capital which terminated the efforts for its removal, and started it on the way to become a stimulus to the patriotic pride of every American and an object of universal admiration.

It is regrettable that the statue erected in his honor in front of the Municipal Building, and dedicated on May 3, 1909, represents him at an age when physical decay had begun to depict its inroads upon his countenance, and the symmetry of his person had become impaired by corpulence. The work to which he owes his celebrity was performed from his 36th to his 39th year, when he was ideally comely in person, with a broad forehead which does not appear in his statue, and which was the most impressive feature of his countenance.

His statue should show him at the height of his physical and mental powers, as they were during his terms as Vice-President of the Board of Public Works and Governor; an Apollo in form, a giant in strength, with the lineaments of an able and dominating mind, illumined by a kindly, steadfast soul.

On January 22, 1872, a memorial signed by 1,000 citizens and taxpayers was presented to the House of Representatives, charging the Board of Public Works and other officials with extravagance and mismanagement. It was referred to the Committee on the District of Columbia. The Committee made a lengthy investigation which resulted in a majority and a minority report (H. R. Report No. 72, 42nd Congress, 2nd Session). The former was signed by H. H. Starkweather, Chairman, and six other members of the Committee, and was strongly in favor of the policies and acts of the defendants, and summed its opinions as follows: (page XIII, Investigation 1872.)

"In passing upon the conduct of the gentlemen comprising the board of public works, whose high character is already known to the people of the District, and in finding all charges of corruption, misconduct, or serious mismanagement not proved, the committee do not wish to be understood as asserting that they have not made mistakes. The new government has but recently been organized. There was a universal demand for extensive improvements during the first season, which the board naturally determined to attempt to comply with. But the injunction sued out against their proceedings, together with the early, cold, and long winter, were unforeseen obstacles, which rendered it impossible to fully carry out the plans for 1871.

"On the other hand, however, it must be remembered that the District has realized the benefit of a very favorable negotiation of its four million loan, at a rate advantageous in itself, and which has raised the credit of the District to a high point, as shown by the negotiation of its waterbonds at par. The governor and members of the board are, on the whole, entitled to the favorable judgment of Congress, and are to be commended for the zeal, energy, and wisdom with which they have started the District upon a new career of improvement and prosperity; and the District itself is entitled to fair and generous appropriations from Congress, in some manner corresponding to the valuation of the property owned by the United States." The minority report was signed by Robert B. Roosevelt and John M. Crebs, and concluded with the following suggestions:

(Page XX, ibid.)

"Without going further into the facts which we believe the evidence sustains, we have arrived at the conclusion that the powers assumed and exercised by the board of public works are dangerous to the best interests of the District, and that the reckless extravagance of all departments of the District government ought to be checked; and while we do not feel authorized to recommend an entire change of government for the District, (as the present one is an experiment only, as yet,) but we feel assured that all officers of the government should be made directly responsible to the people for their acts. We therefore recommend the adoption of the following resolution:

"Resolved, That the Committee on the District of Columbia be, and they are hereby, instructed to report forthwith to the House a bill so changing the organic act as to make all the officers elective by the people, except the governor; and requiring the board of public works to give bond and security for the faithful performance of their duties, and placing them directly under legislative control. And that until said act can go into effect and a board elected, that they be by law prohibited from drawing any money from the District treasury; but that payments shall be made by warrants on the treasury, as contemplated in the thirty-seventh section of its organic act; and that they be required to furnish quarterly statements of all expenditures made by them, giving the name of the person to whom paid, and for what purpose, which report shall be made to the treasurer of the District and be open for public inspection." Early in 1874, in compliance with a petition of W.W. Corcoran and many other leading property owners in the District, who charged the officers of the District government with unlawful conduct, extravagance and mismanagement, a Joint Select Committee of the Senate and House of Representatives was appointed by a resolution which originated in the House of Representatives on February 2, 1874, and was concurred in by the Senate on the 5th of that month, and consisted of Senators William B. Allison, Allen G. Thurman, and Wm. M. Stewart; and Representatives Jeremiah M. Wilson, Jay A. Hubbell, Lyman K. Bass, H. J. Jewett and Robert Hamilton, to investigate the conduct and efficiency of the Board of Public Works and other features of the District government.

The investigation conducted by this Committee showed a complicated and apparently insolvent condition of affairs which seemed to call for a readjustment of the municipal situation by disinterested hands. The Committee made a report on June 16, 1874, in the course of which it said:

"Your committee, therefore, recommend the abolition of the executive, the secretary of the District, the legislative assembly, the board of public works, and the office of Delegate in Congress. They do not mean, by recommending the abolition of the legislative assembly, to preclude the idea that there should not be some representative body in the District of Columbia; but they believe the one now existing, with the powers conferred, is not such a one as is contemplated by the Constitution, or as the wants of the District require; and, inasmuch as the next assembly will be elected before the next session of Congress, they think it unnecessary to incur the expense of electing a legislative assembly, which, if not abolished now, would likely be abolished at the next session. From what has already been said, we think it clear that the board of public works, as now organized, has powers, or at least has exercised powers, that ought not to be committed to anybody or board. The committee have permitted the present Delegate in Congress to continue until the close of the next session, in order that the District might have a representative on the floor to make such criticisms as he might deem necessary upon the form of government which they have raised a committee to provide for and report upon.

"The committee recommend the appointment of a commission to manage the affairs of the District, under limited and restrained powers, because there is not sufficient time to prepare a proper system of frame-work for the government of the District, and have it fully discussed and passed upon at the present session of Congress. The committee have placed the repair, improvement, and control of the streets under the management of an officer of the Engineer Corps of the Army, because they believe, under such officer, whatever work is done will be well done, and by an officer responsible to the Executive and to Congress. "

"Your committee have unanimously arrived at the conclusion that the existing form of government of the District is a failure; that it is too cumbrous and too expensive; that the powers and relations of its several departments are so ill defined that limitations intended by Congress to apply to the whole government are construed to limit but one of its departments; that it is wanting in sufficient safeguard against maladministration and the creation of indebtedness; that the system of taxation it allows opens a door to great inequality and injustice, and is wholly insufficient to secure the prompt collection of taxes; and that no remedy short of its abolition and the substitution of a simpler, more restricted, and economical government will suffice. Your committee have, therefore, reported a bill for a temporary government, until Congress shall have time to mature and adopt a permanent form."

The recommendations of the Committee were embodied in a bill abolishing the Territorial government and providing for a temporary form of government to wind up its affairs. It further recommended the appointment of a committee to devise a permanent form of government for the District and submit the same at the next session of Congress, this committee to settle and determine also the proportion of expenses to be borne by the District and United States respectively. The report also recommended an audit of the finances of the District with a view of funding its indebtedness into a bond payable at a remote period and bearing a low rate of interest.

CHAPTER VIII.

The Temporary Commission Government; 1874-1878

The recommendations of the Allison Committee were put into effect by the speedy passage of the Act of Congress, approved June 20, 1874, which abolished the Territorial form of government and provided for a Commission of three members to be appointed by the President of the United States by and with the consent of the Senate. This Commission was to exercise much the same power and authority as had been vested in the Governor and Board of Public Works under the Territorial government. To co-operate with and assist the Commission, the President was by this act authorized to detail an officer of the Engineer Corps of the Army who, under the general supervision of the Commissioners, was to have control of the engineering work of the municipality.

The first three Commissioners appointed and confirmed under this law were William Dennison, of Ohio, John Henry Ketcham, of New York, and Henry T. Blow, of Missouri. President Grant nominated Alexander R. Shepherd as one of the temporary Commissioners, but the Senate refused to confirm the nomination, deeming it advisable to administer the new policy by new agents.

Commissioner Dennison had been governor of Ohio during the greater part of the Civil War, and near the close of the war had been appointed by President Lincoln to be Postmaster General, in which capacity he served through part of President Johnson 's term. As District Commissioner under the temporary government he served from July 1, 1874, to July 1, 1878.

Commissioner Ketcham was born in Dover, N. Y., December 21, 1832. He served two terms as town supervisor, member of the State Assembly and State Senator and entered the Union Army as Colonel of the 150th New York Volunteer Infantry, being promoted in 1862 to Brigadier General and after the close of the war being brevetted Major General. He was elected to Congress from New York, to serve in the 39th, 40th, 41st, 42nd and other Congresses until his death which occurred in New York City, November 4, 1906. He took office as District Commissioner on July 3, 1874, resigning June 30, 1877, in order to be a candidate for re-election to Congress.

General Ketcham was forceful, physically and mentally, and during his service as a Commissioner, dominated the management of the affairs of the District Government through the energetic, thorough and constant attention which he gave them. It was fortunate for the District that an administrator so well equipped, so resourceful and devoted to his task, had been entrusted with the complicated and responsible duty of bringing order out of the municipal chaos which existed at the time of his appointment.

Commissioner Blow was born in Southampton County, Virginia, July 15, 1817. He removed to Missouri in 1830 and was graduated from St. Louis University, afterwards serving four years in the State Senate of Missouri. In 1861 he was appointed Minister to Venezuela, from which post he resigned in less than a year. He was elected to Congress from Missouri in 1862 as a Republican, and re-elected in 1864, serving also as a delegate to the Baltimore Convention in the latter year. From May 1, 1869, to February 11, 1871, he represented the United States as Minister to Brazil. He went into office as District Commissioner July 1, 1874, but owing to ill health resigned December 31, 1874, his death occurring September 11, 1875, at Saratoga, New York.

The Engineer officer detailed to assist the Commission was Lieutenant Richard L. Hoxie, who had been named by the President and confirmed by the Senate as engineer officer with the Board of Public Works a few days prior to its abolishment. He met once or twice with the Board but took no part in its official proceedings. He acted as such assistant to the temporary board of Commissioners, form July 2, 1874, until July 1, 1878.

Lieutenant Hoxie, who afterwards become Brigadier General Hoxie, of the Corps of Engineers of the United States Army, was born in New York, and removed during his youth to Iowa. He served in the First Iowa Cavalry during the Civil War, and on July 1, 1864, entered the United States Military Academy from which he was graduated on June 15, 1868.

This Commission held its first meeting on the afternoon of Saturday, July 3, 1874, in the H Street parlor of what was then the Arlington Hotel at the northwest corner of H Street and Vermont Avenue. At that meeting the Commissioners appointed William Birney assistant attorney and Dr. William Tindall Secretary. Among those present and advising the Commissioners was Senator Allen G. Thurman of Ohio.

The afternoon of that day is memorable for the violent tempest which occurred towards evening doing immense damage to trees and houses.

The Commissioners held their sessions at the Arlington on the 6th, 7th and 8th of July; on the 9th in the office of the former Governor, located in the second story of the building at the northwest corner of 17th Street and Pennsylvania Avenue, northwest, and thereafter in the building called the Columbia Building or Morrison Building on the west side of John Marshall Place, then Four-and-a-Half Street, three doors above Pennsylvania Avenue.

Commissioner Blow's term under the temporary government was completed by Captain Seth Ledyard Phelps, a native of Ohio, and a graduate of the Naval Academy, who had served with credit in the Mexican War and in connection with the Chili Astronomical Survey. During the Civil War he was assigned to the command of a gunboat in the western river flotilla where he made the friendship of General Grant. After the war Captain Phelps became President of the Pacific Mail Steamship Company and in connection with its affairs spent several years in China and Japan, returning to America and resigning his position with the Company in 1873. He entered upon his duties as temporary Commissioner on January 18, 1875.

Commissioner Phelps was of a genial, generous temperament, and was by nature and training well equipped for the admirable service which he rendered during his term of office.

An interval of five months elapsed following the resignation of General Ketcham before his successor took office. This was due to the determined opposition, led by Mr. William Birney, to the confirmation of Judge Thomas B. Bryan who was nominated by President Hayes for the position. Judge Bryan's nomination was, nevertheless, finally confirmed, and he took office on December 3, 1877, and held until July 1, 1878, when the permanent Board succeeded to the duties of the temporary Board.

Judge Bryan was a lawyer, linguist and author of national reputation, but had little opportunity during his brief term of office to render any noteworthy service in his official capacity.

Pursuant to the recommendations of the Allison Committee, Section 6 of the Act creating the temporary Board of Commissioners provided for a Board of audit to consist of the first and second Comptrollers of the Treasury of the United States. The function of this Board was to audit for settlement the unfunded or floating debt of the District, including that incurred by the Board of Public Works, and to issue to creditors whose claims should be established, certificates of indebtedness which were to be convertible by the Sinking Fund Commissioners created by the seventh Section of the Act into bonds bearing 3.65 per cent interest, payable in fifty years and guaranteed by the faith of the United States.

The principal function of the temporary Board of Commissioners was to close up the affairs of the Board of Public Works and put them on a systematic basis. Incident to the accomplishment of these purposes, it was necessary for the Commissioners to complete and in some cases to extend the contracts made by the Board of Public Works in order to prevent deterioration of work partially done. Under their alert and judicious administration, the District also developed normally in all branches of its government.

Section 5 of the act creating the temporary form of government provided for a joint select committee to consist of two Senators and two Ex-Representatives whose duty it should be to prepare a suitable form of government for the District with proper drafts of statutes to be enacted by Congress to carry it into effect. This Committee was also to submit a statement of the proper proportion of the expenses of the District which should be borne by the District and by the United States respectively.

On December 7, 1874, the joint committee, through its Chairman, Senator Lot M. Morrill of Maine, made a majority report (No. 479, 43rd Congress, 2nd session), accompanying Senate Bill No. 963, which contemplated a department of the United States Government strictly limited to the affairs of the District, at the head of which should be a board of general control, designated the Board of Regents. This Board was to consist of three members to be appointed by the President, which should have power to appoint such subdivisions and bureaus of the municipal government as should be necessary, except as to the Board of Education, part of whose members were to be elective.

On January 11, 1877, Senator Spencer, of Alabama, submitted a minority report (No. 572, 44th Congress, 2nd session), which recommended the creating of a local government to be derived from the free suffrage of the people of the District.

Neither of these reports was adopted. So well did the temporary Commission accomplish the ends for which it had been created that when Congress came to consider the establishment of a permanent government the main features of the temporary Commission were adopted, and a permanent Board of three Commissioners to be appointed by the President, two from civil life and one from the Engineer Corps of the Army, was provided for. This action on the part of Congress was in a great measure the result of the influence of a volunteer committee of one hundred citizens who by united and organized effort did much towards inducing Congress to enact the much needed legislation; but more especially of the earnest public spirited efforts of Honorable J. C. S. Blackburn of Kentucky, who had charge of the measure in the House of Representatives.

In less than two years after the temporary board of Commissioners had assumed its duties, it too became the object of an investigation by the Committee of the House of Representatives on the District of Columbia, which propounded a series of interrogations as to the manner in which those duties had been discharged.

This investigation related principally to the manner in which the Commissioners had adjusted the number and compensation of official personnel with regard to the most economical service, and the extent and authority for work under extensions of contracts of the board of public works. These questions the Commissioners answered in full on April 4th and 10th, 1876, and obviously to the refutation of any direct or implied imputation upon their honor or judgment, as Congress took no action adverse to them in the matter.

The Board of Audit was also investigated pursuant to a resolution of the House of Representatives adopted on January 31st, 1876. The result of this investigation was the summary repeal on March 14, 1876, of the law establishing that board, and the transfer of all of its records to the custody of the Commissioners.

CHAPTER IX.

The Permanent Commission Government; 1878.

The act creating the permanent Board of Commissioners was approved June 11, 1878. This act declared that all the territory ceded by the State of Maryland for the permanent seat of Government of the United States, should "continue to be designated as the District of Columbia," and that the District of Columbia should "remain and continue a municipal corporation."

By the terms of this act the two civil members of the Board of Commissioners were required to have been residents of the District for three years next preceding their appointment. Their salary was fixed at $5,000 per annum. The first appointment was to be one Commissioner for one year and one for two years, after which their successors were to be appointed for three years. The Engineer Commissioner was required to be above the rank of Captain, though later, in order to make possible the appointment of Captain William T. Rossell, then one of the Assistants to the Engineer Commissioner, the law was amended to permit of the appointment, as Engineer Commissioner, of a Captain in the Corps of Engineers who had held that rank for fifteen years. The salary of the Engineer Commissioner when the position was first created, was to be the same as his regular pay as an officer in the Army but was later fixed at $5,000.

The act of Congress which provides for the appointment of a Captain, as Engineer Commissioner, was approved December 24, 1890.

Representative — afterwards Senator — Joseph C. S. Blackburn, of Kentucky, who was the Chairman of the committee which prepared the draft of the Act creating the permanent Commission government, inserted in the draft a clause directing that the Commissioners to be appointed from civil life should belong to different principal political parties; but President Hayes, through Representative — afterwards President — Garfield, requested Mr. Blackburn to omit this requirement as it would be in the nature of a reflection upon the President's impartiality. Mr. Garfield orally assured Mr. Blackburn that the President would be governed by the policy indicated in the intended proviso, and on the strength of that assurance Mr. Blackburn withdrew the objectionable clause from the bill.

This Act gives the Commissioners plenary powers, under certain prescribed regulations, in administering the affairs of the District, except so far as they may be controlled by Congress. It abolished the Board of Metropolitan Police and transferred all its powers to the Commissioners. It abolished the Board of School Trustees and provided for the transfer of its functions to a board of nineteen persons to be appointed by the Commissioners. By a subsequent Act jurisdiction over the public schools has been placed in the Board of Education of nine members, three of them to be women, appointed by the Judges of the Supreme Court of the District. The "Organic Act" abolished the Board of Health and transferred its duties to a Health Officer to be appointed by the Commissioners.

The Act, in addition to defining the general powers and duties of the Commissioners and establishing the details of the District Government, provided that after the Commissioners had in each year submitted their estimates of the work proposed to be undertaken and of the cost of the government during the ensuing fiscal year, Congress should, to the extent to which it should approve the same, appropriate the amount of fifty per centum thereof and that the remaining fifty per centum should he assessed upon the taxable property and privileges in the District other than the property of the United States and of the District of Columbia.

The incorporation of this provision was in large measure due to the activities of the committee of one hundred previously mentioned, a subcommittee of which submitted to Congress on November 21, 1877, an address signed by J. M. Wilson, Joseph Casey, C. F. Peck, Joseph Shillington, S. V. Niles, Josiah Dent, W. S. Cox, C. B. Church, B. G. Lovejoy, W. H. Clagett, W. W. Corcoran, S. H. Kauffman, W. M. Dixon, A. Y. P. Garnett, L. A. Gobright, M. W. Gait, A. T. Britton, Thos. P. Morgan and Win. Stickney.

This address concluded with the following passage:

"As in the beginning, the Federal City was without population or resources to which its founders could look for its development and improvement, so also, at the present time, it is wholly without means, either of wealth or industry, to meet the enormous outlays, necessitated by the magnificence of its plan. It has no business except what is based upon the wants of its citizens and of the government service; one-half of its property, and the best half, is owned by the United States, and pays no taxes; and the other half is now mortgaged for more than one-fourth of its value by the debt contracted in exhausting and paralyzing efforts to make it what its patriotic founders designed it to be, a National Capital, worthy of the name it bears. Several millions of dollars are now required to renew its decayed and almost impassable streets. Where shall its already overburdened taxpayers look for aid and relief except to the Congress of the United States? From the facts here presented, the inference is plain that the United States and our own taxpaying citizens, as part owners or tenants in common, are bound, respectively, to contribute a just and equal share of the funds necessary to develop and improve the common property; and that the United States, having exclusive and absolute title to the streets and avenues of the city as well as to the public grounds and buildings, (which alone give value to the property of citizens), and being clothed by the Constitution with plenary and exclusive power of control and administration, the Government is under special obligation to furnish its share.

"It is equally clear, that the taxpayers of the District have already and in fee simple contributed more than their equal share of these improvements. Will not the Government, with equal fidelity to its high trusts, discharge the obligations required alike by its Constitutional relations to the District, and by justice to its citizens?" The chief credit, however, for the determination of Congress to recognize a liability on the part of the National Government for one-half the cost of the government of the Capital City was the report of the Committee on Judiciary of the House of Representatives submitted by its Chairman, Mr. Luke Poland, on June 1, 1874.

While the Allison Committee had been investigating the Board of Public Works the House Committee on Judiciary had been directed to inquire into and report upon the legal relations between the Federal Government and the local government of the District, and the extent and character of the mutual obligations in regard to municipal expenses; and further to inquire and report whether some accurately defined basis of expenditures could be prescribed and maintained by law.

The report of this committee ranks with the report made by Senator Southard in 1835, as a classic in its appreciation and presentation of the responsibilities of the National Government towards its Capital.

After reviewing the conception of the founders of the city as evidenced by the "observations" set forth in L 'Enfant 's plan, the report continues:

"The committee believe there can be no question, in laying out such a city as is here described, that it was fully contemplated by Government that the extent of expenditures would keep pace with the magnificence of the plan to be ultimately carried out. The founders of the capital city evidently did not believe that in their time this plan could be consummated, but they were establishing the permanent seat of government. It was as the Supreme Court said in Van Ness vs. The City of Washington: ' The grants were made for the foundation of a Federal city, and the public faith was necessarily pledged when the grants were accepted to found such a city. ' And again in the same opinion, ' that the city was designed to last in perpetuity — capitoli immobile saxum.'

"The Federal city was to be a temple erected to liberty, toward which the wishes and expectations of all true friends of every country would necessarily be directed; and, considered under such important points of view as evidently controlled the minds of the founders, it could not be calculated on a small scale. Everything about it was to correspond with the magnitude of the object for which it was intended. It foresaw a far distant future when it was to be the center of a continent under one form of government looking to it for its laws and for its protection. It was to be a city where all improvements made and expenses incurred were to be for the benefit of the whole people.

"Viewing the capital city in this national aspect, we may well understand the motives which governed its founders in imposing upon all who were to come after them such duties and responsibilities toward it as would be peculiar to the capital city alone, and which would fully justify a liberal if not a munificent policy in expenditures.

"As to the mutual obligations of the Federal Government and the citizens to defray these expenses, the committee find little difficulty. It is clear, if this national capital was founded for the use of the United States, and was placed under its exclusive government and control, and upon a scale of magnificence appropriate only for a national capital, it never could have been contemplated that the burden of expenditures should fall upon those citizens of the United States who might temporarily or permanently take up a residence at the capital. Originally we know there was no population here to which the Government could look for contributions toward these expenditures; and as the city was not to become one of trade and commerce and manufactures, the local population could not be looked to in the future as being sufficient, either in numbers or wealth, to carry out the magnificent intentions of the founders. Nor, indeed, would it have been just to impose this burden upon them; for, upon the theory upon which the capital was founded, all these expenditures would ultimately be for the benefit of the whole people, and justice would dictate that the burden should fall upon the whole people." As to the basis of contribution between the United States and the District toward the expense of the local government, the report says:

"Aside, then, from all questions of sentiment or patriotism or pride in the national capital, your committee are impressed with the belief that the Federal Government sustains at least such relation toward the citizens and the local government as would require it to contribute to municipal expenses an amount bearing the relation to the whole amount required, which the interest of the Federal Government here bears to the interest of the local government; and this they believe to be at least one-half."

The Act of June 11, 1878, is commonly referred to as the "Organic Act" or "Constitution" of the District. In the case of Eckloff v. D. C. (135 U. S. 240) Mr. Justice Brewer, speaking for the Supreme Court of the United States, applies both of those terms to it, saying:

" The Court below placed its decision on what we conceive to be the true significance of the Act of 1878. As said by that court, it is to be regarded as an organic act, intended to dispose of the whole question of a government for this District. It is declared by its title to be an Act to prove 'a permanent form of government for the District. ' The work permanent is suggestive. It implies that prior systems have been temporary and provisional. As permanent it is complete in itself. It is the system of government. The powers which are conferred are organic powers. We look to the Act itself for their extent and limitations. It is not one act in a series of legislation, and to be made to fit into the provisions of the prior legislation, but it is a single complete Act, the outcome of previous experiments, and the final judgment of Congress as to the system of government which should obtain. It is the constitution of the District, and its grants of power are to be taken as new and independent grants and expressing in themselves both their extent and limitations. Such was the view taken by the court below, and such we believe is the true view to be taken of the statute. "

When the "Organic Act" went into effect on July 1, 1878, President Grant re-appointed Commissioner Seth L. Phelps, who had been a member of the temporary Commission, and added Josiah Dent, as civil Commissioner and Major William J. Twining, as Engineer Commissioner, to complete the Board.

Commissioner Dent was a native of Maryland who removed to the District after the war and married the daughter of Mr. E. M. Linthicum, taking up his residence in Georgetown. He was a lawyer by profession and served actively as a member of the Citizens' Committee of One Hundred to secure legislative justice from Congress. His term as Commissioner extended from July 1, 1878, to July 17, 1882.

Commissioner Twining was born at Indianapolis, Ind., and was graduated from the Military Academy July 1, 1859. He was brevetted Captain on December 16, 1864, for gallant and meritorious services in action during the siege of Nashville, Major and Lieutenant Colonel of Volunteers on January 26, 1865, for gallant and meritorious services in the campaign in Georgia and Tennessee, and Major General on March 3, 1865, for gallant and meritorious services during the war. He resigned his volunteer commission August 30, 1865, was made Captain of Engineers, December 28, 1865, and Major, October 16, 1877. The service of Commissioner Twining, the first of the Engineer Commissioners, terminated with his death on May 5, 1892.

He was succeeded by Major Garrett J. Lydecker who served from May 11, 1882 to April 1, 1886. Commissioner Lydecker was born in "English Neighborhood," New Jersey, November 15, 1843. He was graduated from the United States Military

Academy in 1864 and was brevetted captain on April 2, 1865, for gallant and meritorious services in the siege of Petersburg, and after the Civil War he was engaged in river and harbor work at Galveston, Michigan City, New Orleans, Chicago and Detroit.

Major Lydecker was succeeded by Col. Wm. Ludlow whose term commenced April 1, 1886 and terminated January 27, 1888. Commissioner Phelps served until November 29, 1879, on which date he was succeeded by Thomas P. Morgan, who served until March 8, 1883, and was in turn succeeded by James B. Edmunds, who served from March 3, 1883, to April 1, 1886. Commissioner Edmunds was succeeded by Samuel E. Wheatley whose term began on April 1, 1886 and ended May 21, 1889.

Commissioner Morgan who succeeded Commissioner Phelps was born near Alexandria, Virginia, then a part of the District, on November 2, 1812. He was elected to the Common Council of the City of Washington in 1847 and to the Board of Aldermen in 1851, and again to the Common Council from 1859 to 1861. During the Civil War he held the position of Quartermaster's Agent in charge of transportation, having been fitted for that duty by his previous connection with the business of water transportation. From March 21, 1873, to March 22, 1878, he served on the Board of Fire Commissioners as the representative of the United States Government under appointment by the President. He was appointed Major of Police February 2, 1878, and held that office until November 29, 1879, when he resigned to take the office of District Commissioner.

Commissioner Edmunds was born in Saratoga County, New York, in 1833. He practiced law a short time in Oswego, New York, and then moved to Iowa City, Iowa, where he practiced law for twenty years. He came to Washington in 1878.

Commissioner Wheatley was born in Washington City, March 29, 1844. He was educated at Hallowell's High School in Alexandria, Virginia. At the age of twenty he went into the lumber business with his father and with his three brothers took charge of the business on his father's retirement in 1866. He was for some time President of the Potomac Boat Club and active in the Episcopal Church.

Commissioner Dent served one term of one year and a second term of three years, his last term expiring July 17, 1882. He was succeeded by Joseph R. West, who held office from July 17, 1882, to July 22, 1885. Commissioner West was succeeded by William B. Webb whose term began on July 22, 1885 and ended with that of Commissioner Wheatley on May 21, 1889.

Commissioner West was born at New Orleans, La., September 19, 1822. He attended the University of Pennsylvania, served in the Mexican War as Captain of Volunteers and moved to California where he engaged in newspaper work in San Francisco. At the outbreak of the Civil War he entered the Union Army as Lieutenant Colonel of the 1st California Infantry. He was brevetted Major General January 4, 1866, for faithful and meritorious service. After the War he moved to Texas and later to New Orleans. He was elected to the U. S. Senate as a Republican, serving from March 4, 1871, to March 3, 1877. He held office as District Commissioner from July 17, 1882, to July 22, 1885. He died in Washington City October 31, 1898.

Commissioner Webb was born in Washington City in 1825. He was graduated from Columbian (now George Washington) University in 1844, and three years later, at the age of twenty-two, he was admitted to the bar. In 1861 he became

171

Superintendent of Police and devoted some years to organizing the police force of the city.

On May 21, 1889, Commissioners Webb and Wheatley were succeeded by John W. Douglass, whose term expired February 28, 1893, and Lemon G. Hine, whose term expired September 30, 1890.

Commissioner Douglass was born in Philadelphia, October 25, 1827. He was admitted to the bar at Erie, Penn., about 1850. From 1862 to 1869 he was Collector of Internal Revenue for the 19th Pennsylvania District. During the years of 1869 to 1875 he was First Deputy and Commissioner of Internal Revenue. Thereafter he engaged in practice of law in Washington until taking office as Commissioner.

Commissioner Hine was born at Berlin Heights, Ohio, April 14, 1832. He studied law at Ann Arbor, Michigan, until the outbreak of the Civil War when he enlisted in the Northwest Rifle Regiment, afterwards 44th Illinois, and served through the War. After the War he came to Washington and formed a law partnership with former governor of Ohio Ford and later with Mr. Sidney T. Thomas. He served in the City Council for several terms. Later he became interested in typesetting machinery and in 1887 retired from practice to take the presidency of the National Typographic Association.

Commissioner Ludlow was born on Long Island, New York, November 27, 1843, and was graduated from the Military Academy June 13, 1864. On July 20, 1864, he was brevetted Captain for gallant and meritorious services in laying a bridge over Peach Tree Creek, Georgia, under severe fire. He was brevetted Major, December 21, 1864, for gallant and meritorious service in the campaign through Georgia and Lieutenant Colonel March 13, 1865, for gallant and meritorious service in the campaign in the Carolinas. He took a conspicuous part in the Cuban Campaign of 1898, being promoted to the rank of Major General of Volunteers for gallant services at Santiago. He died August 30, 1901, of illness contracted in the line of duty in the Philippine Islands.

Col. Ludlow was succeeded by Major Charles W. Raymond who served from January 27, 1888 until February 3, 1890, and who was succeeded by Lieut. Colonel Henry M. Robert whose term extended from February 14, 1890 to October 14, 1891.

Commissioner Raymond was born at Hartford, Connecticut, January 14, 1842. He was graduated from the United States Military Academy June 23, 1865. He was active in various river and harbor improvement undertakings in various parts of the country previous to his appointment as Engineer Commissioner of the District.

Lieut. Col. Henry Martyn Robert was born in South Carolina. He was graduated from the Military Academy July 1, 1857 and served throughout the Civil War in the Union Army. He was retired March 2, 1901, being then Brigadier General and Chief of Engineers. He has been justly accorded a large degree of prominence as the author of " Robert 's Rules of Order. "

The period covered by the terms of the Commissioners who have just been enumerated extended from the establishment of the permanent Commission Government, roughly to the beginning of the decade from 1890 to 1900.

To these early Boards of Commissioners fell the task of carrying to completion the work of improvement which had been so vigorously begun by the Board of Public Works, and practically the replacement of all the wood pavements laid by that Board, with more durable material.

Chief among the notable public works undertaken during the early years of the permanent Commission government were the extensions of the sewer and water systems of the city.

In 1879 work was begun on the New York Avenue sewer. This sewer, starting at Seventh Street and New York Avenue, follows New York Avenue to 15th Street; thence down 15th Street to Pennsylvania Avenue, and from there cuts diagonally across the White Lot to 17th and B Streets, where it empties into the Tiber sewer.

In 1880 the Northeast Boundary sewer was commenced. Beginning at 7th Street and Florida Avenue this sewer follows Florida Avenue to 15th Street, northeast; thence down 15th Street to G Street, northeast; thence eastward to the neighborhood of 18th and E Streets, northeast, where it empties into the Eastern Branch. This sewer occupied about six years in its construction.

The Q Street sewer was constructed in 1885 and runs from 17th and Q Streets, northwest, westwardly along Q Street to Rock Creek.

The Northwest Boundary sewer was constructed in 1887 and runs from 14th Street and Florida Avenue, northwest, westwardly along Florida Avenue to a point on Rock Creek near the P Street bridge.

The execution of this extensive sewer extension work in so short a period of time was rendered possible by an appropriation of $500,000 by Congress in 1884. This appropriation was in the nature of an advance conditioned upon the repayment by the District of its one-half, with interest, in annual instalments of not less than $50,000 each. Its procurement was chiefly due to the influence which Commissioner Edmunds had acquired with Congress. Under this appropriation a total of seventeen miles of sewers, large and small were constructed.

The extension of the water system of the city had been made the subject of an investigation by Lieutenant Hoxie under the temporary Commissioners. On May 27, 1878, he made a report recommending the construction of an accumulating reservoir to be located on the heights north of the city, which should be connected by tunnel with the distributing reservoir at Georgetown. As a temporary expedient to increase the water supply of Capitol Hill, Lieutenant Hoxie recommended the erection of an iron stand pipe of 120,000 gallons capacity in the middle of 16th Street extended, upon the brow of Meridian Hill, to be supplied by means of a pumping station to be located on U Street between 16th and 17th Streets, northwest.

Both of these recommendations were adopted. The stand pipe and U Street pumping station were established in the spring and summer of 1878. This stand pipe was removed on February 8, 1894.

Work on the construction of the Seventh Street reservoir back of Howard University and the tunnel connecting it with the Distributing reservoir in Georgetown was begun under the supervision of Engineer Commissioner Lydecker. The tunnel was cut mainly through solid rock and the muffled detonations of the blasting operations incident to its construction were for a long time a feature of life in the then suburban portions of the northwest section of the city.

A matter of pressing importance with which the permanent Commissioners were required to deal was the replacing of the old wooden pavements with permanent paving of an improved character. Of the original area of 1,005,231 square yards of wooden paving, about 480,000 square yards remained, but this for the most part was impassable. So urgent was the need for new pavements that it was made the subject of a special report to Congress by the first permanent Board.

In 1885, the Commissioners, in view of the success of the $500,000 sewer appropriation of the previous year and of the fact that the District then had a large sum to its credit in the United States Treasury, asked in their report for a similar advance of one million dollars for street improvements which were then urgently needed. An appropriation of this character would have meant much to the city at that time, but Congress could not be prevailed upon to grant it.

The first permanent Board in its annual report for the fiscal year 1878 included an interesting statement of the amounts contributed by the several municipalities in the District of Columbia for their expenses as compared with the amounts contributed by the National Government, from 1800 to 1876. This statement shows:

Aggregate amount (of assessments on property in the City of Washington) as reported	$32,007,255.70
Add collections for licenses, rents, etc.	$4,078,626.12
Add water department rents	$626,838.92
Add expenditures by Georgetown	$3,500,000.00
Add expenditures by county	$2,000,000.00
Add expenditures by Alexandria prior to 1846, date of retrocession to Virginia	$1,250,000.00
Add outstanding District funded debt	$8,363,400.00
Add outstanding 3.65 bonds	<u>$13,743,250.00</u>
Total expended by the people of the District	$65,569,370.74

Deducting the amount of the bonded debt above stated from $65,569,370.74 there still remains an absolute paid-up expenditure, as follows:

By the people of the District of Columbia	$43,462,720.74
Expended by the United States	$27,311,950.00

During the years 1878, 1879, 1880 and 1881, the Commissioners under authority of special acts of Congress, spent approximately $80,000 in filling the old Washington Canal from Third Street, west, to its mouth on the Eastern Branch, the canal from Third Street to its western mouth having been converted into a sewer by the Board of Public Works. The filling of the eastern end by the Commissioners was done largely to give employment to the large number of unemployed persons resulting from the financial depression then prevailing throughout the country.

A matter of importance which came to the attention of the early Commissioners was the establishment of a station so located as to permit both branches of the Baltimore and Ohio Railroad to enter the city over one line. Looking with an almost prophetic vision some thirty years into the future, the report for 1878 says: "It is entirely practicable to unite these two lines outside the city and bring them in upon one line of street to a station somewhere north of Massachusetts Avenue." The same report advocated the removal of the Baltimore and Potomac Depot from its old location on 6th and B Streets to a position south of the Mall. The idea of a union station for all steam railroad lines seems to have been first suggested in the report for 1885.

The most important legislative measure affecting the District adopted during the decade from 1880 to 1890, was an Act of Congress approved August 27, 1888, to regulate the subdivision of land within the District of Columbia, which provided that

" No future subdivision of land in the District, without the limits of the Cities of Washington and Georgetown, should be recorded in the Surveyor's Office of the District, unless made in conformity with the general plan of the City of Washington." This law also prescribed that the Commissioners should make and publish general orders to regulate the platting and subdividing of all lands in the District, and that no plats should be admitted to record in the Surveyor's Office without the Commissioners' written order to that effect.

This legislation was especially due to the efforts of Mr. Joseph Paul and Senator John Sherman.

Several efforts were later made to obtain legislation to correct the irregular subdivisions, which had been made in the near environs of the city. While their attempts were not successful, they so directed attention in the need of such action, that the Washington Board of Trade appointed a committee to secure legislation on the general subject of Street Extensions over the entire District outside of Washington and Georgetown. The labors of this committee resulted in the enactment of the Act "to provide a permanent system of highways in that portion of the District of Columbia, lying outside of the city," approved March 2, 1893, and subsequent germane legislation.

On January 14, 1889, Mr. Taulbee introduced in the House of Representatives, the following Resolution which was passed the same day:

"Whereas, It is stated in certain newspapers that the commissioners of the District of Columbia have in recent purchases of real estate within and for the use of the District of Columbia paid to and through certain agents appointed or employed by them prices above that asked or received by the vendors or owners of such property, contrary to law: Therefore,

"Resolved, That the Speaker of the House of Representatives appoint a special committee of five members to investigate the matter of the purchases of real estate by the commissioners of the District, and report to the House in writing, at any time, by bill or otherwise; and that said committee be furnished a stenographer by assignment by the Speaker from the roll of stenographers now in the employ of the House, and that they be authorized to employ a clerk at a compensation of $6 per day, and that said committee be authorized to sit during the sessions of the House and authorized to administer oaths and send for persons and papers. That the expenses of said investigation be paid out of the contingent fund of the House." The investigation which was conducted pursuant to this

resolution resulted in the following legislation in the District of Columbia appropriation act approved March 2 of the same year: "That hereafter the Commissioners in making purchases of sites for schools or other public buildings shall do so without the employment of agents or through other persons not regular dealers in real estate in the District of Columbia, or through such regular dealers who have not had the property for sale continuously from the date of the passage of this act, and in no case shall commission be paid to more than one person or firm greater than the usual commission." October 1, 1890, John W. Ross took office as successor to Commissioner Hine. Commissioner Ross was three times reappointed, his term continuing until the date of his death, which occurred on July 29, 1902. With him as civil members of the Board were associated Myron M. Parker, who served as successor to Commissioner Douglass from February 20, 1893, to March 9, 1894;

George Truesdell, who succeeded Commissioner Parker and served from March 10, 1894, to May 7, 1897; John B. Wight, who succeeded Commissioner Truesdell on May 8, 1897, and served until May 8, 1900; and Henry B. F. Macfarland, whose first term, as successor to Commissioner Wight, began on May 9, 1900.

Commissioner Ross was born at Lewiston, Ill., June 23, 1841. He attended Illinois College and was graduated in law from Harvard University, being admitted to the Board in 1866. In 1869 he was elected to the Illinois Legislature for two terms. In 1873 he came to Washington where he practiced law until appointed Postmaster of that city, in which capacity he served from February 1, 1888, to October 1, 1890, resigning to accept the position of District Commissioner.

Commissioner Parker was born at Fairfax, Vermont, November 7, 1843. He served through the Civil War in the 1st Vermont cavalry. In 1876 he came to Washington and later was graduated from the law department of Columbian (now George Washington) University. For several years he was assistant postmaster of Washington City. He is a prominent mason, and has displayed a leading interest in almost every phase of business enterprise and civil progress in the National Capital during his residence there.

Commissioner Truesdell was born in New York City. He was educated as a civil engineer at the University of Michigan. At the outbreak of the Civil War he enlisted as private in the 12th New York Volunteers and was promoted to Lieutenant and Captain in 1862, being badly wounded at the battle of Gaines Mill and imprisoned in Libbey Prison. When the regiment was mustered out in 1863 he was appointed Major and Paymaster in the regular army and served as such until 1869. He was brevetted Lieutenant Colonel for meritorious services. He practiced his profession in New Jersey for two years after leaving the army and removed to Washington in 1872. In 1888 he organized the Eckington and Soldiers Home Railway Company whose line was the first street railroad operated by electric power in the District, of which he was president for five years. He has been prominent in all measures for civic betterment in the District for many years and was especially active and efficient in efforts to secure the enactment of the law for the extension of the highway system.

Commissioner Wight was born in Washington City, March 3, 1853. He entered the employ of Leo C. Campbell, a hardware merchant in 1867, resigning after nine years to take charge of the business affairs of the Deaf and Dumb Institute at Kendall Green which position he held until February, 1890, when he resigned and went into the real estate and insurance business. From 1893 until appointed Commissioner he held the position of Secretary of the Washington Board of Trade.

During the period covered by the terms of the civil Commissioners who have just been mentioned, the Engineer members of the Board were Captain William T. Rossell, who succeeded Commissioner Robert on October 15, 1891, and served to May 8, 1893; Major Charles F. Powell, who served from May 8, 1893, to March 1, 1897; Captain William M. Black, who served from March 2, 1897, to May 31, 1898; Captain Lansing H. Beach, who served from June 1, 1898, to October 31, 1901; and Colonel John Biddle, who served from November 1, 1901, to May 1, 1907.

Commissioner Rossell was born in Alabama and was graduated from West Point in 1873. He became chief of Engineers.

Commissioner Powell was born in Jacksonville, Illinois, August 13, 1843. At the outbreak of the Civil War he enlisted in the 5th Wisconsin Volunteers and served

176

with that regiment until September 28, 1863, when he was appointed to the Military Academy from South Carolina.

Commissioner Black was born at Lancaster, Pa., December 8, 1855. He attended Franklin and Marshall College from 1870 to 1873 and was graduated from the United States Military Academy in 1877. During the Spanish-American War he served as Chief of Engineers of the Porto Rican Campaign and later as Chief Engineer of the Department of Havana; and from 1900 to April, 1901, as Chief Engineer of the Division of Cuba. He was connected with the Isthmian Canal Commission from April, 1903, to July, 1904.

Commissioner Beach was born in Iowa and was graduated from the Military Academy July 1, 1878.

The period from 1890 to 1900 was characterized by a steady development and improvement of the District through the able administration of the several Boards of Commissioners who served during that period. Commissioner Ross perpetuated his memory by his untiring efforts to secure Congressional sanction, together with suitable appropriations, for the erection of a municipal building. His labors toward this end were recognized by the placing of a bronze tablet to his honor in the vestibule entrance to the present municipal office structure.

Of vital consequence to the District during this period was the action of Congress on two occasions in disregarding the half-and-half principle of the Act of June 11, 1878.

The first instance was the authorization by act of September 26, 1890, of the construction and maintenance of a bathing beach on the Tidal Reservoir near the Washington Monument, for which the sum of $3,000 was appropriated to be payable entirely out of the District revenues.

This proceeding was of little consequence, however, except as a precedent, as compared with the action of Congress taken during the years 1894, 1895, 1896 and 1897, in directing the repayment to the United States Treasury out of the general revenues of the District, of the unpaid balance of the amount advanced to pay the District's half of the expense incurred under the Act of Congress of July 15, 1882, and other acts for the extension of the water supply system of the District, under which the Lydecker Tunnel and Howard University reservoir had been constructed. This act had made the money so advanced repayable in twenty-five annual instalments, entirely out of the revenues of the Water Department. In 1894, thirteen instalments of this loan had been so paid, leaving twelve instalments or $735,364.73 unpaid. The entire interest on this debt, amounting to $254,135.39 was also paid out of the general revenues of the District. Congress by the Acts of August 7, 1894, March 2, 1895, June 11, 1896, and March 3, 1897, required the repayment of this entire sum in four years instead of in twelve years as had been intended when the loan was made, and required it to be paid out of the general revenues of the District instead of out of the revenues of the Water Department as originally prescribed. This, in addition to working an extreme immediate hardship upon the District, constituted a distinct violation of the half and half principle in withdrawing this large amount from the general revenues of the District to which as part of the so-called "appropriation fund," if it had not been withdrawn, Congress under the half and half principle would have been required to add an equal sum for defraying the expenses of the District. The amount, therefore, of which the financial resources of the

District for general purposes were thus deprived was twice the sum of that principal and interest, or $1,978,980.84.

Commissioner Macfarland was twice re-appointed, his term of service covering the period of practically ten years from May 9, 1900, to January 24, 1910. On October 16, 1902, Henry L. West took oath as successor to Commissioner Ross. Commissioner West served two terms, his service terminating with that of Commissioner Macfarland on January 24, 1910.

Commissioner Macfarland was born in Philadelphia, February 11, 1861. Coming to Washington shortly after the Civil War he was educated in the public schools and in Rittenhouse Academy, Washington. Thereafter he read law in the office of the Honorable W. B. Webb. In 1879 he entered the Washington bureau of the Boston Herald, and engaging otherwise as a correspondent and general writer. He was appointed Commissioner of the District by President McKinley. He delivered many addresses in the interest of the District, notably the Capital Centennial Address at the White House, on December 12, 1900, the District of Columbia Address at the Pan American Exposition September 3, 1901, and an address at the Louisiana Purchase Exposition on October 1, 1904.

Commissioner West was born at Factoryville, Staten Island, N. Y., August 20, 1859. Coming to Washington at an early age he began working for the Georgetown Courier when thirteen years old and later became in turn reporter and managing editor on the Washington Post. He was a contributor to several periodicals, writing the political articles in the Forum. He was honored by election to the Presidency of the Gridiron Club. A paragraph which he prepared for the Commissioners' annual report for the fiscal year 1908, was the first official recommendation of the Commissioners for the establishment of a public utilities commission in the District.

Colonel Biddle was succeeded in office by Major Jay J. Morrow, who served from May 2, 1907, to December 21, 1908; Major Spencer Cosby, who served from December 21, 1908, to March 15, 1909; and Major William V. Judson, who served from March 15, 1909, to February 28, 1913.

Commissioner Biddle was born at Detroit February 2, 1859. He was graduated from the United States Military Academy in 1881, and commissioned Captain in 1892. From 1891 to 1898 he was in charge of the river and harbor work at Nashville, Tenn. During the Spanish-American War he served as Lieut. Colonel and Chief Engineer of Volunteers, afterwards serving in Cuba, Porto Rico and the Philippine Islands from 1899 to 1901.

Commissioner Morrow was born in West Virginia and appointed from Pennsylvania to the Military Academy from which he was graduated June 12, 1891. He was commissioned Major of U. S. Volunteer Engineers on September 15, 1898, receiving an honorable discharge from the Volunteers on October 6, 1898.

Commissioner Cosby was born in Maryland October 2, 1867. He was graduated at the head of his class from the United States Military Academy in 1891. At the outbreak of the Spanish-American War he was appointed Major of Engineers in the Volunteer forces. In 1898 he served on the staff of Maj. Gen. Brooke during the operations in Porto Rico and on August 13 was engineer of the column commanded by Gen. Hains to turn the entrenched position of the Spanish on the heights north of Guayamas. From September, 1901, to April, 1903, he was in charge of the river and harbor work near Mobile, Ala., then went to Manila where he served as Engineer

Officer of the Department of Luzon and later in charge of the construction of light houses in the Philippine Islands.

Commissioner Judson was born in Indianapolis on February 16, 1865. He attended Harvard University two years and then entered the Military Academy from which he was graduated in 1888, later attending the U. S. Engineering school at Willets Point, N. Y. He served as Recorder of the Board of Engineers, U. S. A., and as member of the U. S. Board of Engineers for Rivers and Harbors and as Instructor in the U. S. Engineering School. As a Commissioner he was especially active and influential in securing the enactment of the provision in the District appropriation law approved March 4, 1913, investing the Commissioners with the duties of a public utilities commission.

Commissioners Macfarland and West were followed by Cuno H. Rudolph and John A. Johnston, whose terms extended from January 24, 1910, to July 19, 1913. Commissioners Rudolph and Johnston were followed by Oliver P. Newman and Frederick L. Siddons, whose terms commenced July 19, 1913. On February 28, 1913, Colonel Judson was succeeded as Engineer Commissioner by Lieutenant Colonel Chester Harding, who on that date took the oath of office at Gatun Canal Zone but did not report for duty as Commissioner until March 8, 1913.

Commissioner Rudolph was born at Baltimore, June 26, 1860. He came to Washington about 1891 having purchased an interest in the hardware firm of J. H. Chesley and Company, and later became President of the Rudolph and West Company. He was connected with West Brothers Brick Company and the National Metropolitan Bank, and also with the Washington Board of Trade and Chamber of Commerce. He has always taken a strong interest in civic betterment work and has been prominently associated with numerous organizations of that nature, notably the Associated Charities and Washington Play Grounds Association. He is President of the Washington Board of Trade and of the Second National Bank of Washington.

Commissioner Johnston was born in Allegheny, Pa., February 22, 1858. He was graduated from the Military Academy in 1879 and from the Ft. Leavenworth Infantry and Cavalry School in 1883. He attained the rank of Brigadier General in 1903. He saw several years of frontier service and was for some time instructor at Ft. Leavenworth and Jefferson Barracks, Mo. He organized the inaugural parades of President Cleveland in 1893 and President McKinley in 1897 and 1901; also the Grant Memorial parade in 1897, and the military parade at the Louisiana Purchase Exposition. During the Spanish-American War he was in charge of the mustering in and out of the volunteer forces in the Adjutant General's Office and was in charge of the reorganization of the General recruiting service incident to the increase of the Army.

Engineer Commissioner Lieutenant Colonel Chester Harding was born in Mississippi December 31, 1866. When five years old his family moved to Alabama where he resided until 1885, when he was appointed to the United States Military Academy, from which he was graduated in 1889. He was engaged in the harbor improvement work at Chicago, and St. Louis and in the improvement of the Mississippi River. He afterwards was instructor in civil engineering at the Military Academy. From April 16, 1902, until October 1, 1906, he was assistant to the Engineer Commissioner of the District of Columbia and superintended the construction of the new District Building. He afterwards was assigned to duty on the construction of the Panama Canal. He was detailed as a Commissioner of the District of Columbia, while on the latter duty, and took the oath of office as such at Gatun, Canal Zone, on February 28, 1913. He reported for duty as Commissioner on March 8, 1913.

Commissioner Newman was born in Lincoln, Nebraska, April 20, 1877, where he spent his childhood. He is the son of Mr. George C. Newman. He removed to Des Moines, Iowa, in 1884 and attended the public schools and academy there until the spring of 1897 when he was appointed a cadet at West Point. In the fall of 1898, he began to write magazine articles, and has been associated ever since with periodical and journalistic writing. He came to Washington in 1901 and has been, until appointed Commissioner, connected with the Washington Post, Washington Times and other newspaper work. He took the oath of office as a Commissioner of the District of Columbia, and entered upon duty as such, on July 19, 1913.

Commissioner Siddons was born in London, England, November 21, 1864. He is the son of Joachim Heyward Siddons and Mary Agnes Cameron Siddons. His father was an author and journalist and was in London at the time of his son's birth, although he was a citizen of the United States. He was graduated in law from Columbian, now George Washington, University in 1887 and was later employed in the Treasury Department. He was instructor on Constitutional Law, Evidence, and Bills and Notes in the National University Law School. He was also one of the Commissioners from the District of Columbia on Uniform State Laws. He is a member of the American Bar Association and a number of professional and fraternal organizations. He took the oath of office as a Commissioner of the District of Columbia, and entered upon duty as such, on July 19, 1913.

With the incoming of the first decade of the twentieth century, during which Commissioner Macfarland was President of the Board, came a new impulse to the progress of the city so noteworthy in its results that the succeeding period may well be regarded as constituting a distinct era in the history of the District of Columbia. At the beginning of this period the National Capital had no filtration plant; no adequate sewer system; no proper sewage disposal arrangements, all the sewage emptying into the water front of the city; and no District government building. Across the Potomac River, the old Long Bridge over which the troops had marched in the Civil War, caused the lower portion of the city including part of Pennsylvania Avenue, to be flooded at every large freshet. Railway crossings at grade were the cause of many serious accidents and two separate, inadequate and inartistic railroad stations, one of them occupying a central position across the principal park within the old city limits, gave rise to unending complaint.

Rock Creek Park and Potomac Park were just beginning to be developed; the Connecticut Avenue Bridge which now spans Rock Creek Park valley had not been planned, and other smaller bridges, for example, that over the Anacostia River, were, like those now spanning the Potomac in place of the removed Long Bridge, yet to be projected.

No provision had been made for a municipal hospital and a home for the aged poor or a reformatory for the minor offenders. There was no District of Columbia public library building in 1900; no publicly owned manual training or business high school buildings, and no plan for other high school or normal school buildings.

All of these physical needs of the District were supplied during the first decade of the century.

Besides expenditure by the United States and the District of Columbia of over five millions of dollars in connection with the abolition of railway grade crossings and the alteration of streets and the preparation of the plaza, the railroads expended over twenty-two millions of dollars, abolishing absolutely all grade crossings within the City of Washington and beginning the gradual abolition of those outside of the city and within the District; freeing the Mall from the servitude of the railway station and tracks and restoring it to the public park system, and building what was in 1908 the most beautiful railway station in the world, a noble gateway for the National Capital, since surpassed in size but not in beauty by the two new stations in New York City. All this work was done under the direction of the District Commissioners who by law were required to pass upon the plans and to certify to the proper execution of them, before the contribution of the United States and the District of Columbia could be paid over to the railroads.

Some of the largest items of expenditure for these improvements in that decade were new city and suburban sewer system and sewage disposal system, $5,136,373; filtration plant, $3,427,306; extension of high service water system, $2,674,552; District government building, $2,500,000; Highway Bridge across the Potomac River, $1,191,468; extension of 16th Street, $1,000,000; extension of Massachusetts Avenue, $500,000; Massachusetts Avenue Bridge across Rock Creek, $236,847; Connecticut Avenue Bridge and approaches across Rock Creek, $864,499; Anacostia Bridge and approaches, $453,730; Piney Branch Bridge, $125,766; District hospital site and tuberculosis hospital building, $203,259; improving Rock Creek, $100,000; a site and buildings for home for the aged and for a municipal colored industrial school (the first in the country), $265,000.

No account is taken in these figures of the ordinary extension and improvement of avenues and streets nor of the construction of new school buildings large and small, nor of new buildings for the fire and police departments which were all counted in the estimates and appropriations as part of the regular expenses of maintenance, although the cost of these improvements amounted in the aggregate to millions of dollars.

During the decade from 1900 to 1910, the annual appropriations increased from $8,725,946.18 for the fiscal year ending June 30, 1901, to $11,405,698.05 for the fiscal year ending June 30, 1911. These figures illustrate the material progress of the District of Columbia in that decade. There were years during the decade, however, in which larger appropriations were made including those for extraordinary municipal improvements, as for example in the years 1905, $12,374,080.10; 1908, $11,444,442.89; 1909, $12,154,977.04.

The assessed value of real property increased from $176,567,549 in 1900 to $285,153,771 in 1910.

During that period approximately twenty-three millions was expended upon extraordinary municipal improvements.

All these expenditures the taxpayers of the District of Columbia a total population of 278,718 in 1900 and 331,069 in 1910, shared equally with the rest of the population of the United States under the half and half plan of appropriations provided for in the act of June 11, 1878, creating the present form of government of the District of Columbia, just as they shared equally in the annual appropriations for the maintenance of the National Capital. Obviously the local revenues were insufficient to provide currently for such extraordinary expenditures on account of municipal improvements in Washington, or any other city, without unduly curtailing the expenditures necessary for the maintenance of all the ordinary municipal service and institutions. It was necessary, if these extensive municipal improvements were to be executed promptly, that the District of Columbia must borrow money in order to meet its half of the expenditures on that account for the particular year. Congress was, therefore, asked to loan the money from the United States Treasury at two per cent, which was done.

The Commissioners also asked Congress to authorize a gradual repayment of the money borrowed by the District of Columbia from the United States Treasury for the extraordinary improvements over such a period of years and at such a rate as would not necessitate the cutting of the appropriations for maintenance and development of the different municipal departments. They pointed out that the revenues of the District of Columbia were steadily increasing; that with the power of appropriation in its hands Congress could control the whole matter; and that by adopting the plan of gradual payments the United States Treasury would get back its money without any embarrassment to the orderly development of the municipal departments. They advocated a separate statement in the estimates of items for extraordinary municipal improvements and separate statements of the appropriations for that purpose; and a separate Capital account kept on the books of the Treasury where the accounts of the District appropriations were kept.

Congress, however, did not adopt this latter recommendation but made numerous advances aggregating about $10,000,000, at two per cent interest, making it repayable out of the District revenues at a rate so rapid that the entire amount was repaid by 1913.

Meanwhile Congress kept down the expenditures for the municipal services and after 1910 making no large appropriations for extraordinary improvements. If the Commissioners' plan had been followed, the improvements would have continued regularly, year after year, and with the increasing revenues of the District the amounts advanced by the United States Treasury would have been gradually repaid.

On the non-physical side, the District of Columbia advanced quite as remarkably as on the physical side. Its public school system was re-organized. Important improvements were made in the school laws, in the salaries of teachers, in the extension of manual training throughout the schools, as well as in the steady increase in school facilities.

In 1900 also began the re-organization of the public charities system, both with respect to governmental institutions and private institutions, utilized by the District government. The Board of Charities appointed in 1900 upon the recommendation of the Commissioners, took the most modern and enlightened view of public charity work and, supported by the Commissioners, presented recommendations to Congress, which at first, bitterly opposed by private interests and not well received by the Committees, finally prevailed in large measure. The Board of Children's Guardians, founded in 1885, was the only modern institution in the District charities system and while its work was known throughout the country and its example followed in many jurisdictions.

There were no municipal playgrounds in the District of Columbia in 1900. But they were soon recommended to Congress by the Commissioners after their usefulness had been shown by experience by philanthropic citizens in private associations. By the close of the decade the District was well equipped with such playgrounds. The National Playground Association was organized in Washington through the encouragement of Commissioner Macfarland, who especially advocated this form of public education.

The only municipal hospital, the so-called Alms House, was in 1900 between the District work house and the District jail on a tract of ground on the Anacostia at the eastern end of the city. The honest aged, and sick poor were associated with criminals and misdemeanants and inadequate provision was made at best in makeshift structures for the sick poor. The Commissioners obtained from Congress authority and money to buy a municipal hospital site and in 1901 bought for $73,639.40 a thirty-three acre tract on what is now Georgia Avenue, on high ground north of the city, upon which the beginnings of the municipal hospital in the shape of a tuberculosis hospital building, stands. They also obtained the authority and appropriation of Congress to have plans prepared for a general municipal hospital. The Commissioners also obtained from Congress authority and appropriation to purchase a large tract of land at the southeast corner of the District opposite Alexandria on the Potomac River.

Subsequently, Congress acting upon the report of a special penal commission approved by the Commissioners, authorized the Commissioners to provide for a work house and reformatory project on a farm purchased by the Commissioners near Occoquan in Virginia, at which the work of the former work house is carried on according to modern ideas.

All the other public charitable institutions were reorganized and improved, the work of the Board of Children's Guardians was supported and strengthened, and the auxiliary service furnished by private charitable institutions was put on a modern business basis under the supervision of the Board of Charities.

In 1900 there was in the District of Columbia no compulsory education law, no child labor law, no Juvenile Court and probation law, no law for the condemnation of insanitary buildings or widening of alleys into minor streets, no law for the regulation of employment agencies, no effective law for the regulation of the sale of poisons and the pharmacy business, no law for the examination and registration of nurses, no law for the examination of veterinary surgeons, no law for the regulation of savings banks or building associations, no law for the removal of nuisances from the property of non-resident owners, no law for the registration of tuberculosis eases or the free examination of sputum, no effective law against racetrack gambling. In 1910 laws covering all these subjects recommended by the Commissioners had been enacted and are being effectively enforced. There was no provision for the supervision of insurance companies in the District of Columbia in 1900 and the insurance business, without regulation, furnished opportunity to wildcat concerns which damaged the business of reputable companies while imperiling the interests of the insured. In 1902 a Department of Insurance was established which has improved the conditions of the insurance business in the District of Columbia.

Most of the departments of the District government, not already mentioned, were re-organized and put on a modern basis. Special action of Congress was obtained for the re-organization of the police, fire, and electrical departments, with better salaries and better facilities for the men. In 1900 there was no fire prevention inspection and no inspection of electrical installation both of which have been secured, resulting in a great reduction of fire loss.

Especial efforts were made to improve the Health Department with particular emphasis upon the protection of the milk supply and all that the Commissioners could do by calling a "milk conference" of experts in 1905 and using their executive power to carry out its recommendations, was done.

In all these matters the Commissioners advocated model laws for the District of Columbia, not only in its interest but for the sake of the rest of the country. Among their recommendations of that period were two, namely, for the creation of a Public Utilities Commission for the regulation of public utility corporations, and that for the reformation of the excise law and reduction of the number of saloons, which were approved by Congress in legislation in 1913. Other recommendations made then which Congress has not yet approved were for a civil service law to govern the District of Columbia offices; (meantime kept on a merit system by Commissioners' action); for the further improvement of sanitary conditions through the health department and otherwise; and the elimination of alley slums; for the further improvement of the charity system; for the regulation of assessment life insurance and the enactment of a model insurance law, and for the regulation of loan concerns in similar fashion to the regulation of savings banks and building associations.

During the decade from 1900 to 1910, in addition to what was repaid the United States Treasury on advances, ten million dollars was added to the sinking fund for the payment of the old bonded debt of the period preceding 1878.

The taxation of real estate, personal property, corporation franchises and licenses and other minor sources of revenue yielded about six million dollars a year. It meant that the inhabitants paid in round numbers sixteen dollars per capita per annum while all the rest of the United States pay in round numbers six cents per capita per annum for the maintenance and development of the common National Capital.

The Commissioners have for many years advocated a civil service law for the offices of the District government; thus far in vain. However, the Commissioners without express authority of law have maintained a civil service system on the principles of the United States law insofar as this has been possible. By arrangement with the civil service commission, affirmed by the court when it was attacked, examinations have been conducted by that Commission for all applicants for the fire and police departments and for all medical and auditing places under the District government. This has been all that could be done without securing special authority and appropriations from Congress.

This review of the recent advancement in the affairs of the District would be incomplete without some recognition of the interest shown by Congress and an acknowledgment of the services rendered by the members of the committees on the District of Columbia and of the sub-committees on appropriations. The committees an Public Buildings and Grounds, at the urgent request of the District Commissioners, provided the legislative authority for the erection of the District of Columbia government building, including the purchase of the site, costing in all nearly two and a half million dollars. The building was constructed under a commission composed of the District Commissioners and the Secretary of the

Treasury, with Captain Chester Harding, Corps of Engineers, U. S. Army, afterwards Engineer Commissioner of the District of Columbia, as the executive and supervising engineer. This building was formally opened on the Fourth of July, 1908, by appropriate exercises celebrating Independence Day, as well as the consummation of the hopes and efforts of years, and the beginnings of the "safe and sane" celebration of the Fourth of July.

The officers detailed from the Engineer Corps to assist the Engineer Commissioner are required by the Act of Congress of December 24, 1890 (26 Stat. 1113) to perform the duties of the Engineer Commissioner in the event of his absence from the District, or his disability, and many of them have so acted.

The officers who have been so detailed are Capt. Richard L. Hoxie, July 21, 1878 to August 1, 1884; Capt. Francis V. Greene, May 2, 1879 to March 3, 1885; Lieut. C. McD. Townsend, August 1, 1884 to March 6, 1886; Capt. F. A. Mahan, March 25, 1885 to May 27, 1886; Capt. Eugene Griffin, May 27, 1886 to March 6, 1888; Capt. Thos. W. Symons, June 5, 1886 to November 1, 1889; Capt. S. S. Leach, March 6, 1888 to June 2, 1888; Capt. James L. Lusk, June 2, 1888 to March 1, 1893; Capt. Win. T. Rossell, November 1, 1889 until detailed as a Commissioner, District of Columbia, October 15, 1891; Capt. Gustav J. Fiebeger, October 31, 1891 to May 27, 1896; Capt. George McC. Derby, March 1, 1893 to October 8, 1894; Capt. Edward Burr, October 9, 1894 to April 28, 1898; Capt. Lansing H. Beach, October 30, 1894 until detailed as a Commissioner, District of Columbia, June 1, 1898; Capt. William E. Craighill, February 28, 1899 to September 15, 1899; Capt. David Du B. Gaillard, July 21, 1899 to March 6, 1901; Capt. H. C. Newcomer, December 27, 1899 to December 23, 1903; Capt. Chester Harding, April 16, 1901 to October 1, 1906; Capt. Jay J. Morrow, January 4, 1904, until sworn as a Commissioner, District of Columbia, May 2, 1907; Capt. William Kelly, September 29, 1906 to July 2, 1910; Capt. Edward M. Markham, August 14, 1907 to August 28, 1912; Capt. Mark Brooke, June 15, 1910, to; Capt. Julian L. Schley, October 8, 1912, to; Capt. Roger G. Powell, October 15, 1913, to

It is a peculiarity of that law that it only vests the senior and junior officers so detailed with the duty to act as an alternate Commissioner; so that when three assistants are detailed for that duty the one of intermediate rank does not become an acting Commissioner in such event but may be subordinate to his junior in rank. The concurrent detail of three assistants has only occurred twice; the first time from 1894 to 1896, when Captains Fieberger, Burr and Beach were in that position, and the second time in 1913 when Captains Brooke, Schley and Powell were on that detail.

Five of the persons who have been nominated by the President of the United States for the office of Commissioner of the District of Columbia were not confirmed by the Senate. These nominees were John F. Olmstead, who was nominated by President Arthur on the 18th of December, 1882, and his name withdrawn January 13, 1883; William B. Webb who had been Commissioner for one term, was nominated for re-appointment by President Cleveland on January 14, 1889, but he was continued in office until May 21, 1889, when President Harrison issued a recess commission to John W. Douglass as Mr. Webb's successor, and on December 4, 1889, sent Mr. Douglass' nomination to the Senate; Francis P. B. Sands, was nominated by President' Cleveland on February 16, 1897, in place of John W. Ross whose term had then expired. Mr. Sands was not confirmed and Mr. Ross was reappointed by President McKinley. Cuno H. Rudolph and James F. Oyster, who were nominated by President Taft on January 21, 1913.

The omission to confirm the latter two was not based on any personal objections but was due to the sentiment that the incoming President Woodrow Wilson was entitled to the opportunity to select the principal authorities to administer the municipal affairs of the National Capital during his term of office.

CHAPTER X.

Municipal Suffrage

The right to vote in the District of Columbia for President of the United States and other national offices existed at the time the territory embraced in the District was ceded to Congress, and was exercised by the qualified voters in the District in the Presidential election of November, 1800, and remained in force until the first Monday in December, 1800, when the exclusive jurisdiction of Congress over the District took effect.

The qualified voters in the portion derived from Maryland were at that time,

"All free men above 21 years of age having a freehold of 50 acres of land in the county in which they offer to vote, and residing therein, and all free men having property in this State above the value of £30 current money, and having resided in the county in which they offer to vote one whole year next preceding the election, shall have a right of suffrage, etc." (Constitution of Maryland).

When the District ceased to be a part of Maryland, its residents, no longer being residents of any county of Maryland, consequently lost the right to vote in the elections of that State.

The qualification of voters in the portion of the District derived from Virginia at the time of the cession was the possession of a certain amount of real property in the county in which the vote was cast. (Vol. 8, p. 306, Hening's Statutes at Large of Virginia). When that part of the District ceased to be under the jurisdiction of any county of Virginia, that right of suffrage in the District accordingly expired.

The citizens of the District of Columbia were subsequently vested with the right of suffrage in municipal matters, as hereinafter shown: but the residents of the portion of the District of Columbia, outside of the city of Washington and of Georgetown, had no right of suffrage, except at the special election to adopt a code of laws in 1858, from the first Monday of December, 1800, when the Jurisdiction of the United States over the District took effect, until the 20th of April, 1871, when they were vested with that function under the territorial Act of February 21, 1871, and possessed it until June 20, 1874, when the territorial form of government for the District was abolished.

With respect to the purpose of the Constitution in regard to local suffrage at the Seat of Government, the following opinions are of interest.

On a motion in the House of Representatives on December 31, 1800, to recommit a bill concerning the District of Columbia, Mr. Harper, in reply to an observation that the people of the District had continued for one hundred years to live happily under their respective State governments, and therefore it was not necessary for Congress to legislate at all on the subject, said:

"But the provision of the Constitution on this subject had not been made with this view. It was made to bestow dignity and independence on the Government of the Union. It was to protect it from such outrages as had occurred when it was differently situated, when it was without competent legislative, executive, and judicial power to insure to itself respect. While the government was under the guardianship of State laws, those laws might be inadequate to its protection, or there might exist a spirit hostile to the General Government, or, at any rate, indisposed to give it proper protection. This was one reason, among others, for the provisions of the

Constitution confirmed and carried into effect by the acts of Maryland and Virginia, and by the act of Congress. " Mr. Madison stated in the Federalist that:

"The indispensable necessity of complete authority at the seat of government carries its own evidence with it. It is a power exercised by every legislature of the Union, I might say of the world, by virtue of its general supremacy. Without it, not only the public authority might be insulted and its proceedings be interrupted with impunity, but a dependence of the members of the General Government on the State comprehending the seat of the government for protection in the exercise of their duty might bring on the national councils an imputation of awe or influence equally dishonorable to the Government and dissatisfactory to the other members of the confederacy. This consideration has the more weight as the gradual accumulation of public improvements at the stationary residence of the government would be both too great a public pledge to be left in the hands of a single State and would create so many obstacles to a removal of the Government as still further to abridge its necessary independence. The extent of this Federal district is sufficiently circumscribed to satisfy every jealousy of an opposite nature. And as it is to be appropriated to this use with the consent of the State ceding it; as the State will no doubt provide in the compact for the rights and the consent of the citizens inhabiting it; as the inhabitants will find sufficient inducements of interest to become willing parties to the cession; as they will have had their voice in the election of the government which is to exercise authority over them; as a municipal legislature for local purposes derived from their own suffrages will of course be allowed them; and as the authority of the legislature of the State, and of the inhabitants of the ceded part of it, to concur in the cession will be derived from the whole people of the State in their adoption of the Constitution, every imaginable objection seems to be obviated."

The first grant of municipal suffrage in the City of Washington was conferred by the Act of Congress approved May 3, 1802, which provided for "The city council to be elected annually, by ballot, in a general ticket, by the free white male inhabitants of full age, who have resided twelve months in the city, and paid taxes therein the year preceding the election being held." (2 Stat. 196.) The Mayor was appointable by the President of the United States.

An Act of Congress, approved May 4, 1812, qualified the suffrage by conferring it on "every free white male citizen of lawful age, who shall have resided in the city of Washington for the space of one year next preceding the day of election, and shall be a resident of the ward in which he shall offer to vote, and who shall have been assessed on the books of the corporation not less than two months prior to the day of election." These suffragists were entitled to vote for a board of aldermen of eight members, and a board of common council 12 members, who elected the Mayor by joint ballot, on the 2nd Monday of June, (ib. 723).

The election of the Mayor by the qualified voters, instead of by the Councils, was next brought within the right of suffrage, and the right restricted to citizens of the United States, and to those assessed " for the year ending on the 31st day of December next preceding the election," and who "shall have paid all taxes legally assessed and due on personal property." Act approved May 15, 1820.

A property qualification was a prerequisite to the right to vote until the election held on the first Monday in June, 1848, under the Act of Congress approved May

17, 1848. Section 5 of that act modified the right of suffrage, by defining the age of the voter as 21 years, who should be subject to and have paid a school tax, and not be a person *non compos mentis*, a vagrant, a pauper, or have been convicted of any infamous crime.

At the special election in the adoption of a Code of Laws for the District, "Every free white male citizen of the United States, above the age of twenty-one years, who shall have resided in the District of Columbia for one year next preceding the said fifteenth day of February, 1858," was allowed to vote, pursuant to a proclamation of the President of the United States, dated December 24, 1857.

An Act of May 16, 1856, provides that "Whereas native-born citizens, resident of the city of Washington, who arrive at the age of twenty-one years between the thirtieth day of December next preceding the election and the day of election are not allowed to vote at such election. That no person, being naturalized between said day of December and the day of the succeeding election shall be entitled to vote at such preceding election." (11 Stat. 15).

All voters in Washington and Georgetown were required by the Act approved May 20, 1862, to take and subscribe an oath or affirmation of allegiance to the Constitution and Government of the United States.

An Act of Congress, approved June 1, 1864, seems to be the first statute mentioning the registration of voters; but that was a registration simultaneous with the offer to vote, where the person offering to vote had not been registered; and prescribes an oath as to residence. Publicity of lists of voters by posting and newspaper publication prior to elections was first required by an Act of Congress of February 5, 1867.

On November 6, 1865, the feeling against the proposition to grant municipal suffrage to negroes in the District of Columbia, found expression in the Board of Common Council of the City of Washington, by the introduction of a resolution which passed that body on the 13th of that month and the Board of Aldermen on the 20th of the same month and became a law as follows:

CHAP. 203. "Joint Resolution providing for a special election to ascertain the sentiments of the people of Washington on the question of negro suffrage.

"Resolved by the Board of Aldermen and Board of Common Council of the City of Washington, That in the event that any bill be introduced in Congress for the admission of the colored man by this city to the right of suffrage, that the Mayor be, and he is hereby, authorized and directed to call the Councils together within two days' notice, for the purpose of taking into consideration measures for holding a special election to ascertain the sentiments of the people on the subject.

"Approved November 23, 1865." On December 11 the Mayor, in consonance with the spirit of that resolution, reported to the Common Council that a bill had been introduced in both houses of Congress to extend to colored persons the right of suffrage in the District. This report was referred to a special committee of the Common Council which on the 14th of that month reported a joint resolution which resulted in the passage of the following ordinance in which the Board of Aldermen concurred on the same date:

CHAP. 218.

"An Act authorizing a Special Election to ascertain the opinion of the people of Washington on the question of Negro Suffrage.

"Whereas, Several bills have been introduced in Congress having in view the extension of the elective franchise, in this city, so as to confer its privileges upon the negro population; and, whereas, the members of the National Legislature, to whom is committed the protection of the interests of the people of the National Metropolis, should be correctly informed of the sentiments of this community on a question so materially affecting their present and future interests, as well as the interests of the country generally: Therefore,

"Be it enacted by the Board of Aldermen and Board of Common Council of the City of Washington, That the Mayor be, and he is hereby, authorized and directed to cause a special election to be held on Thursday, the 21st day of December, 1865, and cause polls to be opened on that day, and to be kept open from eight o'clock in the morning till six o'clock in the evening, to enable the legal voters of the City of Washington to give expression, in a formal manner, to their opinions on the propriety of extending the elective franchise to the negro population, now residents, or hereafter to become residents, within the limits of this Corporation.

"Sec. 3. The Mayor shall transmit a copy of the returns to the presiding officer of each House of Congress to be laid before those bodies, and cause the same to be published in the newspapers of this city.* * *

"Approved December 16, 1865." In pursuance of this ordinance a special election was held on the 21st day of December, 1865, the result of which is set forth in the following letter from the Mayor to the President of the Senate of the United States:

Washington City, Mayor's Office,
January 6, 1866. Hon. L. F. S. Foster,
President of the Senate of the United States. Sir:

" I have the honor in compliance with an act of the Councils of this city, approved December 16, 1865, to transmit through you to the Senate of the United States the result of an election held on Thursday, 21st of December, to ascertain the opinion of the people of Washington on the question of negro suffrage, at which the vote was 6,626, segregated as follows:

Against negro suffrage 6,591
For negro suffrage 35
Majority against negro suffrage 6,556

"This vote, the largest, with but two exceptions, ever polled in this city, conclusively shows the unanimity of sentiment of the people of Washington in opposition to the extension of the right of suffrage to that class, and that its integrity may be properly appreciated by the Senate, I give the aggregate of the vote cast at the five elections immediately preceding, for Mayor.

"Approved December 22, 1865.

"1856, 5,840; 1858, 6,813; 1860, 6,975; 1862, 4,816; 1864, 5,720.

"No others, in addition to this minority of thirty-five, are to be found in this community who favor the existence of the right of suffrage to the class, and in the manner proposed, excepting those who have already memorialized the Senate in its favor, and who, with but little association, less sympathy, and no community of interest or affinity with the citizens of Washington, receive here from the general government temporary employment, and having, at the National Capital, a residence, limited only to the duration of a presidential term, claim, and invariably exercise the elective franchise elsewhere.

"The people of this city, claiming an independence of thought, and the right to express it, have thus given a grave and deliberate utterance, in an unexaggerated way, to their opinion and feeling on this subject.

"This unparalleled unanimity of sentiment which pervades all classes of this community in opposition to the extension of the right of suffrage to that class engenders an earnest hope that Congress, in according to this expression of their wishes, the respect and consideration they would, as individual members, yield to those whom they immediately represent, would abstain from the exercise of its absolute power, and so avert an impending future, apparently so objectionable to those over whom, by the fundamental law

of the land, they have 'exclusive jurisdiction.'

With much respect, I am, sir,

Your own and the Senate's

Obedient servant,

Richard Wallace, Mayor."

A similar election was held in Georgetown on the 28th day of December, 1865, in pursuance of the following resolution:

A resolution in regard to Negro Suffrage.

"Whereas it is proposed in the Congress of the United States so to amend the charter of Georgetown as to extend the elective franchise to persons of color in said town; and whereas such legislation, in the opinion of this Corporation, is wholly uncalled for, and would be an act of grievous oppression, against which a helpless community have no defense, except by an appeal to the sense of justice of Congress; and whereas it may tend to avert this evil to have an expression of opinion from the voters of the town: Therefore,

" Resolved, That the polls be opened on the twenty-eighth day of December inst., and be kept open on said day between the hours of 9 o'clock a. m. and 6 p. m., at the several precincts of the town, under the direction of the Commissioners of Election, for a special balloting by the qualified voters of the town upon the question whether they are in favor of the extension of the right of suffrage by law to the colored inhabitants of said town or not — those in favor of said extension to vote 'Yes,' and those opposed thereto to vote 'No.'" The result of that election was 712 against negro suffrage and one vote in favor of it.

An Act of Congress, adopted January 8, 1867, which was passed over the veto of President Andrew Johnson, abolished all racial distinctions respecting suffrage in the District, and provided for registration of voters prior to election, and limited the right of voting to those whose names were on the list of registered voters. This law is the first enactment which omits the word "white" as a voter's qualification. But all "distinction of race color or previous condition of servitude" as a qualification of suffrage in the District of Columbia was abolished in terms, by an Act of May 31, 1870. (16 Stat. 14).

The latest right of suffrage in the District of Columbia was granted by an Act of Congress of February 21, 1871, (16 Stat. 421), as follows:

"Sec. 7. And be it further enacted, That all male citizens of the United States, above the age of twenty-one years, who shall have been actual residents of said

191

District for three months prior to the passage of this act, except such as are non-compos mentis and persons convicted of infamous crimes, shall be entitled to vote at said election, in the election district or precinct in which he shall then reside, and shall have so resided for thirty days immediately preceding said election and shall be eligible to any office within the said District, and for all subsequent elections twelve months' prior residence shall be required to constitute a voter; but the legislative assembly shall have no right to abridge or limit the right of suffrage." (18 Stat. 116). The Registration Officers and Superintendents of Elections, the time, place, and manner of conducting the first election under that law, were designated in an undated proclamation by the Governor and Judges of the Supreme Court of the District of Columbia, as directed by section 5 of that law. The first election under that law was held on Tuesday, April 20, 1871, from 8 a. m. until 7 p. m. But the like duty as to subsequent elections was vested in and exercised by the Legislative Assembly and Governor.

The Act of the General Assembly of Maryland, passed December 25, 1789, incorporating Georgetown prescribed respecting municipal suffrage in that town, "that all free men above twenty-one years of age, and having visible property within the state above the value of thirty pounds current money, and having resided in said town one whole year next before the first day of January next, shall have the right to assemble at such place in said town as the said mayor, recorder, and aldermen, or any three or more of them shall appoint, and proceed to elect viva voce," etc.

A property qualification in Georgetown continued until August 11, 1856, when an Act of Congress of that date granted the suffrage to every free white male citizen of the United States who had attained the age of twenty-one years and had resided in Georgetown one year immediately preceding the election and been subject to and paid a school tax for the year.

By the Act of February 21, 1871, above cited, Georgetown became amenable to the same laws respecting suffrage, as the rest of the District.

When the Government created by the Act of February 21, 1871, was abolished on June 20, 1874, all right of municipal suffrage anywhere in the District of Columbia was extinguished and has not been restored.

Although Congress may confer the privilege of self-government upon the people of the District of Columbia, as an administrative expedient, as it has done, to save it from the toil and care which exclusive legislation required by the constitution would involve, or from considerations of policy or sentiment, just as it has since vested the Commissioners with power to make police and other regulations in the nature of the ordinances of other municipalities, it is obvious that local suffrage cannot be granted to the people of the District as a right, without an amendment to the constitution to that effect. In short, Congress has no power to divest itself of complete responsibility for the government of the National Capital.

CHAPTER XI

General History.

At the time of the removal of the Government to Washington in 1800 the population of the city consisted of 2,464 white persons, 623 slaves, and 123 free colored persons; 3,210 persons in all. The population of Georgetown was 2,993. At this time the public buildings consisted of the original north wing of the Capitol — the portion now occupied by the Supreme Court; the President's house; the Treasury building, a plain, two-story brick structure containing thirty rooms, which occupied the site of the south front of the present edifice; and a similar building at the southwest corner of the grounds of the President's house, known at first as the War Office and later as the Navy Department building.

During the first decade of the city's existence the population nearly trebled, the census of 1810 showing it in that year to be 8,208, of whom about 6,000 were whites, about 1,300 slaves, and about 900 free colored persons. The population of Georgetown was in that year 4,948. This decade, which covered the mayoralty of Mr. Brent, witnessed a considerable development in the condition of the city. In 1803 Congress spent $13,466 in the improvement of Pennsylvania Avenue, which at the time of the removal of the Government was almost impassable. This appropriation was largely due to the interest of President Jefferson, who was also responsible for the planting of the double row of poplars which adorned Pennsylvania Avenue from the foot of the Capitol grounds to Fifteenth Street.

The amended charter of 1804 provided "for the establishment and superintendence of schools," and an act of the City Councils of December 5 of that year provided "that the superintendence of public schools within the City of Washington shall be placed under the direction of a board of thirteen trustees, whereof seven shall be annually chosen, by the joint ballots of the Council, from among the residents of the city, and six be annually chosen by individuals contributing to the promotion of schools, as hereinafter provided."

The Board was given power to receive donations for the schools. A small charge was made for pupils whose parents or guardians were able to pay for them, but for those who could not afford tuition fee the board made provision, keeping the knowledge of such free pupils to themselves, that the children should not be mortified by the fact.

It was further provided that so much of the net proceeds of taxes laid or to be laid on slaves, dogs, licenses for carriages and hacks, for ordinaries and taverns, for retailing wines and spirituous liquors, for billiard tables, for theatrical and other amusements, and for hawkers and peddlers up to fifteen hundred dollars should be appropriated as the trustees might decide to be necessary for the education of the poor of the city.

All contributors to the amount of ten dollars, and over, were entitled to meet and elect six trustees for the schools, to remain in office one year. At this election each voter had as many votes as the sums of ten dollars he had contributed. In addition to these six trustees, the City Councils at another meeting, elected seven other trustees, to hold office for one year. President Jefferson was made one of the first trustees and president of the board and accepted the duty in a courteous letter to Mayor Brent, dated August 14, 1805.

The first committee appointed to solicit contributions succeeded in getting $3,782 from 191 persons. President Jefferson contributed $200 of this amount.

The board made a distinction between " poor children " and pay pupils, thus: "In these schools poor children shall be taught reading, writing, grammar, arithmetic, and such branches of the mathematics as may qualify them for the professions they are intended to follow; and they shall receive such other instruction as is given to pay pupils, as the board may, from time to time, direct; and pay pupils shall, besides, be instructed in geography and in the Latin language. " Pay pupils were charged five dollars a quarter for tuition.

Each principal, in connection with the superintending committee, directed his school, but was subjected to intervention by the board. He received $500 a year, payable quarterly. If the number of pay pupils in his school exceeded fifty, his salary might be increased by the board. Out of this salary he was required to pay the rent of the school house, for fuel and other incidentals, as well as for assistant teachers. Fifty dollars a year was allowed for "paper, pens, ink, and books necessary for the instruction of poor children."

Toward the close of the first decade of the century a school society was organized in Georgetown with Thomas Corcoran as its president. This movement resulted in the establishment in 1811 of a school on the Lancastrian system, supported by popular subscription, at the head of which was placed Mr. Robert Ould, an Englishman, who had been recommended by Joseph Lancaster, the founder of this system of schools. In 1812 the corporation provided for an addition to the school building for the accommodation of female pupils.

There were numerous private schools in Washington in its earliest days and Georgetown had several good institutions of learning when Washington was originated. The Reverend A. T. McCormick organized a school on Capitol Hill in 1802, where he taught the common branches of studies. This school was successfully continued for many years.

In 1803 Francis Donnelly opened another school "in a building then lately occupied as an auction store, near the West Market." This same year Mr. J. Sewell opened a school on F Street.

Georgetown, which was a town of importance when the Federal City was born, had several good schools before the Government became established in Washington. The most important of these was established in 1785, by the Reverend John Carroll, First Archbishop of Baltimore, together with five men of influence in the community. These gentlemen established an "Academy at Georgetown, Potomac River, Maryland."

In 1789 this enterprise was furthered by the erecting of the "South East College" building, and in 1791 the school was opened to students. Later the institution was called the "College of Georgetown." In 1815 this college had so grown in efficiency that an Act of Congress was passed, raising it to the rank of a university, which was empowered to confer degrees in the arts and sciences.

In 1803, the Columbian Academy of Georgetown, under the supervision of Reverend David Wiley, was doing good work, with seventy-five pupils in attendance.

A school worthy of special note is one that was built in 1807, the first school established for colored children. George Bell, an ex-slave, was the leader of the movement for this school, and he was greatly assisted by Nicholas Franklin and

Moses Liverpool, who had also been slaves. Bell and his wife had bought the freedom of one another.

This school had a one-story frame building, and was taught by a Mr. Lowe, a white man. The school continued for a few years and then ceased, but in 1818 the building, which had been used as a residence, was again converted into a school house and a school for negro children started in it by the "Resolute Beneficial Society," of which William Costin was President, James Harris, secretary, and George Bell, treasurer. A night school was added and both the night and day schools continued several years. The first teacher of this restored school was a Mr. Pierpont, of Massachusetts, and the next was the first negro to teach in the District, John Adams.

The social life of Washington from the beginning centered largely about the President's house and took its character from the entertainments given there. When the Government was removed to Washington in 1800 it found an established social caste among the old residents of Georgetown and the owners of estates in the surrounding country, both in Maryland and in Virginia. The Georgetown balls or assemblies had been noteworthy events since the Revolution. For some time following the removal of the Government to Washington the dearth of accommodations in the new city caused much of the social activity of the time to continue to center at Georgetown.

Mrs. Adams, on her arrival at the new capital, continued the formal "drawing rooms" which President and Mrs. Washington had inaugurated in Philadelphia; but President Jefferson, on coming into office, threw down the social barriers which his predecessors had established and admitted all classes to his receptions. He, however, maintained a special degree of dignity at the state dinners which were usually presided over by Mrs. Madison, occasionally with the assistance of one of the President's married daughters.

On March 4, 1801, Mr. Jefferson, in company with a number of friends, walked to the Capitol from his lodgings at the northwest corner of C Street and New Jersey Avenue. His entrance to the Capitol was greeted by a salute from the local Artillery Company, and he was accompanied to the Senate Chamber by the heads of Departments and the Marshal of the District of Columbia.

From the meagre accounts of his second inaugural on March 4, 1805, it appears to have been quite as unostentatious as his first, and that he rode on horseback from the White House to the Capitol, attended by his Secretary and groom, along Pennsylvania Avenue.

Washington society received new impetus with the inauguration of the fourth President of the country, James Madison, in 1809. The new mistress of the White House, the charming "Dolly" Madison, who had so often helped Mr. Jefferson to entertain his guests, now had her own way about managing the Capital's social affairs, and she soon caused the simplicity of Jefferson's administration to be forgotten in contemporaneous gaieties.

This change commenced with the inauguration, which was inducted with much ceremony and impressiveness. Militia of Georgetown and Alexandria conducted the new President to the Capitol where, in the Hall of Representatives, Chief Justice Marshall administered to him the oath of office.

In the evening a grand ball was given, the first inaugural ball in Washington. Over four hundred guests attended this fete. It is recorded that the excitement of the day added much animation to Mr. Madison's "pale, student face," and Mrs. Madison, " resplendent in a gown of yellow velvet, her neck and arms hung with pearls, " was the " center of all eyes. "

Two weddings took place in the President's House during the incumbency of President Madison. On March 11, 1811, Lucy Payne, the widow of a nephew of President Washington and sister-in-law of President Madison, was married to Justice Todd, of the Supreme Court; and in 1812 Anna Todd, a cousin of Mrs. Madison, was married to Representative Jackson, a great-uncle of "Stonewall" Jackson.

The most noteworthy incident in the early history of the city was the coming of the British under General Ross and Admiral Cockburn in August, 1814.

Throughout the year 1813 a British fleet had been in control of Chesapeake Bay, and in retaliation for the burning of Newark in Canada by the Americans had committed many barbarities among the towns and inhabitants along its shores. They had, however, for a long time been dissuaded from an attack on Washington by the belief that both the land and water approaches were guarded by fortifications and adequate forces of troops.

In July, 1814, the fleets of Admiral Cockburn and Admiral Cochrane united in the Chesapeake and alarmed by this demonstration the Government made hasty preparations for defense against a possible advance towards Washington. General W. H. Winder, who had seen service in the Northwest but was without much military experience, was authorized to raise 93,000 men by draft. The force actually raised consisted of less than 1,000 regulars, together with a brigade of District militia under General Walter Smith, of Georgetown, numbering about 1,000; a brigade of 2,200 militia from Baltimore under General Stansbury, and two other Maryland regiments and one from Virginia, giving about 1,800 additional men. Included in these forces were eighteen pieces of artillery. The regulars consisted of 520 sailors and marines under Commodore Barney and 300 regular troops under Lieut. Col. Scott. The militia had been raised with the stipulation that they should not be called into service until the British forces had landed and were consequently undrilled and otherwise unprepared for the exigencies of a campaign.

The British sent one fleet up the Potomac as far as Alexandria from which they took away several merchant vessels. The other force pursued Commodore Barney's gunboat flotilla into the Patuxent River, where Barney landed his men and burned his vessels. The British land forces, which arrived at this time from Bermuda, consisted of four thousand of Wellington 's veterans. The entire British force, including the complement of sailors and marines from the fleet numbered about 5,000 men. This force proceeded by leisurely stages as far as Melwood, twelve miles from the city. From this point a feint was made to approach Washington over the Eastern Branch bridge, but the route was then changed to Bladensburg. The American militia had reached the city by forced marches and many of them were exhausted by fatigue and sickness. One regiment, which arrived the night before the battle, was delayed so long in receiving its arms that it did not reach the field.

Upon the near approach of the British, Stansbury's Baltimore brigade was stationed at Bladensburg while General Winder, misled by the British feint, took position with the main body of the American forces at the Eastern Branch bridge.

On the morning of August 24, learning that the British had gone towards Bladensburg, General Winder hastened to that point, arriving at about the same time as the British and taking position about a mile in the rear of Stansbury's brigade. Stansbury's line was quickly driven back by the British who advanced to the main line of the American forces. The latter were demoralized by the Congreve rockets of the British and quickly gave way under General Winder's orders to retire. Commodore Barney's forces, however, maintained their position resolutely until their position was flanked and their commander seriously injured.

Lieutenant Gleig, of the English forces, in his account of the battle said:

"Had they (the American forces) conducted themselves with coolness and resolution, it is not conceivable how the day could have been won. But the fact is, that with the exception of the sailors from the gunboats, under the command of Commodore Barney, no troops could behave worse than they did. The skirmishers were driven in as soon as attacked. The first line gave way without offering the slightest resistance, and the left of the main body was broken within half an hour after it was seriously engaged. Of the sailors, however, it would be injustice not to speak in terms which their conduct merits. They were employed as gunners, and not only did they serve their guns with a quickness and precision which astonished their assailants, but they stood till some of them were actually bayoneted, with fuses in their hands; nor was it until their leader was wounded and taken, and they saw themselves deserted on all sides by the soldiers, that they quit the field."

General Ross reported his loss as 64 killed and 185 wounded and missing, most of his casualties resulting from the attack on Barney's battery. An English authority states this to have been the greatest number in proportion to the men engaged of any which had been inflicted upon English troops in battle. The American loss was 26 killed and 50 wounded.

No stand was made by the American forces until Tenleytown was reached from which point they again retired to Montgomery Court House.

The British followed closely and arrived at the Capitol grounds at six in the evening. That night they burned the Capitol, President's House, Treasury, State and Navy buildings, and a number of private houses on Capitol Hill. While the flames were rising one of the most terrific thunder storms in the history of the city took place and the torrents of rain extinguished the fires in the Capitol and President's House in time to preserve the walls.

Commodore Tingey in command of the Navy Yard, acting under instructions, burned large quantities of material and a vessel which was under construction as well as two adjacent privately-owned rope walks.

A detachment of British soldiers went to Greenleaf's point to destroy the stores at the Arsenal there. All the powder had been thrown into a dry well into which a British soldier threw a lighted torch. An explosion followed which resulted in the killing or wounding of nearly one hundred British soldiers.

Fearing an attack by the militia, the British withdrew the following night, leaving their wounded to the mercy of the Americans.

Just before the arrival of the British in the city, Mrs. Madison, escorted by a party of gentlemen, left the White House and crossing the Long Bridge took refuge in a tavern in Virginia where she was later joined by the President. The burning of the Long Bridge compelled them to make their return by boat.

The residence of the President was then established at the Octagon House at the corner of New York Avenue and 18th Street and in 1815 removed to the residence at the northwest corner of 19th and Pennsylvania Avenue where it remained until the restoration of the Executive Mansion.

After the withdrawal of the British Congress for a time occupied the Blodget Hotel building which had been acquired for the use of the general Post Office, and later moved into a building erected for the purpose by an organization of Washington citizens. This building stood on the southeast corner of First and A Streets northeast. It was for a long time known as the " Old Capitol Building " and was used during the Civil War as a military prison.

On October 18, 1814, the City Councils of Washington voted $300 for a sword to be presented to Commodore Barney " as a testimony of their respect for the gallantry and intrepidity displayed by himself and the officers and men under his command in the defense of the city."

On March 5, 1817, the inauguration of President Monroe took place. On that day the President and Vice-President elect, were escorted by a large body of militia to Congress Hall. There they were met by the ex-President, Senators and Judges of the Supreme Court. From the Eastern balcony the new President delivered his address and took the oath of office, which was administered by Chief-Justice Marshall.

During Mr. Monroe's administration levees at the President's mansion continued, though not so frequently as under his predecessor. Mrs. Monroe, owing to physical disability, did not mingle as much in society as had Mrs. Madison, but she performed the honors of the White House in a creditable manner, assisted by her daughter, Mrs. George Hay. Mrs. Monroe had been a forceful and dignified member of society for years. When abroad with her husband in 1803, while he was United States minister to France, she succeeded in having Madame LaFayette, who was imprisoned at LaForce, set at liberty.

March 20, 1820, witnessed a wedding in the East room of the rebuilt White House, when Maria Monroe married her cousin, Samuel L. Gouverneur, her father's private secretary.

A gloom was thrown over Washington people in the midst of these social activities, caused by the news of the death of Stephen Decatur, who was shot in a duel with Commodore James Barron.

The quarrel out of which this duel grew was the result of the surrender of the frigate Chesapeake by Commodore Barron to a search and the impressment of three seamen by the British frigate Leopard off the capes of Virginia in 1807. Decatur was one of a coterie of officers of the Navy who never forgave Barron for surrendering, and when in 1818 Barron sought the command of the newly constructed ship Columbus, Decatur opposed his appointment so persistently and offensively that under the code of the times Barron after a protracted correspondence with Decatur had little choice but to eventually challenge Decatur to a duel.

The affair occurred at Bladensburg on March 22, 1820. The men fought with pistols at eight paces. Both fell at the first fire; Barron seriously wounded, and Decatur suffering from a shot in the groin from which he died several days later.

In the fall of 1822, ten thousand people attended the races in Washington, to witness a contest between "Eclipse" and "Sir Charles," two famous Virginia racers.

More than a million dollars were staked on this event, some excitable persons staking and losing all they possessed of worldly goods. "Eclipse" proved worthy of his name, outdistancing "Sir Charles," and making a fortune for his owner, including the stake of $5,000 and many thousands more in wagers.

The year 1824 was made memorable by the visit of General Lafayette, who arrived from Baltimore on October 12 of that year and was welcomed by elaborate public ceremonies and an enthusiastic display of popular affection. He was given a municipal dinner at the Franklin House Hotel, and during his stay many social entertainments were given in his honor.

In anticipation of General Lafayette's visit Mayor Smallwood constructed a reception room as an addition to his residence, which is still standing at 324 Virginia Avenue, southeast. It was Mayor Smallwood's expectation to personally entertain the distinguished guest of the city, but his untimely death on September 30, 1824, twelve days before Lafayette's arrival, prevented the carrying out of his plan.

The census for 1820 showed the population of Washington at that time to be 13,247, of whom about three-fourths were white. The slaves, and free colored persons were about equal in number, the former being slightly in the majority. Georgetown had a population in this year of 7,360. The growth and development of the city from this time until 1860 is traced in the annual statements of Mr. John Sessford, an early resident, which were published in the National Intelligencer and have been reprinted in the Records of the Columbia Historical Society.

In his statement for 1822 Mr. Sessford mentions the levelling of the ground on the north front of the State and Treasury Departments, the filling of the low grounds east of 7th Street and south of Pennsylvania Avenue, the completion of the west front of the Capitol and of the original wooden dome of that building. For 1823 he tells of the completion of the south portico of the President's house, the laying of cast iron water pipes from north of G Street to F, along F to 12th and thence to Pennsylvania Avenue, connecting with the K Street Spring near or in Franklin Park, the filling of the low ground between 10th and 12th Streets adjoining Tiber Creek. The compiler recommends the deepening of the river channel to admit the passage of steamboats. He mentions also the erection of an extensive wharf for the accommodation of the Southern Steamboat Line. The first steamboat on the river was the Washington which commenced trips to Aquia Creek in June, 1815. For 1825 he mentions the planting of trees on two squares of the filled low lands south of the Avenue, the completion of the eastern portico of the Capitol, the grading of Pennsylvania Avenue from 17th to 22nd Street, and the completion of the grading of the grounds of the President's House and City Hall. He states that at that time there were about 13 miles of brick paving averaging 13 feet wide. Referring to industrial conditions, he complains of the importation of non-resident slaves to the injury of free labor.

During the second decade of the city's existence, industrial activities began to assume respectable proportions. In December, 1810, Philip Pyfer opened an establishment for the manufacture of hides on Pennsylvania Avenue opposite Center Market. A similar establishment was maintained by John Helmar opposite the house of Dr. Thornton. In 1812, John Achmann commenced the manufacture of fire engines in Washington. Achmann had learned his trade in Europe and invented an engine of his own. His engine is described as having a box of copper, the pumps of brass and the rest of the engine except the carriage of iron. In 1811 the Washington Brewery was established at the foot of New Jersey Avenue by J. W. Colbert and Company for the manufacture of malt liquors. In May, 1813, a factory for the making of spinning and carding machinery was set up by R. Parrot and I. W. Westerman of England, at the foot of Parrot's rope walk on the Eastern Branch.

In 1817 two mills were established for the manufacture of woolen goods, one of them the Washington Knit Stocking Factory under the proprietorship of Isaac Keller, the other the Columbia Mills under the proprietorship of George Jackson. In 1810 or 1811, A. and G. Way established a window glass factory on the bank of the Potomac near the mouth of Tiber Creek, from which was produced an average of 3,000 boxes containing one hundred square feet of glass each per year.

Foxall's Foundry, in which were cast most of the heavy guns used in the War of 1812, was founded in 1800 by Henry Foxall, a former partner of Robert Morris, in the Eagle Foundry at Philadelphia. It was located about a mile above Georgetown near the site of the canal.

The commerce of what is now ordinarily contemplated under the name of the City of Washington, long ante-dates the establishment of the city and goes back to the early history of Georgetown. Long before the Revolution it was the custom of the farmers of the surrounding country to bring their produce to Georgetown from which large quantities of it were shipped to Europe. Chief among the articles of commerce in those days was tobacco which was hauled long distances either in wagons or in hogsheads through which an axle was inserted and the hogshead drawn over the roads by horses, this custom giving rise to the institution known as tobacco roads.

Until about 1800 or even later, two channels were open to Georgetown, one on either side of Analostan Island, and that on the Virginia shore being the shorter was the most commonly used. This channel was closed by the building of a stone causeway across it in 1805. Previous to this time most of the wharves and warehouses at Georgetown were located at the west end of the town but after the closing of the causeway the merchants began to extend their shipping facilities along the banks of the river at the lower part of the town.

Prior to 1822 the tobacco was stored and inspected at Loundes' warehouse, a frame building south of Bridge and between Market and Frederick Streets. So extensive did the tobacco trade of Georgetown become that in 1822, two 3-story fireproof brick warehouses, roofed with slate and with sheet iron doors and shutters, were built by the corporation. These buildings covered three lots situated west of High and south of Bridge Street.

The commerce of Georgetown during the first quarter of the century was greatly stimulated by the operations of the "Potowmack, " afterwards the "Potomac," Company. The Potowmack Company was chartered by identical statutes of the Maryland and Virginia Legislatures in October, 1784. It provided for the taking of subscriptions to five hundred shares of stock in the amount of $222,222.2-9, of which Maryland and Virginia agreed to subscribe fifty shares each. The Company was organized at a meeting held in Alexandria, May 17, 1785.

At the Little Falls was constructed, on the north side of the river, a canal two and one-half miles long with four masonry locks having a total elevation of thirty-seven feet.

At the Great Falls a canal was constructed on the south side of the river twelve hundred yards long with five locks having a total difference of level of seventy-six feet, nine inches, the two lower ones being cut in solid rock.

At Shenandoah Falls, below Harper's Ferry, a canal one mile long was cut. Another, three-quarters of a mile long, was dug at Seneca Falls and another, fifty yards long, was dug at House's Falls, five miles above the one at Shenandoah Falls. Neither of the last mentioned had locks. On the Shenandoah River six canals, with an aggregate length of 2,400 yards, were dug and five locks constructed.

In addition to these improvements much was done in the way of removing obstructions and constructing dikes and wing dams in the Potomac, Shenandoah and Monocacy Rivers. The total expenditures, including original cost and cost of repairs, maintenance and operation, from 1800 to 1822, was $729,387.29.

The boats used in this navigation were shoal draft vessels of about twenty tons capacity. Some of them were of a permanent character and were pushed up the river by poles on the return trips. More frequently they were temporary affairs put together often with wooden dowels, and after reaching Georgetown were taken apart and sold for lumber.

From the opening of the canal upon the completion of the Great Falls locks in 1800, to August, 1826, when the Company was merged in the new Chesapeake and Ohio Canal Company, these boats brought down 1,309,911 barrels of flour, 48,909 barrels of whiskey, upwards of 40,000 hogsheads of tobacco, and more than five hundred tons of iron, besides large quantities of lime from Frederick, and other articles, bringing the total valuation to $10,534,000.

An act of the City Councils, approved July 11, 1818, provided that $1,000 should be appropriated for the Western School, no part thereof to be expended except for the education of poor children; that the Trustees of the First District were authorized to place at a school, for the purpose of receiving a higher grade of instruction, any scholars who should have arrived at such a degree of improvement as to warrant the same, and appropriated $150 to enable them to do so.

On July 30, 1821, the Lancastrian school took possession of an old stable at the corner of Fourteenth and G Streets.

Mr. Ould, Principal of the Western school, tendered a report for the months of June 22, 1824 and June 22, 1825, in which he said:

"One hundred and three scholars are reading O'Neall's Geography, Ramsay's Life of Washington, Murray's Introduction, Reader and Sequel, Terry's Moral Instructor, and Day's Sanford and Merton and spell words in Walker's Dictionary; 62 of them commit daily to memory a portion of Geography, Grammar and Dictionary; 51 are learning to read Scriptural Instructions; 34 are learning to read monosyllables, and 34 are perfecting themselves in the alphabet and in words of from two to four letters.

"Of the scholars learning to write, 154 can write tolerably, and many of them can do the ornamental hands of Old English, German Text, Engrossing, and Roman and Italian Print.

" One hundred and eight are in Arithmetic; 38 of whom are progressing through the first four rules of Arithmetic, Simple, Compound, and Decimal Reduction, Single and Double Rules of Three, Practice, Simple and Compound Interest, on to Exchange." An important incident of the first quarter century of the Capital was the determination of the longitude of Washington reckoned from Greenwich, an

201

achievement which is to be credited to Mr. William Lambert, a clerk in the Pension office.

Mr. Lambert's final calculations were the result of a Joint Resolution of Congress, passed March 3, 1821, authorizing the President to have astronomical observations made to determine the correct longitude of the Capitol Building from Greenwich or from any other known meridian in Europe.

Mr. Lambert continued his calculations throughout the summer of 1821, making frequent observations with the result that he finally reported the longitude of the Capitol as 76° 55' 30.54", and that of the President's House as 76° 57' 05.33" west from Greenwich. In consequence of Mr. Lambert's labors and upon his recommendations, Congress established the Naval Observatory on the site of the present Naval Hospital. Numerous errors were afterwards found to exist in Mr. Lambert's calculations and upon the establishment of the transatlantic cable an additional source of accuracy was obtained. By the report of the United States Coast and Geodetic Survey for 1884, the longitude of the Statue of Freedom on the Capitol Building was given as 77° 0' 33.54".

Twice in its early years the city found opportunity to respond to the distress of its neighbors. In September, 1803, the City Councils authorized the expenditure of $300 for the relief of a number of the inhabitants of Alexandria who had removed here because of the epidemic of yellow fever which was then devastating that town.

On July 26, 1815, an appropriation of $1,000 was made "as a gratuity for the relief of the sufferers by the late destructive and calamitous fire in the town of Petersburg. " The assessment for this appropriation like all others at the time, was apportioned among the several wards.

Just before the close of the first quarter century of the city the first serious attempt to effect the retrocession of Alexandria County to Virginia was made. Meetings for and against retrocession were held in Alexandria in March, 1824. The project being put to vote was defeated by a count of 404 to 286 votes.

Probably the oldest church in the District is St Paul's Episcopal, Rock Creek Parish, which was organized in 1719 as one of a string of Episcopal churches extending from Baltimore to Richmond, with a small chapel on the site of the present church on the Rock Creek Church Road just north of the Soldiers' Home grounds. The present edifices was erected about 1775. The second oldest church in the District is believed to be the German Lutheran Church at Wisconsin Avenue and Volta Place which was first established in a log structure on the present site in 1769. Christ's Church, Episcopal, worshipped from about 1775 until 1807 in what had been a barn, about where New Jersey Avenue and D Street, southeast, now intersect. In 1807 part of the congregation erected the present church on G Street between 6th and 7th, southeast, naming it Christ Church. The West Street Presbyterian Church of Georgetown was organized about 1781, and about 1783 constructed its first building at Washington and Bridge Streets, replacing it with a larger one in 1821. The present Dumbarton Avenue M. E. Church of Georgetown was founded in a cooper shop in 1792, and in 1795 erected a small brick church on Montgomery Street. The present structure was erected in 1849. St. John's Episcopal Church in Georgetown was organized in 1796 and its building completed in 1804. Trinity Church, Catholic, of Georgetown, was organized by Bishop Carroll in 1795 and its building completed in 1797. St. Patrick's, Catholic, with its first building on F Street near 10th was organized in 1797. The First Presbyterian Church was organized in 1795 and met for some time in a carpenter shop used by the workmen on the President's House and for a few months in the north wing of the original Capitol building. In 1812 it moved into a new building on South Capitol Street, and in December, 1827 dedicated its first building on the present site on 4th Street.

The First Baptist Church organized in 1802 with its edifice at 19th and I Streets, where it remained until in 1833 it constructed a new building on the site of Ford's Theatre. The Methodists of Washington first met in one of the "Twenty Buildings" at South Capitol and N Streets in 1802 or 1803. They afterwards occupied Mr. Carroll's barn on New Jersey Avenue, southeast, and in 1811 dedicated a new brick church called Ebenezer on 4th Street between South Carolina Avenue and G Street, southeast, The F Street Presbyterian Church was organized in 1803 and in 1808 constructed its first building at 14th and F Streets, on the site of the New Willard Hotel. In 1808 the Friends erected their first meeting house on the site of the present structure. The Second Baptist Church was organized in June 1810, and occupied a structure near the Navy Yard, being then known as the Navy Yard Baptist Church.

The site and building for Foundry M. E. Church at 14th and G Streets were donated by Henry Foxall, the owner of Foxall's Foundry, in fulfillment of a resolution taken by him at the time of the British invasion of 1814 that he would construct such a church if his foundry should be spared. The church was dedicated on September 10, 1815. St. John's Episcopal Church which was the place of worship of every President from Madison to Buchanan, inclusive, and later of President Arthur, Mrs. Roosevelt and Mrs. Taft, was designed by Benjamin Latrobe and was dedicated on December 27, 1816. St. Peter's Catholic Church at 3rd and C Streets, southeast, was organized May 10, 1820, and its first building completed the following year. All Souls' Unitarian Church was organized in 1820, and its building at 6th and D Streets dedicated June 9th, 1822. Wesley M. E. Chapel at 5th and F Streets was organized in 1823. The Second Presbyterian Church was organized in 1820; the Fourth Presbyterian in 1829; the Central M. P. in 1829; its first frame building. "The Tabernacle, " being dedicated in 1832; Trinity P. E. Church was dedicated in 1829; The First M. P. Church and the Congress Street M. P. Church of Georgetown dedicated their buildings in 1830.

The commencement of the second quarter century of the city's history was marked by the inauguration of President John Quincy Adams on March 4, 1825. This inauguration surpassed any other demonstration in Washington up to that time. The President-elect drove to the Capitol with ex-President Monroe, escorted by the District militia and a cavalcade of citizens.

John C. Calhoun, the Vice-President, took the oath of his office in the Senate Chamber and a little later, in the Hall of Representatives, Chief-Justice Marshall administered the oath to Mr. Adams.

During this administration President and Mrs. Adams held very democratic receptions in the East Room of the White House, where people of many classes and nations were welcomed. One good feature of these entertainment was that guests were required to come early and leave by eleven o'clock, an example then followed by other entertainers of Washington.

In 1826 occurred the bloodless duel between Henry Clay and John Randolph near the Virginia end of the Chain Bridge. Clay, offended at some remark of the offensive character for which Randolph was notorious, had challenged the latter. Clay's shot went wide and Randolph fired in the air, whereupon Clay expressed his gratification' that his opponent had not been injured, and a reconciliation followed.

The year 1827 closed in Washington with a "Fair for the benefit of the Orphan Asylum, " of which Mrs. Margaret Bayard Smith, the wife of the original owner of the National Intelligencer, Samuel Harrison Smith, said, "Every female in the city, I believe, from the highest to the lowest, has been at work for it.

Conveniences for residents were much improved in Washington by the close of 1828, and Mrs. Smith, in a letter to her sister in November of that year, wrote: "Never in my life have I been so comfortably and agreeably fixed. My wishes are completely satisfied. Our house, a delightful one, in the best part of the city, surrounded with good neighbors, good churches and good pavements which enable us to visit both neighbors and churches in all weather. You will recollect the situation of the Department of State, etc. — it is opposite to this. A broad pavement leads one way to Capitol Hill and another to Georgetown, besides cross paved ways in every direction."

Two months later this sprightly woman wrote: " Our city is as alive and bustling as New York." This was at the period closing the administration of John Quincy Adams.

As improvements came and population increased the improvident, unfortunate class known as "the poor," became part of the city's burden, and in the winter of 1829, a severe season, there was much suffering. Mayor Gales appointed at this distressing time, three persons in each city ward to receive contributions for and to visit and distribute necessities to these unfortunates. Citizens were solicited to contribute anything they would for the general relief. Congress contributed fifty cords of wood and the Treasury Department, not permitted to give away government property, sold at cost, fifty cords of wood, for the benefit of the poor.

The White House during the administration of the second Adams was the scene of the wedding of Mary Hellen, the niece of Mrs. Adams, to John Adams, the President's son, on February 20, 1828.

On March 4, 1829, General Andrew Jackson, the first western President, was inaugurated. The campaign between Jackson and John Quincy Adams had been unusually bitter, and as a consequence Mr. Adams refused to take part in the inaugural ceremonies of Jackson.

The President-elect was escorted to the Capitol by a guard of volunteer Revolutionary veterans.

John C. Calhoun of South Carolina, was sworn into the office of Vice-President in the Senate Chamber, after which Congressmen and other dignitaries moved to the East portico of the Capitol. When General Jackson made his appearance there a mighty shout arose from the multitude below, to which Jackson responded by removing his hat and bowing to the people, visibly moved by the honor shown him. He then read his inaugural address, after which the venerable Chief Justice Marshall, whose privilege it had been to administer the oath to so many of the Country's chief executives, now performed that honorable duty for the last time.

After this ceremony the President and his party had difficulty in reaching the street. Mrs. Margaret Bayard Smith relates that the new President mounted a waiting horse and rode to the White House.

The crowd surged down Pennsylvania Avenue to the Executive Mansion, where refreshments were served to thousands of guests.

Social affairs in Washington during Jackson's administration had numerous upheavals. During the first four years the famous Mrs. Eaton, formerly Mrs. Timberlake and previous to that "Peggy" O'Neal, who became the wife of Secretary Eaton of Jackson's Cabinet, caused much disturbance in social circles. Scandal was attached to the name of Mrs. Eaton and social leaders refused to take her to their homes or to visit her. The President espoused the cause of the ostracized woman, his feelings still sensitive by reason of an experience just previous to his election, when his wife's name had been bandied by his political enemies, which cruelty had hastened the death of Mrs. Jackson.

In the case of Mrs. Eaton, Jackson found that being President did not enable him to carry his point. He could order men's actions to a great extent, but the men's wives were not to be ordered, and Mrs. Peggy held sway over a few only. One gathers from reading that she seems to have enjoyed the sensation she caused. She finally brought about dissensions that dismembered the Cabinet, but women of the old Congressional and society set were obdurate to the end and Mrs. Eaton never attained high position in the Washington society circle. Her cause was espoused, however, by the Russian Ambassador, a bachelor, and by Secretary of State Van Buren, a widower. Daniel Webster attributed the election of Van Buren as Jackson's successor to the partisanship he displayed in behalf of Mrs. Eaton.

The social life of the first half of this administration represented a conglomerate society, but during the second half the etiquette of refined society was in large measure restored. Jackson, really fond of intellectual companionship, tired of the motley levees which caused useless expense of money and time, with benefit to no one. As democratic as ever, he felt the necessity of enforcing dignity in social as well as political affairs, and to curb the license of the vulgar, while conforming to polite usages.

During the incumbency of President Jackson the White House witnessed three weddings; Delia Lewis of Nashville was married to Joseph Yver Pagot, Secretary of the French Legation, in 1829; Emily Martin, a niece of the President and Louis Donaldson, a grandson of President Jefferson, were married in 1832; and Mary Eastern, a niece of the President, and Lucien B. Polk, a relative of President Polk, were married in 1837.

President Jackson was the first Chief Executive to undergo the indignity of personal assault, an experience which came to him twice during his term of office. The first of these occurred in May, 1833, when the President was on his way, with a number of distinguished people, to lay the corner-stone of the monument to Mary Washington, the mother of the first President. They were on the steamboat Sidney, and at Alexandria the boat stopped to take on more passengers. One of these, Lieutenant R. B. Randolph, immediately after boarding, went to the cabin where President Jackson sat. There, standing before the President, he pulled off his gloves, ostensibly for the purpose of shaking hands with the distinguished man before him. Observing him, the President put out his hand good-naturedly and said, "Never mind your gloves, sir." Randolph, instead of taking the proffered hand, thrust his own in the President's face and exclaimed, " I came to pull your nose! "

A sensation was immediately created and several gentlemen seized Randolph and hurried him from the cabin. Jackson caught up his cane and made a rush for his assailant, but Randolph, who had been thrust from the boat, hurried off and escaped.

On January 29, 1835, during the funeral ceremonies of Senator Warren R. Davis of South Carolina, at the Capitol, as Jackson stepped onto the portico a man named Richard Lawrence quickly stepped before the President and attempted to shoot him. The pistol only snapped, and the man was seized by several bystanders, but before being under control, he attempted a second shot, when again the percussion-cap failed.

The most noteworthy incident of this period of the city's history was the cholera epidemic which occurred in 1832 during the mayoralty of John P. Van Ness.

Early in the month of August, 1832, the epidemic of cholera which had made its appearance in New York during the month of June, broke out in Washington, and gained rapid headway. The city councils provided for the appointment of extra police commissioners to be associated for a period of four months with the Board of Health. Rigorous measures were adopted looking to the prevention of the spread of the disease, including the prohibition of the sale of liquor for a period of ninety days, as well as the introduction within the city limits of sea food and of nearly all classes of vegetables and fruits. Public theatrical performances and evening religious gatherings were also prohibited. The prohibitions upon the use of the various species of vegetables which were forbidden caused great public dissatisfaction and resulted in a meeting of citizens at the City Hall on the evening of August 21, which adopted resolutions protesting against the enforcement of the regulations adopted by the Board of Health. Another meeting however, endorsed these regulations.

The epidemic reached its height in the early part of September when between 10 and 15 deaths were reported each day, although it is believed that fully double this number were victims of the disease. By the 1st of October, the disease was believed to have departed.

Throughout the continuance of the epidemic the dead carts passing through the city, their drivers ringing a bell and at times blowing a horn and calling " Bring out the dead, " were a daily sight. The total number of deaths as reported to the Board of Health was 459. Of these 269 were males and 190 females; 251 were white and 208 were colored. The highest mortality appeared in those ranging from 30 to 40 years of age. In connection with this event it is of interest to note that in consequence of the yellow fever epidemics in Philadelphia of 1793 and 1798, the latter of which had caused the President, with the administrative offices of both the State and National governments to remove temporarily to Germantown, Congress had by Act approved February 25, 1799, provided that

"In case of the prevalence of a contagious or epidemical disease at the seat of government it shall be lawful for the President of the United States to permit and direct the removal of any or all the public offices to such other places, as in his discretion, shall be deemed most safe and convenient for conducting the public business." The epidemic of 1832 was not of sufficient severity to result in the invocation of this law, and happily no other such visitation has afflicted the nation's Capital.

For 1827 Mr. Sessford tells of the completion of the west section of the City Hall, and of the Penitentiary at the Arsenal; and of the construction of a large Reservoir at

D Street and Indiana Avenue, with 2,500 feet of iron pipe line. He states that in this year there set out daily five stages for Baltimore, one for Frederick, and three for Alexandria; with three each week for Annapolis and two each week for Piscataway. He enumerates two steamboats per day for Alexandria, one daily for Alexandria and Fredericksburg, one every Wednesday for Norfolk, one every Tuesday for Baltimore, and one from Georgetown to Alexandria twice each day.

The census of 1830 showed the population of Washington to be at that time 18,827; an increase of 5,580 during the preceding decade. Of the persons enumerated in 1830, about 13,400 were white; about 2,300 were slaves; and something over 3,000 were free colored persons. This was the first census in which the freedmen were shown to outnumber the slaves. The population of Georgetown in this year was 8,441.

The " Marsh Market, " where the Center Market is now, was the center of business activity, and near it, chiefly on Pennsylvania Avenue, were leading hotels, boarding houses, and business locations. The Avenue was the great shopping district and promenade of Washington's residents. Gambling was a crying evil of the day, and during the sessions of Congress many thousands of dollars were lost in the Pennsylvania Avenue resorts.

In his statement for 1832, Mr. Sessford says that the draw bridges over the Canal at 12th and 14th Streets were raised 15 feet to admit the smaller steamboats to 7th Street, from which it is to be inferred that some of the steamboats of that time were of very meager dimensions. It was in this year that the poplars on Pennsylvania Avenue under President Jefferson were removed and the Avenue graded and paved in the center with nine inches of stone from 3rd to 14th Street.

In 1833 the original Treasury building was destroyed by a fire which occurred on March 4, of that year.

In 1835 the rebuilding of the Potomac Bridge, which had been partially destroyed by flood in 1831, was completed with a draw at the city channel and one at the Georgetown channel. In this year, also, the Baltimore and Ohio Railroad was completed to Washington.

The Baltimore and Ohio Railroad Company had been chartered by the Maryland Legislature in February, 1827. The corner stone was laid at Baltimore on July 4, 1828, by the venerable Charles Carroll of Carrollton, and the road was completed from Baltimore to Point of Roeks by April 1, 1832.

An Act of Congress approved March 9, 1833, authorized the construction of a branch line into the District of Columbia, conditioned upon the commuting of the stock of the Washington and Baltimore Turnpike Company for that of the Railroad Company. On July 20, 1835, the operation of two trains a day to Bladensburg was commenced and on August 25 following, the service to the original station at 2nd Street and Pennsylvania Avenue, west, was inaugurated.

In 1836 iron pipes replacing the former wooden pipes were laid from the Capitol along the north side of Pennsylvania Avenue to 15th Street, with a sufficient number of plugs for cases of fire. From these pipes water was supplied to all stories of the present east wing of the Treasury building, which was then under construction, as were also the present F Street wing of the Patent Office building, a portion of the New Post Office (now the Land Office) building, and the new jail on the Gothic order at the northeast corner of Judiciary Square.

The extent of the paved footways in the year 1837 is stated by Mr. Sessford as aggregating about 24 miles.

On March 4, 1837, Andrew Jackson gave place to another choice of the people, Martin Van Buren.

On the bright cold morning of the inauguration President Jackson and President-elect Van Buren were driven to the Capitol in a carriage reputed to have been made of oak from the old United States frigate Constitution, drawn by four horses. They were escorted by companies of citizens and a volunteer brigade of infantry and cavalry.

In the Senate chamber of the Capitol the two leaders witnessed the taking of the oath as Vice-President by Richard M. Johnson, after which they and all the dignitaries went to the Eastern portico. Here "Old Hickory" received a rousing cheer from the people, showing that his popularity had not decreased with cessation of office.

Mr. Van Buren advanced and read his inaugural address, after which Chief - Justice Taney administered the great oath.

The managers of the Inaugural Ball endeavored to make it the most elaborate given up to that time. The price of admission was ten dollars, but the ball was a crowded affair notwithstanding. The President and Vice-President were seated on a dais, where they received congratulations from many distinguished Americans and foreigners.

In 1838 the entire country was shocked by the news of the killing of Congressman Cilley of Maine by Congressman Graves of Kentucky in a duel at Bladensburg. The contest was with rifles at ninety-two yards. Three shots were exchanged. After each of the first two Congressman Cilley, in line with his attitude throughout, offered to make any reasonable adjustment of the difficulty, but his opponent appeared to be determined to bring about his death. Cilley 's aim was seriously hampered by a strong wind which blew in his face. At the third fire he fell mortally wounded. The affair aroused a widespread popular feeling which resulted in the Act of Congress of February 20, 1839, making dueling unlawful.

During the latter part of President Van Buren's administration the residents of the District were greatly perturbed by the hostile attitude of Congress due in some measure to the prevailing Whig sentiment among the local citizens. This hostility found expression in the refusal of Congress to renew the expiring charters of six of the banks of the District. It was further manifested when application was made for a renewal of the charter of the city of Washington, which by its terms expired in 1840. The select committee of Congress to which the latter subject was referred submitted a proposed charter in which every reference to slaves contained in the expiring charter was so studiously expunged as to indicate a deliberate purpose to abolish the institution of slavery in the city of Washington. The bill passed the third reading but was finally defeated upon a motion to reconsider offered by a southern Senator who with others from the same section had unwittingly voted in favor of it.

The result of the hostile attitude of Congress was a lively interest on the part of the residents of Washington in the presidential election of 1840. During the campaign of that year a log cabin facing Pennsylvania Avenue was erected in the open space in front of the Center Market and maintained as a Whig headquarters. In front of it was placed a platform from which speeches were delivered, and near it was erected a liberty pole one hundred and seven feet high from which was flown a Harrison and Tyler streamer.

The inauguration of President William Henry Harrison took place March 4, 1841. For several days previous to the inauguration General Harrison was the guest of Washington's Whig Mayor, Mr. Seaton. President Van Buren who had been defeated of re-election showed his bigness by dining the President-elect, together with a distinguished company, where politics had no place and the dinner was a genial success.

On the inaugural day General Harrison rode a splendid white horse to the Capitol, accompanied by a distinguished escort and a great throng of admirers. Upon reaching the Capitol he went immediately to the Senate Chamber, where Vice-President Tyler was sworn into office, after which all repaired to the Eastern portico, where the great official read his inaugural address. After this enthusiastically received message General Harrison took the oath of office from Chief-Justice Taney.

President Harrison survived his inauguration ordeal only one month, departing from this life April 4, 1841, much lamented by the entire country, as a man who had given promise of making an excellent executive for the country.

Vice-President Tyler succeeded him, taking the Presidential oath from the Chief Judge of the Circuit Court of the District of Columbia.

The year after entering the Presidency Mr. Tyler lost his wife, a woman who had made herself beloved, in her quiet way, in the Capital city. They had been married twenty-nine years. This sad occurrence threw a gloom over the White House and the city for a time, but later society in Washington attained much brilliancy, the President's daughter and daughter-in-law, especially the latter, Mrs. Robert Tyler, after the marriage of his daughter Elizabeth in the White House to William Waller, on January 31, 1842, usually presiding at the White House entertainments. After the President took a bride to the Executive Mansion in 1844, society endeavored to honor the new White House Mistress in many ways and she was a credit to all compliments, being a charming and cultured woman.

It was after one of the entertainments during this period, when much candle-grease had fallen on gentlemen's coats and ladies' handsome gowns, that it was suggested, and a little later decided to have the rooms lighted with gas, a method of lighting which was then being tried in several places with success. Charles Dickens and his wife visited Washington in 1842, receiving much attention as "Boz" was well known and much beloved by American readers.

On February 23, 1843, Congress passed an act appropriating money for the construction of a telegraph line from Washington to Baltimore. The line was completed on May 24, 1844, and the following day the first message, "What hath God wrought?" was sent over the wires by Miss Annie Ellsworth, whose father was at the time the Commissioner of Patents. Shortly after the question came from Baltimore, "What is the news in Washington?" and the reply was sent back, "Van Buren 's stock is rising. " On May 28th, the news of the nomination of James Carroll for Governor of Maryland and of the nomination of John Tyler for President of the United States, by the Tyler Convention and of a lengthy speech of Benjamin F. Butler in favor of a majority rule in the Convention came over the wire from Baltimore. On Wednesday, the 29th of May, news came from Baltimore of the nomination of James K. Polk for the presidency by the Democratic Convention. This last announcement created so much surprise that the telegraph was discredited until the news had been confirmed by special messenger sent to Baltimore to ascertain the facts.

On February 28, 1844, the gunboat Princeton took a party of 400 invited guests, including President Tyler and his cabinet, on an excursion down the Potomac. On the return, in firing a salute at Port Washington, a gun burst killing Secretaries Upshur and Gilmer, Commodore Kennon, Mr. Virgil Maxey and Mr. Gardner, and wounding 17 seamen. President Tyler was in the Captain's cabin and escaped. A state funeral for all those killed was held from the White House.

The inauguration of President Polk on March 4, 1845, was attended with great display and elaborate ceremonies.

Vice-President Dallas was sworn into office in the Senate Chamber, after which there was the usual retirement to the east portico of the Capitol, where the President-elect read his inaugural address and was sworn into office by Chief-Justice Taney. A levee followed at the Executive Mansion.

The day preceding the inauguration, President Tyler, the retiring incumbent, and his wife gave a reception to their friends, at which Washington citizens showed their appreciation and warm friendship for the retiring President. In the evening General Van Ness, selected by his fellow citizens for the purpose, delivered an address to Mr. Tyler, expressing the regret felt by Washington people at parting from him, to which honor the President replied in his happy and dignified manner.

The day following the inauguration President and Mrs. Polk received at the White House, and Mrs. Polk was immediately accepted as a graceful leader for the Capital city's social affairs, nor was she a disappointment to her new friends. Much later in her husband's administration, after he had made the usual enemies that fall to a President's lot, Mr. Clay said to Mrs. Polk, "that, although some had expressed dissatisfaction with the administration of her husband, not one seemed to have found the least fault with hers."

In 1846 a sentiment among the citizens of the town and county of Alexandria in favor of withdrawal from the District of Columbia culminated in a petition to Congress having this object in view. Congress responded by passing an Act approved July 9, 1846, submitting the question to the voters of the territory affected. The election which was held on the first and second days of September, 1846, resulted in a vote of 763 in favor of retrocession and 222 against it. By proclamation of September 7, 1846, President Polk announced that the portion of the District derived from the State of Virginia was re-ceded to that State.

During President Polk's administration the war with Mexico took place, Washington was represented in the American armies by five companies. Of these the first two to go — the "Washington Volunteers, No. 1" and the "Washington City Riflemen" — constituted respectively companies C and D in the battalion which stormed the forts of Monterey on September 21, 1846, under Lieutenant Colonel William H. Watson, who lost his life in that assault, though Company D was prevented from participation in the attack by being detailed to guard the camp.

The funding of the $10,000,000 war loan authorized by Congress was effected by one of Washington's citizens, Mr. W. W. Corcoran, who afterward became noted through his benefactions.

On February 23, 1848, Ex-President, and at the time Representative, John Quincy Adams, died at Washington.

On Sunday, April 16, 1848, a sailing vessel named the Pearl slipped away from Washington with 77 fugitive slaves. A number of residents of Washington and Georgetown obtained the Steamer Salem which started in pursuit and found the Pearl anchored in Cornfield Harbor at the mouth of the Potomac. Boarding the schooner they fastened down the hatches, bound the captain and hands in charge of the vessel, and towed the schooner back to Georgetown. Captain Edward Sayres of the Pearl was convicted and sentenced to pay 73 times $140, and Daniel Drayton was sentenced to pay 73 times $100, both to stand committed until their fines were paid. They were afterwards pardoned on August 12, 1852. This episode resulted in an attack on the officers of the National Era, occasioned by the supposed endorsement by that paper of the attempted kidnapping of the slaves.

President-elect Zachary Taylor arrived in the Capital February 23, 1849. Here he was met by Mayor Seaton and his reception in the city was one of cordiality and high respect that must have filled his heart with gratitude and love for the people who so honored him.

March 4, coming on Sunday, the inauguration took place on the 5th, when the usual programme was conducted, Vice-President Fillmore being sworn into his office in the Senate Chamber and the President on the platform built in front of the East portico, by Chief-Justice Taney, in presence of a multitude of people.

The retiring President and President-elect had driven to the Capitol together, preceded by twelve volunteer companies and a Whig escort. After the inauguration ceremonies the same procession returned through Pennsylvania Avenue to the White House.

At night there were three balls, one on Judiciary Square, where society was displayed in all its splendor; one at Carusi's, where the military had precedence; and another at the National Theatre. The President appeared at each of these balls during the evening, accompanied by Mayor Seaton, and his entrance into the ball-room each time was the event of the night, bringing enthusiasm that shook the structures.

Mrs. Taylor was not in robust health and did not care for the duties of social leader, so her daughter, who had married Colonel William W. Bliss, filled this honorable position with grace and dignity, during the period of President Taylor's incumbency.

One year and four months after he went into office, President Taylor left governmental and all other earthly tasks to others. He died on July 9, 1850, at the White House, after a short illness, brought on from taking part in a Fourth of July celebration, on a very warm day. Having been a military here, he was given a military funeral, General Scott coming to Washington to superintend the arrangements.

On March 31, preceding the death of President Taylor, John C. Calhoun, had laid down his earthly burdens in the Capital.

The period from 1836 to 1850 was covered by the four-year incumbency of Mayor Force and by the ten-year incumbency of Mayor Seaton and witnessed a very substantial advance on the part of the city.

The census for 1840 showed a population for Washington of 23,364; an increase during the preceding decade of 4,529. Of the total number in 1840, 16,843 were white; 1,713 were slaves; and 4,808, or nearly three times the number of slaves, were free colored persons. The population of Georgetown in 1840 was 7,312, or over eleven hundred less than in 1830.

For 1840 Mr. Sessford mentions that there were erected one, and in 1841 three, four story buildings, making a new class. For 1842 he mentions the completion of the colonnade of the Treasury Building. He states that there were then nine steamboats plying from the city.

In 1843 the old jail was altered and fitted for a Lunatic Asylum.

In 1844 the Naval Observatory was completed; a portion of Maryland Avenue, New York Avenue, 14th and 10th Streets graded and graveled; new lines of iron pipe laid from the spring on C Street down 6th to Pennsylvania Avenue. The old jail, which had been fitted up for a Lunatic Asylum, was given over to the faculty of the Columbian College for a hospital with a large class of students.

In 1845 Pennsylvania Avenue was graded and graveled by the Government from the Capitol to the Navy Yard, and from 6th to 15th Street, west, it was completed by pebble-paving, curbing, and gravelling.

In 1846, the brick "North Market" on K Street between 7th and 8th, was constructed. In Georgetown, a large iron rolling factory adjoining the Aqueduct was nearly completed.

In the latter part of 1846, the first attempts were made at gas illumination in Washington. Mr. Crutchett, of Dayton, Ohio, illuminated Capitol Hill and North Capitol Street with lamps burning " Crutchett 's Solar Gas," which was produced from oil and which gave a very satisfactory and brilliant light. On December 29, 1848, the President's House was lighted with this gas which gave great satisfaction at the time, and in the course of that year the Washington Gas Light Company was formed with the object of manufacturing solar gas for supplying the citizens of Washington.

After an experience of several years, however, it was found impossible to manufacture this gas commercially at a profit, and the company erected a plant for manufacturing gas from coal, east of 4£ Street between Maryland Avenue and the City Canal. This establishment commenced furnishing gas to the population of Washington in 1851, through pipes which were laid from the works up 4th Street to Pennsylvania Avenue and thence both ways on the latter thoroughfare toward the Capitol and President's House. Owing to the scattered condition of the population of Washington at the time this company commenced operations, its first years were not profitable ones. A circular published by the company in 1856 stated that twenty miles of street mains had been laid since the completion of the new works in 1851, with a total of 30 miles of mains and an annual average consumption of 944,000 cubic feet of gas per mile, and added "A line of 6-inch pipe over a mile in length was laid from the vicinity of the Capitol to the Navy Yard, with only one widely scattered row of street lamps, passing many squares with scarcely a dwelling house on each, and double lines of pipe are in that part of Pennsylvania Avenue near Georgetown with quite as uninviting prospect of private consumption."

In 1847 Mr. Sessford tells of the construction of the five-story Winder building at 17th and F Streets; the completion by W. W. Corcoran of a five-story building at 15th and F Streets for some of the Treasury department offices; the enlargement of the old Fuller mansion at 14th and Pennsylvania Avenue to a four-story, 150 room hotel occupied by Messrs. Willard; the erection of a five-story 72 room hotel at 12th and the Avenue which was later opened as the Irving House. In that year gas lights were placed around the terrace of the Capitol and a gas lantern ninety feet high raised above the Capitol dome; the east wing of the Smithsonian building was completed and the west wing commenced.

For 1848 Mr. Sessford speaks of Mr. Easby's shipyard immediately west of the Observatory, at which, he says, many fine vessels had been built. Iron pipes were substituted for the old wooden ones from the spring on 13th Street above I, and from the spring at 3rd and Indiana Avenue. The opening of Indiana Avenue provided for by Congress was begun; 4th Street was graded from Maryland Avenue to the Arsenal and the foundation for the Washington Monument was within three feet of completion to the base of the shaft.

For 1849 Mr. Sessford gives an excellent idea of the extent to which the improvement of Washington's streets had been pushed. In that year the paving of "the road north of the President's House" and of 15th Street in front of the State and Treasury Department building was completed; also 13th Street from New York Avenue to I Street; 10th from K to N; Vermont Avenue from I to M; Ohio Avenue from 12th to 15th; New York Avenue from 7th to North Capitol; and H Street from Massachusetts Avenue to the turnpike gate. The City Hall which had long stood in a rough state was nearly completed on its south front without the wings; the 7th Street wing of the Patent Office was under construction, and the shaft of the Washington Monument had been raised 35 feet above the base.

The progress of the schools of Washington during the periods just covered was substantial but not rapid.

In 1836 Mayor Force endeavored with slight results to arouse interest in this subject. In a message dated June 27 of that year he complained that the support provided for the schools was insufficient, being only that from the interest (and increase) of the $40,000 previously provided by lotteries. "Means from elsewhere are hardly hoped for," said Mayor Force, "and the city has no revenue to apply to their support. None of the public lots in the city, though liberally granted to Colleges in our vicinity, and to other institutions, could be obtained for the endowment of our schools."

In 1841 Mayor Seaton attempted to make the Aldermen and Councilmen realize the importance of work for education by informing them that of 5,200 children of school age in Washington, only 1,200 were in school — public and private.

The next year he advocated either an extension of the then existing system, or the adoption of the New England plan, whereby citizens were taxed for the support of the schools and all children were entered as free pupils.

Several churches attached schools to their work and applications were made to the city government to give aid to certain churches to enable them to widen the scope of free education.

The indifferent attitude of the City Councils towards the schools of the city caused those interested in the cause of education to have reports made by the teachers as to the exact conditions of their schools, and these reports published and editorially commented upon, caused some interest to be aroused in citizens and officials hitherto latent. All white children between the ages of six and sixteen years were declared eligible to the schools, "to be admitted on prepayment of a tuition fee not over fifty cents a month, and furnishing their own school books," although the provision was still made that "children of indigent parents may be taught and supplied with books without charge."

The sum of $3,650 was appropriated for the purpose of building two school houses and for renting rooms suitable for such purposes.

From that time the popularity of the schools increased, and as the city's first half century drew to a close, the city councils became more liberal in providing funds for their support. By 1848 ten new primary schools had been authorized, and several others followed in the next two years, with teachers and assistant teachers for each.

Later all charge for tuition was abolished, and a bill passed for an annual taxation of every male citizen of one dollar, to be used exclusively for the public schools, with the additional provision that the Mayor was authorized, when the school fund proved insufficient, to supply the lack from the General Fund.

The Georgetown schools continued to exist largely by individual subscriptions; but many of the original subscribers died and the burden became too heavy for those left, so the Corporation finally, December 31, 1842, undertook the entire conduct of public education in its city by passing " An Ordinance establishing the Georgetown School."

In 1844, however, need again appears, as parents and guardians of pupils were solicited to make donations to the school.

Funds were so insufficient for the increased demands that it was decided to charge tuition, so that on July 1, 1848, it was resolved that the guardians of the Town School should be directed to charge and receive pay for all scholars whose parents or guardians were in the opinion of a majority of the Board, able to pay not exceeding $1 per month, for the general use of the school.

At the close of this year the School Board came out in debt to the amount of $153.47, which sum was appropriated by the city. The Corporation was also solicited for more ample accommodations for the schools. This call was responded to August 11, following, by an ordinance providing "That for the purpose of procuring a house of ample dimensions for the future permanent accommodation of the Male and Female Free Schools, $1,200 be paid to the Methodist Episcopal Society for their present church; and that a 'sum not exceeding $800 be devoted to the expense of alteration and proper fitting up for the comfortable accommodation of said Free Schools.' "

Columbian College had its inception in 1819 with the formation of a "Literary Association" which had been started in 1817 by Rev. Luther Rice, a returned Baptist Missionary. A tract of 46 ½ acres was purchased at the site of the present 14th and Euclid Streets and in 1820 a building erected at a cost of $35,000. The college was chartered by Congress in February, 1821. Among those who contributed to it financially were William H. Crawford, John C. Calhoun, John Quincy Adams and many members of Congress and residents of Washington, as well as a number of prominent Englishmen. The first President was the Rev. William Staughton, a celebrated English clergyman. The first commencement, which took place on December 15, 1824, was attended by President Monroe, several members of Congress and Cabinet officers and by General Lafayette, who was then on his celebrated visit to America. The medical department was started March 30, 1825, and held its sessions in a building at 10th and E Streets, with the exception of a five years' suspension beginning in 1834, until 1844, when Congress authorized it to use the former jail building on Judiciary Square immediately north of the City Hall which it occupied as a medical school and hospital until the breaking out of the Civil War.

214

The law department was started in February, 1826, with Judge Cranch at its head, but continued only one year and was not revived until after the Civil War.

The medical department of Georgetown University was put in effect on May, 1851.

The Columbia Institute for the Deaf and Dumb was incorporated on February 16, 1857, and the collegiate department with Professor E. M. Gallaudet as President was organized by Act of Congress in 1864. The site was the former estate of Amos Kendall, known as "Kendall Green."

Although Washington and Georgetown were fortunate during their early years in having the services of a number of skilled physicians and surgeons, the regulation of the practice of medicine does not appear to have been attempted until 1817. On September 26, of that year the Medical Society of the District of Columbia was organized with Dr. Charles Worthington as its first President. On February 16, 1819, Congress granted this society a charter which authorized it to examine and license duly qualified physicians to practice medicine within the District of Columbia. This charter was revived in 1838. On January 4, 1833, the Washington Medical Association was formed and on June 6, 1848, the name was changed to the Medical Association of the District of Columbia, and physicians of Georgetown were admitted to membership. In 1830 the Washington Medical Institute was formed to give instruction in Medicine and in 1841 the Pathological Society was organized for the purpose of medical discussions.

Homeopathy was introduced in the District of Columbia by Dr. John R. Piper, who located in Washington in 1849, and practiced here thirty years.

By an ordinance passed in 1853 one physician and one apothecary for the poor was provided for from each ward, the physicians being paid by the city.

The commerce of what is now the capital of the nation during the second quarter century of the existence of the capital city, consisted mainly in that enjoyed by Georgetown.

On July 26, 1824, the inspection of tobacco, which had been the chief article of Georgetown's commerce, was removed from Loundes' warehouse to the new warehouse erected by the corporation. At the height of the business the shipping of tobacco to Europe from Georgetown attained in some years as much as 5,000 hogsheads. The chief tobacco merchants were the firm of Laird and Son. This firm was dissolved on the death of John Laird on July 11, 1833, and with that event the tobacco trade of the town rapidly died away.

The trade of Georgetown was not entirely confined to tobacco, however, and it did a large importing and exporting business with every quarter of the globe. From 1815 to 1835 the value of products exported to foreign markets from Georgetown aggregated $4,077,708. From 1826 to 1835 there were shipped from that port to other American cities nearly a million barrels of flour valued at $4,710,540; 5,400 hogsheads of tobacco valued at $300,000, and other products bringing the total for this period to over $5,000,000. Up to the year 1835, goods arriving at Georgetown from both American and foreign ports reached a total valuation of $3,505,000.

Among the prominent ships which came to Georgetown were the Eagle and Shenandoah and later four ships owned by citizens of Georgetown, the Francis Depau, Southerner, Caledonia and Catherine Jackson. These ships first appeared at Georgetown in 1836, but after several voyages were found too large and were sold.

215

Previous to the building of the Baltimore and Ohio Railroad Georgetown was a distributing point for the upper Maryland territory, but it lost its position with that event and did not regain its commercial prominence until the construction of the Chesapeake and Ohio canal brought with it a large trade in the trans-shipment of Cumberland coal and other products of the upper country. From the time of the completion of this canal, the commercial history of Georgetown is in a large measure identified with that of the canal.

The heavy deposit of silt in the channel of the Potomac River resulting from the cultivation of the country surrounding the upper portions of the river and its tributaries, made its appearance in the early years of the century, and as early as 1833 it became necessary for the first time to dredge the channel. This work was done under a Congressional appropriation by the corporation of Georgetown under contract with E. and T. P. Ellicott of Baltimore, who executed the work by means of a dredging machine. The channel so cut was 4,000 feet in length, 140 feet wide, 15 feet deep at low tide and 19 feet at high tide. Previous to this excavation, the bar below Georgetown allowed at some places a depth of only 10 feet.

The second quarter century of the history of Washington is practically coterminous with the period occupied in the construction of the Chesapeake and Ohio canal.

The difficulties incident to the navigation of the upper Potomac convinced the members of the Potomac Company in 1822 that profitable operations could be carried on only by means of a continuous canal. Accordingly, a charter for the Chesapeake and Ohio Canal Company was obtained from the Legislature of Virginia on January 27, 1824, and on May 16, 1825, the stockholders of the Potomac Company consented to the transfer of the property rights and franchises of that company to the new company in exchange for stock of the latter company. Subscription books were opened October 1, 1827. Congress and the city of Washington subscribed one million dollars each, and the cities of Georgetown and Alexandria $125,000 each. These with private subscriptions brought the total to $3,090,100. Ground was broken on July 4, 1828, President John Quincy Adams turning the first spadeful of earth and Mayor Gales and many other officials and citizens participating.

On July 4, 1831, the canal was completed to the first feeder at Seneca, a distance of twenty -two miles. The continuation of the work from this place to Point of Rocks was delayed by a legal contest with the Baltimore and Ohio Railroad over the question of the right of way to the river bank, but the prior right of the canal company was adjudicated by the Maryland Court of Appeals on May 5, 1831.

From this point on the construction of the canal was made possible almost entirely by the financial assistance rendered by the State of Maryland. In 1835 that State loaned the canal company $2,000,000 in six per cent bonds of the State; in 1836 it made a second loan of $3,000,000 in six per cent bonds, and in 1837 a loan of $1,375,000 in five per cent bonds.

By means of these loans the canal was in 1839 completed to dam No. 6, 134 miles above Georgetown, leaving 50 miles to be completed to carry it to its intended terminus at Cumberland. At this stage the work came to a standstill for several years for lack of funds to complete it. Finally, in 1845, the State of Maryland authorized the company to issue its bonds in the amount of $1,700,000 and in order to make them salable waived the prior lien on the company's property which the State held as security for its own advances. The conditions imposed by the Maryland Legislature upon the issuance of these bonds were very onerous but they were finally negotiated by the contractors, Messrs. Hunter, Harris and Co., who agreed to take the bonds in payment and who were compelled to suspend work on March 11, 1850, as a result of the excessive discount at which they found it necessary to sell the bonds. The work was at that time nearly completed, however, and was finished by Michael Byrne of Frederick County, Maryland, on February 17, 1851, nearly twenty-three years after its commencement.

By an act of Congress approved May 26, 1830, a charter was granted for the continuation of the canal from Georgetown to Alexandria by means of an aqueduct bridge across the Potomac at Georgetown. The work was commenced in 1833 and water was turned into the aqueduct on July 4, 1843. The cost of the aqueduct bridge was $600,000 of which Congress contributed $400,000. The canal to Alexandria with its locks cost $550,000 more.

In 1861 the Government took possession of the aqueduct, drew off the water and used the bridge for the transportation of troops. In 1868 the aqueduct was rebuilt by lessees of the owning company and in 1886 it was sold to the United States Government which replaced it with the present steel bridge constructed upon the original piers.

The census of 1850 showed the city of Washington, after a half-century's existence, with a population of 40,001; an increase of 16,635 during the preceding decade. Of this population 30,000 were white; about 2,100 slaves; and 7,900 free colored. Georgetown, with a population of 8,366, showed a gain of slightly over 1,000 in the preceding ten years. Trade in slaves in the District of Columbia after January 1, 1851, was prohibited by Act of Congress of September 20, 1850.

A graphic description of conditions in the city at the beginning of its second half century is furnished by Mr. James Croggon in the Fiftieth Anniversary Supplement of the Evening Star. "At that period," he says, "perhaps one-third of the platted avenues and streets had not been improved, and not one fourth of the building lots; and of the reservations it may be said they existed only on paper. The lines of the latter had just then been marked. Then the greater portion of the area was wild waste, and land, which included street beds, was fenced in and cultivated. Rhode Island Avenue was practically unknown, as was also New Hampshire Avenue, north of the " Round Tops, " as the neighborhood of Washington Circle was then called. The short cut to Holmead's grave yard was known as the "Road to Holmead's, " not as Connecticut Avenue. Twentieth, 14th and 7th Streets were the only streets cut through to the Boundary, now Florida Avenue. The first was used as a road to Holmead's and Kalorama; the second, to Columbia College, the race course and cockpit; and the third connected with the turnpike to Montgomery bounty, near the old Cross Keys tavern. The entire northeastern portion of the city and much of the Navy Yard section were commons. In the unsettled portions were to be found brick kilns, slaughter houses, grave yards and a few market gardens, with not infrequently a "horse heaven," where the bodies of dead animals were left unburied to furnish prey to carrion birds. Two squares northeast of the court house were the brick kilns and yards where had been made the bricks for the Patent Office building and two squares north of the latter were the potteries of Mr. Burnett, and two others were on the line of 7th Street, one at L Street. Milch cows were allowed to run at large, and many old residents kept them with profit, not being obliged to pay anything for their pasturage. The only mark of improvement in these parts, other than those mentioned was to be found by stumbling over, now and then, a cube of stone, marked with a number, at the southeast corner of the square. Just beyond the city limits were to be found the primeval forests broken by farming land. Indeed, few knew where the city ended and country commenced.

The fire companies at this time were the Union, at 19th and H Streets; the Franklin, at 14th and E; the Northern Liberties, at 8th and K; the Perseverance, at 8th and Pennsylvania Avenue; the Columbia, at New Jersey Avenue and B, southeast; and the Anacostia, at 9th and K, southeast.

The city then owned four district school buildings accommodating about two thousand pupils. The building of the first district was in a remodeled stable opposite the old Foundry Church at 14th and G Streets; the second district building was a two-story brick at 5th and F Streets; the third district building at 3rd and D, southeast, and the fourth district building at 6th and D, southwest, were also of brick.

While the public schools during the first half century of the city's existence received appropriations from time to time from the public funds, the establishment of the special school tax authorized by the new charter of 1848 was practically contemporaneous with the beginning of the second half century. It was provided for by act of the City Councils of May 22, 1848 levying a school tax of one dollar upon every free white male citizen of twenty-one years of age. The Board of School trustees provided for by ordinance of November 12, 1858, consisted of three members from each of the four school districts and had practically unrestricted powers in the matter of fixing the courses of study and appointing teachers.

Private institutions of learning at that time included the Washington Seminary, now Gonzaga College, located on F Street between 9th and 10th; St. Joseph's Academy for girls, at 9th and F Streets; Rittenhouse Academy on Indiana Avenue near 3rd Street; the Rugby Academy, at 14th and K Streets; the Union Academy at 14th and New York Avenue; McLeod 's Academy, on 9th Street between G and H; the Emerson Institute on H between 12th and 13th; the Central Academy at 10th and E and Mrs. Burr's Academy on H near 13th.

Four markets supplied the city with food products, the corner grocery being then little known. The Center or Marsh Market was a small brick building from which two long sheds extended east and west; the Western Market, at Pennsylvania Avenue and 20th Street, had recently been rebuilt of brick; the Northern Liberty Market was at 7th and K Streets, and the Navy Yard, or Eastern Branch Market, was at 5th and K Streets, southeast.

From Mr. Sessford's annals and other accounts of the times it is to be gathered that a number of machine shops, foundries, and lumber mills were in operation. One of the important industrial plants of the period was the yard for the construction of steam vessels established by George Page in 1851 at the foot of 7th Street. Here were built the Champion, the Jennie Lind, the William Selden and a ferry for the Alexandria run. In September, 1851, Page tested the speed of the Selden in a race with a New York built boat, the George Washington, from Piney Point to the city. The Selden won by ten miles, making the run in five hours and forty-six minutes, a record which would be considered remarkable at this date.

With the completion of the Chesapeake and Ohio Canal in 1851, an extensive source of power was available to Georgetown through the utilization of the water of the canal which there had a head 33 feet above the river. This power was employed mainly in the manufacture of flour, the grain being brought to the mills in the boats operating on the canal. The mills of David L. Shoemaker, P. L. Moore, Beall and Shoemaker, William H. Tenney & Sons; James S. Welch, George Shoemaker, Ross Ray & Brother and A. H. Herr had an aggregate capacity of from 150 to 300 barrels of flour per day, the shipments from Georgetown sometimes reaching 300,000 barrels per year. The flourishing condition of the Georgetown flour trade and the popularity of the Georgetown brands was largely the result of the intelligent inspection and grading of the product by George Shoemaker, who annually for 49 years was elected flour inspector for the town.

In addition to the flour mills on the canal was Bomford's cotton factory equipped with 100 looms and 3,007 spindles and employing in the neighborhood of a hundred persons. In 1865 a paper mill was established by George Hill, Jr., at the foot of Potomac Street.

In 1851 the diminutive brick depot of the Baltimore and Ohio Railroad at 2nd Street and Pennsylvania Avenue, with its car shed extending north along the bank of Tiber Creek, which flowed nearly south at this point, was abandoned, and the new station established at New Jersey Avenue and C Street, an event which necessitated a considerable amount of street grading in the neighborhood of the new depot. In 1855 this depot was connected with the north end of the Long Bridge by tracks on 1st Street and Maryland Avenue. The following year the Washington and Alexandria Railroad was completed from Alexandria to the south end of the Long Bridge, and an omnibus service carrying passengers across the bridge was inaugurated, connecting the two lines of railroad.

Passengers and mail for Fredericksburg, Richmond and other southern points were transferred from the 11th Street wharf to the railroad terminus at Aquia Creek by a line of steamers including the Baltimore, Powhatan and Augusta.

Between Washington and Alexandria were at all times two or more steamers making five or six round trips daily, with the fare a "levy" or 12 ½ cents. Among the steamers on this run were the Phoenix, Joe Johnson, Tom Collyer, George Page and Union.

The Columbia made weekly trips to Baltimore, stopping at way points, and the Osceola made semi-weekly trips to Norfolk. The Tom Collyer carried excursions to Mount Vernon, and once each week the Columbia took excursions as far as Indian Head. Two small steamers, the G. W. P. Custis and Arlington Belle, carried picnics to Arlington Spring where Mr. Custis had thrown open his grounds to the public.

In September, 1859, the New York and Washington Screw Steamship Company placed the Steamer Mt. Vernon upon a regular run between New York and Washington. This vessel continued to make her trips until the outbreak of the Civil War, when she was sold to the Government.

Transportation to points outside the city, aside from that furnished by the Baltimore and Ohio Railroad and by the various steamboat lines, continued to be conducted by old-fashioned mail coaches, which connected the city with Rockville, Brookville, Marlborough and Port Tobacco, in Maryland, and Leesburg, Warrenton, Middleburg, and other points in Virginia.

219

Transportation within the city during the years preceding the war was conducted by means of lines of stages or omnibuses seating from twelve to sixteen persons. One line ran from the foot of the Capitol to High Street in Georgetown; another from the Capitol to the Navy Yard; while others ran to North Washington and to the steamboat wharves. The fare was at one time a "fip," or 6 ½ cents, but later came to be six cents or five tickets for a quarter.

In 1858 Congress authorized Gilbert Vanderwerken and others to lay a double track horse car line from the west gate of the Capitol grounds along Pennsylvania Avenue and 15th Street to Georgetown. The promoters succeeded in raising $200,000 for this purpose but the project was not carried through at that time, the first car line not being established until 1862.

The decade preceding the Civil War witnessed a number of important public improvements. In 1851 was commenced the construction of the wings of the Capitol, the erection of the Soldiers' Home building, and the improvement of the Mall, the White Lot and Lafayette Square and the site of St. Elizabeth's Insane Asylum was determined upon. In this year also Brown's and Todd's hotels on Pennsylvania Avenue between 6th and 7th Streets were remodeled and combined as the Metropolitan with its present impressive five-story marble front. In 1855 the old wooden dome of the Capitol was removed, and the following year work was begun on the present dome. This work with the construction of the wings of the Capitol continued practically through the period of the Civil War.

In 1854, the assessed value of the real and personal property was slightly under twenty-five million dollars, yielding an annual revenue of nearly $162,000; and the funded debt was slightly under three-quarters of a million dollars.

During the years just preceding the War a very considerable amount of work was done on the streets, the most interesting at this day being the improvement of 14th Street in 1855 with curbing and sidewalks from K Street to the Boundary and bigrading and flag crossings for a part of this distance.

From 1850 to 1860 the population of Washington increased to 61,122, a gain of 50 per cent. During this period Georgetown's population remained practically stationary, the census of 1860 giving that place 8,733 persons, a gain of less than 400 in the preceding ten years.

As the city advanced in population the churches steadily increased in number. In 1833 Concordia Lutheran Church was organized and built, and the First Baptist erected its new building on the site of Ford's Theatre. The new building of the Fourth Presbyterian Church was dedicated in 1841, and the colored members of its congregation organized in 1842 as the First Colored Presbyterian — now the Fifteenth Street Presbyterian Church in Cooks school building on 15th Street, the site of the present church. St. Matthew's Catholic Church was consecrated in 1842, and the E Street Baptist Church in the same year. Ryland Chapel, McKendree M. E. Church, and St. Paul's Lutheran Church were dedicated in 1844; the Church of the Ascension in 1845; and Union Chapel M. E. in 1846.

In 1847 St. Mary's Catholic Church was dedicated, the land having been donated by John P. Van Ness. It was in this year that the first attempt to organize a Congregational church was made, but after a few years the members disbanded owing to dissension over the slavery issue. In 1849 Dumbarton Avenue M. E.

Church was erected, and the colored members of Foundry organized as Asbury M. E. Church.

In 1851 Trinity P. E. Church removed from its original location, where Henry Clay had been a communicant, to its present edifice 3rd and C Streets. The Sixth Presbyterian Church was organized in 1852, and in that year the Church of the Epiphany and Grace Episcopal Church were dedicated. Fletcher M. E. Chapel, Assembly Presbyterian Church, and St. Johannes' German Evangelical Lutheran Church were dedicated in 1853, in which year also Westminster Presbyterian was organized as the 7th Street Presbyterian Church.

St. Dominic's Catholic Church was consecrated in 1856. Its great bell weighing a ton and a half was installed in 1865. In 1857 Fifth Baptist, then known as the Island Baptist Church, Trinity German Evangelical Lutheran and Western Presbyterian Churches were dedicated. Waugh Chapel was dedicated in 1858, and St. Aloysius' Catholic Church was dedicated in 1859. The Washington Hebrew Congregation, which had organized in 1854 occupied the building which had been for some years occupied by the Congregationalists on 8th between H and I Streets.

After the death of President Taylor in 1850, Vice President Fillmore was called to the Presidency, and on July 10 of that year Judge Cranch of the Circuit Court administered the oath to him in the hall of the House of Representatives. Mrs. Fillmore, a scholarly woman more inclined to study than to society, filled well her position as social leader. To her is given credit for inducing Congress to include a library as part of the equipment of the White House.

The last year of President Fillmore's term was marked by the death, on June 9, 1852, of Henry Clay in his rooms at the National Hotel at 6th Street and Pennsylvania Avenue.

On March 4, 1853, occurred the inauguration of President Franklin Pierce. General Pierce arrived from his home in Concord, New Hampshire, a few days before the inauguration, and engaged rooms at the Willard Hotel. In addition to the military parade, the incoming President had the personal escort of a committee appointed by Congress, consisting of the retiring President and Senators Jesse D Bright and Hannibal Hamlin. He was sworn in on the East Portico by Chief Justice Taney. His inauguration was saddened by the death of his son in a railroad accident on the way to Washington, a circumstance to which in his address he feelingly alluded with the words: "No heart but my own can know the personal regret and bitter sorrow over which I have been borne to a position so suitable for others, rather than desirable for myself."

In consequence of her bereavement, Mrs. Pierce, during the first years of her husband's administration, appeared rarely in public. Later she took a more active part in social life as a duty which she owed to her position.

Many brilliant women graced the social life of the Capital at this time, notable among them being Mrs. Jefferson Davis, and Mrs. Stephen A. Douglas, who before her marriage had been known as "the beautiful Adele Cutts. "

President-elect Buchanan, on arriving at Washington a few days before his inauguration, took lodgings at the National Hotel, where he was waited upon by the Judges of the Supreme Court. On March 4, 1857, he drove to the Capitol with the retiring President, their carriage escorted by a lengthy procession. In the evening the usual ball was given in a hall erected for the purpose on Judiciary Square, fifteen thousand tickets being sold for the occasion.

President Buchanan was the country's first bachelor President. Having no family of his own, he had been as a father to his sister's children, and his niece, Harriet Lane, became mistress of the Executive Mansion. She was well fitted for the position, and it has been said of her that a more beautiful woman has never presided over the White House.

Social conditions in the Capital during the decade preceding the Civil War were marked by the growing rift between the northern and southern factions. Each maintained its own circle. The southern element was particularly exclusive and maintained an attitude of studied aloofness toward their fellow residents from the North. Southerners who were obliged to recognize northern men in their official capacity refused to recognize them or their families socially.

On June 1, 1857, occurred the election riot which resulted in the killing and wounding of a number of persons. This affair arose out of the attempt of the Know-nothing party to prevent the participation of naturalized voters in the election by the importation of rowdies from Baltimore.

The trouble started at about 9:30 in the morning when the "Plug Uglies," a club from Baltimore, attempted to drive all naturalized voters from the polls at the first precinct of the fourth ward. In this affair Ward Commissioner Richard Owens, Justices Goddard and Dunn, Chief of Police Baggot, and officers Degges and Birkhead and F. A. Klopfer, a private citizen, were injured. It resulted in driving most of the naturalized citizens from the polls at this place. An hour later, the imported rowdies made an attack at the lower precinct of the second ward and fired several shots.

Mayor Magruder then appealed to President Buchanan for military assistance. The request was referred to the Secretary of the Navy who ordered out a hundred and ten marines under Major Tyler and Captain Maddox who marched to the polling place of the first precinct of the Fourth Ward where they found a party of the disorderly element awaiting them with a six-pound brass swivel under the shed of the Northern Liberty Market at Seventh Street and Massachusetts Avenue. The Mayor addressed the crowd which numbered some fifteen hundred persons and demanded that the polling places be opened. On this demand being refused, a section of the marines under Major Tyler advanced with fixed bayonets to take the swivel gun which was then abandoned by those in charge of it, who, in retiring threw rocks and fired pistols at the marines, one of whom was wounded. The marines were then ordered to fire with the result that six persons, including an infant and two colored men were killed, and a number of others wounded. The rowdies dispersed hastily, some leaving the city on foot and some catching a train as it was leaving the depot. A force of artillery arrived late in the day from Fort McHenry but no further trouble was experienced.

On February 27, 1859, Daniel Sickels, afterwards prominent as a General in the Union Army, killed Philip Barton Key on Madison Place on the east side of Lafayette Square. The trial of Sickels and his acquittal on the plea of the "unwritten law" are among the famous incidents of the country's legal history. Key was a son of the author of the " Star Spangled Banner." His brother Daniel had been killed in a duel by J. H. Sherburne in 1836.

222

In the fall of 1860 Washington received a visit from the then Prince of Wales — afterwards King Edward VII of England. The Prince had been visiting Canada when he was invited to Washington by President Buchanan. During his stay he made a trip to Mount Vernon where he planted a horse-chestnut tree near Washington's tomb.

At 6:30 o'clock on the morning of February 23, 1861, President-elect Lincoln arrived in the city and was met by Congressman Washburne of Illinois who accompanied him to Willard's Hotel. During the forenoon he paid a visit to President Buchanan with whom he had a lengthy interview.

On February 27, Mayor Berret and the City Councils after paying a farewell call to President Buchanan, proceeded to Willard's Hotel, where the Mayor in a short speech welcomed the President-elect, who is reported to have responded as follows: —

"Mr. Mayor: I thank you, and through you the municipal authorities, by whom you are accompanied, for this welcome; and as it is the first time in my life since the present phase of politics has presented itself in this country that I have said anything publicly within a region of country where the institution of slavery exists, I will take this occasion to say, I think very much of the ill-feeling that has existed, and still exists, between the people from the section from which I came, and the people here, is owing to the misunderstanding between each other, which unhappily prevails. I therefore avail myself of this opportunity to assure you, Mr. Mayor, and all the gentlemen present, that I have not now, and never have had, any other than as kindly feelings toward you as to the people of my own section. I have not now, and never have had, any disposition to treat you in any respect otherwise than as my own neighbors. I have not now any purpose to withhold from you any of the constitutional rights, under any circumstances, that I would not feel myself constrained to withhold from my own neighbors; and I hope, in a word, when we shall become better acquainted, — and I say it with great confidence, — we shall like each other the more. Again I thank you for the kindness of this reception."

As there were rumors of threats against Lincoln's life, General Scott on the day of the inauguration posted soldiers along the Avenue and on parallel streets on the roofs of houses. A little before noon President Buchanan called for Mr. Lincoln at Willard's Hotel, and the two proceeded to their carriage, in which, with Senators Baker and Pearce they rode to the Capitol. A guard of picked soldiers of the regular army formed a cordon about the carriage so dense as to hide it from the people on the streets. A striking feature of the parade was a float representing the Union on which the States and Territories were impersonated by young girls dressed in white and carrying flags.

At the Capitol Mr. Lincoln and President Buchanan went arm in arm to the Senate Chamber where they saw Vice-president Hamlin installed. The party then proceeded to the East portico where, from the platform erected over the steps, Mr. Lincoln was introduced by Senator Baker of Oregon. After this, bowing acknowledgement to the thousands of people before him, he read his inaugural address, concluding: —

"Though passion may have strained, it must not break the bonds of our affection. The mystic cords of memory, stretching from every battlefield and patriot grave to every living heart and hearth-stone all over this broad land, will yet swell the chorus of the Union, when again touched, as surely they will be, by the better angels of our

223

nature." The oath was administered to President Lincoln by the venerable Chief Justice Taney.

That night the inaugural ball was held in a specially constructed frame building north of the City Hall. The affair was attended mainly by northern visitors to the city, as the local social element, on account of its southern sympathies, stayed away. The newspapers of the day contained many sportive allusions to the alleged crudities of deportment on the part of the President's western friends. At eleven o'clock the President and Mrs. Lincoln, and Vice-president and Mrs. Hamlin with their party, arrived and were greeted with an enthusiastic demonstration. The first levee of the administration occurred on March 8.

On Saturday, April 13, 1801, occurred the fall of Fort Sumpter. The following Monday President Lincoln issued his call for 75,000 volunteers. Within thirty days nearly fifty thousand troops had arrived at Washington and were encamped in the vacant fields about and within the city or quartered in the public buildings.

A London correspondent wrote:

'It is about forty miles from Baltimore to Washington, and at every quarter of a mile for the whole distance a picket of soldiers guarded the rails. Camps appeared on both sides, larger and more closely packed together; and the rays of the setting sun fell on countless lines of tents as we approached the unfinished dome of the Capitol. On the Virginia side of the river, columns of smoke rising from the forest marked the site of Federal encampments across the stream. The fields around Washington resounded with the words of command and tramp of men and flashed with wheeling arms. Parks of artillery studded the waste ground and long trains of white-covered wagons filled up the open spaces in the suburbs of Washington."

A grand review of the army was held by General Scott on July 4, 1861, on which day Congress met in response to the President's call for an extra session. On July 17, the army started for the battlefield of Bull Run, accompanied by a large concourse of citizens. Following its disastrous defeat came the establishment of hospitals, the construction of fortifications around the city and the reorganization and enlargement of the army until in October, 1861, 150,000 soldiers were congregated in the city and its environs. Following the Peninsular and Second Bull Run campaigns the city became a vast hospital in which it is estimated thirty thousand sick and wounded were at one time under care and treatment. Ovens, constructed on the present site of the Capitol terrace baked sixty thousand loaves of bread a day, and vast quantities of military stores passed through the city to the armies in the field.

After the battles of Cedar Mountain, Second Bull Run and Chantilly in August, 1862, a trainload of nearly a thousand citizens of Washington endeavored to reach the battle field to care for the wounded, but the destruction of the railroad compelled them to return after reaching Fairfax Court House.

During the succeeding year Antietam, Fredericksburg, Chancellorsville and Gettysburg each in turn sent its quota of wounded to the Washington hospitals, of which upwards of seventy were established.

After every battle near the Capital, people from all directions flocked there to find their dead and wounded and heartrending scenes gave constant proof of the barbarity of war.

Washington ladies were constant visitors to the hospitals, giving of their means and service to the wounded. In this work Mrs. Lincoln seemed to find more congenial occupation than in society. Many Washington people not reconciled to the "Black Republican" President, as he was styled by some, did not graciously receive him and his wife into society, but the President's own worth soon made a welcome place for himself, and Mrs. Lincoln held her own dignity in a commendable manner that made for her strong friends among her new acquaintances.

Abraham Lincoln's second inauguration occurred March 4, 1865, and despite bad weather the fore part of the day, the ceremonies were held in the usual way. The procession was chiefly a military one.

In the Senate Chamber Andrew Johnson was sworn into office as Vice-president, after which Mr. Lincoln was escorted to the east balcony of the Capitol where he delivered the celebrated address closing with the words: "With malice towards none, with charity for all, with firmness in the right as God gives us to see the right, let us strive on to finish the work we are in. "

This time Mr. Lincoln was sworn into office by a Chief Justice of his own appointment, Salmon P. Chase. The inaugural ball was held the Monday night following.

On March 23, 1864, General Grant arrived in Washington from the west to take command of all the Union armies, and on the night of May 3 started with the Anny of the Potomac upon the historic overland campaign. Then followed in quick succession the terrible battles of the Wilderness, Spottsylvania, and Cold Harbor, the crossing of the James, and the siege of Petersburg, a campaign from which unprecedented thousands of sick and wounded were brought back to Washington by rail and boat.

In July, 1864, the city was thrown into consternation by the approach, by way of the upper crossings of the. Potomac, of a Confederate force under General Early. Two divisions of the Sixth Corps were dispatched by General Grant from the army of investment in front of Petersburg, and arrived by boat on the afternoon of July 11, under command of General Horatio G. Wright. They proceeded at once to Fort Stevens on the 7th Street Pike. The following afternoon they attacked the forces of General Early, who, perceiving the impossibility of capturing the city, withdrew into Virginia. During this engagement, President Lincoln was an interested spectator. While he stood on the parapet of Fort Stevens a surgeon was wounded within a short distance from him. It was only in response to the urgent importunings of General Wright that he finally stepped down out of range of the passing bullets.

On April 9, 1865, the city, with the entire North, was thrown into a delirium of joy by word of the surrender at Appomattox. Six days later North and South alike were staggered by the news that President Lincoln had been assassinated.

On the fateful night of April 14, 1865, the President and his wife had gone to Ford's theatre to see Laura Keene in "Our American Cousin." The President's entrance into the theatre was the cause of much commotion. Although the first act had begun, the performance ceased, the orchestra burst forth with "'Hail to the Chief," and the audience rose en masse, waving handkerchiefs and hats and cheering lustily.

All went well until second scene of the third act was reached. The President at the time occupied a box at the south end of the stage. With him were Mrs. Lincoln, a Miss Harris, and Major Henry R. Rathbone. The only actor on the stage at the time was a young man named Harry Hawk.

At about fifteen minutes past 10 o'clock a pistol shot rang out, surprising, though not alarming the audience, as it was first thought to be part of the play. A moment later Mrs. Lincoln screamed and John Wilkes Booth, a young actor of great promise, who had gained access to the President's box, leaped from the box to the stage, flashing a dagger tragically and crying "Sic semper tyrannis!"

As Booth jumped from the box on to the stage, a height of about nine feet, his right spur caught in the blue part of an American flag which was draped around the box and tore out a piece which he dragged half way across the stage. He struck the stage floor with such force that he broke the fibula or small bone in his left leg. Despite this accident he faced the audience, cried "The South is avenged!" and made his escape behind the scenes.

Major Rathbone, when he heard the fatal shot, attempted to seize Booth, who was standing immediately behind the President, and who made a thrust with a dagger at Rathbone 's breast which the latter parried with his left arm receiving a wound several inches deep in that arm between the elbow and shoulder.

When the shot was fired President Lincoln was looking down at some person in the orchestra. The pistol ball entered the back part of the left side of his head just behind his ear and lodged in the front part of the brain a short distance behind the right eye.

President Lincoln was carried across the street to house No. 516 Tenth Street, directly opposite the theatre, the home of a Mr. Peterson, where he died at 7:22 o'clock the next morning.

Booth, upon leaving the theatre, mounted a horse which was being held for him in the back alley running north and south, by a hanger on at the theatre called Peanut John, whom Edward Spangler had sent out for that purpose. He rode up to F Street, thence to 9th Street; down Ninth to E; along E to and through Judiciary Square; down 4th to Indiana Avenue; by way of Indiana Avenue, the Capitol Grounds and Pennsylvania Avenue to Eleventh Street east, and thence to the Navy Yard Bridge, where he was halted by Sergeant Silas T. Cobb, in charge of the Bridge guard. He said his name was Smith, and gave a satisfactory explanation to the sergeant, who passed him across the bridge. A few minutes later, David R. Herold rode up to the bridge, and was also passed by the sergeant.

The two reached the tavern at Surrattsville kept by John K. Lloyd, about midnight and obtained a carbine and some whiskey.

Booth and Herold continued in the bright moonlight toward southern Maryland and stopped a short time before daybreak on Saturday morning at the house of Dr. Samuel A. Mudd, about twenty miles southeast of Washington. The doctor with the assistance of his wife, dressed Booth's fractured leg, which, Booth told him, was caused by his horse falling upon him.

After leaving Dr. Mudd's they were hidden by Samuel Cox in a small isolated pine grove, densely undergrown with laurel and holly, about five miles northeast of Pope's Creek, where they remained for six days in a state of wretched untidiness, on several occasions hearing searching parties of cavalry ride past their place of concealment. They were furnished provisions and information by a farmer named Thomas A. Jones, who visited them seven times, and on the cloudy, foggy night of the next Friday conducted them to the Potomac River to a place called Dent's Meadow, a mile or two north of Pope's Creek, where a small stream entered the

Potomac River. The journey from the pine grove to the river was extremely hazardous, as they had to pass two houses, at one of which a number of dogs were kept. Booth rode a horse on account of his broken leg until within 300 yards from the river, when they came to a fence which they could not remove, and Booth had to walk in extreme torture down the steep bluff to the shore, supported by the others. After putting Booth and Herold in a row-boat, Jones lighted a candle and showed them the way to Virginia by means of a compass which Booth had.

The tide was flooding so strongly that it carried them to Nanjemoy Creek, several miles up the river on the same side from which they started. Here they remained all day Saturday, visiting the house of Colonel J. J. Hughes, who fed them and told them how to reach Mrs. Quesenberry's, near Machodoc Creek on the Virginia Shore, to whom Jones had given them a letter of introduction. Saturday night they crossed the river to Gambo Creek, near the mouth of Machodoc Creek. On Monday they were carried to Port Conway on the Rappahannock River, which they crossed at noon of that day to Port Royal, accompanied by three officers of the former Confederate Army, to whom they caused great concern by telling their names and their crimes. It is of interest respecting the disputes as to Booth's identity that one of these officers named W. S. Jett, testified at the trial that he noticed the initials "J. W. B." on Booth's hand.

Booth and Herold then went to the house of Mr. Richard H. Garrett, about three miles south of Port Royal where they slept Monday night. On Tuesday night they slept in the barn, which was surrounded about one o'clock of that night by Federal cavalry, commanded by Lieutenant E. P. Doherty. Booth refused to surrender but offered to come out if the troops were withdrawn so as to give him a chance. The barn was set on fire and Herold came out and surrendered. Booth, who could easily be seen by the light of the fire through the cracks in the barn was shot with a revolver through one of the cracks, by a soldier named Boston Corbett. The ball entered the right side of his neck a little back of his ear and came out a little higher on the other side. He was taken to Garrett's house and laid on the porch where he died about seven o'clock in the morning. His last words were: " Tell mother I die for my country."

The body of Booth was brought to the city of Washington, and buried in the old penitentiary enclosure at Arsenal Point where the War College buildings are now located, and four years afterwards was exhumed and identified by his dentist in Washington and then removed to the Greenmont cemetery in Baltimore city where it was reinterred and remains.

About the same time that the President was shot, Lewis Payne, whose real name was Lewis Thornton Powell, and who was the son of a Baptist minister in North Carolina, entered the room where Secretary of State, William H. Seward, who resided on Madison Place, where the Belasco Theatre now stands, was lying ill in bed, and stabbed him in the right cheek and in both sides of his neck. In gaining access to the room he met both of the sons of Secretary Seward and assaulted them, fracturing the skull of Frederick, and cutting Sergeant George F. Robinson, the Secretary's attendant, on the forehead with a knife, but none of the wounds which he inflicted resulted fatally.

On April 19, funeral services for the President were held in the East Room of the White House. The body was then conducted at the head of a funeral procession three miles in length, to the Capitol where it lay in state two days before being taken to Springfield, Illinois, for burial.

According to a statement made by Samuel Arnold in 1869 and a remark in a lecture by John H. Suratt in December 1870, a party of seven including Booth, Herold, Atzerott, Payne, Surratt and two others, went in the early afternoon of March 16, 1865, to the Soldiers' Home to abduct the President, who was to attend a play there, but who sent a member of his cabinet in his place. It was their intention to capture him in his carriage and drive it to the Potomac River in southern Maryland and carry him across into Virginia.

David E. Herold, George A. Atzerodt, Lewis Payne, Michael O'Laughlin, Edward Spangler, Samuel Arnold, Mary E. Surratt and Dr. Samuel A. Mudd were tried for conspiracy to assassinate the President and other officers of the Federal Government at Washington. The "Military Commission" by which they were tried was composed of Major-General David Hunter, Major-General Lewis Wallace, Brevet Major-General August V. Kautz, Brigadier-General Albion P. Howe, Brigadier General Robert S. Foster, Brevet Brigadier-General Cyrus B. Comstoek, Brigadier-General T. M. Harris, Brevet Colonel Horace Porter, Lieutenant-Colonel David R. Clendenin, and Brigadier-General Joseph Holt, Judge Advocate and Recorder of the Commission, and held its sessions from May 19th until June 30th 1865, in a room in the northeast corner of the old penitentiary which was located at Greenleaf Point.

Mrs. Surratt, Atzerodt, Herold and Payne were condemned to death, and were hanged on the 7th of July 1865 in the walled yard of the penitentiary.

Dr. Mudd, O'Laughlin and Arnold were sentenced to life imprisonment at hard labor, and Spangler to imprisonment at hard labor for six years and were committed to the Military Prison at Dry Tortugas Island, on the Gulf Coast of Florida. They were pardoned a few years later.

The state of popular feeling at this time, was largely responsible for the execution of Mrs. Surratt, which in the calmer judgment of after years is generally regarded as an act of undue severity. The evidence is convincing, that under the magnetic influence of the melodramatic Booth she was involved in a plot to abduct the President; but her remarks just before the assassination and previously, and her expression of astonishment when she first heard of it, imply a reasonable doubt that she had any complicity in Booth's murderous purpose. The memorandum found on his person, when dead, indicates that his determination to kill the President was a sudden impulse of a few hours inception. The fact that Booth called upon her at her residence a few hours before the murder imports little in view of her statement on the afternoon of the tragedy, to Louis J. Weichman, the principal witness against her at the trial, "Yes, and Booth is crazy on one subject, and I am going to give him a good scolding the next time I see him." Certainly that evidence would have had weight in mitigating her sentence, if given at her trial.

On May 23 and 24, 1865, occurred the grand review of the Union Armies by President Johnson and General Grant. On the first day from 9 in the morning to 3 in the afternoon the troops of the Army of the Potomac, lead by General Meade, marched up the Avenue and past the reviewing stand. The following day the Army of the Tennessee lead by General Sherman, travel worn from the march through

Georgia and the Carolinas, followed the same route as their comrades of the Army of the Potomac had taken the day before.

During the Civil war the District of Columbia furnished 16,534 volunteers to the Union Army. Captain J. R. Smead's company of National Rifles, which crossed the Long Bridge on the night of May 23, 1861, and marched toward Alexandria, was the first body of Union troops to invade the State of Virginia. A considerable number of young men of the District also entered the Confederate Army and rendered meritorious service in its campaigns.

Two results of the Civil War having an important bearing on the property rights of numerous residents of Washington were the Acts of Congress providing for the liberation of slaves and for the confiscation of the property of those who had assisted the Rebellion.

The liberation of slaves in the District of Columbia was brought about by the Act of April 16, 1862 and provided for a commission of three members who should assess the value of all slaves whose owners could prove their loyalty to the Union. This Act was entirely independent of the President's Emancipation Proclamation. Under its provisions the sum of $914,942 was awarded for 2,989 slaves, in addition to which one hundred and eleven slaves were liberated for whom no compensation was paid, though later, on proof of loyalty being made by owners, twenty-eight more were paid for.

Colored persons were made liable to the same penalties for offenses as white persons by Act of Congress of May 21, 1862.

Under the so-called confiscation act, proceedings were brought against a number of residents of the District who had rendered aid to the South during the conflict. In a decision handed down July 24, 1863, Judge Wylie of the Supreme Court of the District, held that the property of Southern sympathizers was liable to confiscation under the Act on the theory that the owners were alien enemies. A considerable amount of property was confiscated under these proceedings — personal property absolutely, but real property, in view of a resolution of Congress only for the life time of the owner.

Vice-President Johnson was inaugurated on the morning of April 15, 1865, being sworn into office at the Kirkwood House.

During Johnson's administration his daughter, Mrs. David T. Patterson, a woman of fine mind, culture and amiability, was mistress of the White House, her mother being an invalid. Mrs. Patterson was a woman of great tact, and although feeling keenly the unpopularity of her father, she filled the difficult position assigned to her in a creditable manner that made for her true and lasting friends and admirers.

The most popular society center in Washington during those years was General Grant's residence. The General and Mrs. Grant gave weekly receptions and these were attended by the elite of the city, as well as by old-time friends of the Grants, known in humbler days.

The inauguration of Grant took place March 4, 1869, and the day was one of the most enthusiastic the Capital City had ever known.

Owing to unfriendliness between Grant and Johnson, the latter did not accompany his successor to the Capitol, his place being taken by General John A. Kawlins.

After the oath was administered to Vice-President Colfax, Chief Justice Chase administered the oath to General Grant on the East portico.

President Grant's second inaugural, which occurred on March 4, 1873, was memorable by reason of the bitter cold accompanied by a violent northwest gale, the thermometer registering two degrees below zero. Extreme suffering was experienced by both the spectators and participants in the parade, which was elaborate and largely military in character. As on the first occasion, General Grant was sworn in by Chief Justice Chase. As on many former occasions the inaugural ball was held in a specially constructed building north of the City Hall. It was an enormous frame structure erected by private contributions at an expense of thirty thousand dollars.

The popularity which General and Mrs. Grant had won during their residence in Washington prior to his election continued throughout both of President Grant's terms of office. During his second term occurred the first White House wedding in thirty -two years; that of the President's daughter, Nellie, to Mr. Algernon C. F. Sartoris on May 21, 1874.

The census of 1870 showed the city of Washington beginning to assume metropolitan proportions with a population of 109,199; a gain of over 48,000 in ten years. Georgetown for the first time since 1820, showed a material gain, with a population for 1870 of 11,384; about 2,500 more than in 1860.

The period immediately following the close of the Civil War was not notable for any extensive public works until the commencement of the operations of the Board of Public Works under the Territorial Government, from 1871 to 1874, as related in a former chapter. The only especially notable improvements during this interim were the introduction of bituminous sidewalk and carriageway pavements and the street parking system during 1868 and 1869, by Mayor Bowen, and the paving of Pennsylvania Avenue from First to Fifteenth Streets northwest with wood blocks under Mayor Emery in 1870.

One important semi-public improvement of a local character, which was the pioneer of the era of modern private enterprise in the District of Columbia, and is yet one of the indispensable market accommodations to the residents of Washington, was the erection of the new Center Market by the Washington Market Company in 1872 on Reservation number 7 on Pennsylvania Avenue between 7th and 9th Streets, northwest, This company was chartered by Congress in 1870 as a result of the insufferable conditions existing in and about the old market which had been maintained by the municipality to that time at the same place. While the new company was making preparations to commence building, the old sheds were destroyed by fire on the night of December 17, 1870. Temporary structures were at once erected and the construction of the present building commenced in the spring of 1871 and completed in the summer of the following year.

As a result of a quarrel between the market company and its stallholders, a number of the latter procured the erection of the Northern Liberty Market, the upper story of which is commonly known as Convention Hall, at 5th and L Streets, northwest. This market took the name which had been for many years held by the old market at 7th and K Streets, and which Governor Shepherd had unceremoniously torn down on September 3, 1872.

By acts passed by the Legislative Assembly in August 1871, and subsequent acts, the sites of the present Western Market at 21st and K Streets, northwest, and Eastern

Market on 7th Street between C Street and North Carolina Avenue, southeast, were acquired and the buildings erected; the former at a cost of about $100,000 for site and building and the latter at a cost of $80,000.

In 1874 the old Jail at the northeast corner of Judiciary Square was torn down by authority of Congress, and its materials sold and the proceeds devoted to the improvement of Judiciary Square. The present Jail on Reservation No. 17, near the Eastern Branch, was authorized by Act of June 1, 1872, and completed about 1876. Of the appropriation of $300,000 for this building, $125,000 was contributed from the revenues of the District.

The decade from 1860 to 1870 is notable for the increase which it witnessed in the transportation facilities of the National Capital.

Through transportation to the south by means of railroad tracks across the Long Bridge was first effected as a result of the military necessities arising out of the Civil War. The Evening Star of January 16, 1862, contains the statement: "Notwithstanding the snow and sleet, five hundred men were at work yesterday, preliminary to the construction of a railroad from Washington to Alexandria, over the Long Bridge. There will be a single track with sufficient turnouts to accommodate the camps in Virginia. It is supposed that the road will be in operation in about three weeks. " The same paper on February 8, 1862, says: "The track over the Long Bridge has been laid, and everything is in readiness to open full connection by rail through this city to our camps in Virginia. A double track is being rapidly laid from the Washington depot to the Long Bridge, and when completed trains can run each way the same time."

The tracks across the Long Bridge connected with those which had been laid in 1855 from the Baltimore and Ohio depot via 1st Street and Maryland Avenue to the north end of the bridge. A passenger station was established at 9th Street and Maryland Avenue. In 1865 the "Great Pennsylvania Route" advertised two through trains to the north and west each day with sleeping cars on all night trains and offered to take discharged and furloughed soldiers home at government rates. The following year the Baltimore and Ohio, which had suffered severely by the military operations of the Civil War, announced that it had re-opened for traffic with its cars and machinery repaired and its bridges and track again in substantial condition; and the Orange and Alexandria Railroad announced two trains daily for the south, leaving the corner of 1st and C Streets. In 1870 the Orange, Alexandria and Manassas advertised "new and elegant sleeping cars from Baltimore to Richmond, its trains leaving from opposite the Baltimore and Ohio depot and from the Maryland Avenue station, from which the Washington and Alexandria was also operating trains to the south.

It was the line of track on 1st Street and connecting the Baltimore and Ohio depot at New Jersey Avenue and C Street with the Long Bridge which Governor Shepherd caused to be torn up in 1871, as related in a former chapter. Shortly after this incident Congress, by Act approved June 21, 1870, ratified the action of the City Councils giving to the Baltimore and Potomac Railroad a right of way into the city by means of a bridge across the Eastern Branch, a tunnel under Virginia Avenue from 11th to 8th Street, southeast, and tracks on Virginia Avenue to 6th Street west, with a location for its station on the Mall at 6th and B Streets, northwest. The tunnel was constructed in 1870.

The Metropolitan Railroad, giving the city direct communication with the west by way of Point of Rocks, was completed in 1870 and entered the city from the north by way of 1st Street, west, with its terminus at the Baltimore and Ohio station at New Jersey Avenue and C Street. It connected with the Baltimore and Ohio by a Y at 1st and I Streets, northwest. This road had its inception in 1853 as a project to connect Point of Rocks with Georgetown and the latter corporation had voted to take $250,000 of its stock. The movement was defeated by Mayor Addison of Georgetown, who in 1856 vetoed an ordinance for the payment of the second installment of $25,000 on the subscription, and who, when the ordinance was passed over his veto, refused to sign the bonds to raise the necessary money for paying the installment. The project was revived by President Lincoln in January, 1863, when he sent a message to Congress calling attention to it as a military measure, with the result that a new charter was granted by Congress, by Act of July 1, 1864.

"With the close of the Civil War steamship transportation facilities received an impetus similar to that which attended the railroads. In 1865 the New York and Washington Steamship Company put the steamers Baltimore, Rebecca Clyde and Empire on the run between New York and Washington with two boats each week leaving the company's wharf at the foot of High Street in Georgetown; and the Atlantic Steamship Company placed the screw boats John Gibson, E. C. Knight and Fairfax on the same run with two boats each week from Georgetown. The latter company in 1870 became the New York, Alexandria, Washington and Georgetown Steamship Company. In 1867 a "new express line" advertised a weekly service between Philadelphia, Washington and Georgetown; and the Baltimore, Alexandria, Washington and Georgetown Steam Navigation Company opened a service twice each week between the cities named in its title.

Between Washington and Norfolk the Lady of the Lake and Jane Mosely were operated by the Plant Line from about 1869 to 1873, about which time the Lady of the Lake burned at her dock in Norfolk. She was rebuilt and the two boats taken over in 1873 by the Inland and Seaboard Coasting Company, a reorganization of the New York, Alexandria, Washington and Georgetown Steamship Company.

On August 8, 1873, the Steamer Wawaset, which operated to the lower river landings, caught fire just above Maryland Point arid was beached near Chatterton's Landing. In the neighborhood of eighty-five persons lost their lives either in the flames or by drowning.

The period from 1860 to 1875 witnessed not only the inauguration but the extensive development of the street railway system of Washington.

Although the company organized in 1858 for the construction of a line from the foot of the Capitol to Georgetown had been unsuccessful in carrying the project to completion, a new company, the Washington and Georgetown Railroad Company, was organized under a charter obtained from Congress under date of May 17, 1862, with authority to construct a line from the Navy Yard to Georgetown with cross lines on 7th Street from the Boundary to the water front and on 14th Street from the Boundary to a connection with the main line at 15th and New York Avenue. This line was completed by the close of 1862. It had a branch line running north of the Capitol on A Street, which then existed as a thoroughfare and passing north and south through the Capitol grounds immediately in front of the east front of the Capitol building.

Two years later the Metropolitan Railroad Company was chartered by Act of Congress approved July 1, 1864, and constructed its line from 11th and East Capitol Streets by way of New Jersey Avenue, D, 5th, F, 14th and H Streets, Connecticut Avenue and P Street, to Georgetown, with, a north and south line on 9th and 4th Streets which terminated at Rhode Island Avenue and 9th Street, and which in 1873 was continued to 7th and Florida Avenue, where it connected with the line which ran on 7th Street to the Rock Creek Church Road, and which the Metropolitan Company acquired.

The Columbia Railway Company was chartered by Act of Congress of May 24, 1870, to operate from New York Avenue and 15th Street, by way of New York and Massachusetts Avenues and H Street, to the Columbia turnpike gate. The Capitol, North Street and South Washington Railway Company was chartered by Act of March 3, 1875. This was generally known as the "Belt Line" by reason of the fact that its tracks constituted a loop. It started at the foot of the Capitol and ran north and west on 1st, G, 4th and Streets and south on 14th, and returned by way of Ohio, Virginia and Maryland Avenues to the starting point.

The Anacostia and Potomac River railroad was authorized by Act of February 18, 1875, to run its line from the north end of the Navy Yard Bridge by way of east 11th Street, south M and N Streets, Water Street, 12th and 14th Streets to 14th and Pennsylvania Avenue.

The period of fifteen years from 1860 to 1875 saw a number of important developments in the matter of public education, not only in the city of Washington, but throughout the entire District of Columbia.

Notable in this connection was the inauguration of a system of colored public schools in the cities of Washington and Georgetown under an Act of Congress approved May 21, 1862, which placed them under the existing boards of public school trustees, and provided that ten per cent of the taxes collected from the negroes of Washington and Georgetown be set apart for their creation and maintenance. On June 11 of the same year Congress created a separate Board of Trustees of Colored Schools for Washington and Georgetown. In 1864 Congress provided that such proportion of all school funds raised in Washington and Georgetown should be set apart for colored schools as the number of colored children between the ages of six and seventeen bore to the whole number of children in those cities. The first colored school under this system was opened in that year. In 1867 five colored schools had been established with four hundred and fifty pupils. By 1875 the reports showed an attendance in the colored schools of nearly five thousand five hundred pupils.

The subject of providing public school education for the children of the County of Washington had been dealt with by Congress in an Act approved August 11, 1856, which submitted the question to a vote of the men and women of that section. The proposition was defeated by a large majority, as property holders were unwilling to be taxed to educate poor children. In 1862, Congress, by Act of May 20 of that year provided for a Board of Commissioners of Primary Schools to consist of seven persons to be appointed by the Levy Court, and authorized a tax of one-eighth of one per cent upon the property of white persons for the support of the white schools, and, in the discretion of the Board, a like tax upon the property of colored persons for the support of colored schools.

In 1871, the Territorial Government, by act of August 21, of that year, created separate boards of trustees of white schools for the cities of Washington and Georgetown and the County of Washington, respectively; and by an Act approved March 3, 1873, Congress provided for a board of nine trustees for the colored schools of Washington and Georgetown to be appointed by the Governor of the District of Columbia. These two boards were consolidated by the temporary Commissioners on August 8, 1874, under authority of an Act of Congress of June 20 of that year, the consolidated board consisting of three members from the cities of Washington and Georgetown and the County of Washington, respectively. By Act of September 9, 1874, Congress increased the number of trustees to nineteen, of whom eleven were to be appointed from the city of Washington, three from Georgetown, and five from the County of Washington.

Notwithstanding the disturbed conditions incident to the Civil War, an unusual number of the city's prominent churches were established during the decade in which that conflict occurred. In 1859 the F Street Presbyterian and Second Presbyterian Churches united under the name of the First Presbyterian Church and the following year the new structure of this church was dedicated. President Lincoln was a member of this congregation, and it was here also that President Cleveland attended services. In 1863 the Washington Hebrew Congregation dedicated its new edifice. In 1865 the Capitol Hill Presbyterian Church commenced services in a small chapel and the buildings of Immaculate Conception, and North Presbyterian Churches were dedicated. In 1866 the new structure of Foundry M. E. Church, St. Paul's Episcopal Church, and Calvary Baptist Church were dedicated. The latter was destroyed by fire in 1867 and rebuilt in 1869. The First Congregational Church was organized in 1865 and its building constructed in 1866 and 1867. The Church of the Incarnation (Episcopal) and Hamline M. E. Church were dedicated in 1867; the First German Reformed Trinity Church, St. Stephen's Catholic Church, Memorial Lutheran Church, and the Gay Street Baptist Church in 1868; and the Mt. Vernon Place M. E. Church (South), Metropolitan M. E. Church, St. Mark's Episcopal, the People's Congregational on Street between 7th and 8th, and the Evangelical Lutheran Church at 32nd and Q Streets, Georgetown, were dedicated in 1869. The latter was built on ground which had been donated for the purpose by Col. Charles Beatty just one hundred years before.

In 1871 the new West Street Presbyterian Church was dedicated; in 1872 Grace M. E. and North Carolina Avenue M. P. Churches were dedicated, Fifteenth Street M. E. Church was organized, and the former Capitol Hill Presbyterian Church, with its name changed to Metropolitan Presbyterian, dedicated its new building at 4th and B Streets, southeast. In 1873 Zion Lutheran Church commenced services in a small frame structure.

The buildings of St. Augustine's Catholic Church, which had occupied a temporary structure since 1866; Mt. Tabor M. P. Church, and Central Presbyterian Church, were dedicated in 1874; Eastern Presbyterian Church, and the Church of the Ascension in 1875; Grace Lutheran and North Capitol M. E. Churches, in 1876; Douglas Memorial M. E. and the new All Soul's Unitarian Churches in 1878. Adams Israel Congregation was organized in 1875. In 1879 the old Friends Meeting House was replaced by the present building.

234

On May 27, 1870, occurred the last of the numerous attempts which have at various times been made in Congress to effect the removal of the Seat of Government from Washington. In the course of debate upon an appropriation bill Mr. Benjamin of Missouri moved to strike out a proposed item for the repair of the Capitol building, and although he disclaimed that his action had any reference to the question of the removal of the seat of Government, such was obviously his motive. By a coincidence, the subject was on the same day brought up in the Senate during the debate upon a bill to appropriate money for the extension of the Capitol grounds. Senator Harlan of Iowa, in speaking against this item, based his argument upon a resolution of the Iowa Legislature approved February 25, 1870 instructing the Senators and requesting the Representatives from that State to oppose all appropriations of public funds for the erection of new buildings or permanent additions to those now in existence or for other permanent improvements in the District of Columbia.

Both of the incidents above related were the outgrowth of a propaganda which at the time was being carried on by a resident of St. Louis named L. U. Reavis looking to the removal of the seat of Government to St. Louis.

Owing to the brief interval available for preparation following the determination of the Hayes-Tilden contest, the inauguration of President Hayes was attended with much less ceremony than was customary on such occasions. As March 4, 1877, came on Sunday, Mr. Hayes was sworn in at 7 o'clock on the evening of Saturday, March 3, by Chief Justice Waite, in the Red Room of the Executive Mansion, in the presence of President Grant, General Sherman, and several others. The inauguration day was overcast but mild. Mr. Hayes rode to the Capitol with President Grant and Senator Morrill. Vice-president Wheeler was sworn in by Senator Ferry, the President pre tempore of the Senate, and the oath was a second time administered to President Hayes on the east portico by Chief Justice Waite. The parade was short and no inaugural ball was held. A torchlight procession closed the day's celebrations.

Mrs. Hayes was a prominent member of the Women's Christian Temperance Union, and consequently during her husband's administration alcoholic refreshments were served at the White House on only one occasion; that of the visit of the Grand Dukes, Constantine and Alexis of Russia. Nevertheless, the social life of the White House was no less elaborate under the Hayes leadership than it had been under that of President and Mrs. Grant, and the diplomatic receptions, particularly, of President and Mrs. Hayes have probably never been exceeded in brilliancy. On June 19, 1878, a White House wedding took place, the principals being Miss Emily Piatt, a niece of the President, and General Russell Hastings, formerly Lieut. Col. of the 23rd Ohio Regiment, of which President Hayes had been the Colonel.

In the forenoon of Monday, September 24, 1877, fire broke out in the roof of the south end of the 9th Street wing of the Patent Office building. Aided by a strong south wind it spread rapidly along the 9th and G Street wings. The entire fire department was called out, and one engine brought from Alexandria and four from Baltimore, while detachments of regulars, marines and militia aided the police force in maintaining order. About 1 o'clock the roof of the 9th and G Street wings fell. The fire was practically extinguished by nightfall. The damage was mainly confined to the roof and upper stories of the 9th and G Street wings.

In consequence of a snow storm the night before President Garfield's inauguration on March 4, 1881, the streets that morning were thinly covered with slush. The sun came out early, however, and the Avenue was dry when the parade started. Mr. Garfield rode to the Capitol with ex-President Hayes and Senators Thurman and Bayard. Vice-president Arthur was sworn in by Mr. Wheeler, his predecessor. In the Senate chamber were President Garfield's mother, who sat with Mrs. Hayes and Mrs. Garfield, General Hancock, who had been President Garfield's opponent, and General Sheridan. The new President was sworn in and delivered his address on the east portico. The inaugural parade, which was elaborate, was under the charge of General Sherman who, in civilian clothes, and wearing a great coat and slouch hat with a gilt cord, was described in the Star as "curbing his horse with a free and experienced hand." The ball was held in the newly erected National Museum building.

Owing to the illness of Mrs. Garfield, the four months of her husband's term of office, previous to his assassination saw little in the way of social life at the Executive Mansion.

On the morning of July 2, 1881, President Garfield was shot while passing through the station of the Baltimore and Potomac Railroad at the southwest corner of 6th and B Streets, northwest, by Charles J. Guiteau, who was concealed behind the B Street entrance. The ball passed diagonally from right to left, through the body of the first lumbar vertebra without injuring the spinal cord, and lodged below the left end of the pancreas, where it became completely and harmlessly encysted. The President was removed to the second story southeast room of the depot. Upon the arrival of Dr. D. W. Bliss he was examined and sent to the White House. An error in the diagnosis led to the overlooking of the track of the ball in the wound, and to the daily injection of antiseptic solutions on the right side, which eventually produced an immense abscess cavity in the vicinity of the gall bladder and a long suppurating channel from the wound to the right groin. He was taken to Long Branch, New Jersey, at 6:30 a. m. on the 6th of September via the Baltimore and Potomac railroad with the hope that the conditions there would be helpful to him, but died there at 10:35 p. m., on the nineteenth of that month; one of the causes of death being attributed to the rupture of one of the mesenteric arteries which had been slightly injured by the passing ball.

The attending surgeons and two experts using an "electrical induction balance," decided on August 1st, after a thorough examination, that "the location of the ball has been ascertained with reasonable certainty and that it lies, as heretofore stated, in the front wall of the abdomen, immediately over the groin, about five inches below and to the right of the navel," which presumed a course directly at right angles to the course actually taken by the ball.

Prayers for the President's recovery were, on the recommendation of the Commissioners of the District of Columbia, offered between 10 a. m. and 12 m., on the 6th of September, in all churches in the District. His body lay in state in the rotunda of the Capitol during the 22nd, and funeral services were conducted there on the 23rd, on the afternoon of which date the body was taken to Cleveland, Ohio, via the Baltimore and Potomac Railroad, and funeral ceremonies conducted at Lake View Cemetery in Cleveland on September 26th.

The assassin, who was obviously mentally unbalanced, was tried in the old City Hall from November 14, 1881, until about 5:30 p. m. January 25, 1882, when the verdict of "Guilty" was rendered. He was hanged in the Jail on the 30th of the following June.

General Arthur was sworn in at his residence in New York City by Justices Brady and Donohue of the New York Supreme Court, at 2:30 a. m. on September 20, 1881. A six months' period followed during which no official functions were held, though the President at times entertained informally and accepted the hospitalities of his friends.

For several months following the death of President Garfield President Arthur occupied the granite house belonging to Hon. B. F. Butler at New Jersey Avenue and B Street, southeast. President Arthur was a widower and during his term the White House was presided over by his widowed sister, Mrs. McElroy. President Arthur was the last President to make use of the building erected as a summer residence for the Presidents at the Soldiers' Home.

On October 14, 1881, the French and German guests of the nation in connection with the dedication of the monument at Yorktown commemorating the surrender of Lord Cornwallis, were officially entertained at Washington. The guests were representatives of families of Rochambeau, Lafayette, Viomenil, de Grasse, de l'Estrade, d'Aboville, de Broglie, and von Steuben, and with them was General Boulanger of the French Army. The ceremonies included a military and civic parade to the Capitol where President Arthur, aided by General Sherman and Secretary of State Blaine, held a reception in the Rotunda in honor of the distinguished visitors. That evening Pennsylvania Avenue was, after some difficulty, illuminated with electricity specially for the occasion.

The weather on President Cleveland's first inauguration day was ideal. President Arthur, Mr. Cleveland, and Senators Sherman and Ransom rode together to the Capitol. Just before Vice-president Hendricks was sworn in by Senator Edmunds, announcement was made, amidst great applause, of the passage of the Grant retirement bill and of President Arthur's message nominating General Grant to fill the vacancy caused by it. President Cleveland's inaugural address was delivered, and the oath administered by Chief Justice Waite, on the east portico. The favorable weather made the parade highly impressive. The ball was held that evening in the newly erected Pension Office building, this being the first of the many which have taken place in that structure.

President Cleveland was the country's second bachelor President, and for the first year of his administration the Executive Mansion was presided over by his sister, Miss Rose Elizabeth Cleveland. On June 2, 1886, the marriage of the President to Miss Frances Folsom, in the East Room brought to the White House one of the most popular of the many lovely women who have graced it. The President's wife was twenty-two years of age at the time of her marriage, and at once became the idol of Washington society. An institution of special interest which she inaugurated was a series of informal Saturday afternoon receptions which she insisted upon holding in order to give the self-supporting women of the city an opportunity to meet the Mistress of the White House.

The inauguration ceremonies of President Harrison on March 4, 1889, were marred by the cold northeast rain which fell all day. General Harrison drove to the

Capitol with President Cleveland and Senators Hoar and Cockrell. In the Senate Chamber the President pro tempore, Senator Ingalls, administered the oath to Vice-president Morton and on the east portico the oath was administered to President Harrison by Chief Justice Fuller. Notwithstanding the inclemency of the weather, the parade was memorable both for its extent and. its character.

At the ball which was held in the Pension building, it was estimated there were twelve thousand persons. The occasion was notable by reason of the absence of all liquors or wines, except Roman punch which was served with the supper.

Mrs. Harrison was assisted in the social functions of the White House by her daughters-in-law, Mrs. Russell Harrison and Mrs. James R. McKee.

The close of the first year of President Harrison's term was marked by a series of tragedies. Dinner invitations to the White House had been issued for February 6, 1890, when the death of the daughter of Secretary of State Blaine on February 2, caused them to be recalled. In the early morning hours of the following day the wife and daughter and the French maid of Secretary of the Navy Tracy lost their lives in the fire which destroyed his residence on I Street facing Farragut Square. The funeral of Mrs. Tracy and her daughter was held from the White House on Wednesday, February 5th. The death of Mrs. Harrison, occurred in the White House on the night of October 24, 1892.

On Sunday, June 2, 1889, occurred the latest and probably the highest of the floods which have at different times inundated Pennsylvania Avenue and other streets in the lower levels of the city. From 2nd to 7th Street the water was up to the floor of the horse cars on the Avenue. Much damage resulted, particularly along the water front. The banks of the Chesapeake and Ohio canal were washed away for great distances and one of the main channel spans of the old Long Bridge was carried out. This flood occurred as a result of the storm which caused the memorable Johnstown disaster. Other floods which have permitted boats to be rowed on the Avenue occurred on February 12, 1881, on November 26, 1887, and on October 1, 1870, when the Chain Bridge was carried away. At the time of the last-mentioned flood the waters reached the seats of the horse cars as they crossed the arched 7th Street bridge over the Tiber canal.

A cold northwest wind with a heavy fall of snow greeted the city's visitors at the occasion of President Cleveland's second inaugural on March 4, 1893. Mr. Cleveland and President Harrison rode to the Capitol unaccompanied. Vice-president Stevenson was sworn in by his predecessor, Mr. Morton, and Mr. Cleveland braved the weather to take the oath, administered by Chief Justice Fuller, on the east portico. The parade was much diminished by the non-participation of numerous organizations which had come to take part but were deterred by the storm. The ball was held in the Pension building.

On the evening of May 19, 1893, the Infanta Eulalie, the daughter and representative of the Queen Regent of Spain, with her husband, Prince Antoine, and a suite of nineteen persons, arrived at Washington on her way to the Chicago World's Columbian Exposition. The following day she was received by President and Mrs. Cleveland in the Blue Room of the White House, and that afternoon received a return visit from Mrs. Cleveland at the Spanish Embassy. Five days were spent by the party in seeing the points of interest in and around Washington and in the enjoyment of many social attentions, among the latter being a formal dinner at the White House on the evening of May 23rd.

On June 9, 1893, occurred the second of the catastrophes with which the name of Ford's Theatre will always be associated. The building was occupied as at present, by the Adjutant General 's office of the War Department. A tunnel in the cellar was being dug, and a pillar in the interior of the building had been undermined by workmen and left without shoring. At 9:30 on the morning of the fatal day the flimsy support of this pillar gave way precipitating an extensive portion of the building into the opening, with the result that twenty-two persons were killed outright or fatally injured.

On the 14th of March, 1894, a self-styled "General" Frye in California demanded of the War Department, transportation to Washington and rations for 800 persons who were unemployed because of the business depression of that period, various groups of whom were formed in western parts of the country. They were variously known as Frye's or Kelley's "Army," Galvia's "Hoste, " Jones' "Boston Contingent" and Morrison's St. Louis "Regiment."

On the 25th of March, Jacob S. Coxey with two hundred such followers called "industrials" left Massillon, Ohio, for the City of Washington. They subsisted en route by begging, by giving exhibitions, and by various forms of charity, and on April 7th forty of these men in an exhausted and almost starving condition arrived at Eckington, on the outskirts of the city, and two days later were taken before the Police Court on charges of vagrancy but were dismissed and admonished not to prolong their stay in the city. On April 29th, Coxey with 300 more arrived and were taken by the police to a camp at Brightwood Driving Park. They were permitted to march the next day on 14th Street to Pennsylvania Avenue, then east to 1st and thence back to their camp.

Coxey and two of his lieutenants, Carl Brown and Christopher C. Jones attempted to test their right to speak from the Capitol steps and were arrested. On May 7th they were adjudged guilty of trespass, and on the 21st of that month sentenced to 20 days in the District Jail which they served. Some of these followers removed to Maryland where they were sent to the House of Correction.

During this period the Frye, Galvin, Randall and Kelley bodies reached the District, but upon learning of the disposition made of the Coxey contingent, went in to camp in Virginia. They were driven away by the militia of that State and became a charge upon the District, at the expense of which, they and others were sent to their former abodes. Owing to the admirable police surveillance no actionable violence occurred from their presence.

A beautiful day, an unprecedented concourse of visitors, and most elaborate preparations combined to render March 4, 1897, the day of President McKinley's first inauguration, memorable in the history of the city. President Cleveland, Mr. McKinley, with Senators Mitchell and Sherman, were escorted to the Capitol by Troop A of Cleveland. Vice-president Hobart received the oath from his predecessor, Mr. Stevenson, in the Senate Chamber, and President McKinley received the oath from Chief Justice Fuller and delivered his address from the east portico. The parade was estimated to be four miles in length. The day was closed with a ball at the Pension building and fireworks at the Monument lot.

239

A number of circumstances combined to produce a dearth of gaiety in the White House during President McKinley's administration. Mrs. McKinley was a sufferer from a nervous trouble, and the President, a man of unusually serious bearing, was weighted with the Cuban difficulty and the threats of and later the actual occurrence of the war with Spain. He was, moreover, the object of probably the most vitriolic newspaper attacks to which any President, in recent times at least, has been subjected. His devotion to his invalid wife was the most noteworthy feature of both the family and social life of the White House, which was at times, however, enlivened by the visits of Miss Mabel McKinley, the President's niece.

During the Spanish-American War the Government maintained a military rendezvous at Camp Alger, a short distance south of Fort Myer. Large numbers of troops were concentrated at that point throughout the summer of 1898. The District of Columbia regiment was stationed at this camp until called to take part in the Santiago campaign. On July 3, 1898, it embarked at Tampa, Florida, in a transport, and on the 11th of that month arrived in front of Santiago, in time to complete the investment of that place, being present at the time of the surrender of the Spanish Army.

On September 9, 1898, the regiment returned from the Cuban campaign, detraining at 3rd Street and Virginia Avenue, and marching up 3rd Street and Pennsylvania Avenue past the White House where it was reviewed by President McKinley. The troops were sadly worn with sickness and fatigue and the marching column was followed by ambulances bearing those too enfeebled to walk.

On the night of September 29, 1896 occurred the most destructive storm that ever visited Washington and on the night of Sunday, February 12, and all day February 13, 1899, occurred the snow storm for which that year is memorable.

On October 2, 1899, Admiral Dewey, on his return to the country after his victory at Manilla, was brought to Washington from New York, in company with a local reception committee of one hundred, on a specially tendered train of the Pennsylvania Railroad Company. A short stop was made at Deanwood, near the District line, where Commissioner John B. Wight tendered to the Admiral an engrossed parchment offering him the freedom of the National Capital. The Admiral was welcomed at the depot with an artillery salute of seventeen guns and driven to the White House where he was received by President McKinley and his Cabinet. The entire party then proceeded to the stand where they reviewed the civic parade by the light of electric illuminations and red fire.

The following day occurred the military parade which followed the Admiral, who in company with the President was driven to the Capitol for the ceremony of the presentation of the sword voted to the Admiral by Congress. The front steps of the east portico were occupied by the sailors and marines of the Olympia wearing the medals voted by Congress for participation in the battle of Manilla Bay. After an address by Secretary of the Navy Long, President McKinley tendered the sword to Admiral Dewey with a few appropriate words, the ceremony was closed with a benediction by Cardinal Gibbons, followed by a review of the procession at the stand by the President, Admiral Dewey and General Miles. A state dinner at the Executive Mansion, and elaborate fireworks with a brilliant search-light display closed the celebration.

On December 12, 1900, the date having been designated by President McKinley, was held the celebration of the one hundredth anniversary of the removal of the seat of Government to Washington. The ceremonies consisted in a reception by the President at the White House to the Governors of the States and Territories, with addresses by Colonel Theodore A. Bingham on the history of the Executive Mansion, Commissioner MacFarland, and Governors Shaw of Iowa and Wolcott of Massachusetts. At 1:30 a civic and military parade took place, ending with a review at the Capitol, after which joint exercises were held in the hall of the House of Representatives, participated in by the members of both houses of Congress, the members of the Supreme Court, the Diplomatic Corps, the Governors of the States and Territories, Lieut. General Miles and Admiral Dewey, and numerous other officials. Addresses were delivered by Representatives James D. Richardson and Sereno E. Payne and Senators Louis E. McComas and John W. Daniel. In the evening a reception was held at the Corcoran Gallery of Art in honor of the Governors of the States and Territories.

For the first time in a quarter of a century a President elect on March 4, 1901, rode to the Capitol as his own successor. On that day Mr. McKinley, accompanied by Senator Hanna and Representatives Cannon and McRae, and escorted a second time by Troop A of Cleveland, drove through a disagreeable rain to receive the oath on the east portico from Chief Justice Fuller, the rain ceasing during this ceremony but starting again before the conclusion of the President's address. Vice-president Roosevelt was sworn in by Senator Frye, President pro tempore of the Senate. The downpour was not sufficiently severe to cause material injury to the inaugural parade in which it was estimated thirty thousand persons took part.

On the evening of September 6, 1901, President McKinley, while holding a reception in the Temple of Music at the Buffalo Pan-American Exposition, was shot through the stomach by Leon F. Czolgosz, a Polish anarchist. He was subjected to a surgical operation soon after but died in the early hours of the morning of September 14, at the home of John C. Milburn the President of the Exposition.

The dead President's body arrived at Washington on the evening of the 16th. The following day, escorted by a procession one and a half miles long, it was taken from the White House to the Capitol, where it lay in state the remainder of the day, and was viewed, it is estimated, by eighteen thousand persons.

Owing to a recently enacted statute prohibiting the draping of public buildings, no black draping appeared on the Capitol or White House. That evening the body started on the trip to Canton, Ohio for interment.

Mr. Roosevelt was sworn in as President by Judge Hazel of Columbus on September 16, at the home of Andrew Wilcox in Columbus, Ohio in the presence of the members of the Cabinet.

The social life of President and Mrs. Roosevelt was characterized by the same intense activity which rendered the administration notable. Mrs. Roosevelt was a woman of remarkable energy and administrative capacity, to which were added social qualities of the highest order. The young ladies of the family, Miss Alice and Miss Ethel Roosevelt furnished a motif for many dances, teas, garden parties and similar affairs for their friends of the younger set, to which were added an exceptional number of dinners, at homes, receptions and luncheons, in addition to the regular public functions. In all, the unprecedented number of one hundred and eighty private

White House entertainments were held during the slightly more than seven years of Mr. Roosevelt's period of office.

Prince Henry of Prussia, the brother of Emperor William, came to America in February, 1902, to take part in the launching of the Emperor's yacht Meteor. He came to Washington for a brief visit on the 24th of that month, calling upon President Roosevelt at the White House and shortly after receiving a return of the call from the President at the German Embassy. He also visited Mount Vernon during his visit. On May 24, of the same year, the representatives of the Rochambeau and Lafayette families, together with representatives of the French Army and Navy, were officially entertained at Washington on the occasion of the unveiling of the Rochambeau statue in Lafayette Square. In August, 1902, President Roosevelt received an official visit from the Crown Prince of Siam; on May 28, 1904, he was visited by a representative of the reigning house of China; and on November 14, 1904, he entertained Prince Sadanura Fushimi, a relative of the Mikado of Japan, then on his way to the St. Louis Exposition.

President Roosevelt's proverbial good luck was in evidence on March 4, 1905, when a clear, beautiful day aided the efforts of those who had arranged one of the most impressive of all the Presidential inaugurals. Accompanied by Senators Spooner and Lodge and Representatives Dalzell, and escorted by three troops of Squadron A of New York, the President was driven in the midst of a hollow square of "Rough Riders" from his old Regiment, to the Capitol where, after Vice-president Fairbanks had received the oath from Senator Frye, Mr. Roosevelt delivered his address, and was sworn in by Chief Justice Fuller. Thirty thousand troops marched up Pennsylvania Avenue in the inaugural parade. The celebration closed with a ball at the Pension Office building and a display of fireworks at the Monument lot.

On February 7, 1906, Alice Roosevelt, the oldest daughter of the President, was married in the East Room of the White House to Representative Nicholas Longworth, of Ohio. Two years later Miss Ethel Roosevelt was formally introduced to society in the White House at an elaborate function given by her mother.

On the misty evening of December 30, 1906, a train of empty freight cars running rapidly toward Washington on the Metropolitan Branch of the Baltimore and Ohio Railroad ran into the rear end of a crowded passenger train just starting from the station at Terra Cotta, in the District, killing forty-three persons and injuring more or less seriously about fifty others, many of the killed and injured being Washingtonians.

The inauguration of President Taft on March 4, 1909, took place immediately following one of the worst snow storms in the history of the Atlantic States. Trains were tied up, wires were down, and the suffering, which was general throughout the afflicted section, worked great hardship upon those who had started to see the inauguration, many of whom were prevented from reaching the city.

While the gale was still raging on the morning of the inaugural day a wide space in the middle of the Avenue was cleared of the snow which had fallen by the municipal street cleaning service; and Mr. Taft rode to the Capitol accompanied by President Roosevelt, and Senators Lodge and Knox and escorted by Troop A of Cleveland.

Mr. Taft was desirous of taking the oath on the east portico, but this was regarded by Congress as imposing too much hardship and danger upon its more elderly members, and a resolution was hastily passed providing for the holding of the ceremony in the Senate Chamber. Vice-president Sherman was sworn in by his predecessor, Mr. Fairbanks, and President Taft by Chief Justice Fuller. Under the circumstances, the parade suffered noticeably. Notwithstanding the severity of the weather a brilliant ball was held in the Pension building and some fireworks, though none of the set pieces which had been designed, were displayed on the Monument lot.

Under Mrs. Taft the public functions of the Executive Mansion were held with the usual frequency and éclat. Mrs. Taft proved herself, also, a most agreeable hostess in the affairs of a private nature which she gave to the more intimate circle of her friends. At one of her lawn parties she introduced the innovation of having the grounds of the White House patrolled by a detachment of United States soldiers, a feature which, owing to public disfavor, was not continued.

On January 25, 1912, the Duke of Connaught, brother of King Edward VII of England and uncle of King George V, paid a brief visit to the Capitol, taking tea at the White House with President and Mrs. Taft, and receiving a return call from the President at the British Embassy.

Propitious weather favored the inauguration of President Wilson on March 4, 1913. On the afternoon of the preceding day five thousand women, with several hundred men, marched up Pennsylvania Avenue to call the attention of the country to the cause of Woman Suffrage, concluding the ceremonies with a series of tableaux on the south portico of the Treasury building.

On the day of the inauguration three thousand students of Princeton University and the University of Virginia lined the way for Mr. Wilson from the Shoreham Hotel to the White House. Mr. Wilson was driven to the Capitol in company with President Taft and Senators Crane and Bacon and escorted by the Essex Troop of New Jersey; Vice-president Marshall being escorted by the Black Horse Troop of Culver Military Academy. After Vice-president Marshall had been sworn in by Senator Gallinger, Mr. Wilson received the oath from Chief Justice White and delivered his address from the east portico. Forty thousand persons took part in the military and civic parade which followed. In deference to Mr. Wilson's wishes the customary ball was omitted. It was estimated that 250,000 people came to Washington for this inauguration.

Two White House Weddings have taken place during the term of President Wilson. On November 25, 1913, the President's second daughter, Jessie Woodrow, was married to Mr. Francis B. Sayre in the East Room; and on May 7, 1914, the President's youngest daughter, Eleanor Randolph, was married in the Blue Room to Mr. William Gibbs McAdoo, the Secretary of the Treasury in President Wilson's Cabinet.

The census of 1880 showed Washington with a population of 147,293, a gain of 38,000 in the preceding decade; Georgetown with 12,578, a gain of a little over one thousand; and the County with 17,753. The total population of the District was 177,624, of whom 59,402 were colored. In 1890 the population of Washington was 188,932; that of Georgetown was 14,046; and that of the County, 27,414. Of the total of 230,392, about one-third, or 75,572 were colored.

By Act of February 11, 1895, Congress decreed that from that date the part of the District of Columbia then constituting the city of Georgetown, which by the Acts creating the Territorial and the temporary commission governments had been given recognition under that name, should no longer be known by the name of the city of Georgetown, but should be known as and constitute a part of the city of Washington, the Federal Capitol. By the census of 1900 the combined population of the two former cities was 247,294, and that of the County 45,973. The total population of the District was 278,718, of which number 87,186 were colored. In 1900 the total population of the District was 331,069 of whom 94,941 were colored.

With the beginning of the last quarter of the 19th century the white public-school system of Washington and Georgetown was divided into five districts, of which Georgetown constituted the fifth. Eleven school buildings of considerable size, and other smaller ones, were owned, but approximately one-third of the school accommodations consisted of rented quarters in churches, private residences, engine houses and public halls, in many cases, being one or two room frame or brick structures. The principal buildings were the Franklin, built in 1869; the Seaton, built in 1871; the Jefferson, built in 1872: the Wallach, built in 1864 the Cranch, built in 1872; and the Curtis built in 1875. In the latter year the old first district building at 14th and G Streets was sold and the proceeds used in acquiring another site. An Act of Congress of June 25, 1864, had made school attendance compulsory upon all children between the ages of six and seventeen, but had been a dead letter from the date of its passage, as the voluntary school attendance exceeded the accommodations. In 1875 the enrollment in the white public schools was 11,241 and in the white private schools, 6,837, making a total white school population for Washington and Georgetown of 18,078.

The public schools at this time were divided into nine grades, of which the first eight comprised the courses ordinarily prescribed for elementary schools, and the ninth the work usually assigned to high schools. The classes in the latter grade were retained in the grammar schools as there was then no high school. The normal schools had been established in 1873.

The colored schools in 1875 had a total enrollment of 5,489, and consisted of ten buildings, one of which was used as a high school.

The construction of school buildings, both white and colored, proceeded vigorously, each year witnessing more or less extensive additions to the number.

The most prolific years were 1883 when six new buildings were constructed; 1887 with seven; 1889 with fourteen; 1891 with six; 1896 and 1897 with five each; 1898 with seven; and 1904 with six. In other years the number built ranged from two to four. A total of 174 buildings for white and colored schools have been erected, all except one, since 1864. With the exception of the Franklin and Wallach schools little attention was paid to the architectural features of the school buildings, which were usually designed in the office of the Inspector of Buildings, until, as a result of the efforts of Commissioner Black in 1897, the present system of obtaining competitive designs from architects was inaugurated.

The first white high school building was the Central, at 7th and Streets, which was constructed in 1883. In 1890 the Curtis building in Georgetown was dedicated to high school purposes as the Western, and in 1891 the Eastern High School was constructed at 7th and C Streets, southeast. The Business High School was organized in 1890 in the old Thompson building. The following two years it was located in the Franklin building and for three years occupied the old Minor building which had

244

formerly been used for the colored normal school. In 1896 it was established in the building owned by Thomas W. Smith on 1st Street between B and C Streets, northwest, which had for some years been occupied by the District Commissioners.

The new Western High School at 35th and T Streets was built in 1898 and destroyed by fire on the night of April 24, 1914. The McKinley Manual Training or Technical High School at 7th and Rhode Island Avenue was built in 1902, and the present Business High School at 9th and Rhode Island Avenue in 1904. The purchase of the site for the new Central High School on Clifton Street between 11th and 13th Streets, was authorized by Congress on March 2, 1911, and its construction authorized in Act of March 4, 1913.

The High School Cadets were organized with two companies in 1882. In 1884 a battalion of four companies was organized; in 1890 a company each from the Business and Eastern High Schools was added; and in 1893 a company from the Western and an additional company from the Central High School were added. The organization first paraded as a full eight company regiment at the second Cleveland inaugural on March 4, 1893. Additional companies have brought the present strength of the regiment to eleven companies organized in three battalions. The first competitive drill was held in 1888, and in 1894 the custom of holding the drill out of doors was inaugurated.

The colored High School on M Street between 1st Street and New Jersey Avenue was erected in 1890. The purchase of the new site on 1st Street between N and O Streets, northwest, was authorized by Act of March 2, 1911. The first company of colored High School Cadets was organized in 1890.

By Act of July 1, 1882, the membership of the Board of Trustees of Public Schools, which had been created in 1871, was reduced from nineteen to nine. On March 1, 1895, the number was increased to eleven in order to allow the Commissioners to appoint two women members. By Act of June 20, 1906, the control of the public schools of the District was vested in a Board of Education to consist of nine members to be appointed by the Judges of the Supreme Court of the District. This Act required that three of the members of the Board should be women and that all should have been for five years preceding their appointment bona fide residents of the District of Columbia.

Since the close of the Civil War the development among the colleges and Universities of the District has been such as to constitute a distinctive and highly important feature of the local history.

In 1865 Columbian College was the recipient from Mr. W. W. Corcoran of a building for a medical school on the present site, and that department, which had been discontinued following the conversion of the old infirmary back of the City Hall into a military hospital, was reestablished. In the same year the old Trinity P. E. Church property on 5th Street between D and E Streets was purchased and occupied by the law department. By Act of Congress of March 3, 1873, the name "Columbian College" was changed to "Columbian University."

A movement to furnish the colored youth of the country opportunities for education comporting with the status in which they had been placed as a result of the Civil War resulted in the establishment of Howard University under a charter granted by Congress on March 2, 1867. The chief actors in this movement were a circle of prominent members of the Congregationalist denomination, notably

General 0. 0. Howard, for whom the institution was named, and Mr. B. F. Morris of Cincinnati. The newly erected building at the head of 7th Street was occupied in November, 1868. The law department was opened on January 1, 1869, and the medical department on October 6 of the same year.

Georgetown University opened its law department in October, 1870, occupying temporarily a number of locations until the erection of the present building on E Street between 5th and 6th Streets in 1891. The magnificent main building of the College, known as Healy Hall, was commenced in 1877 and completed in 1879. In 1882 the medical department was permanently housed in its newly erected building on H Street between 9th and 10th Streets.

In 1882 Columbian University established its preparatory school at 14th and H Streets and the following year sold its property at 14th and Euclid Streets and erected its new college building at 15th and H Streets. The Corcoran Scientific School was established in 1884 and the dental department in 1887.

The National University was incorporated in 1879 and at once commenced instruction with its law department. In 1884 it established medical and dental departments which after some years were discontinued. The Catholic University was incorporated in 1887 and commenced instruction in Caldwell Hall in 1889 Georgetown University established its hospital in 1898, its dental department in 1901 and its training school for nurses in 1903.

In 1897 Columbian University discontinued its preparatory school and established its hospital in the building at 14th and TI Streets which the preparatory school had occupied. In 1898 it erected a handsome three-story building in the rear of its main building at 15th and H Streets for its law department and its newly created School of Comparative Jurisprudence and Diplomacy. In 1900 its new medical building was erected on the site of the old one and the main hospital building was erected in the space between the medical building and the old hospital. In 1904 the name was changed to George Washington University. In 1910 the policy which for some years had involved encroachments upon the principal of certain of the University's endowment funds resulted in a reorganization and a sale of the property at 15th and H Streets, the law department being housed in the Masonic Temple at 18th and H Streets and the college departments in a building on I Street between 15th Street and Vermont Avenue. In 1912 the present quarters of the college department on G Street between 20th and 21st Streets were rented and the following year were purchased by the University.

The Catholic University, following its establishment in 1887, has grown rapidly. Caldwell Hall, the pioneer building has been followed in the order named by McMahon Hall, Albert (formerly Keane) Hall, and in 1912, by Gibbons Hall.

The American University was incorporated under the laws of the District on June 3, 1891, under the auspices of the Methodist Episcopal Church. The site, embracing ninety-two acres at Nebraska Avenue and the Loughborough Road, was acquired at about this time, but the buildings were not completed until the present year. The dedication ceremonies, participated in by President Wilson and Secretaries Bryan and Daniels were held on May 27, 1914.

The last thirty-five years have seen many notable developments in church lines, not only in the establishment of new churches, but in the erection of new, larger and more beautiful structures for the older congregations, and in several cases their removal to more appropriate locations.

The year 1881 was signalized by the dedication of four prominent churches the Church of the Reformation (Lutheran), Tabernacle Congregationalist Church, St. Andrew's Church (Episcopal), and Plymouth and Lincoln Memorial Congregational Churches (Colored).

The Church of Our Father (Universalist) was dedicated in October, 1883. The first steps looking to the formation of this congregation had been taken in 1867. Previous to the erection of the present building the congregation had worshipped in various halls. The Vermont Avenue Christian Church, in which President Garfield had worshipped, was after his death replaced by the present building, erected as a memorial to the Martyred President, which was dedicated in 1884. In that year also the new building of St. Patrick 's Church was dedicated, and St. James' Episcopal Church was erected sufficiently for occupancy. The Church of Our Redeemer (Lutheran) was dedicated in 1885; Grace M. E. Church (South) was organized in 1886 and the building completed soon after; St. Paul's Catholic Church and Independent M. E. Church were dedicated in 1887, the Fifth Congregational Church organized with its place of worship in Milford Hall at 8th and I Streets, and the original Metropolitan Baptist Church was completed in 1888; and the new St. Mark's Episcopal Church was completed in 1889.

The present marble structure of St. Peter's Catholic Church and the new First Baptist Church were erected in 1890. Twelfth Street Methodist Church, St. Joseph's Catholic Church Maryland Avenue Baptist Church, the new building of St. Mary's Catholic Church, Keller Memorial Church (Lutheran), Grace Baptist Church, and the new First German Reformed Trinity Church were erected in 1891. The Church of the Covenant was first occupied in 1885, but not completed until 1892, and the Church of the United Brethren of Christ in the same year. St. Thomas Episcopal Church was organized in 1892 and its building erected soon after.

In 1893 the congregation of Unity Presbyterian Church, which had occupied a brick chapel the site of the present buildings since 1884, erected their new structure under the name of Gunton Temple Memorial Church. In 1896 the Church of the New Jerusalem (Swedenborgian) which had been organized in 1846 and had occupied a number of locations including a church building on north Capitol Street which was burned in 1889, erected its present Gothic structure on the Avenue of the Presidents. The Church of the Sacred Heart was dedicated in 1900. St. Margaret's Episcopal Church was organized in 1897 and constructed soon after.

In 1904 the new building of Foundry M. E. Church on the Avenue of the Presidents was dedicated, the old structure at 14th and G Streets being replaced by the Colorado Building. Ingram Memorial Church was dedicated in 1910. The Chapel of the Nativity, the first portion of the Protestant Episcopal Cathedral to be constructed, was dedicated in 1912, as was also the new building of the Metropolitan Baptist Church. In 1913 St. Matthew's and St. Martin's Catholic Churches and the First Church of Christ, Scientist, were dedicated. The Central Presbyterian Church was dedicated in 1914.

The local branch of the Young Men's Christian Association was organized in 1852 by William J. Rhees, Rev. Thomas Duncan, and Rev. William C. Langdon. It was incorporated by a special Act of Congress in 1864. Various locations were

247

occupied from time to time until 1900, when the building of the Columbia Athletic Club on G Street between 17th and 18th Streets was purchased. This proving inadequate to the needs of the Association, the adjacent property was acquired and the new building erected in 1905 adjoining the old. The Association has established a branch for railroad men at the Union Station, and branches for soldiers at Fort Myer, Washington Barracks, and Marine Barracks. A branch for colored men is located at 1816 12th Street, northwest. It has a total membership, in all branches of more than six thousand five hundred.

The regulation of the practice of medicine appears to have remained chiefly with the Medical Society of the District of Columbia until 1874. By an Act of June 23 of that year Congress directed the Board of Health to make regulations looking to the recording of vital statistics. One of the regulations so established required all persons practicing medicine in the District to be registered with the Board of Health; and the Commissioners by an order dated August 28, 1874, provided that physicians who should be entitled to registration should include such as had received licenses from some medical society or those holding diplomas from medical schools or institutions. No further regulation of practice was attempted until the enactment of the so-called Medical Practice Act of June 3, 1896, which was passed in recognition of a demand from physicians that some more stringent regulation than had formerly existed be established. This Act provided for the creation of three boards of medical examiners representing respectively the regular, the homeopathic and the eclectic schools of practice, which should examine applicants for licenses to practice and report to the Board of Medical Supervisors consisting of the presidents of the three boards of examiners. The Board of Dental Examiners had been created by Act of June 6, 1892. By Act of May 7, 1906 a Board of Pharmaceutical Examiners was created and its president merged with the former Board of Medical Supervisors in a Board of Supervisors in Medicine and Pharmacy. An Act of April 29, 1902, created an Anatomical Board to regulate the distribution of bodies among the various medical schools of the District.

Mention was made in a former chapter of the agitation resulting in the passage of the Act of March 2, 1893, relative to the establishment of a permanent system of highways in that portion of the District lying outside of the cities of Washington and Georgetown. This Act directed the Commissioners to prepare a plan for the extension of the highways over the territory mentioned, subject to certain stipulations as to width of streets; the work to be done in sections as occasion should demand; and that the maps of the sections as laid out should be subject to the approval of a commission consisting of the Secretaries of War and Interior and the Chief of Engineers. The Commissioners were further given authority to lay out circles and reservations at the intersections of the principal avenues and streets, corresponding in number and dimensions with those existing at such intersections in the city as originally laid out. This monumental task was accomplished between the years 1893 and 1898 by Mr. William P. Richards of the District Engineering Department, who had immediate charge of the work. Mr. Richards was largely aided by Captain, afterwards Commissioner, Lansing H. Beach, who as one of the assistants to the Engineer Commissioner during the greater part of this period gave the project his special attention. By a provision in the Act of March 2, 1893, as well as by subsequent provisions in Acts of June 30, 1898, and February 16, 1904, the Commissioners were empowered to name the streets, avenues, alleys, highways, and reservations so laid off. By an order of August 6, 1901, the Commissioners adopted an elaborate system to be followed in giving names throughout the entire highway extension system, and by an order dated October 15, 1904, and numerous orders subsequent thereto have given names to various streets and reservations under the system so adopted.

The nomenclature of the streets of Georgetown was changed to make it conform as nearly as possible to that of the streets of Washington by an order of the Commissioners of October 4, 1880. This was an arbitrary order and was without authority from Congress, which, however, by the Act of February 11, 1895, abolishing the separate designation of the city of Georgetown, directed the change in the nomenclature of the streets of Georgetown to be made. Nothing was done by the Commissioners in compliance with this requirement until eleven years after the passage of the Act, when, by an order dated November 24, 1909, they validated their former action.

The first telephone service installed in the City was the National Telephone Exchange which was established by George C. Maynard and William H. Barnard in 1879, and which was succeeded in December 1 of that year by the National Capital Telephone Company. The latter company was succeeded by the Chesapeake and Potomac Telephone Company, a New York corporation, in August, 1883. No specific authorization by Congress of any telephone company to do business or lay wires in the city appears ever to have been granted, the only legislation on the subject being in the form of direction to the Commissioners in various appropriation bills not to allow other than existing companies to lay wires in the streets and limiting the height of wires and length of conduits.

In the fall of 1881 the first attempt at the introduction of electric lighting in the City of Washington took place in connection with the ceremonies attending the dedication of the statue to General Thomas in Thomas Circle. It was planned to string a temporary row of arc lamps over the middle of Pennsylvania Avenue from the Peace Monument to the Treasury Department by means of guys stretched across the street, the current to be obtained from a dynamo connected with the engine of a saw mill on 13th street. This attempt was not a success but as an immediate consequence of the interest awakened by it, the Heisler Electric Light Company was incorporated by Messrs. Stilson Hutchins, D. B. Ainger, Wm. Dixon, Moses Kelly and George A. Kelly. A small experimental plant was established in the Washington Post Building supplying current to a small number of lights in the neighborhood of Pennsylvania Avenue and 10th Street. On October 14, 1882, the United States Electric Lighting Company was incorporated under the laws of West Virginia, with a capital of $300,000, and took over the property of the Heisler Company. This company vigorously extended its system throughout the city, its first large contract being with the Baltimore and Ohio Railroad. In 1884 it laid an underground conduit on Pennsylvania Avenue and other streets, being one of the pioneers of underground conduit construction, in which its expensive system was regarded as a model. The company's plant was burned down on the night of July 16, 1885, but within two weeks the company was again in operation and the following September consolidated with the Brush Electric Light Company. The present building at 13th and B Streets was completed in 1887.

On November 27, 1898, the city post office was established in the unfinished General Post Office building on Pennsylvania Avenue between 11th and 12th Streets, after more than a century of migration from one location to another. Mr. Madison Davis, in a paper read before the Columbia Historical Society in 1902, gives an interesting account of its various homes, from which the following information is gathered: from July 17 to December 31, 1795, the city post office was located at the home of Thomas Johnson, Jr., the first postmaster on the north side of F Street between 13th and 14th; from January 1, to September 30, 1796, at the home of Christ. Richmond, at the southeast corner of 13th and F Streets; from October 1, 1796 to January 29, 1799, on 1st Street between East Capitol and A Streets, northeast; from January 30, 1799, to June 19, 1800, on the north side of F Street between 13th and 14th, probably the same as its first location; from June 11, 1800 to June 30, 1801, at the northwest corner of 9th and E Streets; from July 1, 1801, to March 31, 1802, on F between 14th and 15th Streets; from April 1, 1802 to June 30, 1810, in the "Southwest Executive Building, then occupied by the State War and Navy Departments on 17th Street, southwest of the President's House; from July 1, 1810, to October 31, 1812, in a building somewhere on Pennsylvania Avenue west of the President's House; from November 1, 1812, to June 30, 1829, in Blodget's Hotel on E between 7th and 8th Streets; from July 1, 1829, to December 15, 1836, in an extension of the Blodget building on 7th and E Streets; from December 16, 1836, the date of the destruction of the Blodget building by fire, to December 30, 1837, in Sceaver's house on the west side of 7th between D and E Streets; from December 31, 1837, to June 28, 1839, in the old Masonic Hall, which is still standing, at the southwest corner of 4£ and D Streets; from June 29, 1839, to September 30, 1841, at the present site of the Raleigh Hotel, at Pennsylvania Avenue and 12th Streets; from October 1, 1841, to September 22, 1843, in the large rooms under Carusi's saloon, which was then a place of entertainment for the fashionable people of the city, at 11th and C Streets; from September 23, 1843 to July, 1857, in two brick buildings on the west side of 7th street between E and F, just north of the south portion of the uncompleted General Post Office, now the Land Office building; from July, 1857, to November, 1879, in the 1st floor of the F Street front of the completed General Post Office building; from November, 1879, to May 31, 1892, in the former Seaton House on the south side of Louisiana Avenue between 6th and 7th Streets; from June 1, 1892 to November 26, 1898, in the Union building on the north side of G Street between 6th and 7th Streets.

In July, 1908, the new Municipal Building on Pennsylvania Avenue between 13th and 14th Streets, was occupied by the District government. The first permanent headquarters of the District government, following the abolishment of the Territorial government, were in the Morrison building on the west side of 4th Street just above Pennsylvania Avenue, which it occupied from July, 1874, to June 28, 1887. It then moved to the remodeled lumber warehouse of Mr. T. W. Smith on 1st Street between B and C Streets, which it occupied until May, 1895. It then removed to 464 Louisiana Avenue, opposite the old City Hall, where it remained until it removed to the newly completed Municipal Building.

Among the principal railroad developments of the last decade of the nineteenth century were the entrance into the city of the Chesapeake and Ohio Railway Company on April 1, 1891, and the consolidation of southern lines into the Southern

Railway Company on July 1, 1894. The coming in of the new century has been rendered memorable by the construction of the Washington Passenger Terminals and the Union Station.

The Union Station was the result of an insistent demand for the removal of grade crossings, and of the desirability of removing the railroad tracks and station of the Baltimore and Potomac Railroad Company from the Mall, as well as of the convenience and artistic results to be gained from the establishment of a single station in which due regard should be had to esthetic considerations.

Agitation against grade crossings dates back practically to the coining into the city of the Baltimore and Potomac Railroad in 1872. The first legislation on the subject consisted in two separate Acts of Congress, both dated February 12, 1901, dealing respectively with the Baltimore and Ohio and the Baltimore and Potomac Railroad Companies.

With respect to the first named company, Congress by this legislation provided for a station near the site of the present Union Station with an overhead viaduct from the north. With respect to the latter company it provided for a new station on the site of the old one on the Mall between 6th and 7th Streets, with an overhead viaduct across the Mall and on Maryland and Virginia Avenues, a new steel railroad bridge in place of the old Long Bridge, and a new steel highway bridge five hundred feet above the location of the old Long Bridge.

The efforts of the Park Commission of 1901 looking to the removal of the railroad tracks and station from the Mall, the fact that Mr. Burnham of that Commission was the architect for the Pennsylvania Railroad Company, and to some extent, the formation of a community of interest in the ownership of the Pennsylvania and Baltimore and Ohio Railroads, resulted in the passage by Congress of the Act of February 28, 1903, providing for the erection of the Union Station on its present site at the intersection of Delaware and Massachusetts Avenues, at a cost of not less than four million dollars, with overhead viaducts from the north which should connect with the Maryland and Virginia Avenue tracks of the Baltimore and Potomac Railroad by a tunnel under the Capitol grounds approximately on the line of 1st Street, east. The passenger traffic of the Pennsylvania Railroad was to come into this station over a line connecting at Magruder Station, Maryland, with its existing line.

To compensate them for the rights and property surrendered and for the expense incident to the construction of the new terminals, Congress provided for the payment of one and a half million dollars each to the Baltimore and Ohio and Pennsylvania companies; the payment to the former to be borne in equal shares by the general Government and by the District of Columbia, and the payment to the latter to be borne entirely by the United States.

The Acts of Congress above mentioned authorized the creation of a terminal company for the purpose of constructing and operating the terminals and station, and accordingly The Washington Terminal Company was incorporated on December 6, 1901, its stock being taken in equal shares by the Baltimore and Ohio and Pennsylvania companies. The Union Station was designed by Daniel H. Burnham and Company, of Chicago. The first train came into the new station on October 23, 1907.

The tracks controlled by the terminal company extend from Florida Avenue to the south portal of the tunnel and are used by the other roads entering the city under special trackage contracts. The terminal company handles only passenger traffic, each of the several railroad companies maintaining its own freight yards.

Other less important developments in the way of rail communication with points outside of the city were the completion of the Washington and Chesapeake Beach Railway in 1892; the Washington, Alexandria and Mt. Vernon Electric now the Washington and Virginia, Railway in 1894; and the trackage arrangement of April 15, 1907, whereby the Washington, Baltimore an Annapolis Electric Railway Company enters the city over the tracks of the Washington Railway and Electric Company.

An event of importance to Georgetown was the establishment of direct steam railroad connection with the Baltimore and Ohio system. This was accomplished by the building of a line along the Georgetown water front under a charter to the Georgetown Barge, Dock, Elevator and Railway Company granted in 1888, the work being completed in 1890. The line for some distance up the river was constructed by the Washington and Western Maryland Railroad Company in 1909; and the line from the point where it crosses the Chesapeake and Ohio Canal to a connection with the Metropolitan Branch of the Baltimore and Ohio at Chevy Chase Station, was constructed by the Metropolitan Southern, a subsidiary company to the Baltimore and Ohio, in 1910.

The beginning of the last quarter of the nineteenth century found most of the water transportation business of Washington in the hands of four companies; the Inland and Seaboard Coasting Company, the Clyde Line, the Washington Steamboat Company, Ltd., and the Potomac Steamboat Company.

The Inland and Seaboard Coasting Company continued for a number of years to operate the John Gibson and E. C. Knight on the New York run. The Knight was sunk in collision with a schooner off Hog Island in 1883, and the Gibson was sold when the line was abandoned in the following year. This company continued to operate the Lady of the Lake and Jane Mosely on the run to Norfolk until 1892, when the advent of the more modern steamers of the Norfolk and Washington Steamboat Company forced the older vessels off the route. The Inland and Seaboard Coasting Company built the John W. Thompson, named after its first President, about 1878, and placed her on the run to the lower river landings. After the breaking up of the company she was sold to E. S. Randall and her named changed to the Harry Randall.

The Clyde Line started about 1876 with the small side-wheel steamer Sue on the run between Washington and Baltimore, with stops at the lower river landings. About 1887 the Sue was bought by Charles Lewis, who for some time had been operating the John E. Taggart on the same run, and who in October, 1894, sold out to the Weems Line, which at once replaced the Taggart with the iron screw steamer Potomac. This line in 1900 replaced the Sue with the screw boat Northumberland; in 1902 it replaced the Potomac with the Calvert; and in 1905, it replaced the Calvert with the Anne Arundel. In 1907 the line was purchased by the Maryland, Delaware and Virginia Railway Company, which replaced the Anne Arundel with the Three Rivers.

In 1878 the Express, which was operated by a rival of the Clyde Line was wrecked in a storm on Chesapeake Bay, near the mouth of the river, with the loss of several lives.

The Washington Steamboat Company operated the Wakefield and T. V. Arrowsmith on the lower river route from 1878 to 1895, when these boats were acquired by the Randall Line, which added to the fleet the former John W. Thompson, re-named the Harry Randall. In 1906 the line was bought by the Chesapeake and Potomac Steamboat Company which has since continued to operate it on the old run, to the lower river, and which changed the name of the Harry Randall to the Capital City.

The Potomac Steamboat Company under the management of George E. Mattingly operated the George Leary and Excelsior between Washington and Norfolk from about 1876 until March, 1891, when the line was taken over by the Norfolk and Washington Steamboat Company. The Excelsior had been built to ferry cars to the Richmond and Fredericksburg Railway terminus at Aquia Creek; and after the construction of the track from that terminus to Quantico, on the Potomac, was used to carry passengers from Washington to Quantico until the construction of the railroad from that place to Alexandria in 1872 completed the through rail connection between Washington and Richmond. She was exceptionally fast, with double boilers and a superstructure so high as to completely hide her walking beam.

The Norfolk and Washington Steamboat Company commenced operations in the Spring of 1891 with the palatial screw steamers Washington and Norfolk, to which in 1895 was added a larger boat, the Newport News, and in 1905 and 1912, respectively, the still larger vessels Southland and Northland. This line since its inauguration has been under the management of Mr. D. J. Callahan, with Mr. E. B. Bowling as General Agent.

The steamer W. W. Corcoran commenced making trips to Mount Vernon about 1870 and continued to do so until replaced by the Charles Macalester in 1890. She was burned at her dock in September, 1891. About 1876, and for some years after, the Arrow, a small fast steamer, also took excursions to Mount Vernon. The Mary Washington, a flat-bottomed steamer, equipped with a centerboard, was operated by E. S. Randall as an excursion boat to White House and Occoquon from about 1873 to 1882.

In the early eighties Mr. E. S. Randall commenced running the Pilot Boy on excursions to River View, later adding the Samuel J. Pentz and Harry Randall. During the late nineties the Macalester was aided on the Mount Vernon and Marshall Hall run by the River Queen, a fast ante-bellum boat, which had been used as a transport during the Civil War, and on which President Lincoln made his visit to the Union Army in front of Petersburg in 1865. After being used on the Marshall Hall run for several years the River Queen was employed for a number of seasons in carrying colored excursions to Notley Hall and Glymont. Colonial Beach was established as a summer resort during the late eighties, since which time a number of steamers have been engaged in the extensive excursion traffic to that place; among them the T. V. Arrowsmith, the Jane Mosely, the Harry Randall, and since 1906, the St. John's of the Chesapeake and Potomac Line.

In connection with the history of the water front, it is of interest to mention that the first patrol boat was the small steam launch Joe Blackburn which was put in service in 1888. She was replaced by the Vigilant in 1897.

The first fire boat was the Fire fighter which went into service October 31, 1905. The provision for her in the District Appropriation Act of 1905 was the result of the personal and practically unaided efforts of Mr. M. I. Weller.

The development and improvement of the horse car lines of the city until they were superseded by the cable and electric methods of propulsion, were in large measure the result of the competition of the chariot and herdic lines.

The so-called chariots, were put in service on Pennsylvania Avenue by Mr. John B. Daish on March 5th, 1877, the day of President Hayes' inauguration. Fifteen of these vehicles operated from 22nd and Pennsylvania Avenue, via G Street, and the Avenue, to the foot of the Capitol. Subsequently twenty more were put on a route from 32nd and M Streets in Georgetown to 4th and Pennsylvania Avenue, southeast. To meet this competition the Washington and Georgetown Railroad Company placed on Pennsylvania Avenue from 17th Street to the Peace Monument a line of so-called bobtail one horse cars, with a three cent fare. The chariot line, which had a fare of five cents or six tickets for a quarter, accepted the tickets of the street railway companies and resold them at a discount in large quantities to the Government, and to the department stores and other purchasers, a course which was necessitated by the refusal of the street railway companies to redeem them. The chariots were continued for two and a half or three years, when, the adventure not proving profitable, the equipment was sold to the Washington and Georgetown Railroad Company.

The Herdic Phaeton Company in December, 1879, commenced carrying passengers in vehicles which took their names from their designer, Peter H. Herdic, of Wilmington, Delaware. This company commenced operations with a line of one-horse vehicles from 22nd and G Streets, northwest, by way of G Street and Pennsylvania Avenue, north of the Capitol, to the Navy Yard gate. To meet this competition the Washington and Georgetown Railroad Company reestablished the line of one-horse cars with a three cent fare from 17th Street and Pennsylvania Avenue to the Capitol, with which it had fought the chariot line, but so large a proportion of the traffic took advantage of these ears that the railroad company was compelled to discontinue them and meet the competition of the herdics with a more frequent two-horse car service.

In 1883 the herdic company established a line from 11th and East Capitol Streets to 15th and T Streets, northwest, by way of East Capitol Street, Pennsylvania Avenue and 15th Street. This line passed through the Capitol grounds, and around the Capitol to the north, the vehicles passing under the steps of the Senate wing to discharge passengers, and in inclement weather doing the same at the House wing. To meet the competition resulting from the 15th Street portion of this line, the Washington and Georgetown Railroad Company in 1884 replaced its old one-horse cars on the 14th Street line with two-horse ears, and instead of stopping them at 15th Street and New York Avenue, continued them on Pennsylvania Avenue, part going up to the east front of the Capitol from the south, and part replacing the branch line which had been maintained from the Peace Monument to the old Baltimore and Ohio depot at New Jersey Avenue and C Street. Soon after this the herdic company moved its route from 15th to 16th Street. About this time it installed an entire new equipment of two-horse coaches.

In 1886 the herdic company established a line on I and K Streets to 13th and north on 13th to T Street, northwest; and another line west on I Street to 17th, on 17th to N and on N to 21st Street, northwest, using on the latter some of its old one-horse coaches.

In 1887 the herdic company discontinued that part of its service from the Capitol to the Navy Yard gate, as well as its ends at 13th and T Streets, and 21st and N Streets, and placed a. two-horse line from 22nd and G Streets northwest, to the Toll Gate at 15th and II Streets, northeast, by way of G, 15th, F, 5th, and H Streets, running in competition with the Columbia Railway Company 's one-horse car line. To meet this competition the Columbia Railway Company replaced its one-horse with two-horse cars and later inaugurated a system of reciprocal transfers with the Metropolitan Railroad Company at 14th and New York Avenue and at 9th and New York Avenue.

The change from one-horse to two-horse cars on the Metropolitan line took place in 1886 and 1887, being effected first on the F Street line and afterwards on the 9th Street line. This change however, had no connection with the activities of the herdic company.

It was in large measure due to the efforts of the herdic company that Congress by Act of May 25, 1894, required all street car and herdic tickets to be printed in sheets of six each, and compelled the acceptance of each other's tickets by all lines, and provided for monthly settlements between the various companies; at the same time forbidding the reissue of the tickets after being once used. Previous to this the tickets were resold as long as they held together, and before they were retired became very soiled and filthy. The herdic company sold the street car tickets received by it in lots of one hundred for $3.90 and later issued books of its own tickets at the same rate. Many of its passengers then adopted the custom of sitting by the ticket receptacles, there being then no conductors on the herdic line, and taking all fares, whether cash or tickets, of the street car lines, and depositing herdic company tickets in the receptacles. This course soon threatened to prove disastrous to the herdic company which then obtained the passage of the law above mentioned in order to compel the railway companies to accept its tickets.

The herdic company continued to run its vehicles until the death of Commodore Potts of Philadelphia, the principal stockholder, in 1896, when it ceased operations for some months. Through the efforts of Mr. Edgar A. Nelson, who had been superintendent of stables practically since the inauguration of the company, and who secured an option on part of the equipment, the concern was reorganized as the Metropolitan Coach Company with Mr. S. Dana Lincoln as its President, and on May 1, 1897, commenced operating a line from 16th and T Streets to 22nd and Gr Streets, under a reciprocal transfer arrangement with the Metropolitan Railroad Company at 15th and H Streets. In 1909 it replaced its horse-drawn coaches with gasoline motor vehicles, experimenting with four different types, and re-equipping its entire line in February, 1913. In May, 1914, it extended its line, which then operated from 16th and U Streets to 15th Street and New York Avenue, on Pennsylvania Avenue to 9th Street, west.

After the construction of the last of the horse car lines in the early seventies, no important extensions were made in the street car systems of the city until the late eighties, when the need for some more rapid method of travel, together with the coming into use in other cities of the cable and various electric systems, resulted not only in the speedy abandonment of horses as a means of propulsion on the existing lines, but in the construction of numerous new lines both in the city and in its suburbs.

Several interesting experiments were made at this time with a view to discovering some practicable substitute for horses. One which was tried on a short stretch of track on 7th Street north of Florida Avenue in about 1890, consisted of two parallel tubes six or eight inches in diameter installed in an underground conduit and caused to revolve by compressed air engines stationed about five hundred feet apart, which imparted motion to the car by means of staggered wooden wheels which pressed against them. On the first attempt to operate this system the pipes supplying the air to the engines froze and the attempt was abandoned. Another system tried out without success by the Anacostia line on a stretch of track three blocks long consisted of magnets set at regular distances along the track, and supplied with current by a wire, which were expected to attract and repel the car as it passed over them. The Metropolitan line tried storage battery cars on its F Street line for a year about 1890 in conjunction with its horse cars, but with little success.

The Eckington and Soldiers' Home Railway Company and the Rock Creek Railway Company were both chartered in 1888 and put in operation about 1891. The former started at 7th Street and New York Avenue, running east on the latter to 3rd Street and thence northward to Brookland. As originally constructed it used the overhead trolley and was the first road in the city to be equipped with electric motive power. Shortly afterwards this line constructed a branch connecting with its main line at New York Avenue and 5th Street, and running south on 5th Street, Louisiana Avenue and 6th Street to Pennsylvania Avenue. This line was operated for a short while with storage battery cars, which however, proved so heavy and expensive that the batteries were removed and horses substituted.

The Rock Creek Railway Company started with an overhead trolley equipment at 18th and U Streets and ran to the District line by way of 18th Street, the Rock Creek bridge, and Connecticut Avenue, extended. From 18th and U it ran east on U Street to 9th Street with an underground trolley known as the Love system, which employed a wheel for purpose of contact instead of the sliding shoe which later came and still remains in general use throughout the city. The cars were equipped for both overhead and underground connection, the change from one to the other being made at the junction of the two systems at 18th and F Streets.

Tn the District Appropriation Act of 1890 Congress authorized the street railway companies then employing horses to change their motive power to electricity, either by storage or underground wire, or to cable. The Act required that in making such change the company should replace the old projecting rails with flat, grooved rails.

Under authority of this Act the Washington and Georgetown changed the motive power on all its lines to cable, the 7th Street line going into operation under the new power on April 12, 1890, and the 14th Street and Pennsylvania Avenue lines on August 6, 1892. The Metropolitan Railroad Company was required by Act of August 2, 1894, to change its motive power to an underground electric system and within the two years fixed by that Act had installed its present shoe contact underground system under patents owned by the General Electric Company. This system had been inaugurated in Budapest, Hungary.

On September 21, 1895, the Rock Creek Railway Company purchased the Washington and Georgetown Railroad Company, and under authority of Act of Congress of March 1 of that year changed its name to The Capital Traction Company. On the night of September 29, 1897, the power house which operated the 14th Street and Pennsylvania Avenue cables of this company, and which stood on the present site of the Municipal building, burned down, thus throwing the Pennsylvania Avenue and 14th Street cables out of service. It was determined to substitute the underground electric system which had been adopted by the Metropolitan line and the work was promptly started on all the Capital Traction Company's lines, horses being used on Pennsylvania Avenue and 14th Street during the installation of the new system. The old cable conduits were used and operation was at no time suspended. The 14th Street division went into operation under electric power on February 27, 1898; the Pennsylvania Avenue division on April 20, 1898; and the 7th Street division on May 26, 1898. In the Spring of 1899 the company changed the Love system on its U Street line to the shoe contact system and extended the latter to its present terminus at Rock Creek Bridge.

The Columbia line changed from horses to cable on March 28, 1895, and from cable to underground electric on July 22, 1899. The Anacostia and Potomac River line, which had been extended from F Street north to Florida Avenue on 11th Street, changed from horses to underground electric in April, 1900.

During the period just discussed a number of electric lines came into existence, most of them of a suburban or interurban character, which outside the city employed the overhead trolley. Most, if not all, of them are mentioned in the following account of the formation of the Washington Railway and Electric Company.

In 1897 certain northern financial interests entered upon a project to consolidate the electric power and railway systems of the District of Columbia. They acquired the Potomac Light and Power Company, changing its name to Potomac Electric Power Company, and the United States Electric Lighting Company, but were deterred for the time from attempting to acquire any street railway lines by the policy which Congress at about that time indicated of refusing to permit overhead trolleys in the city. In 1899, however, the movement was revived by the organization of the Washington Traction and Electric Company, the purpose of which was to acquire a controlling interest in the stocks of the various lines of the District, and which shortly after succeeded in obtaining control of the following lines:

The Anacostia & Potomac River Railroad Company, which had previously absorbed the Belt Railway Company; formerly the Capital, North Street and South Washington Railway Company; the Brightwood Railway Company; the Capital Railway Company; the City & Suburban Railway of Washington, a consolidation of the Eckington & Soldiers' Home Railway Company, Maryland & Washington Railway Company, and the Columbia & Maryland Railway Company of Maryland; the Columbia Railway Company; the Georgetown and Tennallytown Railway Company; the Metropolitan Railroad Company, embracing the Connecticut Avenue & Park Railway Company, Union Railroad Company, and the Boundary & Silver Springs Railway Company; the Washington & Glen Echo Railroad Company; the

Washington & Great Falls Electric Railway Company, which had previously acquired the West Washington & Great Falls Electric Railway Company of Montgomery County; the Washington & Rockville Railway Company; and the Washington, Woodside & Forest Glen Railway & Power Company.

The Washington Traction and Electric Company was a holding, rather than an operating company, but it was hoped, by the resulting co-operation among the companies under its control, to so reduce operating expenses and increase traffic as to quickly put the concern on a profitable basis. These expectations, however, were not met, the dividends on the stock of the profitable companies being insufficient to pay the interest on the bonds covering the entire system, of which some of the lines were in a very poor financial condition. At the end of two years the Washington Traction and Electric Company defaulted the interest on its bonds and went into the hands of a receiver.

Notwithstanding the failure of this effort at consolidation, the benefits to the public which had resulted from the standardization of the various lines, the interchanging of transfers and the improved facilities for bringing suburban patrons directly into the city prevailed upon Congress to consent to a second effort to bring about the desired consolidation, with the result that by an Act approved June 5, 1900, it authorized the Washington and Great Falls Electric Railway Company to acquire the stock of the various roads which had been under the control of the Washington Traction and Electric Company. This stock was acquired on February 4, 1902, by the Washington and Great Falls Electric Railway Company, which under authority of the above Act, changed its name to the Washington Railway and Electric Company. An important feature of the Act authorizing this consolidation was a clause giving the various companies the right to make contracts for the use of each other's tracks, under which the bringing of suburban and interurban traffic into the heart of the city has been greatly facilitated.

An attempt during the year 1912 to bring about a still more extensive consolidation of power and street railway companies in the District resulted in a recommendation by the District Commissioners on December 5, of that year in response to which Congress in the District Appropriation Act of March 4, 1913, included a provision known as the "Anti-merger Law" which prohibits any public utility corporation doing business in the District from transferring its stock to another company without specific authority from Congress to do so. Another clause of the same Act created the Public Utilities Commission consisting of the three District Commissioners with power to supervise and regulate every street railroad or other common carrier, gas company, electrical company, water power company, telegraph or telephone company, and pipe line company operating in the District. This legislation was drafted by Corporation Counsel Edward H. Thomas in collaboration with Commissioner William V. Judson, who zealously urged its introduction, and Senator Jacob H. Gallinger, who as Chairman of the Senate Committee on the District, earnestly furthered its enactment.

On March 30, 1914, Representative Robert Grosser introduced in Congress a bill directing the District Commissioners within ninety days after its passage to institute proceedings with the Public Utilities Commission for the condemnation of all the street railway lines doing business wholly or in part within the District of Columbia, the District to issue its thirty year 3.65% bonds to raise funds for paying the condemnation awards. The bill further authorized the Commissioners to purchase such portions of the street railways mentioned as extend outside the District. The United States was not to be liable for either the principal or interest on the bonds, nor was any payment made or debt incurred by the District on account of such condemnation to be a basis of contribution by the United States toward the maintenance of the District Government. The passage of this bill has been recommended by District Commissioners Newman, Siddons and Harding.

The sightseeing traffic of the city originated in the latter part of 1902 when the American Sightseeing Car and Coach Company commenced operating sightseeing street cars on the tracts of the Washington Railway and Electric Company from 6th Street and Pennsylvania Avenue. In 1904 large sightseeing automobiles came to the city, since which time a number of companies have gone into the business of enabling visitors to the National Capital to see its numerous points of interest with the least possible waste of time.

The so-called taxicabs came to the city in 1908. On March 17 of that year the Commissioners passed an order setting aside a number of stands exclusively for the use of those vehicles.

While a number of causes have contributed to retard the development of the District of Columbia as an industrial center, nevertheless the increase in the number of industrial establishments in recent years has been of a character not to be ignored. Without going into great detail, it may be said that there are at present upwards of five hundred industries located in the District, among which are in the neighborhood of 150 printing and publishing concerns; over seventy bakeries, five malt liquor factories, about twenty-five foundries and machine shops, ten lumber factories, fifteen stone works, and seven flour and grist mills.

The new century has witnessed notable developments in both the retail and wholesale commerce of Washington. Through a spirit of co-operative enterprise among the merchants of the city, not only has the widespread custom which once prevailed among many local residents of doing their shopping in Baltimore, Philadelphia and New York been checked, but Washington has in turn become the shopping center for a territory extending forty miles to the east and north and for several hundred miles to the west and south. The city's retail establishments today number some twelve department stores; eighty dry goods stores and more than fifty hardware stores.

The extension of Washington 's wholesale trade has kept pace with that of its retail trade, particularly in supplying the needs of an extensive territory to the south and west, with the result that new establishments have sprung up and old ones have been compelled to increase their facilities. The city has now eight large wholesale grocery houses, fourteen wholesale lumber merchants, thirty-three electrical machinery and supply firms, four wholesale paper firms, two wholesale drug firms, and sixty-five commission merchants.

The extent of the growth of the District of Columbia as a business center, generally, in recent years may be gathered from the fact that the bank clearings increased from $129,000,000 in 1900 to $392,000,000 in 1912.

For many years during the latter part of the nineteenth century, probably dating back at least to the close of the Civil War, an important feature of the commercial life of the District consisted in the bringing of ice from the Kenebec River to

259

Georgetown in coasting vessels which carried back to New England ports cargoes of Cumberland coal. The manufacture of artificial ice has within the past decade resulted in the entire abandonment of this traffic.

The civic, commercial and industrial development of Washington in recent years owes much to the many citizens, merchants and other like associations organized for presenting the needs of various localities to Congress and to the Boards of Commissioners. Preeminent in this direction, however, has been the organization commonly known as The Washington Board of Trade which was incorporated on December 11, 1889, as "The Board of Trade for the District of Columbia" by twenty-seven prominent citizens of Washington, and was largely due to the complaint by members of Congress that there was no representative body which could present impartially to that body, the needs of the District as a whole. The principal function, therefore, of the Board of Trade has been the advancement of every branch of civic betterment largely through the comprehensive and vigorous presentation to Congress of matters which concerned the welfare of the National Capital at large.

The Washington Chamber of Commerce was formed by the merger in 1907 of the Jobbers' and Shippers' and Business Men's Associations. Its purpose has been the exploitation of Washington's commercial advantages, in addition to which it has made a particular effort to attract conventions to the Nation's Capital. In 1909 and 1910 it raised a fund of $25,000 for this purpose; and its efforts have within the past four years resulted in bringing thousands of visitors and millions of dollars to the city.

The debt of the District of Columbia on May 31, 1871, when the Territorial government went out of office, was $3,256,382.48 of which $900,403.80 was floating, and $2,355,978.68 bonded indebtedness. Of the total, the city of Washington owed $2,966,693.27, the city of Georgetown $261,463.37, and the Levy Court $28, 825.84.

To offset this debt the city of Washington held a credit of $60,000, with accumulated interest, on account of bonds of the Alexandria and Washington Railroad Company to that amount which it had been compelled to pay on account of its guarantee of an issue of $150,000 on February 8, 1855. About $60,000 of this debt was afterwards collected by the city in a suit against the railroad company. In addition Washington held $50,000, and Georgetown $25,000, of the bonds of the Chesapeake and Ohio Canal Company which those cities had subscribed in April, 1847, to assist the company to complete the canal to Cumberland. These bonds, with accrued interest and two certificates of indebtedness amounting to $9,000, with interest from 1867, are still due.

On July 1, 1878, when the permanent Commission government went into effect the debt of the District was $22,106,650, which was shortly thereafter increased by the issue of $1,254,050 in 3.65% bonds on account of claims arising from the operations of the Board of Public Works. On July 1, 1914, this debt had been reduced to $6,939,150.

CHAPTER XII

Public Buildings and Grounds

The story of the erection of the north wing of the original Capitol Building by the original Commissioners provided for by the Act of Congress of July 16, 1790, establishing the permanent seat of government at Washington, has been treated in the chapters bearing upon the establishment of the city by those Commissioners.

In 1803 President Jefferson placed the construction of the south wing in charge of Benjamin Henry Latrobe, a young Englishman who had met President Washington shortly after his arrival in this country in 1796, and who had attained some success in Philadelphia as an architect and engineer. The south wing was finished under the superintendence of Mr. Latrobe in 1811, and the two wings were connected by a wooden gallery or bridge occupying the place of the present rotunda. The structure had at that time the appearance of two separate buildings and was in this condition when the interiors of both buildings were destroyed by the British in 1814.

The reconstruction of the building was in 1815 placed in charge of Mr. Latrobe, who was in 1817 succeeded by Mr. Charles Bulfinch, a native of Massachusetts, who restored the north and south wings, reconstructing the Senate and House of Representatives chambers — now the Supreme Court and Statuary Hall respectively — and the west projection which enclosed the original quarters of the Congressional Library. Mr. Bulfinch also completed the rotunda with a low wooden dome. In 1827 the building as thus reconstructed was declared complete. The entire cost of the building up to this time, including both the original construction and the reconstruction, was $2,433,814.

In 1850 Congress determined to enlarge the Capitol. Much discussion resulted as to the method by which this was to be done. To the influence of President Fillmore is largely due the adoption of plans contemplating extensions in the form of wings in conformity with the general architectural character of the original portion of the building as designed by Dr. Thornton. The wings and dome were the design of George U. Walter, of Philadelphia, who had designed the Girard College in that city, and under whose designs the Patent Office and Treasury Department buildings had been completed. The cornerstone of the south wing was laid on July 4, 1851, by President Fillmore, assisted by the Grand Lodge of Masons of the District of Columbia, the Grand Master wearing the regalia which President Washington had worn as Grand Master pro tern of Alexandria Lodge when he laid the cornerstone of the original building in 1793. The orator of the occasion was Daniel Webster.

The Statue of Liberty crowning the dome was modeled by Thomas Crawford, in Rome, Italy, and cast by Clark Mills in his foundry, near Brookland, D. C.

The exterior of the original Capitol Building is constructed of sandstone brought from Aquia Creek, Va. This was so badly disfigured by smoke at the time of the destruction of the building by the British in 1814 that it was necessary to obliterate the marks of the smoke by painting, which practice it has been necessary to continue ever since. The walls of the north and south wings were constructed of Massachusetts marble, and the monolithic columns are of marble from Cockeysville, Maryland. The result has been that the exterior of the building as a whole is not of uniform appearance.

The new Hall of the House of Representatives was first occupied on December 2, 1857, and the new Hall of the Senate on January 4, 1859, though the colonnades and porticos of these additions were not completed until shortly after the close of the Civil War. The dome of the Capitol, which had not been commenced until 1856, was completed August 26, 1864. The work of completing the building was carried on during the Civil War at the instance of President Lincoln, who believed that its continuance would have a powerful moral effect upon the country, and particularly upon those Union soldiers who had occasion to pass through Washington.

The bronze doors at the east entrance to the rotunda are the design of Randolph Rogers, who was specially commissioned by Congress to design them. They were cast at Munich, Bavaria, in 1861, and were designed and modelled at Rome. The bronze doors at the entrances to the Senate and House wings were designed by Thomas Crawford.

The total cost of the Capitol up to July 15, 1870, was $12,256,150.

The original construction of the President's House has been detailed in the chapters dealing with the establishment of the city.

James Hoban's design contemplated a central building with wings or terraces. It is uncertain just when the original east and west terraces were constructed, but they were probably completed during the administration of President Jefferson, whose office was on the site of the present Executive Offices opposite the entrance to the Navy Department.

After the destruction of the interior of the building by the British in 1814, it was rebuilt within the original walls which like those of the Capitol were painted white to obliterate the marks of the fire. The new building was completed in 1818. In 1819 Congress appropriated $8,137 "for enlarging the offices west of the President's House." The south portico was added about 1823, and the north portico about 1829. In 1848 gas lighting was installed and in 1853 a system of heating and ventilating was put in effect. About 1857 the west terrace was used to support a greenhouse which remained until the restoration of the building in 1902. The original east terrace was removed some time prior to 1870.

By Act of June 20, 1902, Congress appropriated $540,641 for the complete renovation and restoration of the building and the construction of a separate temporary office for the President. The work was placed in charge of Messrs. McKim, Mead and White, architects, of New York, and occupied about four months.

The alterations made were very extensive as the size of the appropriation will indicate. They involved the removal of the greenhouse, the restoration of the terraces, with a public entrance at the end of the east terrace and the President's office at the end of the west terrace. Many structural changes were made in the main building the chief purposes of which were: "to put the house in the condition originally planned but never fully carried out; to make the changes in such a manner that the house will never again have to be altered; that is to say, the work should represent the period to which the house belongs architecturally, and therefore, be independent of changing fashion; to modernize the house in so far as the living rooms are concerned, and provide all those conveniences which are now lacking. "

In its restored condition the mansion approaches architecturally as nearly as possible the intentions of the founders, while the interior accommodations have been skillfully adapted to the needs of the times.

In the chapters on the establishment of the city mention is made of the construction of the Treasury Department building, erected in 1799 by the original Commissioners. This building was destroyed by the British in 1814 and a new building was speedily erected in its place. This was destroyed by fire on March 31, 1833. By Act of Congress approved July 4, 1836, the President was authorized to select a site and construct a new fire proof building for this Department. This Act carried an appropriation of $100,000 and was the beginning of the present structure. It is commonly told that President Jackson, tiring of delay in the selection of the site, walked over the ground one morning and planted his cane in the northeast corner of the present site with the words: " Here, right here, I want the corner stone laid." At any rate, Robert Mills, the architect for the building, testified before a committee of Congress in 1838 that "The precise position of the building had been determined by the positive directions of the late President. " The investigation at which this testimony was given was the result of vigorous criticism to the location, design and materials of the building and resulted in the employment of Thomas U. Walter of Philadelphia to supervise the completion of the work.

This portion of the building was completed in 1842 at a cost of $660,773. It extended 340 feet along 15th Street and was 170 feet deep.

By Act of March 3, 1855, Congress appropriated $300,000 for extending the building upon plans prepared by Mr. Walter. Under this act the south wing was completed in 1861, and the west wing in 1864. The site of the present north wing of the building was then occupied by the brick building of the State Department. This building was torn down in November, 1866, and the construction of the north wing of the Treasury building begun in April of the following year. This wing was finished in 1869. The total building as thus completed cost $6,127,465.32. The original east wing was faced with sandstone from Aquia Creek and ornamented with thirty drum columns of the same material. The other wings were faced with granite and ornamented with granite monolithic columns quarried from Dix Island, near Rockland, Maine, and brought to Washington in sailing vessels.

The work of replacing the sandstone facing and drum columns of the east wing with granite facing and monolithic granite columns was commenced in May, 1907 and completed in the latter part of 1908. The stone for this work was quarried at Milford, New Hampshire.

The Patent Office building was begun in the fall of 1836 under an Act of Congress appropriating $108,000 out of the Patent Fund. The part of the building erected at this time was that facing F Street. The body of the building was Virginia sandstone and the front was faced with split granite. It is' said that the proportions of the portico on F Street are exactly those of the Parthenon at Athens. This wing was completed in 1840 at a cost of $422,011.65.

The east wing fronting on 7th Street was begun in 1849 and completed in 1852 at a cost of $600,000. The 9th Street wing was begun in 1852 and completed in 1856 at a cost of $750,000. The north wing on G Street, which completed the building, was begun in 1856 and completed in 1867, at a cost of $575,000. The 7th, 9th and G Street wings were of granite, with exterior facings and columns of marble.

The massive granite building of the State, War and Navy Departments, located at the southeast corner of Pennsylvania Avenue and 17th Street, west of the Executive Mansion, was designed by Mr. A. B. Mullett, the Supervising Architect of the Treasury Department. It is 567 feet by 342 feet, covering an area of 4.920 acres, with a height of 145 feet. Its construction was completed in 1888, at a cost of approximately $11,000,000.

Previous to the construction of this building the War Department had been partially housed in the old Winder Building at 37th and G Streets, northwest, and the State Department, after the demolition of 1866 of the building occupied by it on the site of the present north front of the Treasury Building, had occupied the building now used as the Washington Orphans' Home at 14th and S Streets, northwest. The Navy Department and part of the War Department occupied two plain brick buildings on the site of the present State, War and Navy Department building. These buildings were erected in 1815 and 1820 respectively and were demolished in 1879.

The Pension Office was completed in 1885. It stands on the northwest corner of Judiciary Square, and is a brick structure, 400 by 200 feet in size, covering 1.84 acres of ground. It was designed by General Montgomery C. Meigs and was modeled after the Farnese Palace at Florence, Italy. Its cost was $1,000,000. The most noteworthy feature of the exterior is the frieze of terra cotta relief work, three feet wide, extending around the building at the height of the first story, representing a military and naval procession. The interior is remarkable for the extensive open space which is used for inaugural balls, and for the enormous brick columns supporting the roof.

The former General Post Office building now occupied by the General Land Office, covering the square bounded by E and F, 7th and 8th Streets, was first erected in 1839 on the plans prepared by Robert Mills and was enlarged in 1855 on the plans of Thomas U. Walter. This building replaced the old Blodget Hotel building which had been purchased by the Government for a post office in 1810, and which was burned on December 15, 1836.

The present structure, which is an adaptation of the Corinthian order of architecture, has much artistic merit, but fails of its proper effect in consequence of its proximity to the massive elements of the Patent Office building.

The Post Office Department building, which occupied about two years in its construction, was completed in 1899, at a cost of $2,585,835. The site was acquired at a cost of $655,490.77. The building was designed in the office of the Supervising Architect of the Treasury, and in style is an adaptation of the Romanesque. It is constructed of gray granite. The tower is 315 feet high.

The new City Post Office, adjacent to the Union Station, was authorized by Act of May 13, 1908. The site cost $450,189, and the building when completed will have cost approximately $3,000,000. It is to be occupied about July 1, 1914. This marble structure which is characterized by an Ionic colonnade on its south front, was designed by the office of the Supervising Architect of the Treasury, in collaboration with the firm of D. H. Burnham and Co., of New York, the designers of the Union Station.

The site of the Customs House on 31st Street between M and N Streets in Georgetown was purchased March 27, 1857, for $5,000. The building was completed early the following year at a cost of $55,368.15.

The Winder Building at the northwest corner of 17th and F Streets, northwest, was constructed in 1848 by W. H. Winder and was rented by the Government until 1854, when it was purchased for the sum of $200,000. It was occupied by the War Department and the Second Auditor's office (now the Auditor for the War

Department) until 1888, when the war Department was removed to the new State, War and Navy Building. It has since then been occupied by the office of the Auditor for the War Department.

The site of the Old Bureau of Engraving and Printing building was purchased July 7, 1878, for $27,536.50. The original portion of the building was completed July 1, 1880, at a cost of $310,000. In 1880 additional land was purchased and in 1891, the wing at the southwest corner was erected at a cost of $80,000. In 1895 additions were made at a cost of $50,000, and in 1900 the completing wing was constructed at the northwest corner. The new building for the Bureau of Engraving and Printing on 14th Street just south of the old building was commenced in December, 1911 and completed February 24, 1914. The plans were drawn in the office of the Architect of the Treasury under Mr. James Knox Taylor. The design was mainly the work of Mr. W. B. Olm stead, at that time the draftsman in charge, subject to some modifications suggested by the Commission of Pine Arts.

The original building for the Department of Agriculture was erected in 1868 at a cost of $140,420. It is a brick building 170 by 61 feet, three stories high above the basement, with mansard roof, and stands near the south edge of the Mall on the line of 13th Street.

The new building for the Department of Agriculture was authorized by Act of Congress of February 9, 1903, the cost to be limited to $1,500,000. The money appropriated was expended by Secretary of Agriculture James Wilson in the erection of two separated wings so arranged as to permit of the later erection of an impressive central structure connecting them. These wings were completed in February, 1908 and stand on the Mall just east of 14th Street with their rear projections abruptly terminating on B Street, south, apparently in anticipation of the closing of this street as suggested in the plans of the Park Commission of 1901, and the erection of a south portion of this building across the present line of this street, completing a hollow square. The present completed wings are of marble facing, and are the design of Rankin, Kellogg and Crane, Architects, of Philadelphia.

The beginning of the Library of Congress was a collection of nine hundred and seventy -three volumes gathered in London in 1800 by Albert Gallatin, Dr. Mitchell and others. The first Congressional appropriation for the purchase of books for the Library was made in the session of 1805-1806 and authors were requested to leave copies of their works with it.

At the time of the British invasion in 1814 the Library possessed three thousand volumes. These were destroyed with the burning of the Capitol buildings in which they were kept.

The nucleus of a new library consisted of the collection of Mr. Jefferson of seven thousand volumes which was purchased for $23,950. The Capitol as reconstructed contained rooms designed for the Library in which the books were placed on the completion of the building in 1824. On December 24, 1851, the Library, which then contained fifty-five thousand volumes, lost thirty -five thousand volumes, as well as Gilbert Stuart's paintings of the first five presidents, by a fire. Under Thomas U. Walter, the Library rooms were re-constructed at an expense of $72,500, the new quarters taking up the entire western projection of the Capitol building and being fitted with iron cases and ceilings.

In 1866, through the efforts of Hon. Rutherford B. Hayes, then Chairman of the House Committee on Library, the collections of ex-Mayor Peter Force were purchased for $100,000, and the same year the Smithsonian Library was consolidated with the Congressional Library. In 1882, the library of Dr. J. M. Toner of Washington, was added.

The construction of a building for the accommodation of the Library was authorized by Acts of Congress approved April 15, 1886, October 2, 1888, and March 2, 1889. The Library of Congress Building was completed in 1897. Its cost, not including the site, which cost $585,000, was $6,375,000, much of which was spent in its art works.

The building is of Italian Renaissance, topped by a gilded dome. It was originally designed by the architectural firm of John L. Smithmeyer and Paul J. Pelz, but their plans were modified by Brigadier General Thomas L. Casey, Chief of Engineers, U. S. A., and the building was erected according to the plans as so modified, under the supervision of General Casey and Mr. Bernard R. Green. The scheme of the interior architecture and decoration is that of Edward Pearce Casey, of New York, and it was under his supervision that commissions for the mural paintings and sculpture were allotted. The building throughout is the product of American artists and artisans.

The Senate office building was erected under the direction of the Superintendent of the Capitol Building and Grounds acting under the supervision of a commission consisting of Senators Shelby M. Cullom, of Illinois, Jacob H. Gallinger, of New Hampshire, and Henry WL. Teller, of Colorado. The consulting architect was John M. Carrere of New York. Proceedings for the condemnation of the site were begun August 10, 1904. On March 15, 1905, the demolition of the buildings on the site was commenced and on March 5, 1909, the building was completed. This building stands on the square bounded by B Street, Delaware Avenue, First Street and C Street, northeast, and occupies three sides of the square, that on First Street remaining open. The site for this building was acquired at a cost of $746,111; the construction of the building cost $3,594,761; the furnishing $300,500; and the approaches $123,000; total $4,764,372.

The House of Representatives office building was erected under the direction of the Superintendent of the Capitol Building and Grounds, acting under the supervision of a commission consisting of Representatives Joseph G. Cannon, of Illinois, William P. Hepburn, of Iowa, James D. Richards, of Tennessee, and Walter I. Smith, of Iowa. Thomas Hastings of New York was the consulting architect. The demolition of the buildings on the site commenced February 1, 1904, and the building was completed November 9, 1907. It stands on the square south of the Capitol bounded by B Street, New Jersey Avenue, First Street, and C Street, southeast, and occupies all four sides of the square. The amount appropriated for the construction of the building was $3,100,000; for the acquisition of the site $743,635.55; for the approaches $132,500; and for the furnishing $300,500; total $4,276,635.55.

The Senate and House office buildings are intended to unite with the Capitol to form one composition: the B Street fronts of the office buildings being identical in size and design and having the same cornice line as the Capitol. The office buildings were kept simple in design, without pediments, domes, or other accentuated features, in order to subordinate them to the Capitol. The general division of parts is suggestive of that in the Gardes Meubles on the Place de la Concorde, Paris. The end pavilions are modeled after those of the Colonnade du Louvre. The B Street colonnades are each made up of 17 "bays" separated by 16 pairs of Roman Doric columns, with a single column at each end. The Senate building is faced with Vermont marble, the House building with marble from Georgia and South Dover, N. Y.

The Senate office building seriously mars the vista of the Capitol from the Union Station. This objection would have been obviated if Congress had included the site of the building in the proposed Plaza connecting the Capitol and Union Station and located the office buildings east of First Street.

The practice of housing the offices of the government of the District of Columbia in rented buildings in various parts of the City of Washington, which prevailed for more than thirty years after the abandonment of the old City Hall, was regarded by both citizens and officials as a source of civic reproach, which could not too soon be removed.

The efforts of the Territorial government to have a municipal building erected on Reservation No. 17, north of the Washington Market Company's buildings, was the first tangible movement in that direction, but it failed because of the demand for all the District's available funds to meet the more urgent needs to improve the streets and provide for the requirements of current administration. Those efforts resulted in the appropriation by Congress in the deficiency Act of March' 3, 1873, of not exceeding $75,000 for the purchase by the United States of the interest of the District of Columbia in the City Hall, of which mention has been made in the chapter on the Territorial government.

No building was begun in pursuance of that law, and the subject was practically dormant until 1890, when the Commissioners in their report for that year made an urgent appeal to Congress that provision be made for an adequate home for the government of the District.

In their estimates for 1892 they included an item of $150,000 to begin such a building to cost between $300,000 and $500,000; and in their annual report for 1891 recommended the use of the site in front of the Washington market for that purpose. The need for a structure for the purpose was annually urged by them upon Congress, but nothing resulted from the recommendations except a favorable report by the Public Buildings Committee of the House, on H. R. 7651 of the 53rd Congress, on July 6, 1894. The Commissioners had about despaired of impressing Congress with the importance of the subject, when to their surprise section 6 of the public building law of June 6, 1902, was enacted and provided for the purchase, at a cost not to exceed $550,000, which was the price paid for it, of Square 255, upon which the power house of the Capital Traction street railway had stood before its destruction by fire on September 29, 1897, and for the erection thereon of a fireproof building for the accommodation of the municipal and other officers of the District of Columbia, at a cost not to exceed $1,500,000, payable half by the District of Columbia and half by the United States. E Street between that square and Pennsylvania Avenue was made part of that square for the site of the building. The Secretary of the Treasury and the Commissioners were directed by that law to act jointly in contracting for and erecting the building.

The building was designed by Cope and Stewardson, architects, of Philadelphia, whose plan was submitted and accepted in competition with a number of other architects.

The immediate supervision of the construction of the building was placed in charge of "an officer of the Government especially qualified for that duty to be appointed by the President of the United States." Captain Chester Harding, of the Corps of Engineers, then an assistant to the Engineer Commissioner, was appointed to that position, and continued on that duty until the summer of 1907, when he was assigned to assist in the construction of the Panama Canal and was succeeded on July 20 of that year by Captain William Kelly, of the same Corps, under whose supervision the building was completed.

The maximum expenditure for the building was fixed at $2,000,000, and the title to the site transferred to the District of Columbia, by the public building Act of March 3, 1903. Its actual cost was about $1,950,000. The material of the building is white marble obtained from South Dover, New York.

The building was begun on June 17, 1904. It was dedicated in connection with the morning celebration of the one hundred and thirty-first anniversary of the Declaration of Independence, by the citizens of the District, under arrangements made by a committee appointed by the Washington Board of Trade and the Washington Chamber of Commerce, of which Mr. John Joy Edson was chairman. The exercises were held on the steps of the main entrance, and consisted of addresses by the Speaker of the House of Representatives, the Secretary of the Treasury, Mr. A. B. Browne, representing the Washington Board of Trade, and Mr. Chapin Brown, representing the Washington Chamber of Commerce, and Hon. Henry B. F. Macfarland, the President of the Board of Commissioners of the District of Columbia; Chairman John Joy Edson presiding and making brief introductory remarks. The United States Marine Band furnished the music. An American flag presented by the Washington Chamber of Commerce was unfurled, to an appropriate salute.

The municipal offices were moved into the building during June and July of 1908.

The Police Court building is situated at the northwest corner of 6th and D Streets, northwest, on the site of the old Unitarian Church, which was purchased by the District out of an appropriation of $20,000 made June 4, 1880 for that purpose. The building was constructed and the site enlarged out of an appropriation of $38,000 made April 27, 1904. While the building was in course of erection the court held its sessions in a rented building on 15th Street between D and E Streets, northwest.

The building occupied by the Court from its inception until its removal to the Unitarian Church building was numbered 466 C Street, northwest.

The Smithsonian Institution is the outgrowth of the provision in the will of James Smithson, an Englishman, who died at Genoa, Italy, June 27, 1829, whereby a legacy of practically his entire property was after the death of a nephew without issue, bequeathed "to found at Washington, under the name of the Smithsonian Institution, an establishment for the increase and diffusion of knowledge among men." On the death of Mr. Hungerford, the nephew who held a life interest in Mr. Smithson's estate, the estate became available for the purposes of the institution in 1835. After some correspondence between the English solicitors for the estate and John Forsyth, Secretary of State, President Jackson transmitted the entire matter to Congress on the 17th of December, 1835, for such measures as might be deemed necessary. The result was that Congress decided to act in the capacity of *parens patriae* of the District of Columbia for the purpose of appearing in the courts of England and maintaining the claim of the City of Washington as trustee for the intended institution to be located in that city.

By Act approved July 1, 1836, the President was authorized to appoint an agent to prosecute for and in behalf of the United States in the courts of England the right of the United States to the legacy bequeathed by Mr. Smithson 's will. Under authority of this Act President Jackson appointed Richard Rush, of Pennsylvania, agent to recover the funds. After some contest a decision was made by the English Chancery Court on May 9, 1838, the net proceeds of which amounted to £106,370 7s 3rd, equal to $508,314.46 in American money. Of this sum the Secretary of the Treasury under authority of Congress, invested $499,500 in the purchase of bonds of the State of Arkansas, and $8,270.67 in bonds of the State of Michigan. Other small investments of the fund were made as it grew.

The question of the means to be adopted in disposing of this fund agitated Congress for eight years after the receipt of the money. Ex-President John Quincy Adams, then a member of Congress, continually urged action. After considering many plans, including that which had many advocates — the returning of the money to England, Congress finally, by Act approved August 10, 1846, authorized the establishment of the Smithsonian Institution on land to be selected from that part of the Mall west of 7th Street, and providing that the Institution to be so established should be devoted to agriculture, horticulture, rural economy, chemistry, nature history, geology, architecture, domestic science, astronomy and navigation.

At this time the fund aggregated more than $800,000, though a considerable amount of interest due from the States to which it had been loaned was in default. This amount was appropriated by the Act for the establishment of the Institution since the bonds in which the original fund had been invested, had some years yet to run.

The present building was shortly afterwards commenced and was completed in 1855. It is of Byzantine architecture and is constructed of red sand stone from quarries on the upper Potomac. It extends 426 feet east and west. The building was designed by James Ren wick, Jr., and was the first non-ecclesiastical building of this style of architecture erected in this country. Immediately on its completion it was made the repository of the national collections which dated back to the United States Exploring Expedition around the world from 1838 to 1842.

The Chancellors of the Institution have been the Justices of the Supreme Court of the United States and the Secretaries of the Institution. The first Secretary was Professor Joseph Henry, who served until May 13, 1878. He was succeeded by his assistant, Professor Spencer Fulton Baird who served until his death, August 19, 1887. Professor Baird was succeeded by his assistant, Professor Samuel P. Langley, who served until his death in 1906, and was succeeded by Professor Charles D. Walcott, the present Secretary.

The original National Museum building was begun in 1879, as a consequence of the crowded condition of the Smithsonian Institution building and was completed in 1881. It is a one-story brick building just east of the Smithsonian building, covering slightly more than two acres of ground.

269

In 1883 the need for additional space induced the Board of Regents of the Smithsonian Institution to apply to Congress for a third building, but, notwithstanding the continued repetition of this request, nothing was done until 1902, when Congress authorized the preparation of plans. All the important museum buildings of Europe and America were visited for ideas to be embodied in the new structure. The architects were Messrs. Hornblower and Marshall of Washington. The construction of a building with granite fronts to cost not exceeding $3,500,000, under the supervision of Bernard R. Green, Superintendent of Buildings and Grounds of the Library of Congress, was authorized by the Sundry Civil Act for the year ending June 30, 1904.

Ground was broken on June 15, 1904, by Secretary Langley of the Smithsonian Institution; the cornerstone was laid October 15, 1906; and the building was completed June 20, 1911. The portico is of the Roman Corinthian order, and the capitols of the two rows of columns supporting the entablature are patterned after those of the Temple of Jupiter Stator at Rome.

The erection of the George Washington Memorial Hall with a seating capacity of 6,000, was authorized by Act of Congress of March 4, 1913, to be begun upon the raising of a building fund of $1,000,000, and an endowment fund of $500,000. The building will be administered by the Board of Regents of the Smithsonian Institution and will be located on the site of the old Baltimore and Potomac Railroad Depot at Sixth and B Streets, northwest. The plans of Tracy and Swartwont of New York were accepted in competition on May 4, 1914.

The Carnegie Institution of Washington was founded by Mr. Andrew Carnegie, January 28, 1902, with an endowment of ten million dollars to which on December 10, 1907, he added two million dollars, and on January 19, 1911, another ten millions, making in all to the present time twenty-two million dollars. The Institution was first incorporated on January 4, 1902, under the laws of the District of Columbia, as the Carnegie Institution. It was reincorporated by Act of Congress of April 28, 1904, as the Carnegie Institution of Washington.

The Executive Offices of the Institution are contained in the handsome three-story Ionic building of Bedford limestone at Sixteenth and P Streets, northwest, and are under the direction of Professor Robert S. Woodward. To the present time ten departments of investigation have been organized, with numerous experiment stations, plants and reservations throughout the country, including the non-magnetic auxiliary brig "Carnegie."

The National Geographic Society was established January 27, 1888, by a small band of explorers and scientists, "for the increase and diffusion of geographical knowledge." In 1899 the Society entered upon the project of popularizing geographical research through the columns of its magazine. In 1902 the heirs of Hon. Gardner Greene Hubbard built Hubbard Memorial Hall at the corner of Sixteenth and M Streets, northwest, as a home for the Society and a memorial to its first President. This is now used for the accommodation of the board rooms and library. The administration building adjoining was constructed by the Society in 1913 on the plans of Arthur B. Heaton. It is of Italian Renaissance architecture. The materials are white brick trimmed with white limestone.

The project of establishing a public library was first agitated in the newspapers and by the Board of Trade, the School trustees, and various workingmen's and citizens' organizations in 1894 as a supplement to the public schools. The establishment of such a library was authorized by Act of Congress approved June 3, 1896 and was largely the result of the efforts of Mr. Theodore W. Noyes, Chairman of the Committee on Library of the Board of Trade. In 1898 Congress appropriated $6,720 for salaries of a librarian and two assistants and for other expenses. A three-story building at 1326 New York Avenue was rented and 15,000 volumes acquired by private donation were installed. For the purchase of books Mr. Crosby S. Noyes contributed, $1,000, the firm of Woodward and Lothrop $1,000, Charles C. Glover, $250, John R. McLean, $250, and many others smaller amounts. James T. Dubois created a fund of $2,000 which he promised to increase to $5,000 to be known as the Henry Pastor Memorial Fund, the interest on which was to be used in the purchase of scientific periodicals. The largest book contribution was the incorporated Washington City Free Library. The estate of Anthony Pollock contributed fifteen hundred books.

On January 12, 1899, Mr. Andrew Carnegie and Mr. B. H. Warner, Vice President of the Board of Trustees of the Library, met by accident at the White House. The needs of the Library were mentioned by Mr. Warner, whereupon Mr. Carnegie offered to donate $250,000 for a building if a suitable site could be obtained and if Congress would appropriate for the maintenance of the institution. Shortly after he increased the donation to $350,000.

On March 3, 1899, President McKinley signed an act of Congress setting aside Mount Vernon Square as the site for the building. Under this act the construction of the building was entrusted to a commission composed of the District Commissioners, the officer in charge of public buildings and grounds and the President of the Board of Trustees of the Library. The design of Messrs. Ackerman and Ross of New York was chosen and on June 21, 1900, the contract for the foundation was signed. The cornerstone was laid on April 24, 1901. The royalties on the book stacks, amounting to $530 were donated by Mr. Bernard R. Green, the Superintendent of Construction, by whom the stacks were patented. On December 13, 1902, the completed building was accepted by the Commission. It was formally dedicated to the public with elaborate ceremonies on January 7, 1903.

The original building of the Corcoran Gallery of Art at the northeast corner of Seventeenth Street and Pennsylvania Avenue was designed by Mr. James Renwick and begun in 1859. In 1861 it was occupied by the Quartermaster General's Department of the Army which remained in it until 1869. On May 10, 1869, its owner, Mr. William Wilson Corcoran, deeded the ground, building and contents, and an endowment fund to a board of nine trustees "to be used solely for the purposes of encouraging American genius in the production and preservation of works pertaining to the fine arts and kindred objects," with the condition that it should be open free to visitors at least two days each week.

The institution was incorporated and exempted from taxation by Act of Congress of May 24, 1870. The building was reconstructed in 1871 and Mr. Corcoran 's private art collection placed in it. The picture galleries, Octagon Room and Hall of Bronzes were opened privately on January 19, 1874, and the entire building thrown open to the public in the following December.

Owing to the demand for additional space and the impossibility of acquiring the necessary ground adjoining the old building the trustees on April 3, 1891, determined upon the purchase of a part of square 171 on 17th Street, between E Street and New York Avenue, northwest, which was subsequently acquired.

On January 9, 1892, the erection of a gallery on the new site was decided upon and Mr. Ernest Flagg of New York was selected as the architect. Ground was broken on June 26, 1893, and the cornerstone laid May 10, 1894. The building was completed January 8, 1897, and formally opened on the evening of February 22 of the same year, nearly three thousand invited guests, including President and Mrs. Cleveland, being present. The building fronts 259 feet on Seventeenth Street and is 133 feet deep. It is constructed of Georgia marble with a basement of Milford pink granite and is on the Neo-Grecian style of architecture. The bronze lions at the entrance were cast from molds made over the famous lions by Canova which guard the tomb of Clement XIII in St. Peter's, Rome.

The Memorial Continental Hall which occupies the 17th Street frontage of the block between C and D Streets, northwest, facing the White Lot from the west, was erected by the National Society, Daughters of the American Revolution, in memory of the patriots of the American Revolution, both men and women. The purchase of the site was decided upon by the Memorial Continental Hall Committee on June 4, 1902, and the ground soon after acquired at a net cost of $50,266.17. On June 4, 1903, the Committee employed Mr. Edward Pearce Casey of New York City, to be the architect of the proposed building, and on January 8, 1904, Mr. Casey's plans and preliminary sketches were accepted.

The cornerstone of the building was laid on the afternoon of Tuesday, April 19, 1904. The following April, the 14th Continental Congress was held in the central portion of the building. The Memorial portico was dedicated by the 16th Continental Congress on the afternoon of Wednesday, April 17, 1907. The entire building was completed and much of the mahogany furniture donated by the various States installed in time for the holding of the 19th Continental Congress, April 18-23, 1910. The total cost of the building was somewhat over $500,000.

The building is designed upon the general style of the homesteads of Revolutionary times and is constructed of Vermont marble. The south portico and all the interior furnishings and decorations of the buildings are the gifts of various individuals, societies and States.

The building for the Pan-American Union is located on the block between B and C Streets on 17th Street, northwest, facing the White Lot from the west and is the result of a gift of $750,000 by Mr. Andrew Carnegie, to which the twenty-one American Republics added the sum of $250,000, which was used in the purchase of the site. The square upon which this building and its grounds are located was formerly the site of the residence of David Burnes, one of the original proprietors of the land occupied by the City of Washington, and of the Van Ness mansion, built by Mr. Burnes' son-in-law, John P. Van Ness.

The designs for the building were the joint product of Mr. Albert Kelsey of Philadelphia, and Mr. Paul P. Cret, Professor of Design at the University of Pennsylvania, a native of France and a graduate of the Ecole des Beaux Arts of Paris.

The colossal groups on either side of the entrance representing North and South America are respectively the work of Gutzon Borglun and Isidore Konti. These sculptors are also respectively the designers of the historic bronze panels in low relief representing General Washington bidding farewell to his Generals and the meeting of San Martin and Bolivar. The Eagle and the Condor are the work of Solon Borgun and the panel in the concourse above the portico arches is the work of Konti.

The laying of the foundation for the building commenced on April 13, 1908. On May 11, 1908, elaborate public ceremonies in connection with the laying of the cornerstone were held. The dedication of the building occurred on April 26, 1910, and was participated in by President Taft, Secretary of State, Knox, Mr. Andrew Carnegie, Ambassador Francisco Leon De la Barra, the Mexican Ambassador, who spoke on behalf of the Latin-American Republics, Senator Elihu Boot, Cardinal Gibbons, Bishop Harding, Mr. Albert Kelsey, the architect, and Director General Barrett of the Pan-American Union.

The row of semi-public buildings on 17th Street will be completed by the so-called Red Cross building to be located on the block facing 17th Street between E and F Streets, filling in the present gap between the Memorial Continental Hall and the Corcoran Art Gallery. This building was provided for by Act of Congress approved October 22, 1913, appropriating $400,000 on condition that at least $300,000 additional should be raised by private subscription. It is intended to commemorate the services and sacrifices of the women of the United States, north and south, for the sick and wounded in war.

The ground breaking for the towering classic temple of the Ancient and Accepted Scottish Rite of Freemasonry at the southeast corner of 16th and S Streets, northwest, took place on May 31, 1911, the 110th anniversary of the establishment of the Supreme Council for the Southern jurisdiction of the United States, the mother council of the world, at Charleston, South Carolina, May 31, 1801. The informal ceremony was presided over by Hon. James D. Richardson, the Grand Commander of the Order.

The design of this structure, by John Russell Pope of New York, and Elliott Woods, the Superintendent of the Capitol, is strikingly similar to the commonly accepted restoration of the Mausoleum at Halicarnassus, one of the ancient Seven Wonders of the World.

Early in the 19th century Professor Hassler constructed at New Jersey Avenue and C Street, southeast, a small brick building with iron doors and windows, intended to be fireproof, for the storage of engraved plates and other records and property of the Coast Survey. This was occupied until 1874.

On August 2, 1832, the Survey occupied a building on the west side of New Jersey Avenue, south of the present building, built by Thomas Law about 1800, and a house adjoining it on the north. These are now included in the Hotel Varnum.

In 1871 the Survey moved into the present Richards building, a brick structure on the east side of New Jersey Avenue just south of the Butler Building and extending through to South Capitol Street. This building was purchased for the Survey on September 21, 1891, for $155,000.

On April 10, 1891, the three Cape Ann granite buildings on B Street, South Capitol Street and New Jersey Avenue, erected by General Benj. F. Butler in 1873-4, were purchased by the Treasury Department for $275,000. The one fronting on B Street, which had at one time been occupied by President Arthur as the Presidential residence and office was assigned to the Marine Hospital Service, now the Public Health Service. The other two were assigned to the Coast and Geodetic Survey. A brick structure to the rear of the Survey is occupied by it for chart printing purposes.

The first structure used as a naval astronomical observatory was erected on Capitol Hill in 1834 under Lieutenant Wilkes of the Navy as a naval depot of charts and was equipped with a number of astronomical instruments. In this building a series of observations was made from 1838 to 1842 by Lieutenant James M. Gillis of the Navy, which did much to bring about the eventual establishment of a permanent observatory.

John Quiney Adams, while a member of the House of Representatives, was an ardent advocate of the project to establish such an observatory, and when the Smithsonian fund became available he repeatedly urged as chairman of the committee on that fund, an appropriation from it for his favorite object. The personal opposition of the friends of President Jackson defeated Mr. Adams' wishes so far as the Smithsonian fund was concerned, but Congress, under the guise of establishing a depot of charts and instruments for the Navy, initiated the observatory by an Act approved August 31, 1842, authorizing the construction of buildings to cost not more than $25,000 on a site to be selected by the President.

The site chosen was as area of about seventeen acres on the eminence known as "Observatory Hill" in west Washington, then bounded by the bank of the Potomac River, E Street, 23rd and 25th Streets, northwest. It now overlooks the site of the Lincoln Memorial, and its buildings are occupied by the Naval Hospital.

The original buildings were constructed under Lieutenant Gillis who went to Europe and consulted foreign astronomers with regard to plans for them. They were completed in September, 1844.

The new Naval Observatory was begun on its present site north of Georgetown in January, 1889 and was officially occupied May 15, 1893.

The United States Army Medical Library and Museum is located in a three-story brick building at the corner of Seventh and B Streets, southwest. This Library originated with the medical books is the office of the Surgeon General of the Army, which began to attain considerable numbers under Surgeon General Joseph Lovell in 1836. At the outbreak of the Civil War it was greatly enlarged for the use of the army surgeons by Surgeon General William A. Hammond. At the close of the Civil War the results of the medical and surgical experience gained by the Army Medical Corps during that conflict were collated in six enormous volumes under the title of "The Medical and Surgical History of the Civil War." This work was the first of its kind and made a great impression, particularly in Europe. Together with the then existing library of the Surgeon General's office, it formed the nucleus of the present Army Medical Library.

Following the close of the Civil War, Dr. John S. Billings, Colonel, Medical Corps, U. S. A., obtained appropriations from year to year for the purchase of medical publications for this library, and entered upon the work of indexing them. In 1887 the present building, which had been authorized by Congress as the result of the efforts of Dr. Billings, was completed for the accommodation of this library and of the Army Medical Museum, which possessed a valuable collection of specimens, particularly of gunshot wounds.

The Army Medical Library now has upward of 500,000 volumes and pamphlets and 5,000 portraits. It is the largest medical library in the world and has been the inspiration for numerous similar institutions which have been established throughout the United States.

The reservation on Greenleaf's or Arsenal Point has been in use as a military post since 1797, this being one of the reservations provided for in the laying out of the city of Washington. It originally contained something over 28 acres, but additional land was acquired by purchase in 1857, and the limits have been extended by filling in the shores until the tract now contains approximately 87 acres. Upon this reservation was erected the old penitentiary building, still standing, in the yard of which took place the execution of the persons convicted c conspiracy in the assassination of President Lincoln. This building was erected under authority of Act of Congress of May 20, 1826, at a cost of $40,000.

The Army War College located on this reservation was authorized by Congress in 1899 in response to the urgent recommendation of Secretary of War Elihu Root, who based his recommendations upon the report of Brigadier General Emory Upton — famous as the leader of the charge at Spottsylvania Court House on May 10, 1864 — who, after the close of the Civil War, had been sent by General Sherman, with two associates, around the world to study the armies of Europe and Asia. General Upton's report relating to the reorganization of the Army had for years lain dormant in the archives of the War Department when it was brought to the attention of the country by Secretary Koot.

The grounds and buildings of the College were planned by the architectural firm of McKim, Mead and White of New York. The cornerstone of the College building was laid February 21, 1903, with Masonic ceremonies, the gavel used being that used by President Washington in laying the cornerstone of the Capitol in 1793. The building was completed in 1907. The statue of Frederick the Great of Prussia, which stands at the northwest approach to the building, was presented to the College by Emperor William of Germany and was unveiled November 19, 1904.

In the original plan of the city of Washington provision had been made for the Navy Yard, to which a tract including slightly over 37 acres had been assigned. In addition, the United States on March 17, 1800, purchased of the Commissioners who laid out the city, two additional squares — Nos. 883 and 884 — for the sum of $4,000, the deed being executed by Commissioners Scott and Thornton. The establishment of the Yard was provided for by Act of Congress of February 25, 1799, in response to the recommendations of Benjamin Stoddert, Secretary of the Navy under President Washington, and was due to the French aggressions upon the commerce of this country. The Act referred to authorized the construction of six frigates and appropriated $1,000,000 for the establishment of six navy yards at New York, Philadelphia, Boston, Portsmouth, Norfolk and Washington respectively.

The Yard was laid out on the plans of Benjamin H. Latrobe under the direction of Captain Thomas Tingey, its first Commandant. Under the peace policy of President Jefferson a number of vessels were laid up in ordinary at the Yard in 1802; and the activities of the Yard were for a number of years confined to overhauling and repairing. The sloop of war Wasp was built at the Yard in 1805, and the schooner Lynx in 1814.

On August 24, 1814, the Yard was destroyed by Captain Tingey, under orders from the Secretary of the Navy, in order to prevent its stores from falling into the hands of the British. The loss caused by this event was estimated at $417,475 and included the frigate Columbia and sloop of war Argus, which were under construction at the Yard.

Following the War of 1812, the Yard was the scene of Robert Fulton's experiments with the naval torpedo, which, for want of financial support, were unproductive of practical results.

In March, 1819, the 74-gun ship Columbus was launched at the Yard and following this the schooner Shark was launched May 17, 1821; the 44-gun Potomac and the schooner Grampus in 1822; the 44-gun Brandywine in June, 1825; the sloop St. Louis in 1828; and the 64-gun frigate Columbia on March 9, 1836. The sloop St. Mary's was launched at the Yard November 24, 1844; a small iron steamer, the Water Witch, at about this time; the steamer Union on December 5, 1846; and the Minnesota shortly before the Civil War.

In 1847 Lieutenant John A. Dahlgren was ordered to ordinance and equipment duty at the Yard. His experiments to ascertain and standardize the ranges of the different classes of naval guns then in use were productive of great improvement in the gunnery of the Navy and resulted in the numerous improvements in gun manufacture and design which have made their inventor famous.

On April 21, 1861, Secretary of the Navy Gideon Welles directed the Commandant of the Yard, Captain Buchanan, to equip for war service the steamers Baltimore, Mount Vernon, Philadelphia and Powhatan. On receipt of this order Captain Buchanan resigned his commission and joined the Confederate service. Commander Dahlgren was at once appointed in his place. Shortly afterwards the 71st New York Volunteers was assigned to the Yard for its protection.

During the early period of the War the Yard was actively engaged in outfitting the Steamers Pawnee, Keystone State, Anacostia, Mt. Vernon, Pocahontas, Powhatan, James Gray and Baltimore for keeping the Potomac open to navigation. Throughout the War the Yard was employed in repairing and outfitting the vessels of the Navy but did no construction work. After the War its importance rapidly declined until following the commencement of the rehabilitation of the Navy in the early eighties, Secretary Whitney, by order of August 14, 1886, assigned the Yard to the control of the Bureau of Ordnance. Government Reservations Nos. 326 and 327 lying on the west side of the Yard and containing about two acres of ground were added to it and a railroad track laid on this new portion of the Yard connecting with the Baltimore and Potomac Railroad.

Shortly after this the establishment of the new gun manufacturing plant began. This plant was completed about 1890 and has grown as the needs of the service required. It is now engaged in the manufacture of fourteen-inch guns for the new super-dreadnaughts of the Navy.

The movement looking to the creation of a Home for Aged Soldiers of the United States Army dates back as far as February 27, 1829, when a report was made by the Committee on Military Affairs in Congress upon the subject of establishing " An Army Asylum Fund. " In 1840, Captain Robert Anderson, later of Fort Sumpter fame, set forth the advantages which would result from such an institution, and outlined a plan for acquiring it. The Military Committee of the House of Representatives, embodied this letter in a report dated January 7, 1841, submitting to Congress an appeal containing the substance of General Anderson's suggestions. In 1844, Major General Winfield Scott gave particular attention to this project in his annual report, and on the strength of General Scott's representations, the Committee on Military Affairs began urging the creation of such an establishment. On March 5,

1846, the Committee, acting upon a memorial of the officers stationed at Ft. Moultrie, and a petition signed by the officers of the Second United States Infantry, again called the matter to the attention of Congress, and repeated their recommendations on January 19, 1848, in a report based upon a memorial signed by the officers of the Army then in Mexico. All of these reports of the Committee favored the enactment of the bill which had been reported in 1841.

During the siege of Mexico City, General Scott, in consequence of a breach of truce by the Mexicans, levied a tribute upon the City of Mexico of $300,000. He transmitted $100,000 of this sum to the Secretary of War in 1848, expressing the hope that the money might be placed to the credit of an army asylum. These funds, together with $18,791.19 of the same levy, were, by Act of Congress of March 3, 1851, made available for the support of the desired institution, which was created by that Act. As a source of perpetual revenue the Act of 1851 appropriated to the use of the Home all stoppage and fines adjudged against soldiers by sentence of court martial forfeitures on account of desertion, a certain portion of the hospital and post fund of each station, moneys belonging to estates of deceased soldiers unclaimed for three years, and also a deduction of 25 cents per month from the pay of each enlisted man.

Under the Act of March 3, 1851, providing for the home, temporary asylums were established in 1851 at New Orleans, Greenwood's Island, Mississippi, and in Washington City, the latter in the Winder Building at 17th and G Streets, northwest. The location in the District of Columbia was made the permanent home and in 1851 256 acres were purchased for this purpose. Between that time and 1869 about 16 acres were added at different times and in 1872 the adjoining estate of Hare wood containing 191 acres was purchased from Mr. W. W. Corcoran. Other small tracts have been acquired since that time, making a total of 500 3-4 acres in the entire tract. The total amount paid for the property was $326,354.55.

The principal building on the grounds is the white marble building. The south part is named after General Winfield Scott and the addition on the north after General W. T. Sherman. A short distance west of the Scott Building is a building named after General Robert Anderson in recognition of his efforts for the establishment of the Home. This was the first building occupied by the inmates of the Home and was used by Presidents Buchanan, Lincoln, Hayes and Arthur as a summer residence.

The eastern building is named the King Building in honor of Surgeon B. King who for thirteen years was the attending Surgeon and Secretary and Treasurer of the Home. Northeast of the Scott building is the building named in honor of General Philip H. Sheridan, erected in 1883. The mess hall and dormitory building of white marble named in honor of General U. S. Grant was occupied July 12, 1910.

The Walter Reed General Hospital at Takoma Park, D. C, was established in 1908 as the general army hospital for the territory east of the Mississippi. It occupies 41 acres of land on the former 7th Street Pike, now Georgia Avenue. It is named after Colonel Walter Reed of the Medical Corps of the Army, who acquired fame as the head of the commission which investigated yellow fever conditions in Cuba at the time of the Spanish American War and met his death in that service. The institution is intended for the treatment of particularly serious and difficult cases transferred from the various post hospitals in the territory to which it is assigned.

The buildings now erected and in course of construction represent an outlay of nearly $500,000. The hospital is designed with a view to extensive temporary enlargement in the event of hostilities.

The U. S. Naval Hospital was founded in 1863 and assigned to the Washington Navy Yard, April 6, 1869. The brick building at 9th Street and Pennsylvania Avenue, southeast, was finished in 1865. The new buildings erected on the grounds of the old Naval Observatory at the foot of 23rd Street, southwest, were occupied October 16, 1906. The building at 9th Street and Pennsylvania Avenue continued to be occupied as a hospital until 1911, when it was abandoned and occupied by the Navy Department for office purposes.

The Commission of Fish and Fisheries was established in 1871 as the result of the efforts of the various State fishing authorities and the members of the American Fish Cultural Association — now the American Fisheries Society. Its purpose was to investigate into the diminution in the supply of food fishes of the United States and the means of checking it. The headquarters building of the Commission, a three-story brick structure at 6th and B Streets, southwest, besides housing the executive offices, contains an interesting museum of marine life. This building had previously served an armory for the District militia for which purpose it was erected at a cost of $30,000, under authority of Act of Congress of March 3, 1855.

Arlington Cemetery, on the Virginia shore of the Potomac, opposite the City of Washington, occupies 200 acres of land, part of the original estate of eleven hundred acres belonging to Daniel Parke Custis, the first husband of Mrs. George Washington. The estate was left by President Washington to his wife's grandson, George Washington Parke Custis, who on his death in 1857 left it to his daughter, Mrs. Robert E. Lee, for life and then to his grandsons Custis and Fitzhugh Lee. As it was never the property of General Lee the Government was unable to confiscate it after the Civil War but purchased it in 1864 at a tax sale for $23,000. In May, 1865, it was created the first of 82 national cemeteries. Later a suit was brought by George W. Lee, the oldest son of General Lee, which resulted in the annulment of the tax sale whereby the Government had acquired the property, and the Government thereupon purchased the tract for $150,000.

Over 16,000 dead of the Civil War, as well as many of the victims of the Spanish-American War and other members of the military and naval establishments are buried at Arlington.

On Georgia Avenue, formerly the 7th Street Pike, near the Walter Reed Hospital, is a small national cemetery where are buried a portion of the Union soldiers who were killed in the defense of the City of Washington against the troops of General Early in July, 1864. This cemetery is near the site of Fort Stevens where the fighting occurred.

The system of public grounds and parks of the City of Washington is based upon the original plan of Major L 'Enfant. While many of the areas designated by him for specific purposes have been appropriated to other uses, nevertheless, the parking system of the original portions of the city is approximately as L 'Enfant laid it out. On L 'Enfant 's map was a list of so-called "references" indicating the purposes to which he intended the various parks to be appropriated. At approximately the present site of the Washington Monument L 'Enfant intended to place an equestrian statue of General Washington which had been authorized by Congress in 1783. At

278

the site of Lincoln Square, he proposed to place "a historical column at a distance of a mile from the Capitol, the same to serve as a standard of distances throughout the country." At the foot of 7th Street, he proposed to place a monument to celebrate the rise of the American Navy. At the present site of the Patent Office he proposed to place a church for National purposes such as public prayer, thanksgivings and funeral orations and assigned to the especial use of no particular sect or denomination, but equally open to all. This church he intended also to be a proper shelter for such monuments as had been voted by the late Continental Congress "for those heroes who fell in the cause of liberty and for such others as might thereafter be decreed by the voice of a grateful nation." He proposed to place grand fountains with a constant spout of water to be obtained from local springs, one on a reservation on Pennsylvania Avenue between 20th and 22nd Streets, west, another on New York Avenue between 12th and 13th Streets, another on Pennsylvania Avenue and 9th Street, another on New Jersey Avenue and G Street, southwest, and another on Maryland Avenue and 8th Street, northeast. Owing to changes made by Major Ellicott in L 'Enfant 's plans these areas do not correspond precisely with existing parks but were probably at or near the sites of the present Washington Circle, Franklin Park, Garfield Park and Green Park. At the foot of the Capitol terrace he proposed to place a grand cascade formed of water from the source of the Tiber. This purpose has been carried into effect by the establishment of the fountain now existing at that point. The grounds to the west of the Capitol, L 'Enfant designated as "a public walk through which carriages might ascend to the upper square of the Federal House." The present Mall he designated as "a grand avenue 400 feet in breadth and about a mile in length, bordered with gardens ending in a slope from the houses on each side." This avenue he intended to lead to the Monument of General Washington and to connect "the Congress garden" with "the President's Park," and "a well-improved field" which was to be "a part of the walk from the President's House of about 1800 feet in breadth and three quarters of a mile in length." This latter is the present White House Lot, upon the east and west margins of which he designated in colors the situations which he considered " commanded the most agreeable prospects " and to be "the best calculated for the spacious houses and gardens such as might accommodate foreign ministers, etc." He also indicated a park around the space occupied by the Capitol, though not covering the entire area of the present Capitol Square and extending out East Capitol Street to Lincoln Park. In addition L 'Enfant indicated by coloring them in yellow, 15 parks at the intersections of streets and avenues which he proposed to divide among the several States of the Union for each of them to improve, the centers of the squares to be ornamented with statues, columns, obelisks or such other ornaments as the different States might choose to erect "to perpetuate not only the memory of such individuals whose councils or military achievements were conspicuous in giving liberty and independence to this country, but also those whose usefulness hath rendered them worthy of general imitation to invite the youth of succeeding generations to tread in the paths of those sages or heroes whom their country has thought properly to celebrate." Along the north edge of the Mall, he indicated in red, spots for the location of places of worship. A number of other squares or areas not designated, he indicated as suitable for colleges and academies "in which every society whose object is national may be accommodated. "

279

As related in Chapter V, these appropriations, except as to the grounds for the Capitol and President's House, were all stricken out on Major Ellicott's plan, and later, upon the preparation of Dermott's "Tin Case Map," seventeen public appropriations were indicated which by proclamations signed by President Washington and President Adams were officially declared to be the public areas of the city. At the time the city was established much of these areas was covered with luxuriant growths of forests. This was particularly true of the space occupied by the Mall and President's grounds. The Commissioners who founded the city did little to protect these trees under the authority granted by the deeds of trust, and they were ruthlessly destroyed by the proprietors. This was a source of great regret and vexation to President Jefferson who regarded their destruction as little short of a calamity.

The areas occupied by the Mall, from the Capitol to the Potomac River, the White House Park, and Lafayette Square were laid out as parks in 1852 under the plans of Andrew Jackson Downing, a noted landscape architect of New York.

It is evident from a review of the old city ordinances that even in its early days some system of parking adorned with trees was in existence. As early as March 25, 1803, a fine of $5 was imposed upon any person willfully injuring any of the street trees. On August 3, 1815, an ordinance was passed appropriating $100 per annum out of the funds of the first and second wards for the purpose of keeping in order, tarring or replanting trees planted by the corporation in the public squares, streets and avenues within those wards. On May 26, 1820, an ordinance was passed granting permission to persons who desired to plant trees in any part of a street or avenue opposite their own grounds to enclose such part of the street or avenue as might be necessary for the purpose of protecting the trees so planted, not exceeding six feet, without the curb line. The trees so planted must not be more than 20 feet apart.

The credit for the adoption of the present existing system of street parking belongs to the Board of Public Works under the Territorial Government, which took advantage of an Act of Congress approved April 6, 1870. This Act authorized the City of Washington to set apart as parks to be adorned with shade trees, walks, and enclosed with curbstones, not exceeding one-half the width of any and all avenues and streets in the city, leaving a roadway of not less than 35 feet in width in the center or two such roadways on each side of a park in the center of the same, the cost to be defrayed by special assessments upon the adjoining property. This measure was presented in the Senate by Senator Justin Morrill of Vermont acting on behalf of the Committee on Public Buildings and Grounds. In the course of the debate on this bill Senator Sherman of Ohio remarked that "the ordinary way now in the large cities of the West is to have the parking on either side and the roadway in the center; that is the proper way. "

The original promoter of the movement which resulted in this legislation was Mayor Bowen who was moved to recommend such a system of parking by the inconvenience suffered by the residents of K Street especially between 12th and 16th Streets, northwest, resulting from the dust arising from the carriageway of that street. A broad parking of trees and shrubbery was contemplated as a protection to the residents from this dust. Under the authority of the act of Congress above mentioned, the City Councils authorized the improvement of K Street by the removal of the curbstones and gutters on both sides of the street and the placing of them twenty-five feet nearer the center, the intervening spaces between the old sidewalks and the relocated curbstones to be graded and converted into grass plots, ornamented by shrubbery and a row of trees on each side. The prosecution of this work was entrusted to a commission and its execution was practically the sole work of Mr. Henry A. Willard, one of the members of this commission. This parking was afterwards removed by the Board of Public Works and an area of bituminous carriageway surface substantially as at present existing, was substituted.

Shortly after coming into existence the Board of Public Works under the Territorial Government, along with its other projects for the development and improvement of the city, vigorously entered upon the task of establishing a comprehensive system of street parking. At its meeting on September 4, 1871, the Board of Public Works appointed William Saunders, William R. Smith and John Saul, a commission to report to the Board what trees they would recommend to be planted and the best places to procure them. Mr. Smith was at the time and for many years thereafter continued to be Superintendent of the Botanical Gardens, Mr. Saunders was then and for many years after, the Superintendent of the grounds of the Department of Agriculture and Mr. Saul was a prominent local nurseryman. This commission continued as a purely voluntary body from the date of its authorization by the Board of Public Works throughout all of the succeeding forms of government until broken up by the deaths of its members about the beginning of the new century. On May 11, 1897, Rear Admiral James E. Jouett, U. S. N., was appointed by the District Commissioners to fill the vacancy occasioned by Mr. Saul's decease on January 8, 1898.

This commission was commonly known as the Parking Commission. It was created without authority of law and served without compensation, but it would be difficult to find an instance of public or altruistic service on behalf of any community surpassing in the degree of devotion to the trust accepted or in professional enthusiasm and skill that which was displayed by this commission throughout the period of its existence. To its efforts the nation is indebted for the system of street trees which is so prominent a feature of the Capital City. Nor would reference to this subject be complete without a recognition of the service rendered by Mr. Truman Lanham, who for 25 years has been the superintendent of Trees and Parkings.

For many years a controversy existed between representatives of the local and national governments over the question of the jurisdiction over the sidewalk and other parking spaces in the city. This question was settled by Congress in an act approved July 1, 1898, wherein jurisdiction and control of the street parking in the streets and avenues of the District of Columbia was transferred to and vested in the Commissioners of the District of Columbia, and other parts of the park system of the District of Columbia were placed under control of the Chief of Engineers of the United States Army under such regulations as the President might prescribe through the Secretary of War. The act defined the park system as comprising all public spaces laid down as reservations on a map which accompanied the annual report for 1894 of the Officer in Charge of Public Buildings and Grounds, together with all areas more than 250 feet square between sidewalk lines after the same should have been set aside by the Commissioners of the District of Columbia for park purposes. This act further authorized the Chief of Engineers of the Army to temporarily turn over to private owners of the adjoining lands, to be cared for by such owners under such regulations as he might prescribe, all the parking spaces in the streets set aside by the Commissioners for park purposes.

With the incoming of the 20th century, the urgent need of additional public buildings as well as a tendency towards the construction of buildings of a semipublic character made it apparent to the public as well as to the law-makers of the nation that the establishment of some definite plan for the location of such structures in the future was a matter of imperative necessity in order that harmonious relationships might be established between the various structures. This sentiment took definite shape during the course of the commemorative exercises held in celebration of the 100th anniversary of the removal of the seat of government to the District of Columbia. Throughout the numerous addresses of that occasion was expressed a predominating sentiment favoring the improvement and development of the District of Columbia in a manner befitting it as the Capital of the American nation.

By a fortunate co-incidence the American Institute of Architects was holding its session in the City of Washington at the time these centennial exercises were in progress and at this session the Institute engaged in an earnest discussion of the question of improving and developing the Capital City. A number of prominent architects, sculptors and landscape architects of the country read papers advancing their ideas upon the different features involved in a scheme for the improvement of the District and in consequence of this discussion a committee on legislation was appointed to confer with the Committees of Congress on the District of Columbia relative to the adoption of definite measures looking to the carrying out of some comprehensive scheme of public improvement.

Conferences between this committee and the Senate Committee on the District of Columbia resulted in a resolution adopted by the Senate on March 8, 1901, that the Committee on the District of Columbia be directed to consider the subject and report to the Senate plans for the development and improvement of the entire park system of the District of Columbia, and that for the purpose of preparing such plans the Committee might secure the services of such experts as should be found necessary for a proper consideration of the subject. On March 19, 1901, the sub-committee appointed to give immediate consideration to the purpose of this resolution met with the representatives of the American Institute of Architects and came to an agreement proposed by the latter to the effect that the services of a voluntary expert commission to consist of Mr. Daniel H. Burnham, of Chicago, and Mr. Frederick Law Olmsted, Jr., of Brookline, Massachusetts, be accepted by the Senate Committee, these gentlemen having authority to invite others to assist them in their work. The gentlemen named associated with themselves Mr. Charles F. McKim and Mr. Augustus St. Gaudens of New York City, to act with them in the preparation of plans. Mr. Burnham had been director of works at the World's Columbian Exposition held in Chicago in 1893. Mr. McKim was the architect of the Boston Public Library, the Rhode Island Capitol Building, the new buildings and fences at Harvard University and other structures of monumental character and was recognized as one of the leading American architects. Mr. St. Gaudens was recognized as the premier of American sculpture, from whose criticisms on art subjects it was universally considered there could be no appeal. Mr. Olmsted was probably the most prominent landscape architect in the country, being the consulting landscape architect of the extensive system of parks and boulevards of the city of Boston and its suburbs as well as of other large parking areas in other cities.

Commenting on the spirit with which these men undertook their task the report of the Senate Committee submitted by Mr. McMillan on January 15, 1902, says:

"At the call of their professional brethren and at the request of this Committee, these men virtually put aside their large and profitable private work and for nearly a year devoted their time, their experience, and their technical training to the service of the nation. These sacrifices they had made without pecuniary reward, and at a time in the professional careers of the majority of them when success and fame were already secured. Not only is the nation fortunate in having obtained the ripest talents of three such distinguished men, but also it is a matter for satisfaction that the fourth member of the Commission enters upon the work at an age when he may be expected to have a part in directing and shaping the development of the plans from the beginning to the end. " Speaking of the recommendations made by this Commission in its report of the Senate Committee, Senator McMillan continues:

"The plans prepared by the Commission and submitted to the Senate with this report are the most comprehensive ever provided for the development of an American city. Every portion of the District of Columbia has been studied; in the outlying sections those spaces best adapted for parks, both small and large, have been marked; the most convenient and the most picturesque connections between the various parks have been mapped; the individual treatment which each particular important park should undergo is recommended; an extension of the park system to Great Falls and to Mt. Vernon is discussed; the development of the Mall receives detailed and elaborate treatment; the location of new public buildings, whether legislative, executive or municipal in character, has been arranged according to a rational system of grouping; and those memorials which mark great epochs or great crises in our national history have been brought into harmonious relations with the general scheme of development."

So thoroughly was the work of the Park Commission appreciated both by the public and by Congress that it was determined to create a similar body which should be of a permanent character. This sentiment took definite shape in an Act of Congress approved May 17, 1910, creating the Commission of Fine Arts. This Commission was to consist of seven well qualified judges of fine arts to be appointed by the President and to serve four years each. The Act provided that it should be the duty of such Commission to advise upon the location of statues, fountains and monuments in the public squares, streets and parks in the District of Columbia, and upon the selection of models for statues, fountains and monuments erected under the authority of the United States, and upon the selection of artists for the execution of the same. The Act required all officers charged by law to determine such questions to call upon the Commission for its advice, the only exceptions being in connection with the Capitol Building and the Library of Congress. The Commission was also required to advise generally upon questions of art when called upon to do so by the President or any Committee of either house of Congress. The members of the Commission were expected to serve gratuitously but their expenses in attending meetings at Washington were to be defrayed by Congress.

Under commissions dated June 15, 1910, President Taft appointed as members of the Commission of Fine Arts, Daniel H. Burnham, of Illinois, Frederick Law

Olmsted of Massachusetts, Thomas Hastings, of New York, Daniel Chester French, of New York, Francis D. Millet, of New York, Cass Gilbert, of New York, and Charles Moore, of Michigan. Mr. Moore was for many years clerk of the Committee on the District of Columbia of the House of Representatives in which position he had, through his intense enthusiasm and untiring interest, rendered services of incalculable value to the National Capital. His influence had always been strong with members of Congress in favor of the development of the District upon a noble scale, and his appointment upon the Commission of Fine Arts was a fitting recognition not only of past services but of his preeminent qualifications to pass upon subjects relating to the beautification of the nation's capital.

The Commission of Fine Arts took charge of the plans, drawings, designs and photographs which had been prepared by the Park Commission in 1901. On October 25, 1910, President Taft issued an order to the effect that no plans for any public building to be erected in the District of Columbia for the General Government should thereafter be approved by the office in charge thereof until submitted to the Commission of Fine Arts for its comment and advice.

Mr. Burnham was appointed Chairman of the Commission and at its first meeting Mr. Millet was elected Vice-Chairman. Upon Mr. Millet fell the greater part of the task of organizing the work of the Commission. On returning from a visit of inspection of the American Academy in Rome, Mr. Millet perished in the Titanic disaster on April 15, 1912. Mr. Burnham died in Heidelberg, Germany, on June 1, 1912. Edwin H. Blashfield of New York, was appointed by President Taft on May 31, 1912, to fill the vacancy caused by Mr. Millet's death and Mr. Peirce Anderson of Illinois was appointed on July 5, 1912, to fill the vacancy caused by the death of Mr. Burnham.

The availability of Rock Creek Valley as the site for a park was officially noticed as early as 1866 by Major N. Michler, of the Corps of Engineers to whom had been referred a resolution of the Senate providing for the selection of a site for a public park and a presidential mansion.

Major Michler brought the matter to the attention of a number of prominent citizens of Washington, among them Admiral Lee, and Mr. W. W. Corcoran, but notwithstanding that considerable interest was shown in the project, no definite action was taken toward the acquisition of the necessary land at that time. In 1883, Captain Richard L. Hoxie, then Assistant to the Engineer Commissioner of the District, recommended the establishment of a park embracing the entire Rock Creek Valley within the District of Columbia, including the hilly country as far west as Tenleytown, and as far east as Rock Creek Church Road, an area of approximately 8,000 acres. Captain Hoxie as a detail of his plan, proposed the construction of a dam just above Georgetown of such height as to back the water up the creek for a distance of four miles in order to secure an added water supply for the city.

To the efforts of Mr. Charles C. Glover is due the credit for the first definite action taken toward the establishment of the park. As the result of his indefatigable exertions Congress by an Act approved September 27, 1890, authorized the acquisition of a tract of land upon both sides of Rock Creek beginning at Klingle Ford Bridge and running northwardly following the course of the creek, of a width not less at any point than 600 feet nor more than 1200 feet, including the bed of the creek, of which not less than 200 feet should be on either side of the creek south of

Broad Branch Road and Blagdon Mill Road, and of such greater width north of those roads as the Commissioners designated by the Act for carrying it into effect, might select.

The area of the territory to be so acquired was limited to 2,000 acres and the cost confined to $1,200,000. For the purpose of acquiring this ground the Act created a Commission to consist of the Chief of Engineers of the United States Army, the Engineer Commissioner of the District of Columbia, and three citizens to be appointed by the President. One-half the cost was to be appropriated from the Treasury and one-half from the revenues of the District of Columbia. The Act authorized the Commission in the event it should be unable to purchase the necessary land at reasonable prices, to institute condemnation proceedings and further directed that such real estate within the District as the Commission should find to be directly benefitted by reason of the location of the park should be assessed to the extent of its benefits received therefrom to pay the cost of the land.

On March 11, 1892, a map setting out the tracts which the Commission proposed to include within the park was prepared and the money therefor drawn from the Treasury and paid into the Registry of the Court for the benefit of the owners, whereupon under virtue of the Act authorizing the creation of the Commission, by its Executive Officer, it formally took possession of the land. On December 13, 1894, the park was turned over by the Commission to the Board of Control created by the original Act. This Board consisted of the Commissioners of the District of Columbia and the Chief of Engineers of the Army. The territory acquired contained 1,605.9 acres and the cost of its acquisition including the incidental expenses was $1,174 511.45.

After the acquisition of the land the Commission held a number of meetings for the purpose of determining upon the assessments against adjoining property to pay for the park and made a test case of the Van Riswick property. Mr. T. A. Lambert, representing the property owners, obtained from Judge Cox of the Supreme Court of the District an injunction against the assessment of benefits against this property and this decision was upheld by the Court of Appeals of the District but reversed in the Supreme Court of the United States. The Commission then renewed its hearings for the taking of testimony but after thorough consideration, concluded that the testimony did not show that there was any appreciable increase in the value of the surrounding property resulting from the establishment of the park and so reported to the Supreme Court of the District of Columbia.

In 1904 Mr. Charles C. Glover offered to dedicate an additional strip of ground along the east side of Rock Creek between Massachusetts Avenue and Connecticut Avenue Bridge, and this offer was accepted by a clause in the appropriation act for the fiscal year 1904, authorizing the Board of Control of Rock Creek Park to accept the dedication of land for the purpose of adding to that park. The dedication of this strip leaves only a small space of about fifty feet in the entire stretch from Massachusetts Avenue to the north end of Rock Creek Park on the east side of the creek which is not owned by the government.

By Act approved February 27, 1907, Congress authorized a parkway approach averaging 400 feet wide, to the Rock Creek Park from 16th Street down the valley of Piney Branch, and Congress is now being asked to authorize the further acquisition of the valley of the Klingle Road from Rock Creek Park to the junction of Klingle and Woodley Roads, comprising 28 ½ acres, as well as land necessary to extend Rock Creek Drive and Lovers ' Lane from Montrose Park north of Georgetown to the proposed Klingle Valley Park, thus giving a continuous driveway from Montrose Park to Rock Creek Park of about two miles in length. It is proposed also to extend the Piney Branch Driveway from 16th Street to Georgia Avenue, giving a connection between Rock Creek Park and the Soldiers' Home Grounds. In the 15 years following the acquisition of this park $223,333.98 have been expended in its improvement, making the total cost to date, $1,397,845.43.

On April 30, 1908, the District Commissioners submitted to Congress a report recommending the improvement of Rock Creek Valley from the Zoological Park to the mouth of the creek, by the open valley method as recommended by the Park Commission in 1901. This report, coming to the attention of Senator Wetmore, of Rhode Island, the latter requested the Commissioners to prepare a map of the lands required for carrying out the proposed improvement, and upon the preparation of this map by the Engineer's office, Senator Wetmore introduced a bill which was enacted in the public buildings act of March 4, 1913, and provided that for the purpose of preventing the pollution and obstruction of Rock Creek and of connecting Potomac Park with the Zoological Park and Rock Creek Park, a commission composed of the Secretaries of the Treasury and of War and Agriculture, should acquire by purchase, condemnation or otherwise, the land on both sides of the Creek included within the lines on the map so prepared and authorized the expenditure for this purpose of $1,300,000.

The public buildings act of June 25, 1910, authorized the Secretary of the Interior to acquire by purchase or condemnation the ground included between Euclid Street, Columbia Avenue or 15th Street, W Street or Florida Avenue, and 16th Street extended, containing approximately 437,000 square feet and appropriated the sum of $490,000 for this purpose, one-half of which was to be contributed out of the revenues of the District and be repaid in four annual instalments with interest at 3%. The same act authorized the Commissioners to purchase or condemn the tract of land known as Montrose lying immediately north of Road or R Street and east of Lovers' Lane on Georgetown Heights, containing 16 acres, at an expense of not over $150,000. Both of these parks were acquired by the Commissioners, that on Meridian Hill at the full amount appropriated and Montrose Park at the cost of $110,000.

From 1898 until 1905 Mr. William P. Richards was employed in laying out, grading and macadamizing new roads, building bridges, culverts, fords, etc., in Rock Creek Park. The main work in road construction was the grading of a road along the Creek from its northern to its southern boundary and now known as "Beach Driveway," in honor of Commissioner Lansing H. Beach, who began, and during his entire term of office, took an especial interest in the designing and development of the improvements of the Park, including the celebrated "Boulder Bridge."

The general appropriation act for the District of Columbia approved June 26, 1912, provided for the acquisition of the ground necessary to preserve the sites of Ft. Davis and Ft. Dupont for park purposes, and for providing a highway between them by widening Alabama Avenue to 150 feet, the entire area thus taken comprising 41 ¼ acres of land. This act required that not less than one-third and all in excess of $21,334 should be assessed as benefits against the adjoining property. By the same act the Secretary of War was directed to investigate and report on the question of the present water supply in the District of Columbia and the sufficiency of its source at Great Falls, to supply the future needs of the United States and of the District of Columbia, and also the availability of the water power at Great Falls or vicinity on the Potomac River, or between the Great Falls and the District of Columbia for the purpose of supplying light and power for the use of the United States and of the government of the District of Columbia.

The Zoological Park originated in the custom of the Smithsonian Institution of obtaining living animals for purposes of study of taxidermists engaged in the preparation of skins and skeletons for mounting. These animals, owing to the absence of adequate arrangements for keeping them, were either killed for their skins or if not desired as specimens were sent to the Zoological Gardens at Philadelphia. During the eighties, Mr. William T. Hornaday, the taxidermist of the National Museum, noted both for his skill in his profession and for the results of his travels in Borneo and South America, conceived the idea of retaining these living animals with the idea of accumulating a collection of them for public exhibition. At Mr. Hornaday's suggestion a separate department of the National Museum — that of living animals — was created, and Mr. Hornaday was appointed curator of this department. As the result of his activities, the Museum owned in 1887 and 1888 about 220 living specimens.

The rapid extermination of many forms of wild animal life aroused a general interest in the subject of the preservation of specimens of these animals to posterity. To Mr. S. P. Langley, Secretary of the Smithsonian Institution, occurred the idea of establishing a Zoological Park in which to preserve specimens of wild animals for the double purpose of diffusing zoological knowledge and preserving the various species from extinction.

Mr. Langley 's idea was to place the animals in surroundings as near as possible like those to which they were accustomed in their wild state. This idea was at the time a novel one and had not been adopted in the zoological collections of Europe, owing to lack of space in those crowded cities where such collections existed. Secretary Langley saw the possibilities for such a park which were to be found in the valley of Rock Creek and he solicited the cooperation of numerous public spirited and official gentlemen in the promotion of his project to convert a portion of this valley into a zoological park. Among those who evinced an active interest were Senator Beck of Kentucky and Senator Morrow of Vermont. Senator Beck introduced a bill in Congress on April 23, 1888, providing for a commission to be composed of the Secretary of the Interior, the President of the Board of Commissioners of the District of Columbia, and the Secretary of the Smithsonian Institution to locate and purchase land for a park which should be turned over to the Regents of the Smithsonian Institution, after being so acquired. This bill failed of passage but the following year Senator Edmunds introduced a similar bill as an amendment to the District of Columbia appropriation bill, carrying an appropriation of $200,000. This bill was passed and was approved March 2, 1889. The Commission provided for in the act selected approximately 166 acres of land and after overcoming some difficulties in re-establishing the lines of the owners of the property needed, owing to the obliteration of old land marks, completed the survey on November 21, 1889, and completed the acquisition of the site on November 4, 1890. An Act of Congress approved April 30, 1890, placed the National Zoological Park under the

287

direction of the Regents of the Smithsonian Institution. Dr. Frank Baker was appointed Superintendent, and under Dr. Baker and the Regents of the Smithsonian Institution the work of developing and improving the land which had been purchased was begun. The amount originally available for this purpose was $100,000. The services of Mr. Frederick Law Olmsted were obtained for the purpose of devising the general plan of improvement and after a number of visits Mr. Olmsted outlined plans for developing the park which have in the main been followed so far as the funds at the disposal of the Regents have permitted.

The park has been very popular with the people of Washington. During the first decade of its existence, attendance as high as 10,000 in a day were frequent, but these numbers were greatly exceeded in the following decade, and on Easter Monday, April 13, 1914, the attendance was slightly under 57,000. The advantage of this establishment over similar establishments in Europe lie not alone in the natural beauties of its location, including Rock Creek and the cliffs and forests of its valley, but also in its extent. This park includes 166.48 acres. The Jardin des Plants at Paris in which is located the Paris Zoological Gardens, includes 17 acres, the Gardens of the Zoological Society of London includes 36 acres, and the Berlin Zoological Garden, 63 acres.

Following the close of the Civil War, or even earlier, the problem of disposing of the rapidly accumulating silt in the Potomac River opposite Washington became a serious one. Between 1870 and 1881, $290,000 was spent in dredging channels 16 feet deep and 200 feet wide through the Georgetown and Washington channels and in removing a number of dangerous rocks which obstructed the harbor at Georgetown.

In connection with the problem of keeping the channels open was that of dealing with the extensive flats reaching from the bend of the river at Easby's Point to the forks of the channel opposite the mouth of the Eastern Branch. Under the River and Harbor Act of March 3, 1881, and a resolution of the Senate of December 13, 1881, the Board of Engineers of the Army investigated and reported upon a plan called for by Congress, having for its object the widening and deepening of the channels of the Potomac; the reclamation of the flats by depositing on them the material dredged from the channels; the freeing of the Washington channel of sewage, and the establishment of harbor lines. The flats were to be reclaimed to a height of three feet above the flood plane of 1877, which, although the highest freshet of record to that time, was exceeded by about three feet by the flood of 1889. The engineer's report provided for a tidal reservoir with automatic inlet and outlet gates to insure the flushing of the Washington channel with each tide. In 1890 a training dike on the Virginia shore was made a part of the project.

The work reached a point during the early nineties where the retaining wall around the vast area of the Potomac flats had been constructed and the area reclaimed and planted with a fringe of willows.

By Act of March 3, 1897, Congress declared this area to be a public park under the name of "Potomac Park." About 19,000,000 cubic yards were dredged from the river and deposited on the flats. The area reclaimed is 628 acres exclusive of that of the tidal reservoir of 111 acres. The office of public buildings and grounds has done a considerable amount of improvement on the Potomac Park, particularly in the laying out of a drive along the river bank.

The improvement of the Anacostia River commenced with the authorization in 1890 of the dredging of a channel 20 feet deep and 200 feet wide near the mouth of that stream. In 1902 Congress authorized the improvement of the portion below the Navy Yard Bridge by a channel 400 feet wide and 20 feet deep at the center. The dredged material was deposited behind a stone bulkhead to a height of seven feet above low tide and the reclaimed area is to be surrounded by an earthen embankment fourteen feet above low tide. This work has resulted in the reclamation of about 160 acres. By the District appropriation act of June 26, 1912, Congress appropriated $100,000 for continuing the reclamation and development of the Anacostia River and Flats from the Anacostia Bridge to the District line, this sum to be expended under the supervision of the Chief of Engineers of the Army upon plans to be approved by a board to consist of the Engineer Commissioner of the District, the engineer officer in charge of the improvement of the Potomac River and the officer in charge of public buildings and grounds. Two similar appropriations have since been made. It is proposed to reclaim the entire extent of the Anacostia flats much along the line suggested by the Park Commission in 1901.

CHAPTER XIII

Art, Literature, Music and the Drama

The first public buildings erected in Washington were structures of beauty instead of mere rude habitations such as those with which infant cities usually begin. Although these palaces in the woods, separated by great distances, were themes for the jest of the short-sighted, yet their majestic proportions rising from their sylvan surroundings must have had an inspiring and prophetic effect upon the appreciative. The White House, the Patent Office, the Treasury Building, and the Capitol, follow closely the old Grecian principles, and are worthy of the great Republic whose government they represent. The other government buildings present varying degrees of merit and mediocrity.

In 1816 David Baillie Warden tells that "Mr. Boyle, a painter from Baltimore, collects objects of natural history, to form a museum in a building near the center of the city, which was formerly occupied as a study by Stewart, the celebrated portrait painter. "

In 1845 William Q. Force tells of King's Art Gallery. Mr. Charles King was an artist living in Washington at that time, having his studio and exhibition building on Twelfth between E and F Streets. Mr. Force also recounts that there were in Washington at that time several other portrait and landscape painters, and that the capital city had become somewhat of an art center.

A National Gallery of Art was early advocated but was many years being provided for. When the National Institute was formed one of its provisions was for the advancement of literature and art, although science received the Institute's greatest attention.

In April, 1841, the Institute was given space in the new Patent Office building, and with the scientific collection began one of art, meager at first but by 1845 large enough to be constituted the germ of a National collection.

When the Smithsonian Institution was established in 1846, the small collection of art pieces was transferred with the scientific collection to its management. One of the provisions in the Smithson will required that a fine art collection be part of the effort of the Institution, and the Committee in its report in 1847, suggested the buying of paintings and sculpture for a more extensive exhibit, besides engravings and architectural designs.

The first important collection purchased was the collection of Indian portraits of Mr. George Catlin. These portraits were taken from life and had been exhibited quite extensively in Europe and America. The whole collection comprised over six hundred pictures, and besides portraits contained landscapes and scenes showing sports, religious ceremonies and other customs of the Indians, making it a valuable historical as well as artistic collection. The purchase of plaster casts of some of the classic statues of Europe was also authorized about this time.

In 1849 the Institution purchased the collection of George Perkins Marsh, comprising many fine engravings and etchings, there being several hundred portfolios altogether, in bound volumes and loose.

This acquisition cost the Government $3,000 and was pronounced the choicest collection of its kind in America. Among these engravings and etchings were many from celebrated artists, such as Rembrandt, Durer, Lorraine, Hollar, Leonardo, and others equally celebrated.

Another Indian collection was sent to the Institution in 1852, by J. M. Stanley comprising one hundred fifty-two canvases.

The main section of the Smithsonian building was completed in 1855. The upper story was divided into three rooms, the western of which was devoted to art purposes and known as the National Gallery of Art. Here the collection furnished pleasure and instruction to visitors and students and grew slowly until January 24, 1865, when a disastrous fire destroyed the entire art collection except a few pieces that had been placed on the main floor of the building and were saved.

After this catastrophe the National art possessions were temporarily placed with the Library of Congress and the Corcoran Gallery of Art, and for years it appeared that there was no National Gallery.

In 1903, at the death of Harriet Lane Johnston, the niece of President Buchanan, who was mistress of the White House while he was President, it was found that she had bequeathed her art collection to the Government, when it should establish a National Gallery. After the decision of the courts that the United States already had a National Art Gallery connected with the Smithsonian Institution, the bequest was made over to the Government in 1906.

In 1904 another great art gift came to the Government by the generosity of Charles L. Freer, of Detroit, Michigan, then consisting of 2,250 pieces, and added to since by the donor.

Less than a year later William T. Evans of New York gave to the United States fifty paintings by American artists, which has since been increased to double that number.

The Harriet Lane Johnston collection, after being turned over to the Smithsonian Institution August 3, 1906, was housed in the reception room and office of the Secretary of the Institution building, and remained there until November 20, when it was transferred to the temporary gallery fitted up in the National Museum building. This collection now occupies a room, where all the pieces can be seen to advantage. Among these is a beautiful miniature of President Buchanan, by John Henry Brown; a portrait of the Prince of Wales, presented to Mr. Buchanan by the Prince himself March 29, 1862; a portrait of Mrs. Abington by John Hoppner; one of Sir Thomas Lawrence 's portraits, that of Lady Essex; Madonna and Child by Luini; Sir Joshua Reynolds ' portrait of Mrs. Hammond; George Romney's portrait of Miss Kirkpatrick; a marble bust of James Buchanan; another of Harriet Lane Johnston 's husband, Henry Elliot Johnston, by Rinehart; a marble cupid by the same artist of the little son of Mr. and Mrs. Johnston, Henry E., Jr.; a beautiful bust of the donor herself; and other beautiful and interesting pieces as well as several objects of historic interest.

When the Evans donation was accepted by the Government the Smithsonian had no suitable place for it, so gladly accepted the tender of the atrium of the Corcoran Gallery of Art.

Early in July, 1909, the collection was transferred to the gallery fitted up in the National Museum building, and Mr. Evans has since added other paintings. Some of the gems are: The Black Orchid by Frederick Stuart Church; High Cliff, Coast of Maine, Winslow Homer; September Afternoon, George Innis; My Day Home,

William Henry Howe; Visit of Nicodemus to Christ, John LaFarge; An Interlude, William Sergeant Kendall; A Family of Birches, Willard Leroy Metcalf; The Boy With the Arrow, Douglas Volk; Eros et Musa, by Henry Oliver Walker; and a portrait of the collector and donor, by Alphonse Jongers.

The National Gallery of Art has other acquisitions also, some of which are: Aurora Borealis, by Frederic Edwin Church; Crossing the Ferry, by Adrian Moreau; Indian Summer Day, by Max Weyl; Portrait of Mrs. Price, by William Hogarth; Sir Sampson Wright, by George Romney; Mrs. Towry, by Sir Thomas Lawrence; Duchess of Ancestor, by Sir Joshua Reynolds; Mrs. Rouse, by Sir Peter Lely, lent by Dr. Thomas M. Chartard, and others of equal note.

A valuable historical collection of canvases hanging in this gallery are the paintings of Edward Moran, depicting scenes from the history of America, from the Landing of Leif Erickson in 1001, to the War with Spain during closing years of the Nineteenth Century. "The Ocean — The Highway of All Nations," leads the list and is a most beautiful representation of the sea. There are twelve scenes familiar to all Americans, including "The Santa Maria, Nina and Pinta," standing out in an evening glow; "The Debarkation of Columbus," showing morning light; "First Recognition of the American Flag;" "Iron Versus Wood Sinking of the Cumberland by the Merrimac;" and others as inspiring, as spirited and as beautiful.

The most elaborate art gallery in Washington and that best known, is the Corcoran Gallery of Art. This great public educational institution was the gift of William Wilson Corcoran of Georgetown, in the form of the old building and grounds at 17th Street and Pennsylvania Avenue, an endowment of $900,000, and a private art collection valued at $100,000. The building has been mentioned in the chapter on Public Buildings and Grounds.

Since the original collection of Mr. Corcoran and the first installation of purchases, many pictures have been added. Some of the pictures that attract most attention are: a portrait of Mr. Corcoran by Charles Loring Elliott, painted in 1887; Church's Niagara Falls; George de Forrest Brush's Mother and Child; Sunset in the Woods by George Inness; A Light on the Sea, by Winslow Homer; Woodgatherers by Corot; Charlotte Corday, by Müller; The Open Fire, by Robert Reed; The Helping Hand, by Emile Renouf; a Bull, by Rosa Bonheur; Washington Before Yorktown, by Rembrandt Peale; Caesar Dead, by Gerome, one of the pictures of the original purchase by Mr. W. T. Walters in 1873; Pope Julius II before the Apollo Belvedere, by Becker; Gilbert Stuart's Washington; Lenbach's Bismarck; Sully's full-length portrait of Andrew Jackson; the row of the Presidents of the United States; Benjamin West's Cupid and Psyche; My Daughter, by Frank W. Benson.

The Barye collection of bronzes is an important possession of the gallery. The entire collection was acquired in 1873 by Mr. Walters while in Paris on his mission of selecting art works for the Corcoran Gallery of Art.

The growth of art in Washington has not been alone in its art galleries. Public buildings have had a large share in adding to the growth and in bringing artists to the Capital. For years the Capitol was a center for artists, and in this great building are some of the art treasures of the Country.

As we enter the rotunda we are attracted by the great Rogers bronze doors, the work of Randolph Rogers, an American sculptor who designed and modeled them in 1858, in Rome. They were cast two years later in Munich by F. von Miller. They were brought to America while the war was in progress and remained sometime unused but were placed in their present position at the eastern front of the building, in 1863.

The arched setting of the doors is appropriate and the deep frame into which the doors fit when opened, is ornamented with symbols of the discoverer they commemorate. The lunette at the top is the largest of the bas-reliefs and represents the landing of Columbus upon the newly found world. Under this, on the eight panels of the doors, are other scenes from the life of the discoverer. These are: Columbus Before the Council at Salamanca; Columbus at La Rabida Convent, where he received hospitality; Columbus at the Spanish Court receiving his commission; Columbus departing from Palos on his first voyage; His encounter with the Indians; His Triumphant Return to Barcelona; His arrival after the third journey in chains; and lastly, His Death.

Stepping into the rotunda, and under the lofty dome, which is one of the greatest architectural achievements, in the world, more of the Country's history is told in the large paintings on the walls. Four of those are the famous Trumbull pictures, painted by Colonel John Trumbull after the American Revolution.

High above these pictures is a historical frieze of fresco, (chiaro-oscuro), a work begun by Constantino Brumidi in 1878, representing events in the history of the country. His death in 1880 stopped the work, which was taken up later by his pupil, Castigini, but was never finished by him. A portion of it is still incomplete.

In the canopy of the dome, is the crowning decoration, the Apothesis of Washington, a very difficult, ambitious and well-executed piece of work that took years for completion and cost $50,000. In this concave surface of sixty-five feet diameter, the artist (Brumidi) has placed Washington as the central figure, with Liberty at his right hand and Victory at his left. The thirteen original States are represented by thirteen women, completing the ring from each side of Washington, a ribbon floating between them, on which are the words, "E Pluribus Unum." Another circle of figures around and under these contains the mythological symbolic representations of Liberty, with drawn sword and driving out, with the eagle at her left, Tyranny or Royalty; Minerva, teaching the arts and sciences; Ceres, goddess of the Harvest; Vulcan, the Olympian mechanic; Neptune, the god of Ocean with his trident; and Mercury, the spirited messenger of the gods.

Other decorations of Brumidi's in the Capitol, executed during the more than twenty years of his work there, are the decorations of the President's room; Cornwallis Suing for the Cessation of Hostilities, in the hall of the House of Representatives; decorations in the room of the House Post-office and Post Roads Committee; decorations in the Senate Committee Room of Appropriations; and those in the room of the Senate Committee on the District of Columbia.

As the Government has spent more than $150,000 on art in the interior of the Capitol, there is painting, sculpture, carving, fresco to be seen in all directions. The Battle of Lake Erie, by W. H. Powell, hangs above a staircase landing in the Senate wing of the building and represents Oliver H. Perry just before leaving the flagship Lawrence. On the wall opposite this picture, but higher, is The Recall of Columbus, by A. G. Heaton, bought by the Government in 1884.

Above another stairway landing in this wing is the Battle of Chapaultepec, by James Walker, representing a scene in that battle.

293

The President's room in the Senate wing is the most elaborately decorated of any room in the building, the work being, as before stated, by Brumidi.

The Vice-President's room is also beautifully decorated and in it hangs Charles Wilson Peale's Washington, said by some to be the best portrait of the First President in existence.

The bronze doors of the Senate wing were designed by Crawford and the plaster cast made in this country. The work was done in Chicopee, Massachusetts, by James T. Ames, in 1868.

The two well-known paintings by Thomas Moran, of the Grand Canon of the Yellowstone and a Chasm of the Colorado, are much admired by visitors.

The Electoral Commission, by Cornelia Adele Fassett, is an interesting portrait picture, painted from the commissioners in 1877-1878.; It portrays the presentation of the Florida Case, as it was known, by fifteen committeemen, five of whom were members of the Supreme Court, five of the Senate and five of the House of Representatives, to decide the validity of the electoral votes of Florida, Louisiana, Oregon and South Carolina.

Opposite this hangs a very different picture, showing the fight between the monitor and the Merrimac in Hampton Roads.

Statues and busts are scattered about, notably that of John Hancock, first signer of the Declaration of Independence and Benjamin Franklin, by Powers; busts of numerous presidents, statesmen, etc., all worthy of note. Other notable portraits in the Senate wing are Gilbert Stuart's Washington; John Adams, copied by Andrews from the original of Stuart; Sully 's Thomas Jefferson; Matthews' Patrick Henry; and H. F. Darby's Daniel Webster, Henry Clay and John C. Calhoun.

One of the best portraits in the building hangs in the Supreme Court room and is that of the first Chief -Justice of the United States, John Jay, in his old-fashioned gown. The picture is a copy by Gray of Gilbert Stuart's original.

There are two interesting mosaics of the martyr Presidents, Lincoln and Garfield, made by Salviati, of Florence, Italy, who presented the portraits to the United States Government.

The south wing, that of the House of Representatives, has its art treasures also. Here are frescoes, oil-paintings, sculpture and carving. Many portraits of members have been given prominent space, and some splendid large paintings are to be seen. Of these, "Westward the Course of Empire takes its Way," by the German artist Emanuel Leutz, is a striking scene of early Western emigrants.

On another staircase landing is the " Signing of the Proclamation of Emancipation, " by Frank Carpenter. The history of this picture is very interesting, as Mr. Carpenter spent the months of its execution in the White House, where he had free access to the President and studied him in all moods, attitudes, expressions, etc. In telling of this experience the artist said: " I intently studied every line and shade of expression in that furrowed face. In repose, it was the saddest face I ever knew. "

The completed painting was pronounced by President Lincoln "as good as can be made," and was afterward bought for $25,000, by Mrs. Elizabeth Thompson, who presented it to Congress.

A marble statue of Thomas Jefferson by Powers, is in this wing, a companion to the Franklin in the Senate wing and cost $10,000, as did also Franklin.

The famous full-length painting of Washington by Vanderlyn is on one side of the Speaker's chair in the Hall of Representatives, and that of Lafayette, presented to the United States by Lafayette during his last visit to this country, on the other side.

The old Hall of Representatives, used by the House from 1807 to 1857, excepting for the period just succeeding the burning of the Capitol by the British, is now used as a Hall of Statuary. It was set apart by act of Congress for this purpose in July, 1864. Here each State is allowed the privilege of placing two monuments, the selections to be the choice of the States.

Novelists, poets, philosophers, geographers, geologists, zoologists, botanists, astronomers, mathematicians, scientists of every description, tacticians, financiers, sociologists, metaphysicians, religionists, journalists and historians, whom it would be almost impossible to name, have written in Washington; and among the scientists and historians especially are to be numbered many of the country's greatest names.

One of the earliest books printed in Washington was Samuel Blodget 's " Thoughts on the Increasing Wealth and National Economy of the United States." This is believed to be the first book on economics written in America.

Histories of Washington have been written from time to time since a few years after its beginning. The earliest of these known was written by Tobias Lear, who wrote in 1793, "Observations on the River Potomack, the County Adjacent and the City of Washington. "

In 1816, David B. Warden wrote a "Description of the District of Columbia." This comprehensive little volume was written while he was consulate in Paris, France, and published in that city. Europeans, curious about the new Federal City, read the book with interest, and America gave it a warm welcome. The writer gave a history of the foundation of the city, its early settlement and later growth.

In 1822, a directory of Washington was published by Judah Delano, which contained an alphabetical list of names of Washington residents, the members of Congress, with their residences.

Jonathan Elliot, in 1830, published a little history of "The Ten Mile Square," and it, like its predecessor by Warden, has been a mine for local historians ever since.

Besides "The Ten Mile Square," Jonathan Elliot served his own and future time well by compiling numerous volumes on political and economic science.

"A Picture of Washington," by George Watterston was published in 1841 and the following year the same author published "A Guide to Washington." Mr. Watterston was Librarian of Congress from 1815 to 1829.

One of the most thorough and entertaining of the annalists of events connected with the origin and development of the National Capitol, is Mr. Wilhelmus B. Bryan, whose narratives cover almost every phase of the subject.

Mr. Hugh T. Taggart, has also contributed with skill and profusion to preserve the facts and traditions which are of leading interest and value on the same topic.

Francis Scott Key, author, of "The Star Spangled Banner," was a resident of the District of Columbia for many years and was recognized as a lawyer of great ability and force.

Peter Force, already mentioned as the forceful mayor and friend of Washington, prepared or preserved nine folios of the American Archives and many other historical records, which would otherwise have been lost or at least much scattered.

295

Anne Royal, while figuring chiefly as a journalist, wrote ten volumes of her travels in the United States.

In 1843 Anthony Reintzel compiled and published "The Washington Directory and Governmental Register," a valuable register and reference help of its day.

Another "Picture of Washington," appeared in 1845, written by William Q. Force, containing short sketches of interesting features in and about Washington, and having attached at the back, a Washington guide.

Another Washington directory was published in 1846 by John T. Towers, containing more than any previous publication of the sort, and in 1850 Edward Waite published "The Washington Directory and Congressional and Executive Register. "

Joseph B. Varnum published in 1848, "The Seat of Government of the United States," another valuable little book to historians and readers.

Robert Walsh, whom George A. Townsend said was perhaps "the founder of review literature in America," grew up in Georgetown and Washington.

Joel Barlow, author of "The Columbiad," an epic which won fame for its author, lived for several years in the District, and built the famous home known as Kalorama.

Several who had studied the Indians in their native ways of living, and recorded their savage customs, lived here, notably among them, Schoolcraft, Stanley and Catlin.

In 1857 Colonel John S. Williams published a "History of the Invasion and Capture of Washington," his object being to vindicate the Americans for their defeat at Bladensburg in 1814.

John Burroughs, the great nature lover and nature writer lived here and wrote here for years. Many of his later writings seem imbued with the atmosphere of Nature as manifested in the District of Columbia, and in the adjacent Virginia and Maryland hills. Another of Nature 's loving sons, and whom we think of so often in connection with Burroughs, was Joaquin Miller, who also wrote several of his books here.

It was here too that Harriet Beecher Stowe's famous novel, "Uncle Tom's Cabin," first appeared, in The National Intelligencer.

Walt Whitman was once a Government clerk in the office of the Attorney-general and produced several of his works during that time.

George Bancroft, the historian, lived and wrote here many years. In 1845 he was Secretary of the Navy under President Polk. To him is due credit for the establishment of the Naval Academy at Annapolis. He died in Washington in 1891, at the advanced age of ninety years.

Ainsworth R. Spofford, was Librarian of Congress for many years. His pen was prolific, despite the arduous duties of his position. For many years Mr. Spofford edited "The American Almanac and Treasury of Facts," and among his writings are "The Higher Law Tried by Reason and Authority;" "The Founding of Washington, with Considerations on the Origin of Cities and Location of National Capitals."

Richard P. Jackson published "The Chronicles of Georgetown, District of Columbia."

George W. Sampson wrote, among other things, "Elements of Art Criticism," a voluminous and comprehensive history of art.

Charles Lanman wrote many books of travel and biography.

General Albert Pike, who lived here several years, was a poet of ability, a journalist of wide experience, and wrote several books on Freemasonry and Law.

Dr. Joseph M. Toner wrote a number of histories and scientific books, besides several volumes of lectures.

Helen C. Weeks wrote many stories for children, winning a name surpassed by few other juvenile writers.

Henry Barnard was an educational writer of note.

George Alfred Townsend, an extensive traveler, contributed to many newspapers and magazines, wrote stories, poems and a history of the Capital called "Washington, Outside and Inside."

Benjamin J. Lovejoy wrote here "The Life of Francis Bacon."

Frederick Douglas, the celebrated negro orator who lived in Washington several years, wrote "My Bondage and My Freedom."

Ben Perley Poore, an early journalist in Washington, wrote 'The Rise and Fall of Louis Philippe," and "Reminiscences of Sixty Years."

Charles D. Drake and Charles Nordhoff wrote socialistic and historical books.

George E. Harris, a Mississippian who lived in Washington many years, has written histories of numerous laws, law books and many other things.

William T. Harris wrote educational and philosophic books and "The Spiritual Sense of Dante's 'Divina Commedia.' " Edward A. Fay wrote a concordance to the works of Dante.

Thomas Nelson Page, the well-known novelist and writer of Southern life, has spent a large part of his life in Washington and has written many of his books here.

Ella Lorraine Dorsey has numerous entertaining volumes and sketches to her credit.

George L. Raymond wrote many books on the fine arts and Charles W. Stoddard wrote here many of the fascinating narratives of his extensive travels.

Elizabeth B. Johnston wrote "Original Portraits of Washington," "Washington Day by Day," besides many stories and sketches.

William L. Shoemaker wrote a book on "The Indian Weed," poems and stories.

Mrs. E. D. E. N. Southworth, a novelist widely read in her day, was a native of Washington and spent most of her life, which was a long one, in the District. It is said that her story "Retribution," published in 1843, was the first serial story written in America. For many years she wrote for the Saturday Evening Post, her stories running its subscription up from twelve hundred to thirty thousand. She wrote, it is said, an average of a novel a year for every year of her life.

Mary Clemmer, poet and journalist, a well-beloved writer of her day, wrote " Ten Years in Washington. "

Henry B. F. Macfarland, the noted journalist and orator, has contributed much to general literature.

Henry Litchfield West, is regarded as the most accomplished political analyst of his time, as well as a writer of excellence generally.

Harriet T. Upton wrote "Our Early Presidents" and other books.

Isabella Alden, known as "Pansy," wrote many of her well-known and broadly read books in Washington.

Alexander Graham Bell has been a writer as well as inventor. Some of his works are: "Upon the Production of Sound by Radiant Energy," and several treatises upon the care and training of deaf mutes.

Edward M. Gallaudet, who came to Washington in 1857 to take charge of the Columbian Institute for the Deaf, Dumb and Blind, wrote "The Combined System of Educating the Deaf;" "International Ethics;" and "Manual of International Law."

Alice C. Fletcher wrote "Studies of Indian Music," and other Indian books.

Jeremiah Curtin did much of his translating and other writing in Washington.

W. W. Rockhill wrote of his extensive travels in the East, and "Life of Buddha."

"Recollections of Men and Things in Washington," by Louis A. Gobright is an interesting book by an observant man who was one of the journalists closely associated with President Lincoln. Noah Brooks, another journalist who was not only associated with President Lincoln, but was his friend, wrote, many years after the President's decease, "Washington in Lincoln's Time," gathered from his own observations while resident here.

Notably among the many other lives written of Lincoln, is one by Nicolay and Hay, both John G. Nicolay and John Hay having been residents of Washington. These men were engaged fifteen years in writing this book, their researches being very extensive. Both of these writers did much other excellent literary work.

Charles Lanman, who was private secretary to Daniel Webster, wrote a life of the great New Hampshire statesman. He also wrote of life in Japan, illustrated with his own sketches and prepared the first "Dictionary of Congress."

Gardner Green Hubbard wrote "American Railroads," "Education of Deaf Mutes" and other things.

William Torrey Harris wrote books on education and philosophy.

Emily Edson Briggs, known as "Olivia," won quite a reputation as a journalist and author.

Simon Wolf, the eminent Jewish orator and author, whose literary productions cover almost every phase of human interest resides here.

Judson C. Welliver, has a national reputation as an essayist and editor.

Molly Elliott Seawell wrote several of her novels here, as did Anna Hanson Dorsey. The latter, a native and resident of the District of Columbia, wrote numerous novels. One of them entitled "May Brooke" was quite successful and was republished in Scotland. It was the first Catholic book published in that country since the Reformation.

Elizabeth R. Scidmore wrote of Alaska, the Sitka Archipelago, the Berkeleys, et cetera.

Frances Hodgson Burnett, a native of Manchester, England, came to Washington in 1875, and after making the American city her home, her books became a mixture of American and English life, which have been read with delight in both countries. "Little Lord Fauntleroy" is known to all the reading world and never ceases to charm its readers.

Some of the other numerous worthy historical writers, who lived in Washington various lengths of time, are, Edward McPherson; Charles C. Nott; P. H. Sheridan, who wrote "Personal Memoirs;" William T. Sherman, also author of his own memoirs; Julia Seaton, author of " William W. Seaton; " Frank G. Carpenter; William E. Curtis; Mary S. Lockwoot; Samuel C. Busey, whose "Pictures of the City of Washington in the Past," is a widely consulted volume; Olive Kisley-Seward Reverend J. L. M. Curry; Clara Barton; Mrs. John A. Logan Sir Augustus G. Foster, Minister of Great Britain in 1811 G. T. Poussin, Minister of France in 1848, who wrote several volumes on America; Senor D. F. Sarmiento; Senor Filipe Molina; Baron Kurd von Schlozer, Ambassador from Germany in 1876-1877; Manuel Larrainzar; Matias Romero, Minister from Mexico to the United States for twenty years; Sir Henry Lytton Bulwer, Minister from Great Britain, 1850-1851; and several other ministers and ambassadors.

Mr. Spofford tells us that thirteen Presidents of the United States have been writers of books, namely: " Jefferson, Madison, Monroe, both the Adamses, Van Buren, Buchanan, Lincoln, Grant, Garfield, Harrison, McKinley and Roosevelt." Since the last named, President Wilson, a well-known writer of history, has been added to the list.

Some strong scientific writers not already mentioned are: Clarence E. Button; Henry Gannett; Henry C. Bolton; Simon Newcomb, the well-known astronomer; Robert Fletcher; Florence A. Merriman, the bird-lover; Theodore N. Gill and George Brown Goode, two naturalists of note; Garrick Mallery; Thomas C. Mendenhall; Lester F. Ward; Charles V. Riley; A. W. Greely; Samuel P. Langley; Major J. W. Powell, a voluminous scientific writer, especially on geology; Professor W. G. McGee; Alexander D. Anderson; and many others, some of whom would be quickly mentioned if such a sea of names did not make it so difficult to choose.

As early as 1797 the Washington Library was formed, with Nicholas King, Librarian. In Georgetown a library was established in 1793 or 1794, known as the Columbian Library. In June, 1801, a circulating library was established by Richard Dinmore on Pennsylvania Avenue, and in August following Hugh Somerville opened a second circulating library in his grocery store near the market.

In 1811 another Washington Library was established and this was the chief library of Washington for a great many years.

A library for Congress was early established and had grown to considerable size when the British destroyed it. After that war was ended renewed determination for a library was aroused and we read of how Thomas Jefferson's long-collected library was purchased by the Government.

As art and literature went hand in hand, so music and the drama marched side by side in municipal culture.

Washington had so many serious business problems and so much opposition to combat, that it was some time before theatres could be made to compensate their owners.

Mr. A. I. Mudd, in an interesting paper prepared for the Columbia Historical Society, gives a full and interesting resume of the history of the Washington stage, which dates from the removal of the seat of the National Government to this city. When the Government was moved from Philadelphia there were then existing in the Quaker City two theatres. One of these was known as the "New Theatre," and its season closed while the Government possessions were being removed. The managers, Messrs. Wignell and Reinagle, moved their players to the new Government center and gave performances in part of the " Lottery Hotel, " which had been fitted up for a play-house and was named the "United States Theatre." The new enterprise was unfortunate in its start, as most of the company's scenery was destroyed by a storm at the time of its removal. This misfortune did not prevent the players from opening for a season in June, 1800, and they continued for several months to play to appreciative audiences.

In 1803 some leading citizens agitated the building of a theatre, and subscriptions for the enterprise were pledged, a site selected at the northwest corner of C and Eleventh Streets, northwest, and a building begun.

On November 16, 1804, the new play-house, which was named the "Washington Theatre," was opened with a "Grand Medley Entertainment by the celebrated Mr. Maginnis from London who had performed in most of the Capital Cities of Europe and America."

On September 9, 1805, the theatre was re-opened with the Philadelphia Company, who played "Wives as They Were and Maids as They Are." Prices to these performances were one dollar for the boxes and seventy cents for seats in the "pit," which was then on the first floor.

There was a short season in 1806, after which the Washington Theatre remained dark for nearly two years. In September, 1808, it was opened by the Philadelphia and Baltimore Company with "The Rivals," in which Mr. Joseph Jefferson took the part of Bob Acres. This was the grandfather of the great Joseph Jefferson of Rip Van Winkle fame.

For several years following, the Philadelphia and Baltimore Company, with occasional changes of members, filled a summer engagement in the Capital city, giving such plays as "The Poor Gentleman," "She Stoops to Conquer, "numerous farces; several of Shakespeare's plays, and several patriotic dramas.

The Thespian Society won local distinction for its members, and in the autumn of 1815 this Society gave several performances for the benefit of the poor, which were largely attended by people of all classes, one night being honored by General Andrew Jackson's presence.

Summer engagements of the Philadelphia and Baltimore Company continued until 1818, when the Theatre's management changed and it was opened for the winter and spring season. On February 26, 1818, Charles Incledon, a famous singer of London, was engaged for one night.

Another London favorite was Mrs. Bartley, who came to Washington March 8, 1819, and played for four nights. On the night of the last performance she recited "A Monologue," written especially for her by the Irish poet "Tom" Moore.

April 19, 1820, the Washington Theatre was destroyed by fire. In 1821 the theatre site was purchased by Lewis Carusi, who built on the ground a new theatre which was opened in 1822, as the "Washington City Assembly Rooms."

Another theatre was also erected in 1821 on Louisiana Avenue. This little theatre, called "The Washington Theatre," accommodated seven hundred people and was conducted in first class manner. It is noted that smoking was prohibited and liquor "excluded from the box lobbies." The colored people were also provided for in the new Washington Theatre by having boxes set apart for them.

On the night of August 1, 1822, Washington had for the first time the elder Booth, who had been playing to crowded houses in London.

In the spring of 1824 Washington had opera, when " Clari; or the Maid of Milan," was given. This opera was well received, especially as it had been written by a former actor of the Washington Theatre, John Howard Payne. It is recorded that the singing of "Home, Sweet Home," by Mrs. Waring was tumultuously received.

In the fall of 1826 Hackett and Edwin Forrest made their first appearance in Washington, one in September, in " The Duke of Gloster," and the other in October in "Pizarro."

Mdlle. Celeste, a great favorite of her day, first appeared in Washington March 29, 1828, as Julietta in "The Dumb Girl of Genoa. " She also gave some of her wonderful dances, which had helped to make her famous. Others who appeared that season were Clara Fisher, Cooper, Pearman, Hamblin and Mr. and Mrs. Sloman.

In 1832 Mrs. Drake starred with Edwin Forrest and they appeared in Washington in several plays.

The autumn season of this year commenced in October. Among the actors who came were T. D. Rice, a minstrel whose success with negro songs made him popular, two of his best being "Clare de Kitchen" and "Jim Crow;" the latter with its dancing making a great impression on the then small Joseph Jefferson. The young Jefferson's imitation of Mr. Rice was so pronounced and funny that the comedian conceived the idea of having the little boy of four years sing with him. He took him on the stage in a bag, and during the song emptied the bag, and the two sang and danced alternate stanzas of the song, which so delighted the audience that twenty-four dollars in coins were thrown onto the stage to the little fellow.

In January of 1833, the famous Fanny Kemble and her father made their first appearance before a Washington audience, playing " The Stranger. " The following month the Ravel family came for the first time and became great favorites.

In 1835 a new theatre called "The National Theatre," was built on Pennsylvania Avenue, and was opened December 7, of that year. The play presented was "The Man of the World," with Maywood as Sir Pertinax Macsycophant.

After the transformation of the old Washington Theatre, it was opened December 25, 1835, renamed "The American Theatre."

George Washington Parke Custis, wrote a national drama, placed in Virginia, called "Pocahontas; or the First Settlers of Virginia." This drama was produced in Washington on the night of February 6, 1836 and was repeated several nights with great success.

General Alexander Macomb, Commander of the United States Army, wrote a play, "Pontiac; or The Siege of Detroit," which was presented at the National Theatre March 4, 1836, to an interested audience. This play was staged with great splendor, the United States marines being used as soldiers who fought the Indians.

Celeste, the popular actress who had been to the old Washington Theatre had become the rage with theatre-goers, and in one season she received $50,000 in the United States. She came to the National Theatre in Washington March 9, 1836 and presented "The French Spy; or The Wild Arab of the Desert." She also danced La Bayadere, the operatic ballet from "The Maid of Cashmere." So much in demand was this stage-queen that she was twice re-engaged, and left Washington the most applauded performer who had come to the city up to that time.

Ellen Tree, who made her debut in Washington in 1838 as Rosalind in "As You Like It," made a great impression on Washington audiences in that and other characters.

The next decade brought many old and new favorites, and theatres underwent changes. On January 4, 1840, the American favorite, Virginia Monier, gave "The Merchant of Venice," herself taking the part of Portia. Charles Keen came January

6, after which he and Miss Monier played together in "Hamlet," "Merchant of Venice," "Richard the Third," and "The Iron Chest."

Mrs. Fitzwilliam, who had been starring in the London theatres, came to Washington, making her debut here January 13, as Miss Peggy, in "The Country Girl." Her Irish songs were especially well received, and she was called one of the most brilliant stars of her day.

The American Theatre opened in March, 1840, for a few nights only, but re-opened later under a new management, Messrs. Jackson and Hardy having leased it, themselves forming part of the company of players. "The Iron Chest" and other plays were given.

At the National Theatre, which opened May 25, 1840, appeared Fanny Elssler and Sylvain from the Royal Academy of Music of Paris in July, when Miss Elssler made an impression on her audiences almost equal to that of Celeste.

During part of the year 1844, the National Theatre was used for a circus and performances came rather spasmodically for a while.

March 5, 1845, while a performance was in progress, the National Theatre took fire and in a short while the entire building was in flames. The audience and actors became panic-stricken, but all the people got out safely.

On November 30, 1846, a new theatre was opened on the northeast corner of Pennsylvania Avenue and Four-and-a-Half Street, called the Odeon. The company was a good one and the expense of keeping them and other added expenses caused the manager to double the prices of admission.

The Odeon was small, accommodating only about four hundred people, so in December, 1847, another theatre was fitted up in a building on Pennsylvania Avenue, not far from the Odeon. The new amusement-house was called "The Adelphi," and could accommodate one thousand people. A stock company was formed, of which the managers, Messrs. Brown and Nichols, were members. This theatre became popular and several good plays were rendered on its boards during its first season.

To the Adelphi came in 1849, Julia Dean, Charley Burke, Bellamy, Kate Horn, Mrs. Drake, and the forty-eight members of the Danseuse Viennoises.

Charlotte Cushman made her first appearance in Washington in 1849, as Meg Merriles in "Guy Mannering," and her finished acting brought much enthusiasm. She gave several other plays and was pronounced one of the best players who had ever come to Washington or had been on the stage.

On the night of November 8, 1850, another Booth, then a lad of sixteen, came to the Capital City with his father, when the to-be famous Edwin took the part of Hemeya in 'The Apostate. "

In September, 1850, Jenny Lind, whose singing and acting had created a sensation in Europe, landed in America. The "Swedish Nightingale" became the rage in America as she had been in Europe, and cities that secured engagements from her had difficulty in accommodating the thousands of people who wished to hear the new wonder sing. Washington had no hall large enough to even half-way provide for the crowds, so some enterprising managers erected one on the site of the old National Theatre. This quickly constructed auditorium was named National Hall and could seat three and a half thousand persons.

Miss Lind was engaged for two nights, December sixteenth and eighteenth, and although seats sold for seven, five and four dollars, the hall was filled at both performances. It proved well that a strong building had been erected for the "Nightingale's" performances, for when she appeared before the audience the walls shook from the applause. When she sang the audience was spell-bound and the pieces especially mentioned for their marvelous rendition are the Bird Song, the Echo Song and the flute imitation.

Carusi's Saloon was a popular place of vaudeville entertainment during this season.

In 1852 we find a new amusement house on Pennsylvania Avenue, between Ninth and Tenth Streets, called the Iron Hall Assembly Rooms. Here were studios of teachers of the different arts and the hall was used for occasional concerts and various exhibits for instruction and entertainment. In 1853 this hall was fitted up for a first-class theatre and renamed, Risley's Varietie.

In the year 1856 this theatre again changed hands and became the "People's Theatre, (Late Varieties) " and it was that year the chief theatre, giving numerous popular plays and bringing some good actors. In May it became the Varietie again and under that name staid open for a short time.

November 19, 1855, it again opened with Kunkle and Company, proprietors and John T. Ford, manager. The theatre had been renovated throughout with "Costumes, Scenery and properties unexcelled for tasteful elegance and effect," and with " new and comfortable seats. "

In November, 1853, Ole Bull came to Carusi's Saloon assisted by Adelina Patti, then young in her brilliant career.

1856 and 1857 shows Carusi's still in popular favor, when many musical treats were there given to Washington audiences, as well as high-class readings: but during 1859 the hall's announcements cease.

Circuses appear yearly too, some having other entertainment features than animals. Franconi's Hippodrome gave athletic performances which lasted a week, during which time were represented "The Tournament of the Field of the Cloth of Gold," "classic games of Greece and Rome, and National sports of all countries and all ages. "

In the Smithsonian Lecture Room, which was continually used for scientific lectures and demonstrations, there was an occasional popular entertainment. In May, 1855, was a Grand Vocal and Instrumental Concert by the Musical Convention, under patronage of the Union Choir Association. In May of the following year this hall had a Children's concert, which was well patronized.

Among other halls of the latter part of the decade the Philharmonic and Willard 's halls seemed to divide honors, in both of which were given several high-class concerts, readings, lectures and other entertainments.

On January 5, 1858 the Washington Theatre was opened, under the management of W. Stuart, the lessee. Its first artist was Teresa Rolla, who, with good support, had a run of a number of nights.

The season of 1859 for the Washington Theatre opened September 1, under the management of S. W. Glenn, with "select and strong dramatic company."

The Washington Theatre had crowded houses during the winter of 1859-1860. It had several seasons of Grand Opera and among other recognized singers of the day was Adelina Patti, who was growing in popularity for her wonderful voice, and Washington audiences were among the most appreciative of her genius. Her sister

Carlotta was considered one of the greatest singers of that time. Among the dramatists who came were Maggie Mitchell and Joseph Jefferson.

1861 shows that the Washington had Hackett; The French Zouaves, real French soldiers who had formed a dramatic corps during the Crimean War and were later joined by some "Lady Zouaves; " Sothern; Charlotte Cushman and other celebrities.

In October The Theatre opens a season under the management of Mr. Bland and in December it is again The Washington Theatre with "crowded houses."

September opened with Ada Isaacs Menken, in her first appearance in Washington, where she became popular.

In February of 1863, Maggie Mitchell received a warm welcome from Washingtonians, who called her " Our Maggie. "

In April there was Grand Opera for over a week, followed by John Wilkes Booth in Shakespeare and other tragedies. The Intelligencer described him as "the distinguished young American tragedian."

One of the actors especially attracting attention was Laura Keene, in February, 1864, when she had a very successful engagement. When she left the Intelligencer asserted: "We are almost vexed with her for this elopement," and of her acting, that it "comes so near Nature as almost to rob Art."

In 1862 three theatres and several halls were having almost nightly performances during the autumn and winter but all were closed during the summer following, 1863, except the Washington Theatre, and Canterbury Hall on the south side of Louisiana Avenue, between Four-and-a-Half and Sixth Streets, a variety resort.

In 1862 the National Theatre was rebuilt and opened April 21, Easter Monday, as Grover's Theatre. The following year there was more rebuilding and renovation of Grover's Theatre and it opened October 6, with a company of "eminent dramatic artists. "

In February of 1864 Edwin Booth had a season of Shakespeare and other drama, during which time he received even more than usual praise as a dramatic artist.

In 1861 New Opera House was opened on Tenth Street, near E, in December with Christy's Minstrels for a short season and the following year we find the theatre changed to Christy's Opera House.

On March 19, 1862, under the management of John T. Ford, a new play-house was opened on Tenth Street, between E and F Streets, northwest, called Ford's Theatre. It was well equipped and artistically decorated, offering comfort to patrons. The opening play was " The French Spy, " by Lucille Western and a superior dramatic company.

During the following September, Maggie Mitchell gave a number of attractive plays there, in all of which she seemed to excel.

In March an English Opera Company with Caroline Richings, Peter Richings, Dunn and a full chorus, besides expert and artistic dancers, performed at this theatre.

Ford's began 1865 with Edwin Forrest, well supported, in Damon and Pythias; " Richelieu; " and Shakespeare. In January, J. McCullough, then young in his fame, played there with Forrest and Madame Ponisi.

During the month of February J. S. Clarke, Mrs. Wilkins, Mrs. Bowers and Alice Gray, were warmly welcomed.

In March, there was a Grand Concert with an orchestra of "forty members of first-class talent." Edwin Forrest followed and then another Grand Concert; and later a week of Grand Italian Opera.

April 3, Laura Keene came, supported by John Dyott, J. C. McCollum, Harry Hawk and the stock company of the theatre. They gave "The Workmen of Washington," which comprised three acts and twelve tableaux. This ran until April 10, when "She Stoops to Conquer," was given and it was followed by "The School for Scandal," when "The Workmen of Washington " was repeated by request, after which followed "Peg Woffington." "Our American Cousin" was staged April 14, when President Lincoln was assassinated there, about 10:20 p. m. by John Wilkes Booth, which ended the play and practically closed that theatre as a place of amusement forever.

Orover's Theatre opened the year 1865 with Avonia Jones in " Leah. " She followed this night with " Medea; " " Camille; " " East Lynne "; " Judith "; and several Shakespearean plays with John Wilkes Booth as co-star. Following this season of drama, the Marinetti Opera Troupe gave their first performances in America, at Grover's. With them was a full Italian chorus and grand orchestra. They were followed later in the month by Lucille Western, whose playing and dancing, especially her jigging, won great applause.

In February Barney Williams was a popular attraction and he was followed the last of the month by Chanfrau. Other players came after him up to the night of President Lincoln 's assassination, after which people had no wish for amusement. In April the management of this theatre announced that "in view of the fearful calamity which has befallen our country in the disastrous death of our beloved President," it was considered "essential that the places of amusement of the city should remained closed until the general grief which our community is suffering has fully subsided," and the theatre was closed indefinitely. All attaches of the theatre, belonging as they did, to the host of mourners, immediately consented to annul their engagements.

In September, 1866, Grover's becomes the National Theatre, with Spalding and Rapley, proprietors. The newly fitted up theatre opened with "The Ice Witch," which stayed until October. Among the attractions following were the comedy " Rosedale;" "Temptation;" "Lady of Lyons;" tragedies, comedies and operas.

Joseph Jefferson had a successful season in December, closing with " Rip Van Winkle, " in which play he had made a reputation even at that early date. The National Intelligencer, December 21, gave half a column of editorial praise of this rendition of Mr. Jefferson's.

The regular season was opened in October, "with a great cast and Marine Band in British Uniform. " They gave " Ours" which ran for several nights and was followed by "Black Crook."

1869 began with "Black Crook," which was followed by another spectacular performance, "Undine," with the same ballet troupe.

A new theatre, known as Wall's Opera House, at the intersection of Louisiana Avenue and C Street, northwest, was inaugurated and managed by John T. Ford, September 22, 1866. Its initial performance was Italian Opera for two nights. October 16 the Washington Dramatic Club gave a benefit in this house for the benefit of the poor.

The amusement halls during the sixties did their part toward entertaining Washington people. Conspicuous among these was Metzerott Hall, on the north side of Pennsylvania Avenue, between Ninth and Tenth Streets, where there were many concerts of high order, lectures, oratorios, entertainments of home talent and readings from famous authors. Among the readers was Mark Twain, whose humor drew great crowds.

In 1868 Carroll Hall, at southeast corner of Tenth and G Streets, northwest, held its own with Metzerott, where there were several celebrities of the day besides dramatic readings, concerts, et cetera. Among the readers here was Charles Dickens in January. Th famous "Boz" gave four nights of entertainment during which time he read or recited selections from The Christmas Carol, Pickwick, David Copperfield and Nicholas Nickleby.

Lincoln Hall in 1868 had Carlotta Patti, the renowned singer, in Grand Concert, and the following month, December, Mrs. Scott-Siddons was engaged for a "Night with Shakespeare and Mendelssohn."

In 1866, the Philharmonic Society of Washington was formed, with about fifty members. "St. Paul" was their first oratorio, which was given March 7. On the night of December 25 of that year, this society gave "The Messiah," conducted by Dr. J. P. Caulfield. The sopranos were Mrs. Butts and Miss Paulie C. Ewer; contralto, Mrs. J. P. Caulfield; tenor, Mr. Arthur Mathison; baritone, Mr. L. V. Gannon.

In April the Mendelssohn Quintette Club gave two concerts, which were both classic and well attended.

In 1869 the Choral Society was organized, composed of male singers of the District of Columbia. In a year the membership numbered one hundred eighty active members, with Harry C. Sherman, musical director.

Herr Franz Abt received his first American welcome in Washington, which occurred on the night of May 8, 1872, when he had a grand testimonial concert. This was under the auspices of the Choral Society and two German societies of Washington at Lincoln Hall.

The National continues successful until January 28, 1873, when the theatre was totally destroyed by fire.

After this misfortune to the National the only places of amusement were the Washington Theatre and various halls, which did their duty until February 22, when Wall's Theatre re-opened and became popular.

On December 1, the National, which had been rebuilt, opened under the management of J. G. Saville. The new theatre's initial attraction was Maggie Mitchell and her excellent company.

In December, 1873, Ford's Theatre, or Walls's Opera House, as it was sometimes called, was again opened, and regained its old popularity. Among its stars that season were Joseph Jefferson and Clara Morris, and these two continued to appear there through the seasons following. All the remaining years of the decade it was among the most popular theatres of the city.

In October, 1877, the Redpath Lyceum Course opened in Lincoln Hall. This course opened with a Grand Concert by the Boston Philharmonic Club and during the season were interspersed several other excellent concerts. The lectures included one on "The Stage," by Daniel Dougherty; "Superfluous Women," by Mary A. Livermore; "Art" by W. W. Story; and "bubbling humor" from Josh Billings.

In 1878 "The Talking Phonograph" was exhibited and great crowds of Washingtonians marveled at this new invention. The theatres and halls gave their usual line of attractions.

During 1879 "Pinafore" seems to have been immensely popular and was presented at different times, winter and summer, in nearly every theatre and hall in the city.

The decade of 1880-1890, showed not only the usual appreciation of good drama and music, but a continued improvement in taste. The amateur entertainments are notably good; and the greatest stars of the world visit Washington during that time.

Among the many lecturers were John Fiske; Robert G. Ingersoll; Mary A. Livermore, and Stoddard, with lectures on history and travel.

On February 27, 1885, the National Theatre was again totally destroyed by fire, after which the popular places of amusement were Ford's, Albaugh's Theatre, the Grand Opera House and Herzog's Museum, afterward changed to Herzog's Ninth Street Opera House.

During the summer the National was rebuilt and opened for its fall season October 5, 1885, with comedy.

Band concerts grow in favor and summer out-of-door concerts for the public were encouraged. One of the noted band leaders, Walter Damrosch, widely recognized for his ability as a musical leader, distinguished himself in another way in May, 1890, by marrying Miss Margaret Blaine, daughter of James G. Blaine, the great statesman.

In 1892 a law was passed that all theatres should have exits from the buildings, leading directly into the streets.

Several new theatres came into existence: Kernan's Lyceum Theatre, Columbia Theatre, Lafayette Square Opera House, the Grand Opera House and The Academy.

In 1898 Josef Hofmann caused much enthusiasm among Washington music-lovers, as well as everywhere he appeared, with his wonderful playing. This trip brought him even more widespread fame than had his tour when a child, at which time listeners had marveled at the boy's execution.

Hall Caine's play, "The Christian," made a tremendous "hit" in September and October, 1898, at the National, with Viola Allen. The Star declared that "Nothing approaching the interest that this play has evoked is remembered in this city by the oldest playgoers."

Washington has become a center of culture, where good drama and classic music are appreciated for their worth and each year dramatists and musicians are received according to their proficiency in their art.

Dramatic and musical societies have done much to elevate public taste and encourage local talent, while some of the most talented and finished teachers of drama and especially of music, afford advantages to aspiring professionals and amateurs.

The summer band concerts have been a powerful force in improving musical taste and familiarizing the public with good and even classic music, especially the finished concerts given by the Marine Band, which attained a world wide fame through its relation to its old leader John Philip Sousa, the eminent composer of band marches and other musical works.

CHAPTER XIV

Monuments

On December 21, 1799, just one week following the death of General Washington, Congress, on motion of Mr. Marshall of Virginia, unanimously passed the following resolution:

"That a marble monument be erected by the United States at the Capitol in the City of Washington, and that the family of General Washington be requested to permit his body to be deposited under it: and that the monument be so designed as to commemorate the great events of his military and political life."

This resolution was transmitted by President Adams to Mrs. Washington who promptly replied, expressing her appreciation of the action of Congress and indicating her willingness to comply with the suggestion made. The subject was, however, postponed by the Senate until the next session and was thereafter postponed from year to year for many years without other action than the passing of resolutions by Congress upon the propriety of carrying out the original intention.

Early in the century, popular sentiment, chafing at the delay of Congress, took shape in a movement to raise by public subscription the money necessary to erect a suitable monument in honor of Washington, the plan being to obtain a subscription of one dollar from each family throughout the United States. On October 31, 1833, a meeting was held at which the Washington National Monument Society was organized with Chief Justice Marshall as President; Judge William Cranch, Joseph Gales, Jr., and W. W. Seaton as Vice Presidents; Samuel Harrison Smith, Treasurer; George Watterston, Secretary; and General T. J. Jesup, Colonel James Kearney, R. C. Weightman, Colonel N. Towson, William Brent, Peter Force, Colonel A. Henderson, Thomas Carbery, Thomas Munroe, M. St. Clair Clarke, W. A. Bradley, and J. McClelland as Managers. The President and Vice President and members of the Cabinet were made ex-officio members of the Board of Managers. The collection of funds was arranged for by dividing the United States into four Districts, to which collectors were assigned, their compensation to be ten per cent of the amount collected. Upon the death of Chief Justice Marshall, Ex-President James Madison was appointed President of the Society July 25, 1835.

In 1836, $28,000 had been collected. In that year the Society advertised for designs, no restriction being placed upon the character of the design except that it should "harmoniously blend durability, simplicity, and grandeur." The estimated cost was put at $1,000,000.

Designs for the proposed monument were submitted by Robert Mills of Washington, S. M. Stone and Bennet and Piatt of New Haven, Thomas McClellend of New York, E. Barasius of Baltimore, George Hadfield, William Elliott and others. On November 30, 1844, W. W. Seaton, Peter Force, and George Watterston were appointed a committee to select the design for the monument and confer with the proper authorities with a view to the selection of a site.

Many designs were submitted. That which was selected was by Robert Mills, a prominent architect of the time. The essential features of this design as published at the time were a grand circular colonnaded building, 250 feet in diameter and 100 feet high, from which was to spring an obelisk shaft 70 feet at the base and 500 feet high, making a total elevation of 600 feet. The rotunda forming the grand base of the

Monument was to be surrounded by 30 massive doric columns, 12 feet in diameter and 45 feet high, elevated upon a base 20 feet high, and 300 feet square. The colonnade was to be surmounted by an entablature 20 feet high which in turn was to be crowned by a balustrade 12 feet high.

The entrance to the colonnaded rotunda was to be a portico of four columns in width and three in depth. Over the entrance was to be a triumphal chariot with a statue of Washington. Statues of the signers of the Declaration of Independence were to ornament the interior of the rotunda. The obelisk was terminated by a much flatter cap than as finally completed. In adopting this design the Society did not commit itself to the construction of the pantheonic base and proposed at first to erect the shaft and leave the question as to the remainder of the design for future consideration.

In 1845 the amount of money collected was $55,359.66. The Board of Managers at this time decided to resume their efforts to raise money by collection and to remove the limit of $1 from each contributor. They appointed Honorable Elisha Whittlesey of Ohio, a general agent for this purpose.

On January 31, 1848, Congress passed a resolution authorizing the Society to erect the Monument upon such portion of the public grounds in the City of Washington as should be selected by the President of the United States and the Board of Managers of the Society. The site selected was public reservation No. 3 on the plan of the city, containing upward of 30 acres, for which President Polk executed a deed to the Society on February 22, 1849.

In his original plan of the city, Major L 'Enfant had designated the point of intersection of an east and west line drawn through the center of the Capitol, with a north and south line drawn through the center of the White House, as the site for an equestrian statue of Washington, the erection of which had been recommended by a resolution of Congress in 1783. The Managers of the Monument Association found it impossible to obtain an adequate foundation at this precise point and were compelled to move the location of the monument a short distance east of it upon the center line of the Capitol.

The work of excavating for the foundation was immediately begun and the foundations, were completed by the first of June, 1848.

The foundation as originally constructed was of blue gneiss rock in large blocks. It was 80 feet square at the base, pyramidal in shape with steps and extended 7 feet 8 inches below and 15 feet 8 inches above ground.

The corner stone was laid on the afternoon of June 7. This stone, which had been donated by Mr. Symington from his marble quarries near Baltimore, transported by the Baltimore and Ohio Railroad Company free of charge, was a block of white marble six feet eight inches square, nearly three feet thick, and weighing 24,500 pounds. Joseph H. Bradley was in charge of the ceremonies. Honorable Robert C. Winthrop, of Massachusetts, delivered the oration; Reverend Mr. McJilton of Baltimore, delivered the prayer and Mr. B. B. French, Grand Master of the District of Columbia Masons, delivered the Masonic address. The dimensions of the Monument were reduced from a 70 foot base as designed by Robert Mills to one of 55 feet.

In May, 1849, Mr. D. C. Sayre of Alabama, on behalf of a number of citizens of that State, proposed to quarry and prepare a block of marble from the quarries of

Talladega County, to be placed in the monument. This offer was accepted and suggested to the Board the plan of soliciting similar stones from States, societies and individuals. It is noteworthy that a large portion of the stones contributed bore inscriptions testifying a hope for the preservation of the Union.

Meanwhile, the work of obtaining subscriptions was progressing rapidly and during the year 1850 contributions amounting to over $28,000 were received. By March, 1852, $130,000 had been received, and the Monument had risen to the height of over 100 feet. In the fall of 1852, $20,000 was raised by contributions obtained at the polls at the Presidential election of that year. In 1856, the total amount received was $230,000, which had been fully expended in the raising of the monument to a height of 174 feet. The work was at this time discontinued for a period of twenty years during the troubled times preceding and following the Civil War.

By Act approved August 2, 1876, Congress appropriated $200,000 for the completion of the Monument under a joint commission to consist of the President, the Supervising Architect of the Treasury and the Architect of the Capitol, the Chief of Engineers of the Army and the first vice-president of the Washington National Monument Society. The Act required the reconveyance to the United States of all the property, rights and privileges in the Monument belonging to the Society, which was executed by W. W. Corcoran and Dr. John B. Blake as officers of the Society on January 19, 1877.

The Act also required the examination of the foundations of the Monument, which being found insufficient were ordered by Congress to be strengthened. Lieut. Colonel, afterwards Brig. General, Thomas Lincoln Casey, assisted by Captain George W. Davis and Mr. Bernard R. Green, accomplished this difficult task in the course of which a deflection of 1.4 inches to the northwest due to settling was corrected. To strengthen the old foundation 70 per cent of the earth under it was dug away to a depth of 13 feet 6 inches and replaced with concrete extending 18 feet within and 23 feet 3 inches without the outer edges of the old foundation. The new foundation was 126 feet 6 inches square. The Monument settled two and one-half inches during the placing of the new foundation and four inches during the entire period of its construction.

The pyramidion which caps the Monument was designed by Mr. Bernard R. Green and is a radical departure from and a marked improvement upon the flattened cap provided in the original design.

The cornerstone of the first course of the new construction was laid on August 7, 1880, in the presence of President Hayes. Four similar appropriations were made in the ensuing four years, and the work was completed December 6, 1884, on which day the capstone was set in place with elaborate ceremonies led by President Arthur at which it was estimated twenty thousand persons were present.

In the course of the renewed work a slight twist was given to the Monument to correct a misalignment of the faces of the lower portion with the points of the compass.

All the marble used in the Monument came from Baltimore County, Maryland, except the first 26 feet of the upper portion which came from Massachusetts. The total cost of the structure was $1,187,710.31.

The famous statue of Washington by Horatio Greenough has probably received as much criticism, praise and censure as any statue ever made. Greenough received a commission from Congress for the work in 1832 and devoted his time and energy to it for eight years.

After its completion a war vessel was first sent to bring it to America but could not handle the huge mass which weighed twenty-one tons and an American merchantman, the Sea, was chartered for its accommodation. The monument reached Washington in 1843 and was placed in the center of the rotunda of the Capitol. This was before the large dome had been built and the huge marble seemed greatly out of proportion. It had friends and advocates from the first but did not appeal to the people generally as a suitable representation of Washington and became the butt of much ridicule. It was finally taken from the Capitol building and placed in the east plaza facing the Capitol. There it stayed for a number of years, unsuited to its environment and exposed to the weather, which had not been considered in its making, and from which it received considerable damage. It was finally removed to the Smithsonian building.

The statue represents Washington seated, in a Roman costume, pointing heavenward with his right hand, while in his left he holds a sheathed sword.

This monument was the first colossal marble carved by an American and it cost for making, transportation, setting, etc., $43,000.

The equestrian statue of Washington in Washington Circle, at Pennsylvania Avenue and Twenty-third Streets, is the work of Clark Mills, a self-taught sculptor who had followed the trade of plasterer.

Congress in 1853 appropriated $50,000 for the monument and donated captured cannon as material for its composition. General Washington in this representation wears the uniform he wore at the Battle of Princeton, from which scene, just after he had rallied his troops in that battle, Mills chose to represent the leader. The face is modeled from Houdon's cast.

The statue was unveiled February 22, 1860. President Buchanan dedicated the monument, civic and military organizations taking part. The address of the occasion was delivered by a Virginia Representative, Honorable Thomas S. Bocock.

Clark Mills' earliest work was the rearing equestrian statue of General Andrew Jackson which stands in the center of Lafayette Square. This sculptor's talents attracted so much attention while he was living in Charleston, S. C, that friends contributed a purse to enable him to go to Europe to study. While stopping in Washington on his way for that purpose, he was offered the commission for the Jackson statue. After some deliberation he accepted the task and his European trip was deferred. It is said that Mills had never seen an equestrian statue up to the time he executed this work. He studied his subject diligently, learned all the parts of a horse and rider, taught a horse to rear and stand on its hind legs, that he might study it so and get its equilibrium. The monument is so perfectly balanced that the creator claimed for it the power to stand in its perfectly poised position, without fastening, indefinitely. For safety against high winds or other disturbing force, however, the feet of the horse were fastened to the pedestal.

After conceiving and modeling this unusual statue, the sculptor himself cast it in bronze at his foundry near the present site of the Catholic University. The statue was dedicated with elaborate ceremonies, January 8, 1853, the thirty-eighth anniversary of the Battle of New Orleans.

311

Twelve thousand dollars was first appropriated for this monument but as that amount did not even pay for the expense of the making, Congress made a later appropriation of twenty thousand dollars. Two replicas of this unusual monument have been made, one erected in New Orleans and the other in the Capitol grounds of Nashville, near the home of the hero of New Orleans.

Several monuments have been erected in the city to the memory of the martyr-President, Abraham Lincoln. The first of these is a life-size white marble standing figure of Lincoln by Lot Flannery, who was a local marble cutter, and is erected on a marble pillar twenty-seven feet in height, in front of the Court House. This tribute was paid for by private subscription and cost $7,000. It was dedicated April 15, 1868, President Grant leading in the ceremonies.

On April 14, 1876, on the eleventh anniversary of Lincoln's assassination, another statue to his memory was unveiled in Lincoln Park, a mile from the Capitol. This is known as the Emancipation Monument and represents Lincoln standing with extended hand to help an unshackled slave to rise. This statue, which cost $18,000, was paid for by subscriptions of freed slaves, the first contribution to the fund being five dollars from Charlotte Scott, an ex-slave of Virginia. Congress appropriated $3,000 for the pedestal. The composition is the work of Thomas Ball.

In the seventies the eminent sculptor Henry K. Brown, was commissioned by Congress to make two equestrian statues, one of General Winfield Scott and one of General Nathaniel Green.

These were executed, that of General Scott being completed and turned over to the city in 1874. It is erected in Scott Circle, at the intersection of Massachusetts and Rhode Island Avenues and Sixteenth and N Streets.

Congress appropriated $45,000 for this monument and supplied the metal from which it was cast from cannon captured during the Mexican War.

Another monument to General Scott, executed by Launt Thompson, is the heroic, standing figure, situated in the grounds of the Soldiers' Home. This large bronze figure looks toward the Capital City and, like the Brown statue, shows the General at an advanced age.

At the intersection of Pennsylvania and Louisiana Avenues and Ninth Street, is a statue of General John A. Rawlings by J. Bailey. General Rawlings was Chief-of-Staff to General Grant and later Secretary of War. This monument is made of cannon captured by Grant's army and was erected in 1874. It cost $12,000, which amount was subscribed by friends and admirers of General Rawlings. Congress appropriated $3,000 for the pedestal.

The monument to General James B. McPherson, by Louis T. Rebisso, standing in the center of McPherson Square, was the gift of the Society of the Army of the Tennessee. The monument was unveiled October 18, 1876. The ceremony was opened by General Sherman and the address of the occasion was given by General Logan. The cost of the monument was $23,500. The pedestal was provided by Congress at a cost of $25,000.

The ornate fountain which stands in the Botanical Gardens is the work of Bartholdi, the designer of the Statue of Liberty in New York harbor. It was first exhibited at the Philadelphia Centennial Exposition and was brought to Washington after the close of the Exposition.

In Stanton Square in northeast Washington, stands the bronze equestrian figure of Nathaniel Green, mentioned above, represented in early Continental uniform, by Henry K. Brown.

Two months after the death of General Green which occurred in June, 1786, Congress made an appropriation for the erection of a monument to his memory. This appropriation was never applied, and not until nearly a century later — June 24, 1874 — was another appropriation, of $40,000, made to honor the early hero, and the act put into effect. The work was completed and turned over to the city in 1877.

The Naval or Peace monument stands at the Western entrance of the Capitol grounds, facing Pennsylvania Avenue. This memorial was designed by Franklin Simmons, after a sketched design by Admiral D. D. Porter. The foundation was designed by Edward Clark. The work cost $41,000, half of which was furnished by contributions from the Navy and half by Congress. This monument was dedicated in 1878.

The statue of General George H. Thomas by J. Q. A. Ward, situated in Thomas Circle at the intersection of Massachusetts and Vermont Avenues and Fourteenth and M Streets was a contribution from the Society of the Army of the Cumberland and cost $35,000. Congress appropriated $25,000 for the pedestal and furnished the bronze for the figures.

The unveiling occurred on November 19, 1879, and the inaugural was very elaborate. Buildings were decorated in honor of the occasion and thousands of people thronged to witness the procession and the place of the unveiling exercises. The procession, chiefly military, is said to have taken two hours to pass one point. In addition to Washington military there were organizations from Annapolis, Alexandria, Cantonsville, Norfolk and Richmond, while military bands also came from West Point, Fort Monroe, Columbus, Ohio, David's Island, New York, and Frederick, Maryland, to assist those already here. Besides the music from these bands a choir of fifty selected male voices sang appropriate hymns and patriotic odes. Senator Stanley Matthews of Ohio delivered the oration, and President Hayes accepted the statue in behalf of the people of the United States.

In Farragut Square at Connecticut Avenue and I Street is a bronze figure by Vinnie Ream Hoxie, of Admiral David G. Farragut, which was cast from the guns of the flagship Hartford. The monument was unveiled April 25, 1881. Its cost was $25,000.

In the Smithsonian grounds is W. W. Story's bronze figure of Professor Joseph Henry, the first Secretary of the Smithsonian Institution, erected by Congress at a cost of $15,000. It was dedicated April 19, 1882.

Chief Justice John Marshall, has been honored by the erection of a dignified sedent figure in bronze, executed by W. W. Story. This monument rests midway of the great western double stairway of the Capitol which leads down to Pennsylvania Avenue. It was the gift of members of the United States Bar, and the Government furnished the pedestal. The monument cost $40,000, and it was dedicated in 1884.

In the center of Dupont Circle at Connecticut and New Hampshire Avenues, Nineteenth and P Streets, is a standing figure in bronze by Launt Thompson, of Rear-Admiral Samuel Francis Dupont, dedicated on December 20, 1884. This monument was erected by Congress at a cost of $20,500.

Another monument erected in 1884 is that of Martin Luther, a replica of the central figure of the great work of Rietschel in Germany, at Wurms, cast from the original model. This strong figure, eleven and one-half feet in height, stands on an eleven foot pedestal before the Lutheran church northeast of Thomas Circle, at Fourteenth and N Streets, northwest. Both the church and statue stand as a memorial of the four hundredth anniversary of the birth of the great German reformer. The monument cost $10,000 and was paid for by subscriptions of Lutherans all over the Country.

The Garfield monument was dedicated May 12, 1887 and is the work of J. Q. A. Ward. It stands before the southwestern entrance of the Capitol grounds. The entire monument cost $62,500, $25,000 of which was contributed by the Society of the Army of the Cumberland, and the remainder by the Government.

In front of Kendall Green Chapel, in the grounds of the Columbia Institute for the Deaf and Dumb, is a bronze monument to Thomas Hopkins Gallaudet, the teacher who first opened the way for the intellectual advancement of those born without the sense of hearing. This group of Gallaudet and his first pupil, little Alice Cogswell, is the work of Daniel C. French. The statue was dedicated in 1887, the centennial year of the birth of Gallaudet, and was paid for by deaf students from every State and Territory in the Union.

At Pennsylvania Avenue, Tenth and D. Streets, is a quaint likeness of Benjamin Franklin, designed by Ernst Plassman. The sculptor of the figure of Franklin was Jacque Jouvenal. This memorial was presented to the city by Mr. Stilson Hutchins, January 17, 1889.

General Lafayette has been honored in America's Capital by the handsome bronze monument in Lafayette Square. Congress appropriated $50,000 for this memorial and the commission for its execution was allotted to two French Sculptors, Alexander Falquiere and Antonin Mercie. Below Lafayette, on the pedestal, is America reaching up to hand him the sword of victory. Standing on the pedestal are Rochambeau, Duportail, D'Estaing and De Grasse. This graceful monument was unveiled in 1890.

The remaining three corners of Lafayette Square are also devoted to monuments to foreign heroes of the American Revolution. These are the monuments to Rochambeau, by F. Hamar, for which Congress appropriated $22,500, unveiled May 24, 1902; to Baron von Steuben, by Albert Jaegers, erected by Congress at a cost of $50,000, and unveiled December 7, 1910; and to Kosciusko, by Antoni Popiel, the gift of Polish-American citizens, dedicated May 11, 1910.

In the Smithsonian grounds, is a memorial dedicated by the Photographic Association of America, to the memory of Louis J. M. Daguerre commemorating the first half century of photography, from 1839 to 1889. This monument, surmounted by a granite globe representing the earth with a bronze relief portrait of Daguerre, is the work of Jonathan S. Hartley, and was dedicated August 15, 1890.

At Pennsylvania Avenue and Seventh Street is a monument to General Winfield Scott Hancock, executed by Henry J. Ellicott.

The unveiling took place May 12, 1896, with impressive ceremonies, opened by President Cleveland.

This monument was a gift of the Government, $40,000 having been appropriated by Congress for its cost and that of the pedestal.

A distinguished physician honored in the Capital city is Dr. Samuel D. Gross, whose bronze stands in the Smithsonian grounds. Dr. Gross was a famous surgeon, as well as teacher and author. This statue is the work of A. Sterling Calder, and was presented to the Government May 5, 1897, by the physicians and surgeons of the United States. Congress appropriated $1,500 for the pedestal.

On the west side of Scott Circle is a standing figure of Daniel Webster, the gift of Mr. Stilson Hutchins. It was dedicated January 18, 1900. It is the work of G. Trentanove. The pedestal was erected by Congress at a cost of $4,000.

On the east side of Scott Circle is a semi-circular memorial to the founder of Homeopathy, Christain S. F. Hahneman, by Charles H. Niehaus. The monument was dedicated June 21, 3900. It was the gift of the American Institute of Homeopathy. Congress appropriated $4,000 for the foundation.

In Iowa Circle at Rhode Island Avenue and 13th Street, is a bronze to General John A. Logan by Franklin Simmons. This monument was unveiled April 9, 1901, the ceremony being led by President McKinley. The oration of the day was delivered by Senator Chauncey M. Depew of New York.

This statue cost $65,000, of which sum $50,000 was appropriated by Congress and $15,000 by the Society of the Army of the Tennessee.

At the intersection of Indiana Avenue, Third and D Streets, is a large bronze by G. Trentanove, of General Albert Pike, erected by the Masonic fraternity and dedicated October 23, 1901.

The monument to General William T. Sherman, by Carl Rohl-Smith, in Sherman Park facing the south front of the Treasury Building, was unveiled October 15, 1903. This monument was erected by the Society of the Army of the Tennessee which contributed $11,000, and the United States Government which contributed $80,000. On one side of the high pedestal is War, represented by a woman tearing her garment as she stands over the slain body of a soldier. On the opposite side of the pedestal is a figure of a woman, typifying Peace. At the four corners of the wide base of the statue are figures representing soldiers of the cavalry, artillery, infantry and engineers.

At Twenty-third and E Streets, at the Naval Museum, is a statue of Dr. Benjamin Rush, a signer of the Declaration of Independence. This monument was erected in 1904 by the American Medical Association.

A monument to General George B. McClellan, by Frederick MacMonnies, stands in the little park surrounded by Connecticut Avenue, Columbia Road and California Street. It was dedicated May 2, 1907 and is the gift of Congress which appropriated $60,000 and of the Society of the Army of the Potomac.

At the intersection of Seventh and C Streets, Pennsylvania and Louisiana Avenues, stands the monument to Dr. Benjamin F. Stephenson, the projector of the Grand Army of the Republic, which organization contributed the figures. The obelisk pedestal was erected by Congress at a cost of $10,000. The monument, which was designed by J. Massey Rhind, was unveiled July 3, 1908.

At Connecticut Avenue and M Street is the monument to Henry W. Longfellow. This statue is a sedent bronze figure in a gown, the work of William Couper, and was unveiled May 15, 1909. It is the gift of the Longfellow National Memorial Association. The pedestal was erected by Congress at a cost of $4,000.

The animated equestrian statue of General Sheridan, by Gutzon Borglum, in Sheridan Circle at Massachusetts Avenue and Twenty-third Street, was erected by Congress at a cost of $60,000 and unveiled November 25, 1909.

On the plaza of the Municipal Building, facing Pennsylvania Avenue stands a bronze memorial to Governor Alexander R. Shepherd. This is the work of W. S. J. Dunbar, a local sculptor, and was unveiled May 3, 1909.

William Couper 's statue of John Witherspoon, one of the signers of the Declaration of Independence, stands at the intersection of Connecticut Avenue, Eighteenth and L Streets. It was presented by the Witherspoon Memorial Association and unveiled May 20, 1909. Congress appropriated $4,000 for the pedestal.

A splendid white marble memorial to Columbus stands in front of the Union Station. This monument was erected by Congress at a cost of $100,000. The architectural work was designed by Daniel H. Burnham and the sculptural work by Lorado Taft. It was dedicated June 6, 1912, by the Italian Ambassador.

The idea of erecting this tribute to the great discoverer was originated by the Knights of Columbus.

The work extends seventy feet wide east and west. In the center is a shaft forty-five feet high, surmounted by a sphere representing the world. Before this shaft is the figure of Columbus standing on the prow of a ship. He is wrapped in the folds of a cloak and looks ahead, over the carved head of a woman on the prow of the vessel, representing Discovery. On one side of the shaft is the hulking figure of an early Caucasian, representing the Old World, while the opposite side has the figure of an Indian, which represents the New World. On the side of the shaft opposite Columbus is a medallion containing the figures of Ferdinand and Isabella of Spain.

At the foot of the 17th Street Speedway on the edge of the Tidal Basin has been erected a standing heroic bronze of John Paul Jones, by Charles H. Niehaus for which Congress appropriated $50,000. It was unveiled April 17, 1912.

In Rock Creek Cemetery are several monuments which are notable works of art. The most striking of these is that by Augustus Saint Gaudens, erected to Mrs. Adams. A woman's figure heavily draped, sits on a granite boulder, with closed eyes and saddened face. The work is intended to be symbolic of Grief or Despair.

Near the southeast corner of the new National Museum building in the Smithsonian grounds stands a vase erected by the Pomological Society to the memory of Andrew Jackson Downing who laid out the entire Mall, as well as the grounds of the White House and Lafayette Park in 1852, and who perished in the wreck of the steamer Henry Clay while the work was in progress.

At the time that Congress made its appropriation for the Paul Jones monument, a similar amount was appropriated for the erection of a monument to Commodore John Barry, to stand facing 14th Street at the west end of Franklin Park. This monument was unveiled May 16, 1914. It was designed by John J. Boyle.

One war hero not connected with our own country, Frederick the Great, of Prussia, is commemorated by a statue, presented to America by Emperor William of Germany, which stands in the grounds of the War College, at the Washington barracks.

A graceful little fountain has lately been erected on the northwest margin of the ellipse south of the White House, to the memory of two of the victims of the terrible

Titanic catastrophe of April 15, 1912, Francis D. Millet and Major Archibald W. Butt of the United States Army. Mr. Millet was a member of the Commission of Fine Arts. The little fountain was designed by two members of the Art Commission, Daniel C. French and Thomas Hastings.

The sedent statue of Archbishop John Carroll, the founder of Georgetown University, located in front of the entrance to the main college building was erected by the alumni of the University and unveiled on May 4, 1912. It was the work of Mr. Jerome Conner of Washington.

In the terraced grounds of the filtration plant stands the memorial fountain erected in 1913 by the citizens of Michigan in honor of Senator James McMillan of that State, who died in 1902, and who was for ten years the Chairman of the Senate Committee on the District of Columbia.

Congress has appropriated $240,000 for a monument to General U. S. Grant. The commission for the sculptural work was given to Henry M. Shrady, and that for the architectural work to Edward Pearce Casey. The elaborately planned memorial was begun at the eastern end of the Botanical Gardens in the Mall. The long pedestal has been erected, and on one wing of it has been placed a spirited group of field artillery.

For many years the question of creating some adequate memorial to Abraham Lincoln of a national character has been under consideration by the American people, and numerous and varied projects having this purpose in view, have been from time to time advanced. This problem was thoroughly considered by the Park Commission in 1901 and the results of the deliberations of that body were a recommendation in favor of a memorial structure of a Grecian type to be erected on the west end of Potomac Park on the central line of the Capitol and Washington Monument, the connection between the Monument and the Memorial to be a setting of parkways, basins, fountains, and trees in continuation of the parkway proposed by the Commission to connect the Monument and the Capitol. By act approved February 9, 1911, Congress created the Lincoln Memorial Commission to consist of William H. Taft, then President of the United States, Shelby M. Cullom, Senator from Illinois who had been mainly instrumental in bringing this legislation to a head, Joseph G. Cannon, of Illinois, Speaker of the House of Representatives, Senator Peabody Wetmore, of Rhode Island, Representative Samuel Walker McCall, of Massachusetts, Senator Hernando D. Money of Mississippi, and Representative Champ Clark, of Missouri. This Commission was directed to determine upon a location, plan and design for a monument or memorial in the City of Washington to the memory of Abraham Lincoln to cost not exceeding two million dollars. Senator Cullom was made Resident Commissioner. He died January 28, 1914, and Ex-Senator Joseph C. S. Blackburn was appointed to succeed him. Senator Money died on September 18, 1912, and his place was filled by the appointment of Senator Thomas S. Martin of Virginia.

At its first meeting the Commission passed a resolution calling upon the Commission of Fine Arts to make suggestions to the Memorial Commission as to the locations, plans and designs for the memorial and particularly that it give its advice as to the following locations: the axis of Delaware Avenue at some point between the Capitol and the Union Station Plaza; the axis of the new avenue authorized to be constructed between the Peace Monument and the Union Station

Plaza; some portion of the proposed plaza between the Capitol and the Union Station; the site in Potomac Park recommended by the Park Commission in 1901; and also any other location which they might deem suitable. The Commission of Fine Arts was also requested to make suggestions in connection with each location as to a memorial suited to it and within the limit of cost authorized by the act, and also as to the best method of selecting the artists, sculptors and architects and making and executing the proper designs.

To the questions thus submitted to it, the Commission of Fine Arts gave most attentive study for a period covering four months. In its report, which it submitted on July 17, 1911, the Commission recommended the Potomac Park site. With reference to the type of memorial to be erected the Commission advised that to avoid competition with the Capitol or the Washington Monument, the Lincoln Memorial should not include a dome and should not be characterized by great height but by strong horizontal lines.

Pending the consideration of the questions submitted to the Commission of Fine Arts, the Memorial Commission, on the advice of the former, selected Mr. Henry Bacon, an architect of New York City, to prepare designs for a memorial with the view to its location on the site at Potomac Park, and soon after employed Mr. John Russell Pope, an architect of New York City, to prepare designs contemplating the placing of the memorial on the Soldiers' Home Grounds on the axis of North Capitol Street, and also for a memorial suitable to be located on the crest of 16th Street hill.

In December, 1911, these architects submitted complete designs, including prospective plans and models for the '3 sites mentioned. After the submission of these designs the Memorial Commission on February 3, 1912, adopted the site on the axis of the Capitol and Washington Monument in Potomac Park at a point near the river bank as best suited for the location of the memorial. The two architects above nominated were then requested by the Commission, after conference, to prepare and submit new designs or modifications of those already submitted, all having in view the site in Potomac Park, and in response to this request Mr. Bacon submitted three designs, one of them a slight modification of his first design, and Mr. Pope submitted a modification of his original design for the memorial contemplating the location in the Soldiers' Home Grounds, which he adapted to the site in Potomac Park. Mr. Pope also submitted a number of sketches of alternate designs for the latter site.

These designs were submitted to the Commission of Fine Arts which reported on March 23, 1912, recommending the adoption of one of the three submitted by Mr. Bacon, and recommending also the employment of Mr. Bacon as architect for the memorial. These recommendations were adopted by the Memorial Commission on April 16, 1912. Certain modifications were suggested to Mr. Bacon in the design submitted by him and he prepared a new design embodying these modifications and submitted it to the Commission which unanimously recommended that Congress approve the construction of the memorial upon the Potomac site in accordance with Mr. Bacon's last design.

CHAPTER XV

The Press

The earliest paper published in what is now the District of Columbia is believed to have been the Weekly Ledger, a Georgetown publication which was started in 1790. In 1796, a second Georgetown paper, the Sentinel of Liberty appeared, the publishers being Green, English and Company.

The first newspaper to be published in the City of Washington was the Washington Gazette, a semi-weekly paper first published on June 15, 1796 by Benjamin More, a bookseller. On July 26, 1797, this paper was discontinued for lack of support. It re-appeared on the 16th of the following September as a weekly, but lack of patronage forced its final discontinuance on March 24, 1798.

On October 31, 1800, appeared the first publication of the National Intelligencer. The editor and proprietor was Samuel Harrison Smith and the paper was published in one of a row of brick buildings on New Jersey Avenue, erected by Thomas Law. The paper from its first publication until January 1, 1813, appeared three times each week. It early announced and throughout its career maintained a policy, at variance with the custom of the times, of abstinence from unnecessary personal abuse joined with the fullest publicity concerning public men and measures.

It is due to the enterprise of Mr. Smith that the early debates of Congress have been preserved to posterity. At first Mr. Smith was denied by the Speaker of the House, Theodore Sedgwick, of Massachusetts, permission to publish other than proceedings which had reached a matured state and upon which the House had come to a conclusion. In 1809, however, Mr. Joseph Gales, Jr., afterwards Mayor of the city, removed to Washington from Raleigh, North Carolina, and entered the employ of Mr. Smith as stenographic reporter of the proceedings in Congress. Mr. Gales was shortly afterwards taken into partnership by Mr. Smith, and in September, 1810, he purchased Mr. Smith's interest in the paper. In October, 1812, Mr. Gales associated with himself in the publication of the Intelligencer his brother-in-law, William Winston Seaton, of King William County, Virginia, who had previously been connected with the Virginia Patriot at Richmond, and on the first of the following year the paper came out as the Daily National Intelligencer. Mr. Seaton aided greatly in the work of reporting the debates of Congress, he taking one branch and Mr. Gales the other. Among the famous speeches for which the country is indebted to these men are those which occurred during the debates between Webster and Hayn in 1830.

Owing to the partial destruction of the office of the paper by the British in 1814, the paper was discontinued from August 24 to October 1 of that year.

The paper continued under the ownership of Messrs. Gales and Seaton until the death of Mr. Gales at Eckington, his country home, on July 21, 1860. On August 31 of that year, Mr. James C. Welling, who had been associated with the paper for about ten years, became associated with Mr. Seaton in the editorship of the paper. On December 31, 1864, Mr. Seaton and Mr. Welling were succeeded as editors and proprietors by Messrs. Snow, Coyle and Company. The new proprietors on April 1, 1865, enlarged the paper to a seven-column sheet and later consolidated with it the Express, changing the name to the "Intelligencer and Express." On November 30, 1869, the paper was purchased by Alexander Delmar, then late Chief of the Bureau of Statistics of the Treasury Department. The publication of the paper was discontinued under Mr. Delmar 's ownership on January 10, 1870.

The Intelligencer supported Mr. Jefferson for the presidency to succeed President John Adams. It continued to support the various administrations in power until President Jackson's time, when it opposed President Jackson on account of his political appointments. Although supporting President Harrison, it opposed Tyler on account of his alleged abandonment of the principles on which he was elected and took sides with Henry Clay and the Whig party. It vigorously opposed the annexation of Texas and in consequence incurred the enmity of John C. Calhoun, then Secretary of State. It opposed President Taylor and espoused the cause of Daniel Webster, but upon the succession of Vice-President Fillmore to the presidency after the death of President Taylor and the appointment of Daniel Webster as Secretary of State, the National Intelligencer again became the organ of the administration. It was the last of the Whig organs and with the incoming of President Pierce was succeeded as the representative of the administration, by the Union. In 1860 it supported John Bell for the Presidency against Abraham Lincoln on account of Lincoln's anti-slavery views, and again in 1864 supported General McClellan as against President Lincoln on the same grounds. It was at all times loyal to the Union but advocated the restoration of " the Union as it was " without the abolishment of slavery. Throughout the reconstruction period the Intelligencer was an ardent supporter of Andrew Johnson and championed the reconstruction methods instituted by Johnson until its discontinuance in 1870.

On August 18, 1834, the Washington Mirror was first published by William Thompson, an Englishman. The name was afterwards changed to the Metropolitan, and under the editorship of Rufus Dawes the paper acquired a considerable degree of popularity. In 1836, it was merged into the United States Telegraph which had been established in 1826 by Duff Green. The Telegraph was the organ of the administration during the presidency of Andrew Jackson, though it was said by Thomas H. Benton that it was more the organ of John C. Calhoun than of President Jackson.

The Globe was established in December, 1830, by Franklin P. Blair. Mr. Blair came to Washington and started the paper at the instigation of President Jackson who had been much impressed by a vigorous article against nullification written by Mr. Blair, which had appeared in the Frankfort, Kentucky, Argus. Shortly following its establishment, Mr. Blair took into partnership John C. Rives, and employed Amos Kendall as an editorial writer. Mr. Kendall was the President's spokesman on the Globe, voicing the President's views in the vigorous broadside editorials which immediately became a prominent feature of the paper. For eleven years following its establishment the Globe received the benefit of the public printing and advertising, which was transferred to the National Intelligencer with the incoming of the nomination of James K. Polk, a Democratic candidate for ceived the contracts for printing the Congressional debates. In 1849 the interest of Mr. Blair was acquired by Mr. Rives who continued to publish the paper until his death when it was continued by his sons.

The establishment of the Washington Union was the result of the nomination of James K. Polk, a Democratic candidate for the presidency, over Martin Van Buren. Prior to this event, the Globe had supported Van Buren for the nomination and the

Richmond Enquirer and the Nashville Union had supported Polk. From these last-mentioned papers came to Washington in 1845, Thomas Ritchie and John P. Heiss, who, on May 1, 1845, issued the first number of the Washington Union, and later purchased the Globe. The Union continued to represent the administration until 1849, when the Whig Party returned to power, and under President Fillmore the National Intelligencer was restored to its former position of organ of the administration. The Union was again made the government organ under President Pierce and so continued through the administration of President Buchanan. In 1859 it was sold by Mr. Ritchie to A. J. Donelson who had been Private Secretary to President Jackson, charge d'affaires to Texas, and Minister to Prussia and the Germanic Federation. Mr. Donelson shortly afterwards sold the paper to George W. Bowman who changed the name to the " Constitution." It was purchased in 1860 by William M. Browne who discontinued it on January 31, 1861.

The Republic was established in 1849, immediately after the inauguration of President Taylor. Its first editors were Alexander Bullitt, formerly of the New Orleans Picayune, and John Sargent of the New York Courier and Enquirer. It appears to have been short lived and to have gone out of existence upon the death of President Taylor.

The National Era was an anti-slavery publication which first appeared on January 7, 1847, under the editorship of Dr. Gamaliel Bailey, of Cincinnati, Ohio. The publishers were Martin Buel and William Blanchard. It was established by means of a fund of $20,000 which had been raised by the advocates of freedom headed by Lewis Tappan and represented in a clerical capacity by Lewis Clephane. Dr. Bailey was a prominent abolitionist, having been associated in the editorship of the Cincinnati Philanthropist with James G. Birney, who afterwards, as nominee of the abolition party for the presidency, caused the defeat of Henry Clay. While Dr. Bailey was connected with the Philanthropist that paper had twice been the victim of mobs which had destroyed its office and thrown its type into the Ohio River. The National Era played a prominent part in the abolitionists' movement. Its regular corresponding editor was John G. Whittier. Other contributors were Theodore Parker, Alice Phoebe Cary, Dr. Pierpont, William D. Gallagher and H. B. Stanton, author of "Modern Reformers." A series of sketches of men and things about Washington was contributed by Dr. James Houston, an accomplished Irishman. Later the Era numbered among its contributors Edward Everett Hale, Salmon P. Chase, Charles Sumner, Wendell Phillips, Harriet Beecher Stowe, Gail Hamilton and Mrs. Bailey, the wife of the editor. Through its columns Mrs. Stowe 's Uncle Tom's Cabin first appeared as a serial story in 1851.

In April, 1848, the office of the National Era was attacked by a mob as the result of an attempted escape by a party of slaves in a sloop named The Pearl which succeeded in getting as far as Cornfield Harbor near the mouth of the Potomac. The office of the Era was at this time on 7th Street between F and G Streets. It was afterwards removed to the Tremont House at the corner of 2nd Street and Indiana Avenue, and at this place which was occupied also by the Republican headquarters, the paper was again slightly damaged by a mob following the election of Mr. Lincoln to the presidency.

The National Republican first appeared on Monday, November 26, 1860, under the ownership of a company at the head of which was Mr. Lewis Clephane. During the war the paper vigorously supported the Government. In 1867 or 1868, it was acquired by William J. Murtagh and S. P. Hanscom and was continued under the editorship of the latter. It was subsequently edited in turn by Mr. Harris, formerly of the Patriot, Mr. Connery, and John P. Foley.

The Daily Patriot was started as a conservative Democratic paper by a syndicate of wealthy Eastern men under the editorship of James E. Harvey with Oscar K. Harris in charge of the news department and Ex-Mayor James G. Berrett as business manager. These men were succeeded soon after by A. G. Allen as editor-in-chief and Louis Bagger as local editor under the general managership of Col. W. H. Philip, J. C. McGuire and R T. Merrick.

The Evening Star was established by Capt. J. B. Tait in December, 1852, a specimen issue being put out on the 4th of that month and the regular daily issue first appearing on the 16th. It consisted of four pages with a total of twenty columns, and its circulation slightly more than 800. It was printed on a hand press. Its first office was at the corner of 6th Street and Pennsylvania Avenue. In May, 1854, it was removed to the second story of a blacksmith shop on D Street near 12th Street, northwest, the present site of the Franklin engine house. Soon thereafter Mr. Tait sold the paper to W. D. Wallach and W. H. Hope, Mr. Wallach soon after acquiring entire ownership. In 1854 the office was removed to the southwest corner of Pennsylvania Avenue and 11th Street, the present site of the Post Office Department. In 1855 Mr. Crosby S. Noyes became associated with Mr. Wallach on the paper and in 1863 a Hoe rotary press was installed. In 1867 the paper was sold for $110,000 by Mr. Wallach to a syndicate composed of Crosby S. Noyes, S. H. Kaaffman, A. R. Shepherd, Clarence Baker and George W. Adams. These gentlemen were incorporated into the Evening Star Newspaper Company by a special Act of Congress in 1868. In 1881 the Star acquired the ground and buildings at the northwest corner of Pennsylvania Avenue and 11th Street, the site of its present structure, and installed what was then a modern perfecting press and folding machine. In 1890 the company erected a four-story building on 11th Street adjoining its former building and shortly afterwards acquired the property adjoining its holdings on Pennsylvania Avenue. On April 13, 1892, the paper suffered severely from a fire but its publication was not discontinued on this account. The present building at Pennsylvania Avenue and 11th Street was erected in 1899 and occupied by the Star on July 1, 1900. The Sunday morning edition of the Star was inaugurated on March 26, 1905.

The Washington Critic originated as a theater program. It was published as an independent evening daily from 1868, with the exception of a short period in 1888, when it appeared under the ownership of Stilson Hutchins as the Evening Post, until May 14, 1891, when its equipment and United Press franchise were purchased by the Evening Star Newspaper Company at a receiver's sale. It was owned successively by Ringwalt, Hack and Miller, by Hallett Kilbourn, and by Richard Weightman and his associates.

The Daily Morning Chronicle which had been started in 1861 by John W. Forney of the Philadelphia Press as the Sunday Morning Chronical under the editorship of Joseph A. Ware, became a daily in 1863. It was acquired in 1870 by John M. Morris, formerly clerk of the United States Senate, who was also proprietor of the South

Carolina Republican. In 1882 the Chronicle was acquired by John Q. Thompson and Company.

The Washington Post first appeared on December 6, 1877, under the ownership of Mr. Stilson Hutchins. At that time the morning newspapers of Washington were the National Republican, owned by A. M. Clapp and Company, and printed in what is now the Southern Railway Building, at 13th and Pennsylvania Avenue, northwest; and the National Union, published by ex-Congressman John Lynch, of Maine, in the old Congressional Globe Building on the north side of Pennsylvania Avenue, between Third and Four-and-a-Half Streets. The evening papers were the Evening Star, and the Critic. None of these dailies then had Sunday issues. In the Sunday field were the Sunday Chronicle, the Sunday Gazette, the Sunday Republic, the Sunday Herald, and the Capital. The latter under the ownership of Don Piatt had acquired a national reputation.

The Post was started in the building at 916 Pennsylvania Avenue, formerly occupied by the Chronicle which had gone out of existence some months previously. The Managing Editor was Col. John A. Cockerill, who had previously been the Editor of the Cincinnati Enquirer. On the editorial staff were A. C. Buell, Montague Marks, Captain Charles H. Allen, and, for a time, Joseph Pulitzer, who afterwards acquired the St. Louis Post-Despatch and the New York World.

In May, 1878, Mr. Hutchins purchased the National Union, which he consolidated with the Post, and moved the Post to the Globe Building on Pennsylvania Avenue. Immediately after this Col. Cockerill resigned to become the Editor of the Baltimore Gazette, and Mr. Walter Stilson Hutchins became Managing Editor, in which position he remained continuously, except for several absences due to illness, throughout the period of his father's ownership of the paper.

In 1879 the Post inaugurated a Sunday morning edition and became the first seven-day paper in Washington.

In 1880 Mr. Hutchins bought the building on the Peter Force property at the northeast corner of 10th and D Streets, northwest. This building was destroyed by fire in July, 1885 and was immediately replaced.

In 1887 Mr. Hutchins purchased the National Republican and merged it with the Post, which thus became, and remained until the appearance of the Times in 1894, the only morning paper in Washington. During the later years of the Post under Mr. Hutchins' ownership its staff numbered among other notable men Henry L. West; Captain Page McCarty, who had been one of the principals in the celebrated Mordecai-McCarty duel in 1873, in which the former was killed, the last prominent Virginia duel; Maurice Splain, at present Marshal of the District of Columbia; General George H. Harries; Richard Sylvester the father of the present Chief of Police; Richard Weightman, grandson of former Mayor Weightman; and two afterwards well-known women contributors — Mollie Elliott Sewall and Jeanette Duncan.

On January 1, 1889, the Post was sold to a syndicate headed by Frank Hatton and Beriah Wilkins. About two years later it removed to its present quarters at 1340 E Street, northwest.

In 1888 Mr. Hutchins purchased the Evening Critic and issued it for some months " as the Evening Post. It was later sold and re-established under its former name.

323

In October, 1905, the Post was purchased by John R. McLean. The Post has always been Democratic in politics and for many years was generally recognized as the National Democratic Organ.

The Washington Times was started as a co-operative enterprise in 1894 under the editorship of Herbert J. Browne by a number of union printers who had been thrown out of work by the introduction of linotype machines. Shares were issued at $10 each and a capital of $1,800 subscribed. The first issue appeared on March 17, 1894. The paper was first published in the building formerly occupied by the Washington Post at 10th and D Streets, northwest. After three months of co-operative ownership the paper was purchased by Ex-Congressman C. GL Conn, of Elkhart, Indiana, who removed it to a building at 11th and E streets, northwest, and added an evening and a Sunday morning edition in 1896. In 1897 Mr. Conn sold the paper to Mr. Stilson Hutchins, who took it back to its former quarters, and issued it for four years and a half under the management of Mr. Walter Stilson Hutchins, as a morning, evening and Sunday morning paper. In November, 1901, the Times was bought by Mr. Frank A. Munsey, who discontinued the morning daily edition and changed the Sunday morning to a Sunday afternoon edition. In 1905, the paper removed to its present quarters at 1329 E Street, northwest. The Times has since been published as a one-cent Sunday afternoon paper.

The Washington Herald was started in 1905 through the efforts of Mr. Scott C. Bone, formerly Managing Editor of the Washington Post, who became the first Editor-in-Chief of the paper. Its first issue appeared on October 8, 1906. In 1910 Mr. Henry L. West, on retiring as District Commissioner, acquired a large interest in the Herald and late in 1910 Mr. Bone severed his connection with the paper to take up the editorship of the Seattle Post-Intelligencer. In 1912 Mr. West withdrew from the Herald and in October, 1913, Mr. C. T. Brainard of New York bought a controlling interest in its stock.

The Herald has always been a politically independent morning paper. It was first published on 15th Street, between New York Avenue and H Street, northwest, but soon moved to its present location on New York Avenue between 13th and 14th Streets, northwest.

The Real Estate and Court Record, a daily, has been in continuous existence over a hundred years, the precise date of its establishment not being known. When started it was a single sheet about six by eight inches in size.

The publication of the Congressional Record by the Government was begun in 1841, when, upon the inauguration of President Harrison, the public printing was taken from the Globe which had held it for eleven years.

CHAPTER XVI

History of Banking

The bank of Columbia was established at Georgetown in 1 793 and was the first banking institution within what afterward became the District of Columbia. It was established by Samuel Blodgett, assisted by Mr. Stoddert and Governor Johnson, of Fredericktown. Samuel Hannon was its first cashier. The last legislation by Congress relating to this bank was approved February 25, 1836, by which its charter was extended to March 4, 1839. It was also provided that no discounts should be made except such as might be deemed proper to renew such notes as had already been discounted, and that no more promissory notes should be put in circulation. This legislation also provided that instead of a president and nine directors, as then required by law, a board should be elected on the first Thursday in March, 1836, and each year thereafter, so long as the law itself remained in force, who should elect one of themselves president; and the stockholders were authorized to choose trustees to wind up the affairs. It is probable that this bank ceased to exist about 1839.

Meetings of the president and directors of the Bank of the United States for the election of directors of the office of discount and deposit for the District of Columbia, were held, and such directors duly elected on February 4, 1806; February 3, 1807, February 2, 1808, February 7, 1809, and February 6, 1810. The first directors were Joseph Carleton, Thomas Tingey, William Brent, James D, Barry, John P. Van Ness, Caleb Swan, Thomas Munroe, Joseph Nourse, David Peter, William Stewart, Lewis Leblois, Benjamin Shreve, Jr., and Phileas Janney. On the third of March, John P. Van Ness was elected president of the board and was annually re-elected until the expiration of the charter in 1811.

The election of February 6, 1810, appears to have been the last election of officers for the branch of the Bank of the United States in the District of Columbia; and the Bank itself soon became extinct through the failure of Congress to renew its charter.

After the expiration of the charter of this bank, in 1811, the business of the office of discount and deposit in Washington was conducted for a time by a temporary board of agents, of which John P. Van Ness was chairman. Still later, a committee was appointed to manage the business, with a view of settling its affairs. This having been accomplished, it was soon found desirable to make an attempt to establish another bank in Washington, as there was then but one little bank, on Capitol Hill, which had not funds sufficient for the business of its vicinity.

At a meeting, held in Davis's Hotel, January 3, 1814, of the stockholders of a new bank, which was named "The Bank of the Metropolis, " John P. Van Ness was chosen president of the new bank and Alexander Keer cashier. The location of this bank was at the corner of F and Fifteenth Streets, west of the Treasury building. Toward the close of the War of 1812-15, when General Jackson made an appeal for funds with which to pay the American soldiers, this bank loaned largely to the Government. After General Jackson became President of the United States, he kept his private accounts with this bank, and after the removal of the deposits from the United States Bank this bank was made a public depository. At length, it was organized under the National Banking law as the National Metropolitan Bank, with John B. Blake president and Moses Kelly cashier. Mr. Blake remained president until 1874, when he was. succeeded by John W. Thompson. Mr. Thompson was succeeded in the presidency of this bank by E. Southard Parker, in 1901. Mr. Parker retired from the presidency of the Columbia National Bank in 1897, and became affiliated with the National Metropolitan, first as cashier, then as first vice-president. He was elected president and served as such until the annual election of 1909, when George White was elected to succeed him. At that time a controlling interest in the stock passed into the hands of a new set of financiers and the policy and management of the bank changed. Negotiations culminated in 1904 in which the Citizens' National Bank was absorbed. The name "National Metropolitan Bank" was changed at that time to "National Metropolitan Citizens ' Bank, " which was retained but two years when the original name was restored.

The Metropolitan Bank occupied the building owned by the Citizens' Bank after the merger, until the new bank building which it now occupies was finished.

The Bank of Washington was chartered in 1809 and was the first bank established in the City of Washington. The capital stock was $100,000. Daniel Carroll, of Duddington, was its first president, and Samuel Eliot, Jr., its first cashier.

In January, 1886, this institution was organized as the "National Bank of Washington."

In the early part of 1907, some of the younger stockholders and directors sought to enlarge the capital of the bank and to inject into its management a little larger activity. The bank at that time was ultra-conservative in management, and the younger men affiliated with it feared loss of power and prestige because of its energetic competitor the Central National Bank.

As soon as it was learned that the President and a majority of the old directors were averse to any change in capitalization or departure from the established order of things, negotiations began with President Clarence F. Norment and other affiliated with the Central National Bank, for the purchase of control of the Bank of Washington. This was gradually brought about within a few months, and at the annual meeting of the Bank of Washington, in 1907, new directors were elected by the interests connected with the Central Bank. The actual merger was effected in April, the charter of the Central Bank surrendered, and the two institutions united under the charter of the National Bank of Washington. The merged bank took possession of the banking house of the older bank and the Central Bank building was retained merely as an investment.

In October, 1908, the stockholders voted to increase the capital stock from $700,000 to $1,050,000 which approximately represented the capital of the merged banks with the addition of the surplus of the Bank of Washington. The new stock was practically all taken by the stockholders of the two banks, by exchange and purchase on the basis of $150 a share.

The Union Bank of Georgetown, District of Columbia, was chartered by Congress, March 11, 1811. The capital stock of the bank was $500,000, in $50 shares. For most of the time during the existence of this bank, Robert Beverly was its president, and David English appears to have been cashier during its entire existence. In 1840, it went into liquidation, but its charter was extended from time to time until 1849, to allow its affairs to be fully settled.

The Central Bank of Georgetown and Washington was chartered March 3, 1817, and when organized John Tayloe was president, and A. R. Levering, cashier. Mr. Tayloe resigned the presidency in May, 1818, and was succeeded by Francis Dodge, who remained president during the bank's short existence. March 2, 1821, Congress passed an Act authorizing this bank to pay off its debts and close its affairs, there being then too many banks in the District of Columbia.

The Farmers and Mechanics' Bank of Georgetown was started in 1814, at a meeting held February 15, at Crawford's Hotel. William Marbury was elected president, and Clement Smith, cashier.

April 12, 1834, its board of directors resolved to suspend specie payments, saying, in explanation of their course: "They foresee that the present prostration of business confidence, and consequent derangement of the currency, must eventually reduce them to this course, and they prefer to anticipate the event by yielding at once to the pressure, rather than to avert it by holding out during the short practical period of delay, at the expense of sacrificing the permanent interests of the bank. This measure is of temporary duration. The board see no necessity in the condition of the bank, for extending it beyond the present singular crisis in the banking history of the country, and confidently anticipate the resumption of active business on a specie basis as soon as this crisis shall pass away."

The original charter of this bank was dated March 3, 1817, and it was renewed by Congress from time to time. On January 15, 1872, this bank was organized as a national bank under the name it now bears, "The Farmers and Mechanics' National Bank of Georgetown." At the time of this organization, the following nine directors were elected: Henry M. Sweeney, Philip T. Berry, William C. Magee, Esau Pickrell, William King, Francis Wheatley, John Davidson, Charles M. Matthews, and Evan Lyons. Henry M. Sweeney was continued as president of the bank. William Laird was continued as cashier and served in the same capacity for forty years.

Upon the retirement of Henry M. Sweeney, after nearly forty years' continuous service, S. Thomas Brown was elected president, September 10, 1896. He had been associated with the bank's affairs since 1876 and was made vice-president in 1891. Mr. Brown died February 22, 1913, and William King was elected president on February 27. The building which the bank has occupied for many years on the south side of M Street in the heart of the business section of Georgetown was renovated and practically rebuilt in the spring and summer of 1912. The capital stock of the bank is $252,000.

The Patriotic Bank was established in May, 1815. On June 7, Robert Brent was chosen president, and Overton Carr, cashier. On June 28, 1825, this bank opened its business in its new banking house, at the intersection of Seventh and D Streets, northwest, opposite the office of the National Intelligencer. On June 1, 1829, the capital stock was $250,000 and its total assets $503,133.87. On April 14, 1834, at a special meeting, it was resolved that, in the opinion of the board of directors, the interest of the bank and its creditors required that the payment of specie for its obligations ought to be suspended. This bank resumed specie payment July 10, 1836, by unanimous resolution, but on May 12, 1837, again suspended specie payments in common with the other banks throughout the country. In 1846, this bank opened a savings department, receiving sums of $5 and upward, upon which it paid interest until the money was withdrawn. This was the first savings bank in Washington.

During the war of 1812-15, with Great Britain, the finances of the country fell into confusion; the Government was obliged to borrow money at a ruinous rate of interest, giving $100 for $88, and taking the proceeds in the notes of banks which could not pay specie — the notes being worth from sixty to ninety cents on the dollar. Under such disastrous circumstances, the evils inflicted on the country by Vice-President Clinton's vote against the renewal of the charter of the old National Bank, already referred to, were plainly visible, and the necessity of such an institution was felt. At the session of Congress of 1813-14, Hon. Felix Grundy, of Tennessee, introduced a measure into the House of Representatives looking to the establishment of a national bank. Action upon the question was not taken at that session "for want of time."

The bill, as presented in the House of Representatives, November 14, 1814, named only Boston, New York, Philadelphia, Baltimore, Richmond, Charleston, and Pittsburgh, as places where subscriptions to the capital stock were to be received, thus confining the opportunities to subscribe almost exclusively to the Atlantic cities. This was far from satisfactory to many Western members of Congress, and Lexington, Kentucky, Nashville, Tennessee; Washington, District of Columbia; Raleigh, North Carolina; Savannah, Georgia, and New Brunswick, New Jersey, were also added, and Pittsburgh stricken out.

For Washington, District of Columbia, Robert Brent, Walter Smith, and Thomas Swann were made the commissioners to receive subscriptions. Mr. Lewis made a motion contemplating the location of the principal bank in Washington, but this was opposed by Mr. Fish, of New York, as the Ways and Means Committee had selected Philadelphia for that distinction. On January 2, 1815, the bill, on final action in the House of Representatives, was apparently carried by 81 affirmative to 80 negative votes. But the Speaker, Hon. Langdon Cheves, from South Carolina, called attention to the rule of the House which permitted the Speaker to vote in two cases, of which this was one, and, declaring his conviction that the bill was a dangerous measure, cast his vote against it, and thus made the vote in the House a tie, and then decided that the bill was lost. On January 8, in an amended form, the bill passed the House by a vote of 120 to 38; and passed the Senate by a good majority. But on January 30, President Madison returned it, without his approval, to the Senate.

On April 5, 1816, the bill passed the House of Representatives and the Senate, and on the 10th of the same month was signed by the President. Of those who voted for the bill more than two-thirds were "Republicans" or "Democrats," as they were indifferently called, in contradistinction to the "Federalists" who numbered about three-fourths of those who voted against the bill. But all of those who thus voted were not opposed to a national bank but voted against the bill in the hope of throwing it again into the committee, and thus having an opportunity to eliminate the features which were objectionable to them.

Under this act the president of the bank appointed as commissioners to superintend the taking of subscriptions in Washington, General John Mason of Georgetown, Thomas Swann of Alexandria, and General John P. Van Ness of Washington. Subscription books were opened on Monday, July 1, 1816, and closed on the 23rd of the same month. The amount subscribed here up to that time was $1,293,000, an amount far exceeding what had been anticipated.

On January 27, 1817, the following gentlemen were appointed directors of the Branch Bank of the United States in Washington: Richard Cutts, Thomas Munroe, B. Thruston, R. C. Weightman, G. Bomford, G. Graham, and William Brent, of Washington; Thomas Tudor Tucker, J. Deane, and Thomas Swann, of Alexandria, and W. Smith, W. S. Chandler, and R. Parrott, of Georgetown. Richard Smith was chosen cashier, and the office began business on Saturday, February 8, 1817. General John P. Van Ness was elected president of this branch. This branch bank continued in successful operation until the main bank was slaughtered.

During the Presidential campaign of 1828, at the close of which Andrew Jackson was elected to the Presidency, his elevation was not urged on the ground of the overthrow of the United States Bank; but soon after his inauguration, he became involved in a controversy with the management of that institution.

In his annual message to Congress he took occasion to observe that the time would soon arrive when the question of granting a re-charter to the Bank of the United States would come before that body, and that " both the constitutionality and expediency of such an institution had been well questioned." The portion of the message containing this assertion was referred by the House to its Committee on Ways and Means, of which the Hon. George McDuffie, of South Carolina, was chairman. The entire committee, including its chairman, who were supporters of General Jackson, gave grave consideration to the whole subject, and made a lengthy report, strongly in favor both of the constitutionality and expediency of a national bank.

But President Jackson continued to press the matter upon the attention of Congress. In 1832, a bill passed both Houses of Congress, re-chartering the United States Bank. President Jackson vetoed this bill, but explicitly stated that, if he had been applied to, he would have furnished a plan of a charter which would have been constitutional. An attempt to pass the bill over the veto failed.

In 1819 there was considerable excitement in reference to the suspension of specie payments. But one merchant and banker of Georgetown, named Romulus Riggs, publicly announced that the banks of the District were paying specie for their notes, and also stated that he held himself responsible for the announcement.

A peculiar feature of the monetary history of the District in 1820 was the practice of cutting paper dollars in such a way as to make change. In the latter part of May of this year, the banks adopted a resolution which was calculated to banish from circulation "such an inconvenient and unsightly sort of currency, and to bring silver into use in its place. Those who have cut notes on hand would do well to exchange them for silver before tomorrow evening." This advice was published May 31, so that it appears that June 1 was the last day on which these cut notes were received at the banks.

In 1834, only three of the banks in the District of Columbia suspended specie payments; the others were kept from doing so, by the presidents and directors of each, with the exception of the Bank of the Metropolis — each pledging his individual property as security for the debts of their respective banks. The Bank of the Metropolis had other means of accomplishing the same results.

In 1835, when it was thought the completion of the Chesapeake and Ohio Canal was near at hand, and the commerce of the cities of the District was about to be greatly increased it was plain that the means of carrying on such commerce was at the same time to be restricted. The National Bank, it was conceded, must fall, and of course its branch in Washington, which had furnished from $1,000,000 to $1,500,000 of the circulating medium, must necessarily close its doors. Besides this, the charters of the several banks in the District would expire in March, 1836, and it was at least problematical what disposition Congress would manifest toward them. It was supposed that even if these charters should be renewed they could not supply capital sufficient for the necessities of trade, as they were small institutions, and the competition among them had caused a limited circulation of their notes. In order to meet these difficulties, it was thought necessary to establish a new bank to be called the Bank of the District of Columbia.

In December, 1835, Congress took up the question of the re-charter of the banks of the District of Columbia, but not before it was necessary for them to do so, as the charters of all of them expired March 3, 1836. The bill re-chartering these banks was passed by Congress in June, 1836, their several charters being extended to July 3, 1838. In August, 1836, the Branch Bank of the United States, in Washington, Richard Smith, cashier, advertised its property for sale.

On May 13, 1836, a notice was published in the press by the Bank of Washington, and by the Bank of the Metropolis in almost identical language, to the effect that notwithstanding information had reached Washington of the suspension of specie payments by the banks in New York, as well as by some of those in Philadelphia and Baltimore, they had determined to continue to pay specie.

The determination to suspend specie payments had been arrived at in New York on May 11 and was the result of the peculiar and great stringency of the times.

One of the most instructive features of the times was with reference to the Government itself suspending specie payments. In Philadelphia, on May 12, some of that city's merchants called at the custom house to make payment of bonds, in order to avoid suit for non-payment, and offered notes on the Government deposit bank in payment of the bonds, which were refused, the Government requiring payment in gold or silver. On the same day, the custom house in Philadelphia, having certain liabilities to meet, refused to pay specie. On May 13, a merchant in Philadelphia, having to pay a certain sum to the Government, tendered payment to the Government deposit bank in its own notes, and they were refused, the merchant being told that the Government would receive nothing but gold or silver.

Throughout the country a national bank was the great desideratum. This was the constant and continuous refrain: "Give us a national bank." But that had been destroyed. The result was wide-spread distress. Bank notes in one part of the country were at a great discount, or entirely worthless, and the people in the various cities were busy in fabricating paper representatives of every part of a dollar. In Washington all kinds of paper were in circulation, the extreme limit being reached in the issue of notes by a certain barber, who, upon the presentation of his notes for redemption, said: "I don't want anything to do with them; go and buy something with them!"

May 16, 1837, the Bank of the Metropolis of Washington issued printed notices announcing its suspension of specie payments, and then the Bank of Washington, which had sustained for three days a heavy run upon it for specie, finding itself standing alone in the city, resolved to close its vaults. It was, however, then prepared to redeem its circulating notes to the last dollar; but it was thought that such a course would only tend to embarrass the mercantile classes, without relieving the public. This bank, therefore, also suspended on the 16th, and was thought to be the last bank to suspend in the Union.

A law passed the House March 1, 1837, designed to counteract the evil effects of the specie circular, by providing that, under certain conditions, and in accordance with certain regulations, no duties, taxes, or sums of money payable for lands should be collected or received otherwise than in the legal currency of the United States, or in notes of banks which were payable and paid on demand in said legal currency of the United States, failed through its retention by the President until after Congress had adjourned.

The banks of Washington which had suspended specie payments were requested by resolution of a public meeting, May 20, 1837, to resume, so far as the $5 notes were concerned. To these resolutions each bank replied separately. The substance of each reply was, that while the bank was anxious to comply with the request, it could not be done with safety or with benefit to the public by any one bank or by the banks of any one city. The Chesapeake and Ohio Canal Company, unable to obtain corporation notes of $1 and $2, determined to issue notes of its own in sums of $2, $1 and fifty cents, in order to carry on its business. These notes, while serving the purposes of the company, found their way among the people generally, and "enabled them to transact their little everyday business." An Act was passed by Congress May 25, 1838, which was in part as follows:

"Be it enacted, That the charters of the Farmers and Mechanics' Bank of Georgetown, the Bank of the Metropolis, the Patriotic Bank of Washington, the Bank of Washington, and the Farmers' Bank of Alexandria, and the Bank of Potomac, in the town of Alexandria, be, and the same are hereby, extended to the 4th of July, 1840, provided that said banks, each for itself, shall conform to the following conditions:

"1. To cease receiving and paying out all paper currency of a less denomination than $5, on or before the promulgation of this act.

"2. To redeem all their notes of the denomination of $5, in gold or silver, from and after the first day of August of the present year.

"3. To resume specie payments in full on or before the first day of January, 1839, or sooner if the principal banks of Baltimore and Richmond shall sooner resume payments in full."

These conditions were justly considered very harsh by the banks.

Specie payments were generally resumed early in 1839, but were soon again suspended, because there had been a continual drain upon the banks for specie to ship to Europe to meet a demand on the Bank of England for export in payment for grain because of bad English harvests. The banks, therefore, thought it best to suspend, and thus to keep the gold and silver at home. On the 11th of October, the banks of the District of Columbia, at a meeting of the representatives of several of them, passed the following resolutions:

"Whereas, Information is received that the banks of Philadelphia and Baltimore have suspended specie payments for the present, and it being the opinion of the several banks in the city of Washington here represented that the safety of the banks and the interests of the community will not be promoted by an attempt to sustain specie payments while the suspension of Northern banks shall continue; and

"Whereas, The banks here have abundant means to meet all. their liabilities, yet as a considerable part of these means have become unavailable for the present, as specie funds, by the suspension of the banks of Philadelphia and Baltimore; be it therefore

"Resolved, That it be, and is hereby, recommended to the several banks here represented, to suspend specie payments for the present, with the pledge of said banks to resume as soon as the banks of Philadelphia and Baltimore shall do so."

The Patriotic Bank was not represented at this meeting and did not suspend, as it had some time before reduced its circulation.

On July 1, 1840, the question came up in Congress as to whether the charters of the banks of the District should be continued.

Mr. Halleman introduced a bill to continue the charters of the banks in the District of Columbia for certain purposes: "That the provisions, restrictions, and enactments of the Act of Congress of May 25, 1838, entitled "An Act to Extend the Charter of the Union Bank of Georgetown, in the District of Columbia, be, and the same are hereby, extended to the Farmers and Mechanics' Bank, of Georgetown; the Bank of the Metropolis; the Bank of Washington; the Patriotic Bank, of Washington; the Bank of Potomac, and the Farmers' Bank, of Alexandria. Provided, that whenever in the original act the 4th of July, 1838, occurs, it shall be construed to mean the 4th of July, 1840, and whenever the 4th of July, 1842, occurs, it shall be construed to mean the 4th of July, 1844."

On Friday, July 3, 1840, Mr. Underwood moved to amend the bill by adding:

"That if the said banks, or any or either of them, shall, within ninety days from and after the passage of this act, resume specie payments, then the said banks, or such of them as shall so resume, shall be entitled to all the rights and privileges conferred by their present charters until the 4th of July, 1842, unless Congress shall at any time otherwise direct; but if such banks so resuming shall at any time after such resumption again suspend specie payments, or refuse to pay any of their notes or other obligations in specie, then such suspension or refusal shall operate as a forfeiture of their respective charters, except for the purpose of winding up their affairs, under the provisions and restrictions contained in this act; and provided further, in all cases where the said banks, or either of them, thereafter refuse payment of any of their notes or obligations, there shall be a summary remedy therefor before any justice or judge having jurisdiction of the case by giving five days' notice, wherein there shall be no supersedeas, stay, execution, or injunction, or certiorari allowed, nor any appeal, except upon an affidavit of merits by the president, cashier, or directors."

This amendment was sustained and the bill as thus amended was passed and sent to the Senate. In this body it was reported without Mr. Underwood's amendment; was returned to the House, and there passed by a vote of 124 to 19; again sent to the Senate, and then to the President, for his signature.

When Congress adjourned, July 21, 1840, after having failed to take action looking to a continuance of the corporate existence of the banks, bank privileges were suspended in the District, on July 4. After that day no bank could reissue its notes, make any discounts or loans or incur or receive any new obligation. The result was that bank notes of any kind could scarcely be found in quantities sufficient to transact the daily business of the community. Not long after the result of the election of William Henry Harrison to the Presidency, and of John Tyler to the Vice-Presidency became known, a memorial to Congress was circulated for the signatures of merchants, tradesmen, mechanics, and other citizens of Washington, setting forth, that "the condition of your memorialists resulting from the present state of the incorporate banks in the city of Washington is such as, in their opinion, calls for some effectual and speedy remedy to be applied by your honorable body."

In the meantime, two of the banks of the District, the Bank of the Metropolis, and the Farmers and Mechanics' Bank of Georgetown, resolved to pay all their notes and other obligations in specie, this action being taken on July 6, 1840.

In order to effect a reform in the currency as soon as possible, President Harrison called Congress together in extra session, and at this extra session Congress passed a bill providing for a "Fiscal Bank," which was only another name for a national bank, to be located in the City of Washington. President Harrison died before the opportunity came for him to assist this necessary work for his signature, and the Vice-President, John Tyler, became the President. President Tyler, when the bill establishing the Fiscal Bank was presented to him for his signature, returned it to Congress with his objections, two in number — first, that he was conscientiously opposed to a national bank, because in his view such an institution was clearly unconstitutional, and he had taken an oath to support and defend that sacred instrument. After the veto of the Fiscal Bank bill, Congress attempted to frame one which, as they understood it, was in accordance with the President's views as to what a national bank should be, giving to it the name of a "Fiscal Corporation," to be located within the District of Columbia, with a capital of $21,000,000. The bill providing for this Fiscal Corporation was likewise vetoed by the President, because he was unable to see the difference between a "Fiscal Bank" and a "Fiscal Corporation." If one was unconstitutional, so was the other.

The bankable paper of the District at that time consisted of the notes of the banks of the District, certificates of deposit of those banks, and notes of the banks of Baltimore and of banks in cities north of Maryland. By far the greatest part of the bank circulation, however, was of the Virginia banks, which, for some reason that was not then clear, could not then be made bankable, except at a loss of $3 per hundred to the possessor. Besides this, there was a flood of the notes of the Baltimore and Ohio Railroad Company, of denominations less than $5, which, up to near the latter part of 1841, circulated at par, and then becoming depreciated in Baltimore, they also, of course, settled in Washington to about ten per cent below par. So great was the loss and confusion that was occasioned, that the merchants of Baltimore agreed not to receive them in payment for anything except at their actual value.

In January, 1842, the rates of discount in Washington were as follows: Baltimore and Ohio Railroad notes, 20 to 25 per cent, discount; Virginia notes, from 4 to 5 per cent, discount, specie was from 3 to 3 ½ per cent, above Baltimore bank notes, while the notes of the banks of the District were equal to specie, and the certificates of deposit of the Patriotic Bank were equal to Baltimore bank notes.

The District banks were honestly conducted. They paid specie often when other banks did not, and always when other banks did. They were at that time paying specie and were quite as able to meet their engagements as any banks in the States. But the triumph of the enemies of the District banks was not permanent. In March, 1844, a bill to extend their charters was reported to the House of Representatives, which became a law June 17, 1844. This law, however, did not specific* ally extend the charters of any of the banks in the District of Columbia. It only provided that each of them might be party to a suit at law, by which debts due by or to any of them might be collected.

Mr. William W. Corcoran commenced the brokerage business in the City of Washington, in 1837, in a small store, ten by sixteen feet in size, on Pennsylvania Avenue, near Fifteenth Street. His business here was eminently successful, and in 1839 he moved to the old Bank of the Metropolis building, on the corner of Fifteenth and F Streets. In 1840, he received into partnership George W. Riggs, son of Elisha Riggs, of New York, broker, the firm name being Corcoran & Riggs. In 1845, Corcoran & Riggs purchased the old United States Bank building, at the corner of Fifteenth Street and New York Avenue, together with all its property and effects uncollected. The business of this firm having been successful, Mr. Corcoran settled with all his old creditors of 1823.

About this time, the house of Corcoran & Riggs took on its own account nearly all the loans made by the Government of the United States. July 1, 1848, Mr. George W. Riggs retired from the firm, and Elisha Riggs, also a son of Elisha Riggs, of New York, by another wife, was taken in as a junior partner. He remained in the firm until 1854. On the first of April of this year, Mr. Corcoran withdrew from the firm, and the business was continued by Mr. George W. Riggs, under the firm name of Riggs & Company, until his death, August 24, 1881.

After the death of Mr. George W. Riggs, which occurred on August 24, 1881, the business of the bank was conducted under the same name by E. Francis Riggs, Thomas Hyde, Charles Carroll Glover and James M. Johnston. E. Francis Riggs withdrew from this bank as director and manager in 1904 and became identified with the interests of the Metropolitan Bank. His interests were taken over by John R. McLean.

The Riggs Bank for many years occupied the old brick building at the northwest corner of Pennsylvania Avenue and Fifteenth Street, but purchased the land adjoining on the west, and erected thereon the new building which it now occupies, in 1899.

The Riggs National Bank has a capital stock of $1,000,000 and its individual deposits amount approximately to $7,000,000.

The First National Bank of Washington was organized in September, 1863 under the National Bank law of Congress and opened its doors for business on the 22nd of that month, at the corner of Fifteenth and Gr Streets. H. D. Cooke was president, and William S. Huntington, cashier. During the panic of 1873, it failed, and was placed in the hands of E. L. Stanton, son of the Secretary of War, Edwin M. Stanton, who wound up its affairs.

The Merchants' National Bank was organized in September, 1864, with William Bayne as president, and L. Huyck, cashier. In March, 1866, this bank became involved with a Baltimore firm which failed, the result of which was that the bank itself was discontinued.

The National Bank of the Metropolis was organized in 1865, was located at No. 452 Fifteenth Street, opposite the Treasury, and went into liquidation the latter part of the year 1868.

The National Bank of the Republic, of Washington, was organized in 1865. It purchased the property of the old Patriotic Bank, of Washington, located at the southwest corner of Seventh and D Streets. The National Bank of the Republic went into the hands of a receiver August 11, 1897, for the purpose of liquidation. This action was due primarily to the death of George Lemmon, chief owner of the institution, and the unwillingness of the directors to assume the risk of carrying on the bank. The Lemmon interest in the bank was purchased in the liquidation proceedings by S. W. Woodward and E. Southard Parker.

The Freedman's Savings and Trust Company was incorporated by an act of Congress approved March 3, 1865, with fifty incorporators. The object of the incorporation was to receive on deposit such sums of money as might be, from time to time, offered by or on behalf of persons previously held in slavery, or their descendants, and to invest them in stocks, bonds, Treasury notes, or other securities of the United States. The books of the company were to be open to inspection to such persons as Congress should appoint.

The business of the company was at first, and for some time, conducted in New York City. When the headquarters of the company were removed to Washington, J. W. Alvord became president, D. W. Anderson, vice-president, and W. J. Wilson, cashier. The latter two were negroes. The business of the bank was prosperous and well conducted until the original charter was so amended, May 6, 1870, as to authorize the trustees and officers of the company to make loans to the extent of one-half of the deposits on unencumbered real estate situated in the vicinity of the several branches of the company, to the extent of one-half the value of such real estate. Some of the funds of the bank were recklessly invested, and in 1871 it failed. There were thirty-four branches of the company, in all parts of the country. When it was discovered that the affairs of the company were in an unsatisfactory condition, a board of three commissioners was appointed in 1875 to take charge. These commissioners were John A. J. Creswell, Robert Purvis, and Robert H. T. Leipold. The deposits then in the aggregate had amounted to about $56,000,000, about $53,000,000 had been paid back to the depositors, leaving about $3,000,000 still due to nearly seventy thousand depositors. The original commissioners were relieved of the labor at their own request on March 7, 1881, under the provisions of an act of Congress approved February 21, 1881. Since then, the work has been in charge of the Comptroller of the Currency, who is still administering the banks affairs under the Act of Congress entitled "An Act authorizing the Commissioner of the Freedman's Savings and Trust Company to pay certain dividends barred by the Act of February twenty-first, eighteen hundred and eighty-one, " approved March 3, 1899, which applies to those depositors of the company only who have not received the five dividends, aggregating 62 per cent, of their balances.

The National Safe Deposit Company, of Washington, was chartered by special Act of Congress, approved January 22, 1867, and commenced business July 27, 1867, at the corner of New York Avenue and Fifteenth Street. It is now a branch of the National Savings and Trust Company.

The National Savings Bank was chartered May 24, 1870, and opened for business on November 1, that year. Henry A. Willard was the first president of the bank, William Stickney, vice-president, Lewis Clephane, secretary, and B. P. Snyder, treasurer. The location of the bank was at the northeast corner of New York Avenue and Fifteenth Street.

The savings feature of this company was authorized by special Act of Congress, of May 24, 1870, and under the provisions of that Act the National Savings Bank was organized, practically as a department of this company. In the process of reorganization in 1890 the National Savings Bank was absorbed by the trust company. The company took the title National Safe Deposit Company of Washington, under the charter of incorporation in 1867. This was changed to National Safe Deposit, Savings and Trust Company under the reorganization of 1890, and the present name, National Savings and Trust Company was assumed on January 31, 1907. William B. Hooper is the present president.

The National Capital Bank, of Washington, was organized in September, 1889. It is located at 314 and 316 Pennsylvania Avenue, southeast. John E. Herrell, its first president, died in 1909, and the directors elected Thomas W. Smith to succeed him. Mr. Smith is one of the principal lumber merchants of the city. He was one of the founders of the bank and has been within its councils from the beginning.

The Second National Bank was established about July 1, 1872. It is located at No. 509 Seventh Street, N. W. Mr. McKelden served as president until 1877, when he was succeeded by Matthew G. Emery. Upon the death of Matthew G. Emery, his son-in-law, William V. Cox, was in 1905, made president of the bank. Mr. Cox resigned, and Honorable Cuno H. Rudolph was selected president on December 17, 1913.

The Citizens' National Bank was organized in 1874, occupying the building formerly occupied by the First National Bank, on Fifteenth Street, between F and G Streets, N. W., and was absorbed by the National Metropolitan Bank (q. v.) in 1904.

The Central National Bank succeeded the Metropolis Savings Bank and was organized as a national bank April 11, 1878. For several years it occupied the old Bank of Washington building, but later it purchased and moved into the building at the junction of Pennsylvania Avenue and C Street at Seventh Street, April 1, 1888. Mr. Samuel Norment was the president of the bank from the date of its organization up to the time of his death, March 23, 1891. Upon his death W. E. Clark was elected president and was succeeded to the presidency of the bank by Clarence F. Norment, the son of the first president, who occupied the position until the time of its merger with the Bank of Washington in April, 1907. The details of the merger are related under the history of the National Bank of Washington.

The Washington Safe Deposit Company was incorporated April 25, 1883 and organized with the following officers: W. G. Metzerott, president; John T. Lenman, vice-president, and Samuel Cross, secretary and treasurer. This company's business is conducted at No. 916 Pennsylvania Avenue.

The Columbia National Bank was organized in February, 1887, with a capital of $250,000. Its first officers were B. H. Warner, president; A. T. Britton, vice-president, and E. S. Parker, cashier. This bank is located at 911 F Street, northwest, in a building erected especially for its use, at a cost of $70,000. B. H. Warner retired from the presidency of the bank after it was fairly started and was succeeded by E. Southard Parker, who remained as its executive head until 1897, when he resigned and became president of the National Metropolitan Bank. He was succeeded by Albert F. Fox, who is its president at the present time.

The Washington Loan and Trust Company was organized August 15, 1889, with a capital of $600,000, which, during the first year of its existence was increased to

$1,000,000. The original purpose of its organization was that of " buying, selling, loaning upon and negotiating bonds, stocks, promissory notes, and other property, and of guaranteeing, certifying, registering, endorsing, and supervising the issuance of bonds, stock, and other securities, " etc. The number of directors was twenty-five. This organization was made under the laws of West Virginia. Business was commenced by the company October 1, 1889, with the office located at the northwest corner of Tenth and F Streets, where it worked under the West Virginia charter until December 13, 1890, at which time it reorganized under the Act of Congress providing for the incorporation of trust companies in the District of Columbia, approved October 1, 1890. The Act is entitled, "An Act to Provide for the Incorporation of Trust, Loan, Mortgage, and Certain Other Corporations within the District of Columbia." This Act authorized the transaction of three classes of business, the first of which, and the class conducted by this company, is therein styled, "A safe deposit, trust, loan, and mortgage business." Without much change from its establishment the Washington Loan and Trust Company has gone forward in a prosperous career, under the conservative management of John Joy Edson, who succeeded Mr. B. H. Warner as president, and the coterie of capitalists associated with him.

The American Security and Trust Company was incorporated October 12, 1889, under the general incorporation laws of the State of Virginia. It was incorporated and reorganized November 11, 1890, under the Act of Congress approved October 1, 1890. Its business was conducted, temporarily, at 1419 G Street, northwest, but in the latter part of the year 1891 it removed to a fine new building erected for its own use at 1405 G Street. It executes all kinds of trusts, and acts as executor, administrator, guardian, assignee, receiver, and trustee, and accepts the management of estates and property generally). Money received on deposit is subject to check on demand, and interest is paid on such accounts at a rate agreed upon. It loans money on real estate and approved personal security. It issues its own debenture bonds upon deeds of trust or mortgages of real estate, in series and in sums of $100, $500, or $1,000, payable in a stated period, with quarterly or semi-annual interest, as may be agreed upon. It has a safe deposit feature, and a storage warehouse department. It also acts as financial agents in the matter of countersigning and registering certificates of stocks, bonds, or other obligations of any corporation, association, State, or public authority, and manages sinking funds on such terms as are agreed upon; as agent or attorney for the collection of interest, dividends, and all forms of income, and as attorney in fact for the interest of non-residents and others who may desire to be relieved of the care and attention of property. A. T. Britton was the first president of the company; C. G. Bell, first vice-president; A. A. Thomas, second vice-president; Percy B. Metzger, treasurer and trust officer, and George E. Emmons, secretary. Charles J. Bell became president of the company, succeeding A. T. Britton, in 1903. At that time the corporation was virtually reorganized. The company purchased the site at the northwest corner of Pennsylvania Avenue and Fifteenth Street, and erected the fine granite building which it now occupies. Col. Henry F. Blount has been connected with this company since December, 1890, when he was made director. He was made a vice-president the next year. He has been a vice-president ever since and is the bank's oldest and first vice-president. He was born in Ontario County, New York, on May 1, 1829.

The Lincoln National Bank, of Washington, District of Columbia, was organized February 27, 1890, with a capital of $200,000, and opened its doors for business on March 25. At the end of the first year, at the reorganization of the board, Mr. Prescott and Mr. Johnson resigned their positions as president and vice-president and were succeeded respectively by Mr. Jesse B. Wilson as president, and by Mr. H. Bradley Davidson as vice-president. Jesse B. Wilson retired from the presidency of the bank in March, 1909 and was succeeded by Richard A. Walker. Upon the death of Mr. Walker he was succeeded by Floyd E. Davis, the present president.

The West End National Bank was organized in 1890, with a capital of $200,000. It was originally located at the corner of Nineteenth Street and Pennsylvania Avenue, in the west end of the city, and for this reason was named the West End National Bank; but after a year's experience, it was moved to No. 1415 G Street, northwest. It went into liquidation and was absorbed by the Citizen's National Bank, which was in turn consolidated with the National Metropolitan Bank.

The Traders' National Bank was organized March 3, 1890, with a capital of $200,000, and with the following officers: George C. Henning, president; William A. Gordon, vice-president; Brent L. Baldwin, cashier. By vote of the stockholders of the Merchants and Mechanics Savings Bank, (q. v.), the Traders' Bank was merged with it in April, 1908, and the charter surrendered.

The Ohio National Bank begun business February 24, 1891, at the corner of G and Twelfth Streets, northwest, in a rented building. Most of those concerned in the movement were Ohio men, and hence, in part at least, the name of the Bank. The Ohio National Bank was not a profitable venture. The assassination of President Garfield, and the disintegration of the Ohio interests in the bank which followed weakened the institution, and it was liquidated commencing December 31, 1897.

The private banking firm of Lewis Johnson & Company commenced business February 1, 1858, at the corner of Pennsylvania Avenue and Tenth Street. It was then composed of Lewis Johnson, David Walker, and Lewis J. Davis. The business is now conducted by J. William Henry, A. Mearns and Benj. Woodruff at 1505 Pennsylvania Avenue. Bell & Company are at 1333 F Street and Crane, Paris & Company at 604 Fourteenth Street.

The American National Bank was organized in the early part of 1903 with the idea of supplying banking facilities for the upper end of F Street, a section of the business district not then supplied with such facilities near at hand. The bank was chartered in May, 1903. During the month of February, 1908, the bank was reorganized and R. H. Lynn, who had been cashier for several years, was elected to the presidency of the bank. The present president is William T. Galliher, one of the city's leading lumber dealers, and prominent in all civic affairs.

The District National Bank resulted from the reorganization of the private banking corporation of Harper & Company under the National Bank Act of September 20, 1909. Robert N. Harper, within a few months after his retirement from the head of the American National Bank, started the banking corporation which bore his name. The new concern began business in the building formerly occupied by the West End National Bank and later by the International Banking Corporation, and which now shelters the Washington and Southern Bank. On October 9, 1913, it absorbed the Citizen's Savings Bank.

In 1911 the District Bank occupied the new building erected for its use on the south side of G Street, just above Fourteenth.

The Federal National Bank was organized, received its charter, raised its stock subscriptions and opened for business in the early part of January, 1913. It took over the Small building at the southeast corner of Fourteenth and G Streets and constructed its banking room on the ground floor. John Poole is president of the new bank, N. H. Shea, vice-president, and Charles B. Lyddane, cashier.

What are familiarly known as trust companies in Washington are all incorporated under the special Act of Congress, approved October 1, 1890. This Act followed numerous applications to Congress for special charters for such institutions and was enacted only after three of the present trust companies had established themselves under charters taken out in one of the States.

Under Acts of Congress trust companies are placed on a par with national banks, being subject to inspection at least twice each year by a bank examiner and being required to make a report of operations at the call of the Comptroller of the Currency five times a year. These reports must be published in at least one daily paper published in the City of Washington.

The law of 1890 prohibited the operation of any trust company in the District unless incorporated under that law, and shortly after its passage the three corporations doing a trust business in Washington took out certificates of incorporation, under the Act, from the office of the Comptroller of the Currency. Under the operation of subsequent laws the trust companies conduct a general banking business, except making loans on commercial paper, maintain a savings department, and pay interest upon deposits.

In the autumn of 1889, Edward J. Stellwagen and others organized the Union Trust and Storage Company. The charter of this company was given to it on February 3, 1900. It went into business in the bank building adjoining the Willard Hotel in F Street, at 1414. The capital stock was increased $2,000,000 in October, 1906, to provide funds for the new building of the company, which has been erected on the site of Wormley's Hotel, southwest corner of H and Fifteenth Street, N. W. Its name was changed on February 11, 1905, to The Union Trust Company. Its president is Edward J. Stellwagen.

In the autumn of 1906 a new trust company, to be known as the United States Trust Company, was organized. The company received a certificate of incorporation March 18, 1907 and went into business on the east side of Fourteenth Street, between F and G on that date.

About April, 1912, the stockholders voted to accept an offer for the purchase of the Merchants and Mechanics Savings Bank with its several branches. The Fourteenth Street Savings Bank was acquired a month later also by purchase. This gave the company not only the central office, but six branches in different parts of the city, including those at Pennsylvania and Ninth Street, formerly the Traders' National Bank and the original home of the Merchants and Mechanics Savings Bank at Seventh and G Streets.

The company moved its central banking offices to the Southern Building in 1910. It was absorbed on November 21, 1913, by The Munsey Trust Company, (q. v.)

The Continental Trust Company was organized by its president, Nathan B. Scott, formerly Senator from West Virginia, and others, who withdrew from the United

States Trust Company and started the Continental. It occupies the building on G Street vacated by the United States Trust Company when it removed to the Southern Building.

The Real Estate Trust Company grew out of a plan devised by the financiers in control of the United States Trust Company, to organize an institution that should give special attention to real estate operations, and security, guarantee, indemnity, loan and mortgage business, as its main field of activity. It was organized and went into business in April, 1912, in the building formerly occupied by the Union Trust Company in F Street.

The company purchased the Montrose Hotel property at the northeast corner of H and Fourteenth Streets, where it is erecting a twelve-story building. Gist Blair is its president.

The Munsey Trust Company was organized principally through the efforts of Frank A. Munsey, owner of the Washington Times. It was the culmination of a purpose entertained by Mr. Munsey for several years. The company is capitalized at $2,000,000 and was incorporated April 15, 1913 and opened for business on the 15th of the following May. It is the youngest of the Washington trust companies and occupies the banking room provided for the purpose in the Munsey Building.

On November 21, 1913, the Munsey Trust Company absorbed the headquarters and five branches of the United States Trust Company. The headquarters of the latter bank were located in the Southern Building at the corner of Fifteenth and H Streets, northwest. The branch banks were located at Fourteenth and U Streets; Tenth and Pennsylvania Avenue; Seventh and G Streets; Twentieth and Pennsylvania Avenue; and Dupont Circle. At the time of its absorption the United States Trust Company had deposits aggregating $6,500,000.

The branch bank at Seventh and G Streets was afterwards sold by the Munsey Company and became the Security Savings and Commercial Bank. The branch at Tenth and Pennsylvania Avenue was sold and became the Franklin National Bank. The branch at Twentieth and Pennsylvania Avenue was sold and organized as the Exchange Bank.

The officers of the Munsey Trust Company are Frank A. Munsey, president; C. H. Pope, vice-president; and A. B. Claxton, treasurer.

The Commercial National Bank was organized in 1904, receiving its charter October 19, that year. Its president is A. G. Clapham. The building at the northwest corner of G and Fourteenth Streets was selected as its location. In April, 1911, the Commercial Bank absorbed the stock, assets and good will of the National City Bank, increasing the capital stock to $750,000, with a surplus of $533,591.

The National City Bank was organized and received its charter in December, 1905, opening for business on the 15th of the month. The bank went into business in the building on G Street, northwest, adjoining the Commercial National Bank.

During the month of March, 1909, a controlling interest in the bank vested in E. Quincy Smith who represented the F. H. Smith estate, and was practically owner of the Washington Savings Bank, located at Twelfth and G Streets. The two banks were merged into the National City Bank and went into business in the building adjoining the Bond building, in Fourteenth Street. The Union Savings Bank, controlled largely by the same financiers as the National City Bank, occupied one-half of the same banking room.

In April, 1911, the stock, good will and assets of the National City Bank were purchased by the Commercial National Bank and it was merged with that institution.

Savings banks did not make perceptible progress in Washington until after 1890. Following the formation of the Union Savings Bank only two or three such institutions got a foothold until after the turn of the century. Since 1894 the multiplication of these small banks has been very rapid. The later ones were organized and established on smaller capital than would suffice for a national bank, and they serve to provide regional banking facilities.

Under the laws of the District, savings banks are subject to the supervision of the Comptroller of the Currency, though many of them have been organized under charters received from one of the States.

Following are brief descriptions of the older savings banks that have survived, and those later formed and in business at the present time.

The Peoples Savings Bank was organized under the laws of West Virginia, September 14, 1903. Among the principal incorporators being S. J. Masters and J. B. Kinnear. The bank had a brief career and was thrown into liquidation at the order of the Comptroller of the Currency, October 24, 1906.

The Anacostia Bank was organized in 1910 and incorporated under the laws of West Virginia. The bank was promoted and organized chiefly through the efforts of George O. Walson, vice-president of the National Metropolitan Bank, to meet the needs of the business men of that part of the District. W. Walson is president. It does a regular banking business, with a savings department.

Bank of Commerce and Savings was organized and incorporated as the Dime Savings Bank, under the laws of Virginia, in August, 1907. It went into business at that time in the Ouray Building at Eighth and G Streets, northwest. The leading spirit in the organization was Maurice D. Rosenburg.

The directors of the bank in 1909 purchased the building at the northeast corner of Seventh and E Streets, northwest, and rebuilt it for the use of the bank and for office purposes. The original plan of bank fashioned after the Dime Savings Bank in New York, not having worked out to the satisfaction of the founders, the name was abandoned in 1910, and the bank assumed the title of "Bank of Commerce and Savings, " and operating as a general commercial and savings bank under its original charter.

The Citizens Savings Bank was incorporated under the laws of Virginia in March, 1906. James A. Sample, A. P. Crenshaw, Sidney I. Besseliever, Bester R. Walters and others were interested in the venture. The bank was established for business in the Bond Building but outgrew these quarters and in 1912 leased a building on G Street, near Fifteenth Street. It was absorbed by the District National Bank, October 9, 1913.

East Washington Savings Bank was incorporated under the laws of the District of Columbia in May, 1905. It was organized to meet the demand in that quarter for loans upon approved first mortgages on real estate. M. I. Weller and others were interested in its foundation. The bank is located at 312 Pennsylvania Avenue, southeast. M. I. Weller is president.

The Home Savings Bank was incorporated under the laws of Virginia in 1899 and is the second oldest institution of the kind now operating in Washington. The savings feature was made prominent and has held that position, though the bank engages in a constantly increasing commercial business. B. F. Saul is its president.

The North Capitol Savings Bank was organized in the later months of 1912, incorporated under the laws of Arizona, November 2, 1912, and went into business at 731 North Capitol Street the following week. The president is Daniel B. Mulcahy.

The Park Savings Bank was organized by business men and residents of Mt. Pleasant who felt the need of a regional bank in that part of the city, and incorporated under the laws of Alabama, and opened for business at Fourteenth Street and Park Road in October, 1909.

The Potomac Savings Bank was established under a certificate of incorporation obtained from the State of Virginia in 1903, with a view to enlarging the banking facilities of Georgetown.

The bank went into business at 1264 Wisconsin Avenue. It moved to 3157 M Street in December, 1905. It entered the new building erected as the permanent home of the bank at the northwest corner of Wisconsin Avenue and M Street, October 1, 1909. The bank does a general banking business, with the savings feature prominent in its operations.

Seventh Street Savings Bank was incorporated under the laws of West Virginia in July, 1912, and went into business during that month, in a room fitted up for the purpose at the corner of Seventh and N Streets, N. W., for the accommodation of the business interests in that part of Seventh Street and the many residents of the vicinity.

The Union Savings Bank is the oldest of the existing savings banks of the District. It was organized under the laws of West Virginia. At this time the Washington Savings Bank was absorbed. The president is Wade H. Cooper.

The bank practically passed into the hands of the financiers who controlled the National City Bank. Upon the merger of the National City Bank with the Commercial National Bank the financiers of the City Bank remained in control of the Union Savings Bank, which absorbed the Mercantile Bank by purchase of the stock in May, 1912.

The United States Savings Bank was incorporated under the laws of West Virginia in 1906. The institution was organized for the purpose of providing banking facilities at Fourteenth and U Streets.

The Washington Mechanics Savings Bank was incorporated under the laws of Virginia in July, 1906. It was formed to afford a means of deposit and the accumulation of savings for the employees of the United States navy yard and the residents of Southeast Washington.

The Merchants and Mechanics Savings Bank was incorporated under the laws of Virginia in 1904, with a capital stock of $50,000. Its original site was on G Street near the corner of Seventh. About this time it absorbed the Traders National Bank by purchase, and its main offices were removed to that building.

It, with its branches, was absorbed by the United States Trust Company in April, 1912 and was operated as a branch of that institution until November 23, 1913, when that company came under the control of the Munsey Trust Company. On April 4, 1914, it was organized as the Franklin National Bank, with Charles C. Cochran as president.

The McLachlen Banking Corporation, incorporated under the laws of the State of Virginia, in November, 1891, was for many years a private banking establishment, but in 1906, popular subscription to its stock was sought, the institution was placed under the supervision of the Comptroller of the Currency and took on more of the banking character. The bank occupies the first floor of its own building at Tenth and G Streets, N. W., which was rebuilt and refurnished in 1912. The president is A. M. McLachlen, its founder.

The Washington and Southern Bank is a private banking corporation, though under the supervision of the Comptroller of the Currency. The bank was organized in 1912 and went into business in the building formerly occupied by the District National Bank, in April, 1912. It was incorporated under the laws of the State of West Virginia. Its president is J. Selwin Tait.

Banking in the District of Columbia, as it is known today, began with the passage of the National Bank Act, in 1863, amended and extended in 1864. This Act laid the foundation of a national paper currency, which took the place of about 10,000 issues of state, county and private bank issues which had been previously known, and the fluctuating value of which more than anything else precipitated the panic of 1857.

A majority of the banks doing business in the District in 1863 and 1864, took advantage of the provisions of the National Bank Act and incorporated under it. General banks organized since that time have usually incorporated as national banks, and the business in general has gone along under that system. The trust company, formed to meet exigencies in business not provided for in the National Bank Act, and the savings bank, as institutions in Washington, came at a later date.

No national bank in Washington has ever been closed by the Comptroller of the Currency, and the few which have liquidated have paid their obligations in full. One branch of an outside banking concern and one savings bank only have felt the weight of the authority imposed on the Comptroller within the half century of operations since the passage of the National Bank Act.

The present tendency is toward consolidation and stronger financial institutions. The big institutions are endeavoring to unite the small regional banks under one charter as branch banks. Under the National Banking Act an institution cannot have branches.

CHAPTER XVII

The Bench and Bar

The Act of Congress of July 16, 1790, providing for the establishment of the temporary and permanent seat of government, left the laws of Maryland and Virginia in force over the territory of these states respectively within the seat of government until further legislation by Congress. As a consequence, all the litigation arising within the present limits of the District of Columbia from the time of the passage of that law until the passage of the Act of February 27, 1801, creating the Circuit Court of the District of Columbia, was conducted in the courts of Maryland at Annapolis. The records of the Commissioners appointed to establish the seat of government under the Act of 1790, give evidence of a very considerable amount of litigation in which they were involved in their official capacity, both as plaintiffs and as defendants. In most of this litigation they were represented by Philip Barton Key, though occasionally other attorneys were employed.

The Act of Congress of February 27, 1801, divided the District of Columbia into two counties, that on the north of the Potomac River with the islands therein constituting the County of Washington and that on the Virginia side of the City constituting the County of Alexandria, the river in its course through the District being deemed to be within both counties. The Act created a Circuit Court, to consist of a Chief Judge and two Assistant Judges, the court to hold four sessions annually in each of the counties created by the Act. An Orphan's Court was created for each of these counties, and provision was made for the transfer of pending litigation in the courts of Maryland and Virginia to the Circuit Court created by the Act. Various statutes amendatory to this Act were from time to time passed by Congress, the most notable of which prior to 1863 was that creating the criminal court in 1838.

By Act approved March 3, 1863, the Circuit Court of the District of Columbia was abolished, and the Supreme Court of the District of Columbia created in its place. This court as originally created consisted of a Chief Justice and three Associate Justices. Any one of these Justices was empowered to hold a Circuit Court or District Court, with an appeal to the entire court en banc, which right of appeal, however, was abolished in 1893, when by Act approved February 9 of that year, the Court of Appeals of the District of Columbia was created. A right of appeal from the courts of the District of Columbia to the Supreme Court of the United States has at all times been recognized by various acts of Congress. By the Act creating the Circuit Court of the District of Columbia, appeals to the Supreme Court of the United States were allowed in case involving one hundred dollars. This amount was afterwards raised to one thousand dollars and is now fixed at five thousand dollars.

Upon the creation of the Circuit Court of the District of Columbia, President Adams tendered the position of Chief Justice to Thomas Johnson, who had been one of the original Commissioners appointed by President Washington for laying out the City, and who had been at different times Chief Justice and Governor of Maryland and an Associate Justice of the Supreme Court of the United States. Mr. Johnson declined the appointment, which was then tendered to and accepted by William Kilty. Judge Kilty was born in London in 1757 and moved at an early age with his parents to Maryland. He served in the Continental Army as a sergeant throughout the Revolutionary War, at the close of which he took up the study of law at Annapolis, being soon after delegated by the State to prepare a compilation of the laws of Maryland, and his work "Kilty's Laws of Maryland" is at this day the recognized authority on that subject. He resigned his position as Chief Justice of the Circuit Court of the District of Columbia on January 20, 1806, to accept an appointment as Chancellor of Maryland, which position he held until his death on October 10, 1821. While Chancellor of Maryland he prepared, under a commission from the legislature of that state, a compilation of the English statutes in force in Maryland.

Judge Kilty was succeeded as Chief Justice of the Circuit Court of the District of Columbia by Judge William Cranch, who was one of the original Assistant Justices of that Court. Judge Cranch had served for a period of six weeks in 1801 as successor to Alexander White on the board of Commissioners appointed to lay out the city. He held the position of Chief Justice of the Circuit Court of the District of Columbia until his death on September 1, 1855. It is said of him by his biographer that only two cases appealed from him to the Supreme Court of the United States were reversed. He, for some years, in addition to his judicial duties, reported the decisions of the Supreme Court of the United States, nine volumes of the reports of that court bearing his name. He also reported the decisions of the Circuit Court of the District of Columbia from 1801 to 1841, in six volumes known as " Cranch 's Circuit Court Reports."

Judge Cranch was succeeded on December 7, 1855, by James Dunlop, who filled the position of Chief Justice until the abolishment of the Circuit Court in 1863. Judge Dunlop had previously been the first judge of the Criminal Court upon its organization in 1838 and had been appointed Assistant Justice of the Circuit Court of the District of Columbia in 1845. He was the grandson of Robert Peter, one of the original proprietors of the land on which the City of Washington was laid out. He was graduated at the college of New Jersey at Princeton, had afterwards been associated in partnership with Francis Scott Key and later for some time served as Assistant United States Attorney for the District of Columbia.

The Associate Justices of the Circuit Court of the District of Columbia were James Marshall, appointed March 3, 1801; Nicholas Fitzhugh, appointed November 25, 1803; Allen B. Duckett, appointed March 17, 1806; Buckner Thruston, appointed December 14, 1809. Judge Thruston was born in Virginia and early migrated to Kentucky. He was appointed Federal judge of the Territory of Orleans in 1805, and in the same year was elected one of the original senators from Kentucky upon the admission of that state into the Union, which position he held until his appointment as Justice of the Circuit Court of the District of Columbia.

James S. Morsell was appointed Associate Justice January 11, 1815 and held that office until the abolishment of the court in 1863. He was a native of Calvert County, Maryland, and had practiced law in Georgetown in the early part of the Century and had served in the war of 1812. He died in 1870 at the age of 95 years.

William M. Merrick was appointed December 14, 1855 and continued to be a member of the Court until its abolishment in 1863. Judge Merrick was born in Charles County, Maryland, in 1818 and prior to his appointment had practiced law in Baltimore and Frederick, Md. Upon the abolishment of the Circuit Court of the District, Judge Merrick resumed the practice of law in Maryland, was elected to the Maryland Constitutional Convention in 1867, to the State Legislature of 1870, and to Congress as a member of the forty-second Congress. In 1885 he was appointed by President Cleveland an Associate Justice of the Supreme Court of the District of Columbia.

The judges of the criminal court created in 1838 were Thomas F. Mason, who served for about one year; James Dunlop from 1839 to 1845; Thomas Hartley from 1845 to his death.

With the establishment of the Supreme Court of the District of Columbia the entire personnel of the judiciary was altered. President Lincoln appointed former Congressman David K. Cartter of Ohio, Chief Justice; George P. Fisher, former Congressman and Attorney General of Delaware; Andrew Wylie, of Pennsylvania; and Abraham B. Olin; former Congressman from New York, as Associate Judges.

Judge Cartter filled the position of Chief Justice until his death in 1887. He was succeeded by Edward F. Bingham of Ohio who served until his death in 1903. Judge Bingham was succeeded on April 1, 1903, by Harry M. Clabaugh, formerly one of the Associate Justices of the Court, who held the position until his death on March 6, 1914.

The Associate Justices following the first appointees and the dates of their appointment have been: David C. Humphreys, May 3, 1870; Arthur McArthur, formerly Governor of Wisconsin, who re-established the custom of reporting the decisions of the Court, July 15, 1870; Alexander B. Hagner of Maryland, January 21, 1879; Walter S. Cox of the District of Columbia, who was largely instrumental in the preparation of the Code of the District of Columbia, March 1, 1879; Charles P. James, of Ohio, one of the compilers of the Revised Statutes of the United States, July 24, 1879; former Justice of the Circuit Court of the District William M. Merrick, May 1, 1885; Martin V. Montgomery of Michigan, formerly Commissioner of Patents, April 1, 1887; Andrew C. Bradley of the District of Columbia, March 23, 1889; Louis E. McComas of Maryland, November 22, 1892; Charles C. Cole of Maine, formerly United States District Attorney for the District, January 28, 1893; Harry M. Clabaugh, formerly Attorney General of Maryland, March 2, 1899; Job Barnard of the District of Columbia, October 1, 1899; Thomas H. Anderson of Ohio, formerly United States District Attorney of the District, April 23, 1901; Ashley M. Gould of Maryland, formerly United States District Attorney for the District, December 8, 1902; Jeter C. Pritchard, formerly United States Senator from North Carolina, April 1, 1903; Daniel Thew Wright of Ohio, November 17, 1903; Wendell Phillips Stafford of Vermont, June 1, 1904.

The Court of Appeals of the District of Columbia was created by Act of Congress approved February 9, 1893.

Richard H. Alvey, formerly Chief Justice of the Court of Appeals of Maryland, was appointed Chief Justice April 15, 1893. He retired in December, 1904. The original Associate Judges were Martin F. Morris of the District of Columbia, who retired in June, 1905, and Seth Shepard of Texas, who was appointed Chief Justice on January 5, 1905.

Charles H. Duell, of New York, formerly Commissioner of Patents, was appointed Associate Justice on January 5, 1905, and resigned in August, 1906. Louis E. McComas, formerly Associate Justice of the District Supreme Court and later United States Senate or from Maryland, was appointed Associate Justice on April 26, 1905, and served until his death in November 10, 1907. The present Associate

Justices are Charles H. Robb of Vermont, appointed October 5, 1906, and Josiah A. Van Orsdell of Wyoming, appointed December 12, 1907.

Owing to the large number of public officials residing at Washington, the courts of the District have naturally been the scene of many trials of nation-wide interest. Among these have been a considerable number of a criminal character. Among the early cases of this nature was the trial of Richard Lawrence for an attack made by him upon President Andrew Jackson on January 30, 1835, while the President was coming out of the rotunda of the Capitol from attendance at the funeral of Congressman Warren R. Davis. The case came on to trial before Judge Cranch on April 11, 1835 and resulted in an acquittal on the ground of insanity. The evidence established the fact that the defendant was laboring under a hallucination to the effect that he was the King of England and of the United States and that President Jackson was a usurper who prevented the defendant from exercising his right of kingship.

In December, 1836, Richard H. White was tried for setting fire to the Treasury Building on March 30, 1833. His indictment was dated March 30, 1836. His defense was based upon the plea of two years limitations provided for in the act governing the crime, the chief issue at the trial being whether the defendant came without the scope of this limitation by virtue of being a fugitive from justice. At the first trial and at the second trial in April 1837 the jury disagreed, but at the third trial in June, 1837, the defendant was acquitted on the plea of limitations.

The trial of Dr. George A. Gardiner in 1853 attracted great prominence throughout the country. Gardiner had presented evidence before the commission provided for by the treaty of peace with Mexico to adjust claims of American citizens against the Mexican Government and had been awarded $428,000 by the commission on account of the alleged destruction of a mine which he claimed to have owned in the State of San Louis Potosi. Gardiner was prosecuted on the charge of perjury in the establishment of this claim. The first trial resulted in a disagreement, after which Mr. Henry May who had assisted the District Attorney, Philip R. Fendall, in the trial of the case, went to Mexico and procured additional evidence in the shape of a letter to Gardiner from his brother, which practically established the guilt of the defendant beyond dispute. When the jury returned with a verdict of guilty, the defendant took something from his vest pocket, placed it in his mouth and called for a drink of water. Almost immediately, he fell. Although denying that he had taken poison he died within an hour. He had frequently stated that he would never serve sentence in case of conviction.

Probably the most notable trial of the first half century was that of Congressman Daniel E. Sickles, afterwards General Sickles, for the killing of Philip Barton Key, at the time United States Attorney for the District of Columbia. Key had for a long time been intimate with the wife of Congressman Sickles, who had secured a confession from his wife and had frequently warned Key against continuing his relations with her. On February 27, 1859, seeing a handkerchief signal pass between Key and his wife, Sickles shot Key on Lafayette Place near the corner of Pennsylvania Avenue. Key died on the 7th of March following. The case was tried before Judge Crawford of the Criminal Court and was prosecuted by Robert Could, who had been appointed by the President to succeed Key as United States Attorney for the District. Sickles was represented by Edwin M. Stanton, afterwards Secretary of War under President Lincoln, by Chilton and Magruder and by Daniel Radcliffe. The case was famous as an early instance of the adoption of the defense of the "unwritten law," upon which ground the jury rendered a verdict of not guilty.

The damage suit brought by Hallet Kilbourn against Sergeant at Arms John G. Thompson of the House of Representatives in 1876, resulted from the commitment of Kilbourn by Thompson, under resolution of the House, to the district jail for contempt in refusing to appear before a committee of the House of Representatives to testify concerning certain matters growing out of the failure of J. Cooke & Co. Judge Cartter issued a writ of habeas corpus, and after three days' argument in the House that body by a vote of 165 to 75 directed the Sergeant at Arms to obey the writ. Kilbourn was discharged by Judge Cartter and soon after brought suit against Thompson and others for false imprisonment. A decision by the Supreme Court of the District, upon demurrer denying the right of action, was reversed by the Supreme Court of the United States in 1881. The first trial in April, 1882, before Judge McArthur resulted in a verdict of $100,000, which was set aside by the judge as excessive. A second trial occurred in November, 1883, before Judge Cox, and resulted in a verdict of $60,000, which the Judge set aside as excessive. The third trial in March, 1884, before Judge Hagner, resulted in a verdict of $37,500, which the Judge reduced to $20,000, which sum with interest was appropriated by Congress on March 4, 1885. Kilbourn was represented in this litigation by Judge J. S. Black; Matthew H. Carpenter; General N. L. Jeffries; Honorable D. W. Voorhees; Enoch Totten; C. A. Eldridge; and W. D. Davidge. The government was represented at different stages by S. S. Shellabarger; Judge William Merrick; W. H. Trescott; H. W. Garnett; Honorable Frank Hurd; Walter E. Smith; District Attorney George B. Corkhill; Assistant District Attorney Coyle; District Attorney Worthington; and the firm of Shellabarger and Wilson. On November 14, 1881, Charles J. Guiteau was brought to trial for the murder of President Garfield in the Baltimore and Potomac Railroad depot in Washington on July 2, 1881, the President having died as the result of the shots inflicted by Guiteau on September 19 following. An interesting point as to the jurisdiction of the court to try the case arose by reason of the fact that the President had died in New Jersey. It was held that the court had jurisdiction of the case, regardless of the place where death took place, because of the fact that the act constituting the crime had been committed within the District. The further defense was interposed that the death of the President had resulted not from the necessarily fatal consequence of the shots inflicted, but as the result of malpractice on the part of the physicians who attended him. The chief defense relied upon, however, was that of insanity, on the ground that the defendant acted under the belief that he was doing the will of God in destroying the President. The case was prosecuted by District Attorney George B. Corkhill, the Government being represented by Judge Porter of New York and Walter D. Davidge of Washington. The defendant was represented by George Scoville and Charles Reed of Chicago. The case was tried before Judge Cox, who allowed the utmost latitude to the defense in the introduction of evidence tending to show the insanity of the defendant. The trial lasted until January 20, 1882, when the jury brought in a verdict of guilty.

The Potomac Flats cases, technically referred to as Morris vs. United States, grew out of the Act of Congress of August 2, 1882, providing for the improvement of navigation of the Potomac River, the establishing of harbor lines, and the raising of the flats in the river opposite the city of Washington, and an Act approved August

5, 1886, which directed the Attorney General to institute a suit against all claimants to the land or water affected by the improvements provided for in the former Act, " for the purpose of establishing and making clear the right of the United States thereto." By the latter act the Supreme Court of the District of Columbia was vested with jurisdiction to determine all questions of title, and to annul or confirm all claims, arising or set forth in connection with the suit.

A large number of claimants came into the suit, and after decrees had been rendered in the lower court the case went to the Supreme Court of the United States where three questions were presented: first, that arising out of the claims of the heirs of James M. Marshall and the heirs of former Chief Justice John Marshall, to the ownership of the entire bed of the Potomac River within the limits of the improvement; second, that involving the validity of the United States patent to the tract known as Kidwell's Meadows above the Long Bridge; third, the validity of a large number of claims the determination of which was dependent upon the decision of what constituted the legal water front boundary of the city of Washington.

The claim of the heirs of John Marshall rested upon the charter granted by King James II of England to Thomas Lord Culpepper on September 27, 1688, granting to Lord Culpepper the so-called "northern neck" of Virginia lying between the Rappahannock and Potomac Rivers, to which the claimants set up their claim as successors to the title of Lord Fairfax, the heir-at-law of Lord Culpepper. The Court held that the title to the bed of the Potomac River could never have been included in the Culpepper grant because it had previously been granted by King Charles I on June 20, 1632, to Cecilius Calvert, second Baron of Baltimore, and first Lord Proprietary of the Province of Maryland.

The claim of the heirs of James M. Marshall was based upon the grant to Lord Baltimore, but the Supreme Court held that the Lord Baltimore title to the bed of the river was a trust in the hands of the Proprietary for the common use of the new community, which upon the Revolution passed to the State of Maryland and was, by the cession by that State to the United States of the territory included in the District of Columbia, vested in the United States.

The claim set up under the Kid well patent was rejected on the ground that the Land Office was without authority to issue a patent to the lands overflowed by the tides as were the Kidwell Meadows.

The third and most interesting question determined by the Supreme Court arose out of the contention made by numerous claimants that riparian rights were annexed to the title to the lots and blocks in the city lying adjacent to the river front.

In determining this contention the Court went deeply into the history of the establishment of the city and concluded that from the outset the city was intended to be bounded on the south water front by a street to be known as Water Street, which cut off any claim of owners of property abutting thereon to riparian rights or to rights in reclaimed land lying between that street and the river channel. The Supreme Court laid great stress upon the Dermott or "Tin Case" Map, the history of which has been given in the chapters on the establishment of the city, which the Court held to be the official map of the city, and on which the designation of Water Street for the first time appeared.

An interesting dissenting opinion was written by Mr. Justice White wherein the view was taken that by the conduct of the original proprietors, the Commissioners who laid out the city, and the early purchasers of water front property, it was plainly indicated that riparian rights were deemed to attach to all property lying adjacent to the river front.

The story of the organization of the Bar Association of the District of Columbia is told in the minutes of the organization as follows:

"Room 28, National Hotel, Washington, D. C.

Tuesday Night, May 23rd, 1871.

A number of the members of the bar of the Supreme Court of the District of Columbia having met at the above-named place and time, a meeting was, upon the motion of Mr. Stanton, organized for the transaction of business, and Mr. Merrick was called to the chair.

Upon motion of Mr. W. Y. Fendall, Mr. Stanton was chosen secretary.

The chair then stated that the object of the meeting was the formation of an organization of the members of the bar of the Supreme Court of the District of Columbia, with the design of elevating the tone, increasing the influence, securing and maintaining the rights of the profession, and of regulating the professional intercourse and relations of the members of the bar, with each other and with the court.

After an interchange of views and expression of opinions on the part of several members of the profession present, it was upon the motion of Mr. Mattingly, Resolved

"That the Gentlemen present form a Bar Association."

Upon motion of Mr. Payne it was resolved

" That a committee of five be appointed by the Chairman to prepare and report a plan or organization."

The Committee was upon motion increased to seven, and thereupon the Chair appointed Mr. Davidge, Mr. Carusi, Mr. Payne, Mr. Coombs, Mr. Totten, Mr. F. Miller and Mr. Perry.

The committee, after consultation, presented through Mr. Davidge the following resolutions, as a preliminary report:

"Resolved. That the title of this association shall be 'The Bar Association of the District of Columbia'.

" ' Resolved. That the members of the bar now present in person and represented by proxy viz: present in person, Messrs. Walter D. Davidge, Richard T. Merrick, Joseph T. Coombs, Nathaniel Wilson, Frederick W. Jones, Christopher Ingle, Enoch Totten, Eugene Carusi, L. G. Hine, R. F. Morris, James G. Payne, F. B. B. Sands, Robert K. Elliot, William Y. Fendall, James Hoban, William J. Miller, Francis Miller, Benjamin G. Lovejoy, R. Ross Perry, Richard Harrington, and Edwin L. Stanton.

"Represented by proxy: Messrs. John C. Kennedy, James Hughes, Walter S. Cox, Thomas J. Durant, A. G. Riddle, Charles F. Peck, Robert Leech, Nathaniel Carusi, Bland Washington, John E. Norris, Mahlon Ash ford, Hugh Caperton, John F. Ennis, William A. Gordon, William D. Cassin, John C. Wilson, Arthur Fendall, Reginald Fendall and A. S. Worthington, are hereby declared to be members of the Association.

" Resolved. That the initiation fee shall be twenty dollars. "

The Constitution and by-laws were adopted at an adjourned meeting held in the same place on the evening of May 30, 1871, at which Mr. Walter D. Davidge was elected President, Mr. Richard T. Merrick, 1st Vice-President; Mr. Walter S. Cox, 2nd Vice-President; Mr. B. G. Lovejoy, Secretary; Mr. William F. Mattingly, Treasurer and Messrs. Enoch Totten, Nathaniel Wilson, William B. Webb, James G. Payne, and Joseph J. Coombs members of the Executive Committee.

Soon after organizing, the Bar Association began the accumulation of a library. A large number of books were contributed by various members and paid for as funds became available. In a few years the Association had acquired one of the most complete law libraries in the country. Arrangements were made whereby two large rooms on the second story of the City Hall were put at the disposal of the Association for the accommodation of the library, which has ever since been kept there for the convenience of both the members of the Association and the Courts.

Even since its organization the Bar Association has been an influential factor in the legal affairs of the Capital. It has shaped needed legislation, obtained many reforms in procedure, established rates of minimum fees, brought about the requirement of an examination for entrance to the bar and done much to raise and maintain the standard of ethics in the profession.

www.ingramcontent.com/pod-product-compliance
Lightning Source LLC
Chambersburg PA
CBHW051412090426
42737CB00014B/2633